MW01053956

Two qualities are generally accepted as indicators of whether an ideology (or system of beliefs and values) is considered **left wing** or **right wing**:

1. To what extent does the ideology favour change or tradition?

Radical versus reactionary at the extremes: This quality often refers to democratic versus anti-democratic beliefs and values held by the ideology.

2. To what extent does the ideology favour individual sovereignty or group security?

Libertarianism or anarchy versus totalitarianism at the extremes: This quality often refers to the degree of government activism advocated by the ideology; that is, very little government involvement versus a great deal of government involvement.

Caution should be exercised when using the terms **left wing** and **right wing**. In spite of the qualities presented above, the terms are subject to wide interpretations and often mean something different when speaking about political behaviour than when speaking about economic behaviour.

PERSPECTIVES ON
Ideology

John Fielding • Matt Christison • Craig Harding • John Meston • Tom Smith • Doug Zook

OXFORD
UNIVERSITY PRESS

OXFORD
UNIVERSITY PRESS

70 Wynford Drive, Don Mills, Ontario M3C 1J9
www.oupcanada.com

Oxford University Press is a department of the University of Oxford.
It furthers the University's objective of excellence in research,
scholarship, and education by publishing worldwide in

Oxford   New York

Auckland   Cape Town   Dar es Salaam   Hong Kong   Karachi
Kuala Lumpur   Madrid   Melbourne   Mexico City   Nairobi
New Delhi   Shanghai   Taipei   Toronto

With offices in

Argentina   Austria   Brazil   Chile   Czech Republic   France   Greece
Guatemala   Hungary   Italy   Japan   Poland   Portugal   Singapore
South Korea   Switzerland   Thailand   Turkey   Ukraine   Vietnam

Oxford is a trade mark of Oxford University Press
in the UK and in certain other countries

Published in Canada
by Oxford University Press

Copyright © Oxford University Press Canada 2009

ISBN 978-0-19-542776-9

The moral rights of the author have been asserted

Database right Oxford University Press (maker)

First Published 2009

The publisher has endeavoured to meet or exceed industry standards in the
manufacturing of this textbook. The spine and endpapers of this sewn book
have been reinforced for extra binding strength, and the cover material is a
premium polymer-reinforced material designed to provide long life and
withstand daily classroom use. The text pages have been printed on Forest
Stewardship Council certified paper, harvested from a responsibly managed
forest, which contains a minimum of 10% post-consumer waste.

Printed and bound in Canada.

1 2 3 4 -- 12 11 10 09

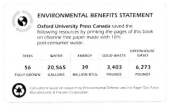

ENVIRONMENTAL BENEFITS STATEMENT

Oxford University Press Canada saved the
following resources by printing the pages of this book
on chlorine free paper made with 10%
post-consumer waste.

TREES	WATER	ENERGY	SOLID WASTE	GREENHOUSE GASES
56	20,565	39	3,403	6,273
FULLY GROWN	GALLONS	MILLION BTUs	POUNDS	POUNDS

Calculations based on research by Environmental Defense and the Paper Task Force
Manufactured at Friesens Corporation.

Alberta Education
Oxford University Press would like to express its thanks to the
30-1 team at Alberta Education and to the 30-1 Resource Review
and Diploma Examination Piloting Team of Alberta teachers and
students for their dedication to social studies education in Alberta
and the Perspectives on Ideology project in particular. Special
thanks are extended to all 30-1 team leaders and project
managers for their efforts.

Editorial Team
Oxford University Press would like to acknowledge the valued
contribution of the editorial team: Jessica Pegis (Project Manager);
Monica Schwalbe, Linda Masci Linton (Managing Editors);
Jodi Lewchuk (Assistant Managing Editor); Margaret Hoogeveen
(Program Manager); Doug Panasis (Project Consultant);
Jonathan Furze, Judith Dawson, Laura Edlund, Sonya Irvine,
Tanjah Karvonen, Leanne Rancourt (Developmental Editors);
Leslie Saffrey (Production Editor); Deborah Cooper-Bullock
(Copyeditor); Maria DeCambra, Monika Schurmann, and
Paula Joiner (photo research and permissions); Jin Tan (Indexing).

Layout and art: VISU*Tron*X

Perspectives on Ideology

Table of Contents

Features

ExCite

When you see this icon on pages of this book, go to the
Learn Alberta site (www.LearnAlberta.ca) and click on the
Perspectives on Ideology learning object for fully interactive learning
scenarios entitled ExCite (Exploring Citizenship). These scenarios
enhance learning of concepts and issues in the student resource.
Supportive of the curriculum's four Related Issues, each scenario
encourages critical thinking and analysis of issues related to ideology
in the context of Canada and different countries around the world.

Identity and Ideology

Trying to define yourself is like trying to bite your own teeth.

—Alan Watts

Pablo Picasso, Jacqueline Rocque (1954), oil and charcoal on canvas, Picasso Estate. © Pablo Picasso Estate / SODRAC (2009)

Only you can be yourself; no one else is qualified for the job.

**—anonymous,
"Bits and Pieces"**

Pablo Picasso, Jacqueline Rocque (1954), oil and charcoal on canvas, Private Collection. © Pablo Picasso Estate / SODRAC (2009)

Pablo Picasso, Jacqueline (1960), oil on canvas, Private Collection. © Pablo Picasso Estate / SODRAC (2009)

Postscript: Jacqueline Rocque was Picasso's model who married him when he was 79 and she was 37.

Each of the works shown here was painted by Pablo Picasso (1881–1973), a famous European artist of the 20th century. Each work is also a portrait of a woman named Jacqueline Rocque. Each painting tries to capture the essential quality of this woman—her identity. Picasso's works often present far more than a mere photo-like image of his subjects, so you may be able to guess at some of the qualities of Madame Rocque.

Who was this person? What kind of person was she? What were her beliefs and her values? Interestingly, our guesses about Madame Rocque— the kind of person she was, how she felt about her life, and her place in the world—would probably reveal as much about ourselves as about her.

If we see a confident woman, at peace with herself and comfortable with her role in life, does that reflect our own comfort and sense of hope? If we see a confused person, lonely, unhappy, or fragmented in some way, does that reflect our own loneliness and confusion? In any case, we can agree that everyone recognizes a fellow human in the paintings—a person with an identity. Whether we think very much about it or not, we also have an identity, and this identity is both the face we present to the world and also the filter through which we see the world.

Visit the Learn Alberta site www.LearnAlberta.ca and click on the *Perspectives on Ideology* learning object for fully interactive learning scenarios entitled ExCite (Exploring Citizenship). These scenarios related to issues and concepts in the Student Resource enhance learning.

ExCite

This book is called *Perspectives on Ideology*. It rests on the notion that our identity is closely related to how we see the world and our beliefs and values about the world around us—our ideology. The Key Issue for this course is ***To what extent should we embrace an ideology?*** Part 1 of this book begins to answer this question with a study of identity. Who am I? What factors helped to make me who I am? To what extent am I a product of my environment, family, language, gender, culture, religion, spirituality, and nation? How have all these factors influenced how I see myself and how I see the world? How might my identity influence me towards certain ways of responding to, and acting in, the world?

The Related Issue for Part 1, ***To what extent should ideology be the foundation of identity?*** explores the relationship between identity and ideology and examines how our identity may cause us to favour the general ideological positions of individualism or collectivism.

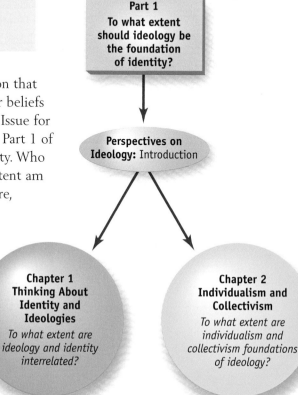

Part 1
To what extent should ideology be the foundation of identity?

Perspectives on Ideology: Introduction

Chapter 1
Thinking About Identity and Ideologies
To what extent are ideology and identity interrelated?

Chapter 2
Individualism and Collectivism
To what extent are individualism and collectivism foundations of ideology?

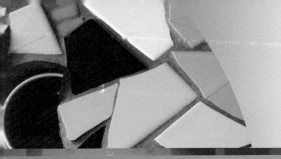

Perspectives on Ideology

Any group of people—a society—that has ever had the luxury of being able to think about its existence eventually arrives at a general understanding of how the world is and how the world ought to be. Such an understanding can be called an *ideology*. Ideologies grow out of the honest and serious contemplation of several fundamental questions:

- What are humans like, and why do they act as they do?
- What is the nature of society?
- What is the role of the individual in society?

You will find many different answers to these questions in this book—some answers given by individuals and some found in ideologies. Your task will not be to decide which one is "right," but to think carefully about whether or not any given ideology is the best way to understand the world. To accomplish this, you will examine and consider the results of ideologies that people have embraced in the past and today. By the time you finish this book, you will be in a position to reassess your own relationship with society and consider to what extent you should embrace an ideology as a way to guide your decisions and actions as a citizen.

Figure I-1 ▶

How does ideology affect the choices you make?

Points of View and Perspectives

As you make your way through this book, you will come across various points of view and perspectives regarding ideology. Keep in mind that, for the purpose of common understandings in this resource, a **point of view** represents an individual's opinion and is based on that individual's personal experience; a **perspective** reflects the outlook of a particular group of people with the same age, culture, economics, faith, language, or other shared quality. Exploring a variety of points of view and perspectives on ideology will help you recognize and develop your own point of view. It will also give you a more comprehensive understanding of ideology than you would have if you studied it from only one perspective.

The mission of Social Studies is to make sense of the human condition. Social Studies asks, "Why do people do the things they do with each other, for each other, and to each other?" Social Studies tries to unravel the central human concerns about the purposes of life, the best ways of living with others, and the best ways of relating to the world around us.

Social Studies: An Issues-Based Discipline

Social Studies is an issues-based discipline. This means that it begins its study at the point where differences of opinion or interpretation emerge. People often take their perceptions to be reality, and yet different people frequently have different perceptions of the same events. There may be disagreements and seemingly irreconcilable views of how things should be. However, it is essential to the project of Social Studies that we carefully, thoughtfully, and respectfully listen to these differences and study the many possible ways to address these concerns. This involves, in part, developing the habit of mind that withholds judgment, remains open for more information, and strives for deeper understandings of the social creature we call "human."

With this general description of Social Studies in mind, teachers and students of Social Studies are reminded that when controversy arises in the classroom, it is important to respect the views of fellow students, be sensitive to the effects of our words on others, empathize with the potential pain of others around us, and identify with others. The well-known phrase "walking in another person's shoes" is well known for a reason: it is essential not only to be aware of our differences but also to acknowledge our common humanity. We are all vulnerable. We are all social creatures who need one another. Mutual respect must colour all aspects of our study of Social Studies.

Why So Many Quotes?

Because Social Studies focuses on these very differences and perspectives, you will notice that quotations from many thinkers are included in this book. Their quotes are meant to show, first of all, the universality of these fundamental questions. The concerns of this course may be new to some but they have been the concerns of people across the ages and throughout many cultures. The words of these thinkers are also meant to invite a response— your response. On occasion, they will provoke you and encourage you to think more deeply about the issues raised in this textbook.

Inquiry-Based Learning

Every chapter following this introduction is built around a Chapter Issue related to ideology. To aid you in exploring this issue, each chapter is divided into sections. Each section offers you an opportunity to answer a Question for Inquiry related to the Chapter Issue and provides you with exploration of some key concepts to help you explore these questions. Some key supporting terminology is also provided to help you understand the key concepts and questions presented. The inquiries you pursue in this book will help you come to your own informed opinions about issues related to ideology. By the end of the book, you will be ready to develop an informed position on the Key Issue for this course: **To what extent should we embrace an ideology?**

In each of the four parts of this book, you will also explore a Related Issue that will help you take an informed position about the Key Issue for this course. Read each of the four issues in the diagram on the opposite page. Which one do you think will interest you most? Which one do you think is most relevant to your life?

As you read through each chapter, you will find many cross-references to concepts, people, or events you were introduced to earlier. Use these cross-references to assist in your inquiry and to see the interrelated nature of issues and concepts throughout the resource. Two extensive indexes are also provided at the back of the book. One index lists and locates all the important terms, concepts, and people in the resource; the other provides a list of the names of organizations, institutions, and people mentioned in the resource. These indexes are meant to help you locate information quickly as you engage in the various tasks and activities throughout your Social Studies course.

Each chapter ends with a section designed to extend the inquiry of that chapter. The tasks suggested are often extensive research inquiries or preparations for debates or other presentations. These activities may require significant time commitments. You will not be expected to complete all these activities. Your teacher will determine which assignments are most suitable and viable for your class.

Finally, keep in mind that Social Studies is as much about developing the skills of inquiry, critical thinking, participation, and communication as it is about acquiring concepts and developing informed positions. Some of the essential skills required of active and responsible **citizenship** are addressed in the Skill Path feature of each chapter. Each Skill Path assignment is designed to give you opportunities to refine essential skills related to the Chapter Issue and the Questions for Inquiry for that chapter.

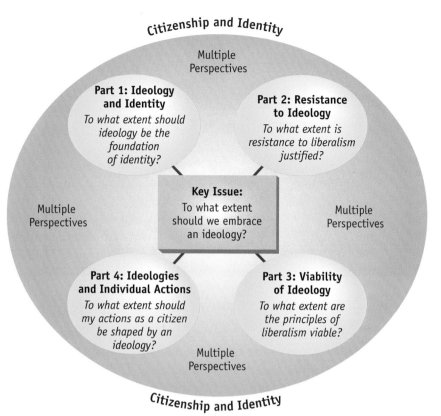

Citizenship and Identity

Multiple Perspectives

Part 1: Ideology and Identity
To what extent should ideology be the foundation of identity?

Part 2: Resistance to Ideology
To what extent is resistance to liberalism justified?

Multiple Perspectives

Key Issue:
To what extent should we embrace an ideology?

Multiple Perspectives

Part 4: Ideologies and Individual Actions
To what extent should my actions as a citizen be shaped by an ideology?

Part 3: Viability of Ideology
To what extent are the principles of liberalism viable?

Multiple Perspectives

Citizenship and Identity

PAUSE AND REFLECT

Our country is based on ideologies that accept certain ideas: freedom of speech, the democratic process, the right to associate with whomever you choose, and so on. How important are these ideas to you? Can you imagine living in a country that did not uphold these ideas?

The Power of Ideologies

In the mid-20th century, two novels appeared that have had a great influence on discussions about human nature and the role of ideology in modern society. Both novels describe dystopias—fictional societies that are deliberately portrayed as negative—where ideology is used to control an unwitting population.

War is Peace, Ignorance is Strength, Freedom is Slavery

In George Orwell's novel *Nineteen Eighty-Four* (1949), "War is Peace, Ignorance is Strength, Freedom is Slavery" are the three slogans of the government of Big Brother. In this fictional world where there are only three countries, Oceania, Eurasia, and Eastasia, Oceania is a totalitarian society led by Big Brother that censors people's behaviour, even their thoughts.

Figure I-3 ▶

Winston Smith, the central character in *Nineteen Eighty-Four*, works under the watchful eye of Big Brother as he changes old newspaper records to match the new truth as decided by the Party.

1. When Postman talks about the fears of Orwell and Huxley, he is talking about two very different views of human nature. What are they?

2. The mottoes of the two societies (in *Nineteen Eighty-Four* and *Brave New World*) are deliberately ironic. What do these mottoes tell you about the way Orwell and Huxley think society should or should not be run?

3. If you were to write the great dystopian novel of the future, what would it be about? How would your society operate? Think about the trends in society that you would want to satirize and criticize. What would your novel say about your view of human nature?

Community, Identity, Stability

In Aldous Huxley's novel *Brave New World* (1932), "Community, Identity, Stability" is the motto of the utopian World State. Here everyone is provided for and there is no violence. Thinking, art, originality, and philosophy are simply forbidden. Instead, people take a drug to ensure that they never feel depressed, and the government strictly controls reproduction.

American social critic Neil Postman compared the respective dystopias of Orwell and Huxley:

What Orwell feared were those who would ban books. What Huxley feared was that there would be no reason to ban a book, for there would be no one who wanted to read one. Orwell feared those who would deprive us of information. Huxley feared those who would give us so much that we would be reduced to passivity and egoism. Orwell feared that the truth would be concealed from us. Huxley feared the truth would be drowned in a sea of irrelevance. Orwell feared we would become a captive culture. Huxley feared we would become a trivial culture, preoccupied with some equivalent of the feelies, the orgy porgy, and the centrifugal bumble puppy.* As Huxley remarked in Brave New World Revisited, *the civil libertarians and rationalists who are ever on the alert to oppose tyranny "failed to take into account man's almost infinite appetite for distractions." In* 1984, *Orwell added, people are controlled by inflicting pain. In* Brave New World, *they are controlled by inflicting pleasure. In short, Orwell feared that what we fear will ruin us. Huxley feared that what we desire will ruin us.*

*pleasant distractions and amusements in *Brave New World*

—"Foreword", from *Amusing Ourselves to Death* by Neil Postman, copyright © 1985 by Neil Postman. Used by permission of Viking Penguin, a division of Penguin Group (USA) Inc.

Understanding Humans and Societies through Ideologies

What are humans like, and why do they act the way they do? What is the nature of society? What is our role as individuals in society? These are big questions, but they are not new questions. For centuries people have spent time thinking about these questions and, quite often, their responses take the form of an ideology. In the words of British literary critic and Marxist activist Terry Eagleton,

What persuades men and women to mistake each other from time to time for gods or vermin is ideology. One can understand well enough how human beings may struggle and murder for good material reasons—reasons connected, for instance, with their physical survival. It is much harder to grasp how they may come to do so in the name of something as apparently abstract as ideas. Yet ideas are what men and women live by, and will occasionally die for.

—**Terry Eagleton, *Ideology: An Introduction* (London: Verso, 1991), p. xiii.**

Ideas are important because they are, as the quote above suggests, the reason why people act in certain ways. In order to become an informed, responsible, and active citizen, you need to be able to understand and evaluate government policies and actions, and develop informed responses to local, national, and global issues. Studying the various ideologies and responses to ideologies that will be presented to you throughout this text is your opportunity to "try them on" to see if they fit you.

Consider the following quotes about humans:

Humans can learn to like anything, that's why we are such a successful species. You can drop humans anywhere and they'll thrive—only the rat does as well.

—**Jeannette Desor (research scientist at General Foods), quoted in Ellen Ruppel Shell, "Chemists whip up a tasty mess of artificial flavors." *Smithsonian*, 17, 2 (May, 1986): pp. 78–85.**

An individual has not started living until he can rise above the narrow confines of his individualistic concerns to the broader concerns of all humanity.

—**Martin Luther King Jr, American civil rights leader, winner of the 1964 Nobel Prize for Peace**

Snapshots

"I understand *how* I was born; I want to know *why*."

Figure I-4 ▲

One view of what really makes humans human is the awareness of their own existence. "Why do we exist?" and "What is the meaning of life?" are questions people have thought about throughout the ages. What would your initial response be to this boy's statement?

It has been said that man is a rational animal. All my life I have been searching for evidence of this.

—Bertrand Russell, British philosopher, mathematician, political activist and social reformer, winner of the 1950 Nobel Prize for Literature

Man is a goal-seeking animal. His life only has meaning if he is reaching out and striving for his goals.

—Aristotle, Greek philosopher of the 4th century BCE, made important contributions to the development of logic and the sciences, tutored Alexander the Great

The belief in a supernatural source of evil is not necessary; men alone are quite capable of every wickedness.

—Joseph Conrad, late–19th-century sea captain and writer, celebrated for his novels and short stories about colonialism and human nature

These quotes are attempts at capturing an ideology in a few words, sometimes humorously. Based on your present opinions and beliefs, organize the quotes from what you consider the most true to the least true.

- Why did you put them in that order?
- What is it about each quote that you agree with or do not agree with?
- Try to write your own ideology about human nature in one or two sentences.
- What did other students in your class write down?
- Can you come up with a class ideology?

What Are Humans Like?

Have you ever read a newspaper article, or seen something in a movie or television show, that made you wonder, "How could someone do that to another human being?" History is full of cases of inhumanity—the Crusades, the Holocaust, the actions of the Ku Klux Klan—and barbaric behaviour still goes on today. But history is also full of acts of kindness and compassion. There have always been people such as Mahatma Gandhi or Norman Bethune who have devoted themselves to helping others and there are many charities devoted to helping others in various ways. Each person or group acts based on its ideology, and every ideology attempts to answer the question "What are humans like?"

Mark Twain wrote, "Man is the only animal that blushes. Or needs to." Why do you think Mark Twain thought this way about people? Write down a list of all the qualities or characteristics that you think make

◀ **Figure I-5**

What views about human nature are explicit and implicit in this cartoon?

humans human. How many of these characteristics are ideological, and how many are biological?

Thinking about what humans are like and what they are capable of is something that people have done for centuries. Philosophers, scientists, politicians, religious leaders, comedians, singers, writers, and others have offered us their ideas about humanity. Consider the following quotes:

Peace by persuasion has a pleasant sound, but I think we should not be able to work it. We should have to tame the human race first, and history seems to show that that cannot be done.

—Mark Twain, popular 19th-century American writer and satirist

Men are cruel, but Man is kind.

—Rabindranath Tagore, early 20th-century Bengali poet, novelist, and lyricist, winner of the 1913 Nobel Prize for Literature

It is human nature to think wisely and act foolishly.

—Anatole France, French writer, member of the French Academy, and winner of the 1921 Nobel Prize for Literature

Our true wealth is the good we do in this world. None of us has faith unless we desire for our neighbours what we desire for ourselves.

—Mohammed, prophet of Islam, 6th to 7th century CE

- What is the message in each of these quotes?
- Which of these quotes do you agree with most?

Clearly there is no easy answer when considering what humans are like, but ideologies are a way to explore the possible answers to this question.

What Is the Nature of Society?

The definition of a free society is a society where it is safe to be unpopular.

**—Adlai E. Stevenson, United States Ambassador
to the United Nations**

Our modern society is engaged in polishing and decorating the cage in which man is kept imprisoned.

—Swami Nirmalananda, Hindu Swami

These two quotes both address the question "What is the nature of society?" There are many answers to this question, and you have only to read newspapers from around the world to figure out that there are many different versions of society out there. Some societies are built on the principles of peace and goodwill, while others are built on tyranny and fear. Ideologies are the foundations on which all societies are structured, for better or for worse, because ideologies are ways of understanding how we should interact with one another.

Part of examining the nature of society is determining whether you view it from an individualist or a collectivist standpoint. **Individualism** is a current of thinking that values the freedom and worth of the individual over the security and harmony of the group. **Collectivism** is a current of thinking that values the goals of the group and the common good over the goals of any one individual. For example, in most places in Canada it is illegal to smoke in restaurants. Where do you stand on this issue? Is it a bad policy that is unfair to the individual smoker, who should be able to smoke wherever he or she pleases? Or is it a good policy that protects the health and well-being of non-smokers, who shouldn't have to breathe in second-hand smoke? In Chapter 1 you will make a Beliefs and Values Inventory to determine whether you lean toward an individualist or a collectivist viewpoint.

In a capitalist society such as Canada's, the focus is often on personal wealth: How much do you make? What car do you drive? Which designer's clothes do you wear? But capitalist societies always have desperately poor people living among wealthy people. Examining the nature of society means questioning the extent to which this individualist approach or a collectivist approach is best. While studying the various ideologies in this book, you will encounter many people who do not subscribe to the values of materialism. For example, the Mi'kmaq [MIG-mah] people (sometimes referred to as the Mi'kmaw, as seen in the quotation by Battiste and Henderson) have a very different version of society:

Mi'kmaw people share an alternative vision of society. While it is compatible with universally recognized human rights, its stress is on wholeness and relationships, in particular on the responsibilities among families, clans, communities and nations. At the minimal level, Mi'kmaw thought teaches that everyone and everything are part of a whole in which the parts are interdependent on each other. Each person has a right to a personal identity as a member of a community but also has responsibilities to other life forms and to the ecology of the whole. Thus Mi'kmaw thought values the group over the individual and the extended family over the immediate or biological family.

—**Source: Marie Battiste and James Youngblood Henderson, *Protecting Indigenous Knowledge and Heritage: A Global Challenge* (Saskatoon: Purich Publishing, 2000), p. 55.**

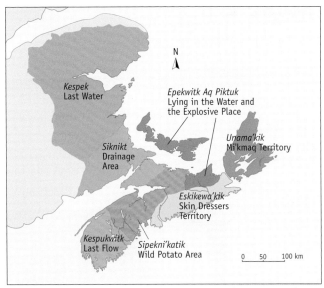

Original source: drawn by Mike Martin for Native Council of Nova Scotia Mi'kmaq Language Program, PO Box 1320, Truro, Nova Scotia B2N 5N2

Figure I-6 ▲

The traditional territory of the Mi'kmaq. How might location and sense of place have shaped the Mi'kmaq's beliefs and values? Analyze some of the place names on the map to guide your response.

Certainly in Canada there are many people who value the community's well-being over their own and devote their time, money, and energy to helping others.

Then again, striving for individualism is not necessarily a bad thing. The influential 19th-century German philosopher Friedrich Nietzsche wrote,

The individual has always had to struggle to keep from being overwhelmed by the tribe. If you try it, you will be lonely often, and sometimes frightened. But no price is too high to pay for the privilege of owning yourself.

However, many people have argued that striving for individual goals alone is not the way to achieve real freedom and progress. Martin Luther King Jr said "An individual has not started living until he can rise above the narrow confines of his individualistic concerns to the broader concerns of all humanity." As an American civil rights leader of the 1960s, King recognized that the cause of his people would be furthered by working together rather than suffering apart. The power of people working together has been proven throughout history, an idea very well put by British musician John Lennon: "If everyone demanded peace instead of another television set, then there'd be peace."

As you read this text and think about the nature of society and how it can be structured, think about the type of society you would make if you were creating an ideal society. Write down some points now, and come back to your list throughout the course. At the end of the course, evaluate how or if your idea of an "ideal society" has changed. Make another list of contributions you can make to the society you live in now that would make it more like your ideal society.

PAUSE AND REFLECT

At this point in your life, which do you value more: individual goal attainment (getting ahead for yourself) or collective well-being (doing things for others)? Write down one pro and one con for each side of the argument. Can there be a balance between the two, or does it have to be one or the other?

Figure I-7 ▼

Which of these images do you identify with? Do any of them capture what you think your role as a citizen is or will be? Are there other aspects of citizenship that are not represented here? Make a list of all the ways someone can be an active, informed, and engaged citizen. Which do you do now? Which do you plan to do in the future?

What Is Our Role in Society?

Look closely at the photographs in Figure I-7. Which one best captures the way you see your future? What is it about that photo that appeals to you? Thinking about our role in society is the third question that ideologies help us answer. It is a complex issue that usually reflects our thinking about human nature and the nature of society. Our society is a democracy, and as such depends on citizen participation. However, in order to participate in a democratic society, people need to understand not only human nature and society, but also what it means to be a citizen and what a citizen's role in society should be.

One of the earliest people to think about our role in society was the Greek philosopher Plato, who lived in the 4th century BCE. Plato believed that the community is best served by each citizen doing whatever it is that he or she does best. The best builders should build; the best farmers should farm; and the best ruler should rule. Plato based his arguments on the belief that humans are not created equal in gifts and talents. Some people are good at making decisions and others are not. Some people are good at guarding, and others are better at making bread. To Plato, your role is determined by your natural abilities.

Your role in society is more than just choosing a career, though. Our roles in society have to do with purpose: What is the purpose we serve in this world? The Dalai Lama has said that "Our prime purpose in this life is to help others." What is your reaction to his position? If helping others is our prime purpose, then there must also be a secondary purpose (and maybe even a third and fourth purpose). The Mi'kmaq people believe that the individual has responsibilities to the collective; that is, the individual's purpose is to better serve the community.

In this collective, each person has both rights and advantages from being part of the whole but also has obligations and responsibilities that define membership and citizenship…As one understands oneself—spiritually, mentally, physically and emotionally—one becomes centered and focussed, and thus becomes a vital force in enabling others to do the same.

—Source: Marie Battiste and James Youngblood Henderson,
***Protecting Indigenous Knowledge and Heritage*, p. 56.**

Both Plato and the Mi'kmaq bring the idea of citizenship into their ideologies. Your role in society, especially a democratic society such as Canada's, is determined in part by what kind of citizen you choose to become. Whatever ideology you subscribe to, you cannot avoid being a citizen of society; that is, having a role in society. Your actions and beliefs shape your purpose, and they have an effect on your society and the people around you.

Ideology in History

Over the centuries, there have been many people who have thought, talked, and written about these three questions, and, in so doing, they created ideologies. Some of these people have had a more profound impact on future generations than others. Plato, for instance, is still one of the most influential philosophers of Western thought—even more than 2000 years after his death! In this section we will look at three other philosophers who have had profound impacts on shaping Western ideologies: Thomas Hobbes, John Locke, and Jean-Jacques

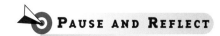

PAUSE AND REFLECT

Do you see any flaws in Plato's theory? Can you think of instances where his theory would not hold true?

Figure I-8 ▲

The Dalai Lama is the spiritual leader of the world's Tibetan Buddhists. He has been a vocal supporter of Tibetan independence from China and is the head of the Tibetan Government in Exile. The Dalai Lama won the 1989 Nobel Prize for Peace.

PAUSE AND REFLECT

What similarities can you see between Plato's and the Mi'kmaq ideologies? How is the well-being of the community served under both views of a person's role in society? How is the individual served?

Rousseau. These men were writers during the Enlightenment, which was a period from the late 17th through the 18th centuries in Europe when the recognition of human reason made human authorship of solutions to human problems seem possible. Western democratic ideas about equality, freedom, and participatory government came out of this time period.

Thomas Hobbes (1588–1679)

Thomas Hobbes was an English philosopher living during the English Civil War. The war was a bitter struggle between the king and Parliament that ended when King Charles I was beheaded. After that, a republic was formed under Oliver Cromwell, a strict Puritan, whose government tyrannized the people and brutally punished anyone who disagreed with its policies.

These events profoundly influenced Hobbes. He believed that human nature is characterized by fear, violence, and dangerous self-interest—in other words, extreme individualism—where people are looking out only for themselves and hurting anyone who gets in their way.

[During the state of nature, people] are in that condition which is called war…In such condition there is no place for industry…no culture of the earth…no arts; no letters; no society; and which is worst of all, continual fear, and danger of violent death; and the life of man, solitary, poor, nasty, brutish, and short.

—Thomas Hobbes, *Leviathan*, Chapter XV, "Of Other Laws of Nature." Great Voyages: The History of Western Philosophy.
http://oregonstate.edu/instruct/phl302/texts/hobbes/leviathan-c.html#CHAPTERXV

Hobbes believed that if everyone is free, then everyone is in danger, and that we all need security more than we need freedom. Hobbes's solution was a society where everyone gave up his or her freedom to one person (a monarch or a dictator) who was responsible for everyone's security. Quite simply, Hobbes did not think it was possible to have both freedom and security.

John Locke (1632–1704)

John Locke, another English philosopher, had a very different view of human nature. Unlike Hobbes, he believed that people are rational, intelligent, and reasonable. Most people living at the time believed that power rested with God and the king (who was chosen by God to rule and therefore had absolute power, a doctrine known as the **divine right of kings**). Locke, on the contrary, believed that the source of power

---

File Facts

Thomas Hobbes (1588–1679)

- studied at Oxford University
- later lived in Paris for several years
- tutored the Prince of Wales (later King Charles II)
- wrote *Leviathan* (1651), a key text in Western political philosophy
- wrote extensively about *social contract* theory and the *state of nature*
- returned to England during the Civil War (1642–1651), fearing persecution from the English royalists in exile
- was banned from publishing any book related to human conduct following the Restoration of the monarchy (1660)

PAUSE AND REFLECT

Do you agree with Hobbes's assessment of human nature? What are the implications of the ideal society Hobbes envisioned? What flaws do you see in his theory?

was people themselves, which was a revolutionary idea in the 17th century. He believed that individuals possess the ability to be reasonable and make rational decisions.

Locke further believed that the only reason governments exist is to protect life, liberty, and property, which is why people give up their natural state of freedom to enter into a civil society. However, Locke believed that any government action had to be justified by popular consent. Take, for example, what Locke said about taxation:

[The government is allowed to tax the people, but] it must be with his own consent—i.e., the consent of the majority, giving it either by themselves or their representatives chosen by them; for if any one shall claim a power to lay and levy taxes on the people by his own authority, and without such consent of the people, he thereby invades the fundamental law of property, and subverts the end of government.

—John Locke, *The Second Treatise of Civil Government*, Chapter 11, "Of the Extent of the Legislative Power," 1690.

File Facts

John Locke (1632–1704)
- studied philosophy and medicine at Oxford University
- wrote about *social contract* theory, like Hobbes, as well as consciousness, identity, liberty, and government
- prepared writings on individual rights that later became key ideas in the ideology of liberalism

Figure I-9

Thomas Hobbes, John Locke, and Jean-Jacques Rousseau all talk about humans in a *state of nature* (that is, prior to the existence of an organized society), but their ideas about this position were very different. Whom do you agree with? Why? Take a look at the photos shown here—people walking to raise money for AIDS awareness and others clashing on the ice rink. What have your experiences taught you about human nature? How does that affect the way you see yourself and others?

The notion of popular consent is what sets Locke apart from most thinkers of his time. In essence, Locke believed in democracy, which is why his theories were used by American revolutionaries almost 100 years later as the basis for their new government.

Thinking about Identity and Ideologies

 Figure 1-1 ▲ ▶

How do my actions reflect my ideology and identity?

KEY SKILL

Analyzing, organizing and evaluating the underlying assumptions of positions

KEY CONCEPTS

Exploring influences on individual and collective beliefs

Key Terms

Ideology
Worldview

The following news story introduces a movement called The Compact. Some people would say that those who join The Compact are acting on their personal ideologies. As you read the story, try to decide whether or not you could be a member of this group. Does your decision indicate something about your ideology? How important is it to act on your ideology?

Shunning materialism saves money

Candice Choi, The Associated Press, July 19, 2008

NEW YORK—Give up worldly goods and help save the Earth. Oh, and save lots of money.

As the economy worsens, one group of Americans is turning to an Earth-friendly way of life as a hardline strategy for saving. The Compact started a few years ago in San Francisco as a group of people who vowed to shun consumer culture for a year in the name of conservation. Now it has over 9 000 members and spinoff groups are sprouting up across the country…

It seems what's good for the Earth is good for the wallet. Since joining in January, The Compact has turned a flood light on [Julia Park Tracey's] family's frivolous spending—scented lotions, flavored lattes, iPod accessories. Now they no longer dry clean their clothes and even make their own cat food.

"All that was money out the window. We could not keep going like that and make ends meet," said Julia Park Tracey, whose budget is being stretched thin by escalating food and gas prices.

What makes The Compact compelling for average Americans is that there are no hard-and-fast rules…Members simply try to conserve the best they can. When necessary, they borrow, barter or buy second hand. Food and hygienic purchases are OK, but the idea is to cut back there too.

The goals sound a lot like those of a growing population of Americans squeezed by inflation. "People are coming for all different reasons, with credit card debt or others who say 'my kids are so materialistic and out of control'," said John Perry, founder of The Compact.

Perry didn't start The Compact to save money, but it's one of the lifestyle's intrinsic perks. He saves at least a couple of hundred dollars a month, which leaves more cash for his mortgage, charity and children's savings accounts. Cutting out dry-cleaning and Starbucks alone is saving Tracey's family $250 a month. Biking and walking conserves not just oil, but piles of gas money. Gone too are the mindless drug store sprees where Tracey would blow $100 or more on cosmetics and snacks.

"The real surprise is that it's so much easier than you would think," Perry said. "If you hang on, it's like dieting—the hunger goes away." Since so much of consumerism is on making upgrades—faster gadgets, the newest sneakers—ending such purchases isn't even all that painful, Perry said.

A sudden en masse withdrawal from consumerism might shock the economy at first, but industries would likely adjust and perhaps even become more efficient over time, said Brian Bethune, an economist with Global Insight. Higher fuel prices, for example, are spiking demand for smaller cars and in turn hurting US auto makers, Bethune said. But that means car companies need to adjust their strategies, he said. "I don't see that as being bad for the economy," he said.

The conservation movement is nowhere close to crippling consumerism, however. Even devoted members of The Compact still buy things like shower curtains or kitchen appliances. Tracey's children, for example, may not eat out as often as some of their friends, but they still have cell phones and iPods they either got as gifts from their grandparents or bought second hand.

"There are different levels of adherence. It's what makes sense to your economic or personal conditions," said Rachel Kesel, one of the founders of The Compact.

Kesel, a 27-year-old San Francisco resident who describes herself as "anti-capitalist, anti-corporate" is on the more radical end of The Compact's membership. But many members resemble the average American family.

"It's very low level activism. It can fit into a lot of different scenarios," Kesel said.

Chapter Issue

In this chapter you will explore the concepts of personal and collective identity, and identify the factors that influence the beliefs and values that make up part of your identity. You will also think about how your beliefs and values affect the way you see the world and your place in society in order to better understand the relationship between identity and ideology. You will be considering the Chapter Issue: ***To what extent are ideology and identity interrelated?***

It is important that you think about ideology in terms of your own identity. This chapter will help you identify your own personal beliefs and values and examine their connections with ideology. This chapter will also help you examine the nature of ideologies: their themes and characteristics. We will provide you with quotes, pictures, and examples so that you are aware of what others have said about ideology and identity. But it is up to you to conduct this inquiry and make the decision about the extent to which identity and ideology are interrelated.

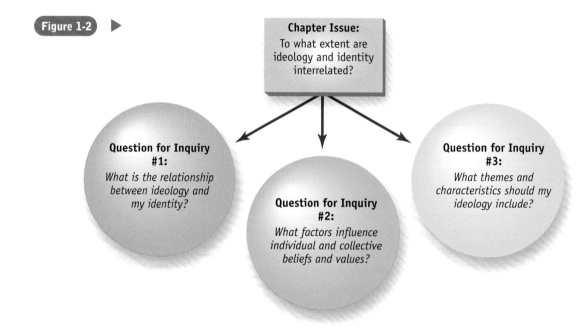

Figure 1-2 ▶

Chapter Issue:
To what extent are ideology and identity interrelated?

Question for Inquiry #1:
What is the relationship between ideology and my identity?

Question for Inquiry #2:
What factors influence individual and collective beliefs and values?

Question for Inquiry #3:
What themes and characteristics should my ideology include?

Understandings of Identity

...the culture of individualism has come to represent not just personal freedom but the essential shape of the social fabric itself. As British prime minister Margaret Thatcher famously summed up this individualist ethos, "There is no society, only individuals and families." In the so-called do-it-yourself society, we are now all entrepreneurs of our own lives.

—Charles Lemert and Anthony Elliott,
Deadly Worlds: The Emotional Costs of Globalization
(Lanham: Rowman & Littlefield, 2006), p. 3.

No man is an island, entire of itself; every man is a piece of the continent, a part of the main...any man's death diminishes me, because I am involved in mankind...

—John Donne, *Meditation XVII*, 1623.

PAUSE AND REFLECT

Do you agree or disagree with the ideas expressed in the quotes?

What is identity? The term *identity* has a wide range of meanings, depending on the context in which it is being used. In a very broad sense, one's identity is *who* or *what* one is. Social scientists and philosophers have described identity as a sense of personal continuity—being the same identifiable individual over the course of time—and an understanding of oneself as unique from others.

Two types of identity frequently discussed in sociology are personal identity and collective identity. **Personal identity** is the idea you have of yourself as a unique individual. It is the collection of traits that you think of as distinguishing you from others. A **collective identity** is one that you share with other people as a member of a larger social group, such as a linguistic, faith, cultural, or ethnic group.

A person's identity may be influenced by such things as gender, religion, language, or culture. If a group of people have the same shared experience, such as a particular religion, then their identities may be influenced in a similar way by that shared experience.

Beliefs and values are important aspects of identity. Just as past experiences and aspects of our lives such as culture and language form our identities, they also help us choose sets of beliefs and values. Although beliefs and values are abstract ideas, they can have real effects on our lives; they influence our behaviour and choices and guide us in our interactions with others.

Different understandings of identity may consider some factors to be more important than others. For example, a holistic Aboriginal perspective like the one on page 25 might stress the importance of community and environment in the formation of one's identity.

Aboriginal worldviews teach that everyone and everything is part of a whole, and each is interdependent with all the others. Each person has a right to a personal identity as a member of a community but also has a responsibility to other life forms and to the ecology of the whole. It is inconceivable that a human being can exist without a relationship with the keepers of the life forces (totems), an extended family, or his or her wider kin.

—Source: James (Sa'ke'j) Youngblood Henderson, "Ayukpachi: Empowering Aboriginal Thought" in *Reclaiming Indigenous Voice and Vision*, ed. Marie Battiste (Vancouver: UBC Press, 2000), p. 269.

Ideology can also influence a person's identity. Political scientists consider an ideology to be a set of principles or ideas that explain our world and our place within it. An individual might embrace a particular ideology because it mirrors certain beliefs and values about the world that the individual already has. Once people consciously embrace an ideology, it may cause them to re-examine and reinterpret their own lives according to the principles of that ideology. Similarly, a group of people may choose to embrace an ideology that reflects its members' shared beliefs and values.

Figure 1-3 ▶

Understandings of identity vary from one society to another, and even from one individual to another. This diagram is one possible illustration of the interrelationship between identity and ideology. Various factors may influence your beliefs and values, as well as your individual and collective identities and personal identity. In turn, your individual and collective identities and beliefs and values can guide you toward an ideology, a way of explaining the world, that is in alignment with your way of seeing the world. What factors do you think have the most influence on your identity?

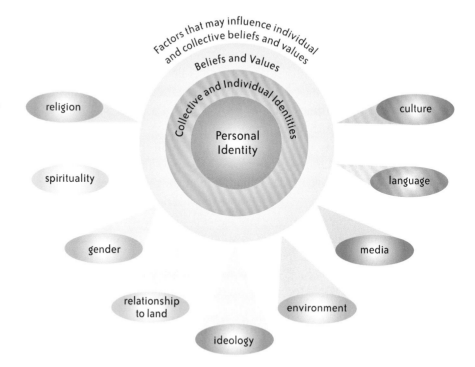

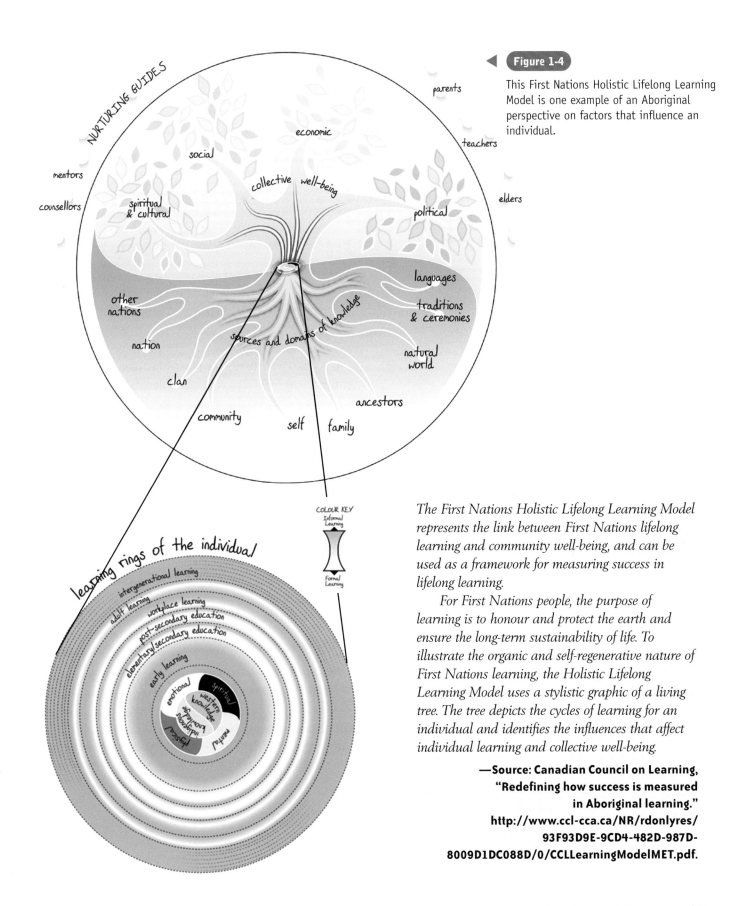

Figure 1-4

This First Nations Holistic Lifelong Learning Model is one example of an Aboriginal perspective on factors that influence an individual.

The First Nations Holistic Lifelong Learning Model represents the link between First Nations lifelong learning and community well-being, and can be used as a framework for measuring success in lifelong learning.

For First Nations people, the purpose of learning is to honour and protect the earth and ensure the long-term sustainability of life. To illustrate the organic and self-regenerative nature of First Nations learning, the Holistic Lifelong Learning Model uses a stylistic graphic of a living tree. The tree depicts the cycles of learning for an individual and identifies the influences that affect individual learning and collective well-being.

—Source: Canadian Council on Learning, "Redefining how success is measured in Aboriginal learning." http://www.ccl-cca.ca/NR/rdonlyres/ 93F93D9E-9CD4-482D-987D- 8009D1DC088D/0/CCLLearningModelMET.pdf.

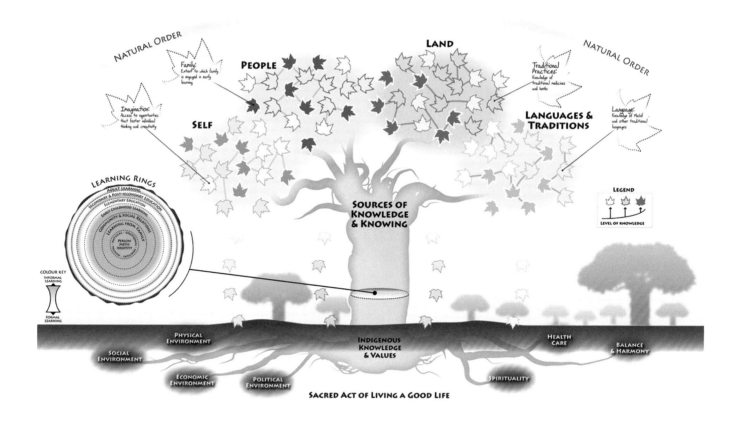

Figure 1-5 ▲

This Métis Holistic Lifelong Learning Model is another Aboriginal perspective on factors that influence an individual.

The Métis Holistic Lifelong Learning Model represents the link between Métis lifelong learning and community well-being, and can be used as a framework for measuring success in lifelong learning.

The Métis understand learning in the context of the "Sacred Act of Living a Good Life," a perspective that incorporates learning experienced in the physical world and acquired by "doing," and a distinct form of knowledge—sacred laws governing relationships within the community and the world at large—that comes from the Creator. To symbolize these forms of knowledge and their dynamic processes, the Métis Holistic Lifelong Learning Model uses a stylistic graphic of a living tree.

**—Source: Canadian Council on Learning,
"Redefining how success is measured in Aboriginal learning."
http://www.ccl-cca.ca/CCL/Reports/RedefiningSuccessInAboriginal
Learning/RedefiningSuccessModelsMétis.htm.**

How do these illustrations (Figures 1-3, 1-4, and 1-5) explain the relationship between identity and ideology?

Conceiving the Self

*Question for **Inquiry***

- **What is the relationship between ideology and my identity?**

◀ **Figure 1-6**

Huxley's *Brave New World* describes a dystopian future society.

In *Brave New World* (1932), English writer Aldous Huxley describes a futuristic society where the state controls human reproduction and uses selective breeding to produce five separate castes, or classes, of people. Each caste is genetically engineered to fulfill a specific range of roles in society. Not only are the individual members of the castes physically and intellectually matched to their prescribed roles in society; they are psychologically conditioned to accept and enjoy their roles. As the director of a laboratory for genetic engineering observes in the book, "that is the secret of happiness and virtue—liking what you've got to do. All conditioning aims at that: making people like their unescapable social destiny" (*Brave New World*, Chapter 1).

The characters in the book are aware that they have been engineered for their particular destinies. Lenina, of the Beta caste, and Henry, of the Alpha caste (the two highest classes), discuss what it might be like to be a member of the Epsilon caste (the lowest class):

"I suppose Epsilons don't really mind being Epsilons," she said aloud.

"Of course they don't. How can they? They don't know what it's like being anything else. We'd mind, of course. But then we've been differently conditioned. Besides, we start with a different heredity."

 PAUSE AND REFLECT

- **What are the similarities or differences between Huxley's fictional world and our world?**

- **Are we born into a way of life and a perspective on the world, or do we choose our future and our outlook? Do we experience anything like the conditioning in *Brave New World* that might lead us to embrace a particular ideology?**

"I'm glad I'm not an Epsilon," said Lenina, with conviction.

"And if you were an Epsilon," said Henry, "your conditioning would have made you no less thankful that you weren't a Beta or an Alpha."

**—Source: Aldous Huxley, *Brave New World*
(New York: Bantam Books, 1932), pp. 49–50.**

Who Are We?

Aldous Huxley was writing about a fictional future society, but can his fictional scenario also be taken as a metaphor for contemporary society? Do the immediate influences of family members, and the more general influence of the culture in which we live, provide us with a predetermined worldview?

There are some aspects of our identities over which we have no control: our cultural background, gender, and family. Nonetheless, an understanding of the influence these things have on our sense of self might allow us to have more control over the choices we make.

The Influence of Our Beliefs and Values

Over time, the events and experiences of living cause us to form and modify our beliefs and values. These new beliefs and values guide our behaviour and help us answer questions such as:

- What is important to me?
- What are human beings like? How should they act?
- Are my concerns restricted to my own self-interest, or do they extend to others as well?
- Should I also be concerned with the well-being of people I do not know?
- What sort of world do I want to live in? What effect can I have on my world, if any?

Every day we interact with a variety of other people, some of them similar to us and others very different from us. The individuals with whom you interact may have beliefs and values similar to your own, or they may have beliefs and values different from yours. If your beliefs are different, if they conflict in some way, what bearing will this have on the possible outcome of your interaction? How do you go about negotiating your differences?

As a set of principles that propose how society should work, an ideology may provide you with answers to some of the questions above. It can provide you with a framework of ideas about what role you should play as an individual in society, and what you can expect from society.

Discovering One's Beliefs and Values: What Lies Beneath?

People sometimes take for granted their beliefs about what human beings are like and what kind of world is desirable or possible. They may make a variety of assumptions about human behaviour and how people *should* live together. Not all of our assumptions are necessarily false; in fact, many of them may be true. The problem with assumptions is that they may not have been tested or examined, so we do not know if they are valid or not. In order to take an informed position on an issue, it is important to first uncover and evaluate one's personal assumptions.

Read one of the ethical statements provided and respond to it (*I agree with this statement because…*). Find another student in the class who holds a different position. Spend a few minutes together identifying and discussing the reasons for your respective positions.

Repeat this process three times with other students who have positions that are different from your own. Note the variety of positions and reasons for supporting them. You can use the guiding questions provided to analyze, organize, and evaluate the underlying assumptions of the positions. These questions will help you explore each position more deeply and allow you to consider each position from the level of some fundamental questions: *What are people like? What is the purpose of life? What kind of society do we want?*

Ethical Statements for Exploration and Response

Earth provides enough to satisfy every man's need, but not every man's greed.

**—Mahatma Gandhi (1869–1948),
Indian civil rights lawyer, activist,
and political and spiritual leader**

Figure 1-7

What assumptions are your beliefs and values based on?

Until and unless you discover that money is the root of all good, you ask for your own destruction. When money ceases to become the means by which men deal with one another, then men become the tools of other men. Blood, whips and guns—or dollars. Take your choice—there is no other.

**—Ayn Rand, *Atlas Shrugged* (1957)
(New York: Dutton, 1992), p. 415.**

If we go on the way we have, the fault is our greed [and] if we are not willing [to change], we will disappear from the face of the globe, to be replaced by the insect.

**—Jacques Cousteau (1910–1997),
French marine explorer and ecologist**

Questions to Guide You

1. What are the different points of view that you and others shared regarding the ethical statements about beliefs and values?
2. What reasons did each of you give for your point of view?
3. What are the factors that cause each of you to hold your respective point of view?
4. How do the reasons for your position reflect your beliefs about the nature of people, the purpose of life, and the nature of society?

Now that you have examined some of your assumptions and beliefs, and those of others, has your point of view changed?

Beliefs and Values Inventory: Where Do You Fit In?

This quiz outlines some of the fundamental beliefs relating to how people define a desirable society. Mark each sentence *often*, *sometimes*, or *rarely*, according to how you feel about it *most* of the time. Your teacher will provide you with a scoring guide.

When you have finished the quiz, work with a small group to come up with three more statements to add to the Beliefs and Values Inventory.

1. I feel that most things run better if planned by a team of people rather than by one person.
2. If you are not in it to win, then you are not in it.
3. Competition causes people to mistrust and fear one another. Co-operation is a much better way to achieve a goal.
4. People should take care of one another. We really are our fellows' keepers.
5. You are a product of all the people you have met.
6. I dislike teamwork. One person always slacks off, and my contribution should not have to make up for someone else's laziness.
7. The buck stops with me. I am responsible for my own actions at all times.
8. As a society, we would not be anywhere if everyone just did as they wanted.
9. My life is directed primarily by what I want to achieve for myself.
10. The most important thing in the world is to be yourself. Even if other people disapprove of your actions, being yourself is worth it in the end.
11. When people agree on something, they can move forward and accomplish anything.
12. What I earn I work hard for. My earnings belong to me. Why should my money go to other people?
13. At home, in school, and in life, it is important to know that rules are for the good of everyone and that we should obey them.
14. If I come across a regulation that is inconvenient to me, I speak up and say why the rule should be changed.
15. It bothers me that just a few people control so much wealth. No wonder there is so much crime. They should share it with others who do not have anything.
16. Working hard and getting somewhere in life is what it is all about.
17. We are only as strong as our weakest link.
18. I decide things for myself. Nobody has the right to make decisions for me.
19. A person's sense of fulfillment comes mainly from personal accomplishments.
20. True personal happiness is found in doing things for others.

Explore the Issues

Concept Review

1 What is identity?

2 What is an ideology?

3 What factors shape an identity?

4 What is the relationship between identity and ideology?

Concept Application

5 Select five statements from the Beliefs and Values Inventory with which you identify or which you feel characterize you best. Based on your five chosen statements, identify the beliefs and values underlying these statements. Work with a small group and compare your essential beliefs and values. Identify the beliefs or values that are shared by more than one member of the group.

- Are there identifiable reasons why some individuals may share the same beliefs and values?
- Are there identifiable reasons why some individuals may have differing beliefs and values?
- What tentative conclusions can you draw from these observations about the relationship between an individual's identity and his or her ideology?

Sources of Identity

Question for Inquiry

- **What factors influence individual and collective beliefs and values?**

It may be tempting to think that our belief system should be universal, that what we hold to be true is true not just for ourselves but for everyone. Many thinkers throughout history have constructed philosophical systems to argue that there *are* universal truths about the world and our place in it. There are also philosophical traditions that hold that there are no universal truths. The fact that there is disagreement over the existence of universal truths—and what those truths might be—means that people must negotiate to some extent with the beliefs and values of others.

What Can We Gain from an Awareness of the Sources of Our Beliefs and Values?

The importance of knowing *where* your beliefs and values come from may not be immediately obvious. The simple fact that you have identified *what your beliefs and values are* may seem sufficient to you to guide your interactions with others.

But considering the origins of our ideas may cause us to examine them further and develop a deeper understanding of them. Thinking about where certain ideas come from may also lead us to accept the validity of the beliefs of others, even if we do not necessarily agree with them.

In his book, *Long Walk to Freedom* (1995), Nelson Mandela wrote the following: "No one is born hating another person because of the colour of his skin, or his background, or his religion. People must learn to hate…"

- What does his statement suggest about the influence of ideology on the beliefs of individuals?

Shaping Identities

In this section you will look more closely at some of the factors, such as family, language, or media, that influence the formation of beliefs and values. As you consider these factors, think about the relative importance of each of them in your own life.

www.CartoonStock.com

Figure 1-8 ▲

How do your beliefs and values affect your interpretation of events in the news or in your own life? What is the cartoonist's perspective on this question?

File Facts

Nelson Mandela

- was born in 1918 in South Africa
- studied and worked as a lawyer
- became involved in the anti-apartheid African National Congress (ANC) after the election of the pro-segregation National Party in 1948
- became the leader of the armed wing of the ANC in 1961, and organized a sabotage campaign against government and military targets
- imprisoned from 1962 to 1990 for his activities
- awarded the 1993 Nobel Prize for Peace
- served as president of South Africa from 1994 to 1999
- was the first president of South Africa elected by **universal suffrage**

Family Influence

Families often have a strong influence on their children's identities. For most people, the earliest influence on their personal beliefs and values is their family.

Many sociologists point to the importance of the family in the formation of identity. According to Ernest W. Burgess, "Whatever its biological inheritance from its parents and other ancestors, the child receives also from them a heritage of attitudes, sentiments, and ideals…" In his book *Family, Socialisation and Interaction Process* (1955), Talcott Parsons argues that "it is because the human personality is not 'born' but must be 'made' through the socialisation process that in the first instance families are necessary. They are factories which produce human personalities."

- What do you think of Parsons's idea that families are "factories which produce human personalities"?

Possibly the most well-known family in North America is the animated Simpson family. Consider Parsons's idea that "families are factories that produce human personalities" as you read the following description of some of the Simpsons.

As for his family, Homer once offers thanks "for the occasional moments of peace and love our family's experienced…well, not today. You saw what happened. O, Lord, be honest! Are we the most pathetic family in the world or what?"

Bart (an anagram for "brat") is their ten-year-old son. Bart is the selfish but good-natured bad-boy, modeled in part on Eddie Haskell from Leave It to Beaver, *the kid that gets away with everything. When Homer prays before a meal, "Rub a dub, dub, thanks for the grub," Bart speaks the unspeakable: "Dear God, we paid for all this stuff ourselves, so thanks for nothing."*

Lisa is a good-hearted and gifted eight-year-old—often the show's conscience. She supports the poor, the powerless and the downtrodden; she is critical of the rich. She questions conventional wisdom, regardless of unpopularity. Asked to sing "The Star Spangled Banner" before a football game, she uses the occasion to announce, "Before I sing the National Anthem, I'd like to say that college football drains funds that are badly needed for education and the arts."

—Reverend John E. Gibbons, "Simpson Family Values"
(Unitarian minister, the First Parish in Bedford, Massachusetts),
excerpt from sermon, October 28, 2001.
http://www.uubedford.org/sermons/JEG-SimpsonsValues-10-28-01.htm

- After reading this quotation, you might conclude that Bart's lack of respect for religious values is in sharp contrast to Lisa's

PAUSE AND REFLECT

What factors do you think have had the most influence on your beliefs and values (for example, your family, gender, or religion)? Do you think any of these factors have led you toward a particular ideology?

respect for others and for social justice. How can you explain how two individuals from the same family would have such different points of view?

- What impact does an individual's family have on his or her beliefs and values? How much influence do you think your parents' ideas have had on your own beliefs and values? Is it possible to explain why two individuals from the same family are often so different?

Relating Gender to Beliefs and Values

The way people understand gender is affected by their experiences—personal, social, cultural—as well as their beliefs and values. How a society perceives gender, sometimes even legislating what is "appropriate" gender expression, can also affect people's view of gender and the freedom to express gender orientation.

Different cultures, for example, may assign specific gender roles to their members. These roles may be based on a variety of factors—economic and religious factors; ideas about family and child security; and traditions. The specific qualities or behaviours that make up a gender role vary from one society to another. They may include particular beliefs and values, such as appropriate public behaviour; which career choices are acceptable for a man or a woman; or what kind of behaviour is expected from a mother or father when raising a child. Gender and gender roles are powerful factors in determining a person's identity.

The quotes below deal with gender roles assigned in western society. Which quote, if any, seems to be most representative of your experience of gender?

Man is the hunter; woman is his game…
Man for the field and woman for the hearth:
Man for the sword and for the needle she:
Man with the head and woman with the heart:
Man to command and woman to obey…

—Alfred Tennyson (1809–1892),
English poet laureate, "The Princess," 1847

Woman is determined not by her hormones or by mysterious instincts, but by the manner in which her body and her relation to the world are modified through the action of others than herself. The abyss that separates the adolescent boy and girl has been deliberately widened between them since earliest childhood…

—Simone de Beauvoir (1908–1986),
French author and philosopher, *The Second Sex*,
[Le deuxième sexe] 1949

Modern invention has banished the spinning wheel, and the same law of progress makes the woman of today a different woman from her grandmother.

—Susan B. Anthony (1820–1906), women's rights activist,
***History of Woman Suffrage*, 1881**

Religion and Spirituality

For what shall it profit a man, if he shall gain the whole world, and lose his own soul?

—The Bible, Mark 8:36 King James Version

When I do good, I feel good; when I do bad, I feel bad. That's my religion.

—Abraham Lincoln (1809–1865), American president 1861–1865

What is the meaning of human life, or of organic life altogether? To answer this question at all implies a religion. Is there any sense then, you ask, in putting it? I answer, the man who regards his own life and that of his fellow creatures as meaningless is not merely unfortunate but almost disqualified for life.

—Albert Einstein (1879–1955), German-American physicist,
received the 1921 Nobel Prize for Physics.
***The World As I See It* (New York: Philosophical Library), 1949.**

In heaven, all the interesting people are missing.

—Friedrich Nietzsche (1844–1900), German philosopher

Say nothing of my religion. It is known to God and myself alone. Its evidence before the world is to be sought in my life: if it has been honest and dutiful to society the religion which has regulated it can not be a bad one.

—Thomas Jefferson (1743–1826),
American president (1801–1809)

A society without religion is like a vessel without a compass.

—Napoléon Bonaparte (1769–1821),
French military and political leader

Religious belief and spirituality take many forms. They are not the same thing, although they may be interconnected. Each plays a role in shaping a person's ideology. An individual may be a practising or non-practising member of a faith community, or adhere to a spiritual tradition without belonging to an organized community. Sometimes people consider themselves to be spiritual without following a defined system of religious belief.

The world's major religions and spiritual traditions share many ideals that teach peace and respect between individuals. Religious or

The Gender Gap?

According to some analysts, the November 2008 election of Barack Obama revealed a difference in the voting behaviour of men and women. This difference is referred to as "the gender gap." In other words, gender seems to be related to how one votes in an election. What factors may influence this gender gap? Do males and females differ in beliefs and values in a ways that could affect decision-making? .

Barack Obama has made a strong showing among women, exceeding the normal Democratic advantage, while fighting a virtually even battle among men, who went heavily Republican in 2004. Mr Obama won 56% of the female vote, compared with 51% of women who voted for John Kerry last time. And he was essentially tied among men, erasing the 55% to 45% advantage that President Bush enjoyed in 2004. Larry Sabato, political science professor at the University of Virginia, says that the Democrat's appeal to women has been one of the most important keys to his success.

> **—Source: BBC News Online, "Who Voted for Obama?" November 5, 2008.**
> http://news.bbc.co.uk/2/hi/americas/us_elections_2008/7709852.stm

In recent years, a great deal of attention has been focused on the gender gap in electoral behavior. The appearance of this gap has both intrigued and puzzled analysts. In seeking to explain it, researchers stumbled upon an even more interesting gender gap, a gap between men and women in policy preferences. Various explanations for the gap in policy preferences have been offered: men and women are socialized differently, or, feminist consciousness has altered opinions. Most such explanations share an underlying theme: the idea that, for whatever reason, women have different values and priorities than men. In effect, it is argued that there is a distinctive woman's perspective that shapes how women view politics.

> **—Source: Pamela Johnston Conover, "Feminists and the Gender Gap",**
> ***The Journal of Politics*, Vol. 50, No. 4 (November 1988): 1004.**

1 The sources suggest that women and men differ in their political attitudes and behaviours, and the second source offers several reasons for these different behaviours. Based on these sources and on your own experience, offer some possible reasons for gender's influence on beliefs and values or a person's decision-making. What other factors could account for gender differences in people's actions, such as actions based on political values?

2 In your experience, do the two sources accurately reflect gender differences?

"You got the job, the family and now the fancy car. But it's not enough, is it? No, my friend, it's never enough."

Figure 1-9

 **PAUSE AND REFLECT**

Do any of your beliefs or values originate in a religious or spiritual tradition? Do these beliefs and values influence how you think society should operate?

spiritual faith can give meaning to people's lives and provide them with a moral system that informs their actions as individuals. Religion or spirituality may also provide people with a set of shared traditions or a sense of community. Adherents to religious traditions may be inspired to express their belief systems through collective action. Organizations such as Habitat for Humanity or Sojourners are examples of groups that engage in collective action based on religious ideals. Nonetheless, armed conflicts can result because of intolerance between different religious groups or belief systems.

Aside from influencing some people's beliefs and values, religion can also inform particular ideologies. Christian Democracy, for example, incorporates many of the principles of Christianity into its political values. Islamism uses the tenets of Islam and Islamic law as the basis for a political system. Many other ideologies are secular, but support the idea of religious freedom in society. Still other ideologies, including some forms of Communism, are opposed to the practice of religion. Karl Marx famously called religion the "opiate of the masses," claiming that the spiritual comfort of religion prevented oppressed peoples from seeking political change.

Spirituality can be expressed outside of religious belief systems and can guide people's beliefs, values and worldview. Spirituality may be expressed individually or collectively and can incorporate many possible spiritual paths. These paths can be pursued and expressed in many ways, including meditation, self-reflection, prayer, shared spiritual traditions and stories, or a sense of purpose.

- To what extent do you think religion and spirituality can influence an individual's or a group's ideology?

Figure 1-10 ▶

Norman Rockwell's painting "The Golden Rule," 1961

◀ **Figure 1-11**

Guests representing 14 faiths join together at the Interfaith Celebration of Edmonton's Centennial at City Hall in Edmonton, Alberta, on Sunday, September 26, 2004.

Environment

Most scientists now agree that human activities are having a significant negative impact on the environment. News stories about global warming and other environmental concerns have become commonplace in the media. A British government study predicted the damage from unabated climate change will eventually cost between 5 per cent and 20 per cent of global gross domestic product each year. Rising sea levels, flooding, and drought may displace as many as 200 million people worldwide by 2050. North Americans produce almost a quarter of the world's greenhouse gases, which are a major cause of climate change.

Concern for the environment is not new. Many modern ecological movements have their origins in the social activism of the 1960s. Since then, organizations such as Greenpeace, founded in Vancouver, British Columbia, in 1971, have fought to raise public awareness about issues such as nuclear weapons testing, nuclear power, overfishing, deforestation, pollution, and, more recently, genetic engineering.

Increasing environmental awareness has had an enormous influence on the lives of many individuals. It has changed their daily habits, with practices such as reuse and recycling becoming more commonplace. It has influenced their behaviour as consumers. It has also influenced how some people vote.

As more and more people realize the importance of their relationship with the natural environment and the impact of their environmental footprint, calls for environmental stewardship are being heard by many national governments. Nonetheless, the December 2007 climate conference in Bali, where 190 countries attempted to agree on how to deal with environmental issues such as climate change,

TRAVEL AGENTS

ESPANA

www.CartoonStock.com

ANYWHERE WITH ICE...A LOT OF ICE

Figure 1-12 ▲

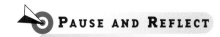

PAUSE AND REFLECT

What impact has environmentalist ideology had on you?

Perspective on Relationship to Land

As energy-producing companies have begun—with the support of local councils—to expand their plants onto prime land, some Canadian farmers have welcomed the move and have benefited greatly by selling their land to these industrial interests. Edmonton-area farmer Wayne Groot represents another perspective on the value of land. Below are two submissions made by Mr. Groot at provincial hearings held to discuss land use.

Farming is in my blood. Our family has been farming for centuries, in Holland and now for over eighty years in Canada. When I walk on a piece of land that I farm I feel a connection, with something that is alive and fruitful. There is a sacredness about it, perhaps similar in ways to the relationship that First Nations have with the creation. This land is certainly not something that I consider a commodity, to be sold to the highest bidder. And yet that is what we are being asked to do…Everything has a price, everyone can be bought. I can understand that in this complex world of ours some sacrifices have to be made for the greater good, but the sad part is that I can see very, very little of anything that contributes to the greater good in this rapid exploitation of our natural resources, or destruction of fertile soil.

Local food production is becoming a more and more important part of our society. We are starting to realize that the cost of transporting food many miles costs much more than the price we pay for it in the store…We are starting to realize that prime agricultural land is worthy of protection…One finds this to be true when one reads the new Land Use Framework that has just been released by the provincial government. I have a letter dated June 9, 2008 from Premier Stelmach indicating that securing Alberta's prime agricultural lands is a provincial priority. It is time we started acting on these priorities.

—Wayne Groot, submission to the Energy Resources Conservation Board, June 2008.

1. In what ways are Mr. Groot's values and beliefs about land similar to and different from some Aboriginal values and beliefs about land?

2. How might a spokesperson for the industrial interests respond to Mr. Groot's submissions? Compare Mr. Groot's values and beliefs with theirs. Why might these values and beliefs differ?

3. Visit the Energy Resources Conservation Board website to determine its beliefs and values regarding land.

demonstrated the great diversity of opinions that countries have about these important issues. These opinions are rooted in specific ideologies. While numerous countries were pushing for significant reductions to be made to greenhouse gas emissions, for example, others were resisting such initiatives. ("Stark Words at Bali Conference: Ban Ki-Moon Warns of Climate Change 'Oblivion'", *Spiegel Online*, December 12, 2007, http://www.spiegel.de/international/world/0,1518, 522929,00.html)

Environmentalism has also spawned the political ideology known as "Green politics". There are Green parties in numerous countries in Europe, Africa, Asia, and the Americas, including Canada. Although the specific policies of Green parties may differ from one country to another, the general principles of Green politics stress environmentalism, ecology, and sustainable economics. Many Green supporters see their ideology as an alternative to more traditional political ideologies such as socialism, conservatism, and **liberalism**, in that it approaches many political issues from an environmental perspective.

- What influence do you think Green politics has on the beliefs and values of individual Canadians?

Relationship to Land

The Great Land of the Inuit is the sea, the earth, the moon, the sun, the sky and stars. The land and the sea have no boundaries. It is not mine and it is not yours. The Supreme Being put it there and did not give it to us. We were put there to be part of it and share it with other beings, the birds, fish, animals and plants.

—**Source: Sam Metcalfe, quoted in *Report of the Royal Commission on Aboriginal Peoples*, Vol. 4, *Perspectives and Realities*, Chapter 3, "Elders' Perspectives", 1996.**
http://www.ainc-inac.gc.ca/ap/pubs/sg/cg/cj3-eng.pdf, p. 2.

The relationship you have to the land you inhabit is another factor that influences your beliefs and values. For example, if your livelihood is connected to land or natural resources, this might exert a strong influence on your identity: a farmer might have a different **worldview** than a journalist living in a city. Many people who live on the prairies rely on the land for their livelihood, as this region has a long tradition of farming and ranching. Small-town fairs and rodeos, or larger ones such as the Calgary Stampede, celebrate this tradition and demonstrate an economic and cultural connection to the land. How we connect to the land and our experiences with our environment determine some of the beliefs and values we hold that shape our identities.

Aboriginal peoples have a long relationship to the lands they inhabit. This relationship has social, cultural, spiritual, and economic aspects. It also involves a responsibility for the environment, as the quote from Sam Metcalfe illustrates. Because many traditional Aboriginal activities are dependent on land, many Aboriginal people have an understanding and respect for the environment and natural resources. Consider the following remarks by Narcisse Blood and Cynthia Chambers:

The notion of repatriation, which is commonly understood to mean the return of ceremonial objects, is offered as a model for authentic participation of Blackfoot in protecting and preserving these sites. Repatriation, as an idea and a practice, acknowledges the Siksikaitapiiksi (Blackfoot) view that places are animate, with whom humans live in relationship. Like any relationship based on interdependence, the one between people and the places that nourish them must be nurtured through unimpeded access, continued use and ceremonies of renewal such as visiting and exchanging of gifts.

It is easy to romanticize Niitsitapiiksi's (Real people, all indigenous peoples of North America) relationship to the land. Leroy Little Bear (Blood and Chambers 2006) points out that Blackfoot relationship to the land has almost become rhetoric. Such a simplistic formula as "Niitsitapiiksi equals ecological" infantilizes, and Disneyfies the vast knowledge Niitsitapiiksi hold collectively and individually about the land; such a stereotype reduces a complex cosmology to simplistic schemata, colour-coded medicine wheels mapping the four directions…

**—Source: Narcisse Blood and Cynthia Chambers,
"Love Thy Neighbour: Repatriating Precarious Blackfoot Sites",
International Journal of Canadian Studies, Issue 39, 2009.**

The importance of land in Aboriginal cultures becomes especially evident when the relationship is disrupted. Consider the impact that bituminous sands projects are having on local indigenous groups in northern Alberta:

Current tar-sands development has completely altered the Athabasca delta and watershed landscape. This has caused de-forestation of the boreal forests, open-pit mining, de-watering of water systems and watersheds, toxic contamination, disruption of habitat and biodiversity, and disruption of the indigenous Dene, Cree and Métis trap-line cultures.

"The river used to be blue. Now it's brown. Nobody can fish or drink from it. The air is bad. This has all happened so fast," says Elsie Fabian, 63, an elder in a Native Indian community along the Athabasca River…

The de-watering of rivers and streams to support the tar sands operations now poses a major threat to the cultural survival of these indigenous peoples. The battle over the tar sands mining comes down to the fundamental right to exist as indigenous peoples.

"If we don't have land and we don't have anywhere to carry out our traditional lifestyles, we lose who we are as a people. So, if there's no land, then it's equivalent in our estimation to genocide of a people," says George Poitras of the Mikisew Cree First Nation.

—**Source: Clayton Thomas-Müller,**
"Tar Sands: Environmental Justice and Native Rights."
Tar Sands Watch, March 25, 2008.
http://www.tarsandswatch.org/tar-sands-environmental-justice-and-native-rights

As treaties were signed between the Canadian government and Aboriginal peoples, some First Nations were forced to leave their traditional lands and relocate in unfamiliar territory. Oscar Kistabish (Osezima) of the Algonquin spoke about the impact of relocation before the Royal Commission on Aboriginal Peoples:

It is on this concept of territory that Aboriginal and non-Aboriginal people do not understand one another. Territory is a very important thing, it is the foundation of everything. Without territory, there is no autonomy, without territory, there is no home. The Reserve is not our home. I am territory. Language is territory. Belief is territory, it is where I come from. Territory can also vanish in an instant…

—**Source: Oscar Kistabish, Val d'Or, Québec, November 30, 1992,**
quoted in *Report of the Royal Commission on Aboriginal Peoples*, 1, 2,
Chapter 11, "Relocation of Aboriginal Communities,"
http://www.ainc-inac.gc.ca/ch/rcap/sg/sg41_e.html

What do these quotes tell you about the Aboriginal relationship to land and resources? What do these quotes tell you about the factors that help shape ideology?

Compare the Aboriginal relationship to the land with remarks made by Floyd Elgin Dominy, the commissioner of the United States Bureau of Reclamation from 1959 to 1969. The Bureau was responsible for developing irrigation in the arid Western states. Dominy stated, "I've seen all the wild [that is, undammed] rivers I ever want to see." He once described the then undammed Colorado River as "useless to anyone."

How do you think someone's views on natural resources might affect his or her ideological beliefs?

Language and Ideology

There is a powerful relationship between language and ideology. Language is one way in which people communicate beliefs and values, worldview, cultural and societal understandings, and sense of self.

Individuals who belong to the majority linguistic group in a society may not give much consideration to the role that language plays in the formation of their identity. When people are surrounded by other

 PAUSE AND REFLECT

How does your relationship to your natural environment inform your beliefs and values? How might your beliefs about people's responsibilities toward their natural environment change if your livelihood was connected to land or natural resources?

The Canadian Charter of Rights and Freedoms was enacted in 1982. Section 16.1 of the Charter, which reflects previous legislation recognizing Canada's two official languages, states:

16. *(1) English and French are the official languages of Canada and have equality of status and equal rights and privileges as to their use in all institutions of the Parliament and government of Canada.*

Do you think the inclusion of section 16.1 in the Charter has had an influence on the identity of Canadians? Explain.

PAUSE AND REFLECT

Francophones make up 2.2 per cent of Alberta's population. How would being a member of a linguistic minority affect an individual's identity?

people who speak the same language—and when their community is surrounded by advertising and other media using that same language—they may take their language for granted or not fully realize its influence on shaping their worldview.

How do you think belonging to a minority linguistic group might affect an individual's conception of language and its importance to identity? Belonging to a linguistic minority means living where a language other than one's own dominates the public space. Language in this situation may be more important to the formation of identity because it is not shared with everyone.

Minority language speakers may also struggle to overcome the forces of linguistic assimilation. For example, in Alberta, one of the stated purposes of Francophone schools is "to reverse assimilation" (Source: *Affirming Francophone Education—Foundations and Directions: a Framework for French First Language Education in Alberta* [Edmonton:Alberta Learning, 2001), http://education.alberta.ca/media/433070/cadreeng.pdf, pp. 17–18).

Spanish scholar Manuel Castells claims that "in a world submitted to culture homogenization by the ideology of modernization and the power of global media, language, the direct expression of culture, becomes the trench of cultural resistance, the last bastion of self-control, the refuge of identifiable meaning." A similar idea can be found in the Canadian Heritage report on *Aboriginal Languages in Canada*: "Preserving Aboriginal languages is an extremely high priority, because of the link between cultural preservation and language—without language, the main vehicle for transmitting cultural values and traditions no longer exists." As a vehicle of cultural transmission, the influence of language on an individual's identity is primal: "It is through language that a student self-realizes himself, as he expresses himself and makes connections with the world around him." (Source: *Cadre commun des résultats d'apprentissage en français langue première* [M-12], 1996, p. ix, translated in Council of Ministers of Education, Canada, *La Francisation: Pour un état des lieux*, Section 2.3 [Toronto: 2002], p. 3.) These beliefs about the importance of language and identity are also shared by Francophones in Canada and play a part in why Francophones have fought to have their official language rights under the Canadian Charter of Rights and Freedoms respected.

- If language can be a means of "cultural resistance", what impact might it have on an individual's choice of ideology?

Francophones have been in what is now known as Canada since the first European settlers arrived around 400 years ago. As members of one of the two official language groups in Canada, Francophones share a linguistic bond that expresses a unique perspective on the world. Both protected and promoted by the Canadian constitution, the French

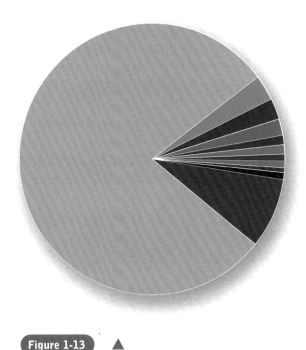

English – 2 576 670

Chinese – 97 275 (including Cantonese, Mandarin and other dialects)

German – 84 505

French – 61 225

Punjabi – 36 320

Tagalog – 29 740 (Philipino)

Ukrainian – 29 455

Spanish – 29 125

Polish – 21 990

Arabic – 20 495

Other languages – 269 555 (including Dutch (19 980), Vietnamese (19 350), Cree (17 215), Italian (13 095), Portuguese (7 205), Greek (3 305), Inuktitut (155), and multiple responses (34 930)

Figure 1-13 ▲

This pie chart shows Alberta's population according to mother tongue based on the 2006 census.

Source: Statistics Canada, "Population by mother tongue, by province and territory (2006 Census)" (Manitoba, Saskatchewan, Alberta, British Columbia) http://www40.statcan.ca/l01/cst01/demo11c.htm[10/21/2008

language is an integral part of a national identity. Efforts to protect the rights of Francophones date back as far as the Québec Act (1774) and more recently include the Official Languages Act (1969) and the Canadian Charter of Rights and Freedoms (1982).

Francophone heritage in Alberta dates to the arrival of French and Canadien explorers and fur traders in the 18th century. In the late 19th century, Alberta's Francophone population grew, mostly due to migration from Québec. In 2008, Francophones in Alberta numbered 65 990, or 2.2 per cent of the population, and the struggle to maintain their language and culture remains an important part of the values and beliefs of many Franco-Albertans.

On a quelque chose, mais on ne sait pas d'où ça vient. On ne sait pas quel prix a été payé, on ne sait pas que ça a duré 100 ans.

Translation: *We now have something (Francophone schools), but people don't know where they [the schools] come from. People don't know what price was paid, or that it took 100 years.*

—**France Levasseur-Ouimet, professor emeritus, University of Alberta, "Fort MacLeod: Une fête pour le cinéma francophone".**
http://www.radio-canada.ca/regions/alberta/2008/04/27/001-cinemagine_n.shtml

> **PAUSE AND REFLECT**
>
> - **In 2001, approximately 7.6 million Canadians, or 22.7 per cent of the population, were Francophone. One million of these people were living outside of Québec. In what ways would a shared language provide Canada's Francophones with a common source of identity?**
>
> - **How would the impact of language on identity differ for a member of an official language minority group, such as Francophones in Canada, and a member of another language minority group, such as a first-generation immigrant Canadian?**

The *Association canadienne-française de l'Alberta* (ACFA), founded in 1926, promotes, defends, and lobbies for the recognition of Francophone rights in Alberta. The ACFA and other community organizations also work to raise the profile of the Francophone community in the province and affirm the diversity of Francophone people.

- Could the desire to protect the rights of a language group be considered an aspect of an ideology?
- How do you think the struggle to uphold their language rights, as found in the Charter of Rights and Freedoms, has shaped identity among Alberta's Francophones?

Media, Beliefs, and Values

Figure 1-14

What influence do the media have on your perception of events?

As new forms of media emerged and spread in the 20th century, many thinkers turned their attention to the effects they might have on individuals and whole societies. Canadian theorist Marshall McLuhan claimed that the "medium is the message"—that the form of the communication was more important than the actual content. According to McLuhan, the predominance of print media prior to the 20th century had favoured the rise of individualism. He thought that the increasing dominance of electronic media would lead to the formation of a "global village"—a trend toward a collective identity shared by all consumers of the same media. McLuhan did not necessarily consider this to be a positive development: he felt that if people were unaware of the effects of electronic media, it could be used against them to establish a form of **totalitarian** control (a totalitarian state is one in which a powerful central government exercises strict control over all aspects of citizens' lives and does not allow political opposition). Some critics of McLuhan disagree with his dismissal of the role of content in media's influence on its audience.

Like McLuhan, many media theorists focus on the potential of media for the establishment of **hegemony**—the political control exerted by one group over others. Edward S. Herman and Noam Chomsky, for example, claim that the content of mainstream media sources reflects the commercial and political interests of the corporations that own them. In the words of Herman,

> *…the dominant media are firmly imbedded in the market system. They are profit-seeking businesses, owned by very wealthy people (or other companies); they are funded largely by advertisers who are also profit-seeking entities, and who want their ads to appear in a supportive selling environment. The media are also dependent on government and other major business firms as information sources, and both efficiency and political considerations, and frequently overlapping interests, cause a certain degree of solidarity to prevail among the government, major media, and other corporate businesses.*

> **—Source: Edward S. Herman,**
> **"The Propaganda Model Revisited."**
> ***Monthly Review* (July, 1996).**
> http://www.chomsky.info/onchomsky/199607--.htm

As a result of hegemony,

> *…producers of a media text design it with a certain meaning in mind. They hope that audiences will decode their text in a certain way—particularly if the text is an advertisement. Preferred readings are those which tie in with hegemonic beliefs—for instance, the idea of beauty and the "ideal" female shape propounded in Western magazines. It is accepted as "natural" that models in women's magazines should be young and drastically underweight. Since the 1960s the preferred reading has been*

PAUSE AND REFLECT

- In your opinion, to what extent do most media sources provide information in an unbiased manner?

- How much influence do you think the media have on people's opinions? Do you think people are fully conscious of the impact of media?

that these women are beautiful. However, there are signs that, as hegemonic belief begins to adapt to the concerns of many that this body shape is actually unhealthy, the preferred reading is beginning to shift...

—Source: Karina Wilson, MediaKnowAll, "Ideology."
www.mediaknowall.com/alevkeyconcepts/ideology.html

- Can you think of specific examples of the media's influence on the beliefs and values of you and your peers?
- Who owns the major sources of news? To what extent do you think the media are used to reinforce the values and ideologies of the most powerful members of society, or can media also provide opportunities to challenge these powerful interests?

Government Shaping Identity

Canada is made up of citizens from diverse cultural backgrounds. Visible minorities make up 13.4 per cent of the population. According to Communications Canada, 85 per cent of Canadians describe Canada as a "multicultural society." Various government policies recognize this perception, by seeking "the preservation and enhancement of the multicultural heritage of Canadians."

Multiculturalism is a manifestation of **pluralism**. A multicultural society comprises diverse cultural, religious, linguistic, or ethnic groups. In a political context, pluralism is a policy that actively promotes the acceptance of diversity in a society. Other manifestations of pluralism in Canadian society include official bilingualism, Charter rights prohibiting discrimination, and the constitutional guarantees of the First Nations, Inuit, and Métis peoples.

The recognition of pluralism has not always been government policy in Canada. Policies such as the head tax on Chinese immigrants and several amendments to the Immigration Act in the first half of the 20th century sought to control the ethnic makeup of Canadian society by excluding immigrants on the basis of ethnic background.

Government efforts to create a more inclusive society based on pluralism and the accommodation of diversity date back to the first Canadian Citizenship Act (1947) and include among other measures the Multiculturalism Policy (1971). The Multiculturalism Act of 1985 states that it is the policy of the Government of Canada to

...recognize and promote the understanding that multiculturalism reflects the cultural and racial diversity of Canadian society and acknowledges the freedom of all members of Canadian society to preserve, enhance and share their cultural heritage...

—Source: Canadian Multiculturalism Act R.S., 1985, c. 24 (4th Supp.).

PAUSE AND REFLECT

In 1965, during the inauguration of Canada's maple leaf national flag, the Honourable Maurice Bourget, Speaker of the Senate, declared, "The flag is the symbol of the nation's unity, for it, beyond any doubt, represents all the citizens of Canada without distinction of race, language, belief or opinion." To what extent do you think it is possible for a symbol such as our national flag to help create a collective identity and a unifying ideology for all Canadians?

- What are the benefits and challenges of a multicultural society? How do Canadians benefit from the diversity of our country's citizenry?
- How do you think the policy of multiculturalism, which is based on pluralism (valuing diversity), has affected Canadians?
- How does it help foster certain collective beliefs among Canadians?

Explore the Issues

Concept Review

1. a) What factors can influence the formation of personal and collective beliefs and values?

   b) For each of the factors, identify a specific example of the influence it has had on the beliefs and values of an individual or a group.

Concept Application

2. Make a list of no more than 10 beliefs or values that you consider to be the most fundamental aspects of your personal identity. Review the factors discussed in this section of the chapter and consider how they have influenced the 10 items on your list. Create a concept web showing the origins of the items on your list.

3. Consider the items on your list, and consider what kind of ideology each item reflects. Are they indicative of individualism, collectivism, or a middle ground between the two?

4. Explore the relationship between identity and ideology. Ask friends and family to talk about their beliefs and values. Encourage them to reflect on factors from this section of the chapter by asking them directed questions. How did they come to form the beliefs and values they hold? What influenced them the most? Do their beliefs and values reflect a conscious choice of ideology?

The Themes and Characteristics of Ideology

Question for Inquiry

• **What themes and characteristics should my ideology include?**

For her wedding to the love of her life, Calgarian Clare Stoeckle wore her mom's circa-1970s wedding dress, "raw, unbleached cotton with little embroidered daisies on it." She borrowed a pair of white leather flip-flop sandals and carried a bouquet of lilacs and daisies, freshly picked by her aunts and bridesmaids.

Her husband, Paul Kelly, rode his bike to the church—a 50-kilometre trip from Calgary to Okotoks—and their guests ate locally grown organic food, including a "cake" made from green tea and banana cupcakes…

…The theme of her bridal shower was "no plastic, no electric appliances," so friends gave no-nonsense gifts such as manual egg beaters and measuring cups.

Instead of a department store gift registry, the couple signed up with Sedmek, a Calgary company specializing in renewable energy systems.

"Now our laundry, hand washing and showers are all heated by the sun, which is wonderful," Kelly says.

Welcome to the world of eco-weddings, planned by and for people who care deeply about the environment.

—**Source: Shelley Boettcher, "Green Wedding: Calgary couples hitch their nuptials to the eco-movement."** *Calgary Herald* **2007.**

Material reprinted with the express permission of: "Calgary Herald Group Inc.", a CanWest Partnership. http://www.canada.com/topics/lifestyle/organicfoodguide/ story.html?id=4601fde8-65ee-4eb4-9170-dee513bde93e&k=3715

PAUSE AND REFLECT

- **How have Clare Stoeckle and Paul Kelly incorporated beliefs and values into their identities? What ideological stance have they adopted?**

- **What impact have their choices had on their social community?**

- **Can you think of specific beliefs and values that have had a direct impact on your identity? Do these beliefs and values reflect a particular ideology?**

As some of the examples in this chapter have illustrated, the beliefs and values that help make up an individual's identity can influence him or her to adopt an ideology that reflects those beliefs and values. Alternatively, an individual's beliefs and values may be part of an ideology that he or she is not even aware of having embraced.

If you embrace a particular ideology, it can have profound effects on your identity. It may influence your actions and choices. It may provide you with a particular perspective on the world. As a blueprint for a society, an ideology can affect groups as well as individuals. It may determine how members of a society relate to one another.

In this section, you will look at some themes and characteristics of a few different ideologies and examine how those aspects of ideology have influenced people's identities and actions.

The Characteristics of Ideology

All ideologies contain a set of beliefs and values about similar things. They are all concerned with the essential questions of life, such as

- What are humans like, and why do they act as they do?
- How should society be organized?
- How has the world worked in the past?
- How should it work in the future?

The answers an ideology provides to these questions form the characteristics of that ideology.

The Nature of Human Beings

Beliefs about human nature—about whether people are essentially good or bad, for example—are fundamental to any ideology. Do you usually trust people until they give you a reason not to, or do you generally approach people with caution? If you approach people openly, it is likely that you believe humans are essentially good. If you are cautious, you likely believe that they are not. This core belief will be part of the way you deal with the world.

For example, consider the following quotation from the Edicts of Ashoka, which were made by the Emperor of India from 273–232 BCE. Ashoka had converted to Buddhism and was determined to spread Buddhism across his empire.

People see only their good deeds saying, "I have done this good deed." But they do not see their evil deeds saying, "I have done this evil deed" or "This is called evil." But this [tendency] is difficult to see. One should think like this: "It is these things that lead to evil, to violence, to cruelty, anger, pride and jealousy. Let me not ruin myself with these things." And further, one should think: "This leads to happiness in this world and the next."

—Source: Ven. S. Dhammika [trans.],
"Seven Pillars Edicts." The Edicts of Ashoka.
www.cs.colostate.edu/~malaiya/ashoka.html

- How might such a view of human nature influence your choice of ideology?

The Structure of Society

Social structures are what bind us together as a society and help the society to function in an orderly fashion. The social structures of any society reflect the beliefs and values of that society.

Economics is an example of a structure of society. For example, there are both wealthy people and people living in poverty in Canadian society, but our provincial governments do have minimum wage laws, meaning that all businesses must pay a minimum amount of money to their workers. Through these means, these governments are trying to maintain the structure of what they perceive to be a fairer society.

There are also informal social structures. Informal social structures are the unwritten rules about acceptable social behaviour and actions. For example, some societies show more respect for people who are elderly and disadvantaged, or place more importance on gender equality, than others do.

Interpretations of History

Interpretations of history, or the past, are another characteristic of ideology, because the events of our pasts tend to influence the beliefs and values that we hold. An individual whose life has been difficult may have a pessimistic view of life and consider that life is a struggle against the odds. Other individuals may grow up believing that it is their duty in life to help people who are disadvantaged because they themselves have been privileged. Their views of the past affect their identities and the way they interpret the world.

Countries also have ideological interpretations of their histories that affect the identities of their citizens. This is sometimes manifested as demonstrations of patriotism, in which the citizens tell their stories to themselves and the world. Remembrance Day ceremonies are an example of such an event, as Canadians pay tribute to the men and women who made sacrifices to protect the liberal democratic traditions of Canada. These stories inform a nation's or a country's historical interpretations, which provide it with an ideology that guides its subsequent actions.

Visions of the Future

Graduating from high school is a sobering experience for many 17- and 18-year-olds. Students getting ready to graduate sometimes experience anxiety about what is in store for them in the future. You most likely have a good idea of what you want your future to look like. If your vision of the future is something like having a job you love, enough money for you to be comfortable, and a happy family, you need to think about the actions you need to take in order to achieve these goals.

The same is true for an ideology, which has a vision of what the world should be like in the future. This vision of the future will help guide the actions of people who embrace the ideology.

The Themes of Ideology

Typical themes of concern to ideologies include nation, class, race, environment and relationship to the land, gender, and religion, among others. Most ideologies talk about, or are concerned with, these themes. In some cases, it may seem as though one or two themes predominate in an ideology—for example, Marxists concentrate heavily on the theme of class, and capitalists emphasize the theme of freedom.

Progressivism is an umbrella term for various ideologies that advocate moderate political and social reform through government action, such as using anti-trust laws to prevent corporations from establishing monopolies in the marketplace. Progressive ideologies generally support social justice and the rights of workers.

The table below displays some of the more important themes of ideologies and examples of each of them.

Theme	Description	Example
nation	a community of people usually occupying a defined territory, often politically independent	The Kurds live in parts of Turkey, Iraq, and Iran and seek self-determination as a nation. Although they number 30 million, the Kurds of Turkey, Iraq, and Iran are not recognized as a nation-state. One aspect of their ideology is to seek self-determination as a nation.
class	a division of society, such as the *middle class*, usually defined by income, wealth, privilege, or role in society	Some ideologies which embrace collectivist values, such as communism, seek to eliminate class distinctions in society through income and wealth redistribution. Other ideologies see class as evidence of a fair distribution of society's resources based on people's talents and initiative.
race	a grouping of human beings distinguished according to biological traits such as skin colour	Some ideologies seek to eradicate racial discrimination; a few ideologies, such as Nazism, have asserted the superiority of one race over others and have sought to separate people along racial lines.
environment and relationship to land	the natural surroundings in which a person lives, and his or her connection to those surroundings	Green ideology espouses, among other things, the principle of *ecological wisdom*, or respect for ecology. Some thinkers believe that the landscape has an influence on how the people of that land see the world. For example, people living in a mountainous region might have a different worldview than those living in on an agricultural plain.
gender	the male or female sex considered as a sociological category	Feminist ideologies are concerned with attaining equal legal and political rights for women.
religion	the worship of one or more deities and acceptance of a particular set of values associated with that worship	Some ideologies, such as liberalism, promote freedom of religion. Other ideologies try to create a society based on the values of a particular religion.

Ideologies in Practice

Read the quotations that follow by three very different thinkers and use a retrieval chart to analyze their ideas. What kinds of themes are addressed in the three speeches? Can you find evidence of beliefs about human nature, beliefs about the structure of society, and visions for the future? Is there evidence of concerns about nation, class, environment, relationship to the land, gender, religion, and change? Which of these themes and characteristics of ideology do you consider most important? Why? Which thinker's ideas are closest to your own? How does this demonstrate the relationship between your personal beliefs and values and your ideology?

Tommy Douglas

Tommy Douglas said the following as he was speaking about his legacy to a New Democratic Party audience in Prince Albert, Saskatchewan, on November 27, 1970:

> *Sometimes people say to me, "Do you feel your life has been wasted? The New Democratic Party has not come to power in Ottawa." And I look back and think that a boy from a poor home on the wrong side of the tracks in Winnipeg was given the privilege of being part of a movement that has changed Canada. In my lifetime I have seen it change Canada.*
>
> *When you people sent me to the House of Commons in 1935, we had no universal old age pension. We have one now. It's not enough, but we have one. We had no unemployment insurance. We had no central Bank of Canada, publicly owned. We didn't have a wheat board, didn't have any crop insurance, didn't have a Canada Pension plan, didn't have any family allowances.*
>
> *Saskatchewan was told that it would never get hospital insurance. Yet Saskatchewan people were the first in Canada to establish this kind of insurance, and were followed by the rest of Canada. We didn't have Medicare in those days. They said you couldn't have Medicare—it would interfere with the "doctor-patient relationship". But you people in this province demonstrated to Canada that it was possible to have Medicare. Now every province in Canada either has it or is in the process of setting it up.*
>
> *And you people went on to demonstrate other things with your community health clinics. You paved the road, blazing a trail for another form of health service, to give people better care at lower cost. You did these things. You have demonstrated what people can do if they work together, rather than work against; if you build a cooperative society rather than a jungle society...*
>
> *Sure things have changed. Hair has gone down and skirts have gone up. But don't let this fool you. Behind the beards and the miniskirts, the long hair, this generation of young people, take it from me, is one of the finest generations of young people that have ever grown up in this country.*

Sure they're in rebellion against a lot of our standards and values and well they might be. They have got sick and tired of a manipulated society. They understand that a nation's greatness lies not in the quantities of its goods but in the quality of its life. This is a generation of young people who are in revolt against the materialism of our society. They may go to extremes at times but this is a generation with more social concern, with a better understanding of the need for love and involvement and cooperation than certainly any generation I have seen in my lifetime...

We ought to expand our economy. There ought not to be one idle able-bodied person in Canada. We need a million new homes in Canada. We need schools. We need recreation centres. We need nursing homes, housing projects, particularly for old people and for people on low incomes. We've got pollution in this country that needs to be cleaned up before we strangle ourselves in our own filth. We need a reforestation program. Many things need to be done. We could put every able-bodied person in this country to work, not just making holes and filling them up but doing useful work. That's the first thing we ought to do.

The second thing we ought to do is to recognize that we haven't had inflation in Canada. What we have had is maladministration of income. What do I mean by that? Well, what is inflation? According to the economic text books, inflation is too much money chasing too few goods. Do you think there is too much money chasing too few goods? Where has this too much money been? Any around here? Do you think the old age pensioners get too much money? Or the unemployed? Or the farmers? Or the fishermen? The Economic Council of Canada says that there are five million Canadians who live below the poverty line. Do you think they've got too much money? That's a quarter of our population, living in poverty.

What about this too few goods? How many supermarkets have you seen close at two o'clock in the afternoon because they haven't got any more goods to sell? We're not short of goods. What we have is inequitable and unfair distribution of income. Raising the old age pension would put money into the pockets of people who spend it. Unemployment insurance of $100 a week would be spent and the economy would begin to move again.

The other thing we could do to redistribute income is to bring in tax reforms. The Carter Commission said that too large a share of the taxes falls on people with incomes of under $10 000 a year. The commission said that if we made the banks, the insurance companies, the mining companies, the gas companies, and those who live off capital gains pay taxes the same as the rest of us do, we would lower the income tax by 15 per cent for everybody with incomes under $10 000 a year and the government would still have $600 million a year more coming in than is coming in at the present time...

—Tommy Douglas, "On His Legacy: to a NDP audience in Prince Albert, Saskatchewan—November 27, 1970." Tommy Douglas Research Institute.

http://www.tommydouglas.ca/speeches/legacy-1970

File Facts)

Milton Friedman

- lived from 1912 to 2006
- won the 1976 Nobel Prize in Economics
- was a prominent member of the Chicago School of Economics
- was a highly influential advocate of free-market economics
- was the economic advisor to former American president Ronald Reagan; his ideas also influenced former British prime minister Margaret Thatcher, former Canadian prime minister Brian Mulroney, and former Chilean dictator Augusto Pinochet

Milton Friedman

This is an excerpt from Milton Friedman's speech "Economic Freedom, Human Freedom, Political Freedom," which he delivered on November 1, 1991:

A free private market is a mechanism for enabling a complex structure of cooperation to arise as an unintended consequence of Adam Smith's invisible hand, without any deliberate design. A free private market involves the absence of coercion. People deal with one another voluntarily, not because somebody tells them to or forces them to. It does not follow that the people who engage in these deals like one another, or know one another, or have any interest in one another. They may hate one another. Everyone of us, everyday without recognizing it, engages in deals with people all over the world whom we do not know and who do not know us. No super planning agency is telling them to produce something for us. They may be of a different religion, a different color, a different race. The farmer who grows wheat is not interested in whether it is going to be bought by somebody who is black or white, somebody who is Catholic or Protestant; and the person who buys the wheat is not concerned about whether the person who grew it was white or black, Catholic or Protestant. So the essence of a free private market is that it is a situation in which everybody deals with one another because he or she believes he or she will be better off.

The essence of human freedom as of a free private market, is freedom of people to make their own decisions so long as they do not prevent anybody else from doing the same thing. That makes clear, l think, why free private markets are so closely related to human freedom. It is the only mechanism that permits a complex interrelated society to be organized from the bottom up rather than the top down. However, it also makes clear why free societies are so rare. Free societies restrain power. They make it very hard for bad people to do harm, but they also make it very hard for good people to do good. Implicitly or explicitly, most opponents of freedom believe that they know what is good for other people better than other people know for themselves, and they want the power to make people do what is really good for them…

If you consider medical care, which is another major problem now, total spending on medical care has gone from 4% of the national income to 13%, and more than half of that increase has been in the form of government spending. Costs have multiplied and it is reasonably clear that output has not gone up in anything like the same ratio. Our automobile industry can produce all the cars anybody wants to drive and is prepared to pay for. They do not seem to have any difficulty, but our government cannot produce the roads for us to drive on. The aviation industry can produce the planes, the airlines can get the pilots, but the government somehow cannot provide the landing strips and the air traffic controllers. I challenge anybody to name a major problem in the United States that does not derive from excessive government...

The important point is that we in our private lives and they in their governmental lives are all moved by the same incentive: to promote our own self interest. Armen Alchian once made a very important comment. He said, "You know, there is one thing you can trust everybody to do. You can trust everybody to put his interest above yours." That goes for those of us in the private sector; that goes for people in the government sector. The difference between the two is not in the people; it is not in the incentives. It is in what it is in the self interest for different people to do. In the private economy, so long as we keep a free private market, one party to a deal can only benefit if the other party also benefits. There is no way in which you can satisfy your needs at the expense of somebody else. In the government market, there is another recourse. If you start a program that is a failure and you are in the private market, the only way you can keep it going is by digging into your own pocket. That is your bottom line. However, if you are in the government, you have another recourse. With perfectly good intentions and good will nobody likes to say "I was wrong" you can say, "Oh, the only reason it is a failure is because we haven't done enough. The only reason the drug program is a failure is because we haven't spent enough money on it." And it does not have to be your own money. You have a very different bottom line. If you are persuasive enough, or if you have enough control over power, you can increase spending on your program at the expense of the taxpayer. That is why a private project that is a failure is closed down while a government project that is a failure is expanded.

—**Milton Friedman, quoted in Micheline Ishay, The Human Rights Reader (New York: Routledge, 2007), pp. 343–346. Used with permission of: The Smith Center for Private Enterprise Studies College of Business and Economics California State University, East Bay** http://thesmithcenter.org

Ovide Mercredi

This is an excerpt from a speech Ovide Mercredi made at the Federation of Saskatchewan Indian Nations' All Chiefs Legislative Assembly in 1992.

It is not easy for me to put a human face to the AFN [Assembly of First Nations]. I am a very private person. I am also a very quiet individual and most of all I am a very serious man.

Part of our job is to make ourselves stronger, to make each other stronger. And I've wondered how we do that myself. I am coming slowly to the realization that you do not become strong by politics.

Power politics in the community, in our organizations, do not heal our people but they create more problems that divide our

File Facts

Ovide Mercredi

- was born in 1946
- became a lawyer specializing in constitutional law
- was the regional chief of the Assembly of First Nations for Manitoba, 1989
- was the national chief of the Assembly of First Nations, 1991–1997
- is the chief of Misipawistik Cree Nation
- is the chancellor of University College of the North, 2007– present
- advocates for non-violent methods for change

people. So we have to do more than just become politicians as leaders. We have to, I think, try to escape the Indian Act and we have to try to operate with the traditions and the values of our society.

The principle of respect, and if you consider it, kindness, a very simple principle, goes a long way to healing people. In our communities, when we grew up, we were taught at least those two basic principles from the time we were crawling until to the time we left home—respect and kindness.

So the challenge for us is not so much the Constitution. The challenge is how we heal ourselves. The challenge is how much faith we have in our own way of doing things and how willing are we to sacrifice our individual advancement for the sake of the community.

You see I am an optimist. I have full confidence in my people. I know we are in pain. I know we are suffering. I know we have problems, social problems. But I also believe that we have the knowledge, we have the talent and we have the strength to change life for the better.

The strongest members of our society are Indian women. Our men, many of our men have fallen and they have fallen because they have lost confidence in themselves. They have fallen because they have given up because there are no opportunities for them and they feel inadequate because they cannot meet the social and economic requirements of their families. But the women have maintained the hope. They have maintained the prospects for a better future and our men are beginning to heal.

That's why I say that I am an optimist about our future because I know that when we come together as men and women, as Elders and children, for the collective good of our people and the advancement of our communities and our societies, not only will we benefit, but Canada as a whole will benefit.

—Ovide Mercredi, quoted in *Saskatchewan Indian*, 21, 3 (May, 1992), p. 7.

Government Responses to Crises—
Evidence of Ideology

Something to Think About: Many people believe that one of the key jobs of governments is to support and care for their citizens. We assume that governments will respond when citizens are in danger or when a natural disaster strikes. How do the actions of a country's leaders in a time of crisis reflect the beliefs and values that underlie their ideology?

An Example: The world was shocked to witness a devastating cyclone smash into an ill-prepared land, and see its government doing nothing. On May 3, 2008, Cyclone Nargis hit the southern delta regions of Myanmar, killing thousands, destroying homes, cutting off electricity, destroying food supplies, and contaminating major agricultural fields with salt water and sewage. One month after the storm, an estimated 100 000 people were dead, 56 000 were missing, and 2.4 million were displaced. In the face of this catastrophe the government of Myanmar reacted by trying to shut out the world, restricting reporters, refusing aid from neighbouring countries, and refusing to issue visas to disaster experts from agencies such as the Red Cross and Médecins Sans Frontières. However, rather than facilitating relief efforts itself, the government put its resources into holding a national referendum on a new constitution.

Many countries immediately offered assistance. Relief teams and aid materials were waiting to be deployed from Thailand, Singapore, Italy, France, Sweden, Britain, South Korea, Australia, Israel, the United States, Poland, Japan, and other countries. The United States had four ships in the area and offered to use helicopters and marines to get food and water to inaccessible areas. Yet only agencies that were in the country before the cyclone were allowed to do what they could to help the situation. No foreign personnel were allowed into the country by the government, which was especially determined to keep foreign military personnel out of the country. Many people died waiting for aid.

Eventually, terrific pressure was put on the government by neighbouring countries and by the United Nations. Myanmar reluctantly agreed to allow food, medicine, and supplies into the country but only if it was distributed by government forces and under government management. Soon stories began to circulate that some areas of the country, those friendly to the government, were receiving supplies, while other areas went without. Other stories surfaced about packages from relief agencies being re-addressed to military generals. The government, according to these stories, was using aid selectively, to reward loyal citizens and punish others. Three weeks after the cyclone struck, very little aid had reached the people who needed it.

File Facts)))

Myanmar (formerly known as Burma)

- In 1948, Burma (formerly a colony of Britain) became independent and almost immediately began to disintegrate as ethnic groups, communists, and Muslims all competed for power.

- In 1962, a left-wing army revolt led by General Ne Win deposed the troubled democratic government and set the country on the path of socialism. Over the next 25 years, the Burmese economy crumbled.

- In 1988, clashes between pro-democracy demonstrators and the military resulted in 3000 deaths in a six-week period.

- In 1989, the government placed Aung San Suu Kyi, the popular pro-democracy opposition leader, under house arrest. Despite her imprisonment, her party scored an overwhelming victory in a 1990 election. The military government did not accept the election results.

- The military regime has brutally suppressed ethnic groups wanting rights and autonomy, and many ethnic insurgencies operate against it. Successive military governments have been accused of corruption, heroin trafficking, and **human rights** violations—including forcible relocation of civilians and use of forced labour. The head of state in 2008 is Senior General Than Shwe.

- Myanmar is the world's second-largest producer of illicit opium, after Afghanistan.

News Stories About the Situation

After several days of praising the work of the United Nations and charities, the regime's official newspaper renewed its attacks on foreign aid and insisted Myanmar could survive without outside help. "The government and the people are like parents and children," the paper said. "We, all the people, were pleased with the efforts of the government."

The paper said that granting free access for aid workers in the delta means donors "are to be given permission to inspect all the houses thoroughly at will."

Myanmar needs 11 billion dollars to recover from the storm, but donors have pledged just 150 million dollars so far, it said.

"Myanmar people are capable enough of rising from such natural disasters even if they are not provided with international assistance," the newspaper said. "Myanmar people can easily get fish for dishes by just fishing in the fields and ditches," the paper said. "In the early monsoon, large edible frogs are abundant." "The people (of the Irrawaddy delta) can survive with self-reliant efforts even if they are not given chocolate bars from (the) international community," it added...

—Source: Sukhpal Singh, "Myanmar condemns foreign aids for linking aid money to have full access in the region." MindTalks.org, May 30, 2008.

http://www.mindtalks.org/misc/myanmar-condemns-foreign-aids-for-linking-aid-money-to-have-full-access-in-the-region.html

On Saturday, [US Defense Secretary Robert] Gates accused Myanmar's military, which has ruled the isolated nation for 46 years, of being "deaf and dumb" to pleas to allow in more foreign aid and relief workers.

Than Shwe's pledge a week ago to allow in "all" legitimate foreign aid workers has yielded more visas for UN relief experts, but red tape is still hampering access to the delta.

Gates contrasted the generals' refusal to accept aid from the US military after Cyclone Nargis struck four weeks ago with the willingness of Indonesia and Bangladesh to accept assistance after natural disasters in recent years.

"With Burma, the situation has been very different—at a cost of tens of thousands of lives," Gates said.

The United States is expected to decide in a few days whether to withdraw its aid-laden ships from waters near Myanmar.

Singapore, one of the biggest foreign investors in the former Burma, said the generals feared giving greater access to foreign aid agencies would show that the regime was incapable of handling the disaster.

However, Myint reiterated that his government was open to all aid provided that it is not politicised.

"In carrying out the relief, resettlement and rehabilitation tasks, we will warmly welcome any assistance and aid which are provided with genuine goodwill from any country or organisation provided there are no strings attached," he said.

—Source: C. Moore (Reuters), "A month after Nargis, junta still under fire." France 24, June 3, 2008.
http://www.france24.com/en/20080603-burma-myanmar-nargis-cyclone-junta-aid

The number of people killed in the storm may never be known. The government has not updated its toll since May 16, when it said 77 738 people were killed and 55 917 were missing.

In a country that has not had a full census in decades, it is not even certain how many people had been living in the area before the storm. Itinerants who worked in the salt marshes and shrimp farms were probably not counted among the dead, aid workers say. But it is clear that in many villages, women and children died in disproportionate numbers, said Osamu Kunii, chief of the health and nutrition section of Unicef in Myanmar.

"Only people who could endure the tidal surge and high winds could survive," Mr. Kunii said. In one village of 700, all children under the age of 7 died, he said.

With only minimal food supplies in villages, aid workers say, delta residents will require aid until at least the end of the year. The United Nations, after weeks of haggling with Myanmar's government for permission to provide assistance, is now using 10 helicopters to deliver supplies to hard-to-reach places and alerting relief experts at the earliest sign of disease outbreaks...

—Source: "Burmese Endure in Spite of Junta, Aid Workers Say." From The New York Times, June 18, 2008 © 2008 The New York Times.

1. Use the Skill Path: Discovering One's Beliefs and Values to answer the following questions: **SKILLS**
   a) How does the information in this Investigation make you feel about the actions of the government of Myanmar? What values and beliefs do you hold that cause you to feel that way?
   b) How would you describe the beliefs and values of the members of the military junta controlling the country? What about the beliefs and values of the foreign countries and organizations who tried to provide aid during the crisis?

2. What are possible reasons the leaders of Myanmar could give to explain their actions in response to Cyclone Nargis?

3. To what extent do countries who disagree with Myanmar's government have a responsibility to help the people of that country?

4. To what extent do individuals like you have a responsibility to help the people affected by Cyclone Nargis or other natural or human-made disasters?

5. One definition of ideology might be, "a system of ideas about how the world is and how it ought to be." Based on your answers to questions 1, 3, and 4, describe your ideology.

Explore the Issues

Concept Review

1. a) Identify the four common characteristics of ideologies.
   b) Identify at least four of the themes of ideologies.
   c) For each of the three speech excerpts in this section, identify what you believe to be the speaker's most important theme.

2. What circumstances would cause an ideology to emphasize one theme of ideology over another?

3. Which of the themes of ideology is most important to you? What beliefs and values account for your selecting this particular theme?

Concept Application

4. In the context of recent historical events, do you think that some ideologies carry some of the themes of ideology to an extreme? Provide evidence for your answer.

Reflect and Analyze

In this chapter you were presented with many perspectives on ideology and identity. You looked at different understandings of identity, and how ideology can influence identity. You considered the factors that influence beliefs and values, such as family, gender, and language. You also explored the characteristics of ideology, such as interpretations of history and visions of the future, and themes of ideology such as nation, class, and race. You can now respond to the Chapter Issue: *To what extent are ideology and identity interrelated?*

Respond to Issues

1 Identify one factor that influences identity. Write a research paper, create a PowerPoint presentation, design a web page, or create some other form of digital product on a historical situation in which that factor had a direct impact on the collective identity of a social group. Consider multiple perspectives on the situation in your response.

Recognize Relationships among Concepts, Issues, and Citizenship

2 Select a medium such as a newspaper or news magazine, a television or radio news program, or an online news source. Examine the news stories presented in this medium and collect data that will show you the extent to which people follow an ideology. You will need to follow this medium for several consecutive days. As you examine this medium, attempt to identify the beliefs and values of the people in the news stories as well as those constructing the story. Include how the themes and the characteristics of an ideology are present along with how these reflect the connections between the people's identities and their ideologies.

Once you have completed gathering the data and have identified the beliefs and values, characteristics, and themes of an ideology, and the connections between identity and ideology, compose a response that demonstrates what you would do to promote or challenge the ideology you have discovered in your inquiry. How is this promotion or challenge an important part of being a citizen in a democratic society?

3 Reread the story of The Compact at the beginning of the chapter. Using the points below to guide you, write a letter to a member of a community group to convince him or her to think about forming a group like The Compact. In your letter, do the following:

* Reflect on the various factors that may have influenced your identity: for example, family, culture, language, media, environment, relationship to the land, gender, and religion and spirituality.
* Consider your answers to the Beliefs and Values Inventory quiz that you took earlier in the chapter. To what extent do your answers reflect aspects of individualism, collectivism, or both?
* Think about the fundamental questions that people have tried to answer: What is the purpose of life? What are people like? What kind of society do we want?

Ideologies of Individualism and Collectivism

Chapter

2

KEY SKILL

Developing, expressing and defending an informed position on an issue

KEY CONCEPTS

Exploring themes of ideologies

Analyzing individualism and collectivism

Evaluating the extent to which personal identity should be shaped by ideologies

Imagine you take a long car trip, and during the trip you observe the bumper stickers on the opposite page. What message is each bumper sticker trying to convey? Is there a sticker you would like to put on a car, or one you would oppose putting on a car? Why? What does each of the bumper stickers suggest about the individuals who chose them and the society in which these individuals want to live?

In previous chapters, you were introduced to the concepts of **individualism** and **collectivism**. When we examine ideologies, we can see that each of them is based on either individualism or collectivism, or a mixture of the two.

Chapter Issue

We cannot escape the fact that, as human beings, we are both individuals and part of a collective. In this chapter you will explore several understandings of individualism and collectivism. Individualist ideologies tend to advocate individual rights, and freedom from government and from collective controls and restrictions. They promote principles such as autonomy, self-interest, personal achievement, and self-reliance. Collectivist ideologies endorse the idea of working co-operatively to solve problems and manage economic and social issues. They hold that collective enterprises, unions, and teamwork can accomplish more than individuals and competition can. They stress social harmony and cohesion over competitiveness. Collectivist ideologies see a positive role for government assistance and control in regard to the economy and social issues, whereas individualist ideologies usually see government as interfering and counterproductive.

You will explore the interaction of individualism and collectivism in society by considering how these two tendencies underlie different ideologies to varying degrees. Can they be reconciled? Are they opposed to each other, or do they complement each other? You will examine the impact of these dynamically linked tendencies on society as well as their influence on personal identity as you deliberate the Chapter Issue: *To what extent are individualism and collectivism foundations of ideology?*

PAUSE AND REFLECT

Compare the bumper stickers on the opposite page. Bumper stickers can express individualist and collectivist perspectives.

Key Terms

Adherence to collective norms
Collective interest
Collective responsibility
Collectivism
Common good
Competition
Co-operation
Economic equality
Economic freedom
Individualism
Individual rights and freedoms
Liberalism
Private property
Public property
Rule of law
Self-interest

Figure 2-1

Chapter Issue:
To what extent are individualism and collectivism foundations of ideology?

Question for Inquiry #1:
What are individualism and collectivism?

Question for Inquiry #2:
In what ways are individualism and collectivism foundations of ideology?

Question for Inquiry #3:
How are individualism and collectivism expressed today?

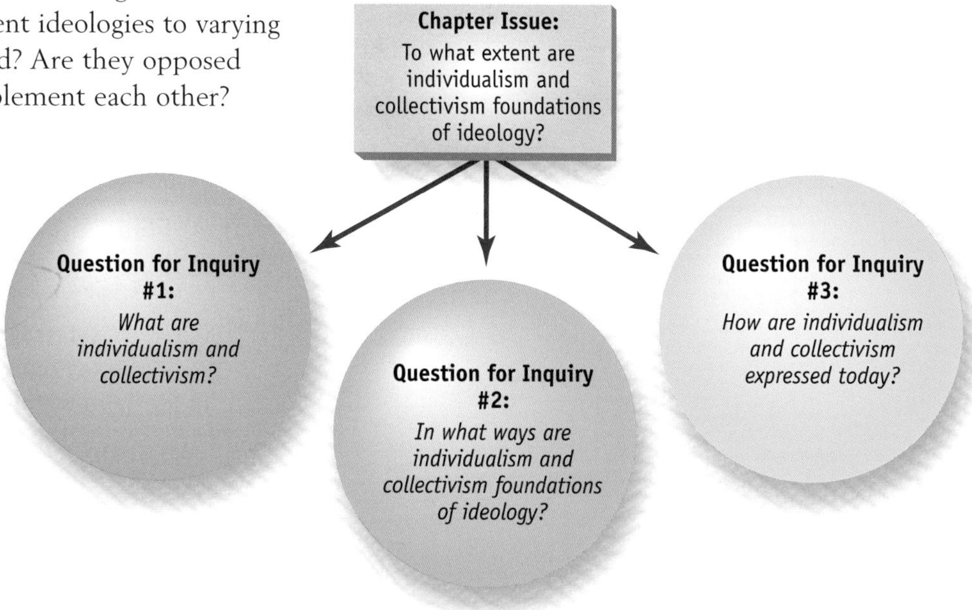

Understanding Individualism and Collectivism

Question for **Inquiry**

• **What are individualism and collectivism?**

One of the dominant characteristics of modern culture is individualism. This individualism prevails not only in the United States but elsewhere, including Korea. In view of such a long human history, it is not easy to define individualism because as a phenomenon it is complex and varied. According to Elwood Johnson, individualism can be defined as "any mode of thought based on the faith that any person may become in himself a prime cause; he may in fact, act his way out of his own history." Similarly, Emil Brunner sees individualism as a "Robinson Crusoe affair" in which the individual is solely important considering his own personality. In this view, society is a coalescence of individuals.

—Yung Suk Kim (theology professor at Virginia Union University), *The Roots of Individualism*.
http://www.youaregood.com/rootsofindividualism.pdf

…it is glaringly apparent that mankind finds itself at present in grave danger. I see the nature of the current crises in the juxtaposition of the individual to society. The individual feels more than ever dependent on society, but he feels this dependence not in the positive sense—cradled, connected as part of an organic. He sees it as a threat to his natural rights and even his economic existence…that which drives his ego is encouraged and developed, and that which would drive him toward other men (a weak impulse to begin with) is left to atrophy.

It is my belief that there is only one way to eliminate these evils, namely, the establishment of a planned economy coupled with an education geared towards social goals. Alongside the development of individual abilities, the education of the individual aspires to revive an ideal that is geared towards the service of our fellow man, and that needs to take the place of the glorification of power and outer success.

—Albert Einstein, "An Ideal of Service to Our Fellow Man," from *This I Believe* (essay collection). David Domine [trans.]. Essay courtesy of the Albert Einstein Archives at the Hebrew University of Jerusalem. This I Believe,
http://www.npr.org/templates/story/story.php?storyId=4670423, May 31, 2005.1954, AEA 28-1067.

More and more, when faced with the world of men, the only reaction is one of individualism. Man alone is an end unto himself. Everything one tries to do for the common good ends in failure.

—Albert Camus, French novelist, essayist, playwright, and winner of the 1957 Nobel Prize for Literature, *Notebooks, 1935–1942*

PAUSE AND REFLECT

Compare the three views of modern society expressed in these quotations. Do you think any of them is an accurate description of Canadian society? Would you prefer to see more or less individualism in our society?

Political philosophy investigates the nature of human communities in order to evaluate their aims and modes of co-operation. One of the key questions of political philosophy is: *What is the relationship between the individual and society?*

In Chapter 1, you read that an ideology can provide you with a framework of ideas about what role you should play as an individual in society and what you can expect from society in return.

There are many different ideologies based on some degree of individualism, and they do not all agree on the best means of organizing society. Nonetheless, most individualistic ideologies have a similar understanding of the individual's place in society and stress the importance of ideas such as personal **autonomy**—a state of individual freedom from outside authority—and **self-reliance**—the quality of being solely responsible for one's own well-being.

Like individualism, collectivism is not a single ideology: many different ideologies are based on collectivist ideas, and these various ideologies may differ in their methods and ultimate goals. All of them, however, stress human interdependence and the importance of a collective, regardless of size, rather than the importance of the individual. The focus of collectivists is the community and society, although families can also exemplify collectivist principles by encouraging members to be responsible for one another rather than simply looking out for themselves. Collectivism emphasizes group goals and the **common good** over individual goals or individual gain.

Early Understandings of Individualism and Collectivism

Some of the principles of individualism have roots in ancient history. For example, Urukagina, the ruler of Lagash in Mesopotamia in the 24th century BCE is thought to have been the first to create property laws: he said that no one could seize another's property. The concept of self-interest was discussed in the 4th century BCE by the Greek philosopher Aristotle in his *Politics*: "That which is common to the greatest number has the least care bestowed upon it. Every one thinks chiefly of his own, hardly at all of the common interest; and only when he is himself concerned as an individual." Other principles of individualism, such as individual rights and freedoms, have become widely accepted only more recently in history.

Examples of collectivism can also be found in ancient cultures. Anthropological studies tell us that most, if not all, the earliest human societies were collectivist, because it was possible to survive only by working and hunting as part of a group. The sense of identity of ancient societies was largely based on membership in a group—usually an extended family.

Collectivism was also practised 2000 years ago by early Christians, as mentioned in the New Testament of the Bible. For example, Acts 2:44–45 states, "And all those who had believed were together, and had all things in common; and they began selling their property and possessions, and were sharing them with all, as anyone might have need." Compare the last part of this sentence with the collectivist maxim popularized by Karl Marx: "From each according to his abilities, to each according to his needs."

Even today, some religious communities embrace collectivist values such as the collective ownership of property. The Hutterites are a Christian community in North America with 45 000 members in approximately 460 colonies, mostly in Western Canada. Hutterite colonies practise a "community of goods" based on an interpretation of the Bible. The members of a colony work together, and all money earned belongs to the colony as a collective. All goods are owned by the colony, rather than by any one individual, including land, houses, and vehicles. When an individual member needs an item, they ask the colony, and the item is bought for them. Members are discouraged from earning personal spending money.

An Aboriginal Understanding of Collectivism

Indigenous peoples such as the Aboriginal peoples in Canada describe their traditional cultures as having a strong sense of the collective. In matters such as land-holding, decision making, and educating and raising children, many Aboriginal cultures emphasize thinking and acting collectively to achieve what is best for the common good. Many of these collectivist traditions are still practised in some Aboriginal communities.

Inuit Elder Mary Anulik Kutsiq describes some of the collectivist aspects of life in traditional Inuit communities—and how some of those traditions have been lost—in the following interview excerpts:

In earlier times, Inuit were very close. They had strong friendships and helped each other through hard times. Today, some people have so much while others have so little and do not bother to share at all. In the earlier days, people shared food even if they didn't have much, as long as there was a little bit of extra food. Pieces of meat were cut up evenly and distributed among the whole community. Bread, bannock and tea were also evenly shared. If there was not enough tea to be divided up for each household, every bit of it was brewed together in a big pot so that everyone could have a cup…

The problem today is that there are too many people in the communities and a lot of them are too self-centred and involved with their own problems to help others. Before this community had so many people, we were all very close and helped each other in times of need. As the population grows, so does the gap between people. We are no longer one big family. We are now separated and we each go our own way…

—Mary Anulik Kutsiq, "An Elder Offers Advice."
Inuktitut Magazine 79 (Fall, 1995): pp. 11, 14–15. www.itk.ca

The Medieval Period (circa 476 to the Renaissance)

Pax Romana, the "Peace of Rome", which had provided structure and security throughout the empire, was replaced by lawlessness and unpredictability. With the collapse of the Roman Empire in 476 CE, Europe was thrown into chaos. Over time, order was restored in small areas under the guidance of local warlords. Small pockets of structure eventually grew into larger and larger areas as warlords joined together and an aristocracy was established. Common people were provided structure and physical security in exchange for loyalty and service to their lords. But the individual life had very little worth. The common person was worth little more than the shrub or the cow on the land owned by the lord.

By 800 CE, most of Europe had converted to Christianity under the Roman Catholic Church. The people of the various European

◀ **Figure 2-2**

During the medieval period, European society had a rigidly hierarchical structure.

kingdoms became subjects of two kingdoms—the worldly kingdom and the spiritual kingdom. Security and order were provided by the earthly rulers. More important, however, was the security and promise provided by the spiritual rulers. If life here on earth was miserable, then at least life after death promised to be glorious. The spiritual ruler—the Roman Catholic Church—held immense power as the gatekeeper of heaven. One result of this situation was that people focused less on the things of the material world and more on the afterlife. Therefore developments in art, science, commerce, and progress in general were not emphasized, and the individual life here on earth mattered very little.

During the medieval period (named from the later perspective of Italian humanists), most people in Europe fit into distinct social categories—peasants, traders, craftsmen, clergy (priests, monks, and other people who performed duties in the Roman Catholic Church), and nobles. What mattered was *how* you fit into your group—*not* your individual identity. For example, if you were lucky, your family might know a stone mason and pay him to take you on as an apprentice. You would work for your master without pay while you learned the craft, then become a journeyman (who could work for pay for any master stone mason), and finally become a craftsman if you were accepted into the guild of stone masons.

During this time, cathedrals were being built all over Europe. These huge building projects, spanning decades and even centuries, would employ many different craftsmen over the years. However, the individual craftsmen were unnamed and received no fame or glory.

Politically, St Augustine of Hippo (354–430) and later Thomas Aquinas (1225–1274) argued that authority was derived from God and divinely instituted natural laws. A king held power through the will of God. This tended to allow for very little individualism in political matters.

The Renaissance (circa 1450–1600)

In contrast to the medieval period, the Renaissance in Europe brought a greater interest in the individual. The term **Renaissance** comes from French and means "rebirth". This period in European history was characterized by a renewed interest in classical Greek and Roman culture. European scholars revived classical ideas about the central importance of life in this world, man's central role in the world, and the appreciation of the worth of the individual.

In 1453, Constantinople, capital of the Byzantine Empire, fell to the Ottoman Empire. Many scholars from cities such as Constantinople fled west, taking with them many Greek manuscripts. Islamic societies in Spain, North Africa, and West Asia had already been reading, translating, developing, and commenting upon Greek scholarship for many centuries, contributing to the growth of these ideas during the Renaissance.

 Figure 2-3 ▲

Bronzino's *Portrait of a Young Man*, 1550

 Figure 2-4 ▲

Michelangelo's *Pietà*, 1498–1499

◀ Figure 2-5

The Basilica di Santa Maria del Fiore, Florence, Italy, built between 1296–1469. Renaissance art reflected the renewed interest in classical philosophy and humanism.

Ancient Greek culture had been very humanistic and very individualistic. According to Greek mythology, the gods on Mount Olympus were anthropomorphic, behaving like people and sometimes interacting with them. In these myths, humans occasionally challenged the gods, and sometimes are depicted as being on equal terms with them. This notion of human potential led the ancient Greeks to focus on the capabilities, strength, beauty, and reason of individual humans. Humans, according to these ancient thinkers and their culture, could be like gods: they could remake their worlds and be the authors of their own fates.

These ideas took hold in the city-states of Italy and quickly changed the thinking and the focus of influential people in Europe. Painters began to study nature and the world around them. They began to use perspective in their works, creating a more three-dimensional depiction of the real world and humans in that world. Sculptures such as Michelangelo's *Pietà*, which depicts a religious scene, celebrated the individual human form. Also, individual artists became known: for example, the *Pietà* was seen as a great personal achievement for Michelangelo, who even carved his name on the sculpture.

Other works of art portrayed real individuals—patrons such as wealthy nobles, merchants, and craftsmen—instead of stylized and archetypical religious subjects. Many works also showed the growing importance of books, education, and the study of nature and natural forces.

▶ PAUSE AND REFLECT

From what you know now, would life in the medieval period or life in the Renaissance suit you better?

The Protestant Reformation (circa 1500–1650)

The Protestant Reformation, partially a product of the growing influence of the Renaissance focus on the potential of the individual in this world, also contributed to the growth of individualism by challenging the authority of the dominant Roman Catholic Church. The Catholic Church interpreted religion for people through both Church tradition and the Bible, while many Protestant Churches claimed to rely on the Bible alone. After the printing press was assembled by Johannes Gutenberg around 1439, the Bible could be translated into many languages and distributed to many more people. In this way, people who could read began to explore, consider, and interpret their faith on a more personal level.

The emergence of individualism in European societies was a process that took several centuries. And while individualism eventually came to predominate in many societies, it has never supplanted collectivism entirely. The two tendencies have existed side by side in a sometimes uneasy relationship that has shaped societies in the past and continues to shape societies today.

Explore the Issues

Concept Review

1. a) Identify three examples of collectivism in history.

   b) Identify two examples of individualism in history.

Concept Application

2. Research and explore understandings of individualism and collectivism other than the ones already presented in this section.

3. Create your own definitions of individualism and collectivism and some examples of how they are expressed by people's actions in society.

4. In groups, discuss whether or not the following things are individualist or collectivist in nature: schools, hospitals, government, and traffic patterns in cities.

Principles of Individualism and Collectivism

- **In what ways are individualism and collectivism foundations of ideology?**

An ideology provides us with a framework or model for society and for the actions of the individuals in that society. In the previous section you looked at general understandings of individualism and collectivism and their respective visions of society. Now you will examine the specific principles of individualism and collectivism on which various ideologies are based.

Principles of Individualism

Individualism is one possible foundation of ideology and is a foundation in particular of liberalism, the prevailing ideology in Western democracy. We will explore the principles of individualism in order for you to understand the roots of what you now find and act within as a citizen or resident of Alberta and Canada.

In this section you will read about the different ways in which the following principles are manifested in society:

- rule of law
- individual rights and freedoms
- private property
- economic freedom
- self-interest
- competition

Rule of Law

A key principle in Canadian life—and in liberal democracies around the world—is the **rule of law**. The principle of the rule of the law has many applications, some of which you will read about in later chapters. In the words of former senator and Canadian constitutional expert Eugene A. Forsey,

What does the rule of law mean? It means that everyone is subject to the law; that no one, no matter how important or powerful, is above the law—not the government; not the Prime Minister, or any other Minister; not the Queen or the Governor General or any Lieutenant-Governor; not the most powerful bureaucrat; not the armed forces; not Parliament itself, or any provincial legislature. None of these has any powers except those given to it by law…

—Source: Eugene A. Forsey, *How Canadians Govern Themselves*, 6th edition. (Ottawa: Library of Parliament, Public Information Office, 2005), p. 32.

In other words, every *individual* is equal before the law. Furthermore, this principle means that citizens are subject to clearly defined rules, rather than the arbitrary power of an individual or group in a position of authority.

In 2007, when Canadian-born British nobleman Conrad Black was found guilty of embezzling in the United States and sentenced in a Chicago court, "Judge Amy St Eve told the former owner of [the newspaper] *The Daily Telegraph*: 'No one is immune from the proper application of law in the United States and that, Mr Black, includes you.'" (Andrew Clark, "'No one is above the law'—Conrad Black gets six years", *The Guardian* online, December 11, 2007, http://www.guardian.co.uk/business/2007/dec/11/conradblack.media business1). Similarly, when Italian prime minister Silvio Berlusconi tried to use Italian immunity laws to avoid bribery charges, he was accused of trying to place himself above the law.

- Would you want to live in a society in which certain members were above the law? Why or why not?
- Are there instances in our society where the rule of law seems to be ignored?

Individual Rights and Freedoms

Individual rights and freedoms are a key principle of individualism and an important feature of liberal democracies. Examples of such rights and freedoms include freedom of religion, freedom of association, and the right to life, liberty, and the security of the person.

One important individual right in liberal democracies is the right to vote. Most early liberal democracies did not extend this right to all citizens. For example, after the American and French revolutions, the right to vote was granted only to some men, mainly property owners. Here are some examples of how voting rights were granted and to whom:

- In England, middle-class men got the vote only in 1832. Working-class men waited until 1885. English women were first able to vote only in 1919—and only if they were over the age of 30.
- In France, all men received the right to vote for the first time in 1789. Various classes of men lost and regained this right until 1848, when all men in France gained the right to vote. Women were granted the right to vote in 1944.

- In the early years of some states in the United States, voters had to be both male and Protestant.
- During the apartheid era, South Africa restricted voting based on race. And Canada, for years, limited the right to vote for Aboriginal people identified as "status Indians."
- Only in 2004 did all prisoners in Canadian prisons become eligible to vote in federal elections.

Now, however, the right to vote has extended in most democratic countries to include all citizens above a certain age, usually 18 or 21.

Guaranteeing individual rights and freedoms can have negative consequences in certain circumstances, and liberal democracies attempt to balance the rights of one individual against the rights of other individuals, the rights of groups, and the needs and goals of the society. For example, in Canada freedom of expression is an individual right protected by the Charter of Rights and Freedoms. However, Article 1 of the Charter stipulates that the rights and freedoms it guarantees are subject to "such reasonable limits prescribed by law as can be demonstrably justified in a free and democratic society." Therefore, we have laws that prohibit the promotion of hatred or discrimination, thus limiting freedom of expression. In one extreme case, an Alberta high-school teacher named James Keegstra was dismissed from his teaching position in 1982 for expressing anti-Semitic views in his classroom and claiming that the Holocaust did not happen. Keegstra was eventually charged with unlawfully promoting hatred against an identifiable group.

From the creation of Canada as a democracy, individual rights and freedoms have been expanded. In the 1960s, social mores were loosening, and this brought about many changes to laws and society in general.

Voices

A Pioneer of Women's Rights

One rare European woman among the Enlightenment thinkers was Mary Wollstonecraft, who wrote *A Vindication of the Rights of Woman* in 1792. Wollstonecraft's daughter Mary Shelley was also a writer and became best known for the original tale of *Frankenstein*, published in 1818, as the Industrial Revolution was changing human lives and economies in a way never seen before. As women in England, neither was able to vote.

The divine right of husbands, like the divine right of kings, may, it is to be hoped, in this enlightened age, be contested without danger...

—**Mary Wollstonecraft, *A Vindication of the Rights of Woman*, Chapter 3, 1792.**

1 What beliefs and values are reflected in this quotation?

Pierre Trudeau was asked in the late 1960s about legal changes (Bill C-150) that granted rights on the issues of sexual preference and reproductive choice. He answered,

Well, it's certainly the most extensive revision of the Criminal Code since the new Criminal Code of [the] early 1950s…it's bringing the laws of the land up to contemporary society, I think. Take this thing on homosexuality. I think the view we take here is that there's no place for the state in the bedrooms of the nation, and I think that, you know, what's done in private between adults doesn't concern the Criminal Code. When it becomes public, this is a different matter.

—**Pierre Elliott Trudeau, Minister of Justice (later Canadian prime minister), December 21, 1967, in response to a reporter's question**

You will examine in greater depth the application of individual rights and freedoms in ideologies such as liberalism in later chapters.

Private Property

The reason why men enter into society is the preservation of their property.

—**John Locke, *The Second Treatise of Civil Government*, 1690, Section 222.**

Modern understandings of property law developed during the Enlightenment period in England. At first, property law was understood to only apply to land (real estate), but it eventually came to apply to three types of property: real estate, other forms of physical possessions, and intellectual property (artistic works, inventions, and so on).

However, the notion of **private property** is only one way of looking at land and property; there are many different perspectives regarding the significance of people's relationships with land. For example, for some First Nations, Métis, and Inuit peoples, land reflects a person's interrelationship with nature and all living things. Some peoples also believe that land cannot actually be owned—cannot be private property—but is rather shared. Some communities also have had a tradition of common property—shared by, worked by, and enjoyed by all. Such differences in perspective on land ownership have sometimes led to conflict among First Nations, Métis, and Inuit peoples, and between Aboriginal peoples and the British and Canadian governments. During the Treaty 7 negotiations among southern Alberta First Nations and representatives of Queen Victoria, prominent Blood chief Medicine Calf remarked, "The Great Spirit, and not the Great Mother [the queen of England], gave us this land." (Source: Alexander Morris, *The Treaties of Canada with the Indians of Manitoba and the North-west Territories* [Toronto: Belfords, Clarke, & Co., 1880], p. 270.)

A more recent example of the important implications of concepts of private and public property is the ongoing dispute over land and resource management between the Barriere Lake Algonquin First Nation and the federal government.

In 1991, Barriere Lake compelled Canada and Québec to sign a groundbreaking land management and sustainable development agreement, after a campaign of civil disobedience that caught international attention.

The Trilateral agreement set important precedents: it would give Barriere Lake decisive say in the management of 10 000 square kilometres of their traditional territory, protect Algonquin land uses, and give them a share in the resource-revenue from logging and hydro projects on their land.

Praised by the Royal Commission on Aboriginal Peoples, the agreement was an alternative to the Comprehensive Land Claims process, which Barriere Lake rejected because it would force them to extinguish their Aboriginal title and rights, among other reasons.

—Source: "A Call for Endorsements and Solidarity."
Barriere Lake Solidarity Collective
Indigenous Community News Network, August 12, 2008.
http://icnn.com.au/index.php?option=com_content&
task=view&id=1593&Itemid=9

As of 2008, the agreement had not yet been implemented, despite ongoing logging and hydro-electric projects, in part because the federal government has not recognized the First Nation's chosen leadership.

The protection of private property can also be a source of conflict in the realm of intellectual property. For example, biotechnology companies expend large amounts of time and money developing and patenting new varieties of plants, such as drought-resistant wheat, that can benefit society as a whole. Farmers who grow these varieties pay royalties to the companies who own the patents. It is not always clear, however, whether newly created plant varieties are significantly different from the existing crops that have been grown for centuries.

In one case, Greenpeace Mexico asked the Mexican government to appeal a patent granted to the DuPont corporation in 2001 by the European Patent Office (EPO). Greenpeace claimed that the corn variety for which DuPont received the patent was too similar to existing corn varieties already grown in Mexico and that the patent could be used to prevent Mexican corn farmers from growing their crops without paying DuPont. The EPO revoked DuPont's patent in 2003. In another case, a US patent was granted in 1999 to Larry Proctor, an American entrepreneur, for a bean variety he developed called 'Enola'. Because 'Enola' is very similar to an existing variety called 'Mayacoba', Mexican bean farmers could no longer export 'Mayacoba' beans to the United States without paying royalties to Larry Proctor. Following an appeal by an agricultural research centre, the United States Patent and Trademark Office revoked Proctor's patent in 2008.

Intellectual Property Rights

As advances in communications technology make it easier to transmit electronic data such as music, films, and software, the definition of intellectual property and the rights consumers have to use what they purchase have become increasingly important topics of discussion. How should government balance the rights of people who create intellectual works with the rights of consumers who purchase those works?

Something to Think About: When you purchase a creative work such as a music CD, movie, or software program, how much control do you have over how you use it? Should you be allowed to share it with someone else? If you receive such a work from someone else, whose property are you enjoying? Are you paying for that? If so, how? If not, why is that?

The following statement is from the Center for the Rule of Law website.

Increasingly, we live in a world where value is generated by creative work, by innovative designs, products and compositions. Especially in advanced economies, economic growth and societal well-being are tied to the incentives to generate new ideas and new technologies and to the ability to put those ideas and technologies into practice. Rights to intellectual property are the foundation for advancing idea-generated growth and the enormous range of improvements in our lives that come from new technologies. Substantial social value is created as well from the software, entertainment, and other copyright-intensive industries, and from the ability of consumers to readily identify quality goods by brand names. Protections for patents, trademarks, copyrights, and trade secrets are essential…International piracy and violations of intellectual property rights abroad present issues of critical importance to our economy.

—Ronald A. Cass, Chairman, Center for the Rule of Law
http://www.ruleoflaw.org/Issues.html

An Example: As file-sharing becomes more widespread, news stories such as the following are more common:

The recording industry won a key fight Thursday against illegal music downloading when a federal jury found a Minnesota woman shared copyrighted music online and levied $222 000 in damages against her.

  Jurors ordered Jammie Thomas, 30, to pay the six record companies that sued her $9250 for each of 24 songs they focused on in the case. They had alleged she shared 1702 songs online in violation of their copyright…

  "This does send a message, I hope, that downloading and distributing our recordings is not OK," said Richard Gabriel, the lead attorney for the music companies…

Record companies have filed some 26 000 lawsuits since 2003 over file-sharing, which has <u>hurt sales because it allows people to get music for free instead of paying for recordings in stores</u>. Many other defendants have settled by paying the companies a few thousand dollars.

—Source: "Woman Faces the Music, Loses Download Case."
The Associated Press, October 4, 2007.
© The Associated Press 2007

Musicians and songwriters appear to be divided on the issue:

Musicians <u>hold mixed views</u> in regards to file-sharing. While reduced CD sales worry artists, the exposure an artist receives through file-sharing can be a valuable promotional tool, especially for lesser known acts. Many feel the tactics of the recording industry are misguided, and believe working with file-sharing technology would increase industry profits.

A survey of 2755 musicians and songwriters on the effects of [file]-sharing was conducted between March and April of 2004. When asked what impact free downloading on the Internet has had on their careers as musicians, 37 per cent said that free downloading has not really made a difference, 35 per cent said that it has helped and 8 per cent said that it has both helped and hurt their career. Only 5 per cent said that free downloading has exclusively hurt their career and 15 per cent of the respondents answered "do not know"...

Some artists publicly den<u>ounce file-sharing</u>. Canadian artists such as The Tragically Hip, Jann Arden, and the Barenaked Ladies take issue with the prevalence of music file-sharing. In 2003, <u>Madonna took aim at file-sharers by deliberately uploading a spoofed file of her release</u>, American Life, in response to the number of music fans sharing her music.

In contrast, Moby, System of a Down, Public Enemy and the Dead, frustrated with the record industry's lawsuits directed at music fans, contend that the record industry's efforts are misguided and that, to succeed in the evolving marketplace, it must work with the new technology instead of against it...

—Source: University of Ottawa, "File-sharing."
Canadian Internet Policy and Public Interest Clinic, June 2, 2007.
http://www.cippic.ca/file-sharing/

QUESTIONS FOR REFLECTION

1. Create a web diagram for each case, on which you note the individual rights involved for those enjoying the music and those creating and selling the music.

2. What is your own experience of hearing or sharing music online? How widespread do you think your experience is?

3. Use the Internet to research the subject of downloading music. Based on your research, experiences, and thoughts about the cases, take a stand on the issue of downloading music and its relationship to <u>individualism</u> in order to prepare and present your opinion in a form you choose.

Economic Freedom

On a personal level, **economic freedom** is the freedom to buy what you want and to sell your labour, idea, or product to whomever you wish. Markets in which consumers and businesses have free choice to buy, sell, or trade, without government interference in those transactions, are called **free markets**. Economic freedom for free-market entrepreneurs would mean that there were no barriers to trade for products they might want to export, and that their customers would not have to pay taxes on their purchases.

The Economic Freedom Index, compiled by the *Wall Street Journal* and the Heritage Foundation, a Washington, DC–based think tank, rates the economic freedom of 157 countries according to the following 10 factors:

- business freedom
- trade freedom
- fiscal (tax) freedom
- degree of government regulation
- monetary freedom
- investment freedom
- financial freedom
- property rights
- freedom from corruption
- labour freedom

In 2008, Canada was ranked 10th on this list, below Hong Kong, Singapore, Australia, the United States, New Zealand, and the United Kingdom. The reason for its ranking is that Canada intervenes in its markets rather than leaving them free from government regulation. After the Great Depression of the 1930s, Canada implemented policies designed to create a "social safety net" for Canadians; the Unemployment Insurance Act (1940), the Canada Pension Plan (1966), the Medical Care Act (1966), and other acts transformed Canada into more of a **welfare state**. A welfare state is one in which the economy is capitalist, but the government uses policies that directly or indirectly modify the market forces in order to ensure economic stability and a basic standard of living for its citizens.

Self-Interest and Competition

Two concepts of individualism closely related to the principle of economic freedom are **self-interest** and **competition**. Supporters of individualism see economic freedom as leading to the most efficient and beneficial economy for the greatest number of people, because it encourages competition and they assume that people generally act in their own self-interest. These ideas were first promoted by 18th-century Scottish philosopher and economist Adam Smith, who saw individual self-interest as an "invisible hand" that guides individuals to contribute for the common good of everyone. You will read more about Smith's views on economics in Chapter 3.

In this view, the forces of supply and demand in the marketplace work to the benefit of the majority. When there is too much supply of a product, the price drops and, eventually, so does the supply. When demand is greater than supply, the price of the product rises, and more entrepreneurs enter the marketplace to profit, eventually causing supply to meet demand once again. Considered another way, each individual buyer's desire to find the best quality product at the lowest price ensures that sellers compete among themselves to provide a variety of products at the lowest prices.

Furthermore, individual entrepreneurs who serve the common good through honesty and reliability may also serve their own self-interest by winning more customers. Essentially, both the buyer's and seller's self-interest works to the benefit of the other.

In such an economy, labour is like any other commodity. If there is an oversupply of labour in a particular area, wages will fall and the workers will look for employment in a sector of the economy where there is a labour shortage. In theory, acquiring a position in politics or economics is based purely on one's ability; the hardest working and brightest people achieve the most economic and political success. Employers will compete to hire these desirable people, and workers will compete to fill the jobs available. It is this drive of individuals working to secure their self-interest that creates economic growth and, in the long term, benefits everyone.

In contrast to this perspective, Canadian-born economist John Kenneth Galbraith argued in the late 1950s that increases in wealth in the United States were concentrated more and more among people with high incomes, and people with low incomes were not earning more. As advisor to several US presidents, he encouraged efforts to reduce this gap—a "war on poverty" and large-scale publicly funded education programs. He also noted that very few industries fit the vision of perfect competition. In Britain, in 2007 a similar gap was seen: the "gap between the rich and poor in Britain has reached its highest level in more than 40 years. Over the past 15 years, more households have become poor, but fewer are very poor—'breadline poor'." (Source: David R. Francis, "Yawning Rich-Poor Gap Could Hobble Economy." *The Christian Science Monitor*, http://www.csmonitor.com/2007/0730/p15s02-wmgn.html?page=2, July 30, 2007.

PAUSE AND REFLECT

What examples in daily life have you seen that support this theory—that market forces benefit everybody? What examples contradict this theory? In October 2006, as many as 9000 people showed up at a job fair in St John's, Newfoundland, looking for work in Alberta. Adam Smith envisioned workers moving between markets of oversupply to markets of demand. What might the impact be of such oversupply on individuals? What might the impact be on society?

Principles of Collectivism

The principles of collectivism are the foundation of ideologies such as communism and socialism. While the principles of individualism formed the basis of the classical liberal ideology that originally guided modern democracies, over time most liberal democracies have evolved and incorporated aspects of collectivism into their political, economic, and social systems. More information about these changes will be presented in Part 2 of this text.

The principles of collectivism you will explore are

- economic equality
- co-operation
- public property
- collective interest
- collective responsibility
- adherence to collective norms

Economic Equality

While the principle of economic equality is common to all collectivist ideologies, its specific meaning varies from one ideology to another. **Economic equality** can mean any of the following, depending on the person or the ideology:

- People with larger incomes should pay more taxes.
- All people should earn equal wages for work of similar value.
- There should be a guaranteed annual income (GAI).
- All people should share in the wealth of the country or the world.
- People should own the means of production (factories or companies that produce goods) collectively.
- Everything should be free. There should be no private property.

Many countries have tried to reform their economic systems to introduce more economic equality. In Canada, for example, the policy of progressive taxation could be seen as an attempt to redistribute wealth. Progressive taxation means that people who earn more money are taxed at a higher rate.

Nonetheless, some thinkers have proposed that amounts of money are not at the heart of economic equality. Mahatma Gandhi was the leader of India's independence movement from Britain in the early 20th century. He thought that economic equality depended on individual need and circumstances:

Economic equality of my conception does not mean that everyone will literally have the same amount. It simply means that everybody should have enough for his or her needs...The real meaning of economic equality is *"To each according to his need." That is the definition of Marx. If a single man demands as much as a man with wife and four children, that will be a violation of economic equality…*

—**Mahatma Gandhi, March 31, 1946,**
quoted in "Economic Equality." Mkghandi.org.
http://www.mkgandhi.org/momgandhi/chap55.htm

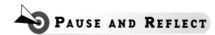

PAUSE AND REFLECT

Do you think we need more economic equality in Canada? Would we have a better society, or would this infringe upon individual freedoms?

Co-operation

All collectivist ideologies emphasize **co-operation**, a principle you are probably already very familiar with. Co-operation can be beneficial to individuals and groups precisely because individuals are unique and have different ideas about how to do things. Co-operation is the means through which members of a group or a collective achieve their common goals. It may involve designating roles, following certain protocols for speaking, or following guidelines for decision making.

One example of collective co-operation is a *co-operative*. Daycare centres, health-care centres, stores, and credit unions are a few examples of enterprises that can be owned and managed co-operatively. Some of the guiding principles of co-operatives include voluntary and open membership, democratic control by members, and economic participation by members.

The principle of co-operation can also influence how members of a society govern themselves. In a recent interview, the Reverend Kathryn Gorman-Lovelady, a moderator at Wolfe Island Aboriginal Interfaith Church, a National Elder on the Canadian Métis Council, a Native Inmate Liaison Officer at the Central North Correctional Centre (Penetanguishene-Lafontaine, Ontario) and an Anishinabek shaman, had this to say about decision making and the traditions surrounding speaking in Aboriginal cultures:

Aboriginal peoples in North America have traditionally approached decisions from a collective base. Prior to contact with Europeans, we evolved an egalitarian "circle" ideology for processing both community and individual decisions. The harshness of daily living, especially in northern climates, necessitated a group of people to hunt and gather, as individuals could not adequately feed a family by themselves. It was too dangerous to hunt by oneself. Everything acquired was collectively rendered into food for present and future use. While heavy emphasis is placed on a person being responsible for their actions (or lack thereof) it was understood that one had easy access to Elders for counsel and life wisdom. The erosion of the collective process (post-contact) has driven many Elders and Aboriginal community leaders to fight for self-government. This is heralded as a return to decision-making as a democratic collective. In this way, every member of the community, young or old, male or female has a

Figure 2-6 ▶

Talking Circle by Leah Dorion. For some First Nations, Métis, and Inuit groups and communities in Canada, there are diverse protocols for speaking. Leah Dorion was raised in Prince Albert, Saskatchewan, and is a Métis artist, author, and filmmaker. In her paintings, she honours the spiritual strength of Aboriginal women and incorporates elements of traditional Aboriginal symbolism, principles, and teachings, such as that depicted here of a talking circle.

right to speak on issues. This may seem to be unwieldy and slow, but ensures that everyone's voice and perspective is included in any decision. Our spiritual practices reflect the beauty of egalitarian collective process— we view all life as equal and sacred in the web of life. It is a practice we continue today.

—Reverend Kathryn Gorman-Lovelady, interview with author, January 7, 2008

Public Property

Public property is anything—land, buildings, vehicles—not privately owned by individuals. Generally speaking, public property is owned by the state or the community, and managed according to the best interests of the community.

Different ideologies support the idea of public property to varying degrees. In a Communist state, all industries could be public property— controlled by the state for the common good of the collective. According to Karl Marx's *The Communist Manifesto* (1848), "the theory of the Communists may be summed up in the single sentence: *Abolition of private property*." Marx and thinkers like him argued that only workers should profit from their own labour, not employers or the owners of the companies. It has been argued that not only is this arrangement fairer for the workers, but it also provides a source of motivation in the absence of financial rewards: because every worker has a stake in the enterprise, they will all have a greater interest in its success.

The concept of public property is also present to a lesser extent in liberal democracies such as Canada. Parks, schools, roads, libraries,

Crown land, and Crown corporations (such as Via Rail or the CBC) are all examples of property that the government manages in the interest of all of society. These properties are maintained with public money raised through taxation.

- What other forms of public property exist in Canada? How do they represent the values of collectivism?
- How would Canadian society be different if all private property were abolished? How would your life be different?

Collective Interest

Collective interest refers to the set of interests that members of a group have in common. More specifically, the principle of collective interest states that while individual members may have individual interests, these interests are often better addressed by making them a common set of interests that the group can address together.

Collective interest is the basis for the organized **labour movement**, which began during the Industrial Revolution. As members of organized trade unions, workers were able to fight successfully for better working conditions and higher rates of pay—successes that individuals could not have realized alone.

Collective interest is also the foundation for social movements and lobby groups, such as human rights groups, professional groups, or international organizations such as the *Organisation internationale de la Francophonie* (OIF) or the Assembly of First Nations (AFN).

The mission statement of the OIF is

The OIF, conscious of the connection created among its members by sharing the French language and universal values, works toward the achievement of peace, cooperation, solidarity and sustainable development. The institutions of the OIF work towards the realization of these objectives.

—Source: *Organisation internationale de la Francophonie.*
http://www.francophonie.org/oif/index.cfm

Article 1 of the AFN's Charter states, in part,

By virtue of their rich heritage, historical experience, and contemporary circumstances, First Nations possess common interests and aspirations to exercise their political will in common and to develop a collective struggle or cause based upon the Indian values of trust, confidence, and toleration.

—Source: *Charter of the Assembly of First Nations.*
http://www.afn.ca/article.asp?id=57

All of these groups represent people with common interests and goals who come together to press for change and reform.

Collective Responsibility

Collective responsibility means holding the whole group responsible for the actions of individuals (or individual groups) within the group. Collective responsibility asserts that there is no individual action for which the group cannot in some way be held accountable.

In her book *Ideologies of Caring: Rethinking Community and Collectivism*, Gillian Dalley describes collective responsibility as the cornerstone of a caring society:

> *At its broadest level, collectivism is about societal responsibility for all members of that society, a moral responsibility that is translated into a practical responsibility. The government is the steward of that responsibility.*
>
> *At a narrower level, responsibility may be held by the local community—the municipality, the neighbourhood, the commune, or by an interest or a functional group such as trade unions, women's groups, or professional associations. Provision of care and support for those who are in any way dependent is clearly part of that responsibility.*

—Source: Adapted from Gillian Dalley,
Ideologies of Caring: Rethinking Community and Collectivism,
2nd edition. (London: Macmillan, 1996), pp. 52–53.

Acknowledgment of collective responsibility is often made in response to deep-rooted social problems that cannot be addressed by targeting

Figure 2-7 ▶

How do campaigns such as Mothers Against Drunk Driving denote collective responsibility?

individuals or a single group. For example, campaigns against underage drinking often state that the cure for this problem must be a collective responsibility. This is how one US government committee examining underage drinking in the United States framed its report, *Reducing Underage Drinking: A Collective Responsibility:*

> *The committee reached the fundamental conclusion that underage drinking cannot be successfully addressed by focusing on youth alone. Youth drink within the context of a society in which alcohol use is normative behavior and images about alcohol are pervasive. They usually obtain alcohol—either directly or indirectly—from adults. Efforts to reduce underage drinking, therefore, need to focus on adults and must engage the society at large.*

—Source: Committee on Developing a Strategy to Reduce and Prevent Underage Drinking, *Reducing Underage Drinking: A Collective Responsibility*, Richard J. Bonnie and Mary Ellen O'Connell (eds.). The National Academies Press, www.nap.edu, 2004.

PAUSE AND REFLECT

Consider how laws are developed: age limits for drinking, voting, and so on. How are the individual's rights sacrificed by belonging to a certain age group?

On the other hand, the idea of collective responsibility does not always guarantee a caring society. Sometimes the idea of collective responsibility is used in totalitarian states such as North Korea, where a strong central government has complete control over most aspects of citizens' lives and does not allow political opposition. In such a society, if one member of a family criticizes the government or its leaders, the whole family might be punished to send a message that the behaviour is not tolerated. Authoritarian governments in particular (see Chapter 11) often claim to be acting on behalf of the "good of all" even when their actions are punitive.

Adherence to Collective Norms

Groups usually impose norms, or standards, on their members as a condition of membership in the group. These norms can relate to conduct, values, or appearance. While they are voluntary, the group members generally see these standards as binding, which makes **adherence to collective norms** important. Sororities and fraternities, political parties, faith groups, trade unions, and professional groups all impose certain standards of conduct on their members. Living up to these standards may be considered a daily responsibility. **Censorship—** deliberately restricting information the public will see—is another example of the imposition of a collective norm. Many media censor themselves informally; however, some governments impose censorship on media.

PAUSE AND REFLECT

What does "protective stupidity" mean? How might the concept of "protective stupidity" apply to your life? Have you ever been in a situation where someone tried to prevent you from thinking for yourself?

A negative view of collective norms can be found in George Orwell's *Nineteen Eighty-Four*. The novel describes how rigidly enforced collective norms can extend so far as to tell people how to think:

A Party member is expected to have no private emotions and no respites from enthusiasm. He is supposed to live in a continuous frenzy of hatred of foreign enemies and internal traitors, triumph over victories, and self-abasement before the power and wisdom of the Party…The first and simplest stage in the discipline, which can be taught even to young children, is called, in Newspeak, crimestop. Crimestop means the faculty of stopping short, as though by instinct, at the threshold of any dangerous thought. It includes the power of not grasping analogies, of failing to perceive logical errors, of misunderstanding the simplest arguments if they are inimical to Ingsoc, and of being bored or repelled by any train of thought which is capable of leading in a heretical direction. Crimestop, in short, means protective stupidity.

—**Source:** *Nineteen Eighty-Four* **by George Orwell (Copyright © George Orwell, 1949). Reprinted by permission of Bill Hamilton as the Literary Executor of the Estate of the Late Sonia Brownell Orwell and Secker & Warburg Ltd.**

While Orwell believed in **democratic socialism**, he saw an extreme version of collectivism being created in the Soviet Union by its leader at the time, Joseph Stalin. You will read more about this period of history in Part 2.

Explore the Issues

Concept Review

1 a) List the principles of individualism. Identify an example of each of these principles in society.

   b) List the principles of collectivism. Identify an example of each of these principles in society.

Concept Application

2 Choose one of the key principles of individualism and one of collectivism, and provide a personal example that illustrates each principle.

3 Based on what you have learned about individualism and collectivism, to what extent do you think Canada is a society based on individualist or collectivist ideologies?

Contemporary Individualism and Collectivism

Question for Inquiry

- **How are individualism and collectivism expressed today?**

Born in 1965, Jeff Skoll grew up in Montréal and Toronto. He pumped gas in a service station to support himself while studying electrical engineering at the University of Toronto. After obtaining a Master of Business Administration at Stanford University in California, Skoll became the first president and full-time employee of eBay. He created a business plan for the online auction company that would lead to its eventual success. When Skoll stopped working full-time at eBay in 1998, his fortune was worth 2 billion dollars.

He has since founded the Skoll Foundation, which encourages social entrepreneurship around the world. He has also become an influential Hollywood movie producer, backing films with socially and politically relevant themes such as Al Gore's environmental documentary *An Inconvenient Truth* (2006). Although his successful business career marks him as the epitome of the "self-made man," he has used his financial success to work toward his vision of the future: "a world of peace and prosperity and sustainability." (Source: Jeff Skoll, Technology Entertainment Design conference, March 2007.)

In reading about the principles of individualism and collectivism thus far in the text, have you come across ideas or values that you share? Do all these values come from only one of these two streams of thinking?

Pause and Reflect

In what ways do you think Jeff Skoll is an example of individualism? In what ways do his actions demonstrate collectivism?

Figure 2-8

Internet entrepreneur Jeff Skoll was an executive producer of Al Gore's environmental documentary *An Inconvenient Truth*.

In speaking about ideologies and the ideas of individualism and collectivism, people sometimes try to suggest that the two viewpoints are incompatible. They argue that the respective values of these two viewpoints are so different that there is no common ground and one must simply choose between them. While it is true that the values of individualism and collectivism are sometimes at odds, there are aspects of the two sets of ideas that can complement each other. In effect, sometimes individualism and collectivism work together for the common good of society.

In this section you will explore a few contemporary examples of individualism and collectivism at work in society. Consider how they compete and how they complement each other.

Attitudes about Individualism and Collectivism in North America

Americans are well-known for their emphasis on the principle of individualism. According to one position, American individualism consists of a characteristic attitude of tough-mindedness toward the claims of others for assistance—not an absolute refusal to help but rather that individuals should first do everything possible before asking others for assistance. The University of Pennsylvania's *International Student and Scholar Handbook* describes one view of this individualism:

> *Since childhood, Americans are encouraged to see themselves as individuals responsible for their own destiny, not as a member of any collective group. Many Americans believe that the ideal person is an autonomous, self-reliant individual. They generally dislike being dependent on other people or having others dependent on them.*

> *Americans have a desire for personal success, both social and economic…Achievement is a dominant motivation in American life and this can lead to not-so-friendly competition.*

—Source: University of Pennsylvania's *International Student and Scholar Handbook.*
http://www.upenn.edu/oip/iss/handbook/like.html

According to a 2004 study by the Pew Research Center, Canadians and Americans have more than a few values in common. For example, almost 65 per cent of Americans and 63 per cent of Canadians think people determine their own success in life. Most Western Europeans, on the other hand, believe that people have "little control over their own destinies." While 91 per cent of Western Europeans think their governments should provide a social safety net (government services such as employment insurance and health care), 77 per cent of Canadians and 73 per cent of Americans believe that their governments should take care of those in need.

PAUSE AND REFLECT

The sources in this section indicate that North Americans tend to embrace the principles of individualism, viewing them through the lens of Western democracy. Other cultures and societies throughout the world, and even some within North America, may embrace the principles of collectivism or a balance of individualism and collectivism. To what extent is the ideology of a culture shaped by the physical location and shared sense of place of that culture?

What is interesting about this study is that in even North American cultures, where a prevailing individualistic point of view sees people as responsible for their own success, the majority of the population believes that government should provide help to those who need it—an idea that is essentially collectivist.

A study that examined levels of consumer spending and happiness found that rich countries, where individualism was more prevalent and consumption was higher, had higher overall levels of *subjective well-being* (that is, a person's perception of their own happiness). However, when people at different income levels within the same country were compared, it was found that, beyond the level at which a person's basic needs can be met, there was little correlation between subjective well-being and income. The author interpreted these findings as follows:

> *…economic development leads to higher levels of national average [subjective well-being] not by increasing consumption…but by creating more individualistic cultures which encourage their members to pursue personal happiness over honor and meeting social obligations. Whether or not this is seen as a socially positive development depends…on the cultural values of the person making the judgement.*

—Aaron C. Ahuvia, "Individualism/Collectivism and Cultures of Happiness."
***The Journal of Happiness Studies* 3, 1 (March, 2002): p. 23.**

In other words, it does not follow that the more money you have the happier you will be. More important is the freedom to pursue you own personal fulfillment. This freedom is what makes you happier.

Other researchers have claimed that increased individualism in a society leads to an increased sense of commitment to the collective. In a study that examined levels of **social capital**—the strength of social relationships between individuals—and individualism, the authors argued the following:

> *In America, the states with a high level of social capital (higher degree of civic engagement in political activity, where people spend more time with their friends and believe that most people can be trusted) were found to be more individualistic. A correspondingly strong association between individualism and social capital was observed in the comparison of different countries. These results support Durkheim's [an early social theorist] view that when individuals become more autonomous and seemingly liberated from social bonds, they actually become even more dependent on society.*

—Jüri Allik and Anu Realo, "Individualism-Collectivism and Social Capital."
***Journal of Cross-Cultural Psychology* 35, 1 (2004): 29–49.**

Such studies seem to indicate that individualism and collectivism are not diametrically opposed concepts. In the following examples, we will look at situations where individualist and collectivist values co-exist.

Entrepreneurialism

Maclean's *magazine and the Northern Alberta Institute of Technology both agree: John Stanton is an outstanding individual. In 2004, Maclean's declared Stanton one of the year's top 10 Canadians "who made a difference." In 2006, NAIT awarded Stanton an honorary diploma "aimed at honoring outstanding individual achievement on a local, national or international level." Born in Edmonton, Stanton turned his new interest in running from a part-time job using a single room to a business of over 60 Running Room and Walking Room store locations and he supports charitable run events as well. Stanton figures he works about 360 days a year—300 of them on the road, visiting stores, giving talks and running with customers. "True success is never knowing if you are working or playing," he says. "I feel pretty successful."*

—Source: Brian Bergman, "John Stanton." ***Maclean's*, July 1, 2004.**
http://www.macleans.ca/article.jsp?content=20040701_83575_83575

John Stanton is a good example of a person who has benefited from the individualist values of economic freedom and self-interest, an entrepreneur who has achieved great success in the capitalist marketplace. But the benefits of entrepreneurship are not necessarily limited to one individual's achievement. Businesspeople also provide economic benefits for others by creating employment, and sometimes even attempt to influence others in positive ways. As well as building a profitable business, John Stanton was able to give back to the community by supporting charitable events and promoting healthy lifestyle choices.

Another entrepreneur, Britain's Anita Roddick, started her own business, selling skin and hair care products, in 1976 to create a livelihood for herself and her two daughters while her husband was away trekking in the Americas. Thirty years later, The Body Shop consisted of 2045 stores serving over 77 million customers in 51 different markets in 25 different languages and across 12 time zones. According to Roddick,

Businesses have the power to do good. That's why The Body Shop's Mission Statement opens with the overriding commitment, "To dedicate our business to the pursuit of social and environmental change." We use our stores and our products to help communicate human rights and environmental issues.

—Source: AnitaRoddick.com
http://www.anitaroddick.com/aboutanita.php

People such as Dr Muhammad Yunus use their own business expertise to help others become entrepreneurs. Dr Yunus was already a

Figure 2-9 ▲

Dr Muhammad Yunus won the 2006 Nobel Prize for Peace. The Grameen Bank is now used as a model for micro-credit institutions in less developed countries around the world.

prominent economist and successful businessman in Bangladesh when he started providing micro-loans to Bangladeshis who wanted to start small businesses, but could not secure loans from traditional banks because of their poverty. His first micro-loan was US $27, provided to a group of 40 furniture makers. By 1983, Dr Yunus's operations had become the *Grameen* (or Village) Bank. As of 2008, Grameen Bank has provided US $7.12 billion in loans to 7.53 million borrowers. The average loan is under US $1000.

> *I did something that challenged the banking world…Conventional banks look for the rich; we look for the absolutely poor. All people are entrepreneurs, but many don't have the opportunity to find that out.*

> **—Dr Muhammad Yunus, quoted in Ishaan Tharoor's "Paving the Way Out of Poverty,"** *Time*, **October 13, 2006.**
> http://www.time.com/time/world/article/0,8599,1546100,00.html

How has Dr Yunus combined values of individualism and collectivism to benefit society?

Social Programs and Public Services

> *In strong and vibrant democracies, a generous social-welfare state is not a road to serfdom but rather to fairness, economic equality, and international competitiveness. [Social welfare refers to government services to help those in need.]*

> **—Jeffrey Sachs, director of the Earth Institute at Columbia University**

A modern liberal democracy such as Canada is a good example of a society in which individualist and collectivist values are used side by side. While Canadian society is characterized by many of the values of individualism such as individual rights and freedoms, the rule of law, and economic freedom, we also benefit from a variety of social programs and public services provided by our government, such as health care, employment insurance, welfare, and public education. These programs can be considered collectivist because all Canadian citizens pay for them through taxation, but not everyone uses them or needs them. Our willingness to pay these taxes, even though we may not use the services provided, demonstrates a commitment to the well-being of the group or collective. While these programs may limit our individual freedoms to some degree—the taxes needed to fund such programs could be seen as a limit on our economic freedom, for example—most Canadian governments have sought to find a balance between individualism and collectivism, rather than excluding one or the other.

Child Care and Ideology

Something to Think About: To what extent is child care the responsibility of the government?

There is an African proverb that states "It takes a whole village to raise a child." This can be interpreted as a collectivist view of child care. How relevant is this view to Canadian society today? Should government be involved in providing child care, or should the responsibility be left to parents?

Child Care Solutions

The demand for daycare has raised the following question: Who should be responsible for providing daycare? Some people argue, on the one hand, that the money spent by government from public taxes results in better child care, because with funding comes more of a standardized approach where all child care is expected to meet a set of criteria. They might also argue that better child care leads to fewer problems later in the child's life; thus, a more collectivist approach is simply good economics because it benefits everyone by achieving a more harmonious society and by producing better citizens.

On the other hand, a more individualist perspective might argue that parents should be more self-reliant and assume complete responsibility for their children. Individualists might also point out that an absence of government involvement would mean lower public spending and thus lower taxes for everyone. There is also evidence that the one-on-one care of an attentive parent or guardian is for most children the best kind of child care. But is this individualistic approach possible in a modern industrialized country?

Views on the Situation

The Canadian Child Care Federation (CCCF) urges Stephen Harper...to work closely with the early learning and childcare community to resolve the childcare crisis in Canada...

"Currently, 70 per cent of mothers with children under six are in the workforce. All of these families require some form of childcare. At the same time, there are only enough regulated childcare spaces for 15 per cent of the children who need it," said Barbara Coyle, CCCF's executive director. "There simply isn't enough quality childcare available. We will be calling on Stephen Harper's government to work collaboratively with us to find solutions."

—Source: Canadian Child Care Federation, "CCCF Urges New Government to Work Together to Solve Child Care Crisis in Canada." January 24, 2006.

http://www.cccf-fcsge.ca/pressroom/pr_32_en.htm

Figure 2-10 ▲

State intervention in the care of children is relatively recent. Child care, as we know it today in Canada, began during the Second World War when many women worked in factories to produce armaments. Since the end of the war in 1945, women have increasingly worked outside the home. Women are no longer expected to single-handedly take responsibility for raising their children, and this has created a demand for daycare centres.

...in 1997, Québec introduced its own day-care system, offering spaces at five dollars a day. [In 2008, the fee was seven dollars a day.]...In October 2004, the Organisation for Economic Co-operation and Development [OECD] released a report that described Canada's childcare system as a chronically underfunded patchwork of programs...[It] holds the Québec system up as a model for the rest of Canada, but the program has had its critics...The Action démocratique du Québec [a provincial political party] called the program a "Soviet-style" service and said the waiting lists are typical of a socialist system. The ADQ's 2003 election platform called for thirty-dollar-a-day vouchers for parents, which they could spend on public or private care. Québec's largest employers' group, the Conseil du patronat, suggested a similar plan that would give families a $5000 allowance for each child to spend as they please.

—Source: CBC News Online, "Day Care." CBC.ca, July 5, 2006.
http://www.cbc.ca/news/background/daycare/

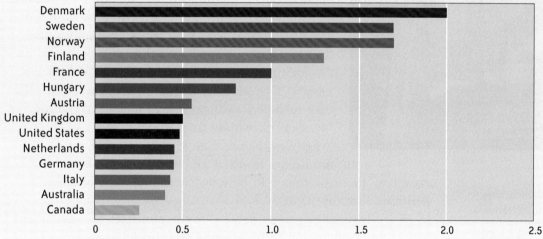

Public expenditure on ECEC services (0-6 years) in selected OECD countries (%)

Source: *Starting Strong II: Early Childhood Education and Care*, Organisation for Economic Co-operation and Development (Paris, 2006), p. 105.

Note: This figure is composed of expenditure extimates, based on replies provided by country authorities to an OECD survey in 2004. The figures provided suggest that Denmark spends 2% of GDP on early childhood services for 0- to 6-year-olds, and Sweden 1.7%. These countries—and Finland—also allocate an additional 0.3% (approximately) to the pre-school class [programs] for children 6 to 7 years.

▲ **Figure 2-11**

This graph shows public spending on early childhood education and care (ECEC) in selected member countries of the Organisation for Economic Co-operation and Development (OECD). What does it indicate about Canada's child-care policy? Should the provincial and federal governments emphasize more of a collectivist approach—more public spending on child care and set standards for daycare centres and staff—or an individualistic approach—leaving child care up to the parents?

QUESTIONS FOR REFLECTION

1 How do the various forms of child-care provision and funding reflect specific principles of individualism or collectivism?

2 Conduct research on the child-care policies of the federal Conservative, the Liberal, and the New Democratic parties. You may also include another party's policy if you wish. Create a chart comparing and contrasting the elements of their respective policies.

3 What is your position on the issue? Consider the issue carefully, and outline the arguments for and against your position. Write a position paper that explores your position and explores the key influences on your beliefs and values that led you to this position.

Figure 2-12 ▲

Kibbutzim (plural of *kibbutz*, meaning "gathering") are communal settlements in Israel, organized according to socialist or collectivist principles such as collective ownership of property, social equality, and co-operation in production, consumption, and education. The kibbutzim have been described as the fulfillment of the communist idea: "From each according to his ability, to each according to his needs."

Kibbutz

Many modern societies founded on the traditional values of individualism have gradually incorporated some degree of collectivism over time. Similarly, some collectivist societies have come to embrace aspects of individualism. The collectivist Israeli communities known as *kibbutzim* are a good example of this.

The first kibbutzim were founded about 40 years before the establishment of the State of Israel (1948), and most were dedicated to agricultural production. Eventually kibbutzim began to engage in industrial production, building factories and other manufacturing facilities. Today, about one-quarter of kibbutz members in Israel work in agriculture and fisheries, and an equal number are working in industry; other kibbutz activities include tourism, finance, and public services. Traditionally, all property on a kibbutz, including tools and clothing, was collectively owned; meals were eaten with the entire community, rather than in the family home; and children were raised by the community. According to the Jewish Virtual Library, "Compared to the past, kibbutzim today offer their members a wider range of individual choices. Members have more latitude in all aspects of their lives, from the selection of clothing and home furnishings to where and how to spend their vacations." (Source: Amnon Rubinstein, "Return of the kibbutzim." *Jerusalem Post* July 10, 2007.)

- Why might a society devoted to the principles of collectivism gradually become more open to the principles of individualism?

Non-Governmental Organizations

I meet people endlessly who have entered into their middle age and suddenly woken up, saying to themselves that yes, they are a success, but they feel awful because they're not doing anything that really interests them. In effect, they wake up feeling bored, which is one of the worst things to happen to a successful human being—it is a sense that you have wasted the first half of your life on the secondary activities. The smart ones get involved and act as citizens. I'm suggesting that you should be getting involved right now. I think a lot of you probably already are, if the

NGO involvement of students is anything to go by. In other words, time is no excuse. Get used to giving public time while you are still poor.

—Source: **John Ralston Saul, "Struggling for Balance: Public Education and Civil Society," a speech given at the University of Calgary, March 25, 2003. Governor General of Canada.**
http://www.gg.ca/media/doc.asp?lang=e&DocID=4026

Non-governmental organizations (NGOs) are another example of a structure founded on both collectivist and individualist values. NGOs are created for the purpose of addressing a social issue such as homelessness, hunger, or economic development. In this sense they are collectivist, since they work together toward a goal that serves the common good within a country or internationally. At the same time, they use aspects of individualism, since they are private initiatives. Habitat for Humanity is one such organization.

Across Canada, and indeed around the world, there are thousands of men, women, and children who are without homes. Some organizations exist to help alleviate this problem. Habitat for Humanity is a non-profit international organization that builds homes for families. In Alberta alone, there are 11 Habitat for Humanity affiliates.

I got involved [with the Jimmy Carter Work Project] for all the wrong reasons. It was out of insecurity and fear in our neighborhood…We were concerned about the devaluation of our houses. But when I saw the whole picture, I was ashamed that I would take such a negative view. Eventually, when I saw Habitat happening, I had to make a statement. I brought biryani (a popular Indian dish) to the site and asked the local gas station to donate bread. We gave it to the [Habitat] homeowners, saying: "This is a small gesture of welcome," because we felt that what they were going to be achieving made them heroes…The thing is, if we can get each person to embrace their neighbor, isn't that what we're supposed to do…?"

—Source: **Stuart Wilson (a South African from the gated community adjacent to Ethembeni, site of the 2002 Jimmy Carter Work Project), quoted on Habitat World**
http://www.habitat.org/hw/june-july04/notes.html

Figure 2-13 ▲

Stuart Wilson (background) helping to build a home in South Africa.

A lot of (the Not-In-My-Back-Yard attitude) has to do with people feeling like islands unto themselves. The whole basis of Habitat is that nobody is. It makes people look beyond the fence of their own homes. Our famous thing is that we break down barriers.

—Source: **Lisa Hartley (executive director, Bergen County, New Jersey, Habitat for Humanity), quoted on Habitat World.**
http://www.habitat.org/hw/june-july04/notes.html

Where Collectivism and Individualism Meet

We have seen that the values of individualism and collectivism are not mutually exclusive. Traditionally, many Aboriginal communities have placed greater importance on the values of collectivism than those of individualism. Today, the Osoyoos Indian Band is integrating values from both of these perspectives in their community.

The Osoyoos Indian Band is a community of 432 members with about 12 950 hectares of reserve lands in southern British Columbia. Over 80 per cent of band members live on the reserve. Through the Osoyoos Indian Band Development Corporation, the band owns and operates 10 different businesses, including a winery, vineyards, a golf course, a construction company, and a cultural centre. They employ 242 people, 89 of whom are band members, and 33 of whom are Aboriginal people from other communities.

One of the driving forces behind the band's success is Chief Clarence Louie, who is both the band chief and the CEO of the development corporation. Chief Louie has gained national attention for his direct approach and his emphasis on economic development and self-sufficiency. He is frequently asked to speak to both Aboriginal and non-Aboriginal groups across Canada about the role of development in Aboriginal communities. Not everyone in British Columbia's First Nations agrees with his views, however.

The Band does not owe its membership dependency. It owes them an opportunity and a chance to become independent.

—Source: Chief Clarence Louie, quoted in the NKMIP Resort Media Kit (NKMIP is run by the Osoyoos Indian Band).
http://www.nkmip.com/assets/files/pdf/20080228%20
Nk'Mip%20Resort%20Association%20Media%20Kit.pdf

Chief Louie made the following comments to the Standing Senate Committee on Aboriginal Peoples. The committee examined the involvement of Aboriginal communities and businesses in economic development activities in Canada:

Why the heck cannot the politicians at all levels of the federal and provincial governments, as well as all the Canadian people, see that when you spend 92 per cent of $8 billion a year on social programs and only 8 per cent on economic development, Aboriginal poverty will always be Canada's hidden shame.

I always say that in Osoyoos we do not look for consensus. I do not believe in consensus; it does not exist any more. The majority rule. We make decisions. We have a vote tomorrow on a $3-million power project going through our reserve, and for all those people who want to vote against it, vote against it. As long as the majority vote for it, this project will go ahead.

I do not attend most AFN [Assembly of First Nations] meetings, I do not attend most Union of BC Chiefs meetings, I do not attend most summit meetings, because in order to be an entrepreneur or businessman, you have to stay home

Children participate in the Nk'Mip Desert Cultural Centre's Rattlesnake Research Program, launched in 2002 by the Osoyoos Indian Band in partnership with the Canadian Wildlife Service. The Rattlesnake Research Program was the recipient of the Aboriginal Tourism British Columbia "Power of Education" award in 2003. The snake pictured here is a Great Basin gopher snake, which is non-venomous. Rattlesnakes, which resemble the gopher snake, are extremely poisonous and should never be touched.

and look after your own. I always feel you should look after your own backyard before going off to try to save all the whales, save all the trees and hug everybody. Stay home and look after the potholes in your own backyard.

—Source: ***Proceedings of the Standing Senate Committee on Aboriginal Peoples***. **Issue 13, "Evidence," meeting on October 26, 2005.**

http://www.parl.gc.ca/38/1/parlbus/commbus/senate/Com-e/abor-e/13evb-e.htm?Language=E&Parl=38&Ses=1&comm_id=1

Half of our businesses are run by First Nations people. Two of those are Osoyoos Indian Band members, but they had to earn those positions. They had to leave the community, go down to the States and get their degree. Even when they came back, they did not immediately get the job. They had to work under the non-Native manager for "X" number of years before they were promoted.

—Source: ***Proceedings of the Standing Senate Committee on Aboriginal Peoples***. **Issue 13, "Evidence," meeting on October 26, 2005.**

http://www.parl.gc.ca/38/1/parlbus/commbus/senate/Com-e/abor-e/13evb-e.htm?Language=E&Parl=38&Ses=1&comm_id=1

1 Construct a chart with two columns: "Principles of Individualism" and "Principles of Collectivism." Identify the main ideas and corresponding evidence in Chief Louie's comments that would go in each column. Based on his comments, do you think Chief Louie favours individualism, collectivism, or a balance of the two?

2 Imagine that you had the responsibility of Chief Louie. What programs would you create for the Osoyoos Indian Band to motivate young people? What businesses would you try to develop in order to inspire young members of the Band to further their education, aspire to good jobs, and so on?

3 Choose a reserve near you, or one that you are interested in finding out more about. Research the economic development activities on this reserve. Alternatively, research a business run on a Métis settlement or an Aboriginal business not on a reserve or Métis settlement. Compare it to the situation of the Osoyoos Band. Are the values of individualism and collectivism being integrated in a similar way? What differences exist between the two situations?

Up in Smoke: Exploring the Characteristics of Ideologies

Debate: Should the government infringe on a smoker's individual freedom in order to promote the well-being of society?

There is no doubt that the anti-smokers are pushing very hard to prohibit the choice to smoke, many times in unscrupulous ways—and that they are using carefully "spun" techniques of instigating intolerance in order to do this.
Our job will be to push back with equal force.

— **Source: Forces Canada (part of the Forces International smokers' rights movement).**
http://www.forces.org/canada/canf.htm

Professional, dynamic advocacy based on solid research and critical thinking have been the hallmark of the NSRA [Non-Smokers' Rights Association] since its inception. Thanks to ongoing efforts in coalition-building with national, provincial and local health and community groups, the association has helped bring about a sea change in Canadian attitudes towards the tobacco industry and its deadly products.

— **Source: Non-Smokers' Rights Association, "What is the NSRA?"**
http://www.nsra-adnf.ca/cms/index.cfm

Questions to Guide You

Use the following questions to guide your exploration of the sources that your teacher will provide, or that you locate on the Internet, about this debate topic.

1. Who wrote the article? What are the author's qualifications to speak on this topic?
2. What is the author's or organization's perspective? What assumptions or judgments about others are being made?
3. What are the different points of view on this issue? What beliefs about the nature of society are represented in the different views? What similarities exist among the various sources?
4. What is your viewpoint on the issue? How does your viewpoint reflect your beliefs and values about the kind of society we should live in? Why is it not ethical to belittle another's position in order to support your own?
5. Now that you can compare your assumptions and beliefs about this issue with others, has your initial position changed? What other evidence might you need to alter your position, if you were inclined to do so?

Explore the Issues

Concept Review
1. a) Identify three expressions of individualist principles in modern society.
   b) Identify three expressions of collectivist principles in modern society.
   c) Identify two examples of individualism and collectivism coexisting in modern society.

Concept Application
2. Compare and contrast an example of individualism from today with one from the past.

3. Compare and contrast an example of collectivism from today with one from the past.

4. Describe a personal example of individualism, and explain whether it was beneficial to you or not.

5. Draw a Venn diagram that shows how the principles of individualism and collectivism overlap. Think of another example, not discussed in this section, of how individualism and collectivism can complement each other, and create a second Venn diagram to show their complementary aspects.

Reflect and Analyze

In this chapter you explored the concepts of individualism and collectivism and the principles upon which they are based. You saw the dynamic relationship between these two concepts, including the ways that they can conflict. You considered the impact of these opposing ideologies in the world as well as their influence on personal identity. You now have a good foundation for responding to the Chapter Issue: *To what extent are individualism and collectivism foundations of ideology?* You can also refine your response to the Related Issue for Part 1: *To what extent should ideology be the foundation of identity?* Think about the extent to which you want individualism or collectivism to influence your personal identity. Discuss this issue with your peers and with your parents or other significant people in your life.

Respond to Ideas

1 a) A U-shape forum promotes open-ended discussions in which participants are encouraged to see the merits of all sides of an issue and to accept positions along a continuum. Use a U-shape forum to discuss the following issue: To what extent should society play a role in child care?

Set up your desks in a U-shape. Students with strongly held views should sit at either tip of the U, while students with mixed views should sit at appropriate spots along the rounded part of the U. As an example, for the question of child care, students who believe that families should find their own solutions rather than relying on government assistance should sit on the right side of the U. Students who believe that the government should run no-fee child care centres funded by taxes should sit on the left side of the U. Students who believe in a compromise between these positions should sit along the rounded part of the U. You are encouraged to move along

the continuum during the discussion as your position on the issue changes. If you decide to move, share your reasons with the rest of the class.

b) When you have completed the U-shape forum activity, create an essay, a poster, a poem, or a PowerPoint presentation answering the following question: *To what extent are individualism and collectivism foundations of your identity?*

Respond to Issues

2 *Play It Out!* In small groups, create a card game that addresses the following issue: *To what extent should ideology be the foundation of identity?*

a) Go back through this chapter and create "principle cards" and "example cards."

b) Decide what kind of card game you will create. An example might be "Go Fish!" where players must match up a principle of individualism or collectivism to an example of that principle. For example, one card of a pair might say "economic freedom," and the other might say "free-market economy."

This card game is intended to act as a review of what you have learned as well as an examination of the influence that ideological values have on people's actions and the structure of societies.

Recognize Relationships between Concepts, Issues, and Citizenship

3 Work in pairs to prepare a one-on-one interview between a news media host and an Aboriginal leader on the following issue: Does a Canadian liberal democratic government conflict both practically and ideologically with traditional Aboriginal worldview? Conduct research to ensure that your questions and answers are well informed.

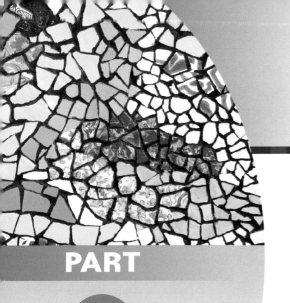

The Origin and Growth of Liberalism

In 1891, the troubled French painter Paul Gauguin fled from Paris to live in the South Pacific paradise of Tahiti. Despite failing health, poverty, and thoughts of suicide, his paintings sought to capture the essence of humanity as he saw it in local life. When a steamer docked in Tahiti in 1897, Gauguin learned of the death of his beloved daughter, Aline. Troubled by the news, he was inspired to create one of his most provocative murals that summed up his thoughts on life and death. The picture's title is based on three questions he scribbled down after learning of Aline's death—*D'où venons-nous? Que sommes-nous? Où allons-nous?*—Where do we come from? What are we? Where are we going?—three questions central to Social Studies.

These three questions also provide the basis for considering the Related Issue for Part 2, ***To what extent is resistance to liberalism justified?*** In Part 2, the question *Where do we come from?* is explored by investigating the emergence of classical liberal ideology during the Enlightenment and the Age of Reason. The complete transformation of the social, political, and economic structures through the political and economic revolutions of the last millennium offers insights into an ideology that continues to evolve and shape our daily lives, our identity, and our conception of the role of a citizen.

The reaction of people within society to this evolving ideology answers Gauguin's question *What are we?* Investigating this question

The only freedom which deserves the name is that of pursuing our own good in our own way, so long as we do not attempt to deprive others of theirs, or impede their efforts to obtain it...Mankind are greater gainers by suffering each other to live as seems good to themselves, than by compelling each to live as seems good to the rest.

—John Stuart Mill,
***On Liberty*, 1859**

Left: Paul Gauguin, "D'où venons-nous? Que sommes-nous? Où allons-nous?" (detail) 1897–1898. Photograph © 2009 Museum of Fine Arts, Boston.

Right: Paul Gauguin (1848–1903), self-portrait, 1889.

gives insights into the concept of identity addressed in Part 1. Answers to this complex question can be seen in the actions of Luddites who smashed machines, Nazis who rejected liberalism, and free market advocates who established a postwar consumer society.

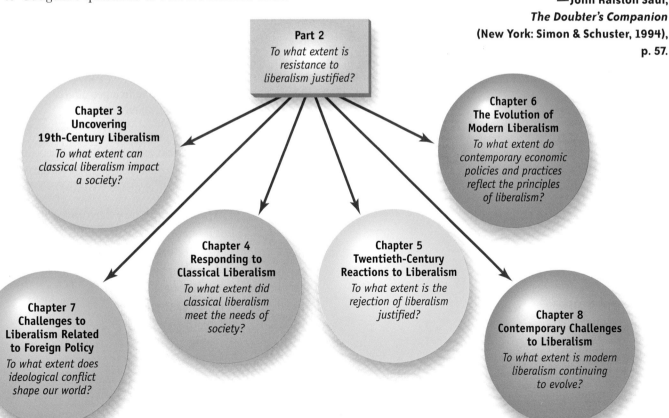

Visit the Learn Alberta site www.LearnAlberta.ca and click on the *Perspectives on Ideology* learning object for fully interactive learning scenarios entitled ExCite (Exploring Citizenship). These scenarios related to issues and concepts in the Student Resource enhance learning.

Much like Gauguin's third compelling question—*Where are we going?*—Part 2 encourages you to consider the past while preparing for the future. You will investigate how others have responded to the economic and social conditions that arose based upon this evolving ideology. This inquiry will provide the basis for you to consider the Key Issue for this course: **To what extent should we embrace an ideology?**

While you read this section, consider how the people quoted here and in Part 2 might respond to Gauguin's questions. Consider also how the current economic and social conditions might cause you to respond to Gauguin's questions or Part 2's Related Issue.

The uniform, constant and uninterrupted effort of every man to better his condition, the principle from which public and national, as well as private opulence is originally derived, is frequently powerful enough to maintain the natural progress of things toward improvement, in spite both of the extravagance of government, and of the greatest errors of administration.

—**Adam Smith,**
The Wealth of Nations,
Book II Chapter III, 1776

But if allowed to run free of the social system, capitalism will attempt to corrupt and undermine democracy, which is after all not a natural state.

—**John Ralston Saul,**
The Doubter's Companion
(New York: Simon & Schuster, 1994),
p. 57.

Part 2
To what extent is resistance to liberalism justified?

Chapter 3
Uncovering 19th-Century Liberalism
To what extent can classical liberalism impact a society?

Chapter 6
The Evolution of Modern Liberalism
To what extent do contemporary economic policies and practices reflect the principles of liberalism?

Chapter 4
Responding to Classical Liberalism
To what extent did classical liberalism meet the needs of society?

Chapter 5
Twentieth-Century Reactions to Liberalism
To what extent is the rejection of liberalism justified?

Chapter 7
Challenges to Liberalism Related to Foreign Policy
To what extent does ideological conflict shape our world?

Chapter 8
Contemporary Challenges to Liberalism
To what extent is modern liberalism continuing to evolve?

Uncovering 19th-Century Liberalism

KEY SKILL

Determining the historical significance of events

KEY CONCEPTS

Examining the history of classical liberalism

Analyzing the impact of the evolution of classical liberalism on society

Key Terms

Class system
Enlightenment
Free market
Industrialization
Laissez-faire capitalism
Limited government
Traditional economy
John Locke
John Stuart Mill
Montesquieu
Adam Smith

Figure 3-1 ▲

Calico printing in a cotton mill. Industrialization and factories transformed life in Britain in the 19th century. To what extent could moving away from agriculture and farm life to working in factories and living in cities affect people's lives or what they individually or collectively value?

The following excerpts provide viewpoints on aspects of what would later become known as the ideologies of classical liberalism and early **capitalism** and their effects on society in 19th-century Britain.

It was a town of red brick, or of brick that would have been red if the smoke and ashes had allowed it; but as matters stood, it was a town of unnatural red and black…It was a town of machinery and tall chimneys, out of which interminable serpents of smoke trailed themselves for ever and ever, and never got uncoiled. It had a black canal in it, and a river that ran purple with ill-smelling dye, and vast piles of building [sic] full of windows where there was a rattling and a trembling all day long, and where the piston of the steam-engine worked monotonously up and down, like the head of an elephant in a state of melancholy madness. It contained several large streets all very like one another, and many small streets still more like one another, inhabited by people equally like one another, who all went in and out at the same hours, with the same sound upon the same pavements, to do the same work, and to whom every day was the same as yesterday and to-morrow, and every year the counterpart of the last and the next.

**—Charles Dickens, *Hard Times*,
Book I, Chapter 5, 1854.**

Oh my friends, the down-trodden operatives of Coketown! [a fictional town in northwest England] Oh my friends and fellow-countrymen, the slaves of an ironhanded and a grinding despotism! Oh my friends and fellow-sufferers, and fellow-workmen, and fellow-men! I tell you that the hour is come, when we must rally round one another as One united power, and crumble into dust the oppressors that too long have battened upon the plunder of our families, upon the sweat of our brows, upon the labour of our hands, upon the strength of our sinews, upon the God-created glorious rights of Humanity, and upon the holy and eternal privileges of Brotherhood!

**—Charles Dickens, *Hard Times*,
Book II, Chapter 4, 1854.**

It always grieves me to contemplate the initiation of children into the ways of life when they are scarcely more than infants. It checks their confidence and simplicity, two of the best qualities that heaven gives them, and demands that they share our sorrows before they are capable of entering into our enjoyments.

**—Charles Dickens, *The Old Curiosity Shop*,
Chapter 1, 1841.**

The natural price of labour is that price which is necessary to enable the labourers, one with another, to subsist and to perpetuate their race, without either increase or diminution…

It is when the market price of labour exceeds its natural price, that the condition of the labourer is flourishing and happy, that he has it in his power to command a greater proportion of the necessaries and enjoyments of life, and therefore to rear a healthy and numerous family. When, however, by the encouragement which high wages give to the increase of population, the number of labourers is increased, wages again fall to their natural price, and indeed from a reaction sometimes fall below it…

These, then, are the laws by which wages are regulated, and by which the happiness of far the greatest part of every community is governed. Like all other contracts, wages should be left to the fair and free competition of the market, and should never be controlled by the interference of the legislature.

**—David Ricardo,
The Iron Law of Wages, 1817.**

The three quotations by Dickens provide a description of conditions in Britain during his lifetime. They are also statements that reveal his point of view. What is his point of view about the impact of classical liberalism on his society? Who would disagree with him, and for what reasons?

Chapter Issue

In this chapter you will look at when and where the ideas of classical liberalism originated, how these ideas evolved into the principles of classical liberalism, and determine some of the impacts of liberalism on society in the 19th century. The main issue for this chapter is ***To what extent can classical liberalism impact a society?***

The scenes of city life described above by Charles Dickens and the values defended in Ricardo's *Iron Law of Wages* were new to the society of 19th-century Great Britain. This was a time of dramatic change for most people. The beliefs and values of classical liberalism, which you will explore in this chapter, helped to bring about this major shift in Western society. Exploring the origins, principles, and influences of classical liberalism will provide you with the necessary background for understanding the role that classical liberal principles have played in the world at large.

Classical liberalism originated in Great Britain and had an immediate impact on its society. Thus many of the examples in this chapter focus on events in Great Britain and North America. Very quickly, however, the principles, beliefs, and values of classical liberalism affected many countries and peoples around the globe. Its impact is still seen today, and its principles continue to shape economic and political decisions in many countries, and between countries, around the world.

Figure 3-2 ▶

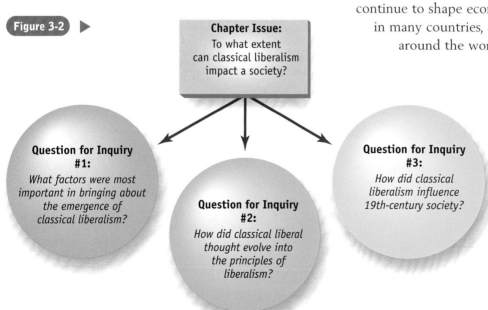

Chapter Issue:
To what extent can classical liberalism impact a society?

Question for Inquiry #1:
What factors were most important in bringing about the emergence of classical liberalism?

Question for Inquiry #2:
How did classical liberal thought evolve into the principles of liberalism?

Question for Inquiry #3:
How did classical liberalism influence 19th-century society?

History of Classical Liberalism

Question for Inquiry

- **What factors were most important in bringing about the emergence of classical liberalism?**

Classical liberalism is an ideology that embraces the principles of individualism about which you read in Chapter 2:

- the rule of law
- individual rights and freedoms
- private property
- economic freedom
- self-interest
- competition

Classical liberalism stresses the importance of human rationality. Just as it values political freedoms, classical liberalism also holds freedom to be the basic standard in economics, and believes the most beneficial economic system to be the **"free market"**: an economy that operates with **limited government** intervention and relies on the choices that rational individuals make in their own self-interest.

A market order based on private property is thus seen as an embodiment of freedom…Unless people are free to make contracts and to sell their labour, or unless they are free to save their incomes and then invest them as they see fit, or unless they are free to run enterprises when they have obtained the capital, they are not really free.

—Source: Gerald Gaus and Shane Courland, "Liberalism", Stanford Encyclopedia of Philosophy (Fall 2008 Edition), Edward N. Zalta (ed.).
http://plato.stanford.edu/entries/liberalism/#DebAboLib

Because more modern schools of liberalism have advocated a greater role for the state in the lives of its citizens, the term *classical liberalism* has been used to indicate the original ideals (or practices or principles) of liberalism.

Figure 3-3 ▼

This timeline outlines the historical development of the European ideas and events that eventually combined to form classical liberalism, a dynamic force for the creation of wealth, industry, and new values, and for the shaping of the modern Western world.

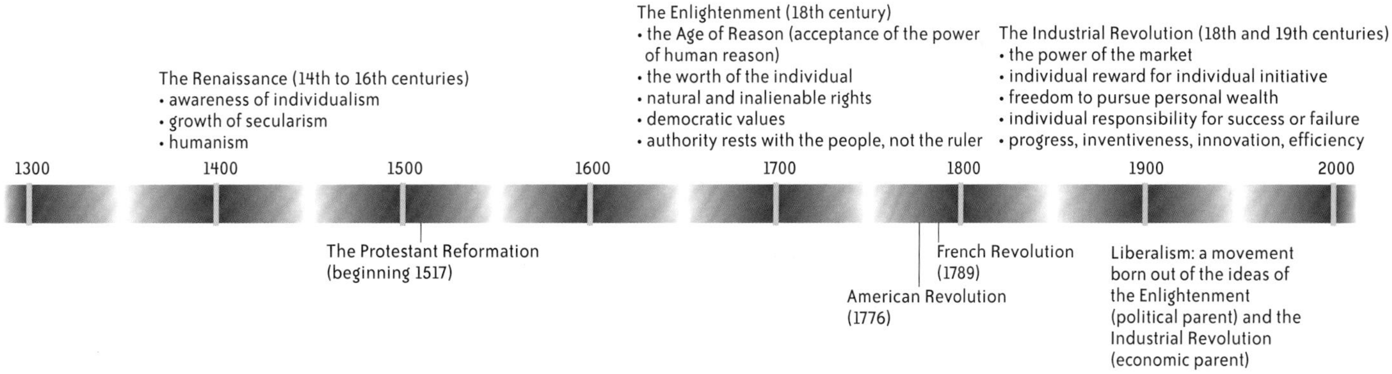

The Enlightenment (18th century)
- the Age of Reason (acceptance of the power of human reason)
- the worth of the individual
- natural and inalienable rights
- democratic values
- authority rests with the people, not the ruler

The Renaissance (14th to 16th centuries)
- awareness of individualism
- growth of secularism
- humanism

The Industrial Revolution (18th and 19th centuries)
- the power of the market
- individual reward for individual initiative
- freedom to pursue personal wealth
- individual responsibility for success or failure
- progress, inventiveness, innovation, efficiency

| 1300 | 1400 | 1500 | 1600 | 1700 | 1800 | 1900 | 2000 |

The Protestant Reformation (beginning 1517)

French Revolution (1789)

American Revolution (1776)

Liberalism: a movement born out of the ideas of the Enlightenment (political parent) and the Industrial Revolution (economic parent)

The beliefs of classical liberalism arose in Europe following the Renaissance and Reformation from the 14th to 16th centuries. The Renaissance sparked a belief in the importance of the individual in society, and the Reformation reflected the belief that reason was as significant as faith for the believer in Christianity. These trends helped promote the rise of the **Enlightenment**, or the **Age of Reason**, beginning in the late 17th century and continuing through the 18th century. In turn, the Enlightenment helped promote the beliefs of classical liberalism that congealed into the liberal ideology of the 19th century.

The Enlightenment had its roots in the 14th-century Renaissance—the revival of Greek and Roman thinking. Thomas Aquinas sought to use the ideas of the Greek scholar Aristotle to support the teachings of the Christian church through the use of logical argument and reason. Other thinkers continued to investigate logic and reason, and starting in the late 14th century a group of thinkers known as the humanists emerged in Italy and France. **Humanists** during this time period believed in the importance of arts and literature alongside faith. They developed an interpretation of history and beliefs about human nature, the structure of society, and the purpose of life, all based on reason rather than religion. Humanists sought meaning and purpose in love, beauty, art, and development of the self. The fields of art, music, literature, science, to name but a few, were now viewed as places to celebrate human accomplishment rather than faith. Along with this came a questioning of the authority, teachings, and practices of the Roman Catholic Church. The Protestant Reformation of the 16th and 17th centuries dramatically altered the political, economic, and social circumstances of Europe through its opposition to the Catholic Church and its hierarchical concentration of religious power and perceived corruption of that power. During the same time period as the Protestant Reformation, faith in the rationality of the individual believer began to grow. Also at this time, Europeans came into contact with other flourishing but non-Christian civilizations (such as Indigenous peoples in North America), further challenging the predominance of established European religious thought about society and the meaning of life.

By the 17th century, Europe was in turmoil as a result of the emergence of new ideas about the role of the individual and the use of reason and logic over faith. Religious wars were rife and contests for imperial expansion dominated the social, political, and economic affairs of Europe. While Enlightenment thinkers believed that these new ideas could lead to freer and more tolerant societies, the ideas were not widely accepted because they challenged the established foundations of society.

Another important trend of the 17th century was the breakdown of the feudal economic order. Cities grew as more and more people became involved in expanded trade overseas. A wealthy middle class emerged. Peasants sought more lucrative work in cities, further eroding

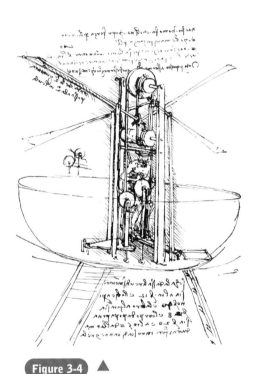

Figure 3-4 ▲

Leonardo da Vinci (1452–1519) was one of the great thinkers of the Renaissance. He is best known for his paintings and his scientific ideas and inventions. Many of his inventions were not practical to construct, but showed an innovative grasp of scientific and engineering principles.

This figure shows a drawing he made in the late 1480s for a type of aircraft called an *ornithopter* (from the Greek for "bird-wing"). A person standing in the bowl-shaped aircraft would operate the wings with various mechanisms, making the wings flap like a bird's.

To what extent could an ideological conflict of reason versus faith impact the structure and foundation of a society and people's lives?

the economic base of the aristocracy, whose wealth was based primarily on agriculture.

In these turbulent times of political struggles for less authoritarian rule, demands for greater economic opportunities, and social movements challenging the status quo, classical liberalism was a political and economic philosophy advocating individual rights and responsibilities and a role for government that was limited to maintaining security and the rule of law. Simply put, classical liberalism focused on allowing citizens the right to freedom in their economic, political, and social lives (although in practice, most of these rights applied primarily to the newly empowered entrepreneurial class). One author called classical liberalism

> …the great political and intellectual movement that substituted free enterprise and the market economy for the precapitalistic methods of production; constitutional representative government for the absolutism of kings or oligarchies; and freedom of all individuals from slavery, serfdom, and other forms of bondage.
>
> **—Ludwig von Mises, *Human Action: A Treatise on Economics*,**
> **foreword to the 3rd edition (Irvington-on-Hudson,**
> **NY: Foundation for Economic Education, 1996).**
> http://www.econlib.org/library/Mises/HmA/msHmA.html

Classical liberalism is typically considered to encourage the following principles:

- the primacy of individual rights and freedoms, to be exercised in the individual's self-interest
- the belief that humans are reasonable and can make rational decisions that will benefit both themselves and society as a whole
- economic freedom, involving the ownership of private property and free markets (markets with limited government intervention)
- the protection of civil liberties
- constitutional limitations on the government

The very close relationship between individual freedom and private property is addressed in the following quote:

> There can be no freedom of press if the instruments of printing are under government control, no freedom of assembly if the needed rooms are so controlled, no freedom of movement if the means of transport are a government monopoly.
>
> **—Friedrich Hayek, "Liberalism,"**
> ***New Studies in Philosophy, Politics,***
> ***Economics and the History of Ideas***
> **(London: Routledge and Kegan Paul, 1978), p. 149.**

Thinkers whose ideas contributed to the ideology of liberalism—people such as Thomas Hobbes; John Locke; Charles de Secondat, baron de Montesquieu; Adam Smith; and John Stuart Mill—were a disparate group of people who lived at different times and places. They were all writing about the political, economic, and social manifestations of individual rights and freedoms and their ideas gradually developed into an ideology. The impact of classical liberalism was to transform European society. You will be introduced to some examples of these transformations throughout this chapter.

Figure 3-5 ▶

The English Civil War (1642–1651), a conflict between Royalists and Parliamentarians, had a major impact on Thomas Hobbes's thinking. This print depicts a scene from the Battle of Marston Moor, which took place on July 2, 1644.

PAUSE AND REFLECT

What does Hobbes mean by the "selfishness" of human nature?

One of the most important tenets of the ideology of classical liberalism is the belief in the individual—that is, that the individual's well-being is as important as the group's. As you read in the introduction, English philosopher Thomas Hobbes was concerned with the problem of social and political order: how human beings could live together in peace and avoid the danger and fear of civil conflict. Although Hobbes's solution to the state of nature where life is "nasty, brutish, and short" seems to suggest that the individual citizen has no worth, and that only the central authority, or Leviathan, matters, a closer reading of his work suggests otherwise. Because of Hobbes's experience with the horrors of civil war, he saw humans as inherently selfish. This selfishness, if left unchecked, would result in chaos and harm to everyone. By having all people give up their sovereignty and by handing power over to a protecting ruler, the Leviathan, everyone would be secure. Hobbes's goal, then, was the security of all individuals, which could be achieved only at the expense of their individual sovereignty. It should also be noted, however, that the Leviathan could justify its power only if it kept its subjects safe. Again, this places the focus back on the worth of the individual subjects.

John Locke (1632–1704) was a contemporary of Hobbes. As you read in the introduction, Locke deeply opposed the authoritarianism of the Church and the state, and believed that individuals had the right to use their reason and logic to make their own decisions. He said, "Reason must be our last judge and guide in everything."

Locke, along with other thinkers such as Hobbes, believed in a social contract, whereby people give up some of their natural rights to a government in order to receive social order and security for themselves and their property. Unlike Hobbes, Locke believed that the government should be directly accountable to the people. He also placed great emphasis on the concept of private property, or the right of individuals to protect and keep what they owned:

The reason why men enter into society, is the preservation of their property; and the end why they choose and authorize a legislative, is, that there may be laws made, and rules set, as guards and fences to the properties of all the members of the society: to limit the power, and moderate the dominion, of every part and member of the society.

—**John Locke, *Two Treatises of Government*, Book 2, Chapter 19, Section 221, 1690.**

Charles de Secondat, baron de Montesquieu (1689–1755) was an Enlightenment thinker in France who satirized the times in which he lived. Under the theory of the divine right of kings, monarchs had come to believe they were no longer bound by any earthly authority, since their status was determined by God. The Church and the monarchy were the two great authoritarian powers, and society was divided into three classes or estates: clergy, aristocracy, and commoners. In the 1700s, pressures for change began to mount against the French regime, which was attempting to hold on to its feudalistic and absolutist structures. Montesquieu's satiric writings so angered the Catholic Church that it banned his works.

Montesquieu believed in the worth of the individual, the equality of individuals, and the accountability of government. He also believed strongly in the separation of powers—that is, that the government should be divided into three branches: executive, legislative, and judicial. Under this system, the three branches should be both separate from and dependent on one another so that the influence of any one power would not be able to exceed that of the other two.

In order for this system to work, the people needed to be involved in the government—that is, it needed to be a democracy. Montesquieu believed that each citizen had to participate in and be aware of the laws and the workings of government.

Figure 3-6 ▼

The Hall of Mirrors was one of the most sumptuous rooms at the palace of Versailles, the home of the French monarchy during Montesquieu's time. For many of the French people, the palace symbolized the negative aspects of absolutist monarchy. Restored to its original state, it is a major tourist attraction today.

Figure 3-7 ▲

John Stuart Mill, in an 1865 portrait. He had a rather unusual childhood. His father regulated his life in an attempt to create a superior intellect and was fortunate that Mill was something of a child prodigy. Possibly as a result, Mill suffered a nervous breakdown as a young man. He is notable for supporting women's rights in an era when very few did.

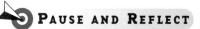

PAUSE AND REFLECT

How does the concept of private property fit into classical liberal theory?

The tyranny of a prince in an oligarchy is not so dangerous to the public welfare as the apathy of a citizen in a democracy.

—Attributed to Montesquieu

It is clear that in a monarchy, where he who commands the execution of the laws generally thinks himself above them, there is less need of virtue than in a popular government, where the person entrusted with the execution of the laws is sensible of his being subject to their direction.

—Montesquieu, *The Spirit of Laws*, Book 3, Part 3, 1748,
Trans. Thomas Nugent. http://www.constitution.org/cm/sol.htm

Montesquieu's separation of powers idea is largely taken for granted in many modern-day democracies. For example, the separation of powers is incorporated into the checks and balances built into the US Constitution, which was written only a few decades after Montesquieu was writing. Like other aspects of classical liberal ideology, however, Montesquieu's idea was radical at the time. It called for the elimination of the three-estate structure of French society (clergy, aristocracy, and commoners) and advocated an unprecedented level of individual involvement in government.

Yet another classical liberal thinker was the English philosopher John Stuart Mill (1806–1873). He was interested in the protection of individual freedom and the promotion of individual decision making as the core of societal institutions. His book *On Liberty* (1859) explores the limits of power that can legitimately be exercised over the individual. He believed that the only limitations that should be placed on an individual were those that would protect the liberty of others—that is, an individual should be able to act as he or she wants, so long as his or her actions would not harm others. Mill also strongly advocated free speech, which he believed was a necessary condition for intellectual and social progress.

If all mankind minus one, were of one opinion, and only one person were of the contrary opinion, mankind would be no more justified in silencing that one person, than he, if he had the power, would be justified in silencing mankind.

—John Stuart Mill, *On Liberty*, Chapter 2, 1859.

The Origins of Laissez-Faire Economics

Around 1750, a dramatic development occurred in Great Britain that changed the world forever. The coming together of new ideas and new conditions resulted in a historical period now known as the Industrial Revolution. The agricultural roots of the British economy were overtaken by industrial ones. Britain's **traditional economy**, which was largely based on subsistence farming in rural areas, shifted to factory work in urban centres. The change was so great that it has been considered a revolution.

Great Britain was unique for several reasons. First, being an island, Great Britain depended on sea trade. This led, over time, to a large commercial fleet, a powerful navy, and the largest empire in the world at that time. Not only did this fill the coffers of the government, it also provided the means for the creation of many personal fortunes for enterprising ship owners and merchants. Many merchants had large amounts of money available for investment.

Second, since the 17th century, the political climate of Great Britain had favoured the development of a parliamentary government and a constitutional monarchy. Power was shared between the king and Parliament—especially the House of Commons, which increasingly consisted of wealthy landowners and merchants. Parliament passed a series of laws called the Enclosure Acts, which served the interests of the merchants and landowners by forcing thousands of low-income farmers away from farmland and into towns and cities. This resulted in an uncommonly large pool of cheap labour.

Third, the world of ideas was being influenced by the writings of Enlightenment thinkers who advocated the primacy of human reason, human initiative, and individual worth.

These three factors came together at this time in Great Britain:

- New ideas about human potential and individual worth (former "commoners" were free to create wealth and achieve status), and the accompanying idea of progress
- A government friendly to business and innovation
- A huge amount of investment capital and cheap labour, and a large number of innovators and inventors who were encouraged by the possibility of reward

Together these resulted in the development of the factory system, the mechanization of labour, the mass production and consumption of consumer goods, the expansion of capitalism and free enterprise, and the shaping of the modern industrialized world. It also produced extremes of wealth and poverty, palatial estates and horrible slums, excess and starvation, child labour, worker abuse, and the degradation of the environment.

The French term *laissez-faire*—leave (people) alone to do (as they wish)—was definitive of capitalism at this time and referred to a reduction of government involvement in the economy. Individual actions and achievements were deemed to be more productive in economic decision making than government actions. Laissez-faire capitalism emerged from the theories of the **physiocrats**. The physiocrats were a group of Enlightenment philosophers in France who critiqued the prevailing economics of **mercantilism**. The mercantilist system held that the aim of all economic pursuits should be to

Figure 3-8 ▲

The Bank of England was formed in 1694. The impact of the new ideology of classical liberalism and the resulting increase in trade is reflected in its building opened in 1748 on Threadneedle Street in London, England. The bank's nickname is "The Old Lady of Threadneedle Street."

strengthen the power and wealth of the state. Physiocrats such as Anne-Robert-Jacques Turgot and François Quesnay took the concept of human agency and applied it to the creation of wealth. They promoted the concept of laissez-faire, which advocated that government should leave business entrepreneurs alone to follow their natural self-interest. Like their successor Adam Smith, about whom you read in Chapter 2, the physiocrats believed that the pursuit of this self-interest in economic affairs would benefit everyone.

The physiocrats' ideas exemplify a notion of progress: human activity in society continually improves the conditions for people. Their notion of laissez-faire reflects their beliefs that

- individuals need to be given freedom to make their own decisions
- individuals' selfishness and competitiveness will inadvertently improve their own societies

Adam Smith (1723–1790) was a Scottish political economist. Smith spent time in France with the physiocrats, and they influenced his thinking. He disagreed with the existing mercantilist economic system, and it is important to realize how radical Smith's ideas were at the time. The mercantilist system increased the wealth of the state but not the wealth of the majority of people within that state, and very few people enjoyed the benefits of the labour that fed the state's wealth. Smith's ideas were in stark contrast to this. He believed that if people worked first and foremost for themselves, everyone—including the state—would be better off. In 1776 he published *The Wealth of Nations*, in which he described a system where individuals work for their own self-interest in a free-market system. Smith insisted that individual self-interest in a free market would lead to a stronger economy and would therefore benefit most people in society.

Every individual necessarily labours to render the annual revenue of the society as great as he can. He generally, indeed, neither intends to promote the publick [sic] interest, nor knows how much he is promoting it…He intends only his own gain, and he is in this, as in many other cases, led by an invisible hand to promote an end which was no part of his intention.

—Adam Smith, *An Inquiry into the Nature and Causes of the Wealth of Nations*, Book IV, Chapter II, 1776.

The idea of the invisible hand, Smith's justification for self-interest as an economic motive, can be stated quite simply: by having every individual look after his or her own best interests, he or she unwittingly ends up helping everyone else, by providing jobs and cheaper products.

Furthermore, Smith believed that the government's role should be limited to maintaining the rule of law, to ensuring contracts were followed, and to providing some public works (such as primary education and road maintenance). Smith's work provided the foundation for much of the capitalist system. These essential concepts—the free market and a limited role for government—became the basis of laissez-faire capitalism, the economic system associated with classical liberalism.

Explore the Issues

Concept Review

1 Fill in the chart below.

Concept Application

2 Which thinkers best represent your own viewpoints and why?

3 In what ways did the principles of classical liberalism help the development of the Industrial Revolution?

4 Explain the concept of the social contract. Use an example of a social contract in your own life.

5 a) Create a concept web based on the principles of classical liberalism that best reflects potential impacts of classical liberalism on society.

b) Which factors were most significant in the emergence of classical liberalism? Identify the factors and give criteria for your idea of "most significant".

Thinkers	Beliefs	How Their Ideas Were Radical at that Time	How Their Ideas Are Related to Classical Liberalism
Hobbes			
Locke			
Montesquieu			
Smith			
Mill			
Ricardo			
Dickens			

To What Extent Did Aboriginal Ideas Influence Liberalism in North America?

Some historians believe that the Haudensaunee (Iroquois) peoples influenced liberal thought in North America. The Great Law of Peace, or the Constitution of the Haudenosaunee Confederacy, outlined the path to harmony and unity among the nations, divided powers between different levels of government, and established the equal participation of the people, including women, in the government. It also guaranteed certain rights and freedoms, including the freedom of speech and the rights of individuals.

Historian Bruce Johansen notes that as early as 1744, Benjamin Franklin, a publisher, who would later co-write the American Constitution, printed the words of the Haudenosaunee leader Canasetoga as he gave advice to American colonists about their dissatisfaction with British rule:

Our wise forefathers established union and amity between the five nations. This has made us formidable. This has given us great weight and authority with our neighboring nations. We are a powerful Confederacy, and by your observing the same methods our wise forefathers have taken you will acquire much strength and power; therefore, whatever befalls you, do not fall out with one another.

—**Bruce E. Johansen,** *Debating Democracy: Native American Legacy of Freedom.* **Santa Fe: Clear Light Publishers, 1998.**

Tom Axworthy, Chair, Centre for the Study of Democracy, writes:

Canada, too, has a tradition of participatory governance, one especially enshrined in the history of our First Nations…Long before the European settlement, Aboriginal people had developed sophisticated mechanisms of government and international relations and the basic principle of this system —consensus decision-making—is of continuing relevance to the modern age.

—**Tom Axworthy, "How our democracy evolved",** *The Kingston Whig Standard, September 27, 2008.*

Dr. John Mohawk, a Seneca leader and scholar, has stated:

I'm fairly certain that the structure of the United States government descends from a confederacy…I don't think it's an accident that the first proposal for a government for the colonies looks strikingly like the structure of the Confederacy of the Six Nations of the Iroquois, even down to the number of representatives and what their powers and limitations would be and all that. It's impossible to imagine that all of those could be coincidences. It seems as though the Americans were watching, especially Benjamin Franklin, who took a big interest in the Indians.

—**Dr. John Mohawk, in "Haudenosaunee Culture: The Great Law as a Model for US Democracy", background notes for** *A Warrior in Two Worlds: The life of Ely Parker.* **WXXI Public Broadcasting Council in Rochester, New York,** *first broadcast 6 April, 2000.*
http://www.pbs.org/warrior/content/modules/great.pdf

1 Based on the sources, what evidence is provided to support the idea that the Great Law of Peace may have had an influence on the American Constitution?

The American Revolution

John Locke had a profound influence on the American revolutionaries of 1776. His ideas, along with those of other early liberal thinkers, inspired the American colonists to declare independence from the British crown and establish a **republican** form of government where governing authority was invested in the hands of its citizens and not a ruling monarch. Examine the following quotes to determine to what extent Locke's ideas were part of the thinking of individuals who shaped the formation of the United States.

For all men being originally equals, no one by birth could have a right to set up his own family in perpetual preference to all others for ever.

—Thomas Paine, "Of Monarchy and Hereditary Succession,"
***Common Sense*, 1776.**

...every Man who comes among us, and takes up a piece of Land, becomes a Citizen, and by our Constitution has a Voice in Elections, and a share in the Government of the Country.

—Benjamin Franklin, letter to William Strahan, August 19, 1784,
quoted in *The Life and Writings of Benjamin Franklin*
(Philadelphia, PA: McCarty and Davis, 1834), p. 582.

The spirit of resistance to government is so valuable on certain occasions, that I wish it to be always kept alive. It will often be exercised when wrong, but better so than not to be exercised at all. I like a little rebellion now and then. It is like a storm in the atmosphere.

—Thomas Jefferson, letter to Abigail Adams, February 1787,
quoted in Paul Finkelman, *Encyclopedia of American Civil Liberties*
(New York: Routledge, 2006), p. 846.

We hold these truths to be self-evident, that all men are created equal, that they are endowed by their Creator with certain unalienable Rights, that among these are Life, Liberty and the pursuit of Happiness.—That to secure these rights, Governments are instituted among Men, deriving their just powers from the consent of the governed,—That whenever any Form of Government becomes destructive of these ends, it is the Right of the People to alter or to abolish it, and to institute new Government, laying its foundation on such principles and organizing its powers in such form, as to them shall seem most likely to effect their Safety and Happiness.

—Source: United States Declaration of Independence
www.yale.edu/lawweb/avalon/declare.htm

❶ What specific aspects of liberalism were built on and/or adopted by these individuals in the American Revolution?

❷ How would the comments be interpreted by various groups in American colonial society? Would every group be supportive of these ideas?

❸ Examine Canada's Constitution Act, 1867 and the Canadian Charter of Rights and Freedoms to determine the extent to which liberal principles influenced the writers of Canada's constitution. How acceptable would these principles be to other societies? How acceptable are these principles to you?

Get to the Source

Follow the links that your teacher will provide to read the entire Declaration of Independence and the Charter of Rights and Freedoms.

Get to the Source

Follow the link that your teacher will provide to read the entire Declaration of the Rights of Man and of the Citizen.

4. *Liberty consists in the freedom to do everything which injures no one else; hence the exercise of the natural rights of each man has no limits except those which assure to the other members of the society the enjoyment of the same rights. These limits can only be determined by law.*

6. *Law is the expression of the general will. Every citizen has a right to participate personally, or through his representative, in its foundation. It must be the same for all, whether it protects or punishes. All citizens, being equal in the eyes of the law, are equally eligible to all dignities and to all public positions and occupations, according to their abilities, and without distinction except that of their virtues and talents…*

11. *The free communication of ideas and opinions is one of the most precious of the rights of man. Every citizen may, accordingly, speak, write, and print with freedom, but shall be responsible for such abuses of this freedom as shall be defined by law…*

—**Source: The Declaration of the Rights of Man and of the Citizen.**

The recognition of many of these rights would significantly alter the status quo. If these articles were to be implemented, what impact might they have on the clergy, nobles, middle class, and peasants in France?

Explore the Issues

Concept Review

1 Using a chart format, connect each of the five principles of classical liberalism listed on page 105 with the eight sections of the Declaration of the Rights of Man and of the Citizen listed on pages 115 and 118.

Concept Application

2 Reread the excerpts from the Declaration of the Rights of Man and from the Citizen and from the Declaration of Independence and identify common themes of liberalism in the two documents.

3 Name three classical liberal thinkers discussed in the first section of this chapter who you think influenced the writers of the Declaration of the Rights of Man and of the Citizen. Show how their thoughts are linked to the five principles of classical liberalism on page 105. Why did you pick those three? How many of the articles of the Declaration are evident in modern-day Canada?

4 Many popular movies portray aspects of the French and American revolutions. Either via your teacher or from your own research, view a movie based on the French or American Revolution. After viewing the movie, respond to the following questions:

a) Whose perspectives are shown in the film?

b) Whose perspectives are not shown? Could these missing perspectives influence the way the events are interpreted?

c) How does the film illustrate the effects of liberalism on the society it depicts?

d) What kinds of resistance to liberal principles are shown in the film? How are these depicted—positively or negatively? How does this portrayal reinforce the film's message with respect to individualism and the ideology of classical liberalism?

e) Create a film poster that shows your understanding of how the film represents responses to liberal principles. Present your poster to the class and then use appropriate parts of the Skill Path on pages 125–126 to examine the historical significance of the film chosen for this inquiry.

Liberal Principles in Action

Question for Inquiry

• How did classical liberalism influence 19th-century society?

The principles of classical liberalism had become widespread in Western societies by the 19th century. The principles were the culmination of the political, economic, and social dynamics of the previous centuries. In Great Britain, classical liberalism tended to be an economic concern that used liberal principles as a springboard to implement laissez-faire economics. The tension between the reality of the market system and the continued awareness of fundamental liberal principles eventually led to the evolution of classical liberalism into modern liberalism. In this section of the chapter you will examine the ramifications of liberalism in terms of capitalism, **industrialization**, the class system, and the role of government, and explore the following question: How did classical liberalism influence 19th-century European society?

The Industrial Revolution (circa 1750–1900)

We began this chapter with a quick study of the origins of classical liberalism and its connection to the Industrial Revolution. Most of the impacts of liberalism we will be discussing in this section—capitalism, the class system, and so on—are linked to the Industrial Revolution. As one scholar put it, the Industrial Revolution was

the most far-reaching, influential transformation of human culture since the advent of agriculture eight or ten thousand years ago…The consequences of this revolution would change irrevocably human labor, consumption, family structure, social structure, and even the very soul and thoughts of the individual.

—Richard Hooker, "The Industrial Revolution." 1996
***The European Enlightenment*, Washington State University**
http://www.wsu.edu/~dee/ENLIGHT/INDUSTRY.HTM

"Industrial Revolution" describes the transition of Britain from an agricultural and mercantile society to a modern industrial one. It provided the impetus by which capitalism became the dominant economic force in Europe. Through the transformation of agriculture, industry, and economics, great wealth was created for some, along with great poverty for others. In the next quotation, Samuel Smiles (1812–1904), a doctor turned political reformer, embodies the kind of liberal ideas that drove the wave of industrialization that characterized the 19th century in Western societies, largely in Europe and North America.

All experience of life, indeed, serves seems to prove that the impediments thrown in the way of human advancement may, for the most part, be overcome by steady good conduct, honest zeal, activity, perseverance, and above all, by a determined resolution to surmount difficulties...

—Samuel Smiles and Charles A. Gaskill,
***Happy Homes and the Hearts That Make Them*, 1889.**

The influence of liberalism on capitalism is intertwined with the development of industrialization in the 19th century. The principles of classical liberalism, especially those dealing with economics (economic freedom, individual freedom, private property, self-interest, and competition) had a powerful effect in freeing up enterprising individuals. The technological developments that led to the mechanization of agriculture and industry were buttressed by these liberal principles as individual entrepreneurs and inventors tried to become more efficient and profitable. The value of the individual and the desire for minimal government involvement in economic affairs helped spur on the Industrial Revolution among the middle and upper classes, making for an ideal environment in which innovation could flourish.

Changes in Agriculture: Enclosure

Prior to the 18th century, agriculture in Britain's traditional economy retained many of its medieval aspects. Small farmers practised subsistence farming on small plots of land carved out of three or four large fields that were held in common. As early as the 12th century, some of these fields were enclosed—that is, the common land became the private property of an individual (an **enclosure**), and the small

Figure 3-10 ▶

In feudal times, the land belonged to a lord and was worked in small strips by his tenants. Immediately prior to the Industrial Revolution, the fields were held in common but small farmers often owned their own particular plots of land. The lord was able by law to force the land's sale.

farmers were dispossessed. The Church denounced this practice, and it became relatively infrequent. However, the growth of sheep farming and the invention of new agricultural technologies, such as the seed drill, required large enclosed fields to be effectively employed, so pressure mounted for enclosure in the 18th century. This time the pressure was accompanied by liberal beliefs in the sanctity of private property, and, in 1801, the British government passed the Inclosure (Consolidation) Act. Farmers received minimal compensation for their small strips of land, and far fewer agricultural labourers were needed on mechanized farms; thus the farmers forced off the land became a large workforce for the new factories.

Commercial and Industrial Revolutions

As a result of the European voyages of discovery in the 15th and 16th centuries, an influx of gold and silver from the Americas stimulated a money economy and the development of financial institutions in Britain. This discredited the government-regulated mercantilist system in favour of free trade, and provided **capital** (money) for the building of factories, made desirable by the new technologies that allowed machinery to replace hand labour. Gradually, the commercial entrepreneur emerged along with the trading merchant.

The factory was created during the 18th century as an expanding and wealthier population demanded more and better goods and as the use of steam engines and many other inventions made large-scale production possible. Large-scale production began in the textile industry. Machines such as the fly shuttle, spinning jenny, water frame, and power loom changed textile production from a cottage industry to a factory industry. The same process eventually occurred in all manufacturing industries.

Classical liberal ideology was inextricably woven into these developments in agriculture and commerce and provided the foundation for the capitalist society.

	Population in 1800	Population in 1900
London	800 000	6 500 000
Paris	500 000	3 000 000
New York	60 000	4 200 000

Source: UN-Habitat, "Today's Slums: Myths versus Reality," January 2007. http://www.unhabitat.org/downloads/docs/Press_SG_visit_Kibera07/SG%2012.pdf.

Figure 3-11

Before the Industrial Revolution, most people lived in small towns where they did manual labour on a very small scale, providing goods and services for their immediate communities. During the Industrial Revolution, numerous people moved to cities to work in factories.

Figure 3-12 ▶

A textile factory, 1835. Before the Industrial Revolution, textiles were hand-produced by a variety of artisans working from their homes.

The Industrial Revolution's Impact on 19th-Century Society

One of the most profound impacts of the Industrial Revolution on 19th-century society was the change in the **class structure** that took place. Previously, wealth had been primarily derived from land ownership, and the aristocratic class that controlled the land dominated the social structure. As industrialization progressed, a new class of factory owners, bankers, retailers, lawyers, engineers, and other professionals arose. These groups gained substantial wealth and came to challenge the aristocratic classes for power and position in society. They were the **nouveau riche** (the newly wealthy), and they were not afraid to show off their wealth with ostentatious homes and lifestyles.

The demonstration of their wealth was a confirmation of the values that they held, but pursuing their own interests economically had obvious consequences. While the nouveau riche enjoyed tremendous economic gains, the labourers working in their factories endured horrible working conditions and were paid insufficient wages to meet their basic needs.

Émile Zola (1840–1902) was a French novelist who attempted to capture the ordinary, often tragic lives of the working class in his writing. The excerpt below is from his 1885 work *Germinal*, where Zola depicts the miserable working conditions in European mines of the late 19th century.

The four cutters had stretched out one above the other across the sloping coal face…Maheu was the one who suffered most. High up where he was the temperature was as high as 95° [35°C], the air did not circulate, and eventually you would suffocate. In order to see clearly he had had to hang his lamp on a nail near his head; but this lamp broiled his skull, making his blood seethe. His torture was worsened above all by the damp. Water kept flowing over the rock above him a few inches from his face; and huge drops kept rapidly, continuously, in a maddening rhythm, falling, always on the same spot. It was no use twisting his neck or bending his head, the drops fell on his face, beating at him, splattering endlessly…He didn't want to stop cutting and gave huge blows which jolted him violently between the two rocks, like a flea caught between the pages of a book, threatened by being completely crushed.

—**Émile Zola, *Germinal*, Part 1, Chapter 4, trans. Havelock Ellis.**

Ibiblio, www.ibiblio.org/eldritch/ez/germinal.html

Figure 3-13 ▲

John Jacob Astor was the first multi-millionaire in the United States. This illustration depicts his descendants taking tea in the family home in 1875. Why did industrialization result in such poor living conditions for some and such luxurious conditions for others? Which of the liberal thinkers' ideas that you have examined might help explain this reality? Why might some liberal thinkers argue against government intervention in the poor conditions of workers?

Women and the Industrial Revolution

Many women had to find work to help support their families during the 19th century. Below are two very different versions of how the Industrial Revolution affected women. Ivy Pinchbeck (1898–1982) argued in her text *Women Workers and the Industrial Revolution, 1750–1850* (1930) that women were better off during the Industrial Revolution than previously. As a reviewer explains, according to Pinchbeck, women were better off for two reasons:

First, many women withdrew from the labor force and were able to enjoy more leisure and higher social standing. Pinchbeck sees the opportunity to specialize in housework as a privilege, and thus she sees withdrawal of some married women from the labor force as an improvement…The second way in which women were better off in 1850 was in improved working conditions for those women who remained in the labor force. Pinchbeck notes that, while contemporaries thought factory conditions were bad, these conditions were actually better than the conditions in alternative employments in domestic industry.

—Joyce Burnette, "A Pioneer in Women's History: Ivy Pinchbeck's ***Women Workers and the Industrial Revolution, 1750–1850,"* **2000.**
Economic History Services
http://eh.net/bookreviews/library/burnette

The following is testimony given before a government commission addressing conditions for women working as seamstresses in 19th-century England.

The common hours of business are from 8 A.M. til 11 P.M in the winters; in the summer from 6 or half-past 6 A.M. til 12 at night. During the fashionable season, that is from April til the latter end of July, it frequently happens that the ordinary hours are greatly exceeded; if there is a drawing-room or grand fete, or mourning to be made, it often happens that the work goes on for 20 hours out of the 24, occasionally all night…The general result of the long hours and sedentary occupation is to impair seriously and very frequently to destroy the health of the young women. The digestion especially suffers, and also the lungs: pain to the side is very common, and the hands and feet die away from want of circulation and exercise.

—quoted in Erna Olafson Hellerstein, Leslie Parker Hume,
and Karen M. Offen, ***Victorian Women: A Documentary Account of Women's Lives***
in Nineteenth-Century England, France and the United States
(Stanford, CA: Stanford University Press, 1981), pp. 324–325.

The governments of the day followed the principles of classical liberalism and resisted legislation that would restrict the economic freedom of employers. It would be several decades before laws were passed to curtail the extreme abuse of workers.

1 What might explain the different views provided by each source? Do you think women were better off during the Industrial Revolution based on these two sources?

2 To what extent do these sources reveal the impact of liberalism on society? What other kinds of sources would be useful in more fully exploring this impact?

Figure 3-14

Jacob Riis took photos of the people and neighbourhoods in New York City to illustrate his book. Riis's book was instrumental in convincing Theodore Roosevelt (then New York City police commissioner, later president of the United States) to initiate a variety of reforms to improve conditions for people of low income.

Elizabeth Gaskell (1810–1865) was a writer living in Manchester, England, who wrote about the difficult circumstances the working classes experienced, and the wealthier classes' perceptions of them. The excerpt below is from her novel *North and South* (1855). When the mother of a factory owner is asked why workers at her son's factory are threatening to strike, she responds as follows:

"For the mastership and ownership of other people's property," said Mrs. Thornton, with a fierce snort. "That is what they always strike for. If my son's work-people strike, I will only say they are a pack of ungrateful hounds. But I have no doubt they will…The truth is they want to be masters, and make the masters into slaves on their own ground."

—**Elizabeth Gaskell, *North and South*, 1855.**

The living conditions of the working class were as difficult as their working conditions. Because of enclosure, the mechanization of agriculture, and the availability of jobs in factories, large segments of the population migrated to the cities in the 19th century in a process of **urbanization**. This led to overcrowding and unsanitary living conditions in the cities, with tenants sometimes being exploited by unscrupulous landlords.

Like other writers of the period such as Charles Dickens, Danish immigrant Jacob August Riis took up the cause of those living in urban poverty. A job as a police reporter in New York gave him first-hand knowledge of his subject. He described the horrendous conditions of low-income New Yorkers in his book *How the Other Half Lives*.

There are numerous examples of tenement-houses in which are lodged several hundred people that have a pro rata *allotment of ground area scarcely equal to two-square yards [1.67 square metres] upon the city lot, court-yards and all included.*

—**Source: New York Health Department, quoted in Jacob A. Riis, *How the Other Half Lives: Studies among the Tenements of New York*, Chapter 2, 1890.**

Explore the Issues

Concept Review

1 Identify principles of classical liberalism found in the Industrial Revolution. How well were these principles received by various individuals and groups within society?

Concept Application

2 Identify key characteristics of laissez-faire economics, and create a concept web to illustrate them. How would these characteristics have affected 19th-century society?

3 Explain the relationship between the enclosure movement and private property rights.

4 How did classical liberalism influence 19-century society? Explain which of these changes were beneficial and which were detrimental. From whose perspective do you decide the beneficial or detrimental nature of these changes?

What Makes History Significant?

If the past is everything that has ever happened, how do historians decide what to write about? One answer is that they look for events that seem to be more important than others because they had an impact beyond the immediate circumstances of the event. They may have caused or contributed to major changes in a society or fit into a larger pattern of events. This is called *historical significance*. Determining historical significance will help you explore the question for this chapter: **To what extent can classical liberalism impact a society?**

As you have seen, the Industrial Revolution is considered to be a significant historical event. Here are some passages about the Industrial Revolution. All the authors agree that it was historically significant, but the reasons they give for its significance differ.

Your Task: As you read each excerpt below, think about the consequences each author is examining. Form a group of three or four students, and rank the excerpts from most significant to least significant, providing reasons why you put the excerpts in that order. Use the Questions to Guide You for assistance.

Excerpt 1

The changes brought by the Industrial Revolution overturned not only traditional economies, but also whole societies. Economic changes caused far-reaching social changes, including the movement of people to cities, the availability of a greater variety of material goods, and new ways of doing business. The Industrial Revolution was the first step in modern economic growth and development. Economic development was combined with superior military technology to make the nations of Europe and their cultural offshoots, such as the United States, the most powerful in the world in the eighteenth and nineteenth centuries.

—**Source: "Industrial Revolution." Microsoft Encarta Online Encyclopedia 2008.**
http://encarta.msn.com/encyclopedia_761577952/
industrial_revolution.html

Excerpt 2

The Industrial Revolution started in England around 1733 with the first cotton mill. A more modern world had begun. As new inventions were being created, factories followed soon thereafter. England wanted to keep its industrialization a secret, so they prohibited anyone who had worked in a factory to leave the country. Meanwhile, Americans offered a significant reward to anyone who could build a cotton-spinning machine in the United States. Samuel Slater, who had been an apprentice in an English cotton factory, disguised himself and came to America. Once here, he reconstructed a cotton-spinning machine from memory. He then proceeded to build a factory of his own. The Industrial Revolution had arrived in the United States.

—**Source: "IRWeb: Information Page." Oracle Education Foundation ThinkQuest.**
http://library.thinkquest.org/4132/info.htm

Excerpt 3

The era known as the Industrial Revolution was a period in which fundamental changes occurred in agriculture, textile and metal manufacture, transportation, economic policies and the social structure in England. This period is appropriately labeled "revolution," for it thoroughly destroyed the old manner of doing things; yet the term is simultaneously inappropriate, for it connotes abrupt change. The changes that occurred during this period (1760–1850), in fact, occurred gradually. The year 1760 is generally accepted as the "eve" of the Industrial Revolution. In reality, this eve began more than two centuries before this date. The late 18th century and the early nineteenth century brought to fruition the ideas and discoveries of those who had long passed on, such as, Galileo, Bacon, Descartes and others.

—**Joseph A. Montagna, "The Industrial Revolution." Yale-New Haven Teachers Institute.**
http://www.yale.edu/ynhti/curriculum/
units/1981/2/81.02.06.x.html

Questions to Guide You

1. Significance depends on point of view. The writer of history will decide what is or what is not significant depending on his or her point of view. What is the point of view of each author? Which perspectives or points of view are missing that could be important to building an informed position?

2. Read the three sources again to determine whether each point of view is primarily political, economic, or social. In addition, determine the writer's rationale and purpose. Fill out a chart similar to the following, and be prepared to defend your answers.

3. Significance depends on purpose. The significance of the event depends on its role in the larger narrative or story that the historian is telling. What purpose is each author using the Industrial Revolution to achieve? That is, why are they writing about the Industrial Revolution in the first place?

Source	Point of View (political, economic, or social)	Rationale	Purpose

Reflect and Analyze

In this chapter you have explored the Chapter Issue, ***To what extent can classical liberalism impact a society?*** You considered where the ideas of classical liberalism originated, how these ideas developed into the principles of liberalism, and some of the effects of liberalism on society in the 19th century.

In the first section of the chapter you were asked to consider the contributions of such individuals as Hobbes, Locke, Montesquieu, Smith, and Mill. While many of their ideas are commonplace in society today, they were radical notions that met with much resistance during the era in which they emerged.

The examination of the French and American revolutions in the second section of the chapter provided you with an opportunity to consider how classical liberal theory could be applied to 18th-century societies and how the ideas of classical liberal theory evolved into an ideology. Responses to classical liberalism resulted in new social, economic, and, specifically, political structures that significantly changed French, American, and other Western societies.

The third section of the chapter explored the social effects of classical liberalism through the Industrial Revolution and laissez-faire capitalism. While the conditions of the working classes during the Industrial Revolution were deplorable, the middle and upper classes accrued enormous economic benefits.

Respond to Issues

1. The Chapter Issue asks how classical liberalism can impact a society. Apply what you have learned from this chapter to determine the short- and long-term impacts of classical liberal ideas and principles as they evolved and were interpreted by the societies that adopted them.

Recognize Relationships among Concepts, Issues, and Citizenship

2. Conduct a search to locate sources that represent 19th-century popular culture (for example, literature, newspapers, dramas, sporting events, cartoons). Examine each source to determine how it expresses the prevalent ideologies of the day. Compile these sources into a PowerPoint presentation that demonstrates how popular culture was affected by classical liberal ideas. The presentation should represent various perspectives and demonstrate the positive and negative reactions to 19th-century liberalism.

KEY SKILLS

Determining relationships among varied sources of information

KEY CONCEPTS

Analyzing the evolution of classical liberalism

Analyzing ideologies that developed in response to classical liberalism

Key Terms

Classical conservatism
Command economy
Communism
Feminism
Human rights
Labour standards
Labour unions
Marxism
Mixed economy
Progressivism
Socialism
Universal suffrage
Welfare capitalism

Responding to Classical Liberalism

Figure 4-1

Children, called "hurriers", taking a load of coal out of a mine in Britain, 1842. Is child labour like this still present today? Where?

Figure 4-2

Children donating their time and energy to paint a house as part of a United Way program.

It is a very frequent thing at Mr. Marshall's [at Shrewsbury] where the least [youngest] children were employed (for there were plenty working at six years of age), for Mr. Horseman to start the mill earlier in the morning than he formerly did; and provided a child should be drowsy, the overlooker walks round the room with a stick in his hand, and he touches that child on the shoulder, and says, "Come here." In a corner of the room there is an iron cistern; it is filled with water; he takes this boy, and takes him up by the legs, and dips him over head in the cistern, and sends him to work for the remainder of the day...

—evidence given to Sadler's Committee, which investigated conditions in the textile mills and produced "The Sadler Committee Report of 1832."
www.thecaveonline.com/APEH/19centurydocuments.html

Our government recognizes the importance of quality, affordable child care and the need to sustain the significant progress achieved to date...Over the past two years more than 4270 licensed child care spaces have been created in Toronto. This is helping more parents balance the demands of work and family, while giving their children access to early childhood education.

—Ministry of Children and Youth Services, "McGuinty Government Strengthens Ontario's Child Care System", July 5, 2007.
ogov.newswire.ca/ontario/GPOE/2007/07/05/c3977.html?lmatch=&lang=_e.html

The quotations above reveal the vastly different beliefs and values between classical liberalism and modern liberalism. During the 19th century, classical liberals had achieved great success in implementing their ideas. Industrialization and laissez-faire capitalism had transformed many Western societies, but not everyone benefited equally from this transformation. Some people were excluded from the benefits of the transformation, and many were aware of injustices arising from the huge differences between the few very wealthy and the vast majority who lived in poverty. From a perspective of people who are underprivileged, classical liberalism was a failure. Some spoke of the benefits of pre-Industrial Revolution beliefs and values, while others felt that classical liberalism had resulted in a society that exploited the many for the benefit of the few. Life had changed for everyone.

Chapter Issue

Ideologies are evolutionary; they adapt and change in response to the political, economic, and social conditions and pressures of the societies in which they exist. By examining ideologies that developed as a reaction to classical liberalism and the ways that liberalism itself evolved in response to its critics, this chapter will assist you in answering the following issue: **To what extent did classical liberalism meet the needs of society?**

One way to explore this question is to consider some of the ways in which people responded to the promotion of classical liberal ideas and practices. This will enhance your understanding by providing several perspectives on liberalism and will help you determine your own response to the question of how and why modern liberalism evolved.

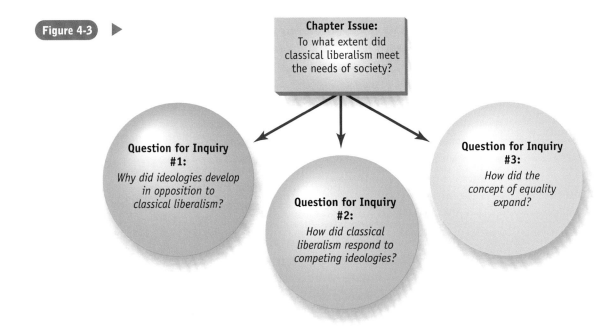

Figure 4-3 ▶

Chapter Issue:
To what extent did classical liberalism meet the needs of society?

Question for Inquiry #1:
Why did ideologies develop in opposition to classical liberalism?

Question for Inquiry #2:
How did classical liberalism respond to competing ideologies?

Question for Inquiry #3:
How did the concept of equality expand?

Opposition to Liberalism

*Question for **Inquiry***

- **Why did ideologies develop in opposition to classical liberalism?**

Classical liberalism and the Industrial Revolution transformed British society. A society based on agriculture and the landed classes, interventionist government, and humanitarianism became a society based on industry and the middle classes, laissez-faire government, and the pursuit of industrial efficiency.

The entrepreneurial ruling elite that flourished under classical liberalism may have lived more democratically than the old landed ruling elite, but the new ideology of laissez-faire capitalism was primarily concerned with industrial efficiency and the accumulation of wealth. These goals were considered to be more important than equality. Factories and businesses were designed to facilitate industrial processes, and workers were viewed as one component of production. Decent wages and working conditions did not lead to increased efficiency (or profits), and were therefore not considered. Government had no responsibilities in this area because it was not expected to play a role in the economy. Thus not all people saw the Industrial Revolution and classical liberalism as positive developments.

The opponents of liberalism flourished in these circumstances, and a number of new ideologies arose in opposition to classical liberalism. In this section of the chapter you will consider these new ideologies. They include Luddism, Chartism, Socialism (Utopian and moderate or democratic), Marxism, classical conservatism, welfare capitalism, the welfare state, and Keynesianism.

Grassroot Movements

Protests against the effects of classical liberalism and capitalism were many and varied. Not all of these developed into complete ideologies, but they reflected the general discontent of the times among various groups of people.

Luddites

By the early 19th century, skilled textile artisans were being replaced by machines operated by cheap, relatively unskilled labourers. The replaced workers formed a protest movement. Claiming to be led by Ned Ludd, who was thought to have been the first person to have destroyed industrial machinery in 1779, disgruntled textile workers formed the Army of Redressers in 1811. Over a six-year period, various

Figure 4-4

Figure 4-4 ▶

Why do you think the Luddites chose to attack the machines being invented during this time? What did the machines represent?

PAUSE AND REFLECT

In its actions against the Luddites, what main principle of classical liberalism was the British government protecting through the use of force and the law?

Armies of Redressers broke into factories and destroyed over 200 of the machines that would make their labour redundant and threaten their employment. The first attacks occurred in Nottingham. The idea quickly caught on, and the movement known as **Luddism** spread across the textile industry.

The government responded by declaring machine-breaking a capital offence—punishable by death—and ordered 12 000 troops into the areas where Luddites were active. A typical attack occurred on April 20, 1812, when several thousand men attacked a mill near Manchester. The mill owner, Emanuel Burton, had known that his purchase of power looms would anger the weavers, so he had hired armed guards, and these guards killed three of the Luddites. The Luddites returned the following day for another attempt. Failing to break into the factory, they burned Burton's house. When the military arrived, it killed seven men.

Violent confrontations continued throughout textile-producing areas until 1817, when the government finally managed to suppress the movement through the use of force and the law. Many more Luddites were killed or captured. Those captured were either executed or transported to penal colonies.

Chartists

Chartism was a working-class movement in Britain that focused on political and social reform. Flourishing from 1838 to 1848, Chartism got its name from the People's Charter of 1838, which outlined the six essential goals of the movement:

- universal suffrage for all men over 21
- equal-sized electoral districts
- voting by secret ballot

- an end to the need for property qualifications for Parliament
- pay for Members of Parliament
- annual elections

The electoral system had been reformed in Britain in 1832, at which time the vote had been extended to some of the male middle classes but not to members of the working class. The right to vote was considered the key to all kinds of improvements for the working class, and a variety of organizations, both moderate and radical, united in their support of Chartism as a way to modify what they considered the undesirable effects of classical liberalism.

The major initiative of the Chartists was presenting the Charter to Parliament in 1839, with 1.25 million signatures. The House of Commons rejected the Charter by a vote of 235 to 46. When some of the Chartist leaders threatened to call a general strike, they were arrested and imprisoned in Newport, Wales. Their supporters marched on the prison demanding the release of their leaders, at which point troops opened fire on them, killing 24 people and wounding 40. A second petition with 3 million signatures was rejected in 1842. The rejection of a third petition in 1848 ended the movement, and many of the Chartists then channelled their efforts into socialist movements.

The significance of the Chartists lies in their demonstration of the discontent that gripped Britain at the time. The government saw them as an unruly mob reminiscent of the French Revolution, but most of their demands were eventually implemented in the Reform Acts of 1867 and 1884.

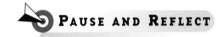

PAUSE AND REFLECT

For what main principle of liberalism were the Chartists fighting to have recognized?

Socialist Ideologies

The term *socialism*, when used generally, refers to any ideology that believes that resources should be controlled by the public for the benefit of everyone in society and not by private interests for the benefit of private owners and investors. Socialist supporters value economic equality among citizens. This equality is achieved by providing income security for all through guaranteed employment and guaranteed living standards. Co-operation is favoured over competition. The implementation of these beliefs is dependent on a high degree of state involvement in the control and direction of the economy.

The great wealth produced by industrialization in 19th-century society was recognized by many people as a wonderful achievement. What was lacking, however, was a fair and just distribution of wealth to all who contributed to it, especially the workers.

The starting point for socialist ideologies was the reform of the political, social, and economic structures of 19th-century liberal society. Socialists rejected the lack of equality and humanitarianism in classical liberalism and deplored the social injustices that resulted. They were concerned with the same ill effects that the Luddites and Chartists were, but unlike those movements, various forms of socialism became effective ideologies.

Utopian Socialists

In 1516, Sir Thomas More wrote a book called *Utopia*, which outlined his concept of the ideal society. The word *utopia* has since been used to refer to any imaginary, perfect world meant to serve as a model for real life. In the 19th century, Utopian socialism was applied to a school of socialist thought that emerged in opposition to classical liberalism.

The **Utopians** were essentially **humanitarians** who advocated an end to the appalling conditions of the average worker in the industrial capitalist countries of the time. Idealistic rather than pragmatic, Utopian socialists did not intend to overturn the basic political, economic, and social systems. Individuals such as Robert Owen in Great Britain, Charles Fourier and Claude Saint-Simon in France, and Horace Greeley in the United States believed that education and improved working conditions could peacefully eradicate the worst aspects of capitalism and lead to an ideal socialist society where everyone would live happily. Saint-Simon is credited with advocating the idea of a "science of society," in which the natural laws of society, just like the natural laws of the sciences, would be used to guide progress.

Robert Owen (1771–1858) believed that the harshness of life under laissez-faire capitalism corrupted human nature. Apprenticed at the age of 10 to a draper, Owen exemplified the classical liberal belief that individuals could realize their potential if they were free to pursue their own inclinations. By the age of 19, Owen had opened his own business. In 1800, Owen became mill manager of the Chorton Twist Company in New Lanark, Scotland, the largest cotton-spinning business in Britain. He subsequently bought the business with several partners. Owen used this opportunity to put his beliefs into practice. New Lanark became a model community to demonstrate his utopian principles.

What ideas individuals may attach to the term "Millennium" I know not; but I know that society may be formed so as to exist without crime, without poverty, with health greatly improved, with little, if any misery, and with intelligence and happiness increased a hundredfold; and no obstacle whatsoever intervenes at this moment except ignorance to prevent such a state of society from becoming universal.

—Robert Owen, "Address to the Inhabitants of New Lanark," January 1, 1816.

www.robert-owen.com

Believing that education was the key to a humane society, Owen established the Institute for the Formation of Character, which was really a community education centre. Infants were cared for while their parents worked, and children attended school until the age of 10 (rather than 5 or 6 as was usual). At 10 years of age, they worked a 10-hour day (shorter than the usual 13-hour day), leaving them time to continue their education in the evening. Adult education was also available. In addition, the Institute sponsored free medical care, concerts, and dancing.

Owen also improved the living conditions of the workers. Existing houses were renovated, and new ones were built with an eye to comfort rather than economy. The streets were paved and regularly cleaned. Company shops with reasonable prices replaced private ones charging high prices. The village was landscaped so that the villagers could enjoy outdoor activities in their leisure time. Fines were imposed for disruptive social behaviour such as drunkenness. Owen wanted to improve all aspects of the workers' lives, including their moral character.

Owen's main interest in improving working conditions related to the hours of work and child labour. The mills were still horrific workplaces by modern standards, but he fostered a co-operative spirit between management and labour, and introduced incentives to reward good employees. The behaviour of the workers was recorded by supervisors who displayed a coloured marker by each person's workstation: black for bad behaviour, blue for indifferent, yellow for good, and white for excellent. The system was very effective and slowly the number of yellow and white markers increased.

Robert Owen devoted his life to publicizing his beliefs, writing books and journals, speaking all over Britain, and proposing factory reform to Parliament. He summed up his vision of society in 1841:

It is therefore, the interest of all, that every one, from birth, should be well educated, physically and mentally, that society may be improved in its character, that everyone should be beneficially employed, physically and mentally, that the greatest amount of wealth may be created, and knowledge attained, that everyone should be placed in the midst of those external circumstances that will produce the greatest number of pleasurable sensations, through the longest life, that man may be made truly intelligent, moral and happy, and be thus prepared to enter upon the coming Millennium.

—Robert Owen
www.robert-owen.com

Unlike the Utopians, who wanted only to modify classical liberalism, other socialist ideologies contemplated fundamental changes to society's structure. According to these socialists, the great evils in society were perpetuated by the concept of private property, which allowed industrialists to control the economy. The socialist intent was to encourage governments and the institutions of capitalism—banks,

Figure 4-5 ▲

New Lanark has been restored and became a UNESCO World Heritage Site in 2001.

industry, commerce, and services—to rethink their purposes and consider replacing the liberal ideology of individualism and limited government.

Socialist thought ranged from moderate and democratic social reform to radical revolutionary Marxism. Socialists agreed on the following beliefs and values:

- Private ownership of the means of production permits exploitation.
- The state should direct the economy to achieve economic equality for all citizens.
- Society should be classless.

While sharing common views, socialists differed greatly in the methods they advocated for achieving their goal of transforming liberal capitalist society.

Marxism

The term **Marxism** was never used by Karl Marx (1818–1883). A group of French socialists, among them Jules Guesde and Benoît Malon, coined the term in the 1880s. Karl Marx himself, on hearing about some of the things these so-called followers were doing, proclaimed that he was not a Marxist. Marx spent three years in France and wrote about the ideas of Jean-Jacques Rousseau and other early socialists, but rejected these ideas for not being scientific enough.

Marxism is a radical form of socialism, often called **scientific socialism** or **communism** to distinguish it from other socialist ideologies. Marx developed a theory that history is the story of evolving class warfare. According to Marx, the only way to overthrow capitalism was by means of a class struggle between the proletariat (workers) and the bourgeoisie (owners). He argued that this workers' revolution was necessary before any significant changes could be made in society.

Marx collaborated with Friedrich Engels to write *The Communist Manifesto* in 1848. Marx believed that economics was the foundation of society and the means of production, such as factories, needed to be in workers' hands. Marx and Engels elaborated many of the principles of scientific socialism, albeit briefly, in this document, outlining how the proletariat would gain the means of production.

1. *Abolition of property in land and application of all rents of land to public purposes.*
2. *A heavy progressive or graduated income tax.*
3. *Abolition of all right of inheritance.*
4. *Confiscation of the property of all emigrants and rebels.*
5. *Centralization of credit in the hands of the state by means of a national bank with state capital and an exclusive monopoly.*
6. *Centralization of the means of communication and transport in the hands of the state.*

Capitalism emerges from feudalism

Violent conflict occurs between the bourgeoisie and the proletariat; the proletariat wins

The victorious proletariat establishes a Dictatorship of the Proletariat, which is also evolutionary in nature:
• A centrally planned economy is established.
• Income is distributed according to the value of work performed

Economic equality is established

Social classes gradually disappear

People work for societal good rather than personal gain

The state "withers away"

Figure 4-6 ▲

The evolution of society according to Marx

7. *Extension of factories and instruments of production owned by the state; the bringing into cultivation of wastelands, and the improvement of the soil generally in accordance with a common plan.*
8. *Equal obligation of all to work. Establishment of industrial armies, especially for agriculture.*
9. *Combination of agriculture with manufacturing industries; gradual abolition of the distinction between town and country by a more equable distribution of the population over the country.*
10. *Free education for all children in public schools, abolition of child factory labour in its present form. Combination of education with industrial production.*

—Karl Marx and Friedrich Engels, "Proletarians and Communists," *Manifesto of the Communist Party,* **1848.**

http://www.anu.edu.au/polsci/marx/classics/manifesto.html

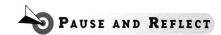

PAUSE AND REFLECT

How are these Marxist ideas a response to classical liberal ideas in society?

The abolition of private property and the centralization of the means of production (such as factories and machinery) in the hands of the state would become essential characteristics of the economy of countries that implemented Marxist ideas and communism. For example, the Soviet Union, China, and North Korea each developed a centrally planned economy or **command economy**. In a free market, competition and the forces of supply and demand determine which goods are produced, how they are produced, and at what prices they are sold. In a command economy, government planners make these decisions.

Politically, socialism struggled to make inroads against classical liberalism. While moderate democratic socialism resulted in some very successful political parties, Marxist parties had much less success in classical liberal societies. The French Communist Party (PCF) is an example of the path that more militant socialist parties took.

Socialism in France split into two movements following the First World War—moderate democratic socialists under Léon Blum, and communists (Marxists) who were affiliated with Moscow-based international communism. The socialists were non-violent in their search for the ideal socialist world, while the communists were more pragmatic and focused on Lenin and the achievement of communism in the Soviet Union through opportunism and revolution. This dichotomy is described in the following quote.

When Léon Blum became the head of the Socialist Party, for reasons of party discipline he accepted the doctrine of Karl Marx...But that does not alter the fact that there is a profound difference between his conception of Socialism, in which he sees a force that will bring about the moral regeneration of mankind, and that of the orthodox Marxists who base their belief purely on materialistic premises and on the determinism of economic forces.

The Voice of Moderate Socialism

The Fabian Society was founded in London, England, in 1884. Many of its original members were prominent intellectuals, academics, and writers: George Bernard Shaw, H.G. Wells, Virginia Woolf, and Emmeline Pankhurst. Later, philosopher Bertrand Russell and economist John Maynard Keynes joined the group. The Fabians were instrumental in the formation of the British Labour Party in 1900, and two of Great Britain's recent Labour prime ministers, Tony Blair and Gordon Brown, are both members of the Fabian Society. Since the society's inception, the Fabians have favoured a gradual and incremental reform of liberalism toward the principles of socialism. The members of the Society have publicized the need for reform through their writings, which deal with prevailing social problems, and through lobbying in the political arena.

The man who pretends that the distribution of income in this country reflects the distribution of ability or character is an ignoramus.

—G. Bernard Shaw, "Socialism and Superior Brains: A Reply to Mr. Mallock," The Fabian Socialist Series, Number 8, 1910.

http://www.marxists.org/reference/archive/shaw/works/brains.htm

In Canada, the Co-operative Commonwealth Federation (CCF) was a moderate and democratic socialist party founded in Canada in 1933, in the depths of the Great Depression, at a time when laissez-faire capitalism seemed to be failing. In reaction to classical liberalism, the CCF stated its ideology in the *Regina Manifesto*. This manifesto was adopted at the CCF's first national convention, which was held in Regina, Saskatchewan, in July 1933. The CCF merged with labour groups to form the New Democratic Party in 1961.

The CCF is a federation of organizations whose purpose is the establishment in Canada of a Co-operative Commonwealth in which the principle regulating production, distribution and exchange will be the supplying of human needs and not the making of profits.

We aim to replace the present capitalist system [classical liberalism], with its inherent injustice and inhumanity, by a social order from which the domination and exploitation of one class by another will be eliminated, in which economic planning will supersede unregulated private enterprise and competition, and in which genuine democratic self-government, based upon economic equality will be possible. The present order is marked by glaring inequalities of wealth and opportunity, by chaotic waste and instability; and in an age of plenty it condemns the great mass of the people to poverty and insecurity. Power has become more and more concentrated into the hands of a small irresponsible minority of financiers and industrialists and to their predatory interests the majority are habitually sacrificed...

The new social order at which we aim is not one in which individuality will be crushed out by a system of regimentation. Nor shall we interfere with cultural rights of racial or religious minorities. What we seek is a proper collective organization of our economic resources such as will make possible a much greater degree of leisure and a much richer individual life for every citizen.

This social and economic transformation can be brought about by political action, through the election of a government inspired by the ideal of a Co-operative Commonwealth and supported by a majority of the people. We do not believe in change by violence.

—**Co-operative Commonwealth Federation,** *Regina Manifesto.*
economics.uwaterloo.ca/needhdata/Regina_Manifesto.html

1 Explain Shaw's critique of classical liberalism.

2 In what ways does the program of the CCF demonstrate opposition to classical liberalism?

3 What connections to the Great Depression exist in the Regina Manifesto?

4 To what extent does the program of the CCF respond to issues in society at that time?

5 How can you tell that the CCF was a democratic socialist party?

This difference is even more marked when one compares the temperament of the Socialists…and that of the Communists. Both want to replace the existing order by another, but…the Socialists believe that Collectivism can come to pass only when the people are prepared to accept it…The Socialists hope that the people will be educated, or educate themselves, into appreciating the advantages of a collectivist society…

—**Raoul de Roussy de Sales, "Léon Blum,"**
***The Atlantic Monthly*, October 1937.**
http://www.theatlantic.com/doc/193710/leon-blum/2

Nonetheless, two socialist factions and the communist party formed a coalition during the 1936 elections, and Léon Blum was elected the first socialist prime minister of France. His coalition government lasted only a year, however, partly because of disagreements over economic policy.

By the 1930s, Marxism had become very popular in France and elsewhere among intellectuals and writers. The Soviet Union enjoyed great prestige as it flourished economically during the Great Depression, which seemed to demonstrate clearly that economic liberalism had failed. Canadian surgeon Norman Bethune, for example, following a visit to the Soviet Union in the mid-1930s, joined the Communist Party. He then went to Spain and to China to help socialists and communists who were involved in armed struggle for political control in their respective countries. Communist ideas and theories remained influential in France of the 1950s and 1960s among intellectuals such as Jean-Paul Sartre and Simone de Beauvoir, and some principles of Marxism found a voice in environmentalism and feminism, but the communist political movement faded away as a major factor in French politics. That said, a number of French presidents and prime ministers in the decades following the Second World War were members of the Socialist Party.

Figure 4-7 ▲

In 1793, King Louis XVI of France was executed, sending shock waves throughout the monarchies and aristocracy of Europe. To what extent do you believe that democratic liberal governments today should have laws related to capital punishment to help provide "law and order" in society?

Classical Conservatism

As you read earlier, Luddites destroyed the machinery of industry in an attempt to preserve the benefits of the world they had previously known. Due to their opposition to industrialization and modernization, the Luddites can be considered reactionary. The word *reactionary* is derived from the French word *réactionnaire*, which came into use at the time of the French Revolution to describe the opponents of the Revolution. Synonyms for *reactionary* are *conservative* or *the Right*, in reference to the political spectrum. All these terms are used to refer to any ideology that supports a return to a previous state of affairs.

The Luddites were not the only reactionaries of the times. The development of **classical conservatism** was also a reaction to classical liberalism. Edmund Burke (1729–1797) viewed the events of the French Revolution from Britain and is identified with the development of the ideology of classical conservatism. Burke was a contemporary of the influential classical liberal Adam Smith, about whom you read in Chapter 3, but Burke came to different conclusions when faced with the same political, economic, and social realities. He did not accept the beliefs and values of classical liberalism, preferring those of the pre-industrial past. He believed that government represented not only the will of the people presently living, but also the legacy of people who had gone before, and the inheritance of those yet to come. Change, therefore, could not be dictated by the whims of the present generation. Change, if it came at all, had to honour the citizens of the past and the future.

Burke was not a political philosopher and never attempted to set out his ideas in an organized way. He reacted to the political issues of the day. Horrified by the extremes of the French Revolution, Burke used these as an example of the flaws of following the values of equality, individualism, and freedom. Burke believed that established institutions, run by the educated people of society, were necessary to control the irrational passions of the uneducated masses. According to Burke, the only reason to make changes to these institutions was to preserve them from the radical or revolutionary change demanded by the masses.

Burke's was one voice among many. Burke and other classical conservatives shared a set of beliefs:

- Society is an organic whole that should be structured in a hierarchical fashion with those best suited to leadership at the top, because people do not have equal abilities.
- Government should be chosen by a limited electorate with special rights, responsibilities, and privileges.
- Leaders should be humanitarian—their role includes the responsibility to care for the welfare of others.

- The stability of society is the paramount concern, to be achieved through law and order and the maintenance of the customs and traditions that bind society together.

While Burke supported established government, he did not support tyranny in any form, whether in a monarchy or in a less organized government structure. He thus viewed the American Revolution (1775–1783), which led to orderly government, quite differently from the French Revolution (1789–1799), which included mass executions, civil disorder, wars against foreign countries, and a failure to establish a stable government. While Burke deplored the conduct of the bankrupt and irresponsible pre-revolutionary French government, he was outraged by the conduct of the French revolutionaries, regarding it as the natural result of liberalism's emphasis on equality and individual freedom. He did not think that all individuals were equally capable of participation in the affairs of the country. According to Burke, uninformed people should not have a say in government; government should be left to those who naturally understood their duties to the country and the people, those with experience and wisdom. Burke predicted that Rousseau's concept of the "general will of the people" was an unrealistic, unnatural, and ultimately dangerous idea that would lead to rule by the mediocre, uneducated, and disinterested. He believed this would end in chaos.

We owe an implicit reverence to all the institutions of our ancestors.

—Edmund Burke, *A Vindication of Natural Society*, 1756.

In a democracy, the majority of the citizens is capable of exercising the most cruel oppressions upon the minority.

—Edmund Burke, *Reflections on the Revolution in France*, 1790.

Classical conservatism, socialism, and communism were responses to classical liberal ideologies and reveal other ideological perspectives that groups of people have held and continue to hold in societies around the world.

PAUSE AND REFLECT

Why would Burke value established institutions and believe that society should value them as well? Why would he be so emphatically opposed to the actions taken in France at this time?

Explore the Issues

Concept Review

1. a) Identify five examples of ideologies that developed in response to classical liberalism.
   b) Create an organizer to outline the similarities and differences between these ideologies.

Concept Application

2. Why did ideologies develop in response to classical liberalism? What classical liberal beliefs and values were challenged by these new ideologies?

3. Did the new ideologies provide the means to a better life for those living in the 19th century? Why or why not?

The Liberal Response

Question for Inquiry

• **How did classical liberalism respond to competing ideologies?**

Figure 4-8 ▶

What is the artist of this cartoon saying about change and adaptation?

Classical liberals gradually came to see the merits of some of their opponents' views and modified the practical applications of some of their values and beliefs. As we examine these developments, keep the principles of classical liberalism—individual rights, private property, economic freedom, and the rule of law—in mind as you develop a response to the Chapter Issue: *To what extent did classical liberalism meet the needs of society?*

Welfare Capitalism

The socialist critique of classical liberalism undermined the political, social, and economic foundations of the classical liberal state. Rather grudgingly, classical liberals began to recognize that some modifications were necessary. The basic premise for these modifications was an acceptance of the notion that laissez-faire capitalists needed to consider the rights of workers and develop a social conscience. Often, especially in the United States, entrepreneurs and industrialists tried to head off the growing demand for **labour unions** and the actions of governments interested in providing social programs, often called a "safety net", for ordinary workers. Many industrialists began to provide their workers with non-monetary rewards to earn their loyalty. For example, George Pullman, the inventor of sleeping cars on trains, built a village for his workers similar to Robert Owen's New Lanark, but Pullman's motivation was not humanitarian: his goal was to prevent labour unrest by responding to some of his workers' complaints. In America, the term **welfare capitalism** referred to these kinds of initiatives by industrialists. In the rest of the industrialized world, however, *welfare capitalism* referred to a classical liberal economic system combined with a government that used legislation to give workers protections such as limited working hours and a minimum wage, and a safety net with features like pensions and medical insurance.

The legislative journey to workers' rights was a long one. Britain, for example, passed a series of Factory Acts, beginning in 1810. Each act gradually improved the working conditions in factories, decreased working hours, regulated the age at which children could be employed, and regulated the number of hours women and children could be required to work. In Germany, the government introduced a law providing leave for illness and maternity in 1883, provided insurance for job-related injuries in 1884, and passed an old-age assistance law in 1889. Over time, many such laws followed in all liberal democratic countries.

From today's perspective, it is easy to look at this kind of government legislation as a logical and acceptable approach to correcting the excesses of classical liberalism. This was not the case at the time, however. Capitalists did not gladly or easily give way to new ways of thinking about society's responsibilities.

American president Theodore Roosevelt (1901–1909) was a reformer who showed his desire to curb the excesses of laissez-faire capitalism early in his presidency. In May 1902, 50 000 United Mine Workers (a union) of northern Pennsylvania walked out, demanding a 10–20 per cent raise, recognition of their union, an 8-hour workday, and fringe benefits. The mine owners refused all their demands and called on Roosevelt to call out the army against the workers. Instead, Roosevelt threatened to call out the army against the owners if they continued to refuse to negotiate. This was an almost unheard-of threat. Roosevelt coined the term *square deal* at this time to signify that both labour and capital must be treated fairly. Roosevelt forced the mine owners into arbitration and a compromise settlement was reached. More information about Roosevelt's responses to laissez-faire capitalism is in Chapter 6.

After his second term as president, Roosevelt went on to found a new political party in 1912—the National Progressive Party—whose platform contained a new kind of liberalism, sometimes referred to as **progressivism**. Roosevelt founded the new party because the Democrats and Republicans were so resistant to change. In the party's platform were the following clauses:

- *The Progressive party, believing that no people can justly claim to be a true democracy which denies political rights on account of sex, pledges itself to the task of securing equal suffrage to men and women alike.*

- *The supreme duty of the Nation is the conservation of human resources through an enlightened measure of social and industrial justice. We pledge ourselves to work unceasingly in State and Nation for:*
  - *Effective legislation looking to the prevention of industrial accidents, occupational diseases, overwork, involuntary unemployment, and other injurious effects incident to modern industry;*

PAUSE AND REFLECT

What are the possible reasons for the different interpretations of the term *welfare capitalism*? In what ways were these differences a reflection of individualist or collectivist ideological positions?

PAUSE AND REFLECT

The National Progressive Party was formed because of an unresponsive political structure in the United States at the time. Identify three principles that this new party hoped to implement that challenged classical liberalism.

– *The fixing of minimum safety and health standards for the various occupations…;*
– *The prohibition of child labor;*
– *Minimum wage standards for working women, to provide a "living wage" in all industrial occupations;*

• *We favor the union of all the existing agencies of the Federal Government dealing with the public health into a single national health service…to perform efficiently such duties in the protection of the public from preventable diseases…*

— **"Progressive Platform of 1912." TeachingAmericanHistory.org.**
www.teachingamericanhistory.org/library/index.asp?documentprint=607

Most of the early legislation based on the principles of welfare capitalism was oriented toward the workplace. Aside from a few exceptions, the legislation did not include non-workplace issues such as child poverty, disability, housing standards, education, or other circumstances where individuals might need some sort of government assistance. In addition, with the onset of the First World War, reforming zeal died down. Governments became preoccupied with the war effort and needed the support of industrialists to ensure sufficient war supplies.

Welfare State

The movement from welfare capitalism to the **welfare state** was spurred by the **Great Depression**. Widespread business failures and impoverishment called laissez-faire capitalism into question in a way never before experienced. It seemed to provide concrete evidence that the existing political, social, and economic order had failed. The Great

Figure 4-9 ▶

Men sharing a room out of economic necessity in Canada in the 1930s during the Great Depression. Many people felt it was imperative to prevent a recurrence of the economic conditions during the Great Depression that created so much suffering for people.

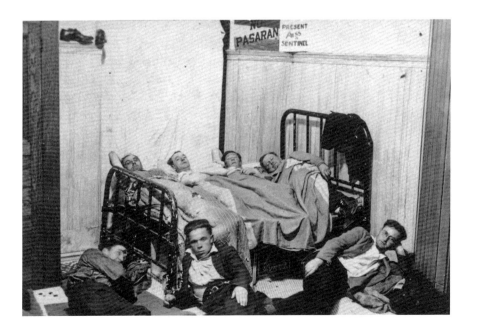

Depression became a catalyst for change, and what began to emerge was **modern liberalism** as we know it today.

The Great Depression was not caused by any single event, but it was a direct result of a free-market economic system. During the 1920s, mass production and consumer spending reached new heights. The 1920s were the years of electrification of the countryside, of communications innovations, of a consumer explosion as people bought new fridges and radios, and of the beginnings of the automobile culture. Unemployment was low, wages were increasing, hundreds of thousands of people were now able to buy their own homes, and it seemed like progress would continue forever.

America had become the breadbasket for Europe during the First World War, because French grain fields had been destroyed by trench warfare. America's western lands were opened to more and more settlers, and grain production was increased dramatically to feed the people of Europe. When the war ended in 1918, American fields continued producing and this continual increase lifted the entire economy. Things were going so well that factories were producing more goods than people could buy. Companies turned to the new tool of advertising to entice people to buy their goods. Many people were buying "on time," that is, paying for their purchases on credit. Credit was used to purchase stocks as well, and the stock market was rife with speculation.

Then, unexpectedly, the grain fields of France began producing again. The world market for grain was flooded and the price of grain crashed. This signalled the beginning of a general rush of people to sell their stocks. In September and October of 1929, the stock market fluctuated wildly. Despite efforts to bolster the market and retain investor confidence, panic selling began on October 24 and the market crashed on October 29.

The stock market crash began an interrelated series of events that resulted in the Great Depression. Banks failed as people withdrew their money. Factories closed, causing unemployment, and unemployment, in turn, resulted in even more factory closures as the unemployed could no longer afford to buy goods. International trade declined as countries instituted tariffs to protect domestic manufacturing.

Influence of the Great Depression on Labour: A Canadian Example

Political leaders in the democracies were baffled by the Depression and were concerned that their citizens would turn increasingly to socialism or, more worryingly, toward communism as the economy sank ever deeper into trouble and more and more workers became embittered. Events seemed to prove these fears well founded when Crowsnest Pass coal workers went on strike in 1932.

Excerpt 2: A newspaper account of the role of the police and labour following the riot

This morning Inspector Bonfield went to Zipp's [Zepf's] Hall, corner of Lake and Desplaines street[s], and closed the saloon and hall. In the building they found several muskets, some red flags and a large mass of socialist documents. There were some books and correspondence which was in German. As far as they have been translated nothing treasonable or opposed to good order was found…

Grief's Hall, at 54 West Lake Street was next visited. A meeting of freight-handlers was in session. After a conference with Inspector Bonfield, the President of the association invited him to address the boys. He went in and was introduced to the striking freight-handlers. The President said: "Men, every one of you raise your right hands and swear that you have no sympathy with the socialists who committed the dreadful crime of last night, and that you deprecate all misrule and will do your level best to keep the peace from being broken, and that you will do your part as good citizens to protect men and property from any harm." Every man raised his hand and emphasized his answer with a lusty "I will." Inspector Bonfield made them a little speech, and advised them to avoid assembling in crowds upon the streets, and especially not to march in procession. He gave them a lot of good advice about avoiding even the appearance of evil, and withdrew…

Source: *Chicago Evening Journal*, May 5, 1886. Eastern Illinois University.
http://www.eiu.edu/~localite/PastTracker/Industry&Labor_1886May6ChicagoTimes.pdf

Excerpt 3: A quote from Samuel Fielden

"The Socialists," he said, "are not going to declare war; but I tell you war has been declared upon us; and I ask you to get hold of anything that will help to resist the onslaught of the enemy and the usurper. The skirmish-lines have met. People have been shot. Men, women, and children have not been spared by the ruthless minions of private capital.

It had no mercy. So ought you. You are called upon to defend yourselves, your lives, your future. What matters it whether you kill yourselves with work to get a little relief or die on the battle-field resisting the enemy? [Applause.] What is the difference? Any animal, however loathsome, will resist when stepped upon. Are men less than snails or worms? I have some resistance in me. I know that you have too. You have been robbed. You will be starved into a worse condition."

Source: Sam Fielden, quoted in "A Hellish Deed: A Dynamite Bomb Thrown into a Crowd of Policemen." *Chicago Tribune*, May 5, 1886, in "The Haymarket Riot and Trial: Selected Newspaper Articles." University of Missouri-Kansas City School of Law.
www.law.umkc.edu/faculty/projects/ftrials/haymarket/haymarketnews.html

Excerpt 4: A newspaper article about the anarchist

The war is over, unless indications are out of joint. The Anarchist has sought his hole and is burrowing as deeply as fear and the police will allow him. His braggadocio is a thing of the past, and when he comes within sight of a blue coat he no longer looks ferocious and shakes his fist; he has an attack of ague and slinks out of sight like a whipped hound. The police enjoy the situation. They feel that the public is on their side and handle their clubs with a vim they lacked a week ago. Woe to the Anarchist who forms the nucleus of a crowd. He is shown no mercy.

Source: "The Anarchists Cowed: Breaking up their Haunts in Chicago." *New York Times*, May 8, 1886, quoted in "The Haymarket Riot and Trial: Selected Newspaper Articles." University of Missouri-Kansas City School of Law.
www.law.umkc.edu/faculty/projects/ftrials/haymarket/haymarketnews.html

Excerpt 5: Trial testimony by August Spies, one of the accused, at the trial in reply to being asked what he had said to the crowd in the Haymarket Square on the night in question

I told the people that for the past twenty years, the toilers, the wage workers, had asked their employers for a reduction of the hours of labor. I told them that there were, according to the statement of the secretary of the National Bureau of Labor Statistics, about two million of strong, physically strong men out of employment. I further told them that the technical development in production, with the machines, etc., the productive capacity had so immensely increased, that by any rational organization of society, all that society required could be produced in a few hours, and that the working of men ten hours a day in such [a] mechanical way as at present was simply another method of murdering them. After having stated that, though every student of social affairs and social phenomena admitted the fact, that society was under the present, under the over-work condition conditions of over-work, retrograding almost, and that the masses were sinking into degradation, demoralization, etc. all on account of the excessive work; that notwithstanding all this their demands had been refused, had not been granted. I proceeded to say that they had asked the Legislators, but the legislators had different interests than those at stake in this question; that they did not so much care about the welfare of society or of any class of society, but that they were looking out for their own interests, and that at least the workingmen had conceived consciously or unconsciously to take the matter in their own hands; that the question was an economic question; that it was not a political question; that the State Legislature nor Congress could not do anything in the premises, that the workingmen could only achieve a normal days work of eight hours or less by their own efforts, by self help.

Source: August Spies, trial testimony, August 9, 1886, quoted in "The Haymarket Riot and Trial: Selected Newspaper Articles."
University of Missouri-Kansas City School of Law.
www.law.umkc.edu/faculty/projects/ftrials/
haymarket/haymarketnews.html

Questions to Guide You

1. What are the different perspectives on the Haymarket Riot?

2. Evaluate the positions.
   a) What evidence can you find to determine the validity of the arguments?
   b) What is the authority of the authors?
   c) Is the information provided accurate?
   d) Are the opinions objective or subjective?
   e) Do the arguments share any commonalities?

3. Place the five positions on a political spectrum of the ideologies discussed in this chapter, similar to the one on page 150. Be prepared to justify your placements.

The Extension of Equality

• **How did the concept of equality expand?**

Initially, the values and beliefs of classical liberalism had brought greater liberty to entrepreneurs—factory owners, mine owners, investors, and other leaders of industry. This freedom for the producers of wealth also resulted in improved products and in better conditions for most members of society as evidenced by the passing of labour laws to establish **labour standards**.

The legislative reforms that benefited the working class were welcomed by workers. However, these reforms were the result of collaboration between government and capitalists, without the participation of workers themselves. Workers wanted more than this. They wanted an equal voice that spoke directly for their interests and reflected their own perspective. More and more people began to believe that liberalism required equal opportunity and equal respect for all members of society.

Labour Standards and Unions

This poem was written in the United States and widely distributed in Canada in the early 1870s. US workers were agitating for an eight-hour workday. Canadian workers were advocating a nine-hour workday. How does it demonstrate workers' sentiments about the situation in which they found themselves?

We mean to make things over;
We're tired of toil for naught
But bare enough to live on—
Never an hour for thought;
We want to see the sunshine,
We want to smell the flowers;
We're sure that God has willed it,
And we mean to have eight hours.
We're summoning our forces,
From shipyard, shop and mill—
Eight hours for work, eight hours for rest,
Eight hours for what we will!

—Source: quoted in Philip S. Foner,
History of the Labor Movement in the United States,
Vol. 2 (New York: International Publishers, 1998), p. 103.

During the 19th century, labourers who wanted to improve their standard of living began to attempt to form unions. What this involved was a recognition of a new right—the right to organize and bargain collectively. If all the workers in one particular trade were united, they could bargain collectively for better hours and wages and threaten to go on strike if their demands were not met. This contradicted the established notion that workers occupied a subordinate place in society. Even if employers took seriously the idea of individual worth, the idea of each individual worker bargaining with a powerful employer was obviously unrealistic and unfair. Unions could give workers the power to collectively negotiate fair wages and decent working conditions—all of which threatened to undermine the capitalist's control of the workplace.

Nevertheless, unions gradually prevailed, and an increasing number of workers gained the right to form unions. The International Labour Organization was formed in 1919, as part of the League of Nations. In 1948, the United Nations incorporated two articles on labour in the Universal Declaration of Human Rights.

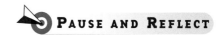

PAUSE AND REFLECT

How would a capitalist or a supporter of classical liberalism likely have responded to the UN Declaration in the 19th century? How does the recognition of this new right to organize demonstrate the extension of equality rights?

Article 23

1. *Everyone has the right to work, to free choice of employment, to just and favourable conditions of work and to protection against unemployment.*

2. *Everyone, without any discrimination, has the right to equal pay for equal work.*

3. *Everyone who works has the right to just and favourable remuneration ensuring for himself and his family an existence worthy of human dignity, and supplemented, if necessary, by other means of social protection.*

4. *Everyone has the right to form and to join trade unions for the protection of his interests.*

Article 24

Everyone has the right to rest and leisure, including reasonable limitation of working hours and periodic holidays with pay.

—Source: The Universal Declaration of Human Rights
© United Nations, 1948. Reproduced with permission.
www.un.org/Overview/rights.html

The following two passages provide two perspectives on unions. The first passage is from the founding convention of the Workers' Party, held on February 18, 1922. The Workers' Party was a socialist movement whose aims were to advocate for Canadian workers.

The trade union movement of Canada in common with the trade union movement of the world is experiencing the gravest crisis in its history.

PAUSE AND REFLECT

To what extent is the Worker's Party supportive of, or a reaction to, classical liberalism?

Already before the world war the policies and structure of the trade unions were being proved inadequate to cope with the growing concentration and solidarity of capital...

...the capitalist class has launched a general offensive for the reduction of the workers' living standards, making at the same time a determined onslaught for the destruction of the trade union movement itself. Utterly unprepared for this attack, the trade unions are almost everywhere in disorderly retreat...Unless the unions begin to understand that the era of conciliation and arbitration in the class struggle is passed...there is danger that the efforts of the capitalist class will succeed.

Under these circumstances the most vital task which confronts the working class is the establishment of a united front to resist the aggressions of the capitalist class.

—Source: "Workers' Party Resolutions on Labour Unions."
http://www.socialisthistory.ca/Docs/Leninist/Trade_Unions_22.htm

The second excerpt is taken from a contemporary article that argues that capitalism and not unions have provided a better living standard for individuals.

...In the U.S. the average work week was 61 hours in 1870, compared to 34 hours today, and this near doubling of leisure time for American workers was caused by capitalism, not unionism...

Of course, this is only true of a capitalist economy where private property, free markets, and entrepreneurship prevail. The steady rise in living standards in (predominantly) capitalist countries is due to the benefits of private capital investment, entrepreneurship, technological advance, and a better educated workforce...Labor unions routinely take credit for all of this while pursuing policies which impede the very institutions of capitalism that are the cause of their own prosperity.

The shorter work week is entirely a capitalist invention. As capital investment caused the marginal productivity of labor to increase over time, less labor was required to produce the same levels of output. As competition became more intense, many employers competed for the best employees by offering both better pay and shorter hours. Those who did not offer shorter work weeks were compelled by the forces of competition to offer higher compensating wages or become uncompetitive in the labor market.

—Source: *How Capitalism Saved America: The Untold History of our Country, from the Pilgrims to the Present* by Thomas J. DiLorenzo, copyright © 2004 by Thomas J. DiLorenzo. Used by permission of Crown Forum, an imprint of Crown Publishers, a division of Random House, Inc.

PAUSE AND REFLECT

What perspective on classical liberalism do DiLorenzo's comments reflect? To whom would each of these points of view on unions seem attractive and to whom would they appear a threat? Which view best informs your own point of view?

Universal Suffrage

Classical liberalism proclaimed the equality of men, meaning the male gender, but in reality only certain men were equal. This becomes obvious when one examines the right to vote. In the 18th century, in countries where voting took place at all, the right to vote was reserved for propertied men with some wealth. In Britain, for example, Parliament was composed of the aristocracy, who held seats in the House of Lords, and landed gentry, who elected one another to seats in the House of Commons. In Canada, which lacked an aristocracy, wealth replaced birth as the qualification for voting. Men had to either own a certain amount of property or pay a certain amount of money in rent or taxes. Women, First Nations peoples, and certain religious and ethnic groups were not allowed to vote.

From 1867 to 1919, the classical liberal idea that voting was a privilege for the few gradually gave way to the modern liberal concept that the franchise was a right, and the various qualifications were eliminated, at first for men only. In Canada, the Dominion Elections Act (1920) extended the federal vote to all citizens of European extraction, both men and women. Non-Europeans had to wait longer for the right to vote. First Nations had to wait the longest—Canada did not extend the franchise to First Nations in a manner that provided them full opportunity to vote without jeopardizing their First Nations status until 1960. The Inuit gained the right to vote in 1950, although it was difficult for them to exercise this right, as polling stations were not generally set up across the North until the 1960s.

PAUSE AND REFLECT

What are the reasons that explain why Canada's First Nations peoples had to wait the longest before winning the right to vote without losing their First Nations status?

Figure 4-14 ▼

What biases were reflected in the restrictions on voting? What other changes to restrictions in voting might be challenged in the future?

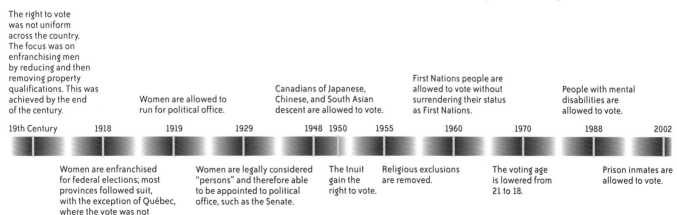

The right to vote was not uniform across the country. The focus was on enfranchising men by reducing and then removing property qualifications. This was achieved by the end of the century.

Women are allowed to run for political office.

Canadians of Japanese, Chinese, and South Asian descent are allowed to vote.

First Nations people are allowed to vote without surrendering their status as First Nations.

People with mental disabilities are allowed to vote.

| 19th Century | 1918 | 1919 | 1929 | 1948 | 1950 | 1955 | 1960 | 1970 | 1988 | 2002 |

Women are enfranchised for federal elections; most provinces followed suit, with the exception of Québec, where the vote was not extended until 1940.

Women are legally considered "persons" and therefore able to be appointed to political office, such as the Senate.

The Inuit gain the right to vote.

Religious exclusions are removed.

The voting age is lowered from 21 to 18.

Prison inmates are allowed to vote.

Get to the Source

To discover more about suffrage in Canada, follow the link that your teacher will provide to Voting in Canada: How a Privilege Became a Right.

Why was there a limited franchise within Canada prior to 1960? How did those wishing to restrict the right to vote justify their position?

Equality Rights for Women in Western Democracies

Feminism, at its simplest, is the belief that men and women are to be treated equally in all respects. Modern feminism had its roots in the Enlightenment thinkers who demanded "the rights of man." Initially, of course, most people took this literally; that is, they considered man to mean men. But classical liberalism did provide a way of thinking about civil liberties that allowed feminism to emerge. Paradoxically, very few of the classical liberal thinkers were willing to concede any rights to women. One French writer of the Enlightenment, Denis Diderot, stated that women were governed by the uterus, "an organ subject to terrible spasms, which rules her and rouses up in her phantoms of every sort." (Source: James F. McMillan, *France and Women, 1789–1914* [New York: Routledge, 2000], p. 5.) Rousseau argued that "…woman was specifically made for man's delight. If man in his turn ought to be pleasing in her eyes, the necessity is less urgent, his virtue is in his strength, he pleases because he is strong. I grant you this is not the law of love, but it is the law of nature…" (Source: Alison Twells, *British Women's History* [New York: I.B. Tauris, 2007], p. 19).

Some women fought against the classical liberal view of women. Mary Wollstonecraft, an early novelist, was a feminist. In *A Vindication of the Rights of Women* (1792) she argued that not only would education make women better wives and mothers, it would also make them the equals of men.

Nonetheless, an ideology of "separate spheres" emerged, and by the 19th century's Victorian era this ideology was firmly in place, reinforcing the inequality of women. At its root was the view of women as clearly inferior to men. Women had no voice in the restrictions placed on them, so most women acquiesced to them, either willingly or under force. Women developed the characteristics of this sphere into their own ideology. They accepted the home, children, and family as their proper sphere and practised the "womanly" virtues of domesticity, child-rearing, religious observance, and charitable activities (if and when they were in a position to do so). Women of all classes worked hard—in fact, they were a supply of cheap labour. The homes of upper- and middle-class women were large establishments, and working-class women performed poorly paid labour that enabled their families to survive. By the 19th century, a number of women viewed their desire to contribute to the larger society as an extension of their feminine sphere. Initially, they ran Sunday schools and established institutions to care for widows, orphans, the elderly, and the ill. Gradually they became involved in the public sphere as they began anti-poverty campaigns and child labour movements or agitated for more equitable divorce and property laws. A public issue that prompted activism by women was the abuse of alcohol. Public drunkenness was common, and it was equally common to have wages spent on the "demon rum" rather than on the needs of the family. Temperance societies sprang up, and women agitated for controls on liquor. By the 1860s, suffragists began to argue for the right to vote, feeling that political power was the only way to achieve their goals. What began as religious and charitable activity evolved into political activity in this first wave of feminism.

As the suffragists had hoped, enfranchisement did lead the way to the extension of other equality rights for women. After a struggle that went all the way to the British government, the Canadian government recognized the right of women to be appointed to public office in 1929. During the 20th century, the government passed laws to accord women more equal rights in the law; in marriage, divorce, and abortion; and in the workplace. In addition, gender equality rights were entrenched in the Charter of Rights and Freedoms.

Suffrage, and in particular women's suffrage, is not universal in the world today. Consider the following situations:

- Lebanon—Partial suffrage. Proof of education required for women, not required for men.
- Saudi Arabia—No suffrage for women. The first local elections ever held in the country occurred in 2005. Women were not given the right to vote or to stand for election.
- United Arab Emirates—No suffrage for men or women. The Parliament is officially appointed, and there are no elections. Neither men nor women have the right to vote or to stand for election although this is expected to change in 2010.

—Source: "The World Factbook: Suffrage"
Central Intelligence Agency.
https://www.cia.gov/library/publications/
the-world-factbook/fields/2123.html, October 23, 2008

Can you suggest why these countries may not be overly supportive of suffrage in general and female suffrage in particular? What connections can you draw between the realities of voting in these places and the countries' relationships to the ideology of modern liberalism, in particular to the liberal ideas of individual rights and freedoms with respect to suffrage?

Figure 4-15 ▲

Mary Wollstonecraft, 18th-century novelist

Visual Voices

Visual images reflect the perspectives of the society that produces them, and act as social commentary. Examine the images below and determine what ideological perceptions of women the images represent.

THE FORCE OF EXAMPLE.

"Now, Jessie, Say your Prayers like a good little Girl!"
"Mamma, dear! why mayn't I kneel down, and hold my Tongue, as Papa does!"

Figure 4-16 ▲

In what way does this 1873 cartoon illustrate the "woman's sphere"?

OUR VILLAGE INDUSTRIAL COMPETITION.

Husband (just home from the City). "My Angel!—Crying!—Whatever's the matter!"
Wife. "They've—awarded me—Prize Medal"—(sobbing)—"f' my Sponge Cake!"
Husband (soothingly). "And I'm quite sure it desery——"
Wife (hysterically). "Oh—but—t' said—'twas—for the Best Specimen—o' Concrete!"

Figure 4-17 ▲

What gender prejudices are being illustrated? What was the political application of these stereotypes?

Figure 4-18 ▲

What is the husband doing in this 1848 cartoon? How is the wife dressed? What was the artist's point of view about women activists' desire for the franchise?

1 How effective do you think each image might be in influencing people living during the 19th century?

2 What changes have modern liberal ideas about equality rights brought to representations of women?

3 Can you think of any contemporary images regarding gender issues (see pages 33–34 and 35) that have a similar impact on people in our society?

Challenging Classical Liberal Beliefs

Most of the women fighting for equal rights in the 19th century were European and in the middle class. They had a good educational background and sufficient leisure time to devote to activities outside the home. But one of the most powerful crusaders for equality was a former slave. Sojourner Truth (c. 1792–1883) escaped from slavery in New York shortly before mandatory emancipation became law in the state in 1827. The following quotation about Sojourner Truth illustrates the struggle to combat classical liberal beliefs and values about women.

The leaders of the movement trembled on seeing a tall, gaunt black woman in a gray dress and white turban, surmounted with an uncouth sunbonnet, march deliberately into the church, walk with the air of a queen up the aisle, and take her seat upon the pulpit steps…A buzz of disapprobation was heard all over the house…

The tumult subsided at once, and every eye was fixed on this almost Amazon form, which stood nearly six feet high [1.8 metres], head erect, and eyes piercing the upper air like one in a dream. At her first word there was a profound hush. She spoke in deep tones, which, though not loud, reached every ear in the house, and away through the throng at the doors and windows.

> *"Wall, chilern, whar dar is so much racket dar must be somethin' out o' kilter. I tink dat 'twixt de niggers of de Souf and de womin at de Norf, all talkin' 'bout rights, de white men will be in a fix pretty soon…*
>
> *"If de fust woman God ever made was strong enough to turn de world upside down all alone, dese women togedder [and she glanced her eye over the platform] ought to be able to turn it back, and get it right side up again! And now dey is asking to do it, de men better let 'em."*

Long continued cheering greeted this…I have never in my life seen anything like the magical influence that subdued the mobbish spirit of the day, and turned the sneers and jeers of an excited crowd into notes of respect and admiration. Hundreds rushed up to shake hands with her, and congratulate the glorious old mother, and bid her Godspeed on her mission of "testifyin' agin concerning the wickedness of this 'ere people."

—Source: Elizabeth Cady Stanton, Susan B. Anthony, and Matilda J. Gage, eds., *History of Woman Suffrage*, Volume I, 1881 (reprint: New York: Arno Press, 1969), pp. 114–117.

In January 1914, the women of Manitoba's Political Equality League staged a hugely successful mock parliament at Winnipeg's Walker Theatre in which Nellie McClung, a leading suffragist, played the premier and other women played the members of the legislative assembly. During the session of the mock

Figure 4-19 ▲

Sojourner Truth, c. 1862. During the Civil War, Truth campaigned for the Union and the establishment of African-American fighting forces.

parliament, a number of men petitioned for the right to vote. McClung answered their request as follows:

If men were all so intelligent as these representatives of the downtrodden sex seem to be it might not do any harm to give them the vote. But all men are not so intelligent. There is no use giving men votes. They wouldn't use them. They would let them spoil and go to waste. Then again, some men would vote too much…Giving men the vote would unsettle the home…The modesty of our men, which we reverence, forbids us giving them the vote. Men's place is on the farm…It may be that I am old-fashioned. I may be wrong. After all, men may be human. Perhaps the time may come when men may vote with the women—but in the meantime, be of good cheer. Advocate and Educate.

—Nellie McClung, quoted in "Suffrage: The Women's Parliament."
Herstory: An Exhibition.

library2.usask.ca/herstory/woparl.html

1 What grounds did Truth use as the basis for women's claim to equal rights? How convincing would her argument be for you if you had lived in this period?

2 How does Truth's speech provide a basis for the modern liberal acceptance of women's rights?

3 What do the narrator's comments reveal about society at the time?

4 What is Nellie McClung's purpose in her quotation?

Explore the Issues

Concept Review

1 Provide five examples of the extension of the concept of equality rights in the late 19th and early 20th centuries.

Concept Application

2 Why did classical liberalism exclude working men, women, and non-Europeans from full participation in Western society? What principles were used to justify ignoring equality rights for these people?

3 Explain the ways in which labour unions, the vote, and the feminist movement are extensions of equality rights that grew out of a reaction to classical liberalism in Western societies.

4 Which of the extensions of equality rights mentioned in Question 2 do you think was most important in satisfying the needs of society? Why?

5 How far should democratic governments go to extend equality rights? Can you see a point where the rights of individuals to choose for themselves might be compromised by the well-being of the community?

6 To what extent was the extension of equality rights the final step in the evolution of classical liberalism to modern liberalism?

Reflect and Analyze

To what extent did classical liberalism meet the needs of society? This question has been a focus for this chapter. Various ideologies developed in opposition to classical liberalism, based on the perceived failure of classical liberalism to create just and equitable political, social, and economic systems.

While conservatism looked to the order and stability of the past, and to government by the educated and privileged, as the ideal society, socialism had a different view of the best possible future. Socialism focused primarily on the idea of equality and imagined a world where humans lived in such harmony and co-operation that eventually government would no longer be necessary. There were, however, divergent beliefs about how this goal was to be obtained.

In the face of the development of new ideologies, classical liberalism itself evolved. First came pragmatic improvements to the working lives of labourers, followed by the acceptance of unions, and the extension of equality rights and the franchise to men, and eventually to women. Fundamental classical liberal values did not change, but the priorities assigned to these values were adjusted to achieve the welfare state. Classical liberalism had begun its transformation into modern liberalism.

Respond to Issues

1 You have been exploring various ideologies that developed in reaction to liberalism and how these ideologies resulted in changes to liberalism. This examination helped you consider your own point of view on contemporary issues in a liberal society and provided a way for you to think about why there may be resistance to an ideology. In considering the issue, *To what extent did classical liberalism meet the needs of society?*, you have analyzed many varied views. Do you agree with the direction that was taken in the evolution from classical to modern liberalism? Do you believe that modern liberalism is the most successful way to meet people's needs? Do you foresee a need for modern liberalism to evolve yet again? Take an informed position on these questions.

Recognize Relationships among Concepts, Issues, and Citizenship

2 Examine the portrayal of labour unions or feminism in the popular media in music and/or film. Choose sources that are contemporary, historical, or both. Do they deal with these issues? Do they encourage or support one particular kind of ideology over another? How convinced are you by their promotion or critique of a specific ideology? How does the ideology promoted or critiqued relate to citizenship in Canada or the world?

Twentieth-Century Rejections of Liberalism

KEY SKILLS

Discerning historical facts from primary sources

KEY CONCEPTS

Evaluating ideological systems that rejected principles of liberalism

Key Terms

Censorship
Collectivization
Communism
Dissent
Fascism
Reactionary
Totalitarianism

Figure 5-1 ▲

The Bloody Sunday incident was a massacre of Russian workers who peacefully marched to petition the czar for rights similar to those in European liberal democracies. This photo is taken from a 1925 film about the massacre, *Devyatoe Yanvarya* (*January 9*). Contrast some of the values held by the people who were responsible for the massacre with the values held by the people who supported the petition.

In January 1905, following massive strikes in St. Petersburg, Russia, unarmed, peaceful demonstrators marched to the Winter Palace to present a petition to Czar Nicholas II, the Russian monarch. Like many industrial workers in Europe, the demonstrators had suffered from the great social inequalities of a laissez-faire capitalist system. Unlike most workers in Europe, however, the Russian workers were a small, unorganized group and had long suffered abuse and neglect at the hands of the Russian aristocracy and an absolute monarchy. Among other things, their petition asked for recognition of basic human rights such as freedom of speech, the press, religion, and conscience; a state-sponsored education system; improved working conditions; fairer wages; a reduction in the workday to eight hours; and a condemnation of the overtime that the factory owners had forced upon their workers.

The protest did not go well. Hundreds were gunned down by the czar's Imperial Guard in an event that came to be known as Bloody Sunday. The Bloody Sunday incident marked a turning point in Russian history. Outraged by the massacre, Russian citizens grew steadily more dissatisfied with their government until the complete transformation that occurred with the Russian Revolution in 1917.

The Russian Revolution was a reaction to the injustices of the authoritarian czarist system and uncontrolled free-market capitalism, in which a small group of people (the bourgeoisie) benefited from the back-breaking working conditions of the peasants and proletariat (working classes). The Bolsheviks (communists), under Vladimir Lenin, sought to destroy this class-based system, reject classical liberal economic principles, and provide better living and working conditions for all.

◀ **Figure 5-2**

"I won the Nobel Prize for Literature. What was your crime?" Boris Pasternak was a highly regarded Russian author who supported the communist revolution through much of his career. Nonetheless, his account of the Russian Revolution, the novel *Doctor Zhivago* (1957), was banned in the Soviet Union, but won him the 1958 Nobel Prize for Literature. This cartoon by Bill Mauldin satirizes the Soviet regime for not allowing Pasternak to accept the Nobel Prize.

Copyright by Bill Mauldin (1958). Courtesy of the Bill Mauldin Estate LLC

Chapter Issue

In previous chapters, you had an opportunity to analyze ideologies that were developed in response to classical liberalism (classical conservatism, Marxism, utopian and moderate socialism, and welfare capitalism). In this chapter you will explore ideologies that completely rejected liberalism in favour of totalitarian systems of government. You may have already formed opinions about communism and fascism, potentially making it more challenging for you to read about them objectively. However, some countries may have numerous reasons—cultural, historical, and even spiritual—for why they might not want to embrace liberalism. It may be instructive to try to view the world through the eyes of the people involved and not only from your own point of view.

Many nations and nation-states throughout modern history have rejected liberalism, including some Indigenous peoples. Soviet Russia and Nazi Germany are two important historical examples that we will explore at this time because they both had dramatic impacts on the events and the ideologies of the 20th century. Therefore, this chapter will examine the ideologies of communism as implemented in the Soviet Union and fascism as practised in pre–Second World War Germany, as well as the ideologies' respective impacts on the lives of the people living in both countries. You will consider the beliefs and values that make up these ideologies and the circumstances that prompted their rise before you make any judgments or draw ethical conclusions as you address the Chapter Issue, ***To what extent is the rejection of liberalism justified?***, and the Related Issue for Part 2, ***To what extent is resistance to liberalism justified?***

Figure 5-3 ▶

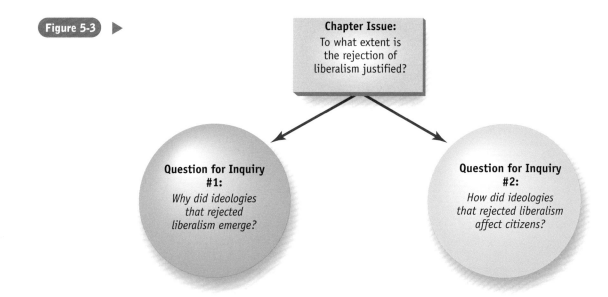

Chapter Issue:
To what extent is the rejection of liberalism justified?

Question for Inquiry #1:
Why did ideologies that rejected liberalism emerge?

Question for Inquiry #2:
How did ideologies that rejected liberalism affect citizens?

Societal Conditions That Led to the Rise of Totalitarianism in the 20th Century

Question for Inquiry

- **Why did ideologies that rejected liberalism emerge?**

The two most influential ideologies that rejected liberalism—**communism** and **fascism**—both utilized totalitarian forms of government. **Totalitarianism** varies in its practice, but as a government system it seeks complete control over the public and private lives of its citizens. It attempts such control by creating a hierarchically organized society with a single political party run by a leader or small elite. The totalitarian Italian state was summed up by fascist dictator Benito Mussolini as follows: "Everything within the state, nothing outside the state, nothing against the state." (Source: Benito Mussolini, quoted in "Politics—That's Me!" *Time* magazine, June 29, 1931.)

In this section we will examine the circumstances and conditions that led to the rise of totalitarian states in Russia and Germany. What effect did the rejection of liberalism have on the lives and the identity of the people who lived under these regimes?

The Nature of Totalitarian Regimes

Totalitarian regimes are responding to what they see as dangerous and destabilizing changes. They consider the existing society in need of a complete transformation. This transformation may be

- **radical**, as in the Soviet Union, where the change desired is a move toward the far left side of the economic spectrum (a classless society with state [public] ownership of property) and a complete rejection of the political and economic traditions of the past, or
- **reactionary**, as in Nazi Germany, where the change desired is a move toward an idealized past and an acceptance of economic inequality (accepting the belief that some people are naturally better than others)

 **PAUSE AND REFLECT**

As you read the following pages and learn about the reasons that the Soviet Union and Nazi Germany had for rejecting liberalism, keep track of the totalitarian methods used by each regime. Make a table as shown below and fill in examples as you read.

	Soviet Union	Nazi Germany
extensive local, regional, and national organization		
youth, professional, cultural, and athletic groups (often forced participation)		
a secret police using terror		
indoctrination through education		
the censorship of the media		
redirecting popular discontent (use of scapegoats)		

Like most ideologies, totalitarian regimes provide an account of the past, an explanation of the present, and a vision for the future. However, the extensive use of propaganda, coercive power, and communications technologies ensure that totalitarian governments maintain strict control over their citizens. Conformity to the state ideology is demanded, and is achieved through such measures as

- extensive local, regional, and national organization
- youth, professional, cultural, and athletic groups (often forced participation)
- a secret police using terror
- indoctrination through education
- the censorship of the media
- redirecting popular discontent (use of scapegoats)

The totalitarianism of the Soviet Union and Nazi Germany were attempts to hold off and reject the beliefs and values of liberalism: a turning away from the worth of the individual and the principle of limited government in favour of a collective, all-powerful state where individuals served the interests of the state. Various factors encouraged both countries to take this route. A long history of authoritarianism in both Russia and the German states; a tradition of communitarianism in Russia; and the defeat of Germany in the First World War by an alliance dominated by liberal democracies all helped to create the conditions needed for the rejection of liberalism in Russia and Germany.

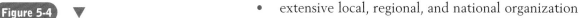

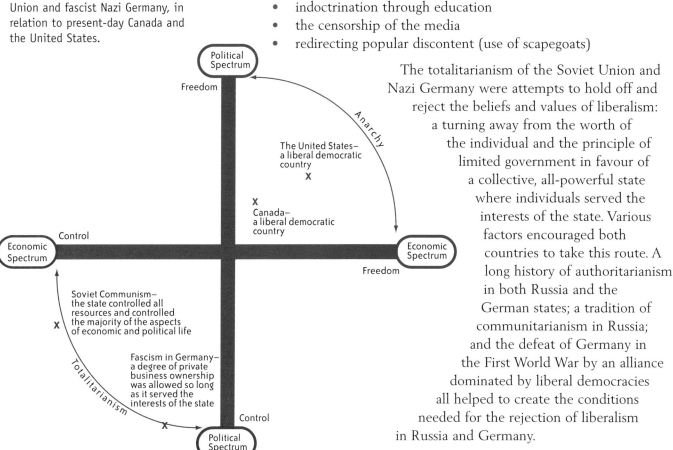

Figure 5-4 ▼

A freedom-control spectrum showing the degree of economic and political freedom in the communist Soviet Union and fascist Nazi Germany, in relation to present-day Canada and the United States.

The Need for Change in Russia

As you read in Chapter 4, the social conditions created by classical liberalism inspired European thinkers such as Karl Marx and Friedrich Engels to come up with ideas for reforming the capitalist system. Ideas such as the worth of every individual, equality, opportunity, and progress were brought into the repressive, feudal empire of Russia in the 19th century, and many groups began movements for change.

Many people in Russia were receptive to the ideas for social reform that sprang up in Europe. At least 80 per cent of Russians were peasants. Some of these peasants were serfs, low-income farmers who worked the land of wealthy landowners, and were legally bound to remain on the lands on which they were born. Czar Alexander II announced the **emancipation**—or freeing—of the serfs in 1861, but the government was slow to implement the new policy. In addition, serfs were obligated to pay for their land for several decades after their emancipation. Thus, Alexander II's reform did little to quell the dissatisfaction in Russian society.

From the 1860s to the beginning of the 20th century, Russian society underwent many dramatic changes. Classical liberal economic policies were adopted, and rapid industrialization occurred that was similar to, but far behind what was already happening in many European countries. In addition, the Russian population doubled from 50 million to 100 million. However, the Russian political structure remained autocratic, as the monarchy did not want to give up control of the country. The limited democratic reforms that were allowed (such as elected local councils in a few Russian provinces) were often implemented many years after they had been announced.

In 1881, the czar was assassinated by a revolutionary group called "Land and Freedom." His son, Czar Alexander III, reacted by imposing stricter political control, and persecuting and exiling liberals and revolutionary groups with the use of a secret police force. Some Russian political **dissidents** (people who disagree with the government) came into contact with Marxism while in exile in Europe, and they would later bring these ideas back to Russia.

Figure 5-5 ▲

Viktor Vasnetsov's *Moving House* (1876). How does this painting depict Russian society not meeting its citizens' needs?

Lenin and the Rise of Communism

The czar's government was inefficient as well as authoritarian. The transportation system was so poorly organized, for example, that food shortages in the cities were commonplace. The czar and the bureaucracy resisted almost any and all suggestions for change, whether from the middle class seeking to introduce liberal concepts such as constitutional monarchy, free speech, and free assembly; from the peasants demanding land of their own; or from the industrial workers demanding unions. The czar's secret police persecuted dissenters of every kind. Discontent and chaos were rife and punishments were severe.

Vladimir Ilich Ulyanov (1870–1924), better known as Lenin, who would later become the leader of the communist Soviet Union, described the conditions in Russia in 1899 as follows:

File Facts

The following terms are used to describe the country of Russia, and vary according to historical time period:

- **Russia** or the **Russian Empire**: The name of the empire located in Eastern Europe and North Asia prior to 1922.
- The **Soviet Union (Union of Soviet Socialist Republics, or USSR)**: The name used between 1922 and 1991 for the communist-led country made up of 15 republics, the largest of which was the Russian Soviet Socialist Republic.
- **Russia** or **Russian Federation**: Since 1992, after the various republics of the USSR had declared their independence, the largest republic, Russia, continues as its own democratic country.

In Russia, not only the workers but all the citizens are deprived of political rights. Russia is an absolute monarchy. The czar alone promulgates laws, nominates officials and controls them. For this reason it seems as though in Russia the czar and the Czarist Government were dependent on no class and cared for all equally. In reality, however, all the officials are chosen exclusively from the possessing class, and all are subject to the influence of the large capitalists who obtain whatever they want—the Ministers dance to the tune the large capitalists play. The Russian worker is bowed under a double yoke; he is robbed and plundered by the capitalists and the landowners, and, lest he should fight against them, he is bound hand and foot by the police, his mouth is gagged and any attempt to defend the rights of the people is followed by persecution.

—V.I. Lenin, *Our Programme*, 1899.
Modern History Sourcebook, Fordham University.
http://www.fordham.edu/halsall/mod/1899lenin-program.html

As Lenin stated, Russian workers were subject to difficult social and economic conditions. Many of these workers gave their support to revolutionary groups. At the beginning of the 20th century, several assassinations of high-ranking politicians were carried out by one of these groups, the Socialist Revolutionary Party, leading to a backlash of repression by the government. In addition, Russia was defeated in a war against Japan in 1905, and this defeat contributed to the Russian citizens' dissatisfaction with their government. The result of this unrest was the Russian Revolution of 1905, fuelled by Russian authoritarianism, the slowness of reform, and events such as Bloody Sunday, the incident you read about at the beginning of this chapter.

Ineffectual Reform

Although the 1905 revolution was eventually suppressed, the czar was forced to allow some reforms, including the following:

- basic civil rights such as the freedom of expression and the freedom of assembly
- universal suffrage
- the creation of an elected legislative assembly called the Duma

These reforms did not satisfy the Russian populace, however, especially since the czar limited the powers of the Duma before its first session, using the Fundamental Laws of 1906. The czar's unwillingness to relinquish political control of the country is evident in the text of these laws. Article 4 states that the czar "possesses the supreme autocratic power. Not only fear and conscience, but God himself, commands obedience to his authority." Article 9 states that the czar "approves laws; and without his approval no legislative measure can become law." (Source: *Svod Zakonov Rossiiskoi Imperii*, 3rd series, Volume 1, Part 1.

[St. Petersburg, 1912], pp. 5–26. http://www.dur.ac.uk/a.k.harrington/
fundlaws.html.) In addition, the czar had the power to dismiss the
Duma and call new elections.

The outbreak of the First World War in 1914 intensified the
problems in the Russian Empire and paved the way for the Russian
Revolution of 1917. During the two years following 1914, food shortages
and strikes were common in Russia, and the poorly led and poorly fed
troops suffered massive losses in the war. Czar Nicholas II, unable to rule
the Russian Empire effectively or deal with the ferment among the
population pushing for reforms in peace time, was overwhelmed by the
pressures of war. In this maelstrom of circumstances, the populace's
discontent grew until February 1917, when mass demonstrations and
strikes coalesced into an outright revolution. The czar abdicated and a
provisional government was declared. Within months, Lenin's communist
Bolsheviks took over the machinery of government in a very well-
organized attack in October 1917.

Communism Is Established

Lenin and the Bolsheviks believed that violent revolution was the only
way to overturn the government and avoid the further development of
liberalism in Russia. Lenin capitalized on the plight of the landless
peasants, the starvation of the low-income workers in the cities, the
dispirited soldiers, and many other groups with his slogan "Land, Peace,
Bread." However, taking power in a time of chaos was easier than
keeping power. A bloody civil war raged for the next five years
between the Red Army of Lenin's Bolsheviks and the White Army, a
loose coalition of forces including supporters of the old regime and
reformers opposed to the Bolsheviks. By 1922, the civil war was over
and communism was established in Russia. By 1924, Russia was
renamed the Union of Soviet Socialist Republics (USSR, or Soviet
Union) and quickly transformed from a land of autocratic czarist rule
to a land of dictatorial rule by the Communist Party.

The emergence of communism in Russia was not an unreasonable
response to the conditions existing for the majority of Russian subjects.
Its interpretation and application, however, complicates any evaluation
of its merit for the lives of the millions of people who were governed
by this ideology. George F. Kennan, a former US ambassador to the
Soviet Union and later a professor, wrote the following assessment of
the Russian Revolution:

*It is, then, according to the relative value one attaches to ends as opposed
to means in human affairs that the positive and negative elements of the
Russian Revolution will stand out through the prism of historical
retrospection. But whichever value predominates—whether one sees this
as a hopeful breakthrough or only as the onset of new misunderstanding,*

Figure 5-6 ▲

Lenin and the Bolsheviks seized control
of the Russian capital, St. Petersburg,
in a single day, causing only two
deaths. The struggle for control of the
rest of the country would be much
longer and more violent.

◣ **PAUSE AND REFLECT**

**What conditions existed for the
majority of Russians that may
have helped the emergence of
communism in Russia?**

conflict and misery—one is obliged to concede to the Russian Revolution the status of the greatest political event of the present century. It deserves this description by virtue of the profound exemplary effect it had across great portions of the globe, of the alteration it produced in Russia's relations with the great powers of the West, and of the changes it brought to the life of one of the world's great peoples.

—George F. Kennan, "The Russian Revolution—Fifty Years After: Its Nature and Consequences." *Foreign Affairs*, **46, 1 (October, 1967): p. 10.**

The Rise of Totalitarianism in Germany

In August 1919, immediately after the First World War, Germany enacted a new constitution. For the first time in its history, Germany would be a republic with a modern, liberal democratic political structure. The German parliament, the Reichstag, was to be elected by universal suffrage. This period in German history has become known as the Weimar Republic, because the new constitution was drafted in the city of Weimar. The constitution provided for several democratic instruments, such as referendums, to ensure that the electorate had a sufficient voice in legislation. Yet within 15 years, Germany would become a totalitarian regime under the fascist Nazi party. A variety of circumstances made the rejection of liberal democracy possible.

Aftermath of the First World War

Germany, allied with the Austro-Hungarian Empire, had been defeated in the First World War. The principal treaty that ended the war, the Treaty of Versailles, was negotiated by the victors of the conflict without German participation. The terms of the treaty provoked a lasting resentment among many Germans. These terms included the following:

- the "war guilt clause," which said that Germany accepted sole responsibility for the war and was thus responsible for all the damage caused by the war
- Germany was to make reparation payments in the amount of US$33 billion
- the Rhineland area of western Germany, which bordered France, Belgium, and the Netherlands, was to be a demilitarized zone
- various European territories that Germany had annexed were given to other countries
- the German Emperor Wilhelm II was to be tried as a war criminal
- the German army was to be limited to no more than 100 000 troops
- the German navy was limited to no more than 15 000 men, with a limited number of vessels

- the manufacture, import, and export of weapons and armaments, including tanks, submarines, aircraft, and artillery, were prohibited

The social democrats and democrats who formed the coalition government of the republic in 1919 had not been involved in the negotiation of the treaty and had little choice but to sign it when Britain, France, the United States, and Italy demanded they do so in November 1919. Nonetheless, much of the German populace blamed the government for the humiliation and economic hardship the treaty would cause for years afterwards. This resentment would undermine many voters' confidence in their liberal democratic government.

Furthermore, many Germans associated liberalism with the victors of the First World War—Britain, France, and the United States: "Fight against liberalism in all its forms, liberalism that had defeated Germany, was the common idea which united socialists and conservatives in one common front." (Source: Friedrich Hayek, *The Road to Serfdom*, [London: George Rutledge & Sons, 1944], p. 185.)

Economic Turmoil

In the years directly following the First World War, the German economy was in ruins. In 1923, Germany declared it could not continue making the reparations payments imposed by the Treaty of Versailles. As a consequence, France and Belgium invaded the Ruhr industrial region of Germany, hoping to claim reparations from the profits of the businesses in the region. The German workers in the region responded with general strikes, and manufacturing came to a halt, causing inflation to skyrocket and further exacerbating the difficult economic situation. The German middle class was quickly becoming beleaguered as it saw its investments and savings become worthless in a matter of months.

From 1923 to 1929, the situation in Germany stabilized to some extent. Economic reforms, including the introduction of a new currency, brought an end to rampant inflation and stabilized the economy. The Dawes Plan, under which American banks lent money to the German government, allowed Germany to continue making reparations payments in accordance with the Treaty of Versailles. However, these measures left Germany with a large debt. The stock market crash of 1929 and the ensuing Great Depression plunged the country into economic hardship once again.

Hitler and the Nazi Party took advantage of the widespread unemployment and desperation this caused in the German populace

Date	Marks for Each American Dollar
December 1918	8.25
December 1919	48
December 1920	73
December 1921	192
December 1922	7 590
June 1923	110 000
September 1923	99 million
October 1923	25 billion
November 1923	2 160 billion
December 1923	4 200 billion

Figure 5-7

The more marks to the dollar, the less the marks are worth. To put this in context, in September 1923, one pint of milk cost 250 000 marks. A pint of milk in the United States at that time cost only US$0.05. Source: Bernd Widdig, *Culture and Inflation in Weimar Germany* (Berkley and Los Angeles: University of California Press, 2001), p. 42.

Figure 5-8

At the height of German inflation, this woman is lighting the morning fire in her stove with money because it is nearly worthless.

Date of Election	Jan. 1919	June 1920	May 1924	Dec. 1924	May 1928	Sept. 1930	July 1932	Nuv. 1932	Mar, 1933
Social Democrats	165	102	100	131	153	143	133	121	120
Communists/Socialists	22	88	62	45	54	77	89	100	81
Centre Party	91	64	65	69	62	68	75	70	74
Democrats	75	39	28	32	25	20	4	2	5
Right-wing Parties	63	157	156	173	134	90	66	83	72
Nazis (National Socialists)	—	—	**32**	**14**	**12**	**107**	**230**	**196**	**288**
Others	7	9	29	29	51	72	11	12	7
Total deputies	423	459	472	493	491	577	608	584	647

Figure 5-9

The number of deputies elected to the Reichstag according to political party, and the rate of unemployment during the same period. What correlation can you see between these statistics?
Source: John D. Clare, *Germany* 1919 - 1939, December 2001, p. 9.
http://www.johndclare.net/Word%20
documents/Weimar%20Germany.doc

	1928	1930	1932
Number of unemployed (in millions)	2	3	6

by declaring that it was the responsibility of the state to provide every citizen with an opportunity to earn a living. The Nazi platform also stated that the profits of industry should be shared by citizens and that everyone should be obligated to work for a living. However, these policies were not strictly followed once the Nazis gained power.

The Legacy of Authoritarian Rule

Since its creation in 1871, the German Empire (as it was known until the end of the First World War) had become a highly industrialized economic power. It did not, however, develop effective liberal political institutions, relying instead on the traditional ruling families and institutions. While it had a parliament elected by limited suffrage, the government was largely authoritarian, with any real political power remaining in the hands of the *Kaiser* (emperor) and the chancellor (prime minister). In the late 19th century, the German government under Chancellor Otto von Bismarck had minimized the appeal of liberal reformers to German workers by adopting social reforms and creating a welfare state under the direction of Bismarck's authoritarian government. These reforms included the introduction of health, accident, old-age, and disability insurance. Thus, many Germans saw the old authoritarian system as benevolent.

Nationalism, Militarism, and Law and Order

Hitler promoted absolute nationalism, which called for the unification of all German-speaking peoples, the use of private paramilitary organizations to stifle **dissent** and terrorize opposition, and the

PAUSE AND REFLECT

React to this statement:
"Democracy is slow in crisis situations—politicians discuss matters at length in parliament, various groups are consulted, any action taken is slow, and often comes too late or is too weak to make any significant change or improvement." How might this idea allow for the rise of a totalitarian leader?

centralization of decision making in a single leader, to whom everyone owed loyalty.

The nationalism of the Nazi Party appealed to many Germans. For much of the 19th century, German territory was a group of states known as the German Confederation, led by Austria. Some areas of Czechoslovakia and Poland had significant German-speaking populations. Thus, many German nationalists saw Austria and other parts of Europe as part of a larger German-speaking nation.

Germany also had a long military tradition. Prior to the creation of Germany, the Kingdom of Prussia had been a strong military power. When Germany became a unified country, Prussia dominated German politics, and the king of Prussia became the kaiser of Germany, and the president of Prussia became the Chancellor of Germany. Thus, militarism remained a dominant force in Germany.

In addition, the Nazis' advocacy of law and order appealed to many Germans who were tired of years of instability. As the First World War ended, the situation in Germany became chaotic. Several violent uprisings occurred, and rival political factions of communists, social democrats, monarchists, and others fought in the streets. Despite the creation of the German Republic and the new constitution, the political violence and occasional armed rebellions would continue for the next few years, sometimes resulting in the deaths of innocent bystanders.

Although much of the violence subsided during the more prosperous years from 1923 to 1929, politically motivated violence became more common with the onset of the Great Depression. Hitler capitalized on the fear this caused Germans by claiming that a stronger government was needed to control the lawlessness. Ironically, much of this political violence was instigated by the Nazi Party's paramilitary organization, the SA, or stormtroopers.

Figure 5-10

The SA (*Sturmabteilung*) intimidated political opponents of the Nazis with physical violence and caused the general population to fear political instability.

The Program of the Nazi Party

In 1919, Adolf Hitler joined the German Workers' Party, which changed its name to the National Socialist German Workers' Party (the NSDAP, commonly known as the Nazi Party) in 1920. The name of the Nazi Party itself was deliberately all inclusive.

The party program of the NSDAP was proclaimed on February 24, 1920, by Adolf Hitler at the first large party gathering in Munich. The national socialist philosophy was summarized in 25 points. The following list includes 10 representative points of the program:

1. We demand the unification of all Germans in the Greater Germany on the basis of the right of self-determination of peoples.

2. We demand equality of rights for the German people in respect to the other nations; abrogation of the peace treaties of Versailles and St. Germain.

4. Only a member of the race can be a citizen. A member of the race can only be one who is of German blood, without consideration of creed. Consequently no Jew can be a member of the race.

6. The right to determine matters concerning administration and law belongs only to the citizen. Therefore we demand that every public office, of any sort whatsoever, whether in the Reich, the county or municipality, be filled only by citizens. We combat the corrupting parliamentary economy, office-holding only according to party inclinations without consideration of character or abilities.

9. All citizens must have equal rights and obligations.

10. The first obligation of every citizen must be to work both spiritually and physically. The activity of individuals is not to counteract the interests of the universality (the community), but must have its result within the framework of the whole for the benefit of all …

12. In consideration of the monstrous sacrifice in property and blood that each war demands of the people personal enrichment through a war must be designated as a crime against the people. Therefore we demand the total confiscation of all war profits.

20. The state is to be responsible for a fundamental reconstruction of our whole national education program, to enable every capable and industrious German to obtain higher education and subsequently introduction into leading positions. The plans of instruction of all educational institutions are to conform with the experiences of practical life. The comprehension of the concept of the State must be striven for by the school [Staatsbuergerkunde] as early as the beginning of understanding. We demand the education at the expense of the State of outstanding intellectually gifted children of low-income parents without consideration of position or profession.

21. The State is to care for the elevating national health by protecting the mother and child, by outlawing child-labor, by the encouragement of physical fitness, by means of the legal establishment of a gymnastic and sport obligation, by the utmost support of all organizations concerned with the physical instruction of the young.

24. We demand freedom of religion for all religious denominations within the state so long as they do not endanger its existence or oppose the moral senses of the Germanic race. The Party as such advocates the standpoint of a positive Christianity without binding itself confessionally to any one denomination. It combats the Jewish-materialistic spirit within and around us, and is convinced that a lasting recovery of our nation can only succeed from within on the framework: common utility precedes individual utility.

1. What are the Nazi Party's views on
   a) who can be a German citizen?
   b) the role of citizens in the new Germany?
   c) the role of the state in the new Germany?

2. What appeal and concerns would the 10 points listed above have had for citizens living in Germany at the time? Which of these points shocks you the most?

3. How and why was the Nazi Party rejecting liberalism? Give specific examples from the points presented here.

Theories of Racial Superiority and the Use of Jews and Others as Scapegoats

Adolf Hitler and the Nazis drew on philosophical ideas already present in German society. Nazi ideology included a racial theory that claimed that Germans formed a superior, "Aryan race"—a race which they claimed was "pure" because it was descended from ancient Indo-European peoples, rather than Jewish or Semitic (Middle Eastern) peoples.

The Nazi Party also used Jews as a scapegoat on which to focus the frustrations of Germans. The Nazis claimed that Jews were the cause of many of Germany's problems, including the Treaty of Versailles, and the exploitation of the working classes by banks and industry. Hitler claimed that Germany's Jewish population—as well as other minorities, such as the Roma (or Gypsies) and people with disabilities—were "diluting the purity" of the "superior" German race. Such claims took advantage of widespread pre-existing anti-Semitism and other prejudices.

Anti-Semitism was not a uniquely German phenomenon. Many people within Christian cultures have blamed Jews for Jesus' crucifixion (see www.remember.org). Anti-Semitism was rampant and even widely accepted in Europe and North America at the start of the 20th century. The Nazis, tragically, openly, and officially rejected some liberal and Christian values in order to advocate for what they believed to be superior beliefs and values, including a belief in their own racial superiority and the scapegoating and persecution of other, non-Aryan peoples.

Explore the Issues

Concept Review

1 a) Identify three reasons for the rise of communism in Russia.

  b) Identify four reasons for the rise of Nazism in Germany.

Concept Application

2 a) Explain how political liberalism and economic liberalism were not evolving simultaneously in Russian society.

  b) For Russia and Germany, which single factor in each country was most responsible for the rejection of liberalism?

3 *Respond to It.* Assume the point of view of a member of the Soviet Communist Party or the German Nazi Party and write a series of newspaper headlines depicting the rejection of liberalism. What role has propaganda had in influencing your point of view? Include your response to liberal ideals and how you support or disagree with them. You will be asked to share your responses with your peers and the teacher.

Understanding Propaganda

Propaganda often exaggerates and misrepresents information to rally support for a cause or issue. Political groups use a variety of propaganda techniques to try to convince the masses that their version of truth and their vision for society is the best one.

Your Task:

1. Examine a source of propaganda from those provided (by your teacher and in Figures 5-11 and 5-12) that in your view best represents a rejection of liberalism. Explain why it is the best.

2. Describe the principles of liberalism being rejected in your example.

3. What techniques does the propaganda use to convey its message?

Figure 5-11 ▲

This German poster is from late 1942. The text at the bottom says "The New Europe cannot be defeated." The rest of the text explains that the plans of the British plutocrats (people of great wealth and influence) and their American allies, as well as the Jews behind them, have failed.

Questions to Guide You

1. Does the example you chose oversimplify the issue? Oversimplification could include omitting information or painting a one-sided picture in which one side of the issue depicted appears all positive and the other side appears all negative.

2. What is the source of the propaganda? Is the information factual or based on opinion? What issues is it responding to?

3. Who is the target audience of the propaganda? Which segments of society would be most convinced by these arguments? Which segments would react most strongly to these arguments?

4. If you had lived during the era of the propaganda you chose, what kinds of responses might you have had to it?

5. Where can you find modern-day examples of propaganda? What issues are they responding to?

Figure 5-12 ▲

Soviet propaganda poster. The text reads "May Day 1920", "On the ruins of capitalism the fraternity of peasants and workers marches against the peoples of the world."

Living with Communism and Nazism

Question for Inquiry

• **How did ideologies that rejected liberalism affect citizens?**

Figure 5-13

Hungarian Jews on the ramp at Birkenau concentration camp. To the left are able-bodied men who are to be sent to the barracks and used for forced labour; to the right are the elderly, women, and children who will be marched in a few moments from the ramp to the nearby gas chamber. Describe the many different ways in which these people were affected by Hitler's reaction to liberalism.

The totalitarian governments of the Soviet Union and Nazi Germany brought major changes to their respective countries. The Soviet Union became an industrialized country with an effective government and assumed an international diplomatic role. Germany escaped the humiliation of the Treaty of Versailles, an unstable government, and economic ruin. These developments, however, were not achieved without devastating costs to many of the people living in each country.

While some citizens in each country benefited, many others suffered or died. Is it reasonable to suggest that the rejection of liberalism can be a dangerous situation for citizens? In this section of the chapter, we will look at how totalitarian ideologies and their rejection of liberalism affected the citizens of the Soviet Union and Nazi Germany.

Communism in the Soviet Union

A follower of Marx and Engels, Lenin nevertheless believed that scientific socialism had to be modified to fit the political, economic, and social context of Russia. Marx and Engels had developed their theories in the context of Western European society, which was very different from that of Russia. As a result, Lenin believed that Marxism must be carried out differently in Russia:

We by no means regard the theory of Marx as perfect and inviolable; on the contrary, we are convinced that this theory has only laid the foundation stones of that science on which the socialists must continue to build in every direction, unless they wish to be left behind by life. We believe that it is particularly necessary for Russian socialists to work out the Marxist theory independently, for this theory only gives general precepts...

—Lenin, Our Programme, 1899. Modern History Sourcebook
http://www.fordham.edu/halsall/mod/1899lenin-program.html

During the course of the Russian Civil War, Lenin and the Bolsheviks attempted to rapidly transform Russia into a communist society. Beginning in 1918, they introduced a group of policies known as "war communism."

In one fell swoop the market was declared illegal. Private trade, the hiring of labor, leasing of land, and all private enterprise and ownership were abolished, at least in theory, and subject to punishment by the state. Property was confiscated from the upper classes. Businesses and factories were nationalized. Surplus crops produced by the peasants were taken by the government to support the Bolshevik civil-war forces and workers in the towns. Labor was conscripted and organized militarily. Consumer goods were rationed at artificially low prices and later at no price at all...

—Sheldon L. Richman,
"War Communism to NEP: The Road from Serfdom."
***The Journal of Libertarian Studies* V, 1 (Winter, 1981): p. 96.**

Figure 5-14 ▶

This chart shows the theoretical organization of a communist society in the first stage of communism, known as the **dictatorship of the proletariat.** As one can see, the economic system would be a centrally planned or command economy. According to Marx and his followers, once this system was fully established and social classes disappeared, there would be no more need for government control and the state apparatus would gradually " wither away."

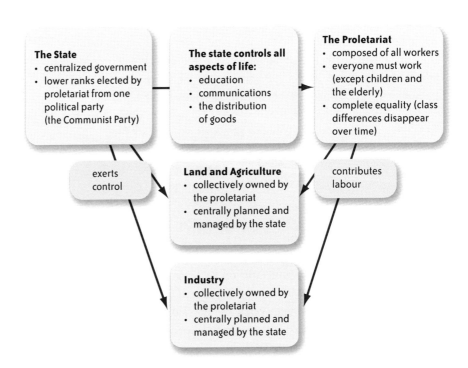

By 1921, however, it was clear that the country could not be transformed as quickly as the government had hoped. The economic disruption of the new policies, as well as the destruction caused by the Civil War (and the First World War immediately before it), led to drops in agricultural and industrial production. Thus, Lenin introduced the New Economic Policy in 1921, which brought back some aspects of capitalism on a temporary basis, in the hope of stimulating the economy.

The New Economic Policy allowed peasants to own farmland and decide what they would produce. Small-business people were allowed to buy agricultural products in the country, and sell them in the cities. Small private businesses were allowed to produce and sell consumer goods. The state retained control of banking, large industry, transportation, and foreign trade.

Stalin: The Five-Year Plans and Collectivization

Upon Lenin's death in 1924, and after a four-year struggle for leadership, Joseph Stalin secured power. The small-scale capitalist practices of the New Economic Policy had been tolerated by the Bolsheviks during and after Lenin's leadership while they consolidated political power. However, the Bolsheviks were concerned that even small-scale private production would encourage capitalism and the accompanying liberal values, and they wanted to continue the transformation of Soviet society into a true communist state. To achieve this, Stalin centralized economic planning and implemented the first of many five-year plans in a new command economy. The plan called for industrial production to increase by about 20 per cent per year in a variety of industries.

Furthermore, to finance this expansion and ensure a sufficient grain supply to feed industrial workers, the government implemented **collectivization**—that is, all land was taken away from private owners and combined in large, collectively worked farms called *kolkhozes*. Farms became food-producing factories with production quotas. Along with collectivization came the persecution of the *kulaks*.

Prior to the revolution, kulaks were a class of prosperous land-owning peasants. After the revolution, new kulaks emerged due to land redistribution and the capitalist aspects of the New Economic Plan. The term *kulak* eventually came to mean not only a prosperous landowner but anyone who employed other workers or owned machinery capable of producing goods. The kulaks who had not already given up their property voluntarily were arrested and deported, or in some cases executed. They became the scapegoats towards whom all the blame for hardships was directed. From 1929 to 1930, the number of peasants working on collective farms increased from 5 million to 70 million.

PAUSE AND REFLECT

What aspects of the New Economic Policy reflect classical liberalism? What aspects of the policy reflect collectivism? What issues was the policy meant to address?

Figure 5-15 ▲

This 1930 poster from the Soviet Union reads "We will keep out kulaks from the collective farms".

Few peasants were satisfied with these changes. Most were not landless, because land had been redistributed following the revolution, so they were losing land they had only recently gained. Because of their resentment, many of them destroyed crops, slaughtered their farm animals, and destroyed equipment, rather than give them up to the state.

All these disruptions to agricultural production led to a major famine in 1932–1933. In Ukraine, the breadbasket of the USSR, Stalin used the famine as a weapon to try to eliminate Ukrainian nationalism and identity. More than 7 million people died in this genocide, which is now known as the Holodomor. One of Stalin's lieutenants in Ukraine noted in 1933 that the famine was a success because the peasants learned "who is the master here. It cost millions of lives, but the collective farm system is here to stay." (Source: "Revelations from the Russian Archives: Ukrainian Famine." United States Library of Congress, http://www.loc.gov/exhibits/archives/ukra.html)

The following excerpt is from a letter sent by the head of a regional board of health, who also quotes the findings of a regional health inspector.

The head of the regional board reports the following: "I have driven around several collective farms [kolkhozes] and consider it necessary to inform you about a few items. I was in various kolkhozes—not productive and relatively unproductive ones, but everywhere there was only one sight—that of a huge shortage of seed, famine, and extreme emaciation of livestock...

The regional health inspector notes the following: "...From my observation of 20 homes in first and second Karpov, I found only in one home, that of a Red Army veteran, a relative condition of nourishment, some flour and bread, but the rest subsist on food substitutes. Almost in every home either children or mothers were ill, undoubtedly due to starvation, since their faces and entire bodies were swollen..."

—Feigin, letter to Sergo Ordzhonikidze, April 9, 1932.
"Revelations from the Russian Archives: Collectivization and
Industrialization." United States Library of Congress.
http://www.loc.gov/exhibits/archives/aa2feign.html

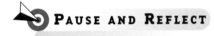

PAUSE AND REFLECT

In what way was Stalin's persecution of the people of Ukraine a rejection of liberalism?

Stalin Eliminates Political Opposition

As a result of the famine of 1932–1933, the drive to industrialization, and the increasingly strict control over the populace, many people within the Soviet Union, although ardent supporters of the socialist cause, became disillusioned with Stalin's leadership. While Stalin felt it was necessary to arrest and execute the dissenters, most of the members of the politburo (political bureau, the ruling elite of the Communist Party) argued against these measures. When Stalin realized that even members of the politburo dared to oppose him, he initiated a period of political repression now known as the Great Purge.

Figure 5-16

Conditions in the camps were harsh, and the mortality rate was much higher in the camps than in the general population. This photo was taken in the Archangelsk region of Russia, sometime between 1921 and 1941.

The Great Purge lasted from 1936 to 1938. The most widely publicized aspects of the purge were three group trials of senior party members and high-ranking members of the armed forces. Most of the surviving "Old Bolsheviks"—members who had joined the Communist Party before the revolution in 1917—were convicted and executed or sent into exile. Most of the highest-ranking officers of the Red Army were also convicted and executed. From the general populace, 1.5–2 million people were arrested for "counterrevolutionary activities" or political reasons. Roughly half of them were executed, and most people in the remainder were sentenced to forced labour camps, collectively known as the Gulag. There were thousands of camps in the Gulag system. They were located in isolated areas such as eastern Siberia. By 1939, there were at least 1.3 million people in the camps.

The following excerpts are from a memoir written by one dissenter, Nadezhda Joffe (1906–1999), who was arrested twice. After her second arrest, she spent 20 years in a labour camp in Siberia.

We wanted nothing for ourselves, we all wanted just one thing: the world revolution and happiness for all. And if it were necessary to give up our lives to achieve this, then we would have done so without hesitating.

I was personally acquainted with many participants in the October Revolution. Among them were people who renounced a calm, comfortable or prosperous life because they fervently believed in a radiant future for all mankind.

Many of those whom Stalin considered to be the Opposition paid with years of exile, prison and camps for fighting him, and for understanding that the socialism which had been built in the Soviet Union was not the same socialism about which the best minds of mankind had dreamed.

**—Nadezhda Joffe, *Back in Time: My Life, My Fate, My Epoch*
trans. Frederick S. Choate (Oak Park, MI: Labor Publications, 1995), p. 237.**

PAUSE AND REFLECT

Consider the following statement: "The socialism which had been built in the Soviet Union was not the same socialism about which the best minds of mankind had dreamed." Do you think that this ideal socialism to which the writer refers currently exists or can exist anywhere in the world? Why or why not?

Stalin Explains Communism

Something to Think About: How did communist leaders defend their ideology to outsiders or those sympathetic to it who wished to learn more?

An Example: Stalin sought to explain communist ideology to a visiting American labour delegation in 1927. Part of the dialogue between Stalin and the Americans was printed in the Soviet newspaper *Pravda*. The following excerpts are from this interview.

Stalin's Interview with the First American Trade Union Delegation to Soviet Russia

QUESTION 3: Since there is legality for one political party only in Russia how do you know that the masses favour Communism?

STALIN: Take the last Soviet elections. In the USSR the whole of the adult population from the age of 18, irrespective of sex and nationality,—except the bourgeois elements who exploit the labour of others and those who have been deprived of their rights by the courts—enjoys the right to vote. The people enjoying the right to vote number 60 millions. The overwhelming majority of these, of course, are peasants. Of these 60 million voters, about 51 per cent, i.e., over 30 millions, exercise their right. Now examine the composition of the leading organs of our Soviets both in the center and locally. Is it an accident that the overwhelming majority of the elected leading elements are Communists? Clearly, it is not an accident. Does not this fact prove that the Communist Party enjoys the confidence of millions of the masses of the peasantry? I think it does. This is another test of the strength and stability of the Communist Party.

QUESTION 12: Can you outline briefly the characteristics of the Society of the future which Communism is trying to create?

STALIN: The general characteristics of Communist society are given in the works of Marx, Engels, and Lenin. Briefly, the anatomy of Communist society may be described as follows: It is a society in which (a) there will be no private ownership of the means of production but social, collective ownership; (b) there will be no classes or State, but workers in industry and agriculture managing their economic affairs as a free association of toilers; (c) national economy will be organized according to plan, will be based on the highest technique in both industry and agriculture; (d) there will be no antagonism between town and country, between industry and agriculture; (e) the products will be distributed according to the principle of the old French Communists: "from each according to his abilities, to each according to his needs"; (f) science and art will enjoy conditions conducive to their highest development; (g) the individual, freed from bread and butter cares, and of necessity of cringing to the "powerful of the earth," will become really free, etc., etc. Clearly, we are still remote from such a society.

With regard to the international conditions necessary for the complete triumph of Communist society, these will develop and grow in proportion as revolutionary crises and revolutionary outbreaks of the working class in capitalist countries grow.

—**Source: Interview between Stalin and the First American Trade Union Delegation to Soviet Russia, *Pravda* September 15, 1927. Marxists Internet Archive**
http://www.marxists.org/reference/archive/stalin/works/1927/09/15.htm

QUESTIONS FOR REFLECTION

1. How do Stalin's responses provide an understanding of his view of the fundamental beliefs and values of communism?

2. Why would American trade unionists be interested in communism?

3. How is communism a rejection of liberal principles? To what extent does Stalin's approach to communism appear to have been successful?

Controlling the Population through Propaganda

One of the goals of totalitarian government is total control over the lives of its citizens. How did the government of the Soviet Union attempt to exert this control? One example can be drawn from the field of art. The government used postcards to promote its emerging ideals. Under the slogan "Bring the Art into the Masses," the Association of the Artists of the Revolution produced titles for some 800 postcards proclaiming such things as the benefits of industrialization and the mechanization of agriculture. Attention was focused on the images of the "new Soviet man" and the "new Soviet woman." Children were depicted playing at their future occupations.

As part of the goal of achieving conformity to the state ideology, fairy tales were abolished or reinterpreted in accordance with the new communist ideology. It was the task of the *Proletkult* (proletarian culture—art without bourgeois influence) to instill the ideals of communism in the young. Children's literature was created so that the new generation would learn the beliefs and values of communism.

For example, in his poem "A Tale about Petia, A Fat Child, and Sima, who is Thin," Russian poet Vladimir Maiakovskii uses a children's fable to critique what he perceives as the excesses of liberalism.

It's clear
even to a hedgehog
this Petia was a bourgeois.

Birds flew by with a song,
they sang
"Sima is a proletarian!"

Maiakovskii goes on to recount that Petia will not share his candy with the other children, and eventually explodes from eating too much. The poem ends with the lines:

Children, learn to love work
as is written here.

Defend
all who are weak
from the clutches of the bourgeoisie.

Then you'll grow up to be
true
strong communists.

—Vladimir Maiakovskii, "A Tale about Petia,
A Fat Child, and Sima, Who Is Thin," quoted in
"What Shall We Tell the Children?", The Voice of the Turtle.
http://www.voiceoftheturtle.org/show_article.php?aid=18

 Figure 5-17 ▲

Builders-to-Be, 1930, postcard by Filosova

 Figure 5-18 ▲

A Woman-Engineer, 1930, postcard by N.I. Shestopalov. Use the Skill Path to assess how these postcards served as propaganda.

Why would it have been so important to the Proletkult to eradicate bourgeois liberal ideas from children's literature? How effective do you think Vladimir Maiakovskii's poem is in promoting the Soviet communist ideology? Does his poem reflect the beliefs of most citizens of the USSR at that time? Do you think children would understand the overt references to communist ideology and the criticisms of liberalism?

Fascism in Nazi Germany

The ideology of fascism in Nazi Germany was in part an expression of Adolf Hitler's deep-seated hatred of liberalism, Jews, and communists. His desire was to rebuild Germany into an empire that would reclaim and increase its international power and influence. He pledged to restore the economic strength and national pride that he and others believed had been lost as a result of signing the Treaty of Versailles, and the machinations of liberals, Jews, and Marxists—in his and his supporters' view—who had undermined the German nation during and after the First World War. For those who chose to wholeheartedly follow the Nazi Party, he promised a much improved but different life.

 Figure 5-19

Features of fascism in Nazi Germany

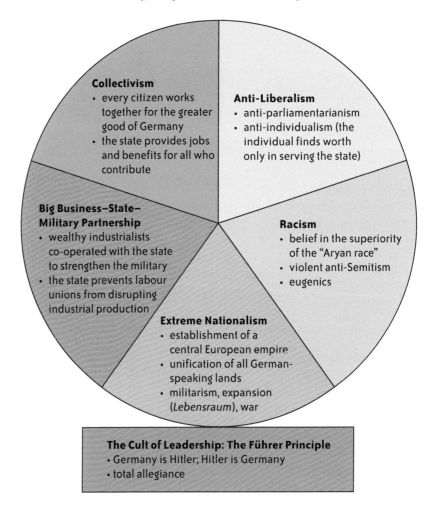

Consolidating Power

In the November 1932 elections, the Nazi party received 33 per cent of the popular vote and about one-third of the seats in the Reichstag. By January 1933, Hitler had been named chancellor. Capitalizing on the situation, Hitler quickly transformed Germany into a totalitarian state.

One month after Hitler became chancellor, a fire destroyed the Reichstag building. A young Dutch communist was soon arrested, and it was claimed by the Nazis that the fire was part of a larger communist plot to take over Germany. Hitler used this communist threat and the ensuing panic it caused in the population to call new elections and pass the Reichstag Fire Decree (1933) and the Enabling Act (1933). These made it possible for the government to

- restrict personal freedom, freedom of opinion, freedom of the press, and freedom of organization and assembly
- eliminate the privacy of mail, telegrams, and telephone conversations
- eliminate the need for warrants to conduct searches
- pass legislation through the office of the chancellor without the approval of the Reichstag
- ban all political parties except the Nazi Party

Through these means, Germany had become a dictatorship by 1933.

On June 30, 1934, Hitler further strengthened his position by ordering the assassination of the leadership of the SA (stormtroopers). As the paramilitary wing of the Nazi Party, the SA had helped Hitler come to power. The SA had become too popular, however, and thus they were seen as a threat to the traditional army's power and Hitler's leadership. The elimination of the SA's leaders removed any remaining challenges to Hitler's leadership within the Nazi Party itself. This purge was known as the "Night of the Long Knives." When President Paul von Hindenburg died on August 19, 1934, Hitler declared himself *Führer*, or leader.

Nazism and the German Economy

While individual rights and numerous social groups suffered under the Nazi regime, the German economy benefited. Six million Germans were unemployed in 1932, due to the Great Depression and the continuing after-effects of the First World War. By 1936, this number fell to fewer than 1 million. The German industrialists, some of whom had helped fund the Nazi Party during its rise to power, benefited from policies such as the ban on trade unions and strikes. The National Labour Service created massive public projects such as the construction of the *Autobahnen* (highways), which provided employment. The re-arming of the German military (prohibited by the Treaty of Versailles) also stimulated industry. Farming and industries were given government subsidies. Moreover, the purchase of farmers' produce was guaranteed, and foreign imports were restricted to encourage consumption of German-made goods. Many of these measures were designed to achieve **autarky** (self-sufficiency or independence from other nations) in the German economy.

But the economic effects of Nazi policies were not entirely positive. Workers had few rights and no legal means to protest to acquire them. Industries were strictly regulated, and access to raw materials and output was controlled. Günter Reimann, a member of the Communist Party of Germany who fled the country prior to the Second World War, wrote about the control the Nazi government exercised over industry:

While state representatives are busily engaged in investigating and interfering, our agents and salesmen are handicapped because they never know whether or not a sale at a higher price will mean denunciation as a "profiteer" or "saboteur," followed by a prison sentence. You cannot imagine how taxation has increased. Yet everyone is afraid to complain. Everywhere there is a growing undercurrent of bitterness. Everyone has his doubts about the system, unless he is very young, very stupid, or is bound to it by the privileges he enjoys.

—**Günter Reimann, *The Vampire Economy: Doing Business Under Fascism* (New York: Vanguard Press, 1939), p. 7.**

Persecution of the Jews and Others

The Nazis used the Jewish people and some minority groups in Germany, including those referenced on pages 177 and 189 of this chapter, as scapegoats for many of the problems in Germany prior to Hitler's ascendancy. The Nazis especially blamed Jewish people for being a part of the government that accepted the Treaty of Versailles, and suggested that Germany's economic problems were due to Jewish control of industry and banking. As a result of these ideas and ideas of their own racial superiority, once the Nazis were in power, they began working toward the systematic elimination of Jews and members of some minority groups from Germany, and eventually all of Europe.

Beginning in 1933, the German government passed a series of laws that sought to exclude people of Jewish ancestry from German society. The following laws are a few examples of this:

- 1933: Jews are barred from working for the government, becoming lawyers, and working as editors. The number of Jewish students in public schools is strictly limited.

- 1935: Jewish officers are expelled from the army. The Nuremberg Laws are passed (see Get to the Source on page 190).
- 1936: Jews are banned from working as tax consultants, veterinarians, or teachers in public schools.
- 1938: Jews are not allowed to change their names or the names of their businesses. Jews must report all property in excess of 5000 *Reichsmarks* (approximately $30 000 in today's dollars). Some Jewish property is confiscated and transferred to non-Jewish Germans. All Jewish businesses are closed. All Jewish students are expelled from public schools.

In a speech before the Reichstag in 1939, Hitler alluded to the coming Holocaust:

If the international Finance-Jewry inside and outside of Europe should succeed in plunging the peoples of the earth once again into a world war, the result will be not the Bolshevization of earth, and thus a Jewish victory, but the annihilation of the Jewish race in Europe.

—**"Combating Holocaust Denial: Evidence of the Holocaust presented at Nuremberg." Holocaust Encyclopedia, United States Holocaust Memorial Museum.**
http://www.ushmm.org/wlc/media_fi.php?lang=en&ModuleId=10007271&MediaId=5700

Eventually, all German Jews and Jewish people in countries that Germany invaded during the Second World War would be detained in concentration camps and ghettos, and often used as slave labour, before being transported to extermination camps. An estimated 6 million Jews died during the Holocaust.

Figure 5-20 ▲

Hitler addresses German troops and Nazi Party supporters at the Nuremberg Rally in 1935. The Nazi Party held mass rallies every year at Nuremberg.

Nazi Eugenics

Under Hitler, Germany became a police state overseen by the Gestapo (secret police) and the SS (*Schutzstaffel*, or elite paramilitary force) who ensured that Germans followed the decrees of the Nazi Party. An important tenet of Nazi ideology was the superiority of the pure Aryan race, and **eugenics**—controlling human reproduction so that desirable genetic traits are encouraged and undesirable traits are eliminated—was practised as a consequence of that belief.

In Nazi ideology, *Untermenschen* (sub-humans) were groups of people deemed racially or socially inferior. Laws ostracizing such groups were enacted, eventually resulting in the murder of Jews (as described earlier), Roma peoples (Gypsies), blacks, Jehovah's Witnesses, homosexuals, people who were mentally ill or physically disabled, Polish peoples and Soviet prisoners of war, and any other group considered Untermenschen. In total, an estimated 9 to 11 million people, including 6 million Jews were killed for these reasons.

way: "We all felt the same, the same happiness and joy. Things were looking up. I believe no statesman has ever been as loved as Adolf Hitler was then. It's all come flooding back to me. Those were happy times." (Source: Quoted in "How did Nazis rule affect Germans?" Greenfield History Site, http://www.johndclare.net/Nazi_Germany3.htm.)

Patriarchy dominated the Nazi ideology. Women were primarily to be in the home, bearing and raising children. The Law for the Encouragement of Marriage, for example, loaned newlywed couples 1000 marks (approximately $6000 in today's dollars), and allowed them to keep 250 marks ($1500) for each child they had. In addition, a woman would receive a gold medal for bearing more than eight children. Professional working women, such as doctors, teachers, and civil servants, lost their employment. Women were forbidden to serve in the armed forces.

Recruiting Youth

Young people were courted by the Nazi government to ensure the future of the thousand-year Reich. Both girls and boys were encouraged to belong to special organizations that, while providing enjoyable activities for children and adolescents, inculcated loyalty to the Nazi regime. Children were encouraged to report any inappropriate—meaning anti-Nazi—behaviour by others, including their parents.

Boys were enrolled in a Cubs program from the ages of 6 to 10 and in the Young German Boys organization from the ages of 10 to 14. At 14, boys became members of the Hitler Youth, and at 18 they went into either the Labour Service or the armed forces. Girls were enrolled in the Young Maidens program at the age of 10 and became members of the League of German Maidens at the age of 14. The programs for boys were focused on future military roles, while those for girls involved domesticity. Resistance to Nazi policies by some of the youth grew as the war advanced, but these youth risked being executed if they were caught.

Figure 5-21 ▶

Some Germans refused to submit to Hitler's will and Nazi Party policies. One of the most famous is Sophie Scholl. Sophie Scholl was a member of a youth resistance group in Germany called the White Rose. Her brother, Hans (left); Christoph Probst (right); Alexander Schmorell; Willi Graf; and Professor Kurt Huber were the core members of the White Rose. This group painted anti-Nazi graffiti on walls and distributed pamphlets telling the German people to resist Hitler and the National Socialist government.

Nazism Reacting to Feminism

Hitler vehemently disagreed with feminist ideas and believed that the German woman's world consisted of "her husband, her family, her children, and her home." In 1933, he appointed Gertrud Scholtz-Klink as Reich Women's Leader of the Nazi Women's League. In one of her many speeches she declared that "the mission of woman is to minister in the home and in her profession to the needs of life from the first to last moment of man's existence." Later in 1938 she stated that "the German woman must work and work, physically and mentally she must renounce luxury and pleasure." (Source: Gertrud Scholtz-Klink, quoted on Spartacus Educational, http://www.spartacus.schoolnet.co.uk/GERwomen.htm.) Due to Hitler's anti-feminist policies, many women joined left-wing political groups.

In 1933, the first concentration camp for women was opened at Moringen. Later in 1938, due to the increasing numbers of women prisoners, a second camp at Lichtenburg in Saxony was built and in 1939, Ravensbrück was opened. What do the following quotations illustrate about the thinking of the role of women in the Nazi state and consequently the implications for women's lives in Germany?

I spent an hour with the principal, a very friendly, neat lady of fifty. She explained that every class in school was built around a course called Frauenschaffen, *activities of women. This general subject was divided into:* Handarbeit *(handwork),* Hauswirtschaft *(domestic science, cooking, house and garden work), and most important, the* Pflege *course (eugenics [encouraging reproduction by persons presumed to have inheritable desirable traits] and hygiene, devoted to a study of the reproductive organs, both male and female, conception, birth, racial purity, infant care, family welfare).*

—G. Zienef, *Education for Death*, 1942, quoted on Spartacus Educational.
http://www.spartacus.schoolnet.co.uk/GERwomen.htm

Young girls from the age of ten onward were taken into organizations where they were taught only two things: to take care of their bodies so they could bear as many children as the state needed and to be loyal to National Socialism. Though the Nazis have been forced to recognize, through the lack of men, that not all women can get married. Huge marriage loans are floated every year whereby the contracting parties can borrow substantial sums from the government to be repaid slowly or to be cancelled entirely upon the birth of enough children. Birth control information is frowned on and practically forbidden.

Despite the fact that Hitler and the other Nazis are always ranting about "Volk ohne Raum" (a people without space) they command their men and women to have more children. Women have been deprived for all rights except that of childbirth and hard labour. They are not permitted to participate in political life—in fact Hitler's plans eventually include the deprivation of the vote; they are refused opportunities of education and self-expression; careers and professions are closed to them.

—**Martha Dodd, *My Years in Germany*, 1939, quoted on Spartacus Educational.**
http://www.spartacus.schoolnet.co.uk/GERwomen.htm

I detest women who dabble in politics. And if their dabbling extends to military matters it becomes utterly unendurable. In no section of the Party has a woman ever had the right to hold even the smallest post.

In 1924 we had a sudden upsurge of women who were interested in politics. They wanted to join the Reichstag, in order to raise the moral level of that body, so they said. I told them that 90 per cent of the matters dealt with by parliament were masculine affairs, on which they could not have opinions of any value. Gallantry forbids one to give women an opportunity of putting themselves in situations that do not suit them.

—**Adolf Hitler, speech given on January 26, 1942.**

1 To what extent do the opinions cited in these sources reflect a rejection of liberalism?

2 How do the points of view expressed compare and contrast with liberal ideas today about the roles of women?

3 What might have been some of the consequences for German society after the Nazi regime ended in 1945 as a result of focusing girls' education solely on their roles as housewives and mothers?

Explore the Issues

Concept Review

1 a) Identify four characteristics of the communist regime in the Soviet Union that were rejections of liberal principles.
b) Identify four characteristics of the Nazi regime that were rejections of liberal principles.

Concept Application

2 a) Knowing what you know about Hitler and his dictatorship, how do you think that it was possible that German people should have had such positive things to say about him?
b) Under what circumstances would people have found the ideologies of communism or fascism appealing?

3 Look at the results of both Stalin's and Hitler's reaction to liberalism. One might qualify each of them as having been the biggest nightmare of the 20th century. From the perspective of the citizens of these regimes, how was the rejection of liberalism a failure?

4 Distinguish between fascist and communist economic policies. Are there elements of either that could be considered liberal?

5 Is authoritarianism a necessary condition for the rejection of liberalism?

Reflect and Analyze

Why did ideologies that rejected liberalism emerge in the Soviet Union and Germany? These totalitarian ideologies sought to exclude liberalism from their societies and enforce all-powerful states, that would supersede notions of individualism. Under what circumstances might ideologies that reject the principles of liberalism, such as totalitarian ideologies, be appealing to a person, a group, or a nation-state?

In Russia, there was a movement from autocracy under Czar Nicholas II to a communist state, first under Lenin and then under Stalin. Germany moved from the German monarchy before the First World War to the Weimar Republic to the Nazi Third Reich under Hitler. The examination of communism and fascism gave you a chance to explore the Chapter Issue: *To what extent is the rejection of liberalism justified?*

1 Working as a class, complete the following activities based on the readings in this chapter.
   a) Construct a list of reasons why a country might reject liberalism. Try to keep these reasons general enough to apply to modern countries.
   b) Working with the list of reasons created by the class, break into groups of four or five students and develop a theory that attempts to explain anti-liberalism. The theory must accurately describe both historical examples from this chapter, and contemporary examples (such as Islamic fundamentalism or a military dictatorship).
   c) Present your theory to the class. Some form of visual medium (such as a poster, PowerPoint presentation, or video) should accompany your presentation.

Respond to Ideas

2 Review the list of the techniques of totalitarianism on page 167 and identify the examples of these techniques as practiced in the Soviet Union and Nazi Germany.

3 The impact of ideologies that reject liberalism is quite diverse. How has your understanding of the reasons why an ideology might reject liberalism been clarified? What impacts can ideologies such as communism and fascism have on their citizens?

Respond to Issues

4 To what extent do you think that the rejection of liberalism by the Soviet Union and Nazi Germany was justified?

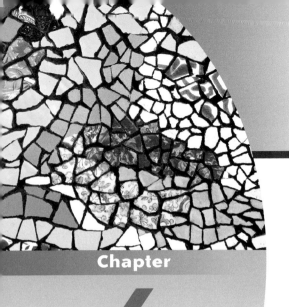

The Evolution of Modern Liberalism

Figure 6-1

A magazine cover depicting the violence of the Homestead Strike (1882). The failure of the strike was the beginning of a long decline for the steelworkers' union. Carnegie steel plants would employ only non-union workers for the next 40 years.

KEY SKILLS

Evaluating the logic of assumptions underlying a position

KEY CONCEPTS

Analyzing the evolution of modern liberalism

Key Terms

Consumerism
Income disparity
Inflation
Monopoly
Social programs
Trickle-down economics
Welfare state

Henry Clay Frick was the late–19th-century's quintessential robber baron—that is, a businessperson who employs hardnosed and sometimes questionable tactics in the free market to amass great personal wealth. A millionaire who made his money supplying coke to the steel plants of Andrew Carnegie, Frick was known for his ruthless business practices.

In response to declining prices of rolled-steel products in the early 1890s, Henry Clay Frick, general manager of the Homestead plant owned by Andrew Carnegie, took a series of bold but miscalculated steps to protect the bottom line. In June 1892, he slashed wages, evicted workers from their company houses, stopped negotiating with union leaders, and threatened to bring in the Pinkertons—a detective agency for hire that amounted to a private army of thugs. When workers called a strike, Frick called on the Pinkertons. On July 6, in the middle of the night, 300 Pinkertons crammed onto barges were towed ten miles up the Monongahela River to Homestead.

Armed workers were waiting on the river bank. At dawn, a pitched battle broke out. After twelve relentless hours, three Pinkertons and seven strikers lay dead.

—**Source: Website of the PBS series American Experience, "Emma Goldman" episode, "People & Events: Henry Clay Frick (1849–1919)", March 2004.**
http://www.pbs.org/wgbh/amex/goldman/peopleevents/p_frick.html

In retaliation for these actions, anarchist Alexander Berkman tried to assassinate Frick two weeks later. Frick survived the attack, and the strike at the Homestead plant collapsed, due in part to the negative publicity generated by the assassination attempt.

Chapter Issue

The economic conditions that made possible the immense fortunes of Frick and other robber barons like him were largely due to the adoption of the principles of economic liberalism in the United States, Canada, Great Britain, and other industrialized countries near the beginning of the 20th century. These economic developments eventually had dramatic impacts on many areas of the world; but because these principles of economic liberalism first arose in Great Britain and North America, this chapter focuses on economic changes in these countries, especially in the United States and Canada.

But the ideology referred to as liberalism has undergone numerous modifications in the last century, so many changes in fact that what we now call modern liberalism might be unfamiliar to Frick. In this chapter you will explore how various historical events and competing ideologies influenced the development of liberalism in the 20th century, and how liberalism then impacted the societies in which it took hold. This exploration will provide you with the background to respond to the Chapter Issue: ***To what extent do contemporary economic policies and practices reflect the principles of liberalism?***

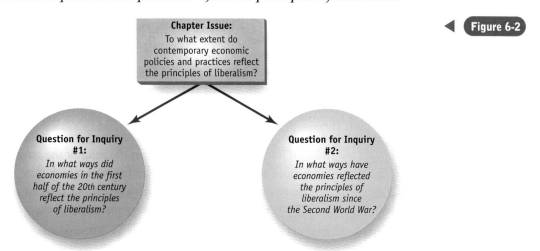

◀ **Figure 6-2**

Chapter Issue:
To what extent do contemporary economic policies and practices reflect the principles of liberalism?

Question for Inquiry #1:
In what ways did economies in the first half of the 20th century reflect the principles of liberalism?

Question for Inquiry #2:
In what ways have economies reflected the principles of liberalism since the Second World War?

Economic Prosperity and Consumerism

After the First World War, North America experienced a brief recession as the booming war-time economy came to an end. This recession ended quickly as factories switched to the production of consumer goods, and the economy continued to grow until 1929. The gross domestic product of the United States increased from $73.6 billion in 1921 to $103.6 billion in 1929. Industrialists such as Henry Ford, founder of the Ford Motor Company, helped spur the economic boom by pioneering techniques such as mass production (using assembly lines and mechanization to produce large volumes of a product at a cheaper price). Ford also used the practices of welfare capitalism (which you read about in Chapter 4); he advocated a minimum wage and a 40-hour workweek in his factories. Ford's motivation was financial, however; he reasoned that if his employees were happier, they would work more efficiently. He also believed that paying them better wages would allow them to buy the products they produced, thus increasing sales. These and other advances in manufacturing (such as the electrification of factories) made a variety of products cheaper, and consumer spending—or **consumerism**—increased dramatically over the course of the decade.

In 1918, for example, 300 000 motor vehicles were registered in Canada. By 1929, this figure had risen to 1.9 million. Similarly, fewer than one in three families in the United States owned a car in 1920; by the end of the decade, four out of five families owned one. The advent of radio and film made mass marketing a powerful influence, thus fuelling consumer spending. The continued spread of technologies such as the telephone and home refrigeration also encouraged consumerism.

Changing Social Values

As the North American free-market economy expanded and rapidly modernized, major social changes occurred. In 1920, women in the United States obtained the right to vote, as Canadian women had, for federal elections, in 1918. There were also greater numbers of women in the workforce. In the United States, Native Americans were granted citizenship by the Indian Citizenship Act (1924). The North American population became more urbanized. For the first time, more people lived in cities than in rural areas.

While greater equality was achieved in some aspects of North American life, there were also many enduring examples of inequality. Following the industrial expansion of the late 19th and early 20th centuries, there was already a noticeable **income disparity**, or difference in earnings, between the rich and the poor. In 1917, for example, the wealthiest 10 per cent of the population of the United States earned

---

> **PAUSE AND REFLECT**
>
> **How do the developments of economic prosperity, mass production, mass marketing, and consumerism reflect the principles of liberalism? How might this affect attitudes in society?**

40 per cent of all the income in the country. During the 1920s, this disparity increased dramatically: by 1928, the wealthiest 10 per cent were earning 49 per cent of the total income. (Source: Emmanuel Saez, "Striking It Richer: The Evolution of Top Incomes in the United States." *Pathways Magazine*, Stanford Center for the Study of Poverty and Inequality [Winter, 2008]: pp. 6–7.)

Anti-immigration sentiment and racial discrimination were bolstered by books such as Madison Grant's *The Passing of the Great Race* (1916) and Lothrop Stoddard's *The Rising Tide of Color Against White-World Supremacy* (1920), which claimed that the "Northern European" character of American society was being threatened by non-European races. The changes to immigration laws in the United States (as noted earlier in this chapter) and Canada during the 1920s reflected this thinking.

The 1930s and the Great Depression

I tried to get a job all over town;
Seven hundred places they turned me down.
They told me six weeks I could get relief,
But I ain't got a bite to eat.

—"Ashes To Ashes, Dust To Dust" written by Woody Guthrie and Hans-Eckardt Wenzel © Copyright Secured WOODY GUTHRIE PUBLICATIONS (BMI) ADMINISTERED BY BUG MUSIC. ALL RIGHTS RESERVED. USED BY PERMISSION

The money changers have fled from their high seats in the temple of our civilization. We may now restore that temple to the ancient truths. The measure of the restoration lies in the extent to which we apply social values more noble than mere monetary profit.

—Source: Franklin D. Roosevelt, Inaugural Address, March 4, 1933, published in Samuel Rosenman, ed., *The Public Papers of Franklin D. Roosevelt*, Volume 2, "The Year of Crisis, 1933" (New York: Random House, 1938), pp. 11–16. History Matters.
http://historymatters.gmu.edu/d/5057/

Following the extended period of prosperity of the 1920s, the world economy suffered the extreme recession now known as the Great Depression. Most economists see booms (periods of economic growth such as the growth in the 1920s) and recessions as normal parts of the free market business cycle. Because of various circumstances, however, the recession of the 1930s was extremely severe. This period would have a long-lasting influence on liberal democratic governments. It led to a growth in government involvement in economies that continues in many forms to this day.

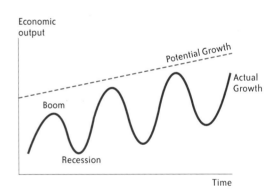

Figure 6-4 ▲

The business cycle refers to the periods of expansion and contraction that free market economies tend to experience, with a single cycle of expansion and subsequent contraction taking place over a period of several years. Many economists argue that this is an unavoidable phenomenon. Some economists, such as John Maynard Keynes (about whom you read in Chapter 4), have argued that the effects of the contractions (or recessions) can be moderated (or reduced, or lessened) through government intervention in the economy.

Thousands of people lost their savings in bank runs during the 1930s. Excessive depositor panic can create a bank run even on a financially stable bank.

The Stock Market Crash of 1929

During the prosperity of the 1920s, the stock prices of successful companies rose. Many people began borrowing money to invest in the stock market on the assumption that prices would continue to rise. These investments further inflated stock prices. When prices on the New York Stock Exchange finally stopped rising in October 1929, people began selling their stocks to take profits before prices dropped further. This profit-taking led prices to drop further, and more investors began selling their stocks. Panic selling caused prices to fall even more quickly. By November 13, the Dow Jones Industrial Average (a measure of the stock prices of the 30 largest publicly owned companies in the United States) had dropped by 48 per cent.

The Aftermath

After the crash, investors who had borrowed money to buy stocks found themselves with large debts and worthless investments. Many consumers in the 1920s had also purchased goods such as automobiles and appliances on credit, creating a high level of debt throughout the economy. Fearing a wider economic downturn after the crash, banks began calling in loans, and many people who had overextended their credit went bankrupt. The crash also caused many people who still had savings to become worried about the security of their deposits in the banks, and this caused several **bank runs**: a situation in which too many depositors try to withdraw their savings from a financial institution, causing it to go bankrupt. A bank run can also force businesses that have borrowed money from the bank to go into bankruptcy.

Some economists also believe that industry and agriculture had become too productive in the 1920s, leading to a glut of products on the market, and a corresponding fall in prices. Marriner S. Eccles, the chairman of the American Federal Reserve from 1934 to 1948, felt this glut was caused in part by an unequal distribution of the profits of the boom.

As mass production has to be accompanied by mass consumption, mass consumption, in turn, implies a distribution of wealth—not of existing wealth, but of wealth as it is currently produced—to provide men with buying power equal to the amount of goods and services offered by the nation's economic machinery. Instead of achieving that kind of distribution, a giant suction pump had by 1929–30 drawn into a few hands an increasing portion of currently produced wealth. This served them as capital accumulations. But by taking purchasing power out of the hands of mass consumers, the savers denied to themselves the kind of effective demand for their products that would justify a reinvestment of their capital accumulations in new plants.

**—Marriner S. Eccles, *Beckoning Frontiers*
(New York: Alfred A. Knopf, 1951), p. 76.**

This is similar to Henry Ford's reasoning for paying his workers high wages. Such arguments would soon be used to justify more government involvement in the economy. In addition, the United States introduced new tariffs in 1930 in an attempt to encourage domestic consumption of American goods; this prompted retaliatory tariffs from other countries, including Canada, and caused some European countries, such as France and Germany, to consume more domestically produced goods, rather than importing them. The result was that international trade slowed down substantially, further hurting economies around the world, and especially those in North America.

These events led to numerous business failures in the early 1930s. In addition, a general loss of confidence in the North American economy caused consumers who still had money to spend less, thus slowing the economy further. By 1933, the unemployment rate in the United States was 25 per cent, and incomes were on average 54 per cent of what they had been in 1929. Figures in Canada were similar. To further exacerbate the situation, North American farmers on the prairies were hit by the Dust Bowl, a series of droughts in the first half of the decade that, after many years of poor farming techniques, destroyed crops and led many people to abandon their farms entirely.

The Great Depression had an impact around the world. In Great Britain, the Depression was known as the Great Slump. France felt the Depression starting around 1931, but not as profoundly as other countries because it was more economically self-sufficient than, for example, Germany. In Germany, the Weimar Republic was hit hard by the Depression and American loans to help the post–First World War economy stopped. As you read in the previous chapter, Germany swung toward political **extremism** during the Depression.

Social Effects of the Depression

The harsh realities of the Depression affected people with low incomes the most, and as the economic crisis continued, they became more numerous. Frustrated with the conditions brought on by the collapse of the capitalist economic system, more people in the United States and Canada began to support political organizations with collectivist ideologies. In Canada, the Co-operative Commonwealth Federation (CCF) was founded in Calgary in 1932 with mixed economic policies such as public ownership of industries and financial institutions.

Unemployment and poverty also led to greater social unrest. Strikes and protests became more common. The On-to-Ottawa Trek and subsequent Regina Riot were two of Canada's better-known incidents. In the early years of the Depression, the Conservative government of Richard Bedford Bennett set up relief camps for unemployed single men. The men were given food and shelter and would work for a small wage on public projects such as building roads. Many workers in the camps, however, felt the pay and conditions were inadequate, and in 1935 a strike was organized in which 1600 workers left their camps and gathered in Vancouver. After two months of protesting, the group decided to take their demands to Ottawa and climbed aboard train boxcars for the ride across the country. They called their journey the On-to-Ottawa Trek.

As the trains stopped in cities across Western Canada, more relief camp workers joined the trek. Finally, Prime Minister Bennnett agreed to meet with a delegation of eight representatives in Ottawa if the rest of the protesters would agree to remain in Regina. The meeting in Ottawa between the delegation and the prime minister went badly, however, and the representatives returned to Regina. Bennett then ordered the RCMP to disperse the protesters, and the Regina Riot ensued. One police officer died and hundreds of people were injured. Bennett's handling of the situation was negatively perceived by many members of the general public. It is believed that the Regina Riot was one of the reasons for the Conservatives' defeat in the 1935 federal election.

The Great Depression and its effects would cause a greater number of people in North America to question the wisdom of the prevailing classical liberal economic system. While some reforms had been undertaken since the unregulated free markets of the 19th century, many North Americans came to believe that government should take on a greater role in the economy to prevent such extreme fluctuations and provide citizens with more economic stability. This signalled a significant shift away from classical liberal thinking toward a mixed economy and a more modern understanding of liberalism.

Roosevelt's New Deal

Franklin D. Roosevelt became president of the United States in March 1933 and offered what he called a **New Deal** for Americans. Roosevelt's policies were influenced in part by the theories of British economist John Maynard Keynes. As you read in Chapter 4, Keynes advocated for a more significant role for government in the regulation of the economy. He felt that in times of prosperity, government should control **inflation** with measures such as raising taxes, using a central bank to raise interest rates, and decreasing government spending. In recessionary times, such as the 1930s, Keynes argued that governments should stimulate the economy by lowering interest rates and taxes and increasing government spending.

Roosevelt's New Deal was a series of programs that focused on relief, reform, and recovery—specifically relief to the unemployed, reform to the economy, and recovery from the Depression. The first wave of programs focused on short-term efforts for all groups in American society. In his inaugural speech, Roosevelt said the following:

Our greatest primary task is to put people to work. This is no unsolveable problem if we face it wisely and courageously. It can be accomplished in part by direct recruiting by the Government itself, treating the task as we would treat the emergency of a war, but at the same time, through this employment, accomplishing greatly needed projects to stimulate and reorganize the use of our national resources.

—Franklin D. Roosevelt, Inaugural Address, March 4, 1933, in Samuel Rosenman, ed., *The Public Papers of Franklin D. Roosevelt*, Volume 2, "The Year of Crisis, 1933" (New York: Random House, 1938), pp. 11–16. History Matters.
http://historymatters.gmu.edu/d/5057/

As well, the banking system was stabilized. The Federal Deposit Insurance Corporation was created in 1933 to insure individual bank deposits.

The second wave of New Deal programs involved essentially redistributing power among businesses, consumers, farmers, and workers. The programs were numerous and far-reaching. Unions were encouraged. The Securities and Exchange Commission (or the SEC, which regulates publicly traded stocks), large-scale public works projects, and a strong social safety net were part of the legacy. The Agricultural Adjustment Act (1933) reduced farm crop and livestock outputs, and thus effectively raised farm prices. Works Progress Administration projects paid people in the arts to act, paint, sculpt, write, and more. The Social Security system was set up to provide financial assistance to people who were elderly and disabled; it continues today, as does the SEC.

Roosevelt's New Deal was an unprecedented, bold response to a crisis. His response was noteworthy in two distinct ways:

- It extended government involvement and intervention in the economy farther than it had ever gone before in the United States and represented an acceptance of government having a very direct role in the economy. The New Deal was an economic response to the inherent instability and the resulting social pain and upheaval of natural market forces. New Dealers felt that government has a responsibility to soften the jagged edges of the market cycles while still preserving the essential freedoms required in the market. There was a perceived need for governments to protect people from the abuses of uncontrolled capitalism.

Figure 6-6 ▲

One of the many back-to-work programs was the Civilian Conservation Corps (CCC). The CCC had young men from unemployed families work in rural areas for $30 per month on such projects as building roads, creating state and national parks, fighting forest fires, or planting trees. The young men pictured here are clearing rocks from a truck trail in Snoqualmie National Forest, Washington, in 1933.

Workers lived in camps, wore uniforms, and were required to send $25 per month home to their families. Most of the men who joined had not finished high school, had had no regular work before, and were malnourished prior to life in the camp. How did the CCC balance the principle of economic freedom against other rights and freedoms? In the circumstances, would you have volunteered to join the CCC?

PAUSE AND REFLECT

How did some of the changes in North American societies during the Great Depression contribute to an evolution of liberalism?

Figure 6-7 ▲

The Tennessee Valley Authority was one of the biggest programs. It involved modernizing a large area, including damming the Tennessee River for electricity. The Fontana Dam seen here opened in 1945 and is 146 metres tall.

PAUSE AND REFLECT

In what ways did Roosevelt's New Deal reject or reflect the principles of liberalism?

- The meaning of "people who matter" broadened. The New Deal showed an understanding that liberal principles apply to more than the rights and freedoms of industrialists; they also apply to the average citizen who needs protection from the vagaries of the market. This is what we mean by the shift from classical liberalism to modern liberalism.

Roosevelt clarified this shift in the understanding of whose interests needed consideration in his "Forgotten Man" speech, among others:

These unhappy times call for the building of plans that rest upon the forgotten, the unorganized but the indispensable units of economic power, for plans...that build from the bottom up and not from the top down, that put their faith once more in the forgotten man at the bottom of the economic pyramid.

—Franklin D. Roosevelt, "The Forgotten Man" (radio address), April 7, 1932. New Deal Network.
http://newdeal.feri.org/speeches/1932c.htm

Roosevelt himself had been born into a family of wealth and privilege, but he was brought up to believe that wealth brought with it a responsibility to those less fortunate. In the Great Depression, which had over 25 per cent unemployment, there were many "forgotten" men, women, and children.

Government Responses to the Depression in Canada

Initially, the Canadian government did not intervene in the troubled economy to the same extent as the Roosevelt administration in the United States. Conservative prime minister Bennett was elected in 1930 on a platform that included make-work projects to provide relief for the unemployed. Bennett's government did establish relief camps, but soon cut government spending, believing that laissez-faire policies would eventually lead the economy out of the crisis. One notable exception to these policies was the creation of Canada's central bank, the Bank of Canada, which took over control of the country's money supply, and began to use interest rates as a means of regulating the economy. Bennett also tried to quell the protests of left-wing groups and used a controversial section of the Criminal Code of Canada to disrupt Communist Party activities in Canada.

Seeing that the economy was not recovering, in 1935 Bennett tried to introduce programs similar to those of Roosevelt's New Deal; however, most of the legislation Bennett introduced, such as the Employment and Social Insurance Act, was later struck down by the courts. Bennett subsequently lost the 1935 election to William Lyon Mackenzie King.

Under Mackenzie King's administration, government became much more involved in the Canadian economy and created many public institutions and **social programs** characteristic of the modern welfare state and a modern **mixed economy**. One of the most important individuals involved in this period of government expansion was C.D. Howe. During the course of his political career, Howe became known to the public as "Minister of Everything." At various times, he served as Minister of Transport, Minister of Munitions and Supply, Minister of Reconstruction, Minister of Trade and Commerce, and Minister of Defence Production. Some of Howe's achievements include the following:

- using unemployed workers in the 1930s to build airstrips across the country, which would soon be used in the rapidly expanding aviation industry
- establishing Trans-Canada Airlines as a Crown corporation in 1937 (it later became Air Canada)
- creating the National Harbours Board, thus centralizing the administration of Canada's ports
- reforming the Canadian National Railway, which was heavily in debt
- helping to create the Canadian Broadcasting Corporation (CBC) in 1936

Perhaps Howe's most important contribution, however, was his work as Minister of Munitions and Supply during the Second World War. Under Howe's direction, the government established 28 Crown corporations to produce goods needed for the war effort. Approximately 80 per cent of this production was exported to other Allied countries. Not only did this contribute to the Allied success in the war, but it also helped the Canadian economy. In the first few years of the war, employment in the manufacturing sector in Canada increased by 50 per cent.

Other public institutions and social programs created during this period include the following:

- the Bank of Canada became a Crown corporation (1938)
- the National Film Board (1939)
- the Unemployment Insurance Act (1940), which created insurance for the unemployed as well as programs to help them find work
- family allowances (1944)
- the National Housing Act (1944) and the Central Housing and Mortgage Corporation (1946), which created public housing programs for low-income families and provided mortgage loan insurance

Interventionist policies were also initiated in the 1936–1939 provincial government of Québec premier Maurice Duplessis, who began a farm credit program, a commission to oversee fair wages, and a benefit program for destitute mothers and visually impaired people. Duplessis also tried to suppress communist activities in Québec by passing the Padlock Law (1937), which allowed the government to padlock any building used for communist meetings or activities for a year.

Explore the Issues

Concept Review

1 Create a chart with three columns. In the first column, list the examples of classical liberal principles and practices covered in this section. In the second column, list the examples of modern liberal principles and practices. In the third column, list the reasons for any specific shift in principles.

Concept Application

2 Think about the principles of individualism and collectivism that you considered in Chapter 2. As you consider influences of these principles, determine who benefited and who did not benefit through the changes brought about by the application of liberal principles. How did changes in government policies in North America reflect shifting attitudes toward principles of individualism and collectivism? How did these principles influence modern liberalism in the first half of the 20th century?

3 Compare government responses to the Great Depression with a government response to a more recent economic crisis in North America. How have governments changed their approaches to economic crises, if at all?

SKILL PATH

Analyzing Government Communications to Determine Perspective

As an Albertan and a Canadian, you experience the implications of market forces, government policy, and government practice; however, you can also take an active role in your community: you can vote in elections (or will soon be able to), you can speak out, and you can "vote" with your dollars in the economy. Whether your goal is to inform yourself, to explore an issue in-depth to develop an opinion, or to take action, you can hone the skill of examining communications to determine perspective and "read between the lines."

Your Task: Using Roosevelt's New Deal era as an example, examine an excerpt of a presidential speech and "read between the lines" for the perspective and the purpose of the communication. Based on your understanding of the context of the communication, examine the message for its underlying beliefs, values, and purpose, and determine how the message is crafted to achieve that purpose. For example, consider how the subject is framed, what words and phrases were chosen, what words were not used, what emotions the text evokes, and the result of all these choices. The Questions to Guide You will help you review the example and apply the Skill Path to other examples in and beyond this chapter.

On September 8, 1933, Franklin D. Roosevelt delivered the following impromptu speech at the 1933 Conference on Mobilization for Human Needs. This was early in the period of the New Deal.

I have been somewhat occupied during the past forty-eight hours with human needs in other parts of the world, outside of our own country—occupied in the hope that the United States would not have to act outside of its own quarters, in the hope that another Republic will be able to solve its own difficulties just as we are seeking to solve our difficulties. And, so, I have no set speech to deliver to you today.

I want to talk to you very simply and very briefly in regard to what might be called "The Whole of the Picture." You are not the whole of the picture and neither am I, but the Nation is. Our task, I think, is to complete the whole of the picture and not leave any unfinished portion thereof.

As you know, the many Governments in the United States: the Federal Government, the forty-eight State Governments, and the tens of thousands of local Governments are doing their best to meet what has been in many ways one of the most serious crises in history. On the whole, they have done well. The Federal Government cannot, by any means, accomplish the task alone. The Government has, during these past months, entered into many fields of human endeavor that it has never participated in before.

I believe we Americans do not wish to see a permanent extension of purely Government operations carried to the extent of relieving us of our individual responsibilities as citizens, and it is with that thought in mind that very early in this Administration we laid down in regard to one portion of this great picture a somewhat simple rule.

When we came to the problem of meeting the emergency of human needs, we did not rush blindly in and say, "The Government will take care of it." We approached it from the other angle first. We said to the people of this country, "When you come to the problem of relief, you

face the individual family, the individual man, woman and child who lives in a particular locality and the first objective and the first necessity are that the citizens of that community, through the churches, the community chest, the social and charitable organizations of the community, are going to be expected to do their share to their utmost extent first."

—Franklin D. Roosevelt, speech at the Conference on Mobilization for Human Needs, September 8, 1933. New Deal Network.

http://newdeal.feri.org/texts/69.htm

Questions to Guide You

1. What is the source of the communication? For example, is it a transcription of a political speech, an official web page, a poster?

2. What is the context? When was the communication made and in what circumstances?

3. Who is the author or speaker? What point of view does this person have on the subject?

4. What is the content? What are the main points? How would you summarize the message?

5. Who is the intended audience for the communication?

6. What is the purpose? What does the speaker or author want the audience to understand or do as a result of this communication?

7. How is the message crafted for this purpose? What keywords and phrases are used and with what impact? What does the speaker or author choose not to say?

Source: Mike Denos and Roland Case, Teaching about Historical Thinking, eds. Peter Seixas and Penny Clark (Vancouver: University of British Columbia, 2006).

The Ebb and Flow of Economic Liberalism Since the Second World War

Question for Inquiry

- In what ways have economies reflected the principles of liberalism since the Second World War?

The Postwar Consensus

In 1942, Sir William Beveridge presented a report to the British Parliament entitled "Social Insurance and Allied Services." In his report, Beveridge recommended that the role of the state be expanded to provide members of society with more security.

Now, when the war is abolishing landmarks of every kind, is the opportunity for using experience in a clear field. A revolutionary moment in the world's history is a time for revolutions, not for patching...

...organisation of social insurance should be treated as one part only of a comprehensive policy of social progress. Social insurance fully developed may provide income security; it is an attack upon Want. But Want is one only of five giants on the road of reconstruction and in some ways the easiest to attack. The others are Disease, Ignorance, Squalor and Idleness.

...social security must be achieved by co-operation between the State and the individual. The State should offer security for service and contribution. The State in organising security should not stifle incentive, opportunity, responsibility; in establishing a national minimum, it should leave room and encouragement for voluntary action by each individual to provide more than that minimum for himself and his family...

—**Sir William Beveridge,**
"Social Insurance and Allied Services,"
November 1942. Socialist Health Association.
http://www.sochealth.co.uk/history/beveridge.htm

In 1948, the Labour Party government adopted several of Beveridge's recommendations and created the National Insurance Act, the National Assistance Act, and the National Health Service Act. This period in British politics, from the end of the First World War until the end of the 1970s, became known as the *postwar consensus* because, despite their political differences, successive governments of the collectivist Labour Party and the individualist Conservative Party maintained the programs that made up the new British welfare state. Not only did countries like Britain, Canada, and the United States implement changes in the role of the state at this time, but a general growth of the principles of liberalism occurred internationally through contacts

Figure 6-8 ▲

Construction of the St Lawrence Seaway began in 1954 and was completed in 1959. The Canadian government paid for approximately two-thirds of the $470 million cost of the project, and the American government paid the remainder.

related to trade, international cooperation, foreign aid, and other programs. The ebb and flow of economic liberalism was in evidence around the world. Many Western democracies followed suit, providing substantial publicly-funded "social safety net" programs such as employment insurance, assistance for people who are elderly, child care, and universal health care.

The Postwar Economy in Canada

As in Britain, most Canadian governments in the three decades following the Second World War created or strengthened social programs. Building on legislation and initiatives passed prior to and during the war, such as Unemployment Insurance and Family Allowances, postwar Canadian governments started several programs characteristic of a welfare state, such as the following:

- the provision of universal health care—Public health care was established in Canada through the Hospital Insurance and Diagnostic Act (1957) and the Medical Care Act (1966).
- the Canada Pension Plan (CPP, 1966)—The CPP, along with Old Age Security, makes up Canada's public retirement income system.
- the Foreign Investment Review Agency (FIRA, 1974)—FIRA was created in the face of concerns over foreign control of Canadian industries with the mandate of screening foreign takeovers of Canadian businesses and the creation of new companies in Canada by foreign investors. The agency was sometimes criticized because it rarely prevented foreign investment in Canadian businesses despite its mandate. In 1984, the name of the agency was changed to Investment Canada, and its mandate was changed to promoting foreign investment in the Canadian economy.
- the Canadian Radio and Television Commission (CRTC, 1968)—The CRTC was established to oversee all aspects of broadcasting in Canada, including licensing, content, and ownership. In 1976, the commission was also given jurisdiction over the telecommunications industry in Canada, at which time its name became the Canadian Radio-television and Telecommunications Commission.
- Atomic Energy of Canada Limited (AECL, 1952)—AECL was created by the federal government to research and develop peaceful uses for nuclear energy. AECL created and markets the CANDU reactor, which is used in nuclear power plants in countries around the world.

In Québec, the provincial Duplessis government undertook ambitious public works projects in the postwar period. Having established its own provincial income-tax program, the Québec government used the funds to expand infrastructure. Duplessis built hydroelectric projects, extended electrification throughout rural Québec, and constructed highways, schools, universities, and hospitals. His government also introduced the country's highest minimum wage and created home ownership assistance acts.

At the same time, Duplessis was a strong opponent of organized labour, and often used provincial police to break up strikers' picket lines. His questionable tactics in dealing with disputes eventually led to the adoption of new provincial labour laws. His anti-communist Padlock Law (1937) was struck down by the Supreme Court of Canada in 1957.

While Duplessis's government was heavily involved in the economy, it was not a strong supporter of most social programs, as it preferred lower taxes. Only after Duplessis's passing, during the Quiet Revolution of the 1960s, would Québec see a strengthening of social programs characteristic of the modern welfare state.

Economic Crises of the 1970s

The 1970s were a difficult period for governments in several liberal democracies. In 1971, the United States withdrew from the Bretton Woods Agreement, which had used the gold standard to set the exchange rates for the currencies of most of the world's industrialized countries since 1945. Soon after, most other countries followed suit, and as world currencies were allowed to freely float on world markets, a period of inflation ensued, slowing economic activity.

Further compounding these problems, Egypt and Syria attacked Israel in 1973, triggering the fourth Arab-Israeli war. In response to American and Western European support of Israel during the conflict, the oil monopoly known as OPEC (Organization of the Petroleum Exporting Countries) imposed a five-month oil embargo on the United States and the Netherlands (among other countries). OPEC also reduced its production of oil. Because of this, the price of oil quadrupled, causing gas shortages and rationing in the United States. This had a double effect of making goods more expensive, thus causing a rise in the rate of inflation, and causing the economy to slow down. When a recession and high inflation occur at the same time, it is known as **stagflation**.

The phenomenon of stagflation also affected the British economy. The economic situation in Britain was so serious that even Prime Minister James Callaghan, whose Labour Party had been responsible for many of the innovations that led to the British welfare state, no longer supported using government spending to help the economy. In 1976, as the British government was forced to borrow US$3.9 billion from the International Monetary Fund, Callaghan said the following in a speech at a Labour Party conference:

Rate of Inflation (%)

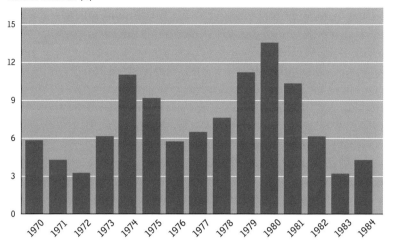

◀ Figure 6-9

Inflation in the United States rose dramatically during the 1970s and early 1980s.

For too long, perhaps ever since the War, we postponed facing up to fundamental choices and fundamental changes in our society and in our economy…We used to think that you could spend your way out of a recession and increase employment by cutting taxes and boosting government spending. I tell you in all candour that that option no longer exists, and that insofar as it ever did exist, it only worked on each occasion since the war by injecting a bigger dose of inflation into the economy, followed by a higher level of unemployment…We will fail—and I say this to those who have been pressing about public expenditure—if we think we can buy our way out by printing "confetti money" to pay ourselves more than we produce.

—James Callaghan, speech at a Labour Party conference, quoted in Michael Starks, *Not for Profit, Not for Sale*, (New Brunswick, NJ: Transaction Books, Rutgers University, 1992) p. 10.

Because of the phenomenon of stagflation, governments in many Western countries found that, while the cost of maintaining the programs of a welfare state was rising due to inflation, the economic slowdown meant that governments collected less tax revenue. This situation would lead to a shift in economic thinking in many countries in the 1970s and 1980s.

Monetarism: Friedman and Hayek

It can be argued that the shift toward classical liberal laissez-faire economics in the form of monetarism—a shift that began in the 1970s—is another swing of an economic pendulum which alternates between interventionism and the free-market economy, reflecting a return to the principles of liberalism. This particular pendulum swing lasted well into the 2000s, and was also promoted in Canada by such figures as premiers Ralph Klein of Alberta and Mike Harris of Ontario, and Prime Minister Stephen Harper. During his time in office, each attempted to undo the interventionist policies of previous governments.

Monetarist theory holds that control of a country's money supply is the best means to encourage economic growth and limit unemployment and inflation. The money supply is controlled through the regulation of interest rates. The economist most closely associated with monetarism is Milton Friedman.

Friedman believed that inflation was primarily the result of an excess supply of money produced by central banks. He argued that when the money supply was increased, consumer spending would also increase, causing demand to rise, and thus inflation to increase (as happened in Germany in the early 1920s). Friedman felt that the amount of money issued by the central bank should be linked to economic indicators such as the rate of inflation.

Another influential economist during this period was Friedrich Hayek. Hayek had been a critic of collectivist thinking since before the Second World War, but his views were not widely popular because of the prevalence of Keynesian economic theory. This began to change in the 1960s and 1970s, and Hayek's theories gradually became more widely accepted.

Hayek believed that, in order for a collectivist society to function, government would have to maintain an extremely high level of control over society. He also felt that excessive government control of economic aspects of life would inevitably lead to government interfering in aspects of citizens' social lives, which he felt was a danger to the liberty of the individual. Hayek also argued that it would be impossible in a centrally planned (that is, collectivist) economy for the central planners to have sufficient information to make rational decisions: although they controlled supply, they could never have enough information about demand (especially in a society the size of modern countries) to make appropriate decisions. Hayek's ideas would have a strong influence on British Conservative prime minister Margaret Thatcher.

Both Friedman and Hayek, like Adam Smith before them, believed that the price system, or the free market, was the only way to balance supply and demand in the economy while maintaining individual liberty.

From my point of view, we in the United States have gone overboard in respect to the extent of regulation and detailed control of labor standards, industry, and the like. It's bad for us…I am in favor of cutting taxes under any circumstances and for any excuse, for any reason, whenever it's possible.

—Milton Friedman, 2006, in John Hawkins "An Interview with Milton Friedman." Right Wing News.
http://www.rightwingnews.com/interviews/friedman.php

The gradual acceptance of monetarism, and the ideas of Friedman and Hayek, was in part a reaction to the inability of governments to deal with the stagflation period of the early 1970s.

Monetarism versus Keynesian Economics

The adoption of monetarism by Great Britain, the United States, and others reflects a swing of the pendulum back to classical liberal principles and away from the interventionist practices of Keynesian economics. The intervention of governments during and after the Depression and the Second World War had established a modified market or a mixed economy—the intervention side of the pendulum swing—but the advice offered by Keynes had been only partially accepted by governments.

Keynes argued that, during recessions, governments should increase the money supply to alleviate the economic downturn and avoid a lasting depression. However, Keynes also maintained that during times of economic prosperity and inflation, governments should cut back on program spending, raise taxes, and raise interest rates, in order to cool off the inflationary economy and offset the government's debt. Some would argue that liberal democratic governments readily accepted Keynes' advice to spend money during hard times, but did not implement his ideas to cut spending during prosperous times because they would be unpopular with voters. This resulted in the massive government debts and stagflation of the 1970s.

While monetarists argue that Keynesian economics were unsustainable in the long term, Keynes' defenders assert that his theories are workable when properly put into practice.

Figure 6-10 ▲

Economist Milton Friedman influenced both British prime minister Margaret Thatcher and American president Ronald Reagan in the 1980s. He followed in the tradition of Adam Smith and felt that government spending and regulation had gone too far.

One key aspect of Reagan's administration was its response to labour. In August 1981, American air traffic controllers were striking and threatening to shut down the airlines. The workers complained about dangerous levels of stress and greater work demands; the issues on the table were wages, hours, and retirement benefits. Reagan was uncompromising; he announced that the strike was illegal and all the striking workers were fired. According to US Attorney General Edwin Meese, Reagan felt it was the "only thing he could do under the law." Source: "The Reagan Years: The air-traffic controllers strike." CNN.com, http://www.cnn.com/SPECIALS/2001/reagan.years/whitehouse/airtraffic.html, 2001.

Reaganomics

Ronald Reagan became president of the United States in 1981. At the time, supporters of Friedman and Hayek argued that stagflation was partly the result of huge national **deficits** from government spending.

[Friedman] believed history "got off on the wrong track" when politicians began listening to John Maynard Keynes, intellectual architect of the New Deal and the modern welfare state. The market crash of 1929 had created an overwhelming consensus that laissez-faire had failed and that governments need to intervene in the economy to redistribute wealth and regulate corporations. During those dark days of laissez-faire, when Communism conquered the East, the welfare state was embraced by the West…[Friedman wrote,] "The major error, in my opinion…was to believe that it is possible to do good with other people's money."

—Excerpted from *The Shock Doctrine: The Rise of Disaster Capitalism* by Naomi Klein, pp. 20–21. Copyright © 2007 Naomi Klein. Reprinted by permission of Knopf Canada.

Reagan was greatly influenced by Friedman's theories. While President Richard Nixon's administration in the 1970s had tried to combat stagflation by setting wage and price controls, Reagan wanted less government involvement and embarked on what was later called **Reaganomics**.

Reagan became president at a time of high unemployment and high inflation. His administration's response included reduced income and business taxes, reduced regulation (controls on business), and increased government spending on the military. These policies are known as supply-side economics, or **trickle-down economics**. Supporters of this perspective maintain that by lowering tax rates, especially among those who are most likely to invest capital (that is, the wealthy), economic growth will be encouraged through increased investment. It was argued that the benefits of increased private investment and government defence spending would "trickle down" through the economy to the working class.

Economic data would not seem to support this theory, however: between 1972 and 1977, the wealthiest 10 per cent of the population of the United States was earning about 33 per cent of all the income in the country. With the advent of trickle-down economics, by 1987 the wealthiest 10 per cent were earning about 41 per cent of the country's total income. (Source: Emmanuel Saez, "Striking It Richer: The Evolution of Top Incomes in the United States." *Pathways Magazine*, Stanford Center for the Study of Poverty and Inequality [Winter, 2008]: pp. 6–7.)

	Date of Election	Spending*	Deficit (−) or Surplus*	Public Debt*
Carter administration	1977	409.2	−53.7	549.1
	1978	458.7	−59.2	607.1
	1979	504.0	−40.7	640.3
	1980	590.9	−73.8	711.9
Reagan administration	1981	678.2	−79.0	789.4
	1982	745.7	−128.0	924.6
	1983	808.4	−207.8	1137.3
	1984	851.9	−185.4	1307.0
	1985	946.4	−212.3	1507.6
	1986	990.4	−221.2	1740.6
	1987	1004.1	−149.7	1889.8
	1988	1064.5	−155.2	2051.6

*all figures in billions of US dollars

Source: Adapted from "Revenues, Outlays, Deficits, Surpluses, and Debt Held by the Public, 1968 to 2007, in Billions of Dollars." United States Congressional Budget Office, http://www.cbo.gov/budget/data/historical.shtml.

◀ **Figure 6-12**

The Reagan administration argued for less government involvement in the economy; however, government spending and debt rose during the 1980s. This was largely due to military spending. Reagan spent more money on military buildup than any previous president; however, increased government spending in the 1980s was somewhat contrary to the path suggested by Friedman and Hayek.

Britain's Thatcherism

Like Ronald Reagan in the United States, Britain's Conservative prime minister Margaret Thatcher (1979–1990), tried to reduce government involvement in the economy and increase economic freedom and entrepreneurship in keeping with classical liberal principles. Under Thatcher, Britain sold much of its social housing in a program that encouraged those who rented council flats (that is, government-owned homes) to buy them. The Thatcher administration also privatized many utility companies, including British Telecom, which had been publicly owned since the 1940s.

Like Reagan, Thatcher took a hard line with labour unions. A coal miners' strike stretched from 1984 to 1985 and, as Naomi Klein describes it, "Thatcher unleashed the full force of the state on the strikers, including, in one single confrontation, 8000 truncheon-wielding riot police, many on horseback, to storm a plant picket line, leading to over 700 injuries." (Source: Naomi Klein, *The Shock Doctrine*, p. 164). In the end, 966 workers were fired and the strike's defeat was a huge symbolic loss to the union movement in Great Britain.

Figure 6-13 ▲

In reference to the coal miners' strike and Britain's war with Argentina over the Falkland Islands, Prime Minister Thatcher said, "We had to fight the enemy without in the Falklands. We always have to be aware of the enemy within, which is much more difficult to fight and more dangerous to liberty." What values are suggested by describing a labour union as the enemy? Source: "Enemies within: Thatcher and the unions." BBC News, http://news.bbc.co.uk/1/hi/uk_politics/3067563.stm, March 5, 2004.)

Blair's Third Way

In contrast to Thatcher and John Major, who followed her briefly as prime minister, Labour Party prime minister Tony Blair ran in 1997 on a platform of a "Third Way": neither the familiar Conservative approach, nor the "old Labour Party" approach that focused on trade unions, public ownership, a strong welfare state, government intervention, and redistribution of wealth. The Third Way was seen as a shift to a more moderate platform that would adopt some Thatcherite and free-market policies, while maintaining some social programs—a new form of mixed economy. It would be a compromise between the Keynesian economics of the postwar period and the more recent monetarism. It was an attempt at balancing the individualist values of monetarism with the collectivist values of social justice.

In the first years of Blair's administration, his approach to the Third Way was described by the BBC as follows:

Put at its most basic the Third Way is something different and distinct from liberal capitalism with its unswerving belief in the merits of the free market and democratic socialism with its demand management and obsession with the state. The Third Way is in favour of growth, entrepreneurship, enterprise and wealth creation but it is also in favour of greater social justice and it sees the state playing a major role in bringing this about. So in the words of one of its gurus Anthony Giddens of the LSE [London School of Economics] the Third Way rejects top down socialism as it rejects traditional neo liberalism.

—Source: "UK Politics: What is the Third Way?"
BBC News, September 27, 1999.
http://news.bbc.co.uk/2/hi/uk_news/politics/458626.stm

During Blair's leadership, the government increased public spending on health care and education from Thatcher's days, and introduced a national minimum wage. At the same time, Blair introduced tuition fees for post-secondary education, which had formerly been free for all students. Since Blair's government, all universities (except one private university) provide undergraduate education for a low tuition fee in the form of a loan that is repayable after graduation when the graduate reaches a certain income level; students from the lowest-income backgrounds have free tuition.

The Netherlands' Polder Model, Kenya's Harambee, and Chad

Other countries have adopted similar compromise approaches that try to find a middle ground between laissez-faire economics and socialist interventionism. Some, such as Britain, refer to the approach as the "third way" or "middle way" between the right and left sides of the economic spectrum. Most of these compromise solutions to economic extremes are not yet clearly defined and can be thought of as works in progress: "One supporter writing to *The Independent* claimed it was a form of benevolent pragmatism—a philosophy that asked of each policy—is it good, does it work?" (Source: "UK Politics: What is the Third Way?" BBC News, http://news.bbc.co.uk/2/hi/uk_news/politics/458626.stm, September 27, 1999.)

The Netherlands has a unique system that plays a significant role in its economy. The system, called the Polder Model, was developed in the early 1980s, after a long period of decline in the Dutch economy. The Polder Model involves employers, unions, and government representatives working together to make decisions, and it helps avoid strikes, thus stabilizing the economy. It also has parallels in the political system:

> *The national identity is reflected in countless advisory and consultative bodies. Each issue where there is a remote danger of disagreement has its own forum in which all interested parties are represented, whether it be [its] traffic issues, defence matters or education affairs.*

> **—Mark Kranenburg,**
> **"The political branch of the polder model."**
> **NRC Handelsblad, July 1, 1999.**
> http://www.nrc.nl/W2/Lab/Profiel/Netherlands/politics.html

Figure 6-14 ▲

The model name comes from the country's *polder,* an interdependent system of dikes that prevent flooding in the Netherlands, much of which is below sea level.

In the wake of devastation resulting from a variety of factors, including colonial occupation, Kenya developed a policy centred on *harambee*—a Bantu word that means literally "let us all pull together." Susan Njeri Chieni says that this term "embodies ideas of mutual assistance, joint effort, mutual social responsibility, and community self-reliance"—and is similar to the concepts of *ujamaa* in Tanzania and *humanism* in Zambia. She also says the following:

> *It is therefore an informal development strategy of the people, by the people (with assistance from external sources, including the government) for the people…Harambee is not new but a traditional principle which existed in every traditional society in Kenya. Each society had self-help or co-operative work groups by which groups of women on the one hand and men on the other organized common work parties, for example to cultivate or build houses for each other, clear bushes, harvesting, etc. The security and prosperity of the group was therefore dependent upon persons being mindful of each other's welfare.*

> **—Susan Njeri Chieni, "The Harambee Movement in Kenya:**
> **The Role Played by Kenyans and the Government in the**
> **Provision of Education and other Social Services." E.G. West Centre.**
> http://www.ncl.ac.uk/egwest/countries/kenya.html

Figure 6-15 ▲

Why would the World Bank impose conditions on Chad's Parliament in order to provide the loan for oil development?

PAUSE AND REFLECT

In this example, what is the level of government involvement? What might be the long-term outcomes of this approach? In what ways does this example represent a middle ground between laissez-faire economics and social justice?

Principles that underlie harambee include the following:

- The product should benefit the public rather than just one individual.
- Projects should maximize the use of local resources that would otherwise be unused or too expensive.

Schools, medical centres, roads, and more have been developed with harambee.

Chad has major oil reserves. Rather than allowing a multinational business to invest in the country and tap these resources (but also create opportunities for local employment and related businesses), Chad and the World Bank "began experimenting with a potentially pathbreaking model…The World Bank agreed to step in and loan the government money to partner with a multinational consortium—led by ExxonMobil—to get the oil flowing. But it also put in place certain conditions. Chad's parliament had to pass a law guaranteeing that 80 percent of the oil revenues would be spent on health, education, and rural infrastructure…" (Source: Fareed Zakaria, *The Future of Freedom* [New York: W.W. Norton, 2004], p. 157.)

Economic Practices and the Principles of Liberalism

Keeping in mind the historical development of liberalism and its expression in economic policy, let's look at a comparison of two different economic systems and how they function.

Sweden and the United States both follow the principles of economic liberalism. However, these countries are clearly different in their economic practices. As you read the article by Lief Utne in this section, think about how economic practices and policies can reflect liberal principles. Consider why such obvious differences occur in these countries.

Sweden and the United States

Countries such as the United States have argued that liberal goals are most effectively achieved by limiting government intervention. In these societies, government provides only the most basic social support while governing over semi-private education and health care systems. For them, the drive to create or produce or acquire wealth arises from self-interest and the need to compete. During times of extreme economic upheaval, these governments may favour more economic intervention, as was the case with Roosevelt's government during the Great Depression of the 1930s.

Other countries such as Canada and Sweden have tended to favour more government intervention in the economy and the lives of citizens. Supporters of this mix argue that economic and social inequality tends to undermine liberalism, as citizens fall prey to fluctuations in the business cycle. Governments that favour this model maintain higher levels of intervention and taxation, but still encourage private property and industry (for example, about 90 per cent of Sweden's industrial output is produced by private companies). Depending on the status of the economy, they believe that liberal growth can take place only with some degree of economic self-reliance and that too much government regulation will impede economic incentive and private entrepreneurs. Such countries are following a compromise model similar to the Third Way approach described earlier.

What does that mean in the daily lives of citizens? Here's one answer from an American writer, Leif Utne, who wrote the following article comparing economic implications of life in the United States and Sweden from his personal point of view. How does your experience as a Canadian compare?

PAUSE AND REFLECT

How do the Polder Model, *harambee* and the economic choices in Sweden compare with your own experience? What beliefs about the individual and the community do they reflect? Which example, if any, would you want to transfer to Canada?

Life Is a Smorgasbord
You can't always get what you want—but in Sweden, you just might find you get what you need.
by Leif Utne

So, will you two ever move here?" That was the question on everyone's mind when my wife, Cilla, and I visited her family in Sweden last Christmas.

"Yes. Probably. Someday," we answered.

Cilla and I met while studying in Chile, one week shy of graduation. We spent much of the next eight months traveling together around Cuba, Brazil, and Scandinavia before coming to live in Minneapolis. We've always assumed that someday we'd live in Sweden for a while.

I've always admired the strong communitarian ethic that is the basis of Sweden's political system. A decade of tough economic times has forced the government to begin dismantling some parts of the country's fabled welfare state, but most of Sweden's social democratic policies remain firmly in place: nearly free university education, universal health care, strong unemployment benefits, and my favorite, a minimum of five weeks vacation for all full-time workers. The chance to live in a society truly dedicated to promoting economic democracy and social justice is one of the great attractions Sweden holds for me. By the time we came home, however, Cilla found herself feeling far less excited by the idea of moving back to Sweden than she had been before.

"After a month in Sweden, you'd feel like you were in prison," she warned me.

Don't get me wrong. Cilla loves her homeland. But she is not a typical Swede. "From the time I was little, my mother always predicted that I'd leave Sweden one day," she tells me. "She said that Sweden was too small for me."

What is it about Sweden that would make Cilla feel claustrophobic, and attract me so strongly? There are many differences between my homeland and hers, but the biggest centers on issues of freedom and choice.

Swedes tend to exercise their freedom of choice in different ways than Americans, emphasizing quality over quantity or diversity. For example, Sweden produces only two kinds of cars, but they're the ultra-reliable Saab and Volvo. Every bathroom in Sweden, it seems, has one of two toilets, water-conserving low-flush models made by Ifö or Gustafsberg, in white or off-white. Few people have cable TV, but the five broadcast networks are known for their high-quality programming. The national liquor monopoly, known affectionately as "The System," is only open till 6 p.m. on weekdays and 2 p.m. on Saturday, but its wine selection is second to none. I mean that literally. The System is the world's single largest wine buyer, and is therefore able to negotiate excellent deals on great wines. Plus, all the clerks have extensive training and are very knowledgeable about wine. And if the bottle you want is out of stock at the local store, they'll find it in another store and have it for you the next day. Cilla lived in London for a short time in the early '90s and says that "there was a liquor store on every corner, but you couldn't find a decent bottle of wine." Despite their grumbling about the limited hours and high liquor taxes, Swedes are proud of The System. Waiting in line at The System on a Friday afternoon is a shared national ritual.

At home, Cilla and I talk about things like this all the time. We both love to travel, speak several languages, and find almost nothing more interesting than exploring cultural differences. In Cilla's case it's a vocation as well as an avocation—she's a professional cross-culturalist who advises executives who are moving from one country to another. So what is it, I asked my resident cross-cultural expert, that makes American and Swedish attitudes toward choice so very different?

Freedom in Sweden, says Cilla, is not only—not even primarily—about economic choices. It's more focused on other factors—the efficiency, beauty, or reliability of goods, the quality of life. Freedom means having leisure time to spend with family and friends, the opportunity to learn and travel. The Swedish idea of choice is to express your individuality in ways that are not tied to your wallet. Although a Swedish grocery store may only carry four brands of soap, Swedes have far more political choices than we do: seven different political parties hold seats in

Parliament in a country of only 9 million.

Like most Scandinavian and continental European nations, Sweden is a far more relationship-oriented society than the United States. Cilla cites Dutch social scientist Geert Hofstede, one of the 20th century's most prominent researchers on intercultural communication, who notes that in a relationship-oriented society, individuals seek affirmation from the group before doing anything and actively avoid standing out from the crowd. This attitude—like the welfare state itself—is consistent with the high value Swedes put on freeing the individual from hardship and discomfort. But it brings consequences that might make Americans snicker, or feel frustrated. An older Swedish woman once told me that the Bosnian refugee family that had recently moved into her apartment building were good people because "they follow the laundry room rules." That was high praise in a culture where every apartment building has a scrupulously clean laundry room with strict rules for reserving a time to do your wash.

The United States, on the other hand, is individualistic in the extreme. Identity in this country, Cilla explains, begins with the individual's sense of self rather than membership in any group. Personal choices in America are about exercising your capacity for individual expression and creativity. Cilla was surprised at how much culture shock she felt moving here. It was a bit like the scene from *Moscow on the Hudson*, a 1984 movie about a Russian saxophonist who defects to the United States. One day he goes into a supermarket to buy coffee, and finds dozens and dozens of varieties. His head begins to spin, he hyperventilates, and ends up in the hospital. After five years in the United States, Cilla's come to terms with American life. It's "the little life," that she enjoys most about this country—owning a single-family house and a car, access to a wide variety of international foods, music. Yet she's conflicted, too. "When I step back, I realize that it's all dependent on this huge, unsustainable apparatus that pollutes the environment and exploits the developing world."

So—will Cilla and I ever move to Sweden? Yes, someday. I'm certain of it. I want to know what it's like to live in a place where freedom has a different meaning than a wealth of choices. And, paradoxically, I feel very fortunate that Cilla and I have that choice.

—Leif Utne, "Life Is a Smorgasbord."
Reprinted with permission from Utne Reader
(May-June 2003); www. Utne.com,
Copyright © 2003 Odgen Publications, Inc.

Economic Liberalism Today

Great Britain, like other liberal democracies, has promoted economic freedom and free trade, and many entrepreneurs have enjoyed the freedom to do business globally. On a grand scale, this means that employers can move their businesses to wherever they find a suitable economic climate. For example, in 2003 the British company Norwich Union announced it would cut 2350 jobs in the United Kingdom and relocate them to India. From 2000 to 2003 "the number of [call centres in India] has risen from 50 to 800 as Western companies have sought to take advantage of cheaper operating costs—estimated to be about 30-40% lower than in the UK." (Source: "Call centres 'bad for India'." BBC News, http://news.bbc.co.uk/1/hi/world/south_asia/3292619.stm, December 11, 2003.)

In addition to the shock of job loss in Great Britain, there were criticisms within India:

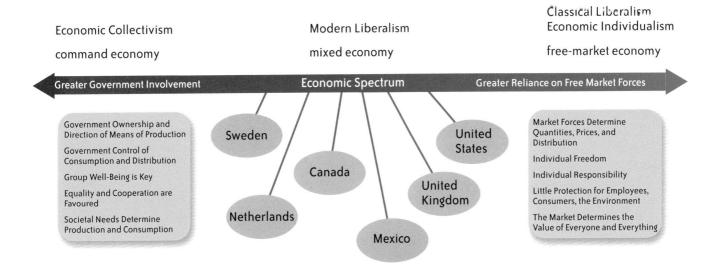

Economic Collectivism

command economy

Modern Liberalism

mixed economy

Classical Liberalism
Economic Individualism

free-market economy

Greater Government Involvement — Economic Spectrum — Greater Reliance on Free Market Forces

Government Ownership and Direction of Means of Production

Government Control of Consumption and Distribution

Group Well-Being is Key

Equality and Cooperation are Favoured

Societal Needs Determine Production and Consumption

Sweden

Canada

Netherlands

Mexico

United States

United Kingdom

Market Forces Determine Quantities, Prices, and Distribution

Individual Freedom

Individual Responsibility

Little Protection for Employees, Consumers, the Environment

The Market Determines the Value of Everyone and Everything

Figure 6-16 ▲

Placing countries on a comparative scale is always an exercise in approximation and perspective. Many factors—traditions, politics, culture, environment, history, and so on—may play a role in the relative economic freedom experienced by people in a country. How a person places countries on the spectrum also depends on the person's point of view and understanding of ideology. Thus, not everyone would agree on the placement of countries on the spectrum in this figure.

In addition, changes in governing parties often lead to changes in economic policy in liberal democracies. Canada, for example, could arguably be placed closer to the United Kingdom and the United States based on recent legislation proposed by the Conservative government. What do you think is the ideal position on the economic freedom-control spectrum?

"[Workers] work extremely long hours badly paid, in extremely stressful conditions, and most have absolutely no opportunities for any kind of advancement in their careers," Mr Bidwai told BBC World Service's One Planet programme.

"It's a dead end, it's a complete cul-de-sac. It's a perfect sweatshop scenario, except that you're working with computers and electronic equipment rather than looms or whatever."

—Source: "Call Centres 'bad for India'" BBC News, December 11, 2003.
http://news.bbc.co.uk/2/hi/south_asia/3292619.stm

Increasing Economic Freedom—Ukraine and Mexico

How can a country that has previously favoured government control of the economy increase economic freedom? When Ukrainian president Leonid Kuchma and American president Bill Clinton met in 1994 (after the fall of the Soviet Union), they discussed how the former communist state could reform its economy by encouraging competition and privatizing.

Years later, in 2002, Ukraine was still reforming its economy to improve the business environment, and the International Centre for Policy Studies (ICPS) evaluated the country as follows: the country's economic legislation became more predictable and addressed competition, foreign trade, taxation, and economic regulation in general. However, the ICPS warned, "Ukrainian authorities should pay more attention to the development of legislation on protecting competition and intellectual property rights." (Source: "Economic legislation in Ukraine becomes more predictable" [ICPS newsletter, #91, December 25, 2000], p. 1: http://www.icps.com.ua/doc/nl_eng_20001225_0091.pdf.)

Closer to home, Mexico joined in the North American Free Trade Agreement (NAFTA) with the United States and Canada to increase economic freedom and improve its economy. NAFTA was implemented in 1994. The following article describes its results as of 2002.

The North American Free Trade Agreement, considered the centerpiece of the new Mexican philosophy, has generated a quarter trillion dollars in cross-border trade with the United States. The treaty helped turn a closed, inefficient economy dominated by state-owned companies into one that was flooded by foreign investment and driven by foreign competition.

But government statistics show that economic liberalization has done little to close the huge divide between the privileged few and the poor, and left the middle class worse off than before. Battered by a series of severe recessions, teachers and engineers, nurses and small-business men, all find themselves swinging above and below the poverty line with the rise and fall of the peso, interest rates and the unemployment rate.

According to a recent government report, in the year 2000 half the Mexican population lived on about $4 a day, with scarcity shifting along with the population from rural regions to cities. Some 10 percent of Mexicans at the top of the income pyramid controlled close to 40 percent of the nation's wealth.

Meanwhile, the 35 percent of Mexico's population that lives in the middle —with average earnings of about $1,000 a month—spirals slowly downward.

The economist Rogelio Ramirez de la O said that in the 1970's, when Mexico's population was 50 million people and the country had begun to enjoy the benefits of an oil boom, some 60 percent of Mexicans were middle and working class. Their numbers and buying power have declined "dramatically" since then, Mr. Ramirez said.

"The promises of economic modernization have not been fulfilled," he added, and Mexico's middle class "now has less buying power than a generation ago."…In an effort to reduce its external debt, the government simultaneously slashed spending for higher education, transportation and health care—all traditional pillars of middle-class life…

It is not a unique predicament in Latin America, a region that has long suffered some of the greatest inequalities of wealth in the world. However, it seems a sorry outcome for a nation that adopted the economic tenets of globalization as gospel. It is particularly bitter for the middle class, the very people who powered the rise of President Vicente Fox, whose election two years ago brought down the dictatorial 71-year regime of the Institutional Revolutionary Party.

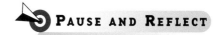

PAUSE AND REFLECT

Mexico joined NAFTA to open its economy and create economic opportunities. What other liberal principles did it have to consider? What was the impact of this choice for Mexico?

Figure 6-17 ▲

The election of Barack Obama to the US presidency in November 2008 signaled for many a time when government ought to taking more control of the economy.

Economic Liberalism and the Global Economy

Towards the end of 2008, two events in the United States seemed to signal a shift in government attitudes regarding liberalism. While the era of increased globalization during the 1990s and up to 2008 reflected a shift towards laissez-faire economic policies, the election of Barack Obama as President of the United States, and the turmoil in the global economy that began with the credit and mortgage crises in the United States in 2008, called these policies into question. The election of Barack Obama was met with an unusual outburst of relief, optimism, and expectancy in many countries. A general euphoria erupted. Change gave rise to hope that a better world was possible. There seemed to be a recognition that governments do indeed have an important role to play in furthering the principles of modern liberalism within their borders and also internationally. The economic meltdown at this time also called into question the wisdom of putting faith in the forces of the unregulated free market. Even conservative governments like those of the United States, France, and Canada in 2008 agreed that government involvement in the economy through the regulation of their national banking systems and the financial markets, and the bailout of important industries, was desirable. The ebb and flow of economic liberalism seems, at present, to be flowing towards the left— towards a greater role of governments in their economies and towards a more cooperative internationalism.

Explore the Issues

Concept Review

1 a) Identify two principles of Keynesian economics, and give examples of their application by governments.

b) Identify two principles of monetarism, and give examples of their application by governments.

Concept Application

2 Review the economic aspects of liberalism as you have explored them in the chapter and create a list of them. In a group, quickly brainstorm ways in which the local, Alberta, or federal government could implement policies that reflect each principle. Then, reflect on each brainstormed policy. Would you be willing to live with the implications of that economic policy? Why or why not?

3 After reviewing the chapter and conducting some additional research, compare the economic challenges faced by two countries: a modern communist state, such as China or Cuba, and one of India, Canada, or the United States. Consider in particular the countries' respective positions on government intervention in the economy, and how liberal principles are reflected in the economic policies and practices of these countries.

4 If you found yourself in the situation of Leif and Cilla, in which country would you choose to live, Sweden or the United States? Why? How is this choice related to the Chapter Issue, the Related Issue for Part 2, and the Key Issue for the course?

Reflect and Analyze

In this chapter you have explored economic principles, policies, practices, and history in order to understand and reflect on the evolution of modern liberalism, and to develop an informed response to the Chapter Issue: *To what extent do contemporary economic policies and practices reflect the principles of liberalism?* This chapter brought together many threads from other chapters and built on your understanding of individualism and liberalism, how they are expressed in economics and politics, and your own beliefs and values. You have seen the expanding concept of the individual on which liberal economies should focus: the merchant, the capitalist entrepreneur, the industrialist, the "forgotten man," or the ordinary citizen. This should further your understanding of the dynamic tension between classical liberalism and modern liberalism.

You have also considered how liberal democratic governments' economic policies have changed over time. You have seen examples of economic policy oscillating between a more collectivist-oriented interventionism and individualist free-market economics in response to various historical events. These shifts demonstrate how interpretations of liberalism vary over time, with particular liberal principles taking precedence over others depending on these interpretations. Now you are ready to respond to the Chapter Issue, *To what extent do contemporary economic policies and practices reflect the principles of liberalism?*, and consider the Related Issue of Part 2, *To what extent is resistance to liberalism justified?*

Respond to Ideas

1. Work with a group of three or four to examine recent actions or announcements of provincial or federal governments in Canada that relate to contemporary economic policies and practices. Analyze these examples, and place them on a continuum from classical liberalism to modern liberalism. Justify your placements and evaluate the viability and desirability of each of these examples from your point of view.

Examine Political Speeches

2. Your teacher will provide you with several examples of speeches from various politicians. Using the Skill Path, examine the speeches and respond to the following questions:
   a) Where would you place each of the speakers on a political spectrum?
   b) Do their positions and policies overlap?
   c) What is the relationship between liberalism and economics in their speeches? How do the speakers use liberalism, and their interpretation and application of it regarding economic policy, to respond to issues in society? What do these speakers seem to value most?
   d) How would the politicians' suggested economic policies affect individuals living in their constituencies?

Challenges to Liberalism Related to Foreign Policy

KEY SKILLS

Analyzing the impact of physical and human geography on history

KEY CONCEPTS

Analyzing how ideological conflict shaped post–Second World War international relations

Key Terms

Brinkmanship
Cold War
Containment
Détente
Deterrence
Expansionism
Liberation movements
McCarthyism
Nonalignment
Proxy wars

Figure 7-1 ▲

The Berlin Wall was a physical manifestation of the iron curtain metaphor used by British prime minister Winston Churchill.

Less than a year after the end of the Second World War, the wartime leader of Britain, Winston Churchill, delivered a speech that popularized the term **iron curtain** to describe the line in Europe between self-governing countries of the West and countries in Eastern Europe under communist Soviet control. The iron curtain became a metaphor for the division between American and Soviet ideologies. Those on either side interpreted the curtain differently: Americans viewed it as a barrier meant to contain those oppressed by communism, a restriction to civil and economic freedoms, and Soviets saw it as a protective measure, a means of protecting themselves from capitalist influences and the potential expansion of fascism.

The following excerpt is from what has become known as the Iron Curtain Speech, which Churchill gave at Westminster College, in Fulton, Missouri, in 1946.

The United States stands at this time at the pinnacle of world power. It is a solemn moment for the American democracy. For with this primacy in power is also joined an awe-inspiring accountability to the future. As you look around you, you must feel not only the sense of duty done, but also you must feel anxiety lest you fall below the level of achievement. Opportunity is here now, clear and shining, for both our countries. To reject it or ignore it or fritter it away will bring upon us all the long reproaches of the aftertime...

I have a strong admiration and regard for the valiant Russian people and for my wartime comrade, Marshal Stalin. There is deep sympathy and goodwill in Britain—and I doubt not here also—toward the peoples of all the Russias and a resolve to persevere through many differences and rebuffs in establishing lasting friendships.

It is my duty, however, to place before you certain facts about the present position in Europe.

From Stettin in the Baltic to Trieste in the Adriatic an iron curtain has descended across the Continent. Behind that line lie all the capitals of the ancient states of Central and Eastern Europe.

Warsaw, Berlin, Prague, Vienna, Budapest, Belgrade, Bucharest and Sofia; all these famous cities and the populations around them lie in what I must call the Soviet sphere, and all are subject, in one form or another, not only to Soviet influence but to a very high and in some cases increasing measure of control from Moscow.

The safety of the world, ladies and gentlemen, requires a unity in Europe, from which no nation should be permanently outcast. It is from the quarrels of the strong parent races in Europe that the world wars we have witnessed, or which occurred in former times, have sprung.

—Winston Churchill, "Iron Curtain" speech, March 5, 1946.
Modern History Sourcebook, Fordham University.
http://www.fordham.edu/halsall/mod/churchill-iron.html

Churchill, speaking right after the Second World War, can be seen as either a messenger who is trying to warn the free world of imminent danger or as an alarmist who is provoking a fight unnecessarily. You will learn more about this historical time period in this chapter. In the meantime, given the context of the quotation above, to what extent do you believe Churchill may have been encouraging conflict with the Soviet Union based on ideology? What information do you already have that might help inform your response?

PAUSE AND REFLECT

Churchill's metaphor—iron curtain—could have many implications on foreign policy. What meanings and implications might be associated with this term?

Chapter Issue

The Cold War (1945–1991) shaped the second half of the 20th century, and it continues to have significant influence not only on international relations, but also on the citizenship and daily lives of people around the world. In this chapter you will investigate and consider the Cold War and related examples of international conflict to explore the Chapter Issue: *To what extent does ideological conflict shape our world?*

During the Cold War, most of the world was split in two camps: those nation-states allied with the Soviets and communism and those allied with the Americans and democratic liberalism. This chapter will help you understand the role that ideology played in the division between these two superpowers, and how ideological conflict shaped international relations after the Second World War. As you explore and investigate the Cold War, use what you have learned in previous chapters to consider how liberalism was affected by this ideological conflict, and how citizens and citizenship were impacted by the promotion of communist and liberal democratic ideologies.

Figure 7-2 ▶

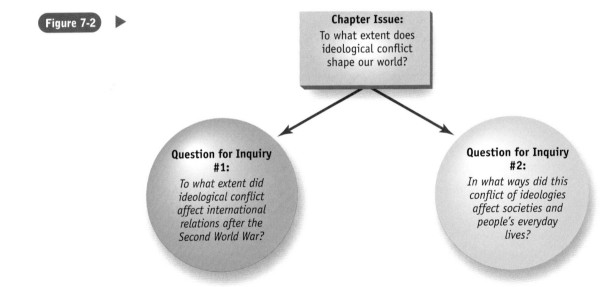

Chapter Issue:
To what extent does ideological conflict shape our world?

Question for Inquiry #1:
To what extent did ideological conflict affect international relations after the Second World War?

Question for Inquiry #2:
In what ways did this conflict of ideologies affect societies and people's everyday lives?

International Relations after the Second World War

Question for Inquiry

- **To what extent did ideological conflict affect international relations after the Second World War?**

In 1927, Joseph Stalin predicted the following:

...there will emerge two centers of world significance: a socialist center, drawing to itself the countries that incline towards socialism, and a capitalist center, drawing to itself the countries that incline towards capitalism. Battle between these two centers for command of the world economy will decide the fate of capitalism and of communism in the entire world.

—Josef Stalin, speech to American workers delegation, 1927, quoted in George Kennan, "Excerpts from *Telegraphic Message from Moscow of February 22, 1946*."
http://academic.brooklyn.cuny.edu/history/johnson/longtelegram.htm

The **Cold War**, which followed the Second World War, was an all-out political, economic, and social struggle between the Soviet Union and the United States: they both wanted victory over not only each other, but also over other countries around the world. Understanding the relationship between these two powerful countries will help you answer the question ***To what extent is resistance to liberalism justified?***

In this chapter we will first look at the political relations between countries with conflicting ideologies, focusing on the United States and the Soviet Union. Then, we will look at the impacts of these conflicts among other countries and in the lives of citizens around the world. As you read this chapter, think about Stalin's prediction and ask yourself to what extent it was correct and what other international tensions have arisen because of competing ideologies.

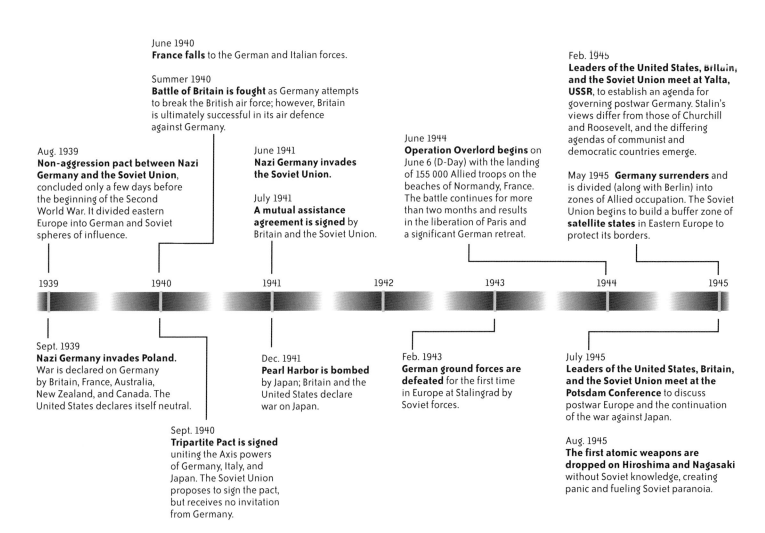

June 1940
France falls to the German and Italian forces.

Summer 1940
Battle of Britain is fought as Germany attempts to break the British air force; however, Britain is ultimately successful in its air defence against Germany.

Aug. 1939
Non-aggression pact between Nazi Germany and the Soviet Union, concluded only a few days before the beginning of the Second World War. It divided eastern Europe into German and Soviet spheres of influence.

June 1941
Nazi Germany invades the Soviet Union.

July 1941
A mutual assistance agreement is signed by Britain and the Soviet Union.

June 1944
Operation Overlord begins on June 6 (D-Day) with the landing of 155 000 Allied troops on the beaches of Normandy, France. The battle continues for more than two months and results in the liberation of Paris and a significant German retreat.

Feb. 1945
Leaders of the United States, Britain, and the Soviet Union meet at Yalta, USSR, to establish an agenda for governing postwar Germany. Stalin's views differ from those of Churchill and Roosevelt, and the differing agendas of communist and democratic countries emerge.

May 1945 Germany surrenders and is divided (along with Berlin) into zones of Allied occupation. The Soviet Union begins to build a buffer zone of **satellite states** in Eastern Europe to protect its borders.

1939   1940   1941   1942   1943   1944   1945

Sept. 1939
Nazi Germany invades Poland. War is declared on Germany by Britain, France, Australia, New Zealand, and Canada. The United States declares itself neutral.

Dec. 1941
Pearl Harbor is bombed by Japan; Britain and the United States declare war on Japan.

Feb. 1943
German ground forces are defeated for the first time in Europe at Stalingrad by Soviet forces.

July 1945
Leaders of the United States, Britain, and the Soviet Union meet at the Potsdam Conference to discuss postwar Europe and the continuation of the war against Japan.

Sept. 1940
Tripartite Pact is signed uniting the Axis powers of Germany, Italy, and Japan. The Soviet Union proposes to sign the pact, but receives no invitation from Germany.

Aug. 1945
The first atomic weapons are dropped on Hiroshima and Nagasaki without Soviet knowledge, creating panic and fueling Soviet paranoia.

Figure 7-3 ▲

This timeline illustrates some of the key events of the Second World War in Europe. Notice some of the shifting alliances that occur. To What extent are these shifting alliances based on ideology?

Yalta

In February 1945, the Allied forces could see that the Second World War would soon end and the "Big Three" met at Yalta (on the Black Sea) to plan both their remaining wartime actions and the future for postwar Europe. One key task for the leaders meeting at Yalta (Roosevelt, Stalin, and Churchill) was, essentially, to re-draw the map of Europe. Their decisions would have implications for many years to come.

The Yalta Accords

A key principle agreed to at Yalta was that, after the war, European countries would be able to have free elections and decide their own futures.

The Premier of the Union of Soviet Socialist Republics, the Prime Minister of the United Kingdom and the President of the United States of America have consulted with each other in the common interests of the peoples of their countries and those of liberated Europe. They jointly declare their mutual agreement to concert during the temporary period of instability in liberated Europe the policies of their three Governments in assisting the peoples liberated from the domination of Nazi Germany and the people of the former Axis satellite states of Europe to solve by democratic means their pressing political and economic problems.

The establishment of order in Europe and the rebuilding of national economic life must be achieved by processes which will enable the liberated peoples to destroy the last vestiges of Nazism and Fascism and to create democratic institutions of their own choice. This is a principle of the Atlantic Charter—the right of all peoples to choose the form of government under which they will live—the restoration of sovereign rights and self-government to those peoples who have been forcibly deprived of them by the aggressor nations.

To foster the conditions in which the liberated peoples may exercise these rights, the three governments will jointly assist the people in any European liberated state or former Axis satellite state in Europe where, in their judgment, conditions require,

(a) to establish conditions of internal peace;

(b) to carry out emergency relief measures for the relief of distressed peoples;

(c) to form interim governmental authorities broadly representative of all democratic elements in the population and pledged to the earliest possible establishment through free elections of Governments responsive to the will of the people; and

(d) to facilitate where necessary the holding of such elections.

—The Yalta Accords, "Part II: Declaration on Liberated Europe," February 11, 1945, quoted in Richard Sakwa, *The Rise and Fall of the Soviet Union*, 1917–1991 (New York: Routledge, 1999), p. 280.

1 Based on this declaration, what choices do you think European countries would make through participation in democratic elections? Why?

2 If any one of the Big Three reneged on any part of this agreement, what impact on international relations would you expect?

After Yalta: The Cold War

Figure 7-4 ▶

This map of Europe illustrates the ideological divisions in Europe following the Second World War. The red-striped countries are Soviet-influenced countries that later aligned themselves militarily with the USSR by signing the Warsaw Pact (1955). How might Soviet occupation of significant areas of eastern Europe in the last months of the Second World War impact the decisions made?

Whether it was ideology or simply the desire for economic and political power that drove the United States and the Soviet Union is open for debate; regardless, the Cold War between the two superpowers caused long-term global tension and disharmony. Numerous events, agreements, and conflicts resulted in the growing tensions among the United States and the Soviet Union and their respective allies. The following are a few examples:

- The postwar treatment of Germany was a major sticking point. The Soviet Union wanted reparations and a weakened Germany as its neighbour; however, the Allies decided that a renewed Western European economy depended on a healthy German economy and a unified Germany.

- US aid to postwar Europe was offered to all European countries but had "strings attached," such as conditions related to economic policies. The Soviet leadership considered this "dollar imperialism" and refused the aid despite the devastation the war had caused in the Soviet Union and its satellite countries, including 25 million homeless Soviet citizens.

- Stalinization began in 1945 with the intention of installing communism in all states liberated from Nazi Germany by the Soviet Union (Bulgaria, Romania, Poland, Hungary, Czechoslovakia, East Germany, Estonia, Latvia, and Lithuania). Ultimately, Stalin aimed for "proletarian internationalism": worldwide communism. Albania, which had declared itself communist at the end of the war, voluntarily allied itself with the Soviet Union.

- Hungary's move toward independence and increased freedoms for its citizens in 1956 followed a denunciation of Stalin by the new Soviet leader, Nikita Khrushchev. This short-lived anti-communist revolution in one of the Soviet Union's satellite states was brutally crushed by the Soviet army.

- When the Second World War was over, the United States and the Soviet Union no longer had common enemies (Nazi Germany and Imperial Japan) to fight. They entered into a period of ideological conflict with each other.

The devastation of Europe and Asia in 1945 left two states—the United States and the Soviet Union—with inordinate influence on the future course of international affairs. These two countries emerged from the Second World War stronger than they were before they entered it. They had mobilized their vast resources for maximum effect: building more weapons and placing more citizens under arms than ever before in either country's history. They had also expanded their territorial control and influence far beyond previous limits. Because of their great influence around the world and economic and military strengths, the United States and the Soviet Union were considered **superpowers**.

In July 1945, when American president Harry Truman and Soviet premier Joseph Stalin met with British prime minister Winston Churchill and his successor Clement Attlee in Potsdam, Germany, most observers recognized that the decisions of these men would determine the future course of world history. As these leaders agreed on such things as reparations to be made and the restructuring of Germany, the undercurrent of the conference was the political and economic division emerging between communist and democratic countries. The British and American leaders were concerned about the extent and growth of Soviet influence, and the Soviets, resentful of the devastating losses they experienced during the war, were concerned with building their influence to protect their borders. During the conference, the leaders warned Japan to surrender or face the consequences, which Truman knew secretly to be the unleashing of a "powerful new weapon," the atomic bomb. Truman did not share his government's plans for a nuclear

PAUSE AND REFLECT

The February 1945 conference was held at Yalta because Stalin insisted that he would go no farther west for the meeting. In your opinion, which countries would have been affected the most by the decisions made at Yalta in 1945? During this time, to what extent did ideology shape the future of these countries?

attack on Japan with the Soviets before bombing Hiroshima and Nagasaki in the week after the conference.

Truman and Stalin sought to avoid another war, but they also recognized each other as rivals for domination over Europe and Asia. Each side feared that the other would convert the resources of the new areas under his control into war-fighting capabilities. Both sides feared a loss of access to traditional markets. Most significantly, both sides feared that the other would win the "war of ideas," convincing the devastated populations of Europe and Asia that liberal capitalism on the one hand, or communism on the other, was the only legitimate system of governance. Ideological conflict between the United States and the Soviet Union, long pre-dating 1945, made the Cold War a contest between worldviews that extended beyond weapons, territory, and economics. The two countries could agree on various measures for geopolitical stability, but their ideological clash made a permanent settlement almost inconceivable.

Expansionism and Containment

In 1927, Stalin referred to the centres "drawing" other countries to themselves, but in fact the superpowers of the Cold War tried to reach out, or expand. **Expansionism**—the attempt to enlarge territorial and ideological influence beyond a country's borders and allies—was what both the Soviet Union and the United States would practise until the end of the Cold War.

At the end of the Second World War, the United States and the Soviet Union began to establish their **spheres of influence** in Europe. Spheres of influence are the territories and countries over which a powerful country dominates. The countries that the western Allies had liberated from Nazi Germany fell under the American sphere of influence, and the countries that the Soviet Union had liberated fell under the Soviet sphere of influence. Each of the superpowers responded to its fears with **containment**: the attempt to thwart another country's expansionism through means other than direct warfare.

Stalin saw postwar Soviet expansionism not only as a way to "command the world economy" (as he had predicted in 1927), but also for specific historical and geographical reasons:

- Stalin wanted to keep Germany divided—a strong, unified Germany had gone to war with Russia twice in the first decades of the 20th century. When the United States, Britain, and France pushed to unify the German zones to help the general economic recovery of Europe, Stalin opposed the idea.
- Stalin wanted to maintain or expand Soviet influence to surrounding countries, including Finland, Poland, and Romania, to create a buffer zone for the Soviet Union's safety.

Expansionism

Looking to the events of the Second World War and to its geography, the Soviet Union asserted its own reasons for expanding its sphere of influence. The United States, however, framed its expansionism in terms of providing other countries with the freedom to choose sides, of defending their freedom to choose a governing ideology. These reasons for extending American influence were described in the Truman Doctrine of 1947, in which President Truman called upon the United States to "support free peoples who are resisting attempted subjugation by armed minorities or by outside pressures." (Source: Harry S. Truman, address before a joint session of Congress, March 12, 1947, http://avalon.law.yale.edu/20th_century/trudoc.asp.) Soviet and American perspectives on expansionism are depicted in the following three quotations.

As a result of the German invasion, the Soviet Union has irrevocably lost in battles with the Germans, and also during the German occupation and through the expulsion of Soviet citizens to German slave labor camps, about 7 000 000 people. In other words, the Soviet Union has lost in men several times more than Britain and the United States together…One can ask therefore, what can be surprising in the fact that the Soviet Union, in a desire to ensure its security for the future, tries to achieve that these countries should have governments whose relations to the Soviet Union are loyal? How can one, without having lost one's reason, qualify these peaceful aspirations of the Soviet Union as "expansionist tendencies" of our Government?

—Joseph Stalin's reply to Churchill, 1946.
Modern History Sourcebook, Fordham University.
http://www.fordham.edu/halsall/mod/1946stalin.html

Reflecting the imperialistic tendency of American monopoly capital, US foreign policy has been characterized in the postwar period by a desire for world domination. *This is the real meaning of repeated statements by President Truman and other representatives of American ruling circles that the US has a right to world leadership. All the forces of American diplomacy, the Army, Navy, and Air Force, industry, and science have been placed at the service of this policy. With this objective in mind broad plans for expansion have been developed, to be realized both diplomatically and through the creation of a system of naval and air bases far from the US, an arms race, and the creation of newer and newer weapons...*

—N. Novikov (Soviet Ambassador to the United States),
telegram to the Soviet Leadership, September 27, 1946.
Cold War International History Project.
http://www.wilsoncenter.org/index.cfm?topic_id=1409&
fuseaction=va2.document&identifier=952E8C7F-423B-763D-
D5662C42501C9BEA&sort=Collection&item=US-Soviet%20Relations
www.cwihp.org

At the present moment in world history nearly every nation must choose between alternative ways of life. The choice is too often not a free one. One way of life is based upon the will of the majority, and is distinguished by free institutions, representative government, free elections, guarantees of individual liberty, freedom of speech and religion, and freedom from political oppression. The second way of life is based upon the will of a minority forcibly imposed upon the majority. It relies upon terror and oppression, a controlled press and radio, fixed elections, and the suppression of personal freedoms. I believe that it must be the policy of the United States to support free peoples who are resisting attempted subjugation by armed minorities or by outside pressures. I believe that we must assist free peoples to work out their own destinies in their own way. I believe that our help should be primarily through economic stability and orderly political process.

—**Harry S. Truman, address before a joint session of Congress, March 12, 1947.**

http://avalon.law.yale.edu/20th_century/trudoc.asp

◣◗ **PAUSE AND REFLECT**

How could the competing viewpoints of Stalin, Novikov, and Truman and the superpowers' competing ideologies create tension in international relations? To what extent was ideology influencing their decision making and people's lives?

Truman Doctrine and Containment

In postwar Europe—and around the world—countries were making exactly the choices that Truman described. Truman wanted to stop Soviet expansionism to contain the communist influence and, rather than resorting to a **hot war** (which includes troops and battles in direct conflict), the United States fought its ideological conflict by creating alliances and giving aid, among other methods. For example, the United States responded with $400 million in aid when the postwar Greek and Turkish governments asked for support in defeating the appeal of communism in their countries. The biggest aid plan, however, was the Marshall Plan, a $13-billion plan to help the recovery of countries ravaged by war in Europe. This offer was for all countries of Europe, communist or democratic. The $13-billion Marshall Plan would be over $100 billion in today's currency.

Over the lifespan of the Marshall Plan (1947–1952), 17 countries in Europe received funds and technical expertise from the United States. Responses from Western Europe included the following:

Churchill's words won the war, Marshall's words won the peace.

—**Dirk Stikker, Foreign Minister, The Netherlands, 1948–1952**

Figure 7-5 ▲

What beliefs and values are represented in this cartoon?

The Marshall speech…was greeted as a great act of statesmanship and as an expression of what we felt was genuine idealism on the part of the United States.

—Halvard Lange, Minister of Foreign Affairs, Norway, 1946–1965
Source: Both quotations from "The Marshall Plan: Rebuilding Europe."
US Department of State International Information Programs.
http://usinfo.state.gov/products/pubs/marshallplan/marshall.htm

The Soviet satellite states rejected Marshall Plan aid due to the diplomatic and political pressure applied by the United States. The Americans required that all recipients of the aid submit to a thorough economic assessment and participate in a unified European economy, conditions that were incompatible with Soviet ideology. Regardless, the offer of aid to the Soviet Union may have been a hollow gesture by the Americans, as it was questionable that the American Congress would approve large sums of aid for countries under the influence of a communist power. As an alternative, the Soviets proposed their own aid package, the Molotov Plan, for Eastern European countries under its influence. The Molotov Plan involved bilateral trade agreements that helped to consolidate the economies of socialist countries such as Poland, Czechoslovakia, East Germany, Hungary, Bulgaria, and Romania, and to solidify the Soviet presence in Europe.

PAUSE AND REFLECT

Using the ideas and quotations presented in this section, determine which perspectives and which rationale would lead the United States to offer aid to all countries, including communist countries.

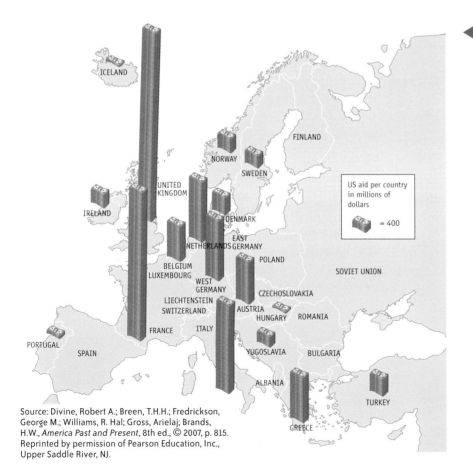

Source: Divine, Robert A.; Breen, T.H.H.; Fredrickson, George M.; Williams, R. Hal; Gross, Arielaj; Brands, H.W., *America Past and Present*, 8th ed., © 2007, p. 815. Reprinted by permission of Pearson Education, Inc., Upper Saddle River, NJ.

◀ **Figure 7-6**

Over 50 years after the Marshall Plan was initiated, the US National Center for Policy Analysis offered the following comments:

Although there is no doubt about the political success of the Marshall Plan, recent economic analyses are more skeptical about its economic impact. Economists today place far more weight on the economic reforms initiated by the Marshall Plan, and much less on the actual aid itself…It is important to remember that Marshall Plan aid was very conditional. Recipients had to agree to balance their budgets, stop inflation and stabilize their exchange rates at realistic levels. They were also encouraged to decontrol prices, eliminate trade restrictions and resist nationalization of industry. In short, the Marshall Plan imposed free market policies on Western Europe in return for aid. This is the reason why the Soviet Union rejected the Marshall Plan for itself and its allies in Eastern Europe.

—National Center for Policy Analysis Idea House, "Marshall Plan: Freer Markets Restored Europe," June 2, 1997. http://www.ncpa.org/pd/pdint140.html

Berlin 1945–1949

When postwar Germany was divided in 1945 into four zones of occupation, the capital was also divided. Berlin consisted of American, English, French, and Soviet sectors but fell 176 kilometres within the Soviet zone of Germany. The Soviets wanted a weaker Germany and a buffer zone between the capitalist West and the communist East. Of the Western Allies, the Americans and British particularly wanted a strong German economy in a revitalized European economy. The Soviets would not allow their zone and sector of occupation to be reunified with the rest of Berlin, thus the result was Bizonia (West Germany, combining the American, English, and French zones) and East Germany, and within communist East Germany, the pocket of Western influence and capitalism, West Berlin.

The Americans' Marshall Plan was eagerly accepted in the western zones of occupation but was rejected by German authorities in the Soviet zone of occupation. In 1948, a new currency called the Deutsche Mark was introduced in Bizonia to replace the occupation currency. Deutsche Marks were also taken into West Berlin where they quickly became the preferred currency. Stalin saw this revitalized West Germany as a threat to the Soviet Union and West Berlin as an unwelcome, capitalist influence in the midst of Eastern communism.

On June 24, 1948, Stalin blocked all road, rail, and canal transportation to West Berlin. The 2.1 million West Berliners were then cut off from all supplies. American General Lucius D. Clay summarized the American attitude toward the city of Berlin: "We are convinced that our remaining in Berlin is essential to our prestige in Germany and in Europe. Whether for good or bad, it has become a symbol of the American intent." Years later, US Secretary of State Warren Christopher stated the following:

In the spring of 1948, Stalin began his campaign to force the Allied powers from Berlin. Hoping to bring the city under communist control, he tried to break the spirit of its people. On June 24, 1948, he imposed a blockade on Berlin. What Stalin failed to judge, however, was the will of the Berliners to defy intimidation, and the resolve of the Allied forces to see them through.

—Warren Christopher, "A tribute to the Berlin airlift,"
US Department of State Dispatch, September 12, 1994.

The Western response was to fly in supplies to the West Berliners. (Agreements made in 1945 did not include ground access to Berlin but did include air access.) Clay spoke with Berlin mayor Ernst Reuter, who assured Clay that Berliners were willing to sacrifice and co-operate with the Allied forces to make the airlift work. The Americans and the British assessed their resources (airplanes, carrying capacity, crews, airports, and so on) and other logistical details at the same time they evaluated the supplies that would be needed. They thought the airlift would last for days or weeks and thus calculated what supplies were needed to meet a set caloric intake per West Berliner per day (including meat, fish, cheese, grains, evaporated milk and whole milk, dehydrated potatoes and other vegetables, coffee, sugar, yeast for baking, and salt).

After the first few weeks of the airlift, the East Berlin newspapers described the Berlin airlift as "the futile attempts of the Americans to save face and to maintain their untenable position in Berlin." (Source: C.V. Glines, "Fifty years ago, a massive airlift into Berlin showed the Soviets that a post-WWII blockade would not work." Indiana Military Organization, http://www.indianamilitary.org/ATTERBURYAAF/History/BerlinAirlift.html.) However, the airlift continued. With the approach of winter, coal and gasoline had to be added to the list of supplies, landing strips were improved, and a new strip was built. The United States and Britain led the effort, with France initially opting out of what it considered a lost cause but eventually joining as well. When it joined, France could offer only its oldest cargo planes as other French military resources were being used in French colonial Indochina (Cambodia, Laos, and Vietnam).

At the height of the Berlin airlift, flights were landing in West Berlin at the rate of one every three minutes. Increasing efficiency was an ongoing concern, and refinements were made to the operations, the American "Operation Vittles" and the British "Operation Plainfare." For example, the flight crews were not allowed to leave their planes in Berlin and crews of local Berliners unloaded the planes as quickly as possible. In September, communists blocked the city elections and Mayor Ernst Reuter spoke before a crowd of Berlin protesters to plead for support: "You peoples of the world. You people of America, of England, of France, look on this city, and recognize that this city, this people must not be abandoned—cannot be abandoned!" (Source: Ernst Reuter, quoted in *The American Experience*, "The Berlin Airlift," PBS, first broadcast January 29, 2007: transcript at http://www.pbs.org/wgbh/amex/airlift/filmmore/pt.html.)

Over a period of 11 months, the American, British, and French forces flew all food and all coal and gasoline needed by the 2.1 million Berliners in a total of 277 804 flights. During the airlift, 17 US and 8 British planes crashed. The official number of casualties was 101. On May 12, 1949, Stalin finally lifted the blockade.

 Figure 7-7 ▼

A 1960s East German poster about the Berlin airlift. Translation: "Air Bridge to West Berlin—a peace-threatening provocation of the Western imperialist powers."

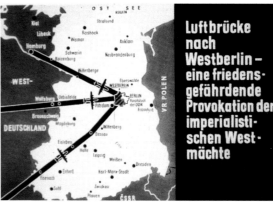

Borders: Physical Boundaries between Ideologies

The physical borders that separated Soviet communist-bloc countries and democratic capitalist countries became increasingly important to

Figure 7-8 ▲

This photo shows Berliners watching an American C-54 land at Templehof Airport in 1948. During the airlift, US pilot Gail Halvorsen started an effort that became known as Operation Little Vittles. After talking with a crowd of children at a Berlin airport, he gave them two sticks of gum and offered to drop some more. He did so by attaching handkerchief parachutes to candy packages. Other pilots joined in, the "operation" became public, candy companies joined in, and American children sent their own candy to help out. Overall, it was considered a major, although initially unplanned, propaganda success.

Figure 7-9 ▶

This map shows the division of Berlin and the wall that was constructed to separate the Soviet sector from the Western sectors of the city.

both Americans and their allies and the Soviet Union. These borders served to divide people by ideological differences, as well as political and economic differences. In a now-divided Germany, where many countries shared an influence, the importance of the borders increased as tensions grew between the superpowers. But what if those who lived on one side or the other of the iron curtain decided to change their ideological points of view? Due to a history of invasion, the Soviets had long been sensitive to the security of their borders, and this increased exponentially with the events of the Second World War. Countries that shared a border with the Soviet Union were under particular pressure to maintain strong political and economic ties with the Soviets, and the Soviets were not receptive to any encroachment of capitalism or democracy.

Fortifying the Border: The Berlin Wall

Because the divided city of Berlin was located in the middle of East German territory, as tensions mounted between the Americans and the Soviets, the city became a hotbed of Cold War tension. At midnight on August 12, 1961, East German troops locked down the border between East Germany and West Berlin, essentially surrounding the city. They tore up the streets and installed barbed wire and fences. From the perspective of the Western powers, the main purpose of this border closure was to stop the flow of East Germans from the Soviet-dominated East Germany into West Berlin where they had access to NATO protection and economic opportunity. The East German government, however, claimed that the wall was meant to protect East Germany from Western aggression. A second fence was later built further inside East German territory, parallel to the original, creating a no man's land between the two walls known as the death strip. The original outer wire

fence was replaced with a concrete wall with watchtowers, bunkers, and trenches. West Berlin became an island of Western values and beliefs within a sea of Soviet-dominated communism.

Breaking Free of the Iron Curtain

Hungary: Revolution of 1956

In fall of 1956, the Hungarian people revolted against their Stalinist government, forming militias and battling the state police and Soviet troops. In less than two weeks, a new Hungarian government was formed, the state police were disbanded, and the first steps were taken toward creating a democratic state. In early November, however, Soviet forces invaded Hungary with a massive show of force, defeated the newly independent country, reversed the changes that came from the revolution and restored a pro-Soviet government. Soviet power in Central Europe was strengthened, and a clear message of the irreversibility of communism in the sphere of Soviet influence was sent around the world.

Czechoslovak Socialist Republic: Prague, Spring 1968

On January 5, 1968, reformist Alexander Dubcek came to power in the Czechoslovak Socialist Republic (CSSR). By April he had granted additional rights and freedoms to its citizens, loosening restrictions on the media, speech, and travel, and limited the powers of the secret police. Dubcek's plan for reformation included a 10-year transition toward democratic elections, emphasized the importance of maintaining good relations with Western countries, and allowed for the possibility of a multiple-party government. Reaction to these reforms by the communist-bloc countries grew increasingly critical, and the Soviets launched talks with the Czechoslovakian government to reach an understanding about the scope and nature of the country's reforms. Ultimately, these talks failed due to division among members of the Czechoslovakian government, and on the night of August 20, 1968, Eastern Bloc armies from four Warsaw Pact countries—the Soviet Union, Bulgaria, Poland, and Hungary—invaded and occupied the CSSR. Within a year, Dubcek's reforms had been reversed.

Yugoslavia: Tito's Defiance

After the Second World War, Yugoslavia elected a communist government and quickly aligned itself with the Soviet Union. However, despite being a member of the communist party, Yugoslavian leader Josip Tito soon began to distance his country from the Soviet Union. Tito ultimately became the first (and only) socialist leader to defy Stalin and reject Soviet demands for absolute loyalty to the Soviet Union. In April 1955, Yugoslavia, under Tito's leadership, became a founding

Figure 7-10 ▲

This map appeared in *Time* magazine on March 10, 1952. How do you think the Soviet Union viewed the strategic importance of those countries with which it shared a border?

member of the Non-Aligned Movement, an international organization of states who consider themselves not formally aligned with or against any major power bloc. Over the years, Tito adopted a more liberal government and fostered relationships with Western countries, creating a political, economic, and ideological division between Yugoslavia and the Soviet Union. This was possible for Yugoslavia and not for other Warsaw Pact countries such as Hungary or the CSSR in part because of its geography: it did not share a border with the Soviet Union.

SKILL PATH

Examining the Interrelationship of Geography and Ideology

A state's political power and actions must be considered within the context of its geopolitical realities: geographic location and features (including resources within and outside of its borders), human geography and interactions, ideological beliefs and values, the political interpretation of those ideologies, and foreign policy.

Your Task: Use the examples from the section "Borders: Physical Boundaries between Ideologies" on pages 245–246 to create a visual representation of how the relationship between geography and ideology can influence international relations. For example, create a map, photo essay, or mixed-media product to illustrate how factors such as geographic location, access to resources, and diversity of people can impact the foreign policy of a nation-state.

As you examine the relationship between geography and ideology in a particular country or region, consider the following:
- geographic features
- natural resources
- population and demographics
- beliefs and values
- neighbouring countries

Afterwards, use the Questions to Guide You to guide an independent or group reflection on the relationship between geography and ideology.

Questions to Guide You

1. With reference to the maps and information provided in the chapter, why was the geographic location of the countries and cities noted important to both the Soviet Union and the United States?

2. Based on the maps provided in the section "Borders: Physical Boundaries between Ideologies" on pages 245–246, what impact do geography, ideology, and a country's history have on a country's foreign policy? Based on the information provided in this exercise, and that regarding the Soviet Union in "Borders: Physical Boundaries between Ideologies" what evidence is there that citizens are affected?

3. How did the location of these countries and their cities affect the respective foreign policies of the Soviet Union and the United States? To what extent is the location of a nation-state an important aspect of its political or economic decision making?

Alignment

In the interests of security, some countries aligned themselves with one superpower or the other. For example, Canada and Great Britain were aligned with the United States, although they did differ on some issues.

Figure 7-11 ▼

Compare these maps. What evidence do you see of expansionism and alignment?

1959

■ USA and its allies	■ Soviet Union and its allies
■ American influence	■ Soviet influence
■ Allied colonies	

1982

■ USA and its allies	□ French military assistance
■ American military assistance	■ Soviet Union and its allies
□ Other Western military assistance	■ Soviet military assistance
■ French military presence	

Figure 7-12 ▲

US president John F. Kennedy, Indonesian president Sukarno, and US vice-president Lyndon B. Johnson. Sukarno tried to protect Indonesia's economy from foreign businesses and to redistribute wealth, working as a nationalist but closely with communist party members. In 1965, the country's General Suharto began to seize power with the support of the US CIA. After Suharto's troops hunted down leftists on their shooting lists, the new Suharto government opened the country for substantial foreign investment.

In other cases, the superpowers influenced or forced countries to choose one ideological side or the other. For example, after the Second World War, the first major covert operation of the US Central Intelligence Agency (CIA) was to influence the Italian election so that a communist-socialist coalition would not win. In countries such as Turkey and Greece, economic aid tipped the balance of support toward the United States. Postwar Czechoslovakia was interested in accepting Marshall Plan aid but the Soviet Union did not allow it to do so. The economic, political, and security benefits of **alignment** encouraged many to choose a side.

Non-Alignment and the Bandung Conference

Rather than following the ideologies of Soviet communism or American capitalism, some countries chose, or tried to choose, their own entirely different ideologies. As the Cold War continued into the 1950s, many countries that had had a long history of European imperialism wanted to step away from the superpower spheres of influence and determine their own futures. In a sense, the Bandung Conference, held in Java, Indonesia, in April 1955, was a direct result of the ideological conflict between the superpowers. At this conference, representatives from 29 African and Asian countries met to promote economic and cultural co-operation and oppose the colonial and imperialist intentions of the superpowers.

At the conference, India's Prime Minister Jawaharlal Nehru declared the following:

If we have to stand alone, we will stand by ourselves, whatever happens (and India has stood alone without any aid against a mighty Empire, the British Empire) and we propose to face all consequences…We do not agree with the communist teachings, we do not agree with the anti-communist teachings, because they are both based on wrong principles.

—Jawaharlal Nehru, quoted in G.M. Kahin,
***The Asian-African Conference* (New York: Cornell University Press, 1956), pp. 64–72.**

In a similar vein, Indonesian President Sukarno said the following:

All of us, I am certain, are united by more important things than those which superficially divide us. We are united, for instance, by a common detestation of colonialism in whatever form it appears. We are united by a common detestation of racialism. And we are united by a common determination to preserve and stabilize peace in the world…Make the "Live and let live" principle and the "Unity in Diversity" motto [be] the unifying force which brings us all together—to seek in friendly, uninhibited discussion, ways and means by which each of us can live his own life, and let others live their own lives, in their own way, in harmony, and in peace.

—Sukarno, quoted in *Africa-Asia Speaks from Bandung*,
(Djakarta: Indonesian Ministry of Foreign Affairs, 1955), pp. 19–29.
Modern History Sourcebook, Fordham University.
http://www.fordham.edu/halsall/mod/1955sukarno-bandong.html

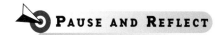

PAUSE AND REFLECT

Based on the two speech excerpts, what were some of the beliefs and values explored and expressed at the conference? How might these be in conflict with those of the superpowers?

The Bandung Conference was the beginning of the Non-Aligned Movement (NAM), a movement that gained influence during the Cold War. From the Bandung Conference emerged the concept of the "Third World": countries that had gained independence from colonialism after the Second World War, which were in the process of industrializing and were committed to choosing their international involvements for themselves. (Note: It is no longer appropriate to refer to these countries as the "Third World." The accepted term is "developing world.") These countries wanted to follow a policy of **non-alignment** with the United States and its allies (the "First World") and the Soviet Union and its allies (the "Second World").

In 1961 in Belgrade, Yugoslavia, leaders from Ghana, Egypt, India, Indonesia, and Yugoslavia officially began the NAM. Despite the NAM's aims for neutrality, Third World countries were pursued by the Soviet Union and the United States, who wanted to include as many countries under their ideological umbrellas as possible. Countries involved with the NAM sought unsuccessfully to use their membership in the United Nations to challenge the hegemony of the United States and the Soviet Union.

Deterrence

Deterrence is a method of cold war, rather than a method of hot war. It involves the building up of one's capacity to fight such that neither opponent will fight because of the expected outcomes. After the 1945 bombings of Hiroshima and Nagasaki and the development of nuclear weapons by the Soviets in 1949, the governments of the world knew that a hot war between the superpowers would mean a nuclear war, one that would kill not only the opponents but also the population of the entire planet. The term for this situation of an unwinnable, nuclear war is **mutually assured destruction (MAD)**. MAD deters each side from entering into direct conflict; hence the concept of "deterrence". Weapons of mass destruction (WMDs) have been key issues in more recent international conflicts, such as those between the United States and North Korea, the United States and Iraq, and the United States and Iran.

In this 1967 speech, Robert McNamara, the US Secretary of Defense, describes mutual deterrence:

...No sane citizen, political leader or nation wants thermonuclear war. But merely not wanting it is not enough. We must understand the differences among actions which increase its risks, those which reduce them and those which, while costly, have little influence one way or another...

One must begin with precise definitions. The cornerstone of our strategic policy continues to be to deter nuclear attack upon the United States or its allies. We do this by maintaining a highly reliable ability to inflict unacceptable damage upon any single aggressor or combination of aggressors at any time during the course of a strategic nuclear exchange, even after absorbing a surprise first strike. This can be defined as our assured-destruction capability.

It is important to understand that mutually assured destruction is the very essence of the whole deterrence concept. We must possess an actual assured-destruction capability, and that capability also must be credible. The point is that a potential aggressor must believe that our assured-destruction capability is in fact actual, and that our will to use it in retaliation to an attack is in fact unwavering. The conclusion, then, is clear: if the United States is to deter a nuclear attack in itself or its allies, it must possess an actual and a credible assured-destruction capability...

Now what about the Soviet Union? Does it today possess a powerful nuclear arsenal? The answer is that it does. Does it possess a first-strike capability against the United States? The answer is that it does not. Can the Soviet Union in the foreseeable future acquire such a first-strike capability against the United States? The answer is that it cannot. It cannot because we are determined to remain fully alert and we will never permit our own assured-destruction capability to drop to a point at which a Soviet first-strike capability is even remotely feasible.

Is the Soviet Union seriously attempting to acquire a first-strike capability against the United States? Although this is a question we cannot answer with absolute certainty, we believe the answer is no. In any event, the question itself is—in a sense—irrelevant: for the United States will maintain and, where necessary strengthen its retaliatory forces so that, whatever the Soviet Union's intentions or actions, we will continue to have an assured-destruction capability vis a vis their society.

—Robert McNamara, September 18, 1967, quoted in "Cold War," CNN Perspectives Series.

http://edition.cnn.com/SPECIALS/cold.war/episodes/
12/documents/mcnamara.deterrence/

Canada in the Cold War

Because of Canada's historical ties to Great Britain, and its shared border with the United States, there was never any doubt as to Canada playing a role in the Cold War. In 1949, Canada was a founding member of the North Atlantic Treaty Organization (NATO), a military alliance designed to defend member countries against attack from the Soviet Union and its allies. Canada also contributed military forces to the defence of South Korea from 1950 to 1953, helping to push back the invading communist forces of North Korea. It was instrumental in implementing a United Nations military force for the purposes of peacekeeping. In fact, peacekeeping was a Canadian idea, first proposed by Prime Minister Mackenzie King in 1945. The idea was not implemented, however, until 1956, during the Suez Crisis—a tense showdown over control of the Suez Canal, with Britain, France, and Israel facing off against Egypt (supported by the Soviet Union). Finally, Canada and the United States cooperated in building a united air defence system along Canada's northern shores. The North American Aerospace Defence Command (NORAD) consisted of the Distant Early Warning Line (the DEW Line), which would give an early warning to the United States of incoming missiles from the Soviet Union. Missile bases and nuclear-armed missiles were also part of the plan, but this has always been a matter of some tension in Canada.

France's Dissuasion Policy

Prior to the Second World War, France was one of the world's leaders in nuclear technology research, influenced first by the breakthrough research of Pierre and Marie Curie and later by the research of their daughter and son-in-law, Irène Joliot-Curie and Frédéric Joliot-Curie, who won the 1935 Nobel Prize for Chemistry.

After the Second World War, France began developing nuclear weapons independently of the United States and Britain, which it used as a deterrent to any countries who might consider mounting an attack on French soil. This policy was called **dissuasion**, the French word for *deterrence*. It differed, however, from the Cold War deterrence policy of the United States and the Soviet Union; France was not developing weapons based on the intimidation of a specific adversary—the policy was designed as a defence from the possibility of attack by any other country.

During the late 1940s, France was excluded from many of the nuclear activities of the United States, Britain, and Canada, due in part to the fact that its High Commissioner for Atomic Energy, Frédéric Joliot-Curie, was an outspoken communist. In addition, France sought to exercise some degree of sovereignty from what it saw as a US-dominated North Atlantic Treaty Organization. Indeed, France withdrew its military participation from NATO in 1966.

PAUSE AND REFLECT

Why do you think France thought it was necessary to develop nuclear weapons as part of its foreign policy?

During the early 1950s, deposits of uranium were discovered in France, providing the country with large quantities of the essential material needed for nuclear weapons and thus allowing France to develop and expand its nuclear program. Through the 1960s and into the 1990s, France conducted numerous nuclear tests. In the 1990s, nuclear arms were still a key component of France's national defence strategy. The French White Paper on National Defence and Security of 1994 says the following:

Nuclear deterrence remains an essential concept of national security. It is the ultimate guarantee of the security and independence of France. The sole purpose of the nuclear deterrent is to prevent any State-originating aggression against the vital interests of the nation wherever it may come from and in whatever shape or form.

—**Source: Présidence de la République, French White Paper on Defense and National Security (Paris, 2008), p. 2, quoted in US Departments of Energy and Defense, *National Security and Nuclear Weapons in the 21st Century*, September 2008, p. 9.**
http://www.defenselink.mil/news/nuclearweaponspolicy.pdf

In the 2000s, France refocused its policy to concentrate on using the threat of nuclear strikes to deter terrorist attacks.

Brinkmanship

Expansionism, containment, and deterrence all came to a head in the Cuban Missile Crisis—a classic example of brinkmanship. **Brinkmanship** is the attempt to push a dangerous situation as far as possible without conceding anything to your opponent.

Fulgencio Batista, who had strong ties to Mafia groups in the United States, was a US-supported dictator who had taken control of the Cuban government by staging a military coup. Batista was a corrupt, pro-capitalist military ruler whose goal was to turn Cuba into the "Latin Las Vegas"—a playground for the wealthy. The Cuban poor, however, had long been ignored and social unrest grew during Batista's regime. From late 1956 to 1959, Cuban lawyer and nationalist Fidel Castro led a socialist revolution, eventually resulting in the overthrow of Batista's government. To address Cuba's long history of wealthy agricultural landowners and poor, often mistreated workers, Castro signed the First Agrarian Reform soon after gaining power. This reform broke up large landholdings, restricted foreign land ownership, and redistributed land to those who worked it, co-operatives, and the state.

The United States grew wary of Castro's socialist ideas and developing relationship with the Soviet Union, and when Cuba agreed to buy oil from the Soviets, American refineries in Cuba refused to process it. In response, Castro expropriated the American refineries, and diplomatic relations between the United States and Cuba were soon broken. In 1960, President Dwight Eisenhower reduced the quota of sugar imported from Cuba by the United States. Cuba responded by nationalizing $850 million worth of American-owned land and businesses. Although the Cuban government offered compensation for the property taken, the American businesses rejected its offer.

In the years after the revolution, the United States received over one million Cuban exiles and encouraged and orchestrated an attempt by a group of these exiles to re-take the island during the disastrous Bay of Pigs Invasion. The Bay of Pigs Invasion was an attack on Cuban soil perpetrated by Cuban exiles trained and supported by the US military. On April 17, 1961, 1511 members of the Cuban Expeditionary Force landed on the southern coast of Cuba, followed by 177 paratroopers. The fighting, which included air strikes, lasted two days before the invaders were forced to retreat. The invasion failed due in part to poor planning, inadequate support from the US military, and the false assumption that rebels in Cuba would be motivated by the attack to rise against Castro. The failed invasion served to increase the popularity of Castro, to generate greater suspicion and mistrust of the United States, and to solidify Cuba's military, political, and economic relationships with the Soviet Union.

The American government became unwilling to trade with Cuba under Castro and, in 1962, imposed an economic, commercial, and financial embargo. In contrast, the Soviets offered Cuba large amounts of financial aid, developed a strong trade relationship, and helped it modernize and strengthen its military. American president John F. Kennedy, aware that Soviet-supported missile bases were being built in Cuba, and that ships carrying missiles that could be armed with atomic warheads were heading across the Atlantic to Cuba, ordered a naval blockade of Cuba. The world watched as the two superpowers came closer and closer to the brink of war. The threat of nuclear war escalated until a diplomatic breakthrough on October 27, 1962. Kennedy agreed not to invade Cuba and to withdraw American missiles from Turkey. In exchange, the Soviet Union would remove its missiles from Cuba. After Soviet leader Nikita Khrushchev ordered his ships to turn around, US Secretary of State Dean Rusk said, "We were eyeball to eyeball, and the other fellow just blinked." (Source: Dean Rusk, quoted in Stewart Alsop and Charles Bartlett, "In Time of Crisis," *Saturday Evening Post* [December 8, 1962].) Ironically, the Cuban Missile Crisis led to a period of relatively peaceful relations between the Soviets and the Americans, as both superpowers realized how close they had come to mutually assured destruction.

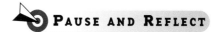

PAUSE AND REFLECT

As you look at the map below, consider why was Cuba perceived as a threat by the United States. Use the Skill Path to think like a geographer about the Cuban Missile Crisis and the positions (geographic and ideological) of Cuba, the United States, and the Soviet Union.

Figure 7-13 ▲

This map was created by the CIA to show the range of missiles being installed in Cuba in 1962.

Figure 7-14 ▶

In September 1959, Soviet leader Nikita Khrushchev visited the United States at the invitation of President Dwight Eisenhower, marking the first time a Soviet leader had set foot on US soil. Seen here (L to R) are US vice-president Richard Nixon and president Dwight Eisenhower, and Soviet premier Nikita Khrushchev.

Figure 7-15 ▼

This timeline highlights some events from the Cold War. Which of these events would lead to increased or decreased tensions? Rank these events in the order of which most lead to an increase or decrease in tensions during this time period.

Détente and Treaties

Because the Cuban Missile Crisis brought the two superpowers to the brink of war, some steps were taken to reduce the tension between the two countries. The cost of the escalating tensions was too great, and the reasons to ease tensions were compelling:

- The Soviet Union was spending billions on the arms race, and the Soviet leadership felt that this was unsustainable.

1963
Hotline
A telephone hotline between the White House and the Kremlin was created to be used in times of emergency. The hotline connected the American president directly to the Soviet premier.

1963
Partial Test Ban Treaty
Signed first by the United States, Britain, and the Soviet Union, this treaty banned the testing of nuclear weapons in the atmosphere, on land, under water, and in outer space. Testing was limited to the underground due to environmental concerns about the effects of the release of nuclear fallout into the atmosphere. These limitations on testing served to slow down the arms race.

1969
Strategic Arms Limitation Talks (SALT)
These talks took place from November to May between the United States and the Soviet Union and resulted in a 1972 agreement to limit the number of missiles acquired, armed, and aimed by the two countries.

1979
Soviet War in Afghanistan Begins
This event resulted in the US government refusing to ratify terms agreed to during the second round of Strategic Arms Limitation Talks (SALT II), and in many liberal democracies of the West boycotting the 1980 Moscow Summer Olympic Games.

1960   1970   1980

1968
Nuclear Non-Proliferation Treaty
This treaty was first proposed by Ireland and ultimately was signed by 189 countries. It covers three key topics:
(1) non-proliferation (a stop to the production, trade, and acquisition of new nuclear weapons),
(2) moving toward disarmament (reducing the number of weapons already acquired), and
(3) the right to peacefully use nuclear technology (for example, nuclear power).

1975
Helsinki Accords
The Helsinki Accords declaration was signed by 35 countries, including the United States and the Soviet Union. It covered topics such as the following:
- respect for the sovereignty of other countries
- refraining from the threat or use of force
- the territorial integrity of states
- the peaceful settlement of disputes
- non-intervention in internal affairs of other countries
- respect for human rights and fundamental freedoms
- equal rights and the right to self-determination
The Soviets were pleased to have their territorial boundaries recognized and respected, and other countries were happy to see the Soviets promise to attend to the human rights issues apparent in communist-bloc countries. The signing of this declaration helped to highlight the values and beliefs that were similar between the ideologies of communist and liberal democratic countries.

Better relations with the United States might open up more trade with Western Europe.

- The American government wanted to spend more money on social programs, and the Vietnam War, in which the United States backed South Vietnam against the Soviet-supported North Vietnam, was becoming a severe strain on the American economy.

The period of reduced tensions, from the mid-1960s to 1979 (when the Soviet Union invaded Afghanistan), was called **détente**. During that time, leaders of the superpowers met at various summits, signed many treaties, and took other measures to reduce tensions. Some of the key diplomatic events of the period of détente are described in the timeline below.

The détente between the United States and the Soviet Union showed how countries with different ideologies can work toward settling their differences through diplomacy. The détente lasted only about 15 years, but the efforts to co-operate rather than compete offered a hopeful example for the future of international relations. During the Reagan years, the Cold War was reignited and billions of dollars were spent on military operations around the world. At this time the efforts of the two superpowers to agree to terms of disarmament were awkward and slow, and were encouraged mostly by the huge economic cost of continuing the Cold War.

1980
President Ronald Reagan is Elected, and the Cold War Heats Up Again
Reagan won the presidency based on a platform that stressed the importance of national security. The Cold War began to escalate again during his presidency as he built up the military and revived the B-1 Bomber program. Reagan was ideologically opposed to communism, and, in a famous address to the British Parliament on June 8, 1982, he called the totalitarian system of the Soviet Union "evil" and said that Marxism-Leninism would be consigned to the "ash heap of history."

1987
Intermediate-range Nuclear Forces Treaty (INF Treaty)
After years of negotiation, the Soviets and Americans signed an agreement to remove INF missile systems (those with a range of 500 to 5500 kilometres) and shorter-range missiles from Europe. As this agreement was a bilateral one between the Soviet and American governments, it did not address the missile deployment of American allies such as Britain or France.

1980   1985   1990

1982
Strategic Arms Reduction Treaty I (START I)
This complex and comprehensive treaty, presented to the Soviets by Reagan, proposed a dramatic reduction in strategic forces, including the number of warheads, limits on heavy bombers and their warheads, and other strategic military systems. Negotiations between the United States and the Soviet Union continued for 10 years before the treaty was signed in 1992. Some people criticized the treaty for being deliberately non-negotiable and deceptively one-sided, even going so far as to suggest that the treaty was designed to sabotage the disarmament process.

1985
Mikhail Gorbachev Becomes Soviet Premier
Beginning in 1987, Gorbachev introduced some liberal reforms through his policies of glasnost (openness) and perestroika (restructuring). Gorbachev signed the 1987 INF Treaty with US president Ronald Reagan, and withdrew Soviet forces from Afghanistan in 1989, followed by the withdrawal of Soviet forces from the satellite states of Eastern Europe. Gorbachev also agreed to the 1990 reunification of East and West Germany and received the 1990 Nobel Peace Prize for his achievements in international relations.

Proxy Wars and Liberation Movements

The United States and the Soviet Union never did descend into a direct hot war but they did have what are called proxy wars. **Proxy wars** are conflicts in which one superpower might fight in another country or provide support to a group which opposes the rival superpower. Aligned countries and countries that remained non-aligned, or unstable countries, for example, in the post–Second World War recovery years, provided opportunities for the superpowers to advance their interests in regions around the world. Each superpower was willing to provide economic or military support to a side that was sympathetic to its ideology.

Liberation movements occur when a country rebels against the country that colonized it or otherwise oppressed it. The group at the centre of a liberation movement fights, militarily and politically, against its perceived oppressor and campaigns for its country's independence, often with a goal of becoming its own sovereign state. Many liberation movements occurred in Latin America, Central America, Africa, and the Middle East from the 1950s through the 1980s. These movements were often funded and supported by one superpower or the other.

Korea and Vietnam

Korea in 1945 and Vietnam in 1954 were both in similar situations: by agreement among world powers, they were each divided into two zones and free elections were to take place. However, the timely elections that were to reunite these countries did not take place as expected. In both cases, the countries became ideological battlegrounds for hot wars between the United States and the Soviet Union. Both Korea and Vietnam sustained high numbers of civilian and military casualties during these hot wars, as well as long-term political and economic setbacks.

Chile

Salvador Allende served as a politician in Chile for almost 40 years and was elected president on a socialist platform in 1970, much to the dismay of the United States. The CIA had interfered substantially in the Chilean elections of 1964, preventing the socialist leader from winning in favour of a pro-Christian democratic candidate. During Allende's presidency, Chile nationalized many industries, started health care reform, renewed diplomatic relations with communist Cuba and the Soviet government, and started to redistribute land wealth. Shortly after Allende came to power, President Nixon authorized millions of dollars in funding for the CIA to create political instability in Chile and ultimately unseat Allende. On September 11, 1973, Allende died during a military coup led by General Augusto Pinochet, who ruled the country as a dictator, implementing free market capitalist economic policies, until 1990. The American government claims it had no direct involvement in the coup; however, it admits to being involved in creating the conditions that led to it.

Afghanistan

The Soviet Union invaded Afghanistan in 1979 to support a pro-Soviet regime, and thus gain a friendly neighbour. In response, the CIA equipped Afghan resistance fighters with rifles from the First World War and other arms in a covert operation that would cost the United States about $5 million a year. Later, Texas congressman Charlie Wilson and CIA agent Gust Avrokotos became convinced that enough money and planning could actually defeat the Soviet Union in Afghanistan. Over time, the operation's annual budget rose to $750 million. When the Soviet soldiers retreated from Afghanistan in 1989, they left behind their allies, the Afghan Army, to fight a strong, well-armed insurgent force (the Mujahedeen), including some commanders who later supported the Taliban regime, Osama bin Laden, and al Qaeda.

The Iran-Contra Affair

During the 1980s, America under President Ronald Reagan was determined to eliminate any socialist (or communist) influence in South and Central America. The United States saw the Americas as being in its sphere of influence. No enemy state could therefore be tolerated within this sphere. Nicaragua's government was considered communist by the Reagan administration, so various US government security agencies funnelled weapons and money to a group of Nicaraguan rebels called the Contras. Congress, however, in 1983, passed legislation making it illegal for the CIA or any other government agency to provide military aid to the Contras. The Reagan administration got around these restrictions by using an agency not named in the legislation, the National Security Council. The NSC secretly obtained funds by selling weapons to moderates in the Iranian government who, it was hoped, would help to get American hostages held in Lebanon released. These dealings with Iran were also illegal. Nevertheless, Oliver North, an operative of the NSC, oversaw the sale of weapons to Iran, the proceeds of which were then funnelled to the Contras in Nicaragua. This new plan was implemented with the approval of NSA Admiral John Poindexter, allegedly without the consent or knowledge of the president.

When news of the American-Iranian-Contra arrangement was made public in an article in a Lebanese magazine, Reagan and other members

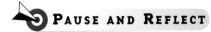
of the American government were confronted and an international scandal ensued. Poindexter resigned, and North was fired. A commission was formed to investigate, and several of the participants were found guilty of charges such as conspiracy and obstruction of justice; however, all convictions were overturned or later pardoned by President George H.W. Bush.

Explore the Issues

Concept Review

1 a) Identify and describe five policies of Cold War strategy.

b) For each policy, provide an example of its implementation.

c) Identify three countries in which proxy wars were waged by the superpowers.

Concept Application

2 In a group, choose and research a key event in American–Soviet relations during the Cold War. Use a variety of sources, and consider multiple perspectives when answering the following questions:

a) What were the key issues faced by the two superpowers that led to the event?

b) How important is this event regarding the extent to which it increased or decreased tensions between the United States and the Soviet Union?

c) What were the choices available to the superpowers during the course of the event?

d) What were the decisions made during the course of the event?

e) What were the reasons for the decisions made during the event?

f) What were the consequences of the event? What does this event reveal about how ideological conflict affected international relations after the Second World War?

3 During tensions in postwar Berlin, Vyacheslav M. Molotov, the Soviet Foreign Minister, noted, "What happens to Berlin, happens to Germany; what happens to Germany, happens to Europe." (Source: Vyacheslav M. Molotov, quoted in D.M. Giangreco and Robert E. Griffin, "Eye of the Storm," *Airbridge to Berlin: The Berlin Crisis of 1948, Its Origins and Aftermath.* Harry S. Truman Library & Museum, http://www.trumanlibrary.org/whistlestop/ BERLIN_A/PAGE_1.HTM.)

To what extent do you agree with Molotov's comments?

Global, Social, and Personal Implications of International Conflict

Question for Inquiry

• **In what ways did this conflict of ideologies affect societies and people's everyday lives?**

Stalin had predicted that all countries would align with either the Soviet state or the American state. Truman believed that every country would need to choose between two alternative ways of life. The ideological, political, and military conflicts of the Cold War had a tremendous impact, not only on governments around the world but also on the beliefs and values of society and on individuals' daily lives.

Ideological conflict played out in political and personal lives. For example, East Germany's Stasi police had 90 000 agents and over 173 000 registered informers. East German citizen Vera Wollenberger joined the peace movement in 1981; due to Stasi harassment, she lost her teaching job and was jailed. After the fall of the Berlin Wall, she was elected as a member of the German Parliament in 1990. She voted in favour of a law giving citizens the right to look at their Stasi files and, on reading her own file, discovered that her husband had been the main informer against her.

Between 1993 and 2008, 1.7 million people requested to see their Stasi files, and the German government is spending millions restoring documents that have been torn to pieces. The German word used to describe the viewing of one's Stasi file is *Vergangenheitsbewältigung*, meaning coming to terms with the past.

Cold War Hysteria

Throughout the Cold War, people around the world experienced the psychological effects of the tensions between the superpowers. Fueled by government-produced propaganda, misinformation, and the threat of a Third World War, mania and paranoia grew among civilians during the late 1940s, 1950s, and 1960s, especially among those living in the United States. For the Soviet people, although equally susceptible to government propaganda, this hysteria was less pronounced due to their recent and historical experiences with war on the home front: they understood what it meant to be attacked or invaded by enemy forces. Americans, however, were facing an unknown. What would happen if they were attacked? How would they deal with an invasion?

In particular, people around the world were afraid of nuclear war, which could produce devastation on a global scale. A preview of this

Figure 7-16 ▲

During the Cold War, especially in the United States, schoolchildren were taught to "duck and cover" in case of a nuclear attack, as in this photo taken around 1955. Some families built fallout shelters in their backyards, and governments built underground bunkers and researched alternative communication systems.

devastation was seen after the atomic bombing of Japan during the Second World War. When the Soviets acquired the atomic bomb shortly after the war and their relationship with the American government deteriorated, Americans grew increasingly worried.

Fallout shelters were built around the world and extensively in the United States. These shelters were meant to protect people from exposure to radiation from a nuclear blast. Fear of a Soviet attack was not limited to the American public. In the 1960s, a large fallout bunker was built just outside of Ottawa to protect Canadian political leaders in the case of an attack. The Diefenbunker, named after Prime Minister John Diefenbaker, is now a Canadian Cold War museum.

The notion of civil defence as a means of patriotism was issued from the top. "Civil defence can serve a deterrent purpose by demonstrating to a potential aggressor that Canada is determined to survive even a nuclear war and carry on as an organized society and united nation in the face of the utmost perils and hardships," said Diefenbaker in 1959. (Source: John Diefenbaker, address to the House of Commons, 1959, shown in *CBC Newsmagazine*, "Calgary Evacuates: Operation Lifesaver," October 9, 1959.)

PAUSE AND REFLECT

Examples of the impact of the American-Soviet ideological conflict span the world. How is this impact depicted in Patria Rivera's poem?

Cold War, 1957
Manila, Philippines   by Patria Rivera

Before we knew how to spell "desk,"
Teacher taught us to duck under one.
Better yet, at the sound of three bell rings,
to line up and down the staircase,
out onto the schoolyard
*to hug the ground under the banaba trees.**
We waited for the H-bomb,
the egg from the sky,
the parachutes
from mainland China.
We waited for the invasion,
Red soldiers in their
full regalia.

As we lay there on the grassy mound,
red ants crept up our shins,
leaving prickly bites.
After so many drills
we came to love the smell of moist earth
and freshly cut grass
on our sweaty shirts.
Sometimes,
we turned over and watched
a congregation of butterflies
sob into the branches,
then spring free from the banaba trees.

(*Note: Banaba trees are indigenous tree to the Philippines. Their leaves are used to make a tea.)

Patria Rivera, "Cold War 1957 Manila Philippines"
in *Puti/White* (Calgary: Frontenac House, 2005).

Voices

The Threat of Nuclear War

One consequence of the American-Soviet struggle was the threat of nuclear war. The following quotations illustrate a variety of perspectives from American, Canadian, French, Japanese, and Russian sources regarding this threat.

A full scale nuclear exchange, lasting less than 60 minutes .... could wipe out more than 300 million Americans, Europeans, and Russians, as well as untold numbers elsewhere. And the survivors—as Chairman Khrushchev warned the Communist Chinese, "the survivors would envy the dead." For they would inherit a world so devastated by explosions and poison and fire that today we cannot conceive of its horrors.

—John F. Kennedy, speech at the Nuclear Test Ban Treaty, July 26, 1963. John F. Kennedy Presidential Library and Museum.
http://www.jfklibrary.org/Historical+Resources/Archives/
Reference+Desk/Speeches/JFK/Nuclear+Test+Ban+Treaty+Speech.htm

Political leaders will decide whether or not a nuclear war actually takes place, yet politicians act as if peace is too complicated for them.

—Pierre Elliott Trudeau (former Canadian prime minister), 1984 Albert Einstein Peace Prize acceptance speech. CBC Digital Archives.
http://archives.cbc.ca/war_conflict/peacekeeping/clips/659-3734/

The Americans and the Russians could destroy the earth 1000 times over. [France] could only do it once—but that is enough.

—Pierre Lacoste (French military strategy advisor, 1966–1972), quoted in "France's Nuclear Weapons Program." Atomic Forum.
http://atomicforum.org/france/france.html

No country without an atom bomb could properly consider itself independent.

—Charles De Gaulle (French president), 1968, quoted in "France's Nuclear Weapons Program." Atomic Forum.
http://atomicforum.org/france/france.html

Humankind continues to face the threat of nuclear annihilation. Today's hesitation leads to tomorrow's destruction...The fates of all of us are bound together here on earth. There can be no survival for any without peaceful coexistence for all.

—Takeshi Araki (mayor of Hiroshima), "Peace Declaration," August 6, 1985. City of Hiroshima, 2001.
http://www.city.hiroshima.jp/shimin/heiwa/pd1985e.html

PAUSE AND REFLECT

Preceding the election of 1964, American president Lyndon B. Johnson's campaign included one of the most controversial television commercials ever made. In the spot, a young girl counts the petals of a daisy as she plucks them. A military countdown takes over and the scene changes to footage of a nuclear explosion. Johnson can then be heard saying, "These are the stakes—to make a world in which all of God's children can live or to go into the dark. We must either love each other, or we must die." (Source: "Peace, Little Girl," first aired September 7, 1964. Conelrad, http://www.conelrad.com/daisy/video.php.) Why might this advertisement be seen as controversial?

In so far as the fear of nuclear war's concerned, I think that probably Russians were less afraid of it than Americans. Maybe it had to do with the fact that Russians knew what war actually was, they'd gone through hell in 1941, '45. Second, there was never the kind of emphasis put on a nuclear attack as imminent. Children in this country were not taught to hide under desks for so-called nuclear drills. There was not this hysteria. There was a very strong feeling that we should never allow war to happen again. We know what war is, we're all against war, our government is against war. We are for disarmament, we will do everything, so that there not be a war. But there never was hysteria, as differing from the United States, and that's a very interesting difference.

—Vladimir Pozner (Russian television commentator), interview for background material for *Red Files*, "Soviet Propaganda Machine," Abamedia and PBS, first broadcast in September 1999. Red Files, 1999.

http://www.pbs.org/redfiles/prop/deep/prop_deep_inter_frm.htm

1 Taken together, what do these quotations reveal about how the threat of nuclear war was perceived by people around the world? What effects might this perception have on people's beliefs and values?

PAUSE AND REFLECT

"We are the first victims of American fascism."
—Ethel and Julius Rosenberg in a letter released by their attorney on the day they were electrocuted for espionage

"Fascism is not defined by the number of its victims but by its way of killing them."
—Jean-Paul Sartre (French philosopher and author), quoted from "Mad Beasts," *Selected Prose: The Writings of Jean-Paul Sartre* (Evanston, IL: Northwestern University Press, 1974), 207-11:
http://snjr.net/snjr/sartre.htm

What role do you think ideology played in the execution of the Rosenbergs?

Espionage

Espionage was a key tool of the Cold War and helped both superpowers in their policies of expansionism and containment. During the Cuban Missile Crisis, for example, espionage was used to strengthen the American position when a spy plane photograph alerted the Americans to the Soviet missiles being installed on Cuban soil. When espionage was discovered and made public, it served to fuel feelings of paranoia and mistrust; however, according to Oleg Kalugin, a retired KGB (Soviet Intelligence) major general, "Intelligence played a tremendous role in keeping the world from the brink, from turning the Cold War into a hot war." (Source: Oleg Kalugin, quoted in CNN Interactive, "Inside the KGB: An interview with retired KGB Maj. Gen. Oleg Kalugin," http://www.cnn.com/SPECIALS/cold.war/experience/spies/interviews/kalugin/).

Julius and Ethel Rosenberg

In 1951, Jewish-Americans Julius and Ethel Rosenberg were tried and convicted of espionage against the American government for delivering secret information to the Soviets about American military weaponry, possibly including the atomic bomb. As an electrical engineer working for the Army Signal Corps, Julius Rosenberg had access to technical information and to people working on military projects. Active communist sympathizers, the Rosenbergs were recruited to work for the KGB and allegedly recruited other spies, including Ethel's brother, David Greenglass. Despite the protests of many American citizens and public figures from around the world, including Pope Pius XII, the

Figure 7-17

In 1946, Soviet schoolchildren presented a carved wooden version of the Great Seal of the United States to the US Ambassador to the USSR, which he then hung in his Moscow study. Six years later, it was discovered that a listening device had been planted in the gift. In the above photo, US Ambassador to the United Nations Henry Cabot Lodge complained to the UN Security Council in 1960 about the incident.

In 1945, Canada experienced its own espionage scandal when Igor Gouzenko, a cipher clerk from the Soviet embassy in Canada, stole documents that revealed a spy ring operating in Canada and presented them to the media.

couple became the first American citizens executed for espionage in the United States. Their highly publicized trial and execution served to fuel investigations into "anti-American" activities by American citizens, including those led by Senator Joseph McCarthy, which are discussed later in this chapter.

1960 U-2 Incident

In the late 1950s, with the permission of the Pakistani government, the American government set up an intelligence installation in Pakistan from which surveillance missions were flown over Soviet territory. On May 1, 1960, an American U-2 spy plane flew over the Soviet Union, taking photographs and measuring the output of uranium-producing plants. The Soviets, however, were aware of the American surveillance, and when the spy plane was spotted, they ordered it to be shot down. His plane severely damaged, American pilot Gary Powers bailed out, parachuted to safety, and was captured. Initially, the American government reported that a weather research aircraft had gone off course and was missing. When the Soviet government reported several days later that an American spy had been captured, and his plane was recovered virtually intact, the Americans were publicly caught in a lie. The East-West summit scheduled for that month was cancelled, leaving American and Soviet relations worse than ever.

The Post–Second World War Red Scare and McCarthyism

Due in part to the devastating effects of the Great Depression of the 1930s, many Americans were drawn to communism as a political and economic ideology, especially those in academic and labour fields.

Figure 7-18 ▲

This 1947 comic book portrays the purported threat of communism to America during the Cold War. What does it reveal about American ideology and feelings toward Soviet ideology at that time?

During and after the Second World War, however, American society experienced a **red scare**, during which an intense fear of communism overcame the majority of the American population, influencing everything from movies and television to national security. This fear was fueled by such things as Soviet espionage and infiltration, the rise of communism in China, the acquisition of the atomic bomb by the Soviet Union, and the development of the Soviet iron curtain that divided Europe.

With the red scare came a strong backlash toward American communists and anyone perceived as being sympathetic toward communism or the Soviets. A movement against all things communist was led by an ex-marine and Republican senator from Wisconsin named Joseph McCarthy. In 1950, McCarthy charged that a number of communist supporters were among those working for the State Department. McCarthy's accusations prompted a hearing to investigate the matter, which ultimately reported that McCarthy's charges were unfounded. Regardless, McCarthy continued to assert that communism had infiltrated the Democratic government and used his accusations to support Republican candidates during the 1950 senate election. McCarthy gained a strong following among many anti-communist Americans and, as chairman of the Senate Subcommittee on Government Operations, he continued to accuse government officials and military leaders of being pro-communist.

On December 2, 1954, the Senate voted to formally reprimand McCarthy due to his zealous and often unfounded accusations. He died three years later, yet the term **McCarthyism** continued to be used to describe the movement to uncover and persecute those with perceived ties to communism, a movement that divided Americans along ideological and political lines. In 2003, when the records of the 1953 Subcommittee on Government Operations led by McCarthy were made public, senators Susan Collins and Carl Levin wrote the following in the preface to the documents:

Senator McCarthy's zeal to uncover subversion and espionage led to disturbing excesses. His browbeating tactics destroyed careers of people who were not involved in the infiltration of our government. His freewheeling style caused both the Senate and the Subcommittee to revise the rules governing future investigations, and prompted the courts to act to protect the Constitutional rights of witnesses at Congressional hearings.

**—Source: Susan Collins and Carl Levin, "Preface,"
Executive Sessions of the Senate Permanent
Subcommittee on Investigations of the Committee
on Government Operations, 2003, p. xi. United States Senate.**
http://www.senate.gov/artandhistory/history/resources/pdf/Volume1.pdf

One of Senator McCarthy's most vocal critics at the time was journalist Edward R. Murrow, who said the following during a 30-minute television news report:

We will not walk in fear, one of another. We will not be driven by fear into an age of unreason if we dig deep in our history and doctrine and remember that we are not descended from fearful men, not from men who feared to write, to speak, to associate and to defend causes which were, for the moment, unpopular. We can deny our heritage and our history, but we cannot escape responsibility for the result. There is no way for a citizen of the Republic to abdicate his responsibility.

—**Edward R. Murrow,** *See It Now*,
"A Report on Senator Joseph McCarthy,"
CBS, March 9, 1954.

House Un-American Activities Committee

During the Second World War, the House Un-American Activities Committee (HUAC) was formed by the US House of Representatives. HUAC delved into suspected threats of subversion or propaganda that attacked "the form of government guaranteed by our Constitution." (Source: HUAC, quoted in "McCarthyism during the Cold War." The War Within, University of California, Irvine Libraries, http://www.lib.uci.edu/libraries/exhibits/warwithin/index.php?page=section_2, 2008.) In 1947, the committee held hearings to investigate communist subversion in Hollywood and the American film industry, after which they "blacklisted" many people who were uncooperative or unwilling to testify. Those blacklisted could no longer work in the entertainment industry; over 300 actors, directors, film screenwriters, and radio scriptwriters were boycotted by the studios. The "Hollywood Ten" famously refused to answer some questions posed by HUAC (citing their First Amendment right to freedom of speech and assembly), and members were found guilty of contempt. Industry members were asked if they were members of the American communist party or sympathetic to it, and furthermore, they were asked to name others who were or might be—including co-workers, friends, and, in one case, even a spouse. Those who were blacklisted had few options: find work in other countries or in theatre, write under pseudonyms or the names of willing friends, or leave the business all together.

PAUSE AND REFLECT

What effects might McCarthyism have had on liberalism in the United States?

PAUSE AND REFLECT

The Internet has its roots in the Cold War. The United States wanted a communication system that could withstand a nuclear attack. ARPANET (Advanced Research Projects Agency Network), created in 1969, enabled packets of information to travel within a decentralized communications network. What other legacies of ideological conflict and the Cold War do you know of?

Cold War Legacies

Something to Think About: Long after economic or military aid ended in regions affected by the Cold War, armaments, military expertise, personal loss, and conflict continued to influence policy and lives.

An Example: The legacy of the Cold War in African countries is described in the following article from Enough Sishi, a researcher at the South African Institute for Security Studies and a contributing writer to *Peace Magazine*.

Read the article and research one country or region mentioned in Sishi's article. Use the Skill Path on pages 248–249 to think like a geographer and respond to the Questions for Reflection on page 269. Assess to what extent the legacy of conflicting ideologies has impacted geopolitical realities in post–Cold War Africa.

Southern Africa is awash with small and light weapons. Most of these weapons are the material legacy of the Cold War. During 1970s, '80s and '90s the superpowers pumped massive amounts of guns and ammunition into this region. Many of these now are controlled by bandits in Mozambique or unemployed demobilized soldiers and black market syndicates in Angola.

These weapons were issued as government grants during the Cold War. The Soviets supported Marxist movements and regimes, while the U.S. supplied pro-capitalists with weapons. The intelligence organizations of the superpowers [KGB and CIA] facilitated this.

Angola

Since Angola got independence in 1975 from Portugal a bloody civil war has dragged on. Throughout this conflict the U.S. pumped millions worth of weapons to the National Union for the Total Independence of Angola (UNITA) and its military component, the National Front for the Liberation of Angola (FNLA) through its military assistance program. U.S. military aid increased from $15 million in 1986 to $300 million in 1992, the year aid was suspended. China was another military supplier of the FNLA. South Africa's capability of supplying weapons to UNITA was boosted by its internal industry, pumping more than $80 million of military aid to UNITA throughout the war until the early '90s.

Russia is said to have supplied most of the military aid through KGB routes to Angola's Marxist-aligned government, the Popular Movement for the Liberation of Angola (MPLA). Available figures state about $2 billion of weapons annually was received from the Soviets, while Cuba supplied $200 million of Soviet arms.

Open military government grants were complemented by covert deliveries, for which statistics were never opened to public scrutiny. It is known that between 1975–76 the CIA secretly supplied anti-Communist insurgents in Angola with mortars, anti-tank rockets, rifles, ammunition and communication equipment. On top of this supply the MPLA and UNITA spent huge amounts on other weapons, with MPLA running a debt of $4 billion.

Mozambique

The superpowers waged the Cold War through proxies, and one such conflict was the Mozambican civil war that broke out in 1975. The Front for the Liberation of Mozambique (FRELIMO) controlled the government and received military support from [the] USSR, while the Mozambique National Resistance (RENAMO) rallied support from anti-communist states. Throughout the 16-year war the FRELIMO government supplied an estimated 1.5 million assault rifles to civilians who supported their cause.

The war ended in 1992, followed by United Nations-sponsored demobilization and disarmament. Unfortunately, the United Nations operation did not destroy the weapons after demobilization. These arsenals were open to corruption and mismanagement after the U.N. had left and some 6 million AK47s are still at large. Up until 1998 South African and Mozambique police continued to recover abandoned arms caches on the borders and inside Mozambique…

The Black Market

The end of the Cold War has dramatically reduced military support in the region, but the weapons themselves have remained and have led to the growth of the black market. In Mozambique, for instance, stockpiles of weapons that were seized during the U.N. disarmament were never destroyed. When the U.N. mission left, corrupt officials sold these arsenals.

In Angola, despite the U.N. instituted arms embargo, UNITA has been able to acquire weapons, allowing the international arms dealers to cash in. Angolans themselves, who are poor and hungry because of decades of war, have been accused by Zambians of illegally crossing the border to Zambia and exchanging their weapons for food. An alliance has emerged between criminal organizations, insurgent groups and ex-soldiers who still retain their weapons of war and who are allegedly engaged in multi-million rand robberies in South Africa. These groups sell guns to each other and exchange other favors. In most Southern African countries wars have brought the economy to its knees. The demobilized soldiers lack job opportunities, so weapons have become their only means of survival. Non-state actors, including criminals, engaging in acts of violence without access to legal arms, create a big demand for light weapons…

—**Source: Enough Sishi, "Small Arms in South Africa,"** *Peace Magazine* **March–April 1998, p. 16.**
http://archive.peacemagazine.org/v14n2p16.htm

QUESTIONS FOR REFLECTION

Using the maps found in Figure 7-11 on page 249, and a current map of Africa from your research, locate the countries mentioned in the article to answer the following questions.

1 Compare the maps from 1959 to 1982. What factors might account for these changing alliances between Angola and Mozambique?

2 In what ways were liberation movements in these African countries impacted by ideological conflicts the Cold War? How and why did the Soviet Union, China, Cuba, and the United States support different liberation movements in Angola and in Mozambique? What were their key motives for supporting these liberation movements?

3 Research these countries in Africa today. To what extent does liberalism impact the political ideology of their current governments?

Explore the Issues

Concept Review

1 Identify five examples of the effects of the Cold War conflict on the everyday lives of citizens in the United States, the Soviet Union, and other countries during the time period of the Cold War.

Concept Application

2 How do differences in ideologies affect citizens' everyday lives, and how can a society deal with such differences? What happens when ideological differences cause conflicts between countries? Using the Skill Path, examine Yugoslavia in 1946–1947, Hungary in 1956, Czechoslovakia in 1968, and another movement for independence during the Cold War. Use a table such as the one below to present your findings.

3 During the Cold War, for example at the time of McCarthyism, some principles of liberalism were abandoned by the United States. This had a profound effect on the lives of many American citizens and left a lasting impression on American society. Create a cause-and-effect chart that shows how the United States came to lose touch locally with the fundamental principles it was trying to defend globally. Discuss the following question in groups: *Do you think that liberal principles have been abandoned in other situations where American democracy has come under stress?* Summarize and present your position to the rest of the class.

Country	Ideological Conflict	Result	Reason for the Result
Yugoslavia (1946–1947)			
Hungary (1956)			
Czechoslovakia (1968)			
Other: _____			

Reflect and Analyze

In this chapter we have been exploring responses to the question: ***To what extent does ideological conflict shape our world?*** You explored how ideological differences, for example those between the United States and the Soviet Union, can cause conflict on a global scale, affecting the lives of people around the world. You have seen how American values such as personal freedom and the importance of the individual were at odds with Soviet values such as egalitarianism and the importance of the working class, causing tensions wherever these two powers met. This conflict led each side to expand its sphere of influence and territory (expansionism) and to attempt to contain the expansion efforts of the other (containment). During the 1950s, the atomic bomb and its destructive power became a strong deterrent for both sides against open warfare and led to a period of détente. The Cold War and its legacy have imprinted the globe, as can be seen in the cultural products, physical borders, and political conflicts that exist today.

As it is likely that people from different countries will continue to have different beliefs and values, what lessons can be learned from the Cold War? On a personal level, what lessons can you take away for dealing with situations in which your own ideologies bring you into conflict with others? What have you learned that can help you address the Key Issue: ***To what extent should we embrace an ideology?***

Respond to Issues

1 On February 10, 2007, Russian Federation President Vladimir Putin threatened to pull out of the Intermediate-Range Nuclear Forces Treaty due to a proposed US missile defence system to be deployed in Poland and the Czech Republic. Is this evidence that the Cold War is not over? In groups, develop and present an argument that supports or refutes the idea that the Cold War still exists today, and decide to what extent an ideological conflict continues to exist between the United States and Russia.

2 Canadians were directly affected by the Cold War. The following are all examples of how Canadians were affected: the spy episode with Igor Gouzenko, membership in NATO, the history of the Avro Arrow fighter jet, UN operations in Korea, the construction of the DEW Line, events in Cuba, actions in the Vietnam War, and family histories. Choose one example of how the Cold War had an impact on Canada and Canadians, and examine it to answer the following questions:

a) What were some specific implications for Canadian citizens and their governments?

b) Given Canada's location relative to the two Cold War superpowers, what strategic role could Canada play in the Cold War? How might the peoples of Canada's North be affected?

c) What role did Canada play internationally?

d) How do these involvements illustrate how resistance to liberalism can or cannot be justified?

Recognize Relationships among Concepts, Issues, and Citizenship

3 Examine how the ideological conflict of the Cold War was portrayed in popular media such as contemporary music and film. In a presentation on the topic, answer the following questions:

a) How do these portrayals reveal how such conflict influenced the culture of the superpowers and/or other countries?

b) How do you think such portrayals influenced Canadian citizens during the Cold War? What examples would you describe as propaganda?

c) How do contemporary music and film reflect the dominant or alternative ideologies in our society today?

d) On what crises, events, or subjects do the examples comment?

e) What popular culture expressions best reflect your own beliefs and values?

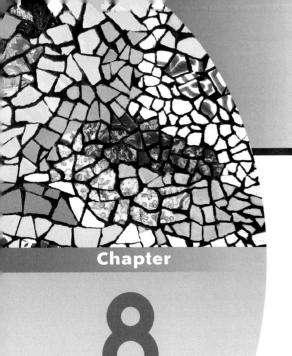

Contemporary Challenges to Liberalism

KEY SKILLS

Evaluating ideas and information from multiple sources

KEY CONCEPTS

Analyzing how modern liberalism is challenged by alternative thought

Key Terms

Civil rights movements

Environmentalism

Neo-conservatism

Whether you support or challenge a particular value of modern liberalism, such as the right to public health care, depends on your vision of what life should be like. What would you write about if you imagined the world 50 or 100 years from now? Science fiction stories in television shows, movies, novels, and computer games explore the possibilities of what life could be like or what the story's creator thinks life should be. An imaginary perfect world is called a utopia. A negative, pessimistic vision of a future world—if, for example, a particular value or principle is taken to an extreme—is called a dystopia. Think of science fiction stories you know. (Recall our discussion of Aldous Huxley's *Brave New World* and George Orwell's *Nineteen Eighty-Four* in the introduction of this book.) Imagine the kind of world that you would want to live in. What is it about this imagined world that you find appealing?

In his book *The Little Prince* (1943), French author Antoine de Saint-Exupéry creates a variety of fictional planets and asteroids to critique characteristics of adult behaviour from a child's point of view. On one asteroid, for example, a businessman spends all his time counting the stars, and claims ownership of them so that he can use them to buy more stars.

Other books describe worlds that resemble our own more closely, except for a few fundamental differences. In *Fahrenheit 451* (1953), author Ray Bradbury describes a country in which the populace voluntarily gives up literature to suppress any subversive ideas that might endanger its "happiness". An authoritarian government then outlaws the possession of books and sets about burning all existing literature.

Similarly, in Lois Lowry's *The Giver* (1993), people convert to "Sameness," giving up individual memories and strong emotions to create a more safe and peaceful society. Eventually, the protagonists in both Bradbury's and Lowry's books choose to forsake the security of their respective societies and struggle to reinstate individuality and freedom of expression.

In these examples, the authors challenge different perspectives of how to organize society and examine the consequences of taking the principles of an ideology to the extreme. What might happen if we based our society solely on economic principles like the businessman who counts stars? What might happen if we gave up all control to the government like the country where books are outlawed? What might happen if we allowed the government to do anything in its power to ensure our security, to the point of sacrificing our individuality?

In a similar way to how Bradbury and Lowry evaluated imaginary societies, Canadians critique aspects of Canadian society and, in doing so, question the role of government: How much do we want or need the government to be involved in our lives, and how much freedom are we willing to give up in exchange for security? Critiques and challenges to how we govern our society can help us see how it might be improved and, in some cases, might lead to changes in the way we live together.

Chapter Issue

As a society evolves, alternative ideas arise that may be embraced or rejected. In some cases, people do not just embrace new ideas, they look to traditional ideas as a way to enrich or counter current ideologies. Why did classical liberalism evolve into modern liberalism? How have new ideas contributed to or challenged modern liberalism? How might modern liberalism evolve further?

In this chapter, you will investigate contemporary currents of alternative thought and explore the challenges they present for liberalism. These examples will help you explore the Chapter Issue: *To what extent is modern liberalism continuing to evolve?* As you consider this question, think about how it fits into the Related Issue for Part 2: *To what extent is resistance to liberalism justified?*

Figure 8-1 ▲

In *Fahrenheit 451*, brigades of "firemen" are employed to find and burn all forms of literature. To what extent should the state intervene to control freedom of thought and expression?

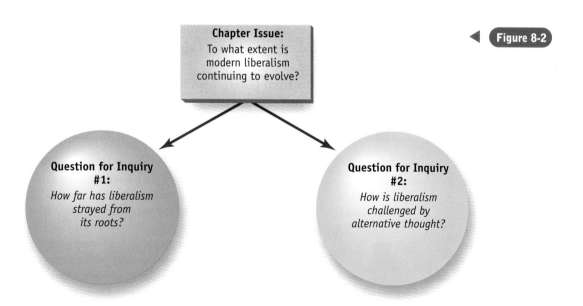

Chapter Issue:
To what extent is modern liberalism continuing to evolve?

◀ **Figure 8-2**

Question for Inquiry #1:
How far has liberalism strayed from its roots?

Question for Inquiry #2:
How is liberalism challenged by alternative thought?

However, for classical liberals, negative freedoms generally meant little more than freedom from government intervention. Citizens in many liberal democracies, such as Canada, possess these negative freedoms. In Canada, fundamental freedoms include

- freedom of conscience and religion
- freedom of thought, belief, opinion, and expression, including freedom of the press and other communication media
- freedom of peaceful assembly
- freedom of association

Figure 8-4 ▶

Modern Liberalism	Classical Liberalism
Positive Freedoms *example: Freedom of expression*	Negative Freedoms *example: Freedom from persecution for following a chosen faith or spirituality*

Classical liberalism proposes that each man has equal political power. Liberals believed that greater political stability would result from greater direct involvement in the political process. Political stability, in turn, would lead to a society that allows individuals to use their freedoms as best they can to achieve social and economic prosperity. In your opinion, are the negative freedoms outlined above sufficient to ensure the well-being of all members of society?

Classical Liberalism and Economics

As you discovered in previous chapters, the 19th century was a period of significant economic growth due, in part, to the Industrial Revolution of the late 18th and early 19th centuries. This economic development coincided with the formation of classical liberal economic theory. Sometimes called **laissez-faire** economics, this ideology supported free markets and an individual's right to own private property. Classical liberals believe that economic markets with little or no government intervention will result in the greatest benefit to all members of society. To prevent intervention, liberals believed that government should be limited to what it can do best, such as developing laws that protect freedoms and private property. Many classical economic liberals did not completely trust popular democracy, however. They feared that the majority of people might not support ideas such as the right to possess private property.

Classical Liberalism and Equality

For classical liberals, a certain amount of inequality is a natural result of protecting property rights and guaranteeing freedoms. This is acceptable to a classical liberal, because the equality valued by classical

PAUSE AND REFLECT

- **Why would some people be opposed to the concept of private property?**
- **Can you think of ideologies you have already explored from the same period that oppose private property? For what reasons did the supporters of these ideologies take this position?**

PAUSE AND REFLECT

Does the modern liberal interpretation of equality refer to equality of opportunity or equality of outcome?

liberals is an equality of opportunity, rather than an equality of outcome, and each individual should enjoy the freedom to take advantage of those opportunities. The classical liberal state remains impartial, allowing citizens to determine their own ideas of good without interference or coercion. All forms of diversity are accepted, including the diverse outcomes based on the choices people make, as long as those choices do not violate the rights of others.

Challenges and Change—Liberalism Evolves

An important belief of classical liberalism is that people will make the choices that are best for them if they are given freedom. Free of government intervention, the classical liberal promise was that the market would spread wealth among those who made wise choices. But what happens if this promise of prosperity is not fulfilled?

During the Industrial Revolution great wealth was being created as laissez-faire economists promoted a transition from the system of mercantilism, the system in which the state had accumulated the wealth. As a result of this transition, the wealth generated from the Industrial Revolution was mostly concentrated in the hands of a small number of society's elite, instead of the hands of the state. Most people remained poorly fed, poorly housed, and poorly educated, and had a short life expectancy. Although laissez-faire economists believed that these problems would correct themselves without government intervention, progressive reformers felt that the suffering should be addressed sooner rather than later. They began advocating change through government intervention.

Enfranchisement Brings Transformation

Beginning in the late 19th century, most Western democracies extended the right to vote to an ever wider group of citizens. As more citizens from the working classes obtained the right to vote, politicians who wanted to be elected had to promise to introduce policies that would meet their needs, such as establishing labour laws, initiating workplace safety standards, and allowing labour unions.

Events of the 20th century contributed to a further evolution of liberal ideology. If the evolving sense of liberalism sought to promote equality, consider how the following events of the 20th century might encourage progressives to urge for greater government intervention:

The late 19th century saw the advent of labour laws protecting the rights of workers. In what way does this represent a shift in thinking from classical liberalism? How would the **enfranchisement** of lower-income workers influence the range of political ideologies embraced by elected governments?

PAUSE AND REFLECT

How might a change of emphasis from equality of opportunity to equality of outcome affect society? To what extent can or should a government address the demand for equal outcomes?

PAUSE AND REFLECT

How do you think a classical liberal might respond to this article of the United Nations declaration?

- the First and Second World Wars
- the Great Depression
- the exclusion of minorities from voting and positions of power
- the change from a rural, agrarian society to an urban, manufacturing society

Modern Liberalism and Positive Freedoms

In Figure 8-4, the continuum illustrating the relationship between classical and modern liberalism and freedoms, one extreme is called *positive freedoms*. Unlike negative freedoms, which are "freedoms from…", positive freedoms can be thought of as "freedoms to…" Progressives (those who supported a shift to modern liberal ideas) believed that certain conditions prevented all members of society from achieving equality. For these people, government intervention was essential to ensure equality of outcome for all people, rather than simply equality of opportunity. One example of this is that taxes were established to provide social programs, such as welfare, for those who were in need of them. Progressives argued that any limits placed on the freedoms of an individual, such as imposing taxes, were justified if they benefited all of society.

The United Nations Universal Declaration of Human Rights contains many examples of positive freedoms. Consider what limitations to liberty the following rights may impose on some people:

Everyone has the right to a standard of living adequate for the health and well-being of himself and of his family, including food, clothing, housing and medical care and necessary social services, and the right to security in the event of unemployment, sickness, disability, widowhood, old age or other lack of livelihood in circumstances beyond his control.

**—Article 25.1 of The Universal Declaration of Human Rights
© United Nations, 1948. Reproduced with permission.**
http://www.un.org/Overview/rights.html

Modern liberals argue that the ability to exercise one's right to freedom depends on the existence of certain conditions. You cannot be free, they claim, if your basic needs are not met, if you are oppressed by unfair labour practices, or if you are subject to discrimination. To ensure freedom, modern liberalism urges government economic and social intervention. At the same time, believing that increased government intervention could result in tyranny, modern liberalism calls for broader social protection and guarantees of civil liberties and equal rights, combined with a more open and transparent government. Civil liberties are the means by which modern liberals seek to maintain dignity and fair treatment for all. Modern liberals seek to ensure greater equality of opportunity through positive rights, such as the right to education, health care, or legal aid.

Human Rights Day, December 10, 2007, marked the start of a year-long commemoration of the 60th anniversary of the Universal Declaration of Human Rights. This photo shows a march in Manila, Philippines on that day. The marchers were protesting alleged human rights violations by the government of Philippine president Gloria Macapagal Arroyo.

Explore the Issues

Concept Review

1 a) Identify three major differences between classical and modern liberalism.

  b) Identify three examples of positive rights and three examples of negative rights.

Concept Application

2 *Compare and Contrast.* The Chapter Issue asks you to consider the extent to which liberalism is continuing to evolve. To help you understand this evolution, work with a partner to compare and contrast how a classical liberal and a modern liberal might respond to the following scenarios:

  a) A family loses its home in a hurricane.

  b) A young person from a low-income household cannot afford to go to university.

  c) A corporation's "glass ceiling" prevents women and visible minorities from reaching the highest levels of management.

3 Do your comparisons of a classical liberal's response and modern liberal's response in Question 2 indicate how far liberalism has moved from its roots? Explain your answer.

4 *Explore Influences.* To what degree is diversity prevalent in liberal democracies today? Does the modern notion of equality refer to equality of opportunity, equality of outcome, or a combination of the two?

5 *Analyze.* The late 19th century saw the advent of labour laws protecting the rights of workers. In what way does this represent a shift in thinking from classical liberalism? How would the enfranchisement of lower-income workers affect the range of political ideologies embraced by elected governments?

Liberalism Evolves

Question for Inquiry

• **How is modern liberalism challenged by alternative thought?**

In the previous section you looked at the origins of liberal principles in classical liberalism, and how these ideas evolved into the ideas of modern liberalism. You have seen how rights and freedoms encompassed by classical liberalism—negative freedoms, or the right to be free from intervention—have been enlarged to include positive rights and freedoms—or the freedom to have the ability and opportunity to seek education, health care, and decent housing, among other things. Some of the ideas now embraced by modern liberalism originated in competing ideologies such as socialism and feminism.

While investigating how modern liberalism is challenged by alternative thought, you will explore the impact that environmentalism, neo-conservatism, religious perspectives, and Aboriginal perspectives have on modern liberalism. These currents of thought have both contributed to the evolution of modern liberalism and challenged the dominant influence of liberal thought on Western society.

In Chapter 2 you looked at how ideologies differed. The main differences were

- interpretations of history
- beliefs about human nature
- beliefs about the structure of society
- visions for the future

Keep these themes in mind as you investigate the following alternative currents of thought and consider how they may have challenged or contributed to the evolution of modern liberal thought.

Environmentalism

Environmentalism has roots at least as far back as the 1800s, but as a political and cultural ideology it gained widespread support primarily in the 1960s. Biologist Rachel Carson's book *Silent Spring* (1962) explained how pesticides enter the food chain and can negatively affect animals and human beings. Carson's book is seen as the initial impetus toward a greater understanding of the impact human activities have on the ecosystem.

Figure 8-7 ▼

The man on the right carrying the detonator is Nobel Peace Prize winner Al Gore. Gore is an advocate of environmental responsibility and a critic of policies that encourage irresponsible economic growth. The detonator represents the Kyoto Protocol, an international agreement aimed at reducing greenhouse gas emissions in an effort to prevent global warming. What does this cartoon say about the relationship between Gore's environmentalism and economic liberalism? What perspectives regarding environmental protection and economic liberalism does this cartoon present?

During the 1970s, organizations such as Greenpeace and Friends of the Earth arose and began pressuring governments to enact laws to protect the environment. Greenpeace has a long list of legal victories: from the 1970s, when France and the United States banned certain types of nuclear weapon tests, through the 1980s and 1990s when the United Nations banned driftnet fishing and countries banned the practice of dumping toxic waste in the oceans. More recently, several major computer manufacturers have agreed to stop using certain toxic chemicals in their products.

The influence of environmentalism has led some political bodies to enshrine the right to a healthy environment alongside the principles of modern liberalism. For example, Article 12 of the United Nations International Covenant on Economic, Social and Cultural Rights recognizes "the right of everyone to the enjoyment of the highest attainable standard of physical and mental health." For individuals to enjoy this right, the Covenant deems necessary, among other steps, improving "all aspects of environmental and industrial hygiene." Section 46.1 of the Québec Charter of Human Rights and Freedoms recognizes that everyone "has a right to live in a healthful environment in which biodiversity is preserved, to the extent and according to the standards provided by law."

Today, environmentalists often speak about the negative impact of many human economic activities. However, free-market economists and skeptics of global warming claim that environmental reform of the economy will do more harm than good. Discussing a recent book that is skeptical of the environmental agenda, Terence Corcoran, editor of Canada's *Financial Post*, describes these concerns:

> …'*The state of humanity has never been better,*' *says Mr. Goklany [Indur M. Goklany, author of* The Improving State of the World: Why We're Living Longer, Healthier, More Comfortable Lives on a Cleaner Planet] *in his book, published by the Cato Institute, backing his claims with detailed findings that show rapid advancement in hundreds of indicators for people all over the world. The conditions that created the great improvements—in health, environment, living standards, mortality, disease control, smog reduction, and human happiness—are the very same conditions the* Financial Post *has typically advocated over a century: growth, technological change, free trade in products and ideas, market forces and personal freedom.*
>
> *…The carbon and chemical economies that green salvationists want to curtail, even eliminate, are in fact the very basis for the world's current and improving conditions. The message in Mr. Goklany's book is that government policy must, above all, preserve the general conditions that have brought us to this state of achievement, not destroy them.*

—**Terence Corcoran, "Good sense to prevail over enviro-alarmism,"** *Financial Post* **March 1, 2007.**
Material reprinted with the express permission of: "The National Post Company", a Canwest Partnership. http://www.canada.com/nationalpost/financialpost/story.html?id=36e9cc22-feea-49ee-a36f-0e4d2b890147

Figure 8-8 ▲

In 1985, Greenpeace's flagship, the *Rainbow Warrior*, was sunk by the French Secret Service en route to France's Moruroa nuclear test site, bringing global attention to the political implications of environmentalism. What impact did the actions of Greenpeace and similar organizations have on the nuclear weapons policies of liberal democracies?

PAUSE AND REFLECT

Imagine that an individual living near a manufacturing plant felt that the waste produced by the plant was adversely affecting his or her environment. How might an individual's right to a clean environment conflict with the economic rights of the plant's owner, or the rights of the plant's employees?

On the other side of the debate are organizations such as the Worldwatch Institute. In its annual report for 2004 entitled "Richer, Fatter, and Not Much Happier," the Worldwatch Institute defies the idea that economic and technological advancement necessarily mean a better quality of life:

Higher levels of obesity and personal debt, chronic time shortages, and a degraded environment are all signs that excessive consumption is diminishing the quality of life for many people. The challenge now is to mobilize governments, businesses, and citizens to shift their focus away from the unrestrained accumulation of goods and toward finding ways to ensure a better life for all.

—Source: Worldwatch Institute, "Richer, Fatter, and Not Much Happier," January 8, 2004.
http://www.worldwatch.org/node/1785

The Worldwatch Institute advocates measures such as increasing taxes on manufacturers, minimizing the impact of production on natural resources through government regulation, requiring manufacturers to take back their products from consumers when they are no longer useful, and encouraging individuals to consume less.

Canada and Carbon Tax

Due to such factors as recent scientific findings regarding global warming, extreme weather events, increasing global temperatures, and the influence of mainstream media such as Al Gore's film *An Inconvenient Truth*, the environment has become an important part of most political parties' platforms in countries around the world. In Canada, environmental issues such as carbon emissions reduction have become key political points, not only for the environmentalist Green Party of Canada, but for parties such as the NDP, Liberals, and Conservatives as well. How these parties address Canadians' growing concerns about the environment, while considering the possible impacts of environmental policies on the Canadian economy and its citizens' pocketbooks, has become a key issue for many Canadians.

Prior to the federal election of 2008, the Conservative Party proposed emissions reduction targets for industry and caps on the emissions of specific pollutants. The NDP's environmental platform was based on a "cap and trade" system, where overall pollution would be limited (or "capped") by the government, and companies that reduced their emissions below the set target would receive credits that they could sell to companies that did not meet their targets. The Liberals proposed a cap and trade system combined with a carbon tax on each tonne of carbon emissions (the tax would be offset by income tax reductions). The Green Party of Canada also proposed a combination of a carbon tax and a cap and trade system. In September 2008, the Sierra Club of Canada, a volunteer environmental organization, graded Canada's political parties on their respective environmental platforms as follows: Green Party, A-; Liberal Party, B+; NDP, B; and Conservative Party, F+. (Source: Sierra Club Canada *Voter's Guide to the Climate Crisis Election*, http://www.sierraclub.ca/national/vote-canada/2008/voters-guide-climate-crisis-election.pdf.)

On July 1, 2008, British Columbia began to phase in a provincial carbon tax, the first of its kind in North America. The tax is designed to discourage the use of fossil fuels and thereby reduce greenhouse gas emissions. According to an opinion poll in May 2008, 72 per cent of Canadians surveyed felt BC's carbon tax was a positive step. (Source: Mike De Souza, "Carbon tax gaining support across Canada: poll." Canada.com, http://www.canada.com/topics/news/story.html?id=c28d5cd4-5404-4ade-a748-0352268d392c, May 25, 2008.) Political debate and legislation related to the carbon tax issue and its prominence in party platforms reveal that politicians are listening to the environmental concerns of Canadians, despite the potential financial implications for consumers and the effects on businesses.

PAUSE AND REFLECT

To what extent should the Canadian government implement policies based on citizens' concerns about the environment?

Balancing Environmentalism and Economics

In this excerpt, Y. C. Deveshwar, Chairman of the India-based Confederation of Indian Industry-ITC Centre of Excellence for Sustainable Development, talks about the "welcome development" of India's economic growth balanced with preservation of the environment. The Centre describes itself as "an institution that creates a conducive, enabling climate for Indian businesses to pursue sustainability goals."

India's new trajectory of high economic growth is a welcome development, providing the wherewithal to secure progressively higher standards of living. For such rapid economic growth to be sustainable it is imperative to include those living at the margin as meaningful participants in the economic process and preserve the capacity of the natural ecosystem to support growth aspirations. I believe that Indian Business needs to enlarge its contribution beyond its primary role of enhancing economic capital, towards also enhancing social capital and natural capital.

—Y.C. Deveshwar, Chairman, CII-ITC Centre of Excellence for Sustainable Development.
http://www.sustainabledevelopment.in/about_csed/chairman_desk.htm

1 Does Deveshwar's point of view reflect classical liberal or modern liberal ideology? Explain.

2 What might be the consequences of adopting Deveshwar's point of view? What might be the consequences of rejecting his point of view?

3 Should governments limit our individual freedom as consumers in society?

Neo-Conservatism

Like other ideologies, any definition of **neo-conservatism** is subject to the interpretation of its supporters. Irving Kristol, a prominent neo-conservative, has noted, "When two neo-conservatives meet they are more likely to argue with one another than to confer or conspire." (Source: Irving Kristol, quoted in Jonah Goldberg, "The Neoconservative Invention." *National Review Online*, May 20, 2003. http://www.nationalreview.com/goldberg/goldberg052003.asp) In fact, many neo-conservatives are former liberals who believe that their liberal policies failed. Some aspects of neo-conservatism challenge modern liberal principles and favour a return to particular values of classical liberalism. Other neo-conservative ideas challenge both classical and modern liberal principles.

Neo-conservatism emerged in the United States during the 1950s and 1960s as a reaction against modern liberal principles that were "taken too far." For example, during this period **civil rights movements** led to affirmative action, a policy in which minorities and women are given greater educational and employment opportunities to address past or current discrimination. This type of policy went against many Americans' ideals of equality and their strong belief in **individualism**. As well, the period of détente between the Soviet and American governments during the 1960s and 1970s, during which the two countries attempted to resolve their differences through diplomacy, was seen by some as a period of weak foreign policy. Neo-conservatives rallied against diplomacy with the Soviet Union in favour of actively promoting capitalism and democracy abroad and fighting against the spread of communism.

Neo-conservatism grew in popularity during the 1980s and was reflected in the economic, social, and foreign policies of American president Ronald Reagan and British prime minister Margaret Thatcher. The Cold War between the United States and the Soviet Union heated up during this time due to the massive funding of American military efforts against communism around the world. When the Soviet Union began to collapse in the late 1980s, many neo-conservatives felt that they had finally won the Cold War. During the 1990s, support for neo-conservatism dropped off and American presidents George H.W. Bush and Bill Clinton drastically reduced military expenditures.

In 1997, the Project for the New American Century (PNAC) was established by neo-conservatives to advocate increasing defence spending, promoting democracy and capitalism abroad, strengthening America's ties to democratic allies, and challenging other governments that are "hostile to [American] interests and values." (Source: Project for the New American Century, "Statement of Principles." http://web.archive.org/web/200708 10113753/www.newamericancentury.org/statementofprinciples.htm.

The principles of the neo-conservative movement are outlined at the Project for the New American Century website. See the Statement of Principles.) Many members of the PNAC became members of President George W. Bush's administration, and after the terrorist attacks on 9/11, a neo-conservative policy of promoting democracy abroad was adopted once again by the White House.

Neo-Conservative Economic Policy

Neo-conservatives generally believe that economic growth can be stimulated by cutting taxes and that government involvement in economic markets should be limited. Supporters of this policy believe that lower taxes in a free-market economy create conditions that provide everyone with the opportunity to prosper. This belief resembles classical liberal economic policy, since it encourages decreased government intervention and focuses on individualism.

Evidence of neo-conservative economic influence can be seen in international organizations such as the World Trade Organization (WTO) and the International Monetary Fund (IMF). These organizations promote free trade and reducing the tariffs, concessions, and regulations by which government involves itself in commerce. Some modern liberals are concerned about neo-conservative efforts to reduce government involvement in the economy, as they believe that governments have a responsibility to regulate trade and industry for the common good and the good of the environment.

As you read in Chapter 6, Milton Friedman, one of the most influential economists in American history, promoted classical liberal policies such as minimizing government involvement in the economy and reducing government regulation of all kinds. Friedman opposed government programs such as public education, public health, and public housing. His views on taxation, privatization, and deregulation were embraced by many neo-conservatives, in particular by President Reagan and Prime Minister Thatcher.

Neo-Conservatism and the Role of Government

Neo-conservatives are not comfortable with the large amount of services provided by modern government and prefer alternative ways of delivering these services. This challenges aspects of modern liberalism and, to a small extent, classical liberalism. Generally speaking, modern liberals believe the government should provide most essential services, such as education and health care. While classical liberals aim to minimize government intervention, they do believe government should be responsible for such things as education.

One example of neo-conservative influence is the establishment of private schools, which are free from many of the rules, regulations, and

Figure 8-9 ▲

Milton Friedman cited Hong Kong prior to its takeover by communist China as an example of an ideal economy: "At the end of the Second World War, Hong Kong was a dirt-poor island with a per-capita income about one-quarter that of Britain's. By 1997, when sovereignty was transferred to China, its per-capita income was roughly equal to that of the departing colonial power, even though Britain had experienced sizable growth over the same period. That was a striking demonstration of the productivity of freedom, of what people can do when they are left free to pursue their own interests." (Source: Milton Friedman, "Hong Kong Wrong." *The Wall Street Journal* October 6, 2006. http://online.wsj.com/article/SB116009 800068684505.html)

British prime minister Magaret Thatcher and American president Ronald Reagan. Thatcher's conservative administration reduced the role of the British government in providing public housing for low-income families. The Housing Act of 1980 introduced a right-to-buy program, in which people who rented government housing were given the opportunity to buy their homes at a price lower than its market value. The proceeds of the sales could not be used by local governments to build more public housing.

government controls that apply to public schools. In the United States, 23 per cent of schools are private, compared to 4 per cent in Alberta and 10 per cent in Québec. Naomi Klein, in *The Shock Doctrine* (2005), criticizes American economist Milton Friedman and his efforts to privatize public education and accuses Friedman and his followers of taking advantage of natural disasters such as Hurricane Katrina in 2005 to fast-track neo-conservative policies. Klein states, "For more than three decades, Friedman and his powerful followers had been perfecting this very strategy: waiting for a major crisis, then selling off pieces of the state to private players while citizens were still reeling from the shock." (Excerpted from *The Shock Doctrine: The Rise of Disaster Capitalism* by Naomi Klein, p. 7. Copyright © 2007 Naomi Klein. Reprinted by permission of Knopf Canada.)

During her time in office, Thatcher formed many government policies based on neo-conservative views. For example, during the 1980s she supported the privatization of state-owned industries; decreased taxes; reduced government programs related to health, employment, education, and social security; and promoted a free-market economy. Ideologically, Thatcher favoured individualism over **collectivism**.

Neo-Conservatism and Foreign Policy

Foreign policy is an area of common ground for most neo-conservatives and includes such ideas as the following:

- Patriotism is good and should be encouraged.
- World government is not a good idea, as it would lead to tyranny.
- A large country has interests that extend beyond its own borders, and thus it needs a strong military.
- Democratic capitalism is a preferable system to others and should be promoted internationally.

Neo-conservative ideology had a strong influence over the foreign policies of the United States and Britain during the 1980s, which fueled the Cold War. After a lull during the 1990s, neo-conservatism once again became a strong influence on American foreign policy in the early 2000s. It was one aspect of the decision to invade Iraq in 2003.

Neo-Conservatism and Morality

Neo-conservatives generally have traditional views about social issues. They are concerned about what they view as the demise of the traditional moral culture and tend to be suspicious of counter-culture movements. Influenced by the Christian Right, many neo-conservatives seek to curtail abortion rights, allow prayer in schools, and urge teaching about creationism in science classes. This is a challenge to both classical and modern liberal principles, as both tend to favour

State of the Union Address, 2002

After the terrorist attacks on 9/11, President George W. Bush addressed the nation and the world in a State of the Union speech that illustrated a renewed neo-conservative influence on American foreign policy. The following are excerpts from this speech.

The men and women of our Armed Forces have delivered a message now clear to every enemy of the United States: Even 7000 miles [11 300 kilometres] away, across oceans and continents, on mountaintops and in caves—you will not escape the justice of this nation…

States like these [Iraq], and their terrorist allies, constitute an axis of evil, arming to threaten the peace of the world. By seeking weapons of mass destruction, these regimes pose a grave and growing danger. They could provide these arms to terrorists, giving them the means to match their hatred. They could attack our allies or attempt to blackmail the United States. In any of these cases, the price of indifference would be catastrophic…

My budget includes the largest increase in defense spending in two decades—because while the price of freedom and security is high, it is never too high. Whatever it costs to defend our country, we will pay.

—George W. Bush, State of the Union Address, January 29, 2002.
http://www.whitehouse.gov/news/releases/2002/01/20020129-11.html

1 What ideas from this speech reflect neo-conservative ideas related to foreign policy?

2 How do these ideas relate to classical and modern liberalism?

keeping religion a private, personal matter. More about the political influence of the Christian Right is covered in the next section.

Religious Perspectives

Religious freedom and freedom of expression are principles supported by most liberal democracies. Consequently, not only are people free to embrace religious values that may conflict with the principles of liberalism, but they are free to express their critique of liberal principles. As you investigate the challenges and opportunities that some people's religious convictions present for liberalism, keep in mind that a wide range of **religious perspectives** exist. Just as the beliefs of different religions vary widely, the specific challenges each religion may present to aspects of liberalism also vary.

Figure 8-11 ▲

Jeane Kirkpatrick, neo-conservative foreign policy advisor to President Reagan and the first female US ambassador to the United Nations (1981–1985), was actually a Democrat when she joined the Reagan administration (the Democratic Party is usually the preferred party of modern liberals). She shared with Reagan and other Republicans, however, at least one key belief: that the United States should have an active role in fighting communism and promoting democracy around the world. She switched to the Republican Party in 1985.

- Can you imagine a situation in which the practices of communitarian groups such as the Doukhobors might conflict with the rights of an individual in one of these communities?

- Can you imagine a situation in which these practices might conflict with the values of the larger community?

Placing the Community Above the Individual

The Doukhobors were a group of immigrants who came to Canada from Russia in the late 19th century to escape persecution. Their beliefs included a form of communitarianism, meaning that they owned and worked land as a community, rather than as individuals owning private property. In addition, the Doukhobors did not recognize the authority of secular (non-religious) government, and so would not swear an oath of allegiance to the Canadian government. Because of these beliefs, the homestead land grants they had initially been given by the government were eventually taken away.

As you read in Part 1, Hutterite communities in Canada also practise community ownership of land and discourage individual ownership of goods. The members of the community, or colony, earn money as a collective, rather than as individuals. The emphasis such religious communities place on the community differs from the classical liberal concept of the individual as the basis of law and society.

Government Limitations on Religious Practices

Frank McKenna, former premier of New Brunswick and former Canadian ambassador to the United States, has stated, "Canada is truly a secular state. Religion and politics do not mix in this country." (Source: Frank McKenna, quoted in Juliet O'Neill, "US a theocratic state, says former Canadian ambassador." *CanWest News Service* June 1, 2007.)

Freedom of religion has long been a central value of liberalism; however, governments will sometimes place limits on religious practices to prevent them from conflicting with the rights of the individual members of a religious community.

For example, protests erupted in Toronto in September 2005 when it was announced that the government of Ontario was considering a proposal to allow Ontario residents to use sharia, or Islamic law, to settle family disputes. Sharia is the Islamic legal framework based on Quran, Sunna (example of the Prophet Muhammad), ijma' (scholarly consensus), and quiyas (reasoning by analogy), starting in the late 8th century. Today, legal codes based on sharia are enforced in some Muslim-majority countries, including Saudi Arabia and Iran, while other countries use sharia primarily to formulate personal status laws for cases involving family matters for Muslims, such as marriage, divorce, or inheritance. Some Muslims living outside of these countries also wish to use sharia law to settle these sorts of family matters. Critics argue that sharia law is incompatible with the Canadian legal system because, they claim, in situations involving family law, such as marriage, divorce, and inheritance, it does not give equal rights to men and women. At the same time, two important principles of liberal democracy are freedom of religion and equality, and at the time of the protests, Ontario allowed faith-based arbitration for members of other religious communities.

Ontario has allowed Catholic and Jewish faith-based tribunals to settle family law matters on a voluntary basis since 1991, but the practice got little attention until Muslim leaders demanded the same rights.

—Source: "Ontario Premier Rejects Use of Shariah Law."
CBC News, September 11, 2005.
http://www.cbc.ca/canada/story/2005/09/09/
sharia-protests-20050909.html?ref=rss

The proposal was later rejected by Ontario premier Dalton McGuinty, who also stated that Ontario would move to ban all religious arbitration, including existing Catholic and Jewish tribunals.

There will be no religious arbitration in Ontario. There will be one law for all Ontarians.

—Dalton McGuinty, quoted in "McGuinty rules out use of sharia law in Ontario." CTV.ca, September 12, 2005.
http://www.ctv.ca/servlet/ArticleNews/story/CTVNews/
1126472943217_26/?hub=TopStories

Although banning Catholic, Jewish, and Muslim faith-based tribunals may prevent some people from adhering to their interpretations of religious traditions in situations such as marriage or divorce, it also ensures that everyone is equal before the law.

Of course, such challenges to modern liberal principles are often limited to specific sects or groups within a particular religion, since religions often include a wide variety of interpretations and practices, as the following quote about Islam by Kristin Norget, an associate professor at McGill University, points out.

The appearance of homogeneity and conformity in Islam is deceptive. Muslims continue to debate the implications of the Koran's teachings for everyday life, and the relation between religious and governmental authority. Taboos and dietary rules are strictly observed in some places and not in others. Women and men have a more equal relationship in some forms of Islam (such as in Sumatra and Indonesia), than is the case in extremist forms of Islam (as in Talibanist Afghanistan)…

Despite Islam's underlying unity, interpretations of the Koran and the particularities of Islamic practices are as wide-ranging across the world as are its followers.

—Kristin Norget, "How Islam Evolved."
CBC News, January 20, 2004. © CBC 2004
http://www.cbc.ca/news/background/islam/evolved.html

How might religious perspectives on health, marriage, divorce, children, or life itself challenge specific liberal principles? How might those conflicts be reconciled? To what extent can modern liberalism accommodate the beliefs of people who live in a liberal society but do not share modern liberal principles?

PAUSE AND REFLECT

To what extent should a government impose liberal principles on religious minority groups?

Political Influence of the Christian Right

Christian Right is a term used to describe a coalition of conservative groups in the United States (and other liberal democracies) that focuses on applying specific Christian beliefs to public policy. The Christian Right could be seen to represent a challenge to modern liberalism, as illustrated in figure 8-12. Members of the Christian Right tend to feel that modern liberal society is straying from religious values and principles that they believe society should follow.

Figure 8-12 ▶

Many members of the Christian Right movement are politically active and lobby the US Congress to support their values and beliefs. They also support candidates they consider sympathetic to their cause. For example, President George W. Bush received a great deal of voter support from members of the Christian Right during the 2000 and 2004 elections.

Christian Right members generally:	Modern liberals generally:
• support the rights of the unborn	• support a woman's right to choose to have an abortion as protected by existing abortion laws
• believe families with heterosexual, married parents create the best environment for children	• favour equal rights for people of all sexual orientations, including their right to marry, and believe that all people equally have the right to parenthood
• support legislation against the use of overt sexual or violent content in television, movies, the Internet, and music	• support the freedom to create and distribute any material that does not infringe on the rights of others and the right for adults to choose the content to which they are exposed
• believe that religion has a place in publicly funded institutions, for example, that prayer should be allowed in public schools	• support secular (non-faith-based) policies and practices in publicly funded institutions
• focus on the need for individuals to take responsibility for their own actions and fulfill their responsibilities as community members	• focus on the need for unequal opportunities in society to be balanced through government intervention, such as affirmative action programs

Source: Grant Wacker, "The Christian Right," Duke University Divinity School, National Humanities Center.
http://nationalhumanitiescenter.org/tserve/twenty/tkeyinfo/chr_rght.htm

◀ **Figure 8-13**

Crowd attending the Washington for Jesus Rally on the Mall in 1988. US president Reagan's administration of that time was strongly supported by some members of the Christian Right.

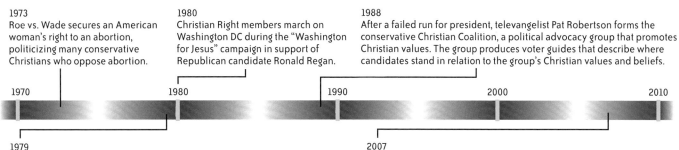

1973
Roe vs. Wade secures an American woman's right to an abortion, politicizing many conservative Christians who oppose abortion.

1980
Christian Right members march on Washington DC during the "Washington for Jesus" campaign in support of Republican candidate Ronald Regan.

1988
After a failed run for president, televangelist Pat Robertson forms the conservative Christian Coalition, a political advocacy group that promotes Christian values. The group produces voter guides that describe where candidates stand in relation to the group's Christian values and beliefs.

1970   1980   1990   2000   2010

1979
Televangelist Jerry Falwell founds the Moral Majority, a Christian Right organization that becomes one of the largest conservative lobby groups in the United States. The Moral Majority campaigns against limiting military arms, state acceptance of homosexuality, abortion, and media that they believe to be "anti-family."

2007
The Family Research Council, a Christian Right lobbying organization, meets in Washington, DC, during the Values Voters Summit. The goal of the summit is to decide on the best presidential nominee for Christian conservatives; all of the top candidates selected are conservative Republicans.

Figure 8-14 ▲

How might the events on this timeline represent a challenge by some members of the Christian Right to modern liberal ideas in the United States?

Religious Traditions and Modern Liberalism

What is the role of religious faith in a society based on modern liberal principles? Critics view some religious principles as incompatible with modern liberal society and express concern about their influence on political and social institutions. Others view religious faith as an important source of community and identity in modern societies, which may lack an explicit set of core principles. Consider the variety of perspectives provided by the following voices.

People are involved with church life in order to escape also from "liberal individualism." Over against mere secularity or privatistic do-it-yourself, pick-and-choose religion, millions are serious about being gathered together. Churches can provide community in a way liberal culture never can.

—Martin E. Marty (religious academic), "Filling in the Gaps of Liberal Culture," book review.
http://www.religion-online.org/showarticle.asp?title=907

Liberal democracy reached an understanding with religion a long time ago: your right, as a citizen, to observe your faith without persecution will be explicitly protected by the state.

In return, you will agree to make your peace with the civil law and respect the rights of others to pursue their beliefs. That's the deal.

—Janet Daley, "Pope's historic visit represents major challenge to all sides", *Daily Telegraph*, London, November 28, 2006.
http://www.independent.ie/opinion/analysis/popes-historic-visit-represents-major-challenge-to-all-sides-70723.html

Secularization is already a reality in the Muslim world. No Muslim society today is governed solely with reference to religious law; religious traditions no longer possess absolute or near-absolute predominance (except perhaps in some remote rural areas); and newly emerging leadership classes are almost everywhere displacing or marginalizing the clerisy of theologico-legal experts who used to control meaning and organization in these societies.

—Abdou Filali-Ansary, "Islam and Liberal Democracy: The Challenge of Secularization." *Journal of Democracy* 7, 2 (1996): pp. 76–80.

1 What issues and questions do these quotations raise for you?

2 To what extent can modern liberalism accommodate institutions and religions that run counter to liberal thought?

Religious Freedom and the Law

Something to Think About: Individual freedom of choice and freedom of religion are central beliefs in modern liberalism. What happens when a group of people within a liberal society uses its freedom to structure a community that embraces illegal behaviour? What role should government play when it is proposed that a religious practice infringes on an individual's rights?

An Example: There is a wide range of religious beliefs in Canada. Even within the same religion, sects have vastly different beliefs. In Bountiful, a town in southern British Columbia, this difference has created a dilemma that governments have not resolved after more than 50 years. An unrecognized, breakaway sect of the Mormon Church, the Fundamentalist Church of Jesus Christ of Latter Day Saints, allows the practice of polygamy, the perceived right of a man to have more than one wife at the same time.

Canada's liberal ideology is confronted with a dilemma. As a liberal society, common beliefs include freedom of religion, freedom of choice, and following the rule of law. Canada has a law against polygamy, but it is rarely enforced. As sects of various religions continue to practise polygamy, Canada must decide if it will grant the freedom to practise polygamy, considering the possible effects of this decision both nationally and internationally.

The following are perspectives on polygamy and the law.

I wish to state categorically that this Church has nothing whatever to do with those practicing polygamy. They are not members of this Church. Most of them have never been members. They are in violation of the civil law. They know they are in violation of the law. They are subject to its penalties. The Church, of course, has no jurisdiction whatever in this matter.

— **Gordon B. Hinckley (president of the Church of Jesus Christ of Latter-day Saints [the church of Mormon]), 1998, quoted in "Polygamy: Questions and Answers With the *Los Angeles Times*." Newsroom, May 31 2006.**
http://newsroom.lds.org/ldsnewsroom/eng/commentary/polygamy-questions-and-answers-with-the-los-angeles-times

A report posted on the Status of Women Canada page on the government of Canada website states:

At the international level, there is a clear movement toward the legal abolition of polygamy to promote the interests of women and children. Canada is widely known for its leadership in promoting the rights of women and the recognition of human rights. Canada should be very reluctant to alter this reputation by decriminalizing polygamy.

—"An International Review of Polygamy: Legal and Policy Implications for Canada." Status of Women Canada, December 19, 2005.
http://www.swc-cfc.gc.ca/pubs/pubspr/0662420683/
200511_0662420683-2_9_e.html#1

An article published in the *Vancouver Sun* in January 2006 says the following:

A new study commissioned by the federal government recommends Canada legalize polygamy and change legislation to help women and children living in plural relationships.

The paper by three law professors at Queen's University in Kingston, Ont., argues a Charter challenge to Section 293 of the Criminal Code banning polygamy might be successful, said Beverley Baines, one of the authors of the report.

"The polygamy prohibition might be held as unconstitutional," she said in an interview Thursday night. "The most likely Charter (of Rights and Freedoms) challenge would be brought by people claiming their freedom of their religion might be infringed. Those living in Bountiful (BC) would say polygamy is a religious tenet…"

Chief author Martha Bailey told The Canadian Press that criminalizing polygamy serves no good purpose. "Why criminalize the behaviour?" she said. "We don't criminalize adultery. In light of the fact that we have a fairly permissive society, why are we singling out that particular form of behaviour for criminalization?"

Baines said polygamy is rarely prosecuted. "No one is actually being prosecuted but the provision is still being used in the context of immigration and refugee stuff. People are not being admitted to the country." She said removing it from the Criminal Code will not force marriage laws to recognize it, but would only remove criminal sanctions.

—Melissa Leong, "Legal experts recommend Canada legalize polygamy." *Vancouver Sun*, January 13, 2006.
Material reprinted with the express permission of:
"The National Post Company", a Canwest Partnership.
http://www.canada.com/vancouversun/news/
story.html?id=e20244cb-63b2-47f9-893e-390453fa5067&k=24668

QUESTIONS FOR REFLECTION

1 What principles of modern liberalism are challenged in this example?

2 What may be the consequences of granting the legal right to practise polygamy to a group based on its members' rights to religious freedom? Whose rights might be compromised if this freedom is granted?

3 Based on this example and others in this section, in what ways can granting religious freedom challenge modern liberal beliefs and values?

Aboriginal Collective Thought

In Canada, some aspects of Aboriginal ways of thinking present an interesting challenge to liberalism, a challenge that has an impact beyond the realities of First Nations, Métis, and Inuit peoples. Several key Aboriginal principles challenge modern liberal ideology.

One of these principles is the importance of the collective. Whereas liberalism is founded on the idea that the individual is the basis of law and society, in many Aboriginal societies greater importance is placed on the collective rather than the individual. Thus, while not all Aboriginal communities are necessarily collectivist, the collective may have a greater influence on the choices individuals make with respect to, for example, natural resource development or economic development.

In addition, the many traditions of Aboriginal peoples seem to provide a different interpretation of progress than that of liberalism. Aboriginal peoples emphasize a connection to the past. Tradition and continuity are important, which is evident from the position of importance that elders have in Aboriginal societies; they are valued for their wisdom, knowledge, and experience. In many Aboriginal societies, group needs are more important than individual needs, and egalitarianism is also emphasized. **Egalitarianism** is a political principle that holds that all people should be treated as equals and allowed equal civil, social, political, and economic rights under the law.

> ### PAUSE AND REFLECT
>
> **How would placing group needs before individual needs present a challenge to modern liberal thinking?**

Nunavut: An Example of Inuit Involvement in Government

In some cases, the values and beliefs of Canada's Aboriginal peoples have had a profound influence on how Canadians are governed.

For example, in Nunavut, voters elect 19 representatives to their Legislative Assembly and none of the candidates belongs to a political party. Once elected, the representatives meet to choose a premier. The assembly blends parliamentary democracy with "the Aboriginal values of maximum cooperation, effective use of leadership resources and common accountability." (Source: "Consensus Government." Government of

Figure 8-15 ▲

Nunavut's Legislative Assembly

Nunavut, http://www.gov.nu.ca/wpc/nunavut.html.) Representatives make decisions using a model of consensus where elders have a crucial advisory role. The government uses traditional Inuit principles to guide its government, laws, and policies. The Nunavut government is guided by Inuit societal values that were outlined in *Pinasuaqtavut: 2004–2009*—a statement of values and priorities that includes four major goals to guide the actions of government: the need for healthy communities; simplicity and unity; self-reliance; and continuing learning. While the need for self-reliance suggests a focus on the individual, from Inuit perspectives it can also be seen as a responsibility to family and community. The Nunavut government also specifies that the number of Inuit employed in the public service be directly proportional to the number of Inuit in Nunavut society; thus, ensuring that the Inuit people are directly involved in the provision of government services. Unlike other provincial and territorial governments in Canada, the Nunavut government works alongside federal government officials in areas such as community planning and development and the environment.

Aboriginal Justice

Another example of a challenge that Aboriginal ideology could present to the principles of liberalism is in the area justice, through the use of sentencing circles in conjunction with western legal structures. Sentencing circles are used to determine the sentence for an offender who has been found guilty of a crime by the justice system. The circle includes the judge from the criminal trial, the offender, the victim, and members of the community, including elders. The group arrives at a sentence by consensus.

Sentencing circles were introduced in part because of a perceived bias in the Canadian justice system against Aboriginal people.

Sentencing circles are being adapted for some non-Aboriginal contexts, such as youth courts; however, most people who pass through the Canadian justice system do not meet the criteria for accessing a sentencing circle or a Peacemaker Circle. While an important value of liberalism is the equality of all individuals before the law, Canada also recognizes the traditional collective values and rights of First Nations, Métis, and Inuit peoples, and that justice is intended to be restorative and healing rather than punitive and retributive. This is also an important basis for other restorative justice programs in Canada, many of which can be accessed by all peoples who meet the criteria for these programs.

PAUSE AND REFLECT

- **What aspects of the Nunavut Legislative Assembly differ from the practices of most liberal democracies?**
- **If party politics are the norm, are non-partisan politics (voting without parties) a challenge to liberal principles?**

File Facts

Under restorative justice, wrongdoers are required to
- recognize the harm they have caused
- take responsibility for their actions
- actively get involved in improving the situation.
- address the damage done to the victims, themselves, and the community

There are several types of restorative justice programs in Canada, including
- victim-offender mediation
- family group conferencing
- sentencing circles
- consensus-based decision-making on the sentence
- victim-offender reconciliation panels

One example of a sentencing circle is the Tsuu T'ina First Nation's Peacemaker Court. Here, elders determined the kinds of cases that should be handled in the court; any case except homicide or sexual assault can be handled here. The court's judge, crown prosecutor, court clerks, and probation officer are all Aboriginal. A peacemaker representing the community is assigned to each case. Four rounds of discussion examine the nature of the wrong committed and its impact, and try to reach agreement on the case. The agreement reached by this court then goes to the Crown prosecutor, who may accept the agreement or simply use it as one consideration before passing judgment on the accused.

Returning Government Powers to First Nations Peoples

In July 2008, several chiefs representing Treaty Six territory began the process of creating a health care system for First Nations peoples outside of the federal government's domain. The following excerpt from an article in Saskatoon's *The StarPhoenix* describes some of the understandings behind this move.

THUNDERCHILD FIRST NATION—*Calling it a solution to government oppression, several chiefs representing Treaty Six territory took the first steps Thursday afternoon toward creating a health system autonomous from the federal government.*

Their vision includes Indian-run hospitals where patients can receive either contemporary or traditional healing methods, the latter relying on holistic and natural medicine from plants and roots, explained Eldon Okanee, a spokesperson for Thunderchild First Nation...

"It's time Indians took control of Indian health much like we did when we took control of Indian education," Okanee said. "Today our education institutions produce hundreds of qualified graduates. We have the same vision for universal health care."

When the Indian Act was created in 1876, First Nations people were prohibited from practising traditional medicine. Their traditional education, culture and languages were also banned as the government tried to assimilate them.

"We're starting to get those things back but we still have to fight," said Okanee, who believes the health-care system could be created by simply redirecting current funding from Ottawa.

—Darren Bernhardt, "Treaty Six chiefs promote Native health-care system." ***The StarPhoenix* July 25, 2008.**
Material reprinted with the express permission of: "Saskatoon Star Phoenix Group Inc.", a Canwest Partnership.http://www.canada.com/saskatoonstarphoenix/news/local/story.html?id=9b26cd92-f104-4953-a367-00a743e106e1

1 Why might a First Nations–run health system for First Nations people experience success where a federally run program has failed?

2 What principles of modern liberalism may be most supported or most challenged by this First Nations initiative?

Explore the Issues

Concept Review

1 Identify at least six specific examples of challenges to modern liberalism from alternative ideologies (for example, the Hutterite practice of collective land ownership).

Concept Application

2 *Gather and Analyze.* Develop a retrieval chart using the information in this section to examine the alternative ideologies presented in this chapter.

3 *Retrieve and Reflect on the Main Ideas.* Look back through this section and at other examples in the chapter to list what you consider to be the three most significant contributions or challenges that alternative currents of thought have made to the evolution of modern liberalism. You could also research additional examples. Discuss your ideas in a small group. Which idea do you think has had the most impact on Canadians? Explain.

	Interpretation of the Past	Vision of the Future	Beliefs about Human Nature	Beliefs about the Structure of Society	Level of Support	Impact on Liberalism
Environmentalism						
Neo-Conservatism						
Religious Perspectives						
Aboriginal Perspectives						

Communication: Analyzing Points of View and Perspectives to Form an Opinion

Throughout this text you are asked to consider the issue **To what extent should we embrace an ideology?** and develop an informed position based, in part, on your analysis of perspectives from a variety of sources.

Your Task: Read the following quotations and imagine that you are listening to each person express his or her point of view on liberalism. After you "listen" to each person, use an organizer such as the one at the end of the Skill Path to analyze the ideas expressed and rate the value of the quotation based on how much it helps you answer the Key Issue. After you have addressed each quotation, write a one-page statement to answer the Key Issue, using the most valued quotations as support. Use the Questions to Guide You for assistance. Note that the following quotations contain some very defined, and potentially controversial points of view about liberalism.

Sometimes the value of a thing does not lie in that which it helps us to achieve, but in the amount we have to pay for it—what it costs us. For instance, liberal institutions straightway cease from being liberal the moment they are soundly established: once this is attained no more grievous and more thorough enemies of freedom exist than liberal institutions! One knows, of course, what they bring about: they undermine the Will to Power, they are the levelling of mountain and valley exalted to a morality, they make people small, cowardly and pleasure-loving—by means of them the gregarious animal invariably triumphs. Liberalism, or in plain English the transformation of mankind into cattle.

— **Friedrich Nietzsche, *Twilight of the Idols*, 1895. English translation: Wordsworth Editions, Ware, Hertfordshire: 2007, p. 71.**

The whole modern world has divided itself into Conservatives and Progressives. The business of

Progressives is to go on making mistakes. The business of Conservatives is to prevent mistakes from being corrected.

— **G.K. Chesterton, *Illustrated London News*, April 19, 1924.**

What do our opponents mean when they apply to us the label "Liberal?" If by "Liberal" they mean, as they want people to believe, someone who is soft in his policies abroad, who is against local government, and who is unconcerned with the taxpayer's dollar, then…we are not that kind of "Liberal." But if by a "Liberal" they mean someone who looks ahead and not behind, someone who welcomes new ideas without rigid reactions, someone who cares about the welfare of the people— their health, their housing, their schools, their jobs, their civil rights, and their civil liberties—someone who believes we can break through the stalemate and suspicions that grip us in our policies abroad, if that is what they mean by a "Liberal," then I'm proud to say I'm a "Liberal."

— **John F. Kennedy, speech to the Liberal Party of New York, September 14, 1960.**

No idea holds greater sway in the minds of educated Americans than the belief that it is possible to democratize governments anytime and anywhere under any circumstances.

— **Jeane Kirkpatrick, "Dictatorship and Double Standards." *The Economist* December 23, 2006, p. 131.**

Liberals feel unworthy of their possessions. Conservatives feel they deserve everything they've stolen.

— **Mort Sahl (American comedian and actor)**

Democrats (I think to myself) are liberals who believe the people are basically good, but that they need government help to organize their lives. They believe in freedom so fervently that they think it should be compulsory. They believe that the poor and ignorant are victims of an unfair system and that their circumstances can be improved if we give them help. Republicans (I think to myself) are conservatives who think it would be best if we faced the fact that people are no damned good. They think that if we admit that we have selfish, acquisitive natures and then set out to get all we can for ourselves by working hard for it, that things will be better for everyone. They are not insensitive to the poor, but tend to think the poor are impoverished because they won't work. They think there would be fewer of them to feel sorry for if the government did not encourage the proliferation of the least fit among us with welfare programs.

—Andy Rooney, "Republican or Democrat." Reprinted with the permission of Scribner, a Division of Simon & Schuster, Inc., from *And More by Andy Rooney* by Andrew A. Rooney. Copyright © 1979, 1980, 1981, 1982, 1986 by Essay Productions, Inc. All rights reserved.

Questions to Guide You

1. To what extent is modern liberalism continuing to evolve? How does each quote represent (or not represent) the evolution of liberalism? Explain.

2. What perspective is evident in each quotation: classical liberalism, modern liberalism, or elements of both?

3. Which person's ideas do you believe are most valid in representing classical or modern liberalism? Rank the ideas from most to least valid and explain your criteria for your rankings.

4. To what extent does each person's statement inform your response to the issue?

Quotation Analysis Organizer	
Speaker: _____	**Date of Quote:** _____
What, if anything, makes what the person is saying powerful, significant, or compelling?	
Do the person's ideas refer to classical or modern liberalism, or other ideologies?	
Is the person supporting or condemning liberal beliefs and values? Which ones? How?	
What ideas do you believe are most valid and can best inform your response? Why?	
What ideas do you believe are the least valid and can least help inform your response? Why?	
How much does this quotation help you answer the Key Issue? Why?	① ② ③ ④ ⑤ (1 = very little, 5 = a great deal)

Reflect and Analyze

In this chapter you explored the following question: *To what extent is modern liberalism continuing to evolve?* The overarching theme of this chapter is that liberalism is not a static, unchangeable ideology. Rather, it is an ideology that evolves—it is open to revision, reprioritization, and reassessment. Historically this has been the case, and liberalism will likely continue to evolve, partly in response to challenges posed by alternative currents of thought.

Liberalism in Canada will continue to evolve, not only as Canadians confront their own political challenges, but also as we are influenced by political developments in other countries such as the United States, where there is both a narrower range of popular ideology and also a stronger tradition of advocating for freedom and rights. In addition, as First Nations, Métis, and Inuit perspectives in Canada gain recognition, Canadians will need to find a way of integrating more completely the concept of collective rights into the framework of modern liberalism. For these reasons, a wide range of sources of alternative thought should be accessed to ensure an inclusive discussion regarding the beliefs and values of our society.

Respond to Ideas

1. Now that you have explored various challenges to liberalism, in a group of three, develop a policy on a specific issue for a political party that you would support. Your policy should include clear justification for the position you have taken; that is, identify the principles that you are using as the basis for your policy. Post your political platform on a bulletin board anonymously, and have your classmates vote on which party's policies they would support in an election. Consider the types of arguments each group makes to support their policies, and the principles on which their arguments are based.

Recognize Relationships among Concepts, Issues, and Citizenship

2. Social programs in Canada are established to create greater equality of opportunity. Develop a list of social programs supported by the federal or provincial governments. Develop an informed opinion on the value and effectiveness of government intervention in these areas. Consider the value of embracing an ideology to address social concerns and note your opinions. Select a format and present your opinions to the class.

The Viability of Liberalism

By this point, you may have developed a tentative response to the Key Issue for this course: ***To what extent should we embrace an ideology?*** You have explored the evolving nature of liberalism and its impact on society and on identity. Your response to liberalism may have grown and evolved as well.

Any photo-essay on world history since the end of the Second World War likely would include some of the images shown here. All of these images present varying perspectives on liberalism. The big ideas to be derived from these images are similar to the ideas that challenge voters during democratic elections, as they decide to what extent they should embrace or reject liberalism. The importance and viability of liberalism continues to be debated in democratic societies. Can an ideology driven by a commitment to open dialogue and progress be embraced as a compelling and viable blueprint for the future?

Noted British philosopher and social advocate Bertrand Russell (1872–1970) observed:

> *The essence of the Liberal outlook lies not in what opinions are held, but in how they are held: instead of being held dogmatically, they are held tentatively, and with a consciousness that new evidence may at any moment lead to their abandonment.*

Signs of the big economic downturn of 2008; Czech citizens press for democratic reform in 1968; poster for *An Inconvenient Truth*, a documentary about global warming

The Spanish-born philosopher, Jose Ortega y Gasset (1883–1955), was a member of Spain's liberal and educated upper class. He once said:

Liberalism is the supreme form of generosity; it is the right which the majority concedes to minorities and hence it is the noblest cry that has ever resounded on this planet.

British statesman and prime minister Winston Churchill (1874–1965) explained:

Any man who is under 30, and is not a liberal, has no heart; and any man who is over 30, and is not a conservative, has no brains.

Part 3 of this course investigates the issue, **To what extent are the principles of liberalism viable?** These are the very concerns and issues suggested by the images and quotations on these pages.

To help you formulate a response to this issue, you will explore how liberal foreign policies have been challenged by both past and current global events. There is no consensus on the viability of liberalism, so attempts to impose this ideology have resulted sometimes in resistance to the principles of liberalism and sometimes in the reformation of liberalism. Exploring domestic and global examples will help you recognize the complexities of liberalism and uncover sources of resistance, to understand how people with alternative or competing worldviews respond to this ideology.

Finally, if liberalism is to remain a viable ideology, it must have a utilitarian purpose—it must provide a solution to a range of contemporary issues confronting people. Exploring the notion of *liberalism as a solution* will provide you with the final piece of the puzzle to help you assess the viability of this ideology

As you explore the topics in Part 3, consider the competing opinions that arise. To help you better resolve this issue, you may want to record the contrasting opinions you read about, as well as the opinions that challenge your current thoughts on liberalism.

Visit the Learn Alberta site www.LearnAlberta.ca and click on the *Perspectives on Ideology* learning object for fully interactive learning scenarios entitled ExCite (Exploring Citizenship). These scenarios related to issues and concepts in the Student Resource enhance learning.

ExCite

Part 3
To what extent are the principles of liberalism viable?

Chapter 9
Imposing Liberalism
To what extent, and for whom, has the imposition of liberalism been successful?

Chapter 12
The Viability of Contemporary Liberalism
To what extent do contemporary issues challenge the principles of liberalism?

Chapter 10
Political Challenges to Liberalism
To what extent should governments reflect the will of the people?

Chapter 11
Complexities of Liberalism in Practice
To what extent should democratic governments promote and protect individual and collective rights?

Aboriginal Experiences of Liberalism in Canada

- **To what extent has the imposition of liberalism affected Aboriginal groups in Canada?**

Figure 9-3 ▶

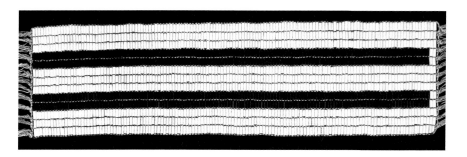

The two-row wampum belt was meant to symbolize the relationship between the Haudenosaunee Confederacy of First Nations and the European settlers as separate yet equal cultures. Do you think the relationship between the two cultures as it is represented in the wampum belt has been maintained since that time? Why or why not?

Differences between First Nations and European cultures were likely evident from the first interactions between European explorers and First Nations peoples. Over time, the Haudenosaunee Confederacy of First Nations in eastern North America (see map in Figure 9-4) proposed and understood that the relationship between themselves and the Europeans was one of sovereign nations that were separate, distinct, and equal. This relationship was portrayed symbolically in a two-row wampum belt marking the Treaty of Fort Albany between the British and the Confederacy in 1664. For the Mohawk Nation, the meaning of the belt is as follows:

From the beginning we realized that the newcomers were very different from any other people who lived on Turtle Island. Consequently, our people proposed a special agreement to be made between the two parties. It is an initial guide for developing relations between ourselves and any other nations. It is the timeless mechanism. Each succeeding generation is taught the importance of the Kaswentha, or Two Row Wampum, for generations to follow.

As you can see, the background of white wampum represents a river. The two parallel rows of purple wampum represent two vessels travelling upon the river. The river is large enough for the two vessels to travel together. In one vessel can be found the Kanien'kehaka [gun-yung-gay-HAH-gah], and in the other vessel the European nations. Each vessel carries the laws, traditions, customs, language and spiritual beliefs of the respective nation.

It shall be the responsibility of the people in each vessel to steer a straight course. Neither the Europeans nor the Kanien'kehaka shall intersect or interfere with the lives of the other. Neither side shall attempt

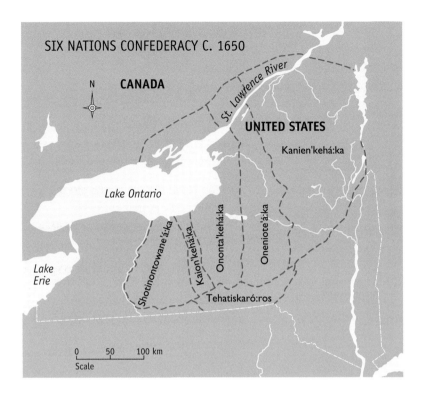

SIX NATIONS CONFEDERACY C. 1650

CANADA

N

St. Lawrence River

UNITED STATES

Kanien'kehá:ka

Lake Ontario

Shotinontowane'á:ka

Kaion'kehá:ka

Ononta'kehá:ka

Oneniote'á:ka

Lake Erie

Tehatiskaró:ros

0   50   100 km
Scale

◀ **Figure 9-4**

The Haudenosaunee Confederacy occupied much of the land in what is now southern Ontario, Québec, and upstate New York. The confederacy was a union of six nations (Mohawk, Oneida, Onondaga, Cayuga, Seneca, and Tuscarora) into a central government under the leadership of the Great Council of Sachems—leaders who were elected from each nation and who were equal in rank and authority. Each nation remained independent in all matters pertaining to local self-government, but the Confederacy transacted business that concerned the common welfare of all six nations.

to impose their laws, traditions, customs, language or spirituality on the people in the other vessel. Such shall be the agreement of mutual respect accorded in the Two Row Wampum.

— **Edward J. Cross (chairman, Kanien'kehaka Raotitiohkwa Cultural Centre, Kahnawake, Québec), quoted in** *Report of the Royal Commission on Aboriginal Peoples*, **Vol. 4, "Perspectives and Realities", Chapter 3, "Elders' Perspectives", 1996, p. 120**
http://www.ainc-inac.gc.ca/ap/pubs/sg/cg/cj3-eng.pdf

Conflicting Ideologies

As the Haudenosaunee had observed, there were many seemingly irreconcilable differences between the respective ideologies of the First Nations peoples and North America's colonial European governments. In the 19th century, the ideology of classical liberalism, and the concept of progress associated with it, became a dominant force in the thinking of many European and North American colonial leaders. This faith in progress became associated with the concept of modernism. Faith in progress had become an ideology, which is still common today.

Despite certain events of the twentieth century most people in the Western cultural tradition still believe in the Victorian ideal of progress, a belief succinctly defined by the historian Sidney Pollard in 1968 as "the assumption that a pattern of change exists in the history of mankind... that it consists of irreversible changes in one direction only, and that this direction is towards improvement."...Pollard notes that the idea of progress is a very recent one—"significant only in the past three hundred years or so"—coinciding closely with the rise of science and industry and the corresponding decline of traditional beliefs...

Our practical faith in progress has ramified and hardened into an ideology—a secular religion which, like the religions that progress has challenged, is blind to certain flaws in its credentials.

—Ronald Wright, *A Short History of Progress* (Toronto: House of Anansi, 2004), p. 3.

The idea of continual progress and the principles of liberalism stood in contrast to many of the ideas of traditional Aboriginal cultures. Although individual First Nations, Métis, and Inuit peoples have their own traditions and conceptions, there are general laws of relationships that are considered common to most Aboriginal cultures. These are the Laws of Sacred Life (including respect for oneself), Laws of Nature, and Laws of Mutual Support. These laws are grounded in the belief that there is a sacred power greater than us, and in the following related principles:

- All parts of creation are interconnected and manifest in the spirit of the Creator.
- Humankind must live in respectful relationship with all that has been created.
- Spiritual forces are gifts intended to aid survival rather than threaten it.

Laws of Sacred Life Each person is born sacred and complete.	Laws of Nature The natural world provides the gifts of life and place.	Laws of Mutual Support People in groups of mutual support are strong. Alone, a person will not survive.
• Each person is given the gift of body with the choice to care for it and use it with respect.	• A people's sense of place and identity is tied to the land/sea which has given the people life.	• Identity comes from belonging in respectful relationships with others.
• Each person is given the capacity and the choice to learn to live in respectful relationships.	• The natural world provides people with the necessities of life.	• Agreement on rules enables cooperation and group strength.
• Each person is given strengths or talents to be discovered, nurtured and shared for the benefit of all.	• People must live in harmony with the laws of nature in order to be sustained by it.	

—Source: Western Canadian Protocol for Collaboration in Basic Education, "The Common Curriculum Framework for Aboriginal Introduction Language and Culture Programs: Kindergarten to Grade 12," June 2000, p. 19.

The various conceptual differences between the traditional ideology of the Aboriginal peoples and the emerging liberalism of the immigrant society would eventually lead to misunderstandings in areas such as land ownership, education, work, and governance.

Conflicting Land-Holding Ideologies

One of the elders from Hobema [sic] says, "When [the Europeans] first came, the people who spoke on [the elders'] behalf told them, 'You see that mountain over there—that's not ours to give you—the land we cannot give you because it's not ours to give, it belongs to the Creator. Those trees and the animals we cannot give you, they're not ours to give. But this is what we'll do. That mountain, that rock, represents our faith and we will treat you in good faith. The animals represent our sharing and our kindness and we will treat you with kindness."

—Source: Rosalee Tizya, "Contact and Resistance: The History of Canada from an Aboriginal Perspective" (Center for World Indigenous Studies, 1999).
http://www.ascwa.com/documents/historyperspective.pdf

This land, over which you now wish to make yourself the absolute master, this land belongs to me, just as surely as I have grown out of it like the grass, this is the place of my birth and my home, this is my native soil; yes, I believe that it was God that gave it to me to be my country forever.

—Mi'kmaq chief in a declaration to the English, who assumed they owned mainland Nova Scotia under the Treaty of Utrecht, 1749, quoted in Report of the Royal Commission on Aboriginal Peoples, Vol. 1, "Looking Forward, Looking Back", Chapter 5, "Stage Two: Contact and Co-operation", 1996, p. 126.
http://www.ainc-inac.gc.ca/ap/pubs/sg/cg/cg5-eng.pdf

One of the ways cultural and ideological differences were most obvious was in the concept of land holding. As you have read earlier in this text, Aboriginal peoples have a unique relationship with the land. While people can control and exercise stewardship over a territory, ultimately the land belongs to the Creator—who gives the land to the people to care for in perpetuity—and the right to inhabit and live from that land is thus inalienable.

As more immigrants arrived from Europe, more land was needed to accommodate them. By 1812, European settlers outnumbered Aboriginal peoples by a ratio of 10 to 1 in eastern Canada. Treaties were negotiated that allowed newcomers to claim the land First Nations inhabited in exchange for promises of compensation in the form of annual payments, social and economic benefits, and the continued use of some land and resources. Many First Nations leaders wanted peace and harmony with the European settlers who were pressing in upon them, but, above all, they wanted to protect and preserve their way of life.

By the time of Confederation in 1867, 123 treaties and land surrenders had already been negotiated in British North America. By 1975 and the James Bay Agreement, there were 500. Many

 **PAUSE AND REFLECT**

What sort of practical problems do you think might arise, given the differences in thinking between Aboriginal peoples and the European immigrant society in Canada?

PAUSE AND REFLECT

- How are the conceptions of land described in these quotes different from liberal ideas of property and ownership?
- Given the differences between these views and principles of liberalism, what potential conflicts might arise over land use?

- **What do you think was at the bottom or the root cause of this attitude that the Europeans brought to treaty negotiations?**

- **How does this difference in understandings of historical agreements between First Nations and the Canadian government help explain the large number of land claims currently being negotiated between various First Nations and the Canadian government?**

contemporary conflicts between individual First Nations and Canadian governments have resulted from some of these agreements. Some of the reasons for these conflicts include the following:

- The British, not trusting oral agreements and traditions, insisted on European-style written and signed treaties. But First Nations societies were often not governed by a hierarchical leadership that could command a population to follow a leader's decisions. Often a chief could sign for his immediate band, but only if its members had been consulted and were in agreement.

- Language was also a problem. Negotiations were conducted through interpreters who not only did not totally grasp both languages but were also sometimes dishonest. Translation was a problem because European concepts such as exclusive land ownership often had no equivalent in First Nations languages.

- European attitudes of cultural superiority called the legal status of the agreements into question, even though they were written documents. The colonizing powers came to believe that the First Nations were not sovereign nations, and thus ceased to consider the treaties valid international agreements.

So far as is known, none of these treaties were put through the procedure in the British Parliament that would have been necessary for such status, nor have Canadian courts made such an acknowledgement. Where "Indian title" was admitted, there was no agreement among colonizers as to what it included. What was agreed was that a "savage" could never validly exercise sovereignty, which was a power that was recognized only for peoples living within organized states. Some further specified that the states had to be Christian.

—Olive Patricia Dickason, *Canada's First Nations* (Toronto: McClelland and Stewart, 1992), p. 177.

Attempts at Assimilation

The great aim of our legislation has been to do away with the tribal system and assimilate the Indian people in all respects with the inhabitants of the Dominion…

—Sir John A. Macdonald, memorandum "Return to an Order of the House of Commons", 2 May 1887.

In their efforts to have Aboriginal peoples adopt liberal ideology and a European way of life (a process known as assimilation), successive Canadian governments used several different means. One of these was the **residential school system** (mandatory boarding schools for Aboriginal children that had the primary goal of assimilating them into Western cultures and traditions), which you likely examined in earlier grades. Others included **enfranchisement** (giving non-Aboriginal rights to First Nations' men to entice them to give up their official Indian status and become part of the mainstream Euro-Canadian society) and various aspects of the Indian Act, both of which will be explored below.

Enfranchisement

The Gradual Civilization Act, passed in 1857, was another example of an attempt to assimilate the First Nations. Any First Nations man who gave up his official Indian status would be considered enfranchised and given 50 acres (0.2 square kilometres) of land on the reserve for his exclusive use. In addition, he would receive his share of any treaty settlements and other band money. When he died, ownership of the land would be given to his children, and land would thus be removed from the band's reserve.

Despite government efforts, only one person with Indian status was enfranchised between 1857 and the passing of the Indian Act in 1876. First Nations people protested against the Gradual Civilization Act and asked for its repeal. Furthermore,

...Indian bands individually refused to fund schools whose goals were assimilative, refused to participate in the annual band census conducted by colonial officials, and even refused to permit their reserves to be surveyed for purposes of the 50-acre allotment that was to be the incentive for enfranchisement.

—Source: ***Report of the Royal Commission of Aboriginal Peoples***,
Vol. 1, "Looking Forward, Looking Back",
Chapter 9, "The Indian Act", 1996, p. 272.
http://www.ainc-inac.gc.ca/ap/pubs/sg/cg/cg9-eng.pdf

Indian Act

To consolidate all the previous colonial laws governing First Nations, in 1876, the government of Canada passed the **Indian Act**. Until the 1982 amendments to the constitution, it was the single most important piece of government legislation affecting First Nations people. It not only defined what First Nations people could and could not do, it imposed a definition of who was a First Nation person. It separated First Nations people from the rest of the people of Canada and was used to control their behaviour and destroy their cultural traditions and customs.

The first Indian Act included an explicit goal of assimilation by which Aboriginal people were encouraged to abandon their Indian status, identity, and traditional cultures to become full-fledged members of Canadian society. Underlying this vision was the belief that Indian people needed to be regarded as children, or wards of the government, as indicated in the 1876 annual report of the Canadian Department of the Interior.

Figure 9-5 ▲

Sir John A. Macdonald (1815–1891) was the first prime minister of Canada. He helped shape Canada's policy on many issues, including Aboriginal relations.

PAUSE AND REFLECT

- **Why do you think only one person agreed to be enfranchised?**

- **Why did the government think that this Gradual Civilization Act would have any appeal to First Nations people in the first place?**

- **How does this policy reflect the imposition of liberalism on Canada's First Nations?**

Consider how different the tone
and language of the Indian Act is
from the tone and language of
the Mohawk explanation of the
two-row wampum belt. In what
ways does this difference in tone
reflect the imposition of
liberalism?

*Our Indian legislation generally rests on the principle that the aborigines
are to be kept in a condition of tutelage and treated as wards or children
of the State…the true interests of the aborigines and of the State alike
require that every effort should be made to aid the Red man in lifting
himself out of his condition of tutelage and dependence, and that is clearly
our wisdom and our duty, through education and every other means, to
prepare him for a higher civilization by encouraging him to assume the
privileges and responsibilities of full citizenship.*

—**Source: Annual Report of the Canadian Department of the Interior,
1876, quoted in *Report of the Royal Commission on Aboriginal
Peoples*, Vol. 1, "Looking Forward and Looking Back",
Chapter 9, "The Indian Act", 1996, p. 277.**
http://www.ainc-inac.gc.ca/ap/pubs/sg/cg/cg9-eng.pdf

The Indian Act represented a marked change from the Royal
Proclamation of 1763 in which Indian persons were recognized as
distinct peoples and nations with the right to negotiate with the
Crown as sovereign nations. Even though this relationship was not one
of total equality, the Crown still could not simply appropriate First
Nations land without negotiating and purchasing the land.

The Indian Act also continued the government's goal of
enfranchisement. It retained the system of voluntary enfranchisement
by which First Nations people could lose their Indian status and gain
full citizenship, and also introduced the compulsory enfranchisement
of any Aboriginal person who received a university degree or became
a doctor, lawyer, or religious minister, whether they desired to be
enfranchised or not. Later amendments also included compulsory
enfranchisement for any Aboriginal woman who married a non-
Aboriginal man, or any Aboriginal person who chose to vote in a
federal election or join the Armed Forces.

Recent revisions to the Indian Act have removed many of these
discriminatory amendments.

The White Paper

In the 1968 federal election, Pierre Trudeau campaigned on a platform
of creating a just society for all Canadians. As a firm believer in
federalism, Trudeau wanted a pluralist society that emphasized a sense
of group cohesiveness and belonging in Canada. For him, this meant
in part bringing Aboriginal peoples into the mainstream. In 1969,
Trudeau's newly elected government issued the **White Paper** that
proposed to abolish treaties, the Department of Indian Affairs, and
everything else that had kept the First Nations and Inuit people
distinct from the rest of the people of Canada. Trudeau believed that
their unique status was preventing the First Nations and Inuit peoples
from integrating into Canadian society. By ending the unique status,

First Nations and Inuit peoples would be able to "catch up" with the rest of society.

The Trudeau government, however, had failed to consult with First Nations and Inuit peoples in any significant way in formulating the White Paper. The paper had a hostile reception from First Nations leaders who saw it as just another attempt to assimilate them into mainstream Canadian culture.

We view this as a policy designed to divest us of our aboriginal, residual, and statutory rights. If we accept this policy, and in the process lose our rights and lands, we become willing partners in cultural genocide. This we cannot do.

—**Source: National Indian Brotherhood, quoted in Olive Patricia Dickason,** *Canada's First Nations* **(Toronto: McClelland and Stewart, 1992), p. 386.**

Taking a Stand against Assimilation: The Red Paper

In response to the government's White Paper, the National Indian Brotherhood published "Citizens Plus," which was also known as the **Red Paper**. In it, they outlined their objections to the government's proposed policy changes. Their observations included the following:

- *The legislative and constitutional basis of Indian status and rights should be maintained until First Nations and Inuit are prepared and willing to renegotiate them.*
- *First Nations and Inuit already have access to the same services as other Canadians, plus additional rights and privileges that were established by the British North America Act, various treaties and governmental legislation.*
- *Only First Nations and Inuit and their organizations should be given the resources and responsibility to determine their own priorities and future development lines.*
- *The government wrongly thinks that the Crown owns reserve lands. The Crown merely "holds" such lands, though they belong to First Nations and Inuit peoples. The government also thinks that First Nations and Inuit peoples can only own land in the Old World, European sense of land ownership. Therefore, First Nations and Inuit should be allowed to control land in a way that respects both their historical and legal rights.*
- *The Indian Act should only be reviewed when treaty rights issues are settled and if there is a consensus among First Nations and Inuit peoples on such changes regarding their historical and legal rights.*

—**Source: "Citizens Plus, also known as the Red Paper, 1970."**
Early Canadiana Online, Library and Archives Canada, Canada in the Making.
Copyright © 1998-2007 Canadiana.org (Formerly Canadian Institute for Historical Microreproductions) http://www.canadiana.org/citm/_textpopups/aboriginals/doc75_e.html, linked from "1951–1981: Aboriginal Rights Movement." http://www.canadiana.org/citm/themes/aboriginals/aboriginals12_e.html#whiteandred.

Figure 9-6 ▲

Harold Cardinal, a member of the Sucker Creek Reserve in Alberta, meets with Prime Minister Trudeau and cabinet ministers in June 1970 to discuss the establishment of an impartial commission to settle treaty claims. In 1968, Cardinal became the youngest elected president of the Indian Association of Alberta. He is best known as the author of *The Unjust Society* (1969). He also helped draft the Red Paper entitled "Citizens Plus" (1970) and authored *The Rebirth of Canada's Indians* (1977).

▶ PAUSE AND REFLECT

- **How does the Red Paper counter the government's attempt to impose liberalism through the policies of its White Paper?**
- **How does the Red Paper establish a new course of thinking and acting by First Nations and Inuit people?**

The federal government withdrew the White Paper and moved on to other concerns, putting First Nations and Inuit issues aside. Nonetheless, the leaders of First Nations and Inuit organizations continued to represent the interests of their members.

Commenting on the government's plan to repeal the Indian Act, Cardinal wrote the following:

> *We do not want the Indian Act retained because it is a good piece of legislation. It isn't. It is discriminatory from start to finish. But it is a lever in our hands and an embarrassment to the government, as it should be. No just society and no society with even pretensions to being just can long tolerate such a piece of legislation, but we would rather continue to live in bondage under the inequitable Indian Act than surrender our sacred rights. Any time the government wants to honour its obligations to us we are more than ready to help devise new Indian legislation.*

> **—Harold Cardinal, *The Unjust Society***
> **(Edmonton: M.G. Hurtig Publishers, 1969), p. 140.**

Contemporary Solutions: Land Claims and the Constitution

> *Business cannot be separated from the environment. The environment cannot be separated from the government. Government cannot be separated from social and economic issues. People cannot be separated from all of the above. Perhaps it is time to recognize this and make efforts to reinstate a whole-life perspective in education.*

> **—Patrick Kelly (Stó:lo [STAH-loh] Nation), quoted in**
> **D. Jensen and C. Brooks, eds., *Celebration of Our Survival:***
> ***The First Nations of British Columbia* (Vancouver: UBC Press, 1991), p. 145.**

Land claims and the non-fulfillment of treaty rights were two other major areas of concern. The government had never signed treaties with many of Canada's First Nations, even though they were dispossessed of their lands. Nations without treaties had been pressuring the government to negotiate land claims for years.

The patriation of the constitution in 1982 was an opportunity to resolve some of the issues. In 1982, the Constitution Act recognized and affirmed existing Aboriginal and treaty rights. Aboriginal rights are those rights that exist simply because Aboriginal peoples have inhabited Canada "from time immemorial." Treaty rights are rights flowing from the various treaties that the government signed over the years with the different First Nations. For the first time, the collective rights and identity of the Aboriginal peoples of Canada entered the laws of the country.

Land claims are slowly being resolved. In 2007, there were 861 unsatisfied claims by 445 First Nations, with a historical pattern of about 60 new claims being filed every year. (Source: Tom Flanagan, "Land Claims Shouldn't Be an Immortal Industry." *The Globe and Mail* June 4, 2007, p. A13.) One particularly troubled claim became a milestone in Canadian history when, on April 13, 2000, Parliament passed the Nisga'a [NIS-guh] Final Agreement Act, a negotiated agreement among the Nisga'a Nation, the government of British Columbia, and the government of Canada.

The **Nisga'a Final Agreement** is primarily a land claims settlement, meaning that the Nisga'a now have complete control over their land, including the forestry and fishery resources contained in it. This does not mean that non-Nisga'a people are forbidden from entering the territory or even living there. The Nisga'a government must make provisions for reasonable public access to the public lands under its control, including access to hunting and fishing on the land. The Nisga'a can, however, make laws that restrict public access in certain situations. In effect, the Nisga'a have complete sovereignty over their land, but there are some strings attached: laws that would severely restrict use of the land or resources by others must be approved by the provincial or federal government.

The most important aspect of the Nisga'a Final Agreement, however, is the measure of self-governance that the Nisga'a now have. Under the Final Agreement, the Nisga'a are required to make a constitution that will govern the Nisga'a people (a referendum must be held where at least 70 per cent of the Nisga'a people approve the constitution). They will have the ability to make laws, create public institutions (such as schools and hospitals), and have a separate police board. This does not mean, however, that they are exempt from provincial or federal laws. In particular, they are still subject to the Charter of Rights and Freedoms and the Criminal Code. And if Nisga'a laws conflict with provincial or federal laws, generally the provincial or federal law will prevail. In addition, the Nisga'a are required to consult with non-Nisga'a inhabitants on laws that will affect them.

The Royal Commission on Aboriginal Peoples and the Healing Fund

Canadians are fair-minded people. They know the situation as we've described in our communities is simply unacceptable.

—Phil Fontaine (Assembly of First Nations National Chief), speaking about the Aboriginal Day of Action (June 29, 2007), a day of national protests that were held to draw attention to government inaction on Aboriginal issues

The only voice that we have is when we start to target those things which disrupt people…, that inconvenience people. That's the only time we seem

Figure 9-7 ▲

A Canada-wide Aboriginal Day of Action was held on June 29, 2007, when some protesters in Ontario blocked sections of Highway 401 and the CN rail lines. They were protesting the federal government's lack of action on resolving important issues for many Aboriginal peoples in Canada.

PAUSE AND REFLECT

Whose point of view do you believe is most informed in their assessment of to what extent people in Canada have clear understandings about important issues for many Aboriginal peoples? Why?

to get the ear of government and the rest of the Canadian public to consider our grievances.

—Shawn Brant (a descendant of Joseph Brant) on the Aboriginal Day of Action, quoted in Sue Bailey, "Veteran native protester vows more militant disruption after day of action." Canadian Press Newswire, June 26, 2007.

As you may have learned in previous grades, the Canadian government formed the Royal Commission on Aboriginal Peoples in 1991 to examine "government policy with respect to the original historical nations of this country" (Source: *Report of the Royal Commission on Aboriginal Peoples*, Vol. 1, "Looking Forward, Looking Back," 1996, p. xxiii) After five years of inquiries and public hearings, the Royal Commission issued a report on its findings.

Among the Commission's recommendations were

- the creation of legislation recognizing the sovereignty of Aboriginal peoples
- the creation of institutions of Aboriginal self-government
- the creation of initiatives to address social, education, health, and housing needs

In the years since the publication of the Royal Commission's report in 1996, many people, including First Nations, Métis, and Inuit leaders, have been critical of what they perceive as a lack of government action to address the Royal Commission's recommendations.

One concrete result of the Royal Commission's recommendations was the creation of the **Aboriginal Healing Foundation** (AHF) in 1998. The AHF is an Aboriginal-managed, Ottawa-based, not-for-profit private corporation with the mission to "encourage and support Aboriginal people in building and reinforcing sustainable healing processes that address the legacy of Physical Abuse and Sexual Abuse in the Residential School system, including intergenerational impacts." (Source: "Mission, Vision, and Values." Aboriginal Healing Foundation website, http://www.ahf.ca/about-us/mission.) To accomplish these goals, the government of Canada awarded 1345 grants worth a total of $406 million to various programs in communities across Canada (including the establishment of healing centres in which counselling and traditional healing activities are available). The AHF was given an 11-year mandate to complete its goals and was disbanded on March 31, 2009. The Assembly of First Nations has called the AHF a "noteworthy success." (Source: Assembly of First Nations, "Royal Commission on Aboriginal People at 10 Years: A Report Card," 2006, p. 4.)

The Potlatch

A specific example of how the Indian Act was used to disrupt traditional First Nations society is the banning of the potlatch, a ceremonial gathering featuring sacred rites, dancing, singing, and gift-giving, which is a significant aspect of many West Coast First Nations cultures. In 1884, an amendment to the Indian Act made participating in a potlatch a criminal offence; appearing in traditional dress and dancing at festivals were also criminalized. The Canadian government considered such traditional practices an obstacle to "civilizing" the West Coast First Nations.

...Indian agents and Christian missionaries equated the custom [potlatch] with a range of vices. However, the objection was ultimately rooted in the Euro-Canadian notion of cultural progress, which opposed the uninhibited distribution of material wealth. [Canadian prime minister Sir John A.] Macdonald accepted the view that, "It is not possible that Indians can acquire property or can become industrious with any good result while under the influence of this mania."

—**"By Executive Decree: Potlatch," Order-in-Council Database, Library and Archives Canada, September 20, 2005.**
http://www.collectionscanada.gc.ca/decret-executif/023004-3062-e.html

Despite the ban, many West Coast First Nations continued to hold potlatches, which sometimes resulted in arrests. In response to one of these arrests, a Nuu-chah-nulth [noo-CHAH-noolth] chief wrote to the *Victoria Daily Colonist* defending the potlatch.

They say that sometimes we cover our hair with feathers and wear masks when we dance. Yes, but a white man told me one day that the white people have also sometimes masquerade balls and white women have feathers on their bonnets and the white chiefs give prizes for those who imitate best, birds or animals. And this is all good when white men do it but very bad when Indians do the same thing...

...I asked a white man to write this in order to ask all white men not to interfere with our customs as long as there is no sin or crime in them. The potlatch is not a pagan rite; the first Christians used to have their goods in common and as a consequence must have given "potlatches" and now I am astonished that Christians persecute us and put us in jail for doing just as the first Christians.

—**Maquinna (Chief of Nootka (Nuu-chah-nulth]),** *Victoria Daily Colonist* **April 1, 1896, p. 6, quoted in Penny Petrone,** *First People, First Voices* **(Toronto: University of Toronto Press, 1984), p. 70.**

Figure 9-8 ▲

Contemporary Namgis [NOM-gees] Nation potlatch

In 1921, Duncan Elliott, deputy superintendent of the Department of Indian Affairs from 1913 to 1932, issued revealing instructions to his agents:

It is observed with alarm that the holding of dances by the Indians on their reserves is on the increase, and that these practices tend to disorganize the efforts which the Department is putting forth to make them self-supporting. … You should suppress any dances which cause waste of time, interfere with the occupations of the Indians, unsettle them for serious work, injure their health, or encourage them in sloth and idleness.

—**Duncan Elliott, quoted in Pamela Williamson and John Roberts,**
***First Nations Peoples* (Toronto: Emond Montgomery, 2004), p. 133.**

Finally in 1951, the Indian Act ban on the potlatch was repealed. Since then, potlatch traditions have been revived in several First Nations.

Namgis Nation Chief Bill Cranmer says the potlatch is once again important in the lives of his people. In the past year alone there have been several potlatches and feasts, bringing hundreds of people into the community. The largest potlatch attracted more than 1500 people. New masks, headdresses and other regalia are being made in the community and worn at the potlatches.

"It's been a real positive for our community to have the cultural centre there," says Cranmer. "The families that weren't practising their culture 30 years ago, are now researching their family history, teaching their kids and their kids are proud of who they are. They are proud to be in the dance. The younger ones are proud to be able to sing the songs."

—**"'Namgis Nation,"** ***Treaty Commission Annual Report***
2006: Six perspectives on treaty making. **Indian and**
Northern Affairs Canada, December 21, 2001.
http://ainc-inac.gc.ca/bc/treapro/mreinf/pub/bctcr6/namgis_e.html

1 What is the hypocrisy that Chief Maquinna sees in the government's actions to stop the potlatch?

2 Why was the government so determined to end the potlatch?

3 How are these actions by the government ideologically driven? Could it be argued that this is an example of imposing liberalism on First Nations people?

Explore the Issues

Concept Review

1 a) Make a list of policies implemented by the Canadian government that can be considered examples of the imposition of liberalism on Aboriginal peoples. Explain each policy.

b) Make a list of actions undertaken by First Nations, Métis, or Inuit peoples to resist the policies and practices of successive Canadian governments.

Concept Application

2 Based on what you have examined thus far, to what extent have the attempts of Aboriginal peoples to resist the imposition of liberalism in Canada been successful? According to the evidence you have examined in this chapter, how viable have the principles of liberalism been for some Aboriginal groups? To what extent have some First Nations, Métis, and Inuit peoples been able to affirm more traditional collective beliefs and values while also working within political and economic systems based on liberalism?

3 Consider the principles of liberalism. Are there any significant differences between some Aboriginal worldviews and the principles of classical liberalism? In what ways has the meeting of these perspectives and ideologies affected Aboriginal groups in Canada?

Whose Perspective on History Is It?

History is the version of past events that people have decided to agree upon.

—Napoléon Bonaparte

The past is everything that has happened and can never be recounted in its totality. History is the telling of what happened and is by nature selective in that telling. In creating that narrative, by identifying what we include and exclude, and by making judgments about the merits of various actions, we make sense of the past and signal what is important to us now. The history we create depends on our present situation and purposes. Thus history, unlike the past, is never static—it changes with emerging values, ideas and audiences. Historical thinking is the act of interpreting and assessing both the evidence from the past that has been left behind and the narratives that historians and others have constructed from this evidence.

—Mike Denos and Roland Case, *Teaching about Historical Thinking*, eds. Peter Seixas and Penny Clark (Vancouver: University of British Columbia, 2006), p. 2.

Appreciating Historical Perspectives on Liberalism

As you consider situations where liberalism has been imposed on a society, it is important to maintain historical perspective. Historical perspective is the ability to consider the past and its observers on their own terms, through the eyes and experiences of those who were there. Historical perspective takes into account the historical context in which the event unfolded—the values, outlook, and circumstances of a society in a particular time and place, and of the observers whose version of events we are considering.

Historical perspective requires us to avoid present-mindedness, or judging the past solely in terms of present-day norms and values. People of the past did not think like we do because their cultures, education, values, and ways of life were different. Perhaps most importantly, historical perspective also requires us to avoid accepting one particular version of events as the only reliable version of events.

Thus, as you look at specific historical events that demonstrate the imposition of liberalism on a people, your understanding of why such an imposition occurred will be aided by keeping in mind questions that reveal historical perspective. For example, consider the following: From whose perspective was the imposition of liberalism beneficial? From whose perspective was it detrimental? Do any accounts of liberalism take a middle ground?

Your Task: Examine the potlatch ceremony discussed in Voices on pages 315–316, and explore the following issue: To what extent were the Canadian government's attempts to suppress the potlatch consistent or inconsistent with the principles of liberalism? Use the Questions to Guide You for assistance.

Questions to Guide You

1. To what extent is the position expressed in the Duncan Elliott quote consistent with the principles of liberalism?

2. In your opinion, how strong is the argument presented in each of the quotes?

3. What is the historical context of each of the quotes? How does this affect the position expressed in each quote?

4. Do the quotes provide an argument based on individualism, on concern for the common good, or on aspects of both of these ideas?

5. Who, if anyone, has the right to impose the principles of his or her ideology on another (think of such ideologies as the protection of private property and the right to a belief system)?

Bringing Liberalism to the World

Question for Inquiry

- **To what extent has the imposition of liberalism today affected people globally?**

PAUSE AND REFLECT

- **The author both admires and is critical of liberalism. What does the author see as the shortcomings of liberalism?**

- **Under what circumstances, if any, is a country justified in imposing its political ideology on another country?**

From a multiculturalist perspective, no political doctrine or ideology can represent the full truth of human life. Each of them—be it liberalism, conservatism, socialism or nationalism—is embedded in a particular culture, represents a particular vision of the good life, and is necessarily narrow and partial. Liberalism, for example, is an inspiring political doctrine stressing such great values as human dignity, autonomy, liberty, critical thought and equality. However, they can be defined in several different ways, of which the liberal is only one and not always the most coherent.

And [liberalism] also ignores or marginalizes such other great values as human solidarity, community, a sense of rootedness, selflessness, deep and self-effacing humility and contentment. Since it grasps only some aspects of the immensely complex human existence and misses out too much of what gives value to life, liberalism, socialism or for that matter any other political doctrine cannot provide the sole basis of the good society. Political doctrines are ways of structuring political life and do not offer a comprehensive philosophy of life. And even so far as political life is concerned, they need to be interpreted and defined in the light of the wider culture and the unique history and political circumstances of the community concerned.

—Lord Bhikhu Parekh (professor of political theory), "What is multiculturalism?" Seminar magazine, December 1999.
http://www.india-seminar.com/1999/484/484%20parekh.htm

Figure 9-9 ▼

Anti-poverty activists and riot police clash in front of the Ontario Provincial Legislature in June 2000. If Canada experienced a decade or more of political and social turmoil, including violent confrontations in the streets, do you think other countries would be justified in intervening and taking over the country to restore order?

Imagine that Canada has experienced a decade of political and social turmoil. Several governments have been dismissed and replaced. There are often political demonstrations in the streets, some of them violent. For a period of time, the Canadian Armed Forces take over the country, claiming that public safety is seriously endangered. Finally, after a series of short-lived civilian governments and military coups, an international force of peacekeepers, led by the United States, invades and occupies the country. A panel of international advisors decides that an unelected interim government should rule the country until law and order are restored. When this has been achieved, the advisors say, the Canadian political system will need to be significantly restructured. How would you react to such a situation? What would be the reasoning behind your reaction?

Such a situation sounds unlikely or even absurd, yet millions of people around the world have experienced a similar situation. Some of those people welcome foreign intervention, while others resent it. Let's look at the reasons for which some countries attempt to impose an ideology, liberalism for example, on other countries. The two biggest reasons are

- **Self-interest**—the imposition of liberalism to eliminate or reduce terrorist threats, or for reasons of economic self-interest

- **Humanitarianism**—the imposition of liberalism for moral or ethical reasons, such as to improve living conditions or stop human rights violations

Imposing Liberalism for Self-Interest

The world understands that whilst of course there are dangers in acting as we are, the dangers of inaction are far, far greater—the threat of further such outrages, the threats to our economies, the threat to the stability of the world.

—Tony Blair (British prime minister), speech to the British people, October 7, 2001.
http://www.pbs.org/newshour/terrorism/combating/diplomacy/blair_10-7.html

The idea of liberal democracies imposing liberalism on another country—by force, if necessary—is not new. American president Woodrow Wilson insisted that democracy be an essential component of the peace treaty with Germany and its allies after the First World War. In a 1918 speech (which would later become the basis for the terms of the German surrender) to the US Congress, Wilson stressed the importance of democracy and self-determination in establishing a lasting peace in Europe. Today, protecting national interests in our increasingly globalizing world is an important part of American foreign policy.

It may be a cliché to say that the world is becoming more interdependent, but it is undeniable that changes in communications technologies, trade flows, and the environment have opened borders and created a more interconnected world. These trends give the United States a greater stake in the fate of other societies, because widespread misery abroad may create political turmoil, economic instability, refugee flows, and environmental damage that will affect Americans…the spread of democracy will directly advance the national interests of the United States.

—Sean M. Lynn-Jones, "Why the United States Should Spread Democracy" Belfer Center for Science and International Affairs, Harvard University, discussion paper, March 1998.
http://belfercenter.ksg.harvard.edu/publication/2830/why_the_united_states_should_spread_democracy.html

Figure 9-10 ▲

On October 7, 2001, British prime minister Tony Blair announced that Britain would be participating in the American military action against targets inside Afghanistan. Blair, a member of the Labour Party, had been Britain's prime minister since 1997. Blair was heavily criticized for his unwavering support of US foreign policies and resigned as prime minister in June 2007 due to pressure from his own party.

One of the most common arguments for establishing liberalism through intervention is economic self-interest. According to this argument, exporting liberal democracy has both economic and security benefits. In this view, if liberalism can be fostered in a country where it is not present, it will benefit the economy of that country, which will in turn encourage trade with other countries, including liberal democracies.

That a process for removing leaders is built into the structure of democracy provides a systematic mechanism for succession that minimizes political crises…Thus, the disruptions of war are avoided and the energies that would be spent in conflict are preserved for economic development. The resulting political stability in democracies…contributes to greater investor confidence, facilitating economic continuity and incentives for long-term asset accumulation.

—Morton H. Halperin, Joseph T. Siegle, and Michael M. Weinstein,
The Democracy Advantage: How Democracies Promote
***Prosperity and Peace* (New York: Routledge, 2004), p. 14.**

http://www.soros.org/initiatives/washington/
articles_publications/publications/halperin_20041217/ch1.pdf

Furthermore, according to this self-interest argument, countries that embrace liberalism are less likely to threaten the security of other liberal democracies. Ever since the September 11, 2001, terrorist attacks on the United States, this argument has been at the forefront of most major military interventions. The "**war on terror**," a military, political, and ideological conflict headed by the United States, was a direct result of these terrorist attacks. The United States and many other countries—including Britain and Canada—invaded Afghanistan in 2001 to remove from power the Taliban, who were known to be supporting al Qaeda, the terrorist group responsible for the attacks. Prime Minister Blair justified Britain's involvement in the US-led attack on Afghanistan on October 7, 2001:

This atrocity was an attack on us all, on people of all faiths and people of none. We know the al-Qaeda network threatens Europe, including Britain, and indeed any nation throughout the world that does not share their fanatical views. So we have a direct interest in acting in our self-defence to protect British lives. It was an attack on lives and livelihoods.

—Tony Blair, speech to the British people, October 7, 2001.
http://www.pbs.org/newshour/terrorism/combating/diplomacy/blair_10-7.html

President George W. Bush has compared the "war on terror" to the Cold War.

It is an ideological struggle with an enemy that despises freedom and pursues totalitarian aims. Like the Cold War, our adversary is dismissive of free peoples, claiming that men and women who live in liberty are weak and decadent—and they lack the resolve to defend our way of life. Like the Cold War, America is once again answering history's call with confidence—and like the Cold War, freedom will prevail.

—George W. Bush, quoted in "Remarks by President Bush on the Global War on Terror" (White House press release, April 10, 2006).
http://www.state.gov/r/pa/ei/wh/rem/64287.htm

The United States extended the "war on terror" to Iraq in 2003, arguing that the country was a threat to the United States because Iraq could begin to use weapons of mass destruction to aid terrorist groups. Unlike the Afghanistan invasion, the war in Iraq did not receive international approval, and Kofi Annan, secretary-general of the United Nations (UN), said the war was illegal from the point of view of the UN. Only the United States and Britain (and small contingents from a few other countries) participated in the invasion. France was one country that did not support the US-led invasion of Iraq, arguing that an invasion would further destabilize the region. As a result, France saw some of its relationships with allies strained. For example, it is estimated that France lost a total of $113 million in wine sales to the United States because of an American boycott over its position. French foreign minister Dominique de Villepin had this to say about the US-proposed invasion of Iraq:

There are two options: The option of war might seem a priori to be the swiftest. But let us not forget that having won the war, one has to build peace. Let us not delude ourselves; this will be long and difficult because it will be necessary to preserve Iraq's unity and restore stability in a lasting way in a country and region harshly affected by the intrusion of force.

Faced with such perspectives, there is an alternative in the inspections which allow us to move forward day by day with the effective and peaceful disarmament of Iraq. In the end is that choice not the most sure and most rapid?…Given this context, the use of force is not justified at this time.

—Dominique de Villepin, speech to the UN Security Council, February 14, 2003. Global Policy Forum.
http://www.globalpolicy.org/security/issues/iraq/unmovic/2003/0214dominiquestate.htm

Imposing Liberalism for Humanitarian Reasons

…Americans should and do feel some obligation to improve the well-being of other human beings. The bonds of common humanity do not stop at the borders of the United States. To be sure, these bonds and obligations are limited by the competitive nature of the international system. In a world where the use of force remains possible, no government can afford to

PAUSE AND REFLECT

What is de Villepin's main argument for not invading Iraq? What does this say about the imposition of liberalism in other countries? What were the repercussions on countries that refused to join the American-led "war on terror"?

- Do you agree or disagree with the justification for foreign intervention expressed in the quote?
- How important do you think the "bonds of common humanity" are in forming the foreign policies of countries such as the United States and Great Britain?

www.CartoonStock.com

Figure 9-11 ▲

The United States has maintained an economic embargo against Cuba in one form or another since 1960, soon after Fidel Castro's new communist government nationalized American-owned holdings. This embargo makes most forms of trade with Cuba illegal for American businesses, and penalizes non-American companies for doing business with Cuba. One of the stated aims of the embargo is to end the communist system and bring democracy to Cuba. Do you think restricting economic activity is a legitimate means of encouraging modern liberal principles in foreign countries?

pursue a foreign policy based on altruism. The human race is not about to embrace a cosmopolitan moral vision in which borders and national identities become irrelevant. But there are many possibilities for action motivated by concern for individuals in other countries. In the United States, continued public concern over human rights in other countries, as well as governmental and nongovernmental efforts to relieve hunger, poverty, and suffering overseas, suggest that Americans accept some bonds of common humanity and feel some obligations to foreigners.

—Sean M. Lynn-Jones, "Why the United States Should Spread Democracy" (cited on p 319).

Apart from national self-interest, another common argument for imposing liberalism on another country is humanitarianism: a belief that a situation demands intervention for moral or ethical reasons, such as the improvement of the living conditions of the population. For example, philosopher John Rawls argues that liberal countries should not tolerate other non-liberal countries that do not observe human rights and that intervention may be justified in such cases. At the same time, he states that liberal democracies cannot intervene in other countries solely because they do not embrace liberalism.

In his account of the foreign affairs of liberal peoples, Rawls argues that liberal peoples must distinguish "decent" non-liberal societies from "outlaw" and other states; the former have a claim on liberal peoples to tolerance while the latter do not. Decent peoples, argues Rawls, "simply do not tolerate" outlaw states which ignore human rights: such states may be subject to "forceful sanctions and even to intervention." In contrast, Rawls insists that "liberal peoples must try to encourage [non-liberal] decent peoples and not frustrate their vitality by coercively insisting that all societies be liberal."

—Source: "Liberalism." Stanford Encyclopedia of Philosophy (cited on p. 105).

The altruistic argument is sometimes used in combination with an argument of self-interest to justify American foreign policy. The "war on terror," for example, was partly based on human rights issues: under the Taliban, Afghani women had virtually no rights, and Saddam Hussein's reign over Iraq was characterized by fear and torture tactics. However, as we will see further on in this section of the chapter, forceful intervention in a foreign country does not always result in improved living conditions for the citizens of that country, regardless of the good intentions of the countries who intervene.

Canada's Involvement in Afghanistan

Canadian troops have been fighting in Afghanistan since 2001, when a US-led coalition of countries began efforts to destroy al Qaeda forces in the country and remove the Taliban regime from power. In the wake of the Taliban's fall, Afghans held democratic elections (their first since 1969) in 2004 and 2005, a process in which women participated as both voters and candidates.

However, coalition forces have not yet defeated the Taliban entirely, and Afghanistan does not yet have its own armed forces capable of maintaining order and protecting its fledgling democracy from an insurgency. Currently, opinion in Canada is divided over the country's involvement in the Afghanistan mission. Here are a few points of view on the situation:

The hard truth is that an ISAF [International Security Assistance Force] retreat from Afghanistan before that country's own forces can defend its security would most likely condemn the Afghan people to a new and bloody cycle of civil war and misrule—and raise new threats to global peace and security... In sum, an immediate military withdrawal from Afghanistan would cause more harm than good.

—Manley panel (group appointed by the Canadian government to review Canada's presence in Afghanistan), quoted in "Extend Afghan mission if NATO sends more troops: panel." CBC News, January 22, 2008.
http://www.cbc.ca/canada/story/2008/01/22/afghan-manley.html

...it's argued that the mission is necessary to protect Canadians from the threat posed by the Taliban and Al-Qaeda. This is a serious argument, but it can be exaggerated. The Taliban do not pose a threat to the existence of Canada. They're not about to invade. Nor are they developing weapons of mass destruction and missiles capable of reaching North America.

The Al-Qaeda elements sheltering behind the Taliban do not pose an existential threat to Canada either. They certainly provide moral and perhaps technical support to aspiring terrorists elsewhere. But if the threat were truly serious, Washington would not have shifted its focus to Iraq. Nor would General Musharraf be allowed to conclude deals with pro-Taliban militants along the border of Afghanistan, while denying NATO forces access to that region.

—Michael Byers, "Afghanistan: Wrong Mission for Canada." The Tyee, October 6, 2006.
http://thetyee.ca/Views/2006/10/06/Afghanistan/

Figure 9-12 ▲

As of August 2007, approximately 2500 Canadian troops were serving in Afghanistan, in order to help the Afghan people rebuild their nation as a "stable, democratic, and self-sufficient society." (Source: "Why are we there?" Canada's Engagement in Afghanistan, Government of Canada, June 9, 2006. http://www.canadainternational.gc.ca/canada-afghanistan/approach-approche/wawt-psna.aspx)

We're not going to fight unless we have to. My soldiers are trained to fight. But they're also trained in humanitarian assistance and peace support, and that's our focus...And we're here to work with the Afghans, to work on those non-fighting aspects, because that's the road to success. That's the road in the future to provide hope and opportunity...The Afghans invited us here...The governors are so happy because they said, "You really are making a difference. You're not coming here to invade us. You're coming here to work with us and respect us by flying our flag."

—Brigadier-General David Fraser (commander of Canadian troops in Afghanistan, commander of coalition troops), quoted in "Cdn. general wants to bring peace to Afghanistan." CTV.ca, February 28, 2006.
http://www.ctv.ca/servlet/ArticleNews/story/CTVNews/20060228/david_fraser_060228/20060228?hub=TopStories

1 Which of the quotes above do you believe is the most realistic assessment of the situation in Afghanistan? What reasons do you have for your choice? Use the guidelines for historical thinking in the Skill Path as you make your assessment.

2 How do you think most Afghan citizens view the presence of foreign troops in their country? How often do you hear accounts of Afghans' opinions about the UN mission in news reports?

3 Do you think Canada has a responsibility to protect the new democratic system in Afghanistan? If so, what limits, if any, should be placed on that responsibility?

Figure 9-13 ▲

Robert Mugabe has led Zimbabwe since 1980, serving as prime minister from 1980 to 1987 and as president since 1987. Mugabe's policies, which have sanctioned killings of Ndebele tribe members and the expropriation of farms owned by white people, have elicited both domestic and international criticism. Since he has been in power, Zimbabwe's economy has spiralled downward, resulting in food and oil shortages that have caused massive internal displacement and emigration.

Reactions to Foreign Liberalism

The British and Americans have gone on a relentless campaign of destabilizing and vilifying my country. They have sponsored surrogate forces to challenge lawful authority in my country. They seek regime change, placing themselves in the role of the Zimbabwean people, in whose collective will democracy places the right to define and change regimes. Let these sinister governments be told here and now that Zimbabwe will not allow a regime change authored by outsiders. We do not interfere with their own systems in America and Britain. Mr. Bush and Mr. Brown have no role to play in our national affairs. They are outsiders and mischievous outsiders and should therefore keep out!

—Robert Mugabe, speech to the UN, September 26, 2007.
http://www.un.org/webcast/ga/62/2007/pdfs/zimbabwe-en.pdf

The imposition of liberalism is not always successful. Democratic elections are often hailed by the political leaders of liberal Western countries as a necessary prerequisite to peace and good governance. However, when they are held in an unstable political climate, elections do not always improve the situation. Elections may even exacerbate existing tensions between conflicting political movements.

Experience indicates that democracy requires a particular combination of institutions and informed public opinion. Outside efforts to impose change typically bring unforeseen consequences that may result in neither stability nor democracy.

—**William Anthony Hay, "Democratization, Order, and American Foreign Policy," April 2006. Foreign Policy Research Institute,**
http://www.fpri.org/enotes/200604.americawar.hay. democratizationorderforeignpolicy.html

PAUSE AND REFLECT

Do you think there are circumstances in which a country's stability and public security are more important than its citizens' right to democratic self-determination? Why or why not?

Foreign governments' insistence on democratic reforms may sometimes ignore the volatility of a particular country's domestic situation. For example, after 20 years of rule under Major General Juvénal Habyarimana, in 1992, the Rwandan regime established a multi-party system and became a coalition government, partly in response to pressure from Western governments. Some observers, such as journalist Robert Kaplan, believe that this coalition government, which was made up of conflicting ethnic groups, eventually created the circumstances that allowed the 1994 Rwandan genocide to take place: ethnic violence that caused the deaths of approximately 800 000 people.

Justifying his own reluctance to hold free elections during a 20-year period of rule, Ugandan president Yoweri Museveni, who has been in power since his military takeover in 1986, made the following comments about the limitations of multi-party democracy in Uganda:

I happen to be one of those people who do not believe in multi-party democracy. In fact, I am totally opposed to it as far as Africa today is concerned…If one forms a multi-party system in Uganda, a party cannot win elections unless it finds a way of dividing the ninety-four percent of the electorate [that consists of peasants], and this is where the main problem comes up: tribalism, religion, or regionalism becomes the basis for intense partisanship.

—**Yoweri Museveni, quoted in Robert D. Kaplan, "Was Democracy Just a Moment?," *The Atlantic Monthly* December 1997.**
http://www.theatlantic.com/issues/97dec/democ.htm

In the next section, we will consider reasons for which liberalism may founder when it is brought in by a foreign power.

PAUSE AND REFLECT

• Do you think it is realistic to expect non-liberal regimes to convert to liberal democracies simply by holding free and fair elections?

• What conditions do you think are necessary for a liberal democracy to survive and flourish?

Haiti's Troubled Democracy

Many citizens of industrialized countries are comfortable with the idea of providing aid to other countries during humanitarian crises such as famines or earthquakes. But opinions tend to be more divided when governments consider intervening in a foreign political crisis. Should industrialized countries avoid getting involved in foreign political situations unless their own security is threatened? Or do countries with political stability and available military resources have a responsibility to maintain or restore liberal democracy in countries where the political system has collapsed?

Something to Think About: Since June 2004, the UN has maintained an international peacekeeping mission in Haiti involving soldiers and police officers from 41 countries, including Canada. As of January 2008, there were 9000 UN peacekeepers in Haiti. Should foreign countries under the leadership of the UN intervene in Haiti to maintain liberal democracy?

Some Background: Haiti is the second-oldest nation-state in the Americas, having declared independence from France in 1804 after a successful slave revolt. Throughout the country's history, Haiti has had a succession of democratically elected presidents and military takeovers.

Haitians elected Dr François Duvalier president in 1957. He declared himself president for life in 1964 and ruled as a dictator until his death in 1971. He was succeeded by his son, Jean-Claude Duvalier, who ruled as president for life until he was deposed in 1986. For the next five years, Haiti was ruled by military governments.

In 1990, Haitians once again elected a president democratically. Jean-Bertrand Aristide was in power for only eight months when he was forced from office by a military coup. The military proceeded to rule the country until 1994, when the United States invaded and occupied the country, restoring Aristide to power.

Aristide's successor, René Préval, was elected democratically to office in 1996. Aristide was once again elected in 2001. He fled the country in 2004 after months of protests against his government, which his critics claimed was violent and corrupt. Months after his departure, the UN peacekeeping mission began. According to the UN Security Council, intervention was (and is) necessary for security and protection during the electoral period and to assist with the restoration and maintenance of the rule of law, public order, and public safety in Haiti.

In 2006, Haiti held its first presidential elections in six years, and René Préval returned to power due to voting that, according to observers, was marred by fraud. Despite the return of the democratic process, and the presence of the peacekeeping force, problems continue.

Here are a few points of view on foreign involvement in Haiti:

The United Nations Stabilization Mission in Haiti, known as MINUSTAH, *along with the help of international aid, has been able to achieve a "measure of political stability" and a "considerable increase in security" in Haiti, [Canada's ambassador to the UN John] McNee said.*

Figure 9-14 ▲

Haitian protestors clash with UN peacekeepers. Many Haitians do not believe the UN should be in Haiti at all. Does an organization such as the UN have an obligation to intervene when a country is experiencing civil unrest, or should the country be left to work it out itself?

But McNee said Haiti needs to find long-term answers to its deep economic problems.

"We were all struck by the developmental challenges in Haiti," he said. "The situation remains fragile. In fairness, we should stress the fragility of it."

The real challenge, he said, is increasing employment in Haiti, and if the economic situation could be improved, then people could be persuaded not to get involved in criminal activity.

—Source: "Haiti in better shape because of UN: Canadian diplomat." CBC News, April 25, 2007. © CBC 2007
http://www.cbc.ca/world/story/2007/04/25/mission-haiti.html

Foreign Affairs Minister Pierre Pettigrew downplayed demands for a Canadian withdrawal from Haiti on Monday, labelling protesters outside his office as "a marginal group of Haitian Montrealers."

Saying the protesters were "fixated on the past and nostalgia," Pettigrew dashed any hopes of a Canadian pullout, expressing his belief that Canada is helping bring stability to the strife-torn Caribbean nation.

The group is among a growing movement in Canada demanding the return of Canadian police officers working to revamp the Haitian National Police. Their voices have become even louder since the December shooting death of retired RCMP officer Mark Bourque, part of the mission in Haiti.

Activists have accused members of the UN stability mission of contributing to the chaos by helping a [supposedly] corrupt Haitian police force support the Haitian elite while targeting the poor majority, many of whom oppose the interim government.

—Source: "Pettigrew: Canada will stay the course in Haiti," CTV.ca, January 3, 2006.
http://www.ctv.ca/servlet/ArticleNews/story/CTVNews/20060103/staying_Haiti_060103/20060103?hub=Canada

By permission of Gary Markstein and Creators Syndicate, Inc.

Figure 9-15 ▲

What do you think this cartoonist's opinion is regarding the political stability in Haiti? Do the sources in this Investigation provide any other perspectives regarding issues in Haiti?

QUESTIONS FOR REFLECTION

1. Why do you think Canada has successful democratic governments whereas Haiti's democratic governments have not worked?

2. Working in a small group, brainstorm reasons why the United States and other industrialized countries, including Canada, sometimes attempt to impose their ideology of liberal democracy on other countries. Come up with as many reasons as you can, and then rank these reasons from the most justifiable reason to the least justifiable reason. The group should come up with a consensus on the ranking. If you cannot come to a consensus, complete the ranking by preferential voting. For example, if your group came up with 10 reasons, each group member would rank the reasons from 1 to 10. A reason ranked 1 (the most justifiable) would get 10 points, and a reason ranked 10 would get 1 point. Add up all the votes cast for each reason and you will have a ranking for your whole group (that is, the reason with the highest number of points will be ranked in first place, and the reason with the least number of points will be ranked tenth).

3. Explore the different ways groups can make decisions. Is voting, as in our democratic tradition, always the best way? What are the strengths and weaknesses of decision making by voting as opposed to other forms of decision making such as authoritarian or one-person rule, consensus, and preferential voting?

Why Can Liberalism Fail?

History has demonstrated that there is no final triumph of reason, whether it goes by the name of Christianity, the Enlightenment, or, now, democracy. To think that democracy as we know it will triumph—or is even here to stay—is itself a form of determinism, driven by our own ethnocentricity.

—Robert D. Kaplan, "Was Democracy Just a Moment?,"
***The Atlantic Monthly* December 1997.**
http://www.theatlantic.com/issues/97dec/democ.htm

Living in a country with a long history of liberal democratic institutions, you may find it strange that some other countries cannot maintain similar institutions themselves once a freely elected government is in power. However, as you have seen in past chapters, liberalism was not adopted overnight by countries such as Canada or the United States. As an ideology, it has evolved over a long period of time, and certain aspects of it have changed as historical circumstances have changed.

As the democratic election of Hitler in Germany demonstrates, liberal democracy has difficulty surviving conditions such as unemployment, inflation, and civil unrest in a country without an existing liberal democratic tradition. In his book *The Future of Freedom*, author Fareed Zakaria discusses a statistical study of the economic conditions necessary for the survival of a democratic political system.

Of course some poor countries have become democracies. But <u>when</u> countries become democratic at <u>low levels of development</u>, their <u>democracy usually dies</u>. (There are exceptions, such as India...) The most comprehensive statistical study of this problem, conducted by political scientists Adam Przeworski and Fernando Limongi, looked at every country in the world between the years 1950 and 1990. It calculated that in a democratic country that has a per capita income of under $1500 (in today's dollars), the regime on average had a life expectancy of just eight years. With between $1500 and $3000 it survived on average for about eighteen years. Above $6000 it became highly resilient. The chance that a democratic regime would die in a country with an income above $6000 was 1 in 500. Once rich, democracies become immortal. Thirty-two democratic regimes have existed at incomes above roughly $9000 for a combined total of 736 years. Not one has died. By contrast, of the 69 democratic regimes that were poorer, 39 failed—a death rate of 56 percent.

—From: *The Future of Freedom: Illiberal Democracy at Home and Abroad* by Fareed Zakaria © 2003 by Fareed Zakaria. Used by permission of W.W. Norton & Company Inc.

When the right conditions for success are not present, some argue, it may even be harmful to another country's security to try to foster liberal democracy prematurely. William Anthony Hay of the Foreign Policy Research Institute makes the following argument:

> No easy path exists to national cohesion and democratic institutions in developing nations. Forcing democratization's pace risks unrest, particularly where deep fault lines exist within societies. Sectarian differences and opposing economic interests can both work against the basic level of consensus that democracy requires, and ethnic conflict introduces another volatile factor that often combines with religion and economic disparities. Rapid change and competition for power within a society exacerbate preexisting ethnic tensions, as seen in post-1989 conflicts from Yugoslavia to Rwanda...

> **—William Anthony Hay, "Democratization, Order, and American Foreign Policy," April 2006. Foreign Policy Research Institute.**
> http://www.fpri.org/enotes/200604.americawar.hay.
> democratizationorderforeignpolicy.html

Referring to Canadian foreign policy, author Tom Keating argues that ultimately, the health of a country's political institutions is dependent on its citizens, regardless of foreign intervention.

> In reviewing Canadian peacebuilding efforts in Africa, Lucie Edwards stated that: "We may be able to offer some help, in the form of financial aid, or advice, or training, or even the temporary stationing of peacekeepers, but in the end, it will be up to Africans to find their own solutions to their conflicts."

> **—Tom Keating, "What Can Others Do? Foreign Governments and the Politics of Peacebuilding," *Dilemmas of Reconciliation: Cases and Concepts* eds. Carol A.L. Prager and Trudy Govier (Waterloo, ON: Wilfrid Laurier University Press, 2003), p. 190.**

This is not a new idea. Philosopher John Stuart Mill expressed the same sentiment 150 years ago.

> ...there can seldom be anything approaching to assurance that intervention, even if successful, would be for the good of the people themselves. The only test possessing any real value, of a people's having become fit for popular institutions, is that they, or a sufficient proportion of them to prevail in the contest, are willing to brave labour and danger for their liberation.

> **—John Stuart Mill, "A Few Words on Non-Intervention," 1859.**

Mill seems to be suggesting that intervention in another country cannot be justified, because the support of the majority of the local population would be necessary for the success of the intervention.

Explore the Issues

Concept Review

1. Complete a table that looks like the one below based on the material you have read in this section.

Arguments for the Imposition of Liberalism	Examples for Each Argument
Arguments against the Imposition of Liberalism	**Examples for Each Argument**

Concept Application

2. What principles of modern liberalism do you think can be successfully fostered in a country by foreign intervention? What principles of modern liberalism can be embraced only through domestic support or instigation? To what extent has the imposition of liberalism today affected people globally? Are there more effective ways of encouraging modern liberalism than those addressed throughout the chapter?

3. Historically, how successful do you think liberal democracies have been in fostering liberalism in other countries?

4. Do Western liberal democracies insist that all their foreign allies embrace liberalism? List examples where they have not done so and why this would be.

5. Are there circumstances in which a country's stability and national security are more important than its citizens' rights to democratic self-determination? Why or why not?

Reflect and Analyze

In this chapter you have explored the question *To what extent, and for whom, has the imposition of liberalism been successful?* and considered how this imposition can have an impact on the viability of liberal principles in democratic societies, notably in North America. First you looked at the effects of the imposition of liberalism on First Nations peoples by North America's colonial European governments and later by the Canadian government on First Nations and Inuit peoples. You considered some of the differences between Aboriginal and European liberal ideologies, and how these differences led to conflicts over issues such as governance and land holding. You also examined attempts to assimilate First Nations, Métis, and Inuit peoples into non-Aboriginal Canadian society and contemporary efforts to resolve some of the issues facing Aboriginal peoples.

Next you broadened the perspective to think about how people in other countries around the world have been affected by the imposition of modern liberalism. You considered some of the arguments used to justify foreign intervention in non-liberal countries, such as self-interest and humanitarianism You also thought about the impact of attempts to impose liberalism and how local populations can be affected by foreign intervention.

Respond to Ideas

1 Reflect on what you have read, thought about, and researched in this chapter. Express your thoughts on the following question: What principles of modern liberalism, if any, can and should be imposed on non-liberal societies? To what extent could the imposition of liberal principles impact the ability of these principles to be successfully embraced and implemented in a society?

Respond to Issues

2 Are there other means of encouraging modern liberalism that would be more successful than those addressed throughout this chapter?

3 Research an example of a First Nations, Métis, or Inuit organization or group that has applied some of the principles of liberalism and its own more traditional approaches to decision making and governance. To what extent has this organization or group succeeded in bridging individual and collective approaches and worldviews in an effort to achieve goals for its people and community?

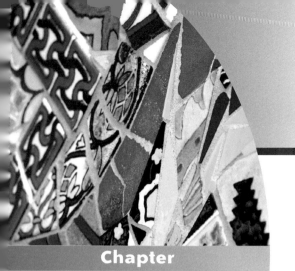

10

Political Challenges to Liberalism

◀ **Figure 10-1**

David Kilgour was first elected to the House of Commons in 1979 as a Progressive Conservative in an Edmonton riding. When he refused to support the introduction of the GST (goods and services tax) in 1990, he was expelled from the Progressive Conservative party, and he became a Liberal. In 2005, he crossed the floor (resigned from the Liberal party) and became an independent because he opposed several Liberal policies.

KEY SKILLS

Integrating and synthesizing argumentation and evidence into an informed position

KEY CONCEPTS

Exploring the extent to which liberal governments reflect the will of the people

Key Terms

Authoritarianism
Consensus decision making
Direct democracy
Military dictatorship
Oligarchy
One-Party state
Party solidarity
Proportional representation
Representative democracy
Responsible government

After almost 15 years as a Liberal MP, and after serious consideration, I concluded last week that I can no longer remain in the party's caucus. My objection to many of the party's new policies...proved painfully decisive.

Calls and e-mails to my office suggest that most constituents support my decision to sit as an independent legislator. Like me, they are concerned by the Liberals' stance on numerous issues.

—**David Kilgour, "Why I left the Liberal Party."**
National Post **April 19, 2005, p. A18.**

Kilgour opposed these party policies because of his own beliefs and the unpopularity of those policies in his riding. He considered that his first duty as a Member of Parliament (MP) was to represent the will of his constituents rather than the will of his party. The tradition of **party solidarity** is a key aspect of Canadian politics: it requires that all party members vote with the party (except in rare instances when party leadership explicitly frees them from this obligation, in what is known as a free vote). Because of the adversarial nature of the parliamentary tradition, party solidarity is enforced.

The party in power can be forced to resign or call an election if

- it loses a vote on an appropriation bill (which authorizes government spending), a taxation bill, or the annual budget
- a motion of confidence (that is, confidence in the government) is rejected by a majority vote
- a motion of non-confidence (that is, non-confidence in the government) is passed by a majority vote

In such cases, the government is considered to have lost its mandate to govern.

The question arises, therefore, as to whether MPs should vote according to the will of their constituents or according to the policy of their party, regardless of their personal beliefs or their constituents' opinions. Most of the time, because of our parliamentary system, party solidarity prevails and each MP votes with his or her party. Occasionally, however, MPs take a stand and refuse to endorse a policy with which they or their constituents disagree. This usually results in the MP either being forced out of the party or leaving voluntarily. MP Kilgour went through both of these situations, first when he disagreed with the Progressive Conservative party in 1990 over the GST, and then in 2005 when he disagreed with the Liberal party's position on several issues.

Chapter Issue

Figure 10-2 ▲

Figure 10-3 ▲

Citizens of a country have a variety of needs and wants. Is it possible for a democratic government to meet the needs of everyone all the time? Should this be the goal of government?

Democracy is never a final achievement. It is a call to an untiring effort.

—John F. Kennedy, speech in Costa Rica, March, 1963.

Liberal democracy stands as a fragile but enduring human experiment to test the hypothesis that ordinary human beings are capable of making wise judgments in matters concerning their own and others' well-being.

According to liberal principles, the ordinary individual citizen (and the aggregated opinions of citizens, referred to as the "will of the people") is central to the shape and workings of government. Ideally, the governing system, its institutions, actions, and legal structures, are designed with the individual citizen's participation and inviolability in mind. This is, of course, an ideal, and the actual practice, even within democratic governments, often falls far short of this ideal. This chapter explores how close to the ideal various systems of government come by asking the question *To what extent should governments reflect the will of the people?*

This exploration will touch on some of the principles central to liberalism, such as individual equality and worth, the rule of law, respecting private property, and ruling through the consent of the governed (the will of the people). It will also help you address the Related Issue for Part 3 of this text: *To what extent are the principles of liberalism viable?*

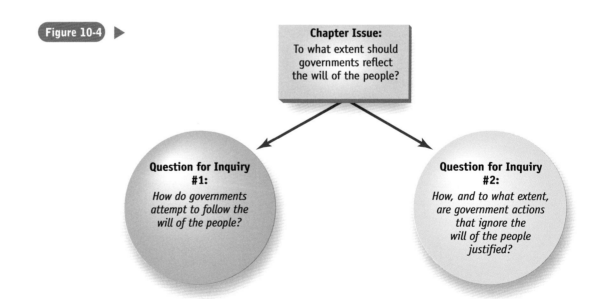

Figure 10-4 ▶

Chapter Issue:
To what extent should governments reflect the will of the people?

Question for Inquiry #1:
How do governments attempt to follow the will of the people?

Question for Inquiry #2:
How, and to what extent, are government actions that ignore the will of the people justified?

Does Government Serve the People or Lead the People?

Question for Inquiry

• **How do governments attempt to follow the will of the people?**

The will of the people…is the only legitimate foundation of any government, and to protect its free expression should be our first object.

—**Thomas Jefferson, 1801**

As we consider the question of whether the liberal principle of following the will of the people is viable in a contemporary world, we will see that this principle is an *ideal* toward which many governments aim, rather than a goal that they consistently achieve. Since liberal democracy was born in the countries of the United States, France, and Great Britain, and then adopted elsewhere, most of the examples in this section will focus on North America and Europe. Nonetheless, this point applies to any and all other democracies, wherever they are.

Some Questions about Democracy

What I want is to get done what the people desire to have done, and the question for me is how to find that out exactly.

—**attributed to Abraham Lincoln (1809–1865)**
(16th president of the United States)

Lincoln's question was a pertinent one: How can a government determine what the will of the people is? Do you believe that Canada, where a party often forms the government even though it receives less than 50 per cent of the votes, is governed according to the will of the people? Is governance by the will of the people even a desirable or realistic goal? Are there circumstances in which a government should act contrary to public opinion? Is public opinion informed opinion?

A 2005 Gallup Poll commissioned by the BBC indicated that 65 per cent of the world's citizens—including 55 per cent of Canadians and Americans—thought that their countries were not governed by the will of the people (that is, by listening to what the people want and trying to enact laws that address those needs and wants). What are some possible reasons that people might feel this way? How might this belief affect people's commitment to getting involved in the affairs of their countries?

Figure 10-5 ▲

Thomas Jefferson was the third president of the United States and was the principal author of the Declaration of Independence. He was instrumental in shaping the democratic system of the new US government.

> ◢ **PAUSE AND REFLECT**
>
> Jefferson's words echo the ideas of John Locke, who put forward the concept of "the consent of the governed." If the will of the people is the foundation of government, in what ways can a government accurately discern the will of the people? What are some possible problems with this principle?

Elections, open, free and fair, are the essence of democracy, the inescapable sine qua non. Governments produced by elections may be inefficient, corrupt, shortsighted, irresponsible, dominated by special interests, and incapable of adopting policies demanded by the public good. These qualities make such governments undesirable but they do not make them undemocratic.

—Samuel P. Huntington, *The Third Wave:*
Democratization in the Late Twentieth Century
(Norman, OK: University of Oklahoma Press, 1993), p. 9.

Several experts on the Middle East concur that the Middle East cannot be democratized. According to this view, democracy is a product of western culture, and it cannot be applied to the Middle East which has a different cultural, religious, sociological and historical background. Similarly, it is argued that the culture of Islam is incompatible with democracy. Basically, this conventional perspective of the Middle East thus contends that democracy in that region is neither possible nor even desirable…On the other hand, it is obvious that the Turkish example demonstrates the invalidity of [this]…I do not subscribe to the view that Islamic culture and democracy cannot be reconciled.

—H.E. Recep Tayyip Erdoğan, prime minister of Turkey, address to Kennedy School of Government, Harvard University, January 30, 2003.

These quotes suggest that democracy is difficult to put into practice, but most would agree with Winston Churchill, who said the following:

Democracy is the worst form of government, except all those other forms that have been tried from time to time.

—Winston Churchill, speech to the House of Commons, November 11, 1947.

It can be argued, as Winston Churchill and others do above, that democracy has its faults and weaknesses. No system of governing is perfect. As you read through the following pages, keep in mind the Question for Inquiry: How do governments attempt to follow the will of the people?

The Will of the People

As citizens of this democracy, you are the rulers and the ruled, the lawgivers and the law-abiding, the beginning and the end.

—Adlai Stevenson (a US politician), speech in Chicago, 1952.

A **democracy** is a form of government in which power is ultimately vested in the people. We will begin by looking at two forms of democracies, direct and representative. The people participate in deciding issues directly (direct democracy) or through elected officials who represent them and make laws in their interests (representative democracy).

The quotation by Jefferson that opened this section states that a government's legitimacy is dependent on popular consent. Many supporters of liberal democracy are likely to agree with this idea. But is it sufficient for governments to win the support of voters during periodic elections, or should they rely on public opinion polls to guide day-to-day and issue-by-issue decisions? How is the will of the people expressed, and does it vary from issue to issue and from time to time? How much influence should the general population have on government policies?

Principles of Liberalism in Direct Democracies

A **direct democracy** operates on the belief that every citizen's voice is important and necessary for the orderly and efficient operation of society. Some economic and political philosophers have argued in favour of this system as an expression of liberal principles. Direct democracy seems practical only with small numbers of people, however, because it requires everyone to get together in one space to discuss issues, then make decisions based on the majority vote. Ancient Athens, the world's first democracy, practised direct democracy with an assembly that may have numbered 5000 or 6000 people.

> *Pure democracies have ever been spectacles of turbulence and contention; have ever been found incompatible with personal security or the rights of property; and have in general been as short in their lives as they have been violent in their deaths.*

> **—James Madison, Federalist Papers, No. 10, 1787.**

Some characteristics of direct democracy are found in the practices of many liberal democracies, however. For example, three important instruments of direct democracy are initiatives, referendums or plebiscites, and recalls.

Citizens in the United States can use *initiatives* to create legislation. To create an initiative, a citizens' group draws up a petition. If the petition is signed by a certain number of citizens, it can force a public vote on an issue. Examples of this form of direct democracy in the 2008 election in California were the following:

> *Proposition 2: to treat food-producing animals (calves, chickens, pigs) more humanely*

Figure 10-6 ▲

In a direct democracy, people vote directly on issues. Such a situation is more practical with small numbers of people, such as in some small towns where the citizens can assemble, discuss issues affecting the community, and arrive at decisions by majority vote.

system (sometimes referred to as the "first-past-the-post" system because, as in a horse race, candidates who pass a certain point in the race with the highest number of votes in each of their ridings win). At present there are 308 Members of Parliament representing all areas of the country in the House of Commons.

Like many government systems, Canada has a bicameral (two-chamber) legislature to provide two different legislative bodies, each based on a different form of representation. Canada's 105-member Senate is based on representation by region rather than on

Figure 10-8 ▶

The number of ridings in each province and territory is generally based on population size (the numbers of electors in each province on the map are as of 2008). Because of the principle of *representation by population*, all of Western Canada has 92 seats in total, and the Atlantic provinces have only 32 MPs. When this is compared to Ontario and Québec, it raises the issue of voter parity: is it fair that over one-third of all MPs come from just one province? Is it fair that urban voters are under-represented in comparison with rural voters? Can you think of reasons why population is the main criterion used in determining ridings? What would happen if all provinces and territories were given the same number of seats? Would this be more fair or less fair?

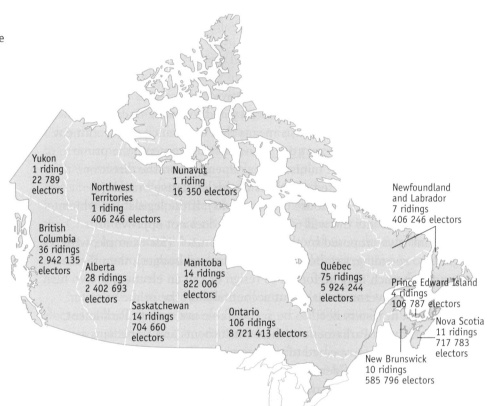

Yukon
1 riding
22 789 electors

Northwest Territories
1 riding
406 246 electors

Nunavut
1 riding
16 350 electors

British Columbia
36 ridings
2 942 135 electors

Alberta
28 ridings
2 402 693 electors

Saskatchewan
14 ridings
704 660 electors

Manitoba
14 ridings
822 006 electors

Ontario
106 ridings
8 721 413 electors

Québec
75 ridings
5 924 244 electors

Newfoundland and Labrador
7 ridings
406 246 electors

Prince Edward Island
4 ridings
106 787 electors

Nova Scotia
11 ridings
717 783 electors

New Brunswick
10 ridings
585 796 electors

Figure 10-9 ▶

In the 2008 federal election, a majority of Canadians who voted, voted *against* the Conservative Party, yet it formed the government. How well do elections reflect the will of the people in a multi-party democracy? Only 59 per cent of eligible voters voted in this election. Do the 37.6 per cent of the 59 per cent who voted (or 22 per cent of the electorate) really represent the will of the people? Is this an indication of something that needs fixing in Canada's parliamentary system?

Party	Seats	Percentage of Popular Vote
Bloc Québécois	49	10.0
Conservative	143	37.6
Green Party	0	6.8
Independent	2	0.7
Liberal	77	26.2
NDP-New Democratic Party	37	18.2

representation by population. Senators are not elected; as a seat becomes vacant in the Senate, the prime minister appoints a new senator—who may remain until age 75—to fill it. Any piece of legislation that has been passed by the House of Commons must also be passed by the Senate before it can become law. It is extremely rare, however, for the Senate to reject a bill that has been approved by the House of Commons. It is, however, common for the Senate to recommend changes (amendments) to bills passed by the House of Commons, and to have the House of Commons consider and pass the bill as amended by the Senate.

Clearly, it can be argued that there are challenges in Canada's system in terms of reflecting the will of the people. Keep these shortcomings in mind as you read the chapter and think about the difficulties they cause and possible solutions to these difficulties.

The United States' Republican Democracy

Unlike Canada, which has a monarch, the United States follows a republican system of government. A republic is a country where the people are sovereign and there is no king or queen. Like Canada, the United States has three branches of government: legislative, executive, and judicial. To ensure that the government adheres to liberal principles, the United States uses a system of checks and balances to make sure that no one branch of the government becomes too powerful. The legislative branch (Congress) has checks over the executive branch (the president and members of the Cabinet) and also over the judicial branch (judges and the court system), and the same is true for the other two branches. For example, the legislative branch can override a presidential veto with a two-thirds vote. The legislative branch also plays a deciding role in choosing individuals to fill vacancies on the Supreme Court, and can remove judges or the president through impeachment. This system was created based on the beliefs that checks and balances would keep the government too weak to override the will of the people, and that the least intrusive government provides more freedom to its citizens.

There are two chambers of the US Congress: the House of Representatives and the Senate. Like Canada, the House of Representatives works on a single-member constituency system and the country is divided into electoral districts based on representation by population. Currently there are 435 members in the House, and the numbers of representatives from each state reflect the relative population of each state. In the United States, the Senate is elected: each state has two senators, regardless of the population of the state. Representatives are elected every two years, and Senators are elected every six years. The elections for the Senate are staggered (one-third of the seats are up for election every two years) to maintain continuity after each election. This system ensures that there are always experienced senators who can carry on the business of Senate, and who can help to initiate new senators into the legislative process.

Figure 10-10 ▶

The breakdown of the Electoral College by state and the District of Columbia, 110th Congress, 2008–2012. There were 538 members in 2008.

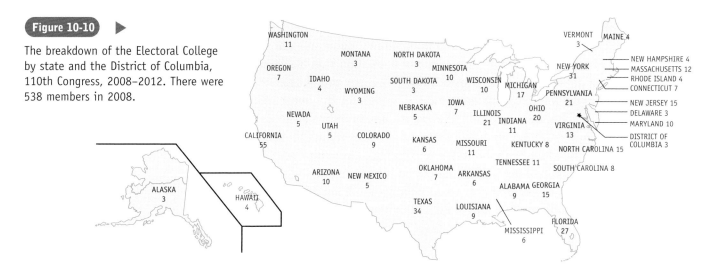

Legislation (a "bill") is voted on in both the House and the Senate; if it passes, it can be signed into law by the president. The president can choose not to sign a bill into law; this is called a veto. A vetoed bill is sent back to the house of Congress where it originated. There, the members of that house can pass a revised bill and submit it again for the president's signature, or they can override the presidential veto with a two-thirds majority vote, thus making the bill into law without the president's approval.

In Canada generally, the party that obtains the most seats in Parliament becomes the government, and its leader becomes prime minister. The process of electing the president in the United States is somewhat different. The people go to the polls and vote for the presidential candidate of their choice by voting for electors pledged to support their choice of candidate. The president is actually elected by a body known as the Electoral College. The framers of the US Constitution were somewhat suspicious of the will of the people and did not want the people to elect the president directly. As a result, they established a process whereby each state and the District of Columbia select electors equal in number to their Congressional representation, and the electors actually elect the president. In all states but two (Nebraska and Maine), it is a winner-takes-all situation: the winner of the popular vote in each state receives all the Electoral College votes for the state. Nebraska and Maine apportion their votes according to the popular vote. The system usually works—that is, the person elected as president usually has a majority of the popular vote; but, it has failed four times—that is, the person elected as president did not have a majority of the popular vote. In the 2000 presidential election, for example, Republican candidate George W. Bush, with 50 456 002 popular votes, won 271 electoral votes. His Democratic opponent, Al Gore, won the popular vote with 50 999 897 votes, but won only 266 electoral votes. Bush was elected president.

The United States has essentially a two-party system, and it is extremely difficult for a third party to win an election. While this has the advantage of stability—there are no three- or four-way votes and no minority governments—it is virtually impossible to challenge the established parties to consider minority opinions. However, the party with the most seats in Congress usually has the support of the majority of voters.

The American system of representational democracy, like Canada's, also has challenges in reflecting the will of the people. Think about this as you continue to search for a way to respond to the Chapter Issue: *To what extent should governments reflect the will of the people?*

Proportional Representation

In Sweden and many other countries, the government uses a different form of representation: **proportional representation**. In this system, citizens vote directly for a party, and then representatives are assigned based on the amount of popular support obtained. The system encourages and legitimizes participation by minority or marginal parties who would not obtain representation in the systems used in Canada or the United States.

Usually, countries using a proportional representation system have many more parties than countries using a single-member constituency system. This often results in coalitions where two or more parties must work together to form the government. On occasion, a minority government might be formed. In Sweden, four major parties have had the most political control and have formed coalition governments for years.

Many people argue that proportional representation is more representative and democratic than a single-member constituency system since the proportion of seats in the legislature more accurately and directly reflects the popular vote (and therefore better reflects the will of the people). It is receiving increasing attention in more and more countries, including Canada. Ontario held a referendum in the 2007 provincial election to see if Ontarians wanted to move to a mixed-member proportional (MMP) system. This means that each voter would vote for a candidate to represent them (as in the single-member constituency system), but would also vote for a party. The Ontario legislature currently has 107 seats; under the MMP system, the constituencies would be rearranged to create 90 ridings for direct representation, and 39 additional seats would be filled based on party votes. The proposed electoral system was voted down by Ontarians, however.

PAUSE AND REFLECT

In the lead-up to the 2007 Ontario referendum on proportional representation, advocates of the reform complained that Elections Ontario had not done enough to inform the public about the proposed changes to the electoral system. Why do you think Ontarians voted against moving to a mixed-member proportional system? Would you be in favour of such a system? What obstacles are in the way of moving to a proportional representation system in Canada?

Figure 10-11

This is only a partial list of countries using proportional representation. This system is common in Europe, especially in the Scandinavian countries, and in South America.

Austria	Germany	Netherlands
Argentina	Greece	Peru
Belgium	Hungary	Portugal
Brazil	Iceland	Scotland
Croatia	Ireland	South Africa
Czech Republic	Israel	South Korea
Denmark	Italy	Sweden
Dominican Republic	Mexico	Turkey
Finland	New Zealand	Venezuela

Examining Proportional Representation

Democracy, loosely translated from its Greek roots, means "rule by the people," or "people power." One of the most important aspects of a democracy is elections: the process by which we choose representatives to sit in Parliament and make laws. As we have seen, there are two predominant types of systems used in democracies to choose representatives, the single-member constituency system and proportional representation.

Your Task: Investigate the results from the 2008 federal election, and determine how the results would have been different if Canada used a proportional representation system. You will form an opinion on the fairness of Canada's system of representative democracy and on whether you think a proportional representation system would be more desirable. You will then find another student in the class who disagrees with you and discuss the issue. Use the Questions to Guide You to for assistance.

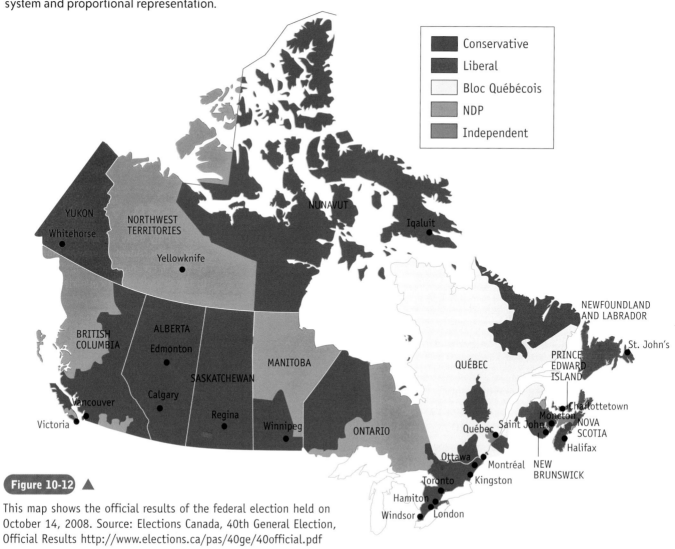

Conservative
Liberal
Bloc Québécois
NDP
Independent

Figure 10-12 ▲

This map shows the official results of the federal election held on October 14, 2008. Source: Elections Canada, 40th General Election, Official Results http://www.elections.ca/pas/40ge/40official.pdf

Party	Number of Votes	Number of Seats
Bloc Québécois	1 379 991	49
Conservative Party of Canada	5 209 069	143
Green Party of Canada	937 613	0
Liberal Party of Canada	3 633 185	77
New Democratic Party	2 515 288	37
Total Votes Cast	13 929 093	

—Source: Elections Canada, Fortieth General Election Official Voting Results.
http://www.elections.ca/scripts/OVR2008/default.html

Figure 10-13 ▲

This table shows the total number of votes cast for each major party and the number of seats each party won during the 2008 election.

Questions to Guide You

1. Calculate the percentage of the popular vote each party received. Round to the nearest decimal place. To do this, divide the total number of votes cast per party by the total number of votes cast.

2. Calculate the number of seats each party would have received under a proportional representation system. To do this, multiply 308 (because there are 308 ridings in Canada) by the percentage you obtained in question 1 (remember to divide your percentage by 100 to arrive at a decimal number that you can use for multiplying). Round to the nearest full number.

3. Answer the following questions:
   a) How many seats would each party have under the proportional representation system? Would the Conservative party still have won the election?
   b) Compare the number of seats you obtained in question 2 to the number of seats each party actually won, shown in Figure 10-13. What is the difference?
   c) How would Parliament be different if the number of seats you calculated in question 2 were the actual distribution of MPs in Parliament? Which parties would gain representation? Which parties would lose MPs?
   d) Which system do you think is more democratic? Which one seems to better represent the will of the people?
   e) How might politics change in Canada if the proportional representation system were adopted?

4. Go online and find the results of another Canadian federal election (you will need to find the total number of ballots cast, and the total number of ballots cast for each party). Work out the results for proportional representation. How does the actual percentage of seats obtained by each party differ from the percentage of seats it would have received under proportional representation?

Challenges to the Will of the People

We have seen that the systems of representative democracy are not perfect methods of reflecting the will of the people, although mechanisms which attempt to do so are in place, such as the concept of responsible government in Canada, the checks and balances in the US republican system, and proportional representation. In addition, in all three types of representative democracy, countries have electorates that select representatives, and in all three, a written constitution exists that serves the interests of the people, outlines and guarantees their rights, outlines the responsibilities of the government, and contains the mechanisms for the system to be changed. What other conditions are necessary to realize the liberal ideal that government should reflect and be shaped by the will of the people?

Some thinkers believe that citizen participation in a democracy requires a kind of civic-mindedness, or a democratic personality. They also believe that this quality can be developed in the citizenry through education.

Any democracy must pay explicit attention to the development of its young people's civic skills, habits, and attitudes. We human beings do not instinctively develop the skills necessary for democracy. We are not automatically capable of working together with others on common problems. We do not naturally understand alternative perspectives. Unless we are taught to care about other people, we are unlikely to show concern from anyone beyond our immediate circle of family and friends.

Citizens are made, not born. Civic education is the process by which we teach young people to be effective and responsible members of democratic communities. Increasingly, we know how to make civic education work in our schools. Nothing is more important to the future health of our democracies.

—Peter Levine, "A blog for civic renewal," October 14, 2005.

http://www.peterlevine.ws/mt/archives/000707.html

Citizen participation is a requisite of any democratic system. Voting—perhaps the most obvious evidence of democracy—is a minimal act. It alone does not define democracy. Democracy requires much more. And if citizens abandon their responsibility, then democracy is in danger of falling into the hands of people who will use the powers of government for their own purposes.

The highest measure of democracy is neither the "extent of freedom" nor the "extent of equality," but rather the highest measure of participation.

—Alain de Benoist (1943–) , French political philosopher

Voter Turnout

Evidence suggests that people are failing to execute even the minimal expectation of democracy by not exercising their right to vote. Voter turnout is generally decreasing. In the 2006 federal election, for example, only 64.7 per cent of eligible voters voted, and in the 2008 election, only 59 per cent of eligible voters voted. This is a problem that plagues all democracies. Some voters are simply indifferent to the issues or to who makes the decisions. This problem creates a challenge to the fundamentals of democracy: If the power resides with the people, what do you do when the people choose not to exercise that power? How does low voter turnout undermine or endanger a democratic system?

PAUSE AND REFLECT

Why do you think voting becomes more likely as people get older? Do young people take their right to vote for granted? What effect do you think voter age has on government policy? Do you think this is something the government takes into account when deciding what laws to pass or where to focus spending?

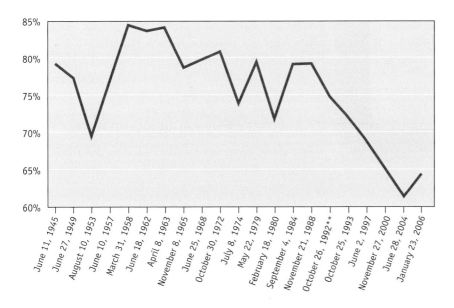

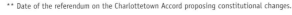

*Official turnout in Canada is based on the number of electors on the final lists of electors.
** Date of the referendum on the Charlottetown Accord proposing constitutional changes.

Figure 10-14

This graph shows the percentage of eligible voters who have participated in federal elections in Canada since 1945 up to the 2006 election.

Source: Elections Canada, Figure 1: Turnout rate in federal elections (1945–2006) in "Estimation of Voter Turnout by Age Group at the 39th Federal General Election, January 23, 2006," p. 2. http://www.elections.ca/loi/res/rep39ge/estimation39ge_e.pdf.

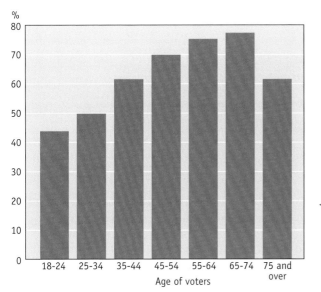

Figure 10-15

This chart shows voter turnout by age in the 2006 federal election.

Source: Elections Canada, "Estimation of Voter Turnout by Age Group at the 39th Federal General Election, January 23, 2006." http://www.elections.ca/loi/res/rep39ge/estimation39ge_e.pdf

Mandatory Voting

Something to Think About: Should voting be compulsory in Canada?

An Example: Voting, as a minimal act of participation, is necessary if a democracy is to function properly. In the 2006 Canadian federal election, only 64.7 per cent of eligible voters turned out to vote. In Australia's 2004 election, there was a 94.5 per cent voter turnout rate. You may wonder why there is such a big difference between the two countries' voting rates. The answer lies in legislation. In Canada, voting is non-compulsory, and since the 1990s, all federal elections have had a voter turnout rate below 70 per cent. In Australia, voting is mandatory by law and the voter turnout rate has not fallen below 94 per cent since 1955. Do you think that voting should be compulsory in Canada?

Canadian senator Mac Harb was interviewed after his speech on mandatory voting to the Frontier Centre for Public Policy in Winnipeg on October 4, 2005.

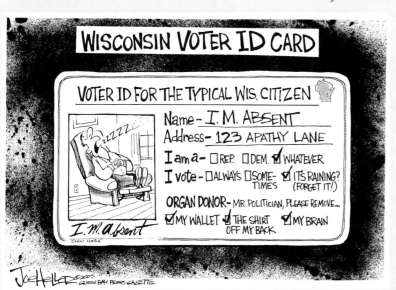

Figure 10-16 ▲

While this cartoon pokes fun at voter apathy in the United States, poor voter turnout is a problem in Canada too. To what extent might an American citizen agree or disagree with the specific messages in this cartoon?

Frontier Centre: Why do you want to make voting mandatory?

Mac Harb: Because of the fact that people, young people in particular, are not participating in the electoral process; less than one out of four bother.

FC: Do you think that policy should apply at all three levels of government?

MH: I believe that all three levels of government should adopt mandatory voting to ensure that all the people vote at all times for those who govern them.

FC: More than thirty countries have mandatory voting but most of them don't enforce the law. Wouldn't we be creating another victimless crime that is a waste of resources to enforce?

MH: Not at all. The mere fact that you have a law creates a deterrent. Seat-belt law is a case in point. Even though we don't do a lot of enforcement of seat-belt compliance, the compliance rate is about ninety percent. I believe that just having the law would by itself have a positive impact.

FC: Should such a provision be embodied in the constitution or in statutory law?

MH: No, it should be a part of legislation or bylaws at the municipal level.

FC: Should voting merely be declared to be a civic duty as in Italy's constitution or established as an affirmative citizen obligation, as in Australia?

MH: I would go with the Australian formula, because their system is very similar to ours.

FC: According to many, Australia has much better government policy than many countries, including Canada. In your opinion, is mandatory voting part of that?

MH: I take the position that, because of the fact that they have mandatory voting, they have more representative government than we do.

FC: Aren't you confusing rights with responsibilities? Classical liberal rights are negative in nature; they only require you to be left alone.

MH: Rights go with responsibilities. We have a right to drink fresh water but we have the responsibility to ensure that we pay taxes in order to keep waterways clean.

FC: In Australia where compulsory voting is at least minimally enforced, they have a problem called the "donkey vote," where unwilling voters exercise their franchise randomly. Wouldn't we be making the process a joke?

MH: That is the question, to do or not to do. In fact you have to look at the lesser of the two evils, and the lesser here is to ensure that everybody votes and then go out and educate those who you believe need education.

FC: Australia's voters also spoil more than five percent of their ballots. Why bother to drag people out if that's what they will do?

MH: The reality of it here is that those who do not vote are close to about thirty percent. As five percent, I would say it was worth the effort for us, for the sake of five-percent waste to reach out to the other twenty-five percent.

—Source: interview between Mac Harb and the
Frontier Centre for Public Policy, October 4, 2005.
Frontier Centre for Public Policy.
http://www.fcpp.org/main/publication_detail.php?PubID=1178

QUESTIONS FOR REFLECTION

1. Do you think mandatory voting would help increase the voter turnout rate in Canada? Use some of the questions and answers in the Mac Harb interview to defend your position.

2. How might mandatory voting in Canada change citizen participation, besides having more citizens voting?

3. Examine the voter turnout graph in Figure 10-14. What other strategies besides mandatory voting might the Canadian government employ to try to increase voter turnout?

© 2006 Brian Fairrington and PoliticalCartoons.com

Figure 10-17 ▲

Is the responsibility of voting too great a burden for the typical voter?

> *The best argument against democracy is a five-minute conversation with the average voter.*
>
> **—Winston Churchill**

▶ **PAUSE AND REFLECT**

How much time and energy would you want to devote to participating in the electoral and democratic process? As a citizen of Alberta, and of Canada, how much do you feel you should know about current issues? Do you care enough about what is going on in your area, the province, and the country to research and keep up to date with the news? Is your opinion an informed opinion?

Elite Theories of Democracy

Some people claim that the needs of a society are best served when one elite group of people, deemed to be better qualified than other citizens, is given the task of making decisions for all. Such a critique of mass participation in democracy is known as the "elite theory of democracy". Voicing criticisms of democracy similar to those of Plato and Thomas Hobbes, economics theorist Anthony Downs has argued that, because a single vote has little weight in a very large group of decision makers, individuals have little or no sense of responsibility for their decision, and are thus less likely to make a rational and well-informed decision.

This theory poses a dilemma for those who favour increased citizen participation in decision making in order to ensure equality of power among citizens: either a small group of well-informed and qualified people make decisions for all of society, and thus there is an inequality of power among individuals; or all members of society have an equal say in the decision-making process but may have little concern for the outcomes of their decisions. Furthermore, it has been argued that, in the second option, ensuring that citizens are well-informed about the decisions they are making is not a viable option, because in order to become well informed about the various decisions, citizens would have to neglect their other duties in society.

Lobbying by Interest Groups

Lobbying is an attempt to influence the direction of governmental policy by groups that represent a particular interest or perspective. These are often well-organized groups designed to raise money to inform and persuade (lobby) representatives or government bureaucrats to consider their perspectives. Frequently, they donate money to representatives' election campaigns, although most democratic governments have limited the allowable amount of their contributions to prevent the actual "buying" of influence. Some lobby groups are self-interested, such as unions, business and development groups, or farmers groups who want specific economic policies that favour their interests. Others lobby in the interests of a particular segment of society, for example, people who are homeless, some Aboriginal peoples, cultural groups, or women. Still others may act to protect the environment, change abortion laws, or protect the right to bear arms.

Whatever the cause, lobby groups spend time and raise money to influence public policy, and some people worry that that this influence may sometimes conflict with the welfare or interests of the voting public. The will of the people may occasionally be overridden by the will of a group of well-organized, vocal, and influential people.

Ethics and the Common Good

Governments may face the following question when considering whether to follow public opinion on a specific issue: Does the will of the people necessarily indicate the right course of action? Is majority public opinion always consistent with the values and principles of a liberal democracy? (The *will of the people* is generally taken to refer to the majority opinion.)

Nineteenth-century thinkers Alexis de Tocqueville and John Stuart Mill used the phrase *tyranny of the majority* to describe one of the potential problems in a democracy: that the will of the majority may be imposed on minorities to the detriment of other liberal principles. In 2005, for example, when the government of Canada introduced legislation into Parliament to recognize same-sex marriages, some Canadians wanted a referendum to be held on the issue so they could express their opinions. Justice Minister Irwin Cotler, however, announced that there would not be a national referendum. Cotler stated that if a referendum had been held to decide whether women were entitled to vote in the early 20th century in Canada, women would likely never have been enfranchised. Was Cotler right in favouring the extension of rights over the will of the people?

Another such example is the abolition of capital punishment. After 109 years and 710 executions, Canadian Parliament abolished the death penalty in 1976. The voting was 131 MPs to 124 in favour of the abolition. Parliament had previously held a vote on abolishing the death penalty in 1966, and it was retained. At that time, 60 per cent of Canadians favoured keeping it, according to polls. A bill to reinstate the death penalty in Canada was introduced and voted on in 1987, but it was defeated. At the time, an Ipsos-Reid poll indicated that 73 per cent of Canadians were in favour of reinstating the death penalty. By 2001, this number had dropped to 52 per cent. Most arguments against the death penalty claim it is unethical, while some also cite the possibility of wrongful convictions as another reason not to use it. Why do you think the majority of MPs voted against the death penalty when polling seemed to indicate that a majority of Canadians were in favour of it?

As Cotler's comments on women's enfranchisement demonstrate, there are times when government claims to be wiser than the people— meaning that the will of the people may not be the best or most ethical course of action. Following are a number of other examples:

- Currently in Canada, juvenile offenders are being tried as minors in the criminal justice system. Following a series of high-profile criminal cases where juvenile offenders committed heinous crimes, many Canadians are starting to feel that minors should be tried in adult courts and sentenced accordingly.

"MY GREATEST ASSET IS I'M SO RICH, I CAN'T BE BOUGHT BY ANY INTEREST GROUP."

Figure 10-18 ▲

- Some Québécois, wishing to preserve their own cultural heritage, language, and customs, have expressed concern to their governments over the degree to which they should accommodate other cultural practices within Québec.
- In Ontario, SUV owners and drivers have faced heavy taxation and even, in certain cases, penalties imposed by government in order to discourage these environmentally unfriendly vehicles.

Do you agree that in these cases the government may be more objective and "wiser" than the people? John F. Kennedy had this to say about the will of the people in a democracy:

The true democracy, living and growing and inspiring, puts its faith in the people—faith that the people will not simply elect men who will represent their views ably and faithfully, but will also elect men who will exercise their conscientious judgment—faith that the people will not condemn those whose devotion to principle leads them to unpopular courses, but will reward courage, respect honor, and ultimately recognize right.

**—John F. Kennedy, *Profiles in Courage*
(New York: Harper & Brothers, 1956), p. 264.**

Practicality versus Popular Opinion

Can you think of a situation in which a decision is made based on practicality or necessity, despite the fact that it contradicts the wishes of the people it affects? For example, shelters for people who are homeless are one of the social services provided by many larger Canadian communities. Most Canadians recognize the necessity of shelters for people who are homeless, given our climate. Those same Canadians, however, may strongly resist a decision by the provincial or municipal government to establish a shelter in their neighbourhoods. Sometimes governments make unpopular decisions because they believe they are necessary for the common good.

Consider the 1987 decision by the federal government to replace the Canadian $1 bill with a coin, which came to be known as the loonie. Economically speaking, the decision was a good one from the government's perspective, because a paper dollar typically wore out within a year, whereas a coin would last 20 years on average. The government expected to save approximately $250 million over the course of the next 20 years. Nonetheless, a year after the coin's introduction, Canadians were not supportive of the decision.

Polling by the mint revealed that the loonie was not embraced by Canadians so long as paper $1 bills were still available. In July 1988, 39 per cent of Canadians said they liked the coin, 25 per cent were indifferent and 36 per cent disapproved of it. But certain groups were *pleased with it, including vending-machine companies, transit authorities, and the visually impaired.*

—Source: "Introducing the loonie," CBC,
first broadcast June 30, 1987. CBC Digital Archives.

http://archives.cbc.ca/IDC-1-73-2325-13535-11/politics_economy/twt/

As you can see, there are many times when a democratic government might form policy that goes against the will of the people. Look back at the Thomas Jefferson quote that opened this section (see page 335). Given the reality of government policy, what does government's willingness to go against the will of the people say about the fundamental principles of liberal democracies? Can you identify any inherent flaws in the principle of the will of the people?

Consensus Decision Making

In **consensus decision making** a group of individuals share ideas, solutions, and concerns to find a resolution to a problem that all members of the group can accept. There are many variations on the process, but most have a similar structure.

1. The question for consideration is presented to the group.
2. All members of the group contribute their opinions on the question.
3. A response to the question is proposed, and the members of the group come to some agreement on the response.
4. If all the members do not agree to the response, those who disagree present their concerns to the group.
5. The proposed response to the question is modified to address the concerns of those who disagree.
6. Another round of discussion is held on the newly modified response. The process repeats until a resolution is reached that all members can accept.

The governments of Nunavut and the Northwest Territories are consensus governments (see chapter 8, pages 294–295). In Nunavut, there are no political parties at the territorial level, which allows each MLA to vote as he or she thinks best. Once the MLAs are elected by the people, they hold a secret ballot to elect a speaker of the Legislative Assembly, a premier, and the cabinet. Approval of any matter before the legislature requires agreement by the majority. They wanted a government that would serve the people's needs as closely as possible. Jack Stagg, a chief federal negotiator of the Nunavut political accord, said "political control is always a better exercise close to the people than far away." (Source: Jack Stagg, quoted on Nunavut 99, http://www.nunavut.com/nunavut99/english/public_gov.html.) A government based on consensus was envisioned as the best way to include the constituents of Nunavut in a more comprehensive way.

One benefit of this system is that the Legislative Assembly is not nearly as adversarial as assemblies and parliaments based on the party system. Certainly, MLAs disagree with one another, and may get upset or critical, but the proceedings in the legislature are, for the most part, calm and respectful. MLAs listen to one another and seldom interrupt. MLA Kevin O'Brien made the following comment about the difference in a consensus legislature:

Nunavut MLAs certainly are not shy about voicing criticism of the cabinet, but they do not criticise and oppose just for the sake of criticism and opposition.

—Kevin O'Brien, "Some Thoughts on Consensus Government in Nunavut." *Canadian Parliamentary Review* **26, 4, 2003.**
http://www.parl.gc.ca/Infoparl/english/issue.htm?param=60&art=26

Another example of consensus can be found in the Quaker-based model. In this model, consensus is grounded in the beliefs and values individuals have about themselves and the group, and the conviction that decision making should reflect the search for truth and goodness. Consensus in this context does not mean unanimity, as the individual's beliefs are always respected. It does, however, mean that "constructive engagement of differences and dissent are integral to the process." (Source: Monteze M. Snyder et al, *Building Consensus: Conflict and Unity* [Richmond, IN: Earlham Quaker Foundations of Leadership Program], 2001.) Differences are resolved by the commitment to carry on the discussion, no matter how time-consuming or difficult.

Proponents of consensus decision making argue that it is egalitarian and inclusive, allowing everyone to participate in a decision, and thereby reflecting more closely the will of the people. As a decision-making process, it aims to find a solution that serves the common good, while taking into consideration the individual and collective beliefs and values of all participants. In addition, the process tends to elicit a high level of commitment to the decision from those involved, and may create a higher quality decision than a majority vote, because it requires more input from those affected.

Like all political systems, however, consensus governments are not without their problems. In Nunavut, MLAs complain that the cabinet does not consult them adequately, that ministers are often unwilling to share critical information, and so on. In addition, voters are not able to vote based on competing sets of policies, since for the most part, they do not even know who will be in the cabinet, and even if they did, they have no way of influencing that process. Others argue that the Nunavut model has little in common with the traditional Inuit consensus decision making on which it was based and that it represents a rejection rather than an affirmation of Inuit culture and values.

PAUSE AND REFLECT

Do you think moving toward a consensus decision-making model would make the Canadian government more representative of the will of the people? What obstacles stand in the way of making Canadian Parliament into a consensus government?

Should Government Rely on the People's Will?

The conservative French thinker Joseph de Maistre once claimed that "every nation has the government that it deserves." Some might see this as a cynical interpretation of the idea that government is an expression of the people's will. Many contemporary thinkers, however, wonder about the reliability of people's choices. Do you think the general population of a country knows what is in the best interests of the country? Consider the following viewpoints on the question.

A vexing problem of democratic theory has been to determine whether ordinary citizens are up to the task of governing a large society. There are three distinct problems here. First, Plato (Republic, Book VI) argued that some people are more intelligent and more moral than others and that those persons ought to rule. Second, others have argued that a society must have a division of labor. If everyone were engaged in the complex and difficult task of politics, little time or energy would be left for the other essential tasks of a society...Third, since individuals have so little impact on the outcomes of political decision making in large societies, they have little sense of responsibility for the outcomes. Some have argued that it is not rational to vote since the chances that a vote will affect the outcome of an election are nearly indistinguishable from zero.

—Tom Christiano, "Democracy." The Stanford Encyclopedia of Philosophy, July 27, 2006.
http://plato.stanford.edu/entries/democracy/

The following is an excerpt of a review of economist Bryan Caplan's *The Myth of the Rational Voter: Why Democracies Choose Bad Policies.*

...Caplan argues that "voters are worse than ignorant; they are, in a word, irrational—and vote accordingly." Caplan's complaint is not that special-interest groups might subvert the will of the people, or that government might ignore the will of the people. He objects to the will of the people itself. In defending democracy, theorists of public choice sometimes invoke what they call "the miracle of aggregation." It might seem obvious that few voters fully understand the intricacies of, say, single-payer universal health care. (I certainly don't.) But imagine, Caplan writes, that just 1 percent of voters are fully informed and the other 99 percent are so ignorant that they vote at random. In a campaign between two candidates, one of whom has an excellent health care plan and the other a horrible plan, the candidates evenly split the ignorant voters' ballots. Since all the well-informed voters opt for the candidate with the good health care plan, she wins. Thus, even in a democracy composed almost exclusively of the ignorant, we achieve first-rate health care.

The hitch, as Caplan points out, is that this miracle of aggregation works only if the errors are random. When that's the case, the thousands of ill-informed votes in favour of the bad health plan are cancelled out by thousands of equally ignorant votes in favour of the good plan. But Caplan argues that in the real world, voters make systematic mistakes about economic policy—and probably other policy issues too.

The role played by citizens in holding leaders to account is a core tenet of all theories of democracy, but most theories seek to satisfy this requirement electorally, through infrequent voting, rather than through continuous feedback such as is now provided by opinion surveys. In part, this is because elections simplify the judgmental task. Competing candidates present themselves as alternative choices for the future, allowing citizens to decide, on whatever basis they find credible, which candidate represents the better option. Choosing among competing candidates is quite another thing from choosing among rival policy proposals, where the complexity of problems, the frequency with which such judgments must be made, and staggering information costs place enormous cognitive burdens on even the policy expert, let alone the typical voter.

—Scott L. Althaus, "False Starts, Dead Ends, and New Opportunities in Public Opinion Research," *Critical Review* **18, 1–3 (2006): 75–104. Reprinted by permission of the publisher (Taylor & Francis Group, http://www.informaworld.com).**

1 In the first quotation of this feature, Tom Christiano notes that one of the problems of democracy is determining whether ordinary citizens "are up to the task of governing a large society." Do you agree? Is voting too big a responsibility for the average citizen?

2 Talk to your parents or other adults about how much they consider political issues before voting. Based on these interviews, do you feel that voters are responsible enough that government should rely on their will? Share your thoughts with the class.

3 How do you think each of the people quoted here would respond to the question *To what extent should governments reflect the will of the people?* Can these views be considered critiques of democracy in general?

4 Technology exists that would make it possible for all citizens to vote on all governmental decisions each day. Would citizens become more informed and responsible if they were required to participate more frequently in decision making?

Explore the Issues

Concept Review

1 a) What are the three types of representative democracies discussed in this chapter?

  b) Which type do you think best reflects the will of the people? Why?

Concept Application

2 Examine Figure 10-7 on page 339. Which mechanisms are the most critical to ensure that governments follow the will of the people? Select the top three and justify your choices.

3 Find three articles about children or teens participating in or influencing democratic processes in Canada or abroad. Each article should represent a different perspective or point of view. Working in small groups with other individuals who have different articles, consider how these young people are fostering change. For each article, with each group of young people in mind, create a short response to the following question: To what extent should governments reflect the will of the people, including young people?

Authoritarianism

Question for Inquiry

• **How, and to what extent, are government actions that ignore the will of the people justified?**

We have seen that liberal democracies sometimes ignore the will of the people in order to implement policies that governments believe serve the common good. Authoritarian systems of government are generally regarded by outsiders as being unconcerned with the will of the people, but this is not necessarily true. In this section of the chapter, we will examine how authoritarian systems of government attempt to discern and respond to the will of the people through non-democratic means. Authoritarian governments may claim that order and security are more important than freedom, and, like a wise father figure, will make decisions in the interests of the people. Some of these governments believe that since they have the best interests of the people at heart, they embody the will of the people, whether the people know it or not. Authoritarian governments may have a detailed vision of a wonderful future—a vision of a world that will be more secure, more morally advanced, and more accurately fitted to the nature of humans—but their vision will require sacrifices and hardship and must therefore ignore the immediate will of the people. We will explore a variety of authoritarian systems to see how they justify their claim to decision-making power. The following section provides understandings of how, and to what extent, actions by authoritarian governments that ignore the will of the people are justified.

Authoritarian Political Systems

The people who cast the votes decide nothing. The people who count the votes decide everything.

> **—Joseph Stalin (leader of the Soviet Union from 1924–1953),**
> **quoted in Helen Thomas, *Thanks for the Memories,***
> ***Mr. President* (New York: Scribner, 2002), p. 197.**

Authoritarianism describes a form of government that vests authority in an elite group that may or may not rule in the interests of the people. Authoritarian political systems take many forms, including oligarchies (Putin's Russian Federation), military dictatorships (Myanmar, formerly known as Burma), ideological one-party states (Cuba), and monarchies (Saudi Arabia). Some of these forms may make reference to the will of the people, or a similar concept, in their

Figure 10-19 ▲

Mao Zedong, better known as Chairman Mao, ruled The People's Republic of China from 1949 to 1976 as the leader of the Communist party. Although revered by many as a hero, his campaign to create a new society and a new citizen resulted in the deaths of hundreds of thousands of the country's citizens.

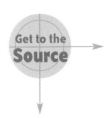
Articles 6 and 7 of the constitution of Saudi Arabia read as follows:

Article 6—Citizens are to pay allegiance to the King in accordance with the holy Koran and the tradition of the Prophet, in submission and obedience, in times of ease and difficulty, fortune and adversity.

Article 7—Government in Saudi Arabia derives power from the Holy Koran and the Prophet's tradition.

The constitution justifies the monarchy as follows:

Article 10—The state will aspire to strengthen family ties, maintain its Arab and Islamic values and care for all its members, and to provide the right conditions for the growth of their resources and capabilities.

How does the Saudi Arabian constitution address the will of the people?

—Source: **"Saudi Arabia–Constitution."**
International Constitutional Law,
http://www.servat.unibe.ch/icl/sa00000_.html, **January 7, 2004.**

laws or constitutions, but their interpretations of the concept differ greatly from democratic traditions.

The central institution of the Saudi Arabian government, for example, is an absolute monarchy. The Basic Law adopted in 1992 declares that Saudi Arabia is a monarchy ruled by the sons and grandsons of King Abd Al Aziz Al Saud, and the constitution asserts that the Quran (also spelled *Koran*) is the basis for all laws of the country. This means that the country is governed on the basis of Islamic law (sharia).

Although it is easy for us to view democracy as "better" than any of the systems presented here—especially since many of the governments that will be discussed are infamous for enforcing their laws through repressive and brutal measures—some of these systems have developed in response to particular historical conditions or as attempts to counter the challenges and problems faced by democracies that this text discussed earlier. Many authoritarian governments also believe that they are serving the best interests of the country.

Some scholars believe that authoritarianism is an expression of collectivism, in opposition to individualism (which, at least theoretically, is favoured by democracies). John Duckitt, in his paper entitled "Authoritarianism and Group Identification: A New View of an Old Construct," argues that both authoritarianism and collectivism subvert individual rights and goals in favour of group goals, expectations, and conformities. Keep this in mind as you read about some types of authoritarian governments.

PAUSE AND REFLECT

Consider the term *guiding parent* with respect to government. How might this term be used to refer to the constitutional relationship between government and citizenry in Saudi Arabia? What, if anything, ultimately checks the power of the leaders in this system? What issues could potentially stem from this distribution of power in society?

Oligarchies

Oligarchy is a form of government in which political power rests with a small elite segment of society. They are often controlled by politically powerful families who pass on their influence to their children. Present-day Russia has been called an oligarchy because of the power that some individuals, previously associated with the Communist party in the Soviet Union, gained after the fall of communism.

It is interesting to note that some scholars believe that any political system eventually evolves into an oligarchy. This theory is known as the "iron law of oligarchy". For example, Robert Michels, in his book *The Iron Law of Oligarchy* (1911), says that he

> *came to the conclusion that the formal organization of bureaucracies inevitably leads to oligarchy…under which organizations originally idealistic and democratic eventually come to be dominated by a small, self-serving group of people who achieved positions of power and responsibility. This can occur in large organizations because it becomes physically impossible for everyone to get together every time a decision has to be made. Consequently, a small group is given the responsibility of making decisions.*

—Robert Michels, from *The Iron Law of Oligarchy*, quoted in Henry L. Tischler, *Introduction to Sociology* (New York: Holt, Rinehart and Winston, 1990), p. 181.

While this may seem to be an exaggeration, some people consider the United States to be an oligarchic democracy, since third-party candidates stand little chance of being elected because of the enormous amounts of capital needed to run for national office. According to this view, in a political system such as the United States, actual differences between political rivals are small, the oligarchic elite imposes strict limits on what constitutes an acceptable and respectable political position, and politicians' careers depend heavily on unelected economic and media elites. These same people would point to the recurrence of two names (of four people) in four recent US election campaigns: Clinton and Bush. Few would argue, however, that the United States is not a democracy. What do you think? Are some modern democracies oligarchic?

One-Party States

A **one-party state** is a type of system where only one party forms the government and no other parties are permitted to run candidates for election. Some of the appearances of democracy exist but the absence of choice and the barriers against change eliminate the liberal democratic principle of the will of the people. One-party states are often communist states, but they describe themselves as a *people's republic, socialist republic,* or *democratic republic* to indicate that they somehow embody the will of the people.

As prime minister of Italy from 1922 to 1943, Mussolini transformed the country into a fascist dictatorship and wielded absolute power. He suppressed individual rights, followed an imperialist foreign policy, and allied Italy with Nazi Germany during the Second World War. Was he simply self-serving and power hungry, or was he driven by a vision of what he thought his country should be (however detrimental that vision may have been to his people)?

Supporters of one-party states often point to the sense of unity, strength, and community that a single-party government can give to a country. They argue that multi-party systems introduce too much division and conflict, which impedes economic and political development; therefore, a single-party state is best for the country as a whole.

Critics say that this system is not truly democratic and does not represent the will of the people, since a choice of only one party is really no choice at all. However, in some single-party states, such as Italy under Mussolini, constituents often could choose for which candidates to vote, although they were all from the Fascist party. One-party systems can easily disregard previous laws or even the constitution, if they so desire. The inclusion of some aspects of democratic government, such as elections, serves as one way to legitimize the government's authority to other countries.

Military Dictatorships

A **military dictatorship**, sometimes known as a military junta, is a form of government in which political power resides with the military leadership. Countries in Latin America, Africa, and the Middle East have presented many examples of military dictatorships. Like any dictatorship, a military dictatorship can be official or unofficial, and sometimes mixed forms exist where the military exerts strong influence over those in power. Military dictatorships often come to power through a coup d'état, in which the existing government is overthrown by military personnel. Examples of such regimes are General Augusto Pinochet's overthrow of Salvador Allende's democratically elected government in Chile in 1973 and General Pervez Musharraf's assumption of power in Pakistan in 1999.

Some military dictatorships have justified their claims to power as a way of bringing political stability to their countries or of rescuing them from "dangerous ideologies." For instance, Pinochet's takeover of Chile was justified as necessary to prevent Allende from creating an authoritarian socialist regime. Military regimes tend to portray themselves as neutral third parties who can provide interim leadership during times of turmoil. This is seen as being better for the people in the long run, even if the will of the people needs to be ignored or undermined in the short term. Musharraf, for example, claimed that the incumbent president of Pakistan was undermining the constitution by abolishing the system of checks and balances. Musharraf claimed that the country had to be saved.

Despite these portrayals, military dictatorships tend to be unwilling to give up power unless forced to do so. Musharraf, for instance, was forced out of power in Pakistan in 2007 because of escalating internal dissension in the country between pro-Islamic and pro-democratic factions, and because he lost the support of the international community. Since the 1990s, military dictatorships have become less common, in part because they have less international legitimacy.

Techniques of Authoritarian Governments

Authoritarian governments use several techniques to first gain power and then maintain it. As you read this section, consider whether the use of these techniques takes into account the will of the people. How then do authoritarian regimes justify the use of these techniques?

Vision

One of the most important aspects of any ideology, including those of authoritarian governments, is a vision: a **vision** of what the country could be if led by a leader who could obtain the vision. Some visions revolve around security—protecting the country from some perceived threat. Adolph Hitler's Nazi party was elected in the early 1930s based on an economic stabilization program, anti-Semitism, and an anti-communist platform. As you read in Chapter 5, Germany at the time was saddled with massive war debts, reparations payments, national humiliation, and political and economic instability. Hitler capitalized on people's fear of communists, and his nationalistic vision of a united, strengthened German Empire in Central Europe appealed to many Germans. Once he became chancellor, Hitler was able to stifle his opponents until the Nazi party was declared the only legitimate party in Germany. When the president died in 1934, at the height of the Depression, the cabinet passed a law transferring the powers of the president to the chancellor—even though the constitution did not allow it. This effectively eliminated any checks or balances on Hitler's power. This move had the approval of 84.6 per cent of the electorate at the time. The people voted for a strong leader with a vision to take them through the years of turmoil. They were not necessarily voting for war or the horrors of the Holocaust to come.

Joseph Stalin consolidated his power in the Soviet Union with a nationalist vision. Instead of following the traditional Bolshevik emphasis on permanent revolution (spreading communism throughout the world by helping other revolutionaries), Stalin instead began a policy known as Socialism in One Country. That is, he focused on improving the country internally. One of the biggest features of this vision was transforming the Russian agrarian economy to an industrial economy. As you read in Chapter 5, Stalin introduced his first Five-Year Plan in 1928. This was a program of agricultural collectivization, which was a means to increase agricultural production to pay for industrialization and to centralize control in a command economy under his leadership. The program met

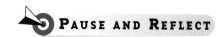

PAUSE AND REFLECT

Virtually all authoritarian governments say that they are working for the best interests of the people; however, many also argue that the will of the people is unimportant because it does not reflect what is best for the country. Is this ever a legitimate justification for ignoring or even subverting the will of the people?

One-Party Systems	Military Dictatorships
China	Burma (Myanmar)
Cuba	Fiji
Laos	Libya
Syria	Mauritania
Vietnam	

Figure 10-21

Here are just a few examples of authoritarian governments in existence as of November, 2008. There are many more that could be added to this list, and even more countries have instances authoritarianism at some point in their histories. Oligarchies are not listed because no country considers itself an oligarchy today, even though some countries, such as Russia, are widely believed to be one.

with intense opposition from the people who owned the land. The collectivization policy and efforts to enforce it and eliminate any resistance to it eventually led to widespread famine, and millions of Soviet citizens, especially in Ukraine, starved to death or were killed. In a meeting during the Second World War, Winston Churchill had the following exchange with Stalin:

Have the stresses of the war been as bad to you personally as carrying through the policy of the Collective Farms?" To which Stalin replied: "Oh, no, the Collective Farm policy was a terrible struggle...Ten million [he said, holding up his hands]. It was fearful. Four years it lasted. It was absolutely necessary...

—**Winston Churchill, *Memoirs of the Second World War* (Boston: Houghton Mifflin Co., 1959), p. 633.**

Propaganda

Another technique most dictatorships—and indeed, most governments in general—use to gain and maintain power is propaganda. Propaganda is the use of a set of messages designed to influence the opinions or behaviours of large numbers of people.

Propaganda is the deliberate, systematic attempt to shape perceptions, manipulate cognitions, and direct behaviour to achieve a response that furthers the desired intent of the propagandist.

—**Garth S. Jowett and Victoria O'Donnell, *Propaganda and Persuasion*, 4th edition. (Thousand Oaks, CA: SAGE Publications, 2006), p. 7.**

Valentina Kulagina, 8 Million Tons of Pig Iron (1931), Lithograph. © Estate of Valentina Kulagina / SODRAC (2009)

Figure 10-22 ▲

This 1931 propaganda poster from the Stalin years promotes the rapid establishment of industries in the Soviet Union. Depictions of happy workers and strong soldiers would have been the norm in propaganda at that time.

As you discovered in your exploration of Nazi and Soviet propaganda in Chapter 5, propaganda is spread through the news media, entertainment media, posters, testimonials, the arts, and a country's education system. The most effective propaganda is done subtly so people are unaware that they are being subjected to a one-sided picture of reality. They have no reason to feel that they are being manipulated.

Propaganda is not always this blatant. The government of the Soviet Union under Stalin, for example, controlled artistic expression. The arts were used for political education, and were meant to shape the will of the people into admiration and acceptance of the regime. The acceptable art form under Stalin was known as Socialist Realism, and its purpose was to glorify the revolution in concrete terms.

Propaganda is never neutral; there is no attempt to equally display both sides of the story. We have, for example, examined the ideological conflict between the United States and Cuba. This conflict is carried out, in part, through a war of words. In 2008, US president George W. Bush called Cuba "a tropical gulag"and "a failed regime". Posters and billboards in Cuba, meanwhile, denounce the United States and its policies, while encouraging Cubans to support the Cuban government.

Figure 10-23 ▲

Figure 10-24 ▲

Controlled Participation

Authoritarian governments also use the technique of controlled participation. The population is allowed to feel as if it is contributing to the country in some ways, for example, by attending rallies, helping to spy on "subversives," preparing for the war effort, becoming the "block boss" for the party—anything that will convince the public to buy into the accepted ideology and prevent the development of contrary opinions. The Nuremberg rallies of Nazi Germany were famous in this respect; they were large, carefully orchestrated events that had a mesmerizing impact on the participants.

Mao Zedong instituted the Cultural Revolution in China in 1966. The revolution was designed to suppress those with liberal leanings, particularly academics. To carry out the revolution, Mao recruited thousands of young people to spread the message of communism throughout the country. Known as Red Guards, these young people went to China's schools and universities to attack traditional culture and spread communism. The media and writers were also targeted. Labelled *capitalists* or *anti-revolutionaries*, thousands of people were hounded from their posts into manual labour or imprisonment. Some were executed. Museums, temples, shrines, old books, and works of art were destroyed. The Red Guards were noted for their propensity for violence and fanatical devotion to Mao. The Cultural Revolution lasted a decade or so, although Mao declared that it was officially over in 1969 because other Communist party members were opposed to the policy.

Directing Public Discontent

Another way of stifling a populace's independent thought consists of directing public discontent. The people are provided with an enemy on which they can safely unleash their frustrations. Their focus can be directed by *show trials*, a foreign threat, or an internal threat. Pro-Islamic forces in the Middle East use the existence of Israel and foreign influence to great effect. Hitler used anti-Semitism.

These are examples of propaganda used in Cuba. The billboard on the left shows former Cuban dictator Fidel Castro and reads "Homeland or Death." The billboard on the right shows a Cuban soldier shouting towards the United States: "Mister imperialists, we are absolutely not afraid." Are any beliefs and values being challenged in these billboards? What are they implying about which values should be most important for Cuban people? To what extent might an American citizen agree or disagree with the specific messages in this billboard?

Stalin used show trials to convict dissidents in the Soviet Union, banishing those convicted to the gulags. To consolidate power and remove anyone who might challenge his authority, Stalin would charge his targets with a manufactured crime and put them on trial. The trials are called *show trials* because the verdict of guilt was assured. On the surface, the trials looked like proper trials, but the charged people who refused to "confess" were tortured, and evidence was fabricated to prove their guilt. These campaigns of repression, which claimed hundreds of thousands of victims in the Soviet Union, were carried out against liberals, writers, the army, and other Communist party members.

Terror

Another means of influencing the will of the people is terror. Some South American governments used quick, brutal, and arbitrary violence to "disappear" dissidents. People simply vanished from everyday life, never to be heard from again. Relatives searched for them in vain, only to discover later that they had been tortured and murdered. The Argentine government carried out such a campaign from 1976 to 1983 following a coup d'état by a military determined to retain power. Some 30 000 people vanished. At times, the dissident's children were given to "acceptable" families for adoption. DNA testing has allowed some of these children to identify their real parents. In 2008, one such child, Maria Eugenia Sampallo Barragan, now 30 years of age, took her adoptive parents to court. The parents were convicted of concealing the identity of a minor and of falsifying documents. The former army captain who had given the child away was also convicted. At a press conference following the trial, Sampallo held up a photo of her adoptive parents and said, "These are not my parents. They are my kidnappers." Sampallo then held up a picture of her biological father and mother and said, "These are my parents." Sampallo's parents are both activists who remain missing. (Source: The Associated Press, "Adoptive parents convicted in landmark Argentine 'dirty war' trial." CBC News, April 4, 2008, www.cbc.ca/world/story/2008/04/04/argentina-trial.html.)

The techniques used by an authoritarian government to enforce its will and negate individual freedoms and the people's will are effective, at least in the short term. If citizens subscribe to the government's vision, if they are soothed by its propaganda, and if they feel they are contributing to the greater good, they may be less aware of the authoritarian nature of the government. The identification of state enemies is a unifying factor, but the use of violence merely drives the will of the people underground. Authoritarian governments are aware of the advantages and disadvantages of these techniques, and use them to varying degrees to meet their particular needs. The premise in all cases, however, is to create the impression that the government is using its authority to protect the country, the interests of the people, and the will of the people, as well as to unify the people behind a vision. People are expected to understand that individuals sometimes need to be sacrificed in the interests of the greater good.

Strengths and Weaknesses of Authoritarianism

Even though many authoritarian governments have sometimes resorted to horrible acts of human rights violations to enforce their power, the fact remains that authoritarianism seems to accomplish many of its goals in many situations. The visions many dictators paint for their countries often address the needs of the people and often result in positive circumstances for many. Many Russians, for example, long for the days of the Soviet Union; under communism they were able to obtain food for their families and heat their homes. Many of the "liberating" market reforms that have come since the collapse of communism have hurt people who were unprepared for a competitive, individualistic lifestyle.

Another interesting example can be found in the Philippines. Ferdinand Marcos, a dictator who ruled the country from 1965 to 1986, was driven from power in a massive, but peaceful, street revolution. He is known to have been extremely corrupt, stealing billions of dollars and stashing the money away in Swiss banks. With recent political and economic instability, however, many in the Philippines are remembering his reign as "better times" because Marcos built roads and hospitals and struck deals with foreign governments to allow Filipinos to work abroad and send home foreign currency, which is now a major feature of the Filipino economy. In fact, the dictator is remembered so fondly now that a nationwide poll in 2005 rated Marcos as the best of the last five Philippine presidents. His rating even topped the rating of the man who organized the revolution that ended his dictatorship. Some say that his greatest achievement was that, even as a dictator, he did listen to the will of the people when it was most important to do so. For example, when the street protest happened, Marcos would not let his guards attack the protestors. Instead, he resigned from power.

Just like democracy, however, authoritarianism has its weaknesses. The willingness by many authoritarian governments to sacrifice individual citizens for the perceived needs of the country is clearly unacceptable on many levels. Most authoritarian governments also seem unable to change leadership in a peaceful manner. This often results in periods of violence and misery during the transition from one leader to another. At other times, authoritarian leaders may be popular leaders whose publics see them as guiding father figures. Later, because of economic circumstances, international pressures, or a general feeling that the leader has become unresponsive, popular support disappears and spontaneous opposition arises. Again, violence is often the result.

Many authoritarian governments have become democracies over the years, partly due to international influence, but also due to the will of the people. Any government, even a dictatorship, will not last if it ignores the people. Such regimes raise difficult questions about why authoritarian leaders are sometimes popularly supported while at other times their popular support disappears. Are there circumstances in which an authoritarian regime can be seen as an expression of the will of the people?

Explore the Issues

Concept Review

1 Create a chart outlining the forms and features of the types of authoritarian political systems that were discussed in this section. Include information on who is in charge, the main features of each system, and a few examples of countries that use that form of government.

Concept Application

2 Given the difficult circumstances some countries find themselves in economically, make an argument that supports an authoritarian political system as a solution to these problems. How could authoritarianism be beneficial to a country with a failing economy? How might the interpretation of the will of the people change in these circumstances? Would it be necessary to ignore it, or could the people's voices be part of the solution? Are there any other examples that you can identify, outside of authoritarian systems, where a group has interpreted what is best for the will of the people differently than the liberal democratic government in power?

3 Choose one of the two assignments below, and for the example chosen, indicate the dictator's perspective on the concept of the will of the people.

a) Find an example of a 20th-century dictator, and conduct research into how he came to power and exercised his power. Write an essay of two to three pages to share your informed response to the issues: To what extent should governments ignore the will of the people, and to what extent are their actions justified?

b) Find an example of a 20th-century dictator who was initially very popular, but who eventually lost the support of his people. What were the reasons for the initial support and the subsequent erosion of popular support? Write an essay of two to three pages to share your informed response to the issues: To what extent should governments ignore the will of the people, and to what extent are their actions justified?

Reflect and Analyze

In this chapter you have explored the question *To what extent should governments reflect the will of the people?* First you looked at democracies and explored how well various types of democracy reflect the will of the people. You also looked at some of the challenges democracies face and how this affects the policies democratic governments follow. You then looked at various types of authoritarian political systems, including some of the techniques authoritarian regimes use to gain and maintain power, as well as some of the strengths and weaknesses of these types of political systems.

Respond to Ideas

1. Reflect on what you have read, thought about, and researched in this chapter. Express your thoughts on the following question: When are governments, whether democratic or authoritarian, justified in ignoring the will of the people?

Respond to Issues

2. Find a country that represents one of the following systems in the 21st century:
   - direct democracy
   - representative democracy
   - military dictatorship
   - ideological one-party state

Find an article discussing a situation in which the government failed to follow the will of its citizens. Write a one- to two-page report on the conflict, answering the following questions:
a) What was the situation in question?
b) What did the people want?
c) What reasons did the government give as to why it did not follow the will of the people?
d) Does the writer of the article have an opinion on the issue (that is, is the article biased)? If so, what is the writer's opinion? What information does the writer share to validate his or her opinion?
e) In your informed response, who was right in this situation, the government or the people? Why?

Recognize Relationships among Concepts, Issues, and Citizenship

3. The need to address HIV/AIDS is a global issue. Its impact reaches every facet of humanity, with children being the victims most dramatically affected. Create a product (for example, a website, brochure, or poster) that persuades people aged 15 to 19 to encourage the Canadian government to take initiative, prevent the spread of this disease, listen to the people affected, and try to find solutions that support the people already involved in this battle. How important should the will of the people be in determining how to address such a global crisis as HIV/AIDS?

Complexities of Liberalism in Practice

KEY SKILL

Communicating effectively to express a point of view

KEY CONCEPTS

Evaluating the extent to which governments should promote individual and collective rights

Key Terms

American Bill of Rights

Anti-Terrorism Act

Canadian Charter of Rights and Freedoms

Emergency and security legislation

Illiberal

Language legislation

Québec Charter of Human Rights and Freedoms

Respect for law and order

Terrorism

Is it ever acceptable for a liberal democracy to suspend the rights of a few to protect the common good? Consider the following example:

Sending a Canadian technology consultant to be confined in a gravelike cell and tortured did nothing to make Americans safer. A Syrian-born Canadian citizen, Maher Arar, 36, was returning home from a vacation in September 2002 when US federal agents detained him in New York City on suspicion of ties to terrorism. Rather than send him to his home and our close ally, Canada, for interrogation, the US government sent him to Syria, a nation with a history of engaging in torture. A year later he was released. Three years later a Canadian commission found no evidence that Arar had any terrorist connection. The commission also concluded that he was systematically tortured and held under horrendous conditions.

The Bush Administration refuses to acknowledge any responsibility, instead offering the tepid explanation that Syrian officials assured the US that Arar would not be tortured. These are the same Syrian officials with whom the US government now says it will not negotiate because they are not trustworthy. Maher Arar's case stands as a sad example of how we have been too willing to sacrifice our core principles to overarching government power in the name of security, when doing so only undermines the principles we stand for and makes us less safe.

—Source: Patrick Leahy, "The Time 100 List: Maher Arar." ***Time* magazine, May 3, 2007.**
http://www.time.com/time/specials/2007/time100/
article/0,28804,1595326_1615754_1616006,00.html

- To what extent do you think the actions of the US and Syrian governments challenged individual or collective rights?

Chapter Issue

Many liberal democracies attempt to reach a consensus over the promotion of individual rights—one of the principles of liberalism—within their state, while at the same time attempting to benefit the common good. Sometimes in their pursuit of the common good, governments ignore the rights of individuals or groups, as the Maher Arar example illustrates. Nonetheless, the struggle for the recognition of individual liberty and collective rights in legislation and the maintenance of the common good is evident in much government legislation. The tension often experienced by governments trying to balance individual and collective rights with the common good highlights the Chapter Issue: *To what extent should democratic governments promote and protect individual and collective rights?* By examining traditional and contemporary approaches taken by liberal democratic governments, you will be able to broaden your understanding of the Chapter Issue. In this chapter you will learn about a broad range of legislation, government action, and citizen initiatives that attempt to address this question.

Figure 11-1 ▲

Maher Arar, a Canadian victim of US **rendition** policies, was selected for *Time* magazine's Time 100 Heroes & Pioneers list.

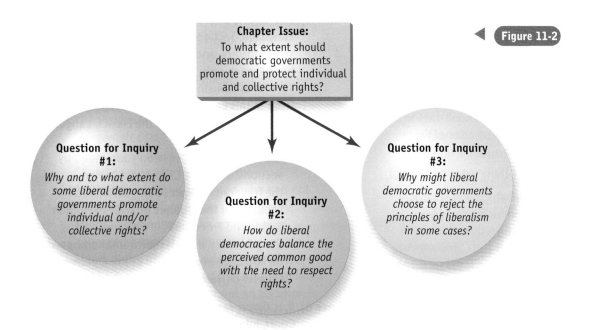

◀ **Figure 11-2**

Chapter Issue:
To what extent should democratic governments promote and protect individual and collective rights?

Question for Inquiry #1:
Why and to what extent do some liberal democratic governments promote individual and/or collective rights?

Question for Inquiry #2:
How do liberal democracies balance the perceived common good with the need to respect rights?

Question for Inquiry #3:
Why might liberal democratic governments choose to reject the principles of liberalism in some cases?

Is the institution of marriage discriminatory? Of course it is, by its very nature. We cannot get married unless we are of a certain age. That is discrimination on the basis of age. We cannot get married if we do not have proper mental capacity. That is discrimination on the basis of disability. We cannot get married unless we are of the proper bloodline [not too closely linked genetically]. That is discrimination on the basis of who our parents are or who our siblings are.

It discriminates against religion because it says we can only have in this country, not in the world but in this country, one spouse: one wife or husband. This is discrimination on the basis of sexual orientation because it says we must marry someone of the opposite sex.

—Tom Wappel, speech in the House of Commons, February 18, 2005.

http://www.tomwappelmp.ca/Speeches/C-38.htm

Mike Boon is a Torontonian who has been maintaining a blog for over five years. On February 1, 2005, he wrote the following:

Earlier today, Justice Minister Irwin Cotler introduced the Liberal government's same-sex marriage bill in the House of Commons. As well as extending the legal capacity to marry for civil purposes to same-sex couples, the package of legislation amends eight other federal acts to extend a variety of marital rights to gay couples, including income tax measures, business and investment benefits and the right to divorce...

At the end of the day, this is still Canada. Because this is Canada, this bill will pass. The Conservative Party will largely vote against it, but the majority of Liberals as well as just about all those from the Bloc Québécois and New Democrat parties will do the right thing. In Canada, all citizens are equal under the law, regardless of skin colour, religion, culture or sexual preference. In Canada, the church and state are indeed separate and our social conscience will remain clear.

I will be a proud Canadian when this bill passes. It's long overdue.

—Mike Boon, "Civil Marriage Act Tabled," February 1, 2005.

http://www.torontomike.com/2005/02/civil_marriage_act_tabled.html

Individual rights are not subject to a public vote; a majority has no right to vote away the rights of a minority; the political function of rights is precisely to protect minorities from oppression by majorities (and the smallest minority on earth is the individual).

**—Ayn Rand, *The Virtue of Selfishness*
(New York: Signet/New American Library, 1964), p. 121.**

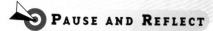

PAUSE AND REFLECT

Summarize Wappel's arguments in your own words. Why does he feel our government should not promote this right?

1 Examine a copy of the Canadian Charter of Rights and Freedoms. Explain how the different arguments presented with regards to same-sex marriage relate to specific sections of the Charter.

2 Canada became the fourth country to legislate same-sex marriage (after the Netherlands [2001], Belgium [2003], and Spain [2005]). In your view, why are these democratic countries explicitly enshrining into their constitutions the right of same-sex partners to marry?

The Promotion of Collective Rights

One responsibility charged to government is the promotion of collective rights and stability. How do collective rights affect your life? How do they affect the lives of people in other countries? As you proceed through this section special attention will be paid to the impact of both active and passive government policy and its impact on citizens.

Group rights are often achieved only by the extension of individual rights. Governments in pursuit of group or collective rights take a wide variety of actions. In the United States, policies known as "affirmative action" were implemented in the 1960s to address inequalities that minorities and women had historically faced. To improve their employment or educational opportunities, the US government introduced hiring and college admissions practices that gave preferential treatment to minorities and women. While not written into the US Constitution as "collective rights," affirmative action programs recognized that in order for all citizens to effectively enjoy equality of opportunity, members of certain groups need to be treated differently. Affirmative action has been challenged in court by those who see it as "reverse discrimination," and a violation of the individual right to equality.

The most certain test by which we judge whether a country is really free is the amount of security enjoyed by minorities.

—Lord Acton, *The History of Freedom in Antiquity*, 1877.

In the context of the Canadian Charter of Rights and Freedoms, "collective rights" refer primarily to the rights of official language groups (Sections 16–23) and Aboriginal peoples (Section 25), and are included to respect laws passed over the course of Canada's history, and to reflect and affirm Canada's bilingual, pluralistic nature. As Supreme Court Chief Justice Beverley McLachlin noted, "Collective rights are the cornerstone on which Canada was built. Without the guarantees made to groups and minorities, it is unlikely that the peoples of Upper and Lower Canada, so different from one another, would have joined to form a country." (Source: Beverley McLachlin, "Democracy and Rights: A Canadian Perspective," *Canadian Speeches, Issues of the Day*, 14:36–45, January/February 2001. http://www.parl.gc.ca/information/library/PRBpubs/prb019-e.htm)

William Kymlicka, a philosophy professor at Queen's University, is a leading expert on collective rights. In his defence of minority rights, Kymlicka argues

...that there are sound principles of justice which require that the rights of citizenship be dependent on cultural group membership; that is, members

Figure 11-5 ▲

Pierre Elliott Trudeau worked consistently to entrench the rights of Canadian citizens during his many years as prime minister. The culmination of these efforts was the Charter of Rights and Freedoms, enshrined in the Constitution Act of 1982. This Act was designed to entrench individual rights; but, at the same time, it included collective rights for Canada's official language groups and Aboriginal peoples.

of certain groups can only be justly incorporated into the political community if "group-differentiated rights, powers, status or immunities, beyond the common rights of citizenship" are accepted.

—**William Kymlicka, quoted in Leighton McDonald, "Regrouping in Defence of Rights: Kymlicka's _Multicultural Citizenship." Osgoode Hall Law Journal_ 34, 2.**
www.ohlj.ca/archive/articles/34_2_mcdonald.pdf

In an address at the Woodrow Wilson International Center for Scholars in Washington, DC, Stéphane Dion, who at the time was president of the Privy Council and Minister of Intergovernmental Affairs in Paul Martin's Liberal government, stated the following:

...collective rights, recognized in the Charter, confirm or establish language rights, Aboriginal rights, and the multicultural character of Canada. The Supreme Court of Canada accords them great importance, to the point that it places respect for minorities among the four fundamental organizing constitutional principles of Canada, alongside federalism, democracy and the rule of law.

Dion went on to say that the inclusion of collective rights was the primary difference between the Canadian Charter of Rights and Freedoms and the American **Bill of Rights**. He also noted that this difference was also due to the time period during which the two documents were written:

The differences between the two texts stem in large part from the fact that they were written in very different historical contexts. In effect, the Bill of Rights is a product of the debates of the Enlightenment, inspired notably by the individual liberalism of John Locke. The Canadian Charter, in contrast, was written in the late 20th century, a time when pure individualism had been modified both by other values and by a more sociological understanding of society. The Canadian Charter was also born in a country that has traditionally heeded the interests of minorities, a tradition grounded in the fundamental political structure of the country.

—**Stéphane Dion, "The Canadian Charter of Rights and Freedoms at Twenty: The Ongoing Search for Balance Between Individual and Collective Rights" (speech given at the Woodrow Wilson International Center for Scholars), April 2, 2002.**
Reproduced with the permission of the Minister of Public Works and Government Services, 2009, and courtesy of the Privy Council Office.
http://www.pco-bcp.gc.ca/aia/index.asp?lang=eng&Page=archive&Sub=speeches&Doc=20020402_e.htm

Collective rights retain the form of individual rights but they are applied to groups rather than individuals. This is the link between individual and collective rights in Canada.

Recognition of Collective Rights

Including collective rights in the Charter on the one hand and having governments in Canada promote or even recognize these rights on the other hand are, however, two different things. Since the Charter came into being in 1982, some groups in Canada have had to fight to have their collective rights respected. For example, you may have studied the case of Francophone schools in Alberta. In the 1980s, some Francophone parents took legal action that went all the way to the Supreme Court of Canada to have the province of Alberta provide Francophone schools and school boards for their children. This collective right was included in Section 23 of the 1982 Charter of Rights and Freedoms (Minority Language Educational Rights), but it took a 1990 Supreme Court decision in favour of the parents before Alberta allowed Francophone school boards to be established to administer Francophone schools.

A similar example stems from the collective rights in Section 25 of the Charter and Section 35 of the Constitution Act, 1982, which recognize and affirm the aboriginal and treaty rights of Canada's Aboriginal peoples (First Nations, Métis, and Inuit). While these rights are constitutionally guaranteed, it has taken many efforts to have certain Aboriginal rights recognized. In the case of hunting or harvesting rights of Canada's Métis people, there continues to be a struggle to have these rights recognized. In 1993, Steve Powley, an Ontario Métis, and his son hunted and killed a moose, and were charged for hunting without a licence. Ten years later, after the case had been appealed through the Ontario court system, the Supreme Court of Canada ruled 9-0 that the Métis of Powley's community in Sault Ste. Marie, Ontario, did indeed have the aboriginal right to hunt, as do "any Métis who can prove a connection to a stable continuous community".

"The highest court of this land has finally done what Parliament and the provincial governments have refused, to deliver justice to the Métis people," said Audrey Poitras, acting president of the Métis National Council.

—**Source: "Ont. Métis community given right to hunt",
CBCnews.ca, September 19, 2003.**
http://www.cbc.ca/canada/story/2003/09/19/metisrule030919.html

However, despite the sections in the Charter and in the Constitution Act and the 2003 Supreme Court decision, many Métis are still fighting to have their Aboriginal right to hunting and harvesting recognized. In 2004 in Manitoba, Métis hunter Will Goodon was charged for duck hunting without a licence. He did have a Métis "harvester" card issued by the Manitoba Métis Federation, but the province of Manitoba refused to recognize the card. In 2008, the Métis

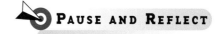

PAUSE AND REFLECT

In Chapter 2 you explored individualism and collectivism and how the values of both underlie, in varying degrees, all ideologies. Individualism favours self-reliance and the protection of individual rights and responsibilities while collectivism favours protecting group goals and the common good. This section of the chapter focuses more closely on the notion of collective rights—those rights claimed by groups to help protect their interests. To what extent do you think collective rights differ from or support the principles of collectivism?

Nation of Alberta took legal action against the Alberta government in order to have the harvesting rights of Alberta's Métis recognized, as charges continued to be laid against Métis hunting without a provincial licence.

As one can see, having collective rights included in the Charter of Rights and Freedoms does not necessarily mean that governments will recognize or promote these rights. What ideological differences might exist that would explain some governments' reluctance to recognize constitutionally guaranteed collective rights?

Explore the Issues

Concept Review

1 Identify and describe three examples from this section of individual and of collective rights protected by government.

Concept Application

2 *You Be the Judge.* Choose from this section an example of an individual or collective right that has been challenged or upheld in a Canadian court, and use the Skill Path to reach a verdict on the issue. Does the issue address how the government is promoting and protecting individual and collective rights?

3 Write a public service announcement (PSA) on behalf of the federal government explaining to all Canadians the differences between individual and collective rights and promoting the importance of these rights and of the role of the Canadian Charter of Rights and Freedoms in Canada. Use clear and effective language and include summaries of a few relevant Charter cases to illustrate your points. You may wish to make your PSA into a short video or multimedia production, a poster including artwork and visuals, or some other format of your choosing.

Balancing Perceived Common Good with Respect for Rights

- **How do liberal democracies balance the perceived common good with the need to respect rights?**

Examine the following newspaper article. What is the relationship between "common good" and "the respect for rights" in the situation described?

Irish pub, French language watchdog battle over vintage signs, service

Sidhartha Banerjee
CP, © 2008 The Canadian Press, 15 February 2008

MONTREAL—It appears a few pints of beer won't be sufficient to douse the latest language tensions brewing in Montreal—this time, Québec's language watchdog is frothing over a popular watering hole cluttered with classic Irish signage and English-only posters.

The wall hangings at McKibbin's Irish Pub include vintage advertisements for Guinness and Harp as well as other traditional fare like Palethorpes Pork Pies.

The owners of the popular hangout say it all just adds to the charm and ambience of the downtown watering hole.

Still, the Office québecois de la langue française says complaints about the English-only signs, an English-only chalkboard menu and English-only service prompted it to send the pub owners a letter wanting answers.

"What we asked them were what measures would be taken to ensure that service would be offered in French because we received two complaints," Office spokesman Gerald Paquette said in an interview Friday.

"If the business says some of those pictures are decorative to give the pub an Irish flavour, it is certain we would exempt them from the charter rules," Paquette said. "But there were other posters also, notably ones about contests and events, that were in English only."

The brewhaha has prompted the pub's co-owners to extend an invite to Premier Jean Charest to stop by for a hearty meal and a pint and inspect the signs himself.

Dean Laderoute and Rick Fon say they'll remove the signs if Charest believes they violate the Québec language law.

"An Irish pub without these decorations is just an empty box," Fon said in an interview. "It's the decor, the pictures, the clutter, it creates the warmth."

Fon also says they have bilingual menus and that his regulars, including a considerable French clientele, all agree the complaints are ridiculous.

"It makes no sense, it's silly," said regular Suzette L'Abbé.

"The staff, if not French-speaking to begin with, get by in French," L'Abbé added.

The pub could face fines as high as $1500 for each infraction.

The pub skirmish is the latest battle over the question of whether there is enough French spoken in downtown Montréal.

The ever-bubbling issue of language has resurfaced in recent months, beginning with a report in Le Journal de Montréal about the ease of obtaining employment downtown with a limited knowledge of French.

Other controversies have included the language of instruction for tots in day care and the use of English on the automated call-answering systems of Québec government departments.

The debate promises to get even more heated next month when the language watchdog releases a study on language trends in the province.

Paquette says McKibbin's has 30 days to come up with answers and if the issue goes further, a legal warning would be sent and Québec's attorney general would decide on penalties and fines.

English-rights activist Gary Shapiro believes the whole language pot started stirring again with the so-called reasonable accommodation debate and has been fuelled since by politicians and a small group of malcontents.

"It's basic harassment," said Shapiro.

"Are they going to come into our homes and our bedrooms next?" Shapiro asked. "Where is it going to end?"

Currently, part of the **language legislation** in Québec requires that "public signs and commercial advertising must be in French. They may be in French and another language provided that French is markedly predominant." According to this requirement, does the Montréal pub seem to be breaking the law?

One of the fundamental freedoms guaranteed to Canadians in the 1982 Charter of Rights and Freedoms is the "freedom of thought, belief, opinion and expression, including freedom of the press and other media of communication." This freedom is not absolute, however. Section 1 of the Charter states that it "guarantees the rights and freedoms set out in it subject only to such reasonable limits prescribed by law as can be demonstrably justified in a free and democratic society." In other words, our rights are limited. In the case of freedom of expression, for example, one must refrain from injuring others' reputations (laws against libel and slander) and from spreading hate against others, which is a crime covered under the Criminal Code of Canada.

But what of language laws in the province of Québec? In 1977, the Québec government passed Bill 101, creating the Charter of the French Language (*La Charte de la langue française*) in order "to make French the common language of Quebecers in all spheres of public life." The Charter of the French language has been challenged and, as a result, amended over the years:

Legislation	Main Provisions	Reactions/Challenges
Bill 101, Charte de la langue française, 1977	*It made French the official language of the state and of the courts in the province of Québec, as well as making it the normal and habitual language of the workplace, of instruction, of communications, of commerce and of business.* "Bill 101", The Canadian Encyclopedia. http://www.canadianencyclopedia.ca/index.cfm?PgNm=TCE&Params=M1ARTA0000744	Court rulings modified this law in order to • allow both French and English in the legislature and courts • allow English-language schooling for students who had begun their education in English elsewhere in Canada • declare that French-only rules for commercial signs were contrary to the right to freedom of expression
Bill 178, an Act to amend the Charte de la langue française, 1988	*It decreed that only French could be used on exterior signs while English would be allowed inside commercial establishments.* Source: CBC Indepth "Bill 101: Language laws in Quebec". CBC News Online, March 30, 2005 http://www.cbc.ca/news/background/bill101/	*In 1993, the United Nations Human Rights Committee ruled that Québec's sign laws broke an international covenant on civil and political rights. "A State may choose one or more official languages," the committee wrote, "but it may not exclude outside the spheres of public life, the freedom to express oneself in a certain language."* Source: CBC Indepth "Bill 101: Language laws in Québec". CBC News Online, March 30, 2005 http://www.cbc.ca/news/background/bill101
Bill 86, an Act to amend the Charte de la langue française, 1993	*Public signs and posters and commercial advertising must be in French. They may also be both in French and in another language provided that French is markedly predominant.* Source: Bill 86, section 58	This bill made the *Charte de la langue française* "constitutionally acceptable as it now complied with the Charter of Rights and Freedoms". Source: "Bill 86", The Canadian Encyclopedia. http://www.thecanadianencyclopedia.com/index.cfm?PgNm=TCE&Params=A1ARTA0009101

For what reason is Québec able to limit people's freedom of expression, as protected by the Canadian Charter of Rights and Freedoms? Primarily, laws protecting and promoting French in Québec are seen to be in the common good of the Francophone majority of that province in order to counter the assimilative forces of English in North America that Francophones in Québec face.

Francophones in Québec form a clear majority within their province, but find themselves, along with other Francophones, in a minority within Canada, and are, so to speak, no more than a drop in an Anglophone ocean, when considering the proximity of the American giant. They feel the pressure of English, which exerts a strong attraction, particularly among immigrants.

—**Stéphane Dion, in a speech delivered at the Symposium on Language Rights, Law Faculty, Université de Moncton, Moncton, New Brunswick, February 15, 2002.**

http://www.pco-bcp.gc.ca/AIA/index.asp?lang=eng&page=archive&sub
=speeches&doc=20020215_e.htm

PAUSE AND REFLECT

To what extent do official language laws in the constitution affirm our Canadian identity?

Figure 11-6 ▲

Examine this political cartoon from 1999. What do the numbers on the blocks refer to? What is holding them up? In other words, upon what grounds are laws that protect and promote the French language in Québec based?

When Government Action for the Perceived Common Good Outweighs Collective Rights

Diana Breti wrote an article entitled "Canada's Concentration Camps—The War Measures Act." In the article, she gives the following example concerning government action to promote the common good. As you read, consider whose rights were promoted and whose were undermined by the government.

In 1942, the Federal government decided it wanted 2,240 acres [over 900 hectares] of Indian Reserve land at Stoney Point, in southwestern Ontario, to establish an advanced infantry training base. Apparently the decision to take reserve land for the army base was made to avoid the cost and time involved in expropriating non-Aboriginal lands.

Figure 11-7 ▲

Commissioner Sidney B. Linden carries a copy of the Report of the Ipperwash Inquiry in Forest, Ontario, on the day of its release.

The Stoney Point Reserve comprised over half the Reserve territory of the Chippewas of Kettle & Stoney Point. Under the Indian Act, reserve lands can only be sold by Surrender, which involves a vote by the Band membership. The Band members voted against the Surrender, however the Band realized the importance of the war effort and they were willing to lease the land to the Government. The Government rejected the offer to lease. On April 14, 1942, an Order-in-Council authorizing the appropriation of Stoney Point was passed under the provisions of the War Measures Act. The military was sent in to forcibly remove the residents of Stoney Point. Houses, buildings and the burial ground were bulldozed to establish Camp Ipperwash. By the terms of the Order-in-Council, the Military could use the Reserve lands at Stoney Point only until the end of World War II. However, those lands have not yet been returned. The military base was closed in the early 1950s, and since then the lands have been used for cadet training, weapons training and recreational facilities for military personnel.

—**Diana Breti, "Canada's Concentration Camps—The War Measures Act."**
The Law Connection, Simon Fraser University, 1998.
http://www.britishcolumbia.com/general/details.asp?id=44
Centre for Education, Law & Society, Simon Fraser University.
www.lawconnections.ca

By 1972, the federal government was well aware of the discontent among the Aazhoodena (Stoney Point First Nation). The Minister of Indian Affairs, Jean Chrétien, wrote to the Minister of National Defence on December 8, 1972:

…They have waited patiently for action. There are signs, however, that they will soon run out of patience. There is bound to be adverse publicity about our seeming apathy and reluctance to make a just settlement. They may well resort

to the same tactics as those employed by the St. Regis [First Nation] at Loon and Stanley Islands in 1970—to occupy the lands they consider to be their own...

—**Source: Ipperwash Public Inquiry Transcript, September 8, 2004. The Ipperwash Inquiry.**
http://www.attorneygeneral.jus.gov.on.ca/inquiries/ipperwash/transcripts/sep_08_04/text.htm

Figure 11-8 ▲

See the timeline below.

1992	*Stoney Point [Aboriginals] serve army with eviction notice. Stoney Pointers are descendants of the original inhabitants of Stoney Point, who reject attempts to join band with nearby Kettle Point.*
1993	*Family members of former residents, including Dudley George, move into Camp Ipperwash.*
July 29, 1995	*Military moves out of military base.*
Sept. 4, 1995	*About two-dozen Stoney Pointers, including George, walk into Ipperwash park, saying they are protecting sacred burial grounds.*
Sept. 6, 1995	*Dudley George, 38, died when OPP (Ontario Provincial Police) members fired on the protesters.*

—**Source: "Ipperwash land returned to Indians", The Toronto Star, December 21, 2007.**
http://www.thestar.com:80/News/Canada/article/287702

The Province of Ontario launched an inquiry into the death of Dudley George on November 12, 2003. The Aazhoodena and the George family made the following statement in their official submission to the inquiry:

Where a First Nations group asserts that it is an independent First Nation with an interest in a land claim or assertion of an Aboriginal or treaty right, the Governments of Canada and Ontario should treat these claims as they would any other formal land claims or assertion of an Aboriginal or treaty right, even if the said First Nations group does not have formal status in Canadian law at the time. The Governments of Canada and Ontario should ensure...an effective process for resolving land claims and disputes over Aboriginal and treaty rights...[The process] should protect the interests of the general public; and...should address systemic disincentives that discourage governments from negotiating settlements in a timely manner.

Negotiations between equally resourced parties should be the primary method for resolving disputes between First Nations and the Governments of Canada and Ontario over land claims or the assertions of Aboriginal and/or treaty rights, with access to a fully independent tribunal to assist the negotiation process where impasses arise between the parties.

—**Source: "Submissions on behalf of the Aazhoodena and George Family Group", The Ipperwash Inquiry, pp. 13, 14.**
http://www.attorneygeneral.jus.gov.on.ca/inquiries/ipperwash/closing_submissions/pdf/AazhoodenaAndGeorgeFamilyGroup_ClosingSubmissions.pdf

❶ Could a suspension of the collective rights of Aboriginal peoples occur today, now that the Charter of Rights and Freedoms has recognized the existence of collective rights for Aboriginal peoples?

❷ Does the provincial government have an obligation to return the Stoney Point lands to the Aazhoodena?

❸ Based on the evidence provided, how do you believe that the federal government and the Aazhoodena would each define "common good"? To what extent did the federal government balance its perceived understanding of the common good with the collective rights of the Aazhoodena?

Efforts to Entrench First Nations, Métis, and Inuit Rights

After centuries of challenges, the struggle of First Nations, Inuit, and Métis peoples for the establishment and recognition of collective rights, equality rights, and governing authority has become a high-profile issue for Canadian governments because First Nations, Métis, and Inuit organizations have conducted campaigns to raise public awareness and pressure governments for these rights. This issue is not confined to Canada. Aboriginal groups from many countries are engaged in the same struggle. Many groups have repeatedly presented cases to the United Nations (UN) for recognition and support while pressuring governments to remedy past wrongs and garner resources to work toward a better future.

Get to the
Source

In Canada this process took a big step forward when the Charter of Rights and Freedoms was enacted as Part I of the Constitution Act in 1982. First Nations, Métis, and Inuit peoples participated in the drafting of the Constitution and the Charter, and are largely responsible for Section 25 in the Charter and Section 35 in Part II of the Constitution that recognize and affirm their collective and treaty rights (rev.3).

25: *The guarantee in this Charter of certain rights and freedoms shall not be construed so as to abrogate or derogate from any Aboriginal, treaty or other rights or freedoms that pertain to the Aboriginal peoples of Canada including:*

a) *any rights or freedoms that have been recognized by the Royal Proclamation of October 7, 1763; and*

b) *any rights or freedoms that now exist by way of land claims agreements or may be so acquired.*

35: *(1) The existing Aboriginal and treaty rights of the Aboriginal peoples of Canada are hereby recognized and affirmed.*

(2) In this Act, "Aboriginal peoples of Canada" includes the Indian, Inuit and Métis peoples of Canada.

(3) For greater certainty, in subsection (1) "treaty rights" includes rights that now exist by way of land claims agreements or may be so acquired.

(4) Notwithstanding any other provision of this Act, the Aboriginal and treaty rights referred to in subsection (1) are guaranteed equally to male and female persons.

—**Source: Canadian Charter of Rights and Freedoms.
Department of Justice Canada,
http://laws.justice.gc.ca/en/charter/.**

▶ PAUSE AND REFLECT

What do the Charter and the Constitution say about governmental responsibility to preserve the collective rights of these three groups? Is legislating these rights sufficient, or do additional steps need to be taken to implement the law?

The Canadian Government and the UN: Differing Perspectives on Collective Rights

Many Aboriginal peoples around the world, including those from Canada, have taken their cases to the UN, a reflection of the fact that Canadian governments have been slow to respond to First Nations, Métis, and Inuit claims. This situation has been gradually changing. The government of Canada is making some progress on addressing Aboriginal land claims and is attempting to speed up the process.

On June 29, 2006, the Human Rights Council of the UN passed the following resolution. Thirty countries voted in favour of the resolution, two voted against, and twelve countries abstained. Canada was one of the two countries to vote against the declaration.

The United Nations Declaration on the Rights of Indigenous Peoples says Indigenous peoples have the right to the full enjoyment, as a collective or as individuals, of all human rights and fundamental freedoms as recognized in the Charter of the United Nations, the Universal Declaration of Human Rights (UDHR) and international human rights law. Indigenous peoples and individuals are free and equal to all other peoples and individuals and have the right to be free from any kind of discrimination, in the exercise of their rights, in particular that based on their Indigenous origin or identity. Indigenous peoples have the right of self-determination. By virtue of that right they freely determine their political status and freely pursue their economic, social and cultural development. Indigenous peoples have the right to maintain and strengthen their distinct political, legal, economic, social and cultural institutions, while retaining their rights to participate fully, if they so choose, in the political, economic, social and cultural life of the State.

—Source: "Human Rights Council adopts the UN Declaration on the Rights of Indigenous Peoples." International Work Group for Indigenous Affairs.

http://www.iwgia.org/sw21486.asp

The Canadian Conservative government voted against the UN declaration for several reasons:

"It contains provisions that are inconsistent with the Canadian charter," Minister of Indian Affairs and Northern Development Jim Prentice said of the deal. "It contains provisions that are inconsistent with the Constitution Act of 1982. It's quite inconsistent with land-claims policies under which Canada negotiates claims."

Prentice said the document would hinder land-claims talks with some aboriginal bands on handing over rights to exploit resources. He said Canada would vote against the document if it remained unchanged.

—Source: "Canada Opposes UN Aboriginal Treaty", CBC.ca, Tuesday, June 20, 2006.

http://www.cbc.ca/world/story/2006/06/20/aboriginal-declaration.html

Regarding the passing of the UN Declaration of the Rights of Indigenous Peoples, Mary Simon made the following statement:

This is a proud day for Inuit and Indigenous peoples around the world. It is also an important day in the progressive evolution of human rights standards for all peoples of the world, indigenous and non-indigenous alike. Today marks the culmination of years of persistent work in achieving this. We celebrate this as a very significant victory for all of humanity.

—Mary Simon, national leader of the Inuit in Canada, on the occasion of the UN Declaration on the Rights of Indigenous Peoples

Treaty Negotiations in British Columbia

STATEMENTS OF INTENT TO NEGOTIATE TREATIES ACCEPTED BY THE
BRITISH COLUMBIA TREATY COMMISSION AS OF MARCH 2007

1 Acho Dene Koe First Nation
2 Allied Tribes of Lax Kw'alaams
3 Carcross/Tagish First Nation
4 Carrier Sekani Tribal Council
5 Champagne and Aishihik First Nations
6 Cheslatta Carrier Nation
7 Council of the Haida Nation
8 Da'naxda'xw Awaetlatla Nation
9 Ditidaht First Nation
10 Esketemc First Nation
11 Gitanyow Hereditary Chiefs
12 Gitxsan Hereditary Chiefs
13 Gwa'Sala-Nakwaxda'xw Nation
14 Haisla Nation
15 Hamatla Treaty Society
16 Heiltsuk Nation
17 a) Hul'qumi'num Treaty Group (Core)
   b) Hul'qumi'num Treaty Group (Marine)
18 Hupacasath First Nation
19 In-SHUCK-ch Nation
20 Kaska Dena Council
21 Katzie Indian Band
22 Klahoose Indian Band
23 K'omoks First Nation
24 Ktunaxa Kinbasket Treaty Council
25 Kwakiutl Nation
26 Lake Babine Nation
27 Lheidli T'enneh Band
28 Liard First Nation
29 Maa-nulth First Nations

30 McLeod Lake Indian Band
31 Musqueam Nation
32 'Namgis Nation
33 Nazko Indian Band
34 Northern Shuswap Tribal Council Society
35 Nuu-chah-nulth Tribal Council
36 Pacheedaht Band
37 Quatsino First Nation
38 Ross River Dena Council
39 Sechelt Indian Band
40 Sliammon Indian Band
41 Snuneymuxw First Nation
42 Squamish Nation
43 Stó:lō Nation
44 Taku River Tlingit First Nation
45 Te'mexw Treaty Association (Bands)
46 Teslin Tlingit Council
47 Tlatlasikwala Nation
48 Tlowitsis First Nation
49 Tsawwassen First Nation
50 Tsay Keh Dene Band
51 Tsimshian First Nations
52 Tsleil-Waututh Nation (Burrard)
53 Westbank First Nation
54 Wet'suwet'en Nation
55 Wuikinuxv Nation
56 Xwémalhkwu Nation
57 Yale First Nation
58 Yekooche Nation

Approximate Boundaries of
Traditional Territories

Nis ga' a Lands

Nass Wildlife Area

Figure 11-9 ▲

Aboriginal groups issued statements of intent to negotiate treaties by the British Columbia government. See reference to the Nisga'a, with whom the province in conjunction with the federal government has already negotiated a treaty. Why might the BC government try to play a leadership role in negotiating treaties alongside the federal government, which generally has jurisdiction in these matters?

Aboriginal land claims in Canada fall into two broad categories:

- **comprehensive land claims**, which are based on the Aboriginal rights recognized by section 25 of the Charter and section 35 of the Constitution Act of 1982, and involve territory and issues which are not yet affected by any existing treaty or other legal agreement. Many of the current land claims cases in British Columbia are in this category.

- **specific land claims**, which involve disputes over the fulfilment or administration of existing treaties or other legal agreements, such as the Indian Act or the historical treaties signed between the Canadian government and various First Nations. Specific claims also include Treaty Land Entitlement claims regarding land allegedly promised through existing treaties, but not delivered. (Source: "Settling Land Claims", Library of Parliament, September 1, 1999, http://www.parl.gc.ca/ information/library/PRBpubs/prb9917-e.htm).

The government of British Columbia states its reasons for conducting treaties:

The reasons for treaty negotiations in British Columbia generally fall into three categories: moral; economic; and constitutional and legal. These are interconnected and need to be resolved in order for British Columbia to prosper both socially and economically.

The moral issue is self-evident. The quality of life for Aboriginal people is well below that of other British Columbians. Aboriginal people generally die earlier, have poorer health, have lower education and have significantly lower employment and income levels than other British Columbians. This is directly related to the conditions that have evolved in Aboriginal communities, largely as a result of unresolved land and title issues, and an increasing reliance on federal support programs.

As well as the obvious issues of the social and economic conditions of Aboriginal people, the courts have told government repeatedly that Aboriginal rights and title exist, and that these rights have significant impact on the way government does its business.

Uncertainty over ownership of land impedes the development of Aboriginal communities and economies, affects the provincial economy and discourages investment. Government has to take that reality into account as it continues to manage the lands and resources of British Columbia.

In order to maximize opportunities for economic development and job creation for all British Columbians, government has to find a way to reconcile the rights and the interests of First Nations with those of the Crown. Treaty negotiations provide for public input and a method for resolution of these issues.

—**Source: British Columbia Ministry of Aboriginal Relations and Reconciliations, "Why We Are Negotiating Treaties."** **Copyright © Province of British Columbia. All rights reserved. Reprinted with permission of the Province of British Columbia.** www.ipp.gov.bc.ca www.gov.bc.ca/arr/treaty/negotiating/why.html

Despite its opposition to the UN Declaration on the Rights of Indigenous Peoples, the Canadian government is making efforts to improve the land claims process. On June 18, 2008, the Specific Claims Tribunal Act was given royal assent. This Act overhauled Canada's land claims process. The new legislation was intended to provide a faster and fairer process for outstanding land claims. Before the legislation passed, a CTV News article quoted Indian Affairs minister Jim Prentice as saying the following:

"It is…time for the government of Canada to initiate full institutional reform, and create a fully independent land claims tribunal, empowered to adjudicate these difficult historic grievances in a binding way," he told the standing committee on Aboriginal affairs. All Canadians, whether Aboriginal or non-Aboriginal, deserve as much.

—**Jim Prentice, quoted in "Ottawa to give more power to land-claims panel." CTV, May 17, 2007.** http://toronto.ctv.ca/servlet/an/local/CTVNews/ 20070517/land_claims_070517?hub=TorontoHome

1 Before approaching this section's readings, had you considered how each level of government could or does impact the promotion of collective rights? identified in the Constitution and Charter and in documents such as the UN Declaration on the Rights of Indigenous Peoples? Can having rights and receiving recognition of those rights sometimes be two different things? Explain.

2 According to the sources you have explored regarding the UN Declaration on the Rights of Indigenous Peoples, section 25 of the Charter of Rights and Freedoms, and Section 35 of the Constitution Act, to what extent can governments in Canada and the United Nations impact the recognition of collective rights for First Nations, Métis, and Inuit peoples? In what ways do the principles of liberalism play a role in government responses to issues of collective rights and land claims in Canada?

Restrictions on Religious Symbolism

In most cases, freedom from discrimination based on religious beliefs is an *individual* right (equality rights, freedom of belief). This right can also be considered a collective right in some countries when a group's freedom of religious practice is in need of protection.

In our globalizing world, you may be quite familiar with symbolism from diverse religious, spiritual, or belief systems. You might openly demonstrate, wear, or share symbols of your own beliefs, culture, spirituality, or religion. Have you ever experienced restrictions on how, when, and where those symbols could be shown, or on your democratic right to freedom of religious expression? Have you ever felt you might be criticized or ostracized for displaying your religious, spiritual, or cultural symbols? To what extent is the individual right to freedom of religious expression important to you and your identity?

As you read in Chapter 3, France became a pioneer of Western democracy when it established itself as a liberal republic in the 18th century following the French Revolution. Although it is one of the oldest liberal democracies, the French government may sometimes act in ways that seem **illiberal**.

In the 1990s, the French government began to restrict the display of religious symbols in public as part of a policy to preserve the secular character of public institutions, including government offices, service desks, and schools. In 2004, the Minister of Education interpreted those restrictions to apply to certain religious symbols, specifically the wearing of hijabs, the headscarves worn by some Muslim women as an expression of modesty, as a symbol of faith, and sometimes as a sign of their commitment to Islamic movements or groups, whether social or political. According to some Muslim scholars, the hijab is mandatory. Under the new interpretation of French law, students who wore a hijab faced expulsion from school. The restrictions expanded to include turbans worn by Sikh males, yarmulkes (skull caps worn by Jewish men), and large Christian crosses.

Taliban forced women to wear hijab and France forced women to remove it; what is the difference as far as the issue of human rights is concerned?... Muslim women in Arab and Muslim states are criticized for staying at home. The French ban is designed to force French Muslim women [to stay] at home.

—Cennet Doganay (a French Muslim student in Strasbourg, France, who was isolated from fellow students for wearing a hijab in 2004), quoted in Hadi Yahmid, "Skin-head Muslim Student Grills France." *Islam Online*, **October 12, 2004.**

http://www.islamonline.net/English/News/2004-10/12/article02.shtml

Figure 11-10 ▲

The hijab is worn by women in many countries, including Canada. How might restrictions on religious and cultural symbols change how people view the relationship between government and individuals?

On September 2, 2004, France's *Loi sur laïcité* (law on secularism) took effect in all state schools. This law reads in pertinent part:

Dans les écoles, les collèges et les lycées publics, le port de signes ou tenues par lesquels les élèves manifestent ostensiblement une appartenance religieuse est interdit.

[Translation:]

In public [primary and secondary schools], the wearing of symbols or clothing through which the pupils ostensibly manifest a religious appearance [or "affiliation"] is prohibited.

The ban on all symbols or clothing that create a religious appearance means that students cannot wear yarmulkes, large crucifixes, Sikh turbans, or of course Islamic headscarves…The word "ostensibly," however, allows pupils to continue the traditional French practice of wearing small Christian crucifixes.

—**Source: "France—Banning Religious Attire—United Sikhs", The Becket Fund for Religious Liberty.**
http://www.becketfund.org/index.php/case/96.html

If there is a protest one day, there will be a counter-protest the next.

—**Nicolas Sarkozy (French Interior Minister at the time of this quote, elected the president of France in 2007, shrugging off further debate on the laws), quoted in "World Protests Against French Hijab Ban."** *Islam Online*, **January 17, 2004**
http://www.islamonline.net/English/News/2004-01/17/article09.shtml

In Britain we are comfortable with the expression of religion.

—**Mike O'Brien (British foreign office minister, providing the British government's response to the French law), quoted in "O'Brien Proud of Britain's Multiculturalism." January 16, 2004.**
http://www.fco.gov.uk/resources/en/pressrelease/2004/01/
fco_npr_170104_obrienreligion

In response to the law, protests were held in France and many countries. Some female students expelled for wearing hijabs and males expelled for wearing turbans sued the French government and were reinstated to their schools. Yet the laws are still in effect, and other countries followed France's lead. The Belgian city of Antwerp passed a law in 2007 that bans the use of "visible symbols of philosophical, religious, political or other opinions" for civil servants who work with the public. (Source: Eva Vergaelen, "City of Fashion Bans the Hijab." *Islam Online*, http://www.islamonline.net/servlet/Satellite?c=Article_C&cid=117715 6198981&pagename=Zone-English-Euro_Muslims%2FEMELayout.)

PAUSE AND REFLECT

Why do you think the French government, as a liberal democracy, would restrict the wearing of religious symbols?

Figure 11-11 ▲

In Canada, the wearing of religious headgear by Sikhs is protected by the Canadian Charter of Rights and Freedoms. If it was Passport Canada's policy to reject applications from Sikhs wearing religious head coverings, would this mean that the government was limiting these Canadians' religious freedom?

Veils, hijabs, and other religious and political symbols are forbidden for nurses, cleaning staff in public buildings, teachers, and clerks, as the people positioned in these roles are to appear "neutral."

France's governmental policies and actions strongly affect its own citizens and also affect people in other countries. How do the restrictions placed on religious symbolism affect the rights of French citizens and those in other liberal democracies?

In a similar vein, some Canadians have been concerned by restrictions placed upon the wearing of certain clothing or headgear during the passport application process:

Passport Canada has upset a British Columbia–based Sikh family by denying its children's passport applications. Passport Canada stated that the religious headgear the children wore in their photos was unacceptable. The children's faces were clearly visible in the photographs.

—Source: adapted from "Sikh passport photos rejected because of headgear." CBC News, August 17, 2007.
http://www.cbc.ca/canada/british-columbia/story/2007/08/17/bc-sikhpassports.html

For security reasons, Passport Canada was trying to impose a certain order on these young citizens that infringed on their freedom of religious expression as protected by the Canadian Charter of Rights and Freedoms. Can you think of other examples where Canadian government agencies have tried to impose order in a situation that threatened to limit citizens' Charter rights?

Explore the Issues

Concept Review

1 Review the examples in this section of the chapter. Create a chart to explain how each example responds to the Question for Inquiry: How do liberal democracies balance the perceived common good with the need to respect rights?

Concept Application

2 *You Be the Judge.* Consider the Supreme Court case *Société des Acadiens et Acadiennes du Nouveau-Brunswick Inc. v. Canada*, about language rights in New Brunswick. Your teacher will provide you with a summary of the case. Use the Skill Path to help you assess to what extent RCMP officers should be required to provide service in both official languages in Canada. If officers are unable to provide service in one of the official languages, is this an infringement of a citizen's official language rights in the Charter?

3 After centuries of being denied basic human rights and the control of their land and government, some First Nations and Métis leaders have advocated violent protests to have their individual human rights and collective Aboriginal rights respected. Research the economic status of First Nations and Métis communities. According to your research, what percentage of the population is experiencing higher, middle, and lower socioeconomic status? Is there a relationship among: economic standing; public education and health; the perception of individual rights and freedoms; and the use of violence? To what extent are the collective rights of Aboriginal peoples under Section 35 of the Constitution being affirmed and recognized in Canada?

Rejecting the Principles of Liberalism

Question for **Inquiry**

- **Why might governments choose to reject the principles of liberalism in some cases?**

The Anti-Smoking movement is promoting the exclusion of 5 000 000 Canadians who consume a legal product and who contribute a significant amount of Tax Revenues to this nation and its provinces. People are being harassed and assaulted by Anti-Smokers and these people seem to feel that they are entitled to do so because the government is backing them.

Our elected representatives do nothing to protect the rights of 20 percent of the population who smoke and who also vote. We feel that this has to stop and that Smokers should be recognized as a Visible Minority in Canada and subject to the same rights and freedoms as other Visible Minorities, most importantly the protection from Hate Crimes and abuse.

— **Source: "Stop Hate Crimes and Social Exclusion of Smokers"(online petition to end government bans on smoking).**
http://www.ipetitions.com/petition/CanadianSmokersRights/

Tobacco users in Canada have found themselves increasingly restricted as to where, when, and how they can use tobacco products legally in Canada. While the purchase of tobacco is legal for adults, its use in public places is not. The rights of smokers and non-smokers have come into competition, with the latter having greater support from both governments and the majority of citizens.

Is it possible to reconcile the rights of smokers with the rights of non-smokers? Should the government favour one side over the other? On what grounds would it do so?

Throughout this section you will have several opportunities to examine historical and contemporary cases where non-liberal government practices have been questioned. You will also explore the reasoning, context, and informational bias of governments at the time of their actions. This information will help you address the following issue: *To what extent should democratic governments promote and protect individual and collective rights?*

Figure 11-12 ▲

Should Liberal Democracies Always Adhere to the Principles of Liberalism?

In what situations is a government justified in imposing secrecy and censorship? Is it ever justified?

In February, 2008, Canadian soldiers fighting in Afghanistan were urged to use caution when using popular websites such as Facebook when communicating with family and friends back home. They were warned to not share photos of themselves in uniform or of the battlefront. According to the Defence Department, "the insurgents could use this information to determine their success or their lack of it…and determine better ways to attack us." However, defence analyst Sunil Ram suggested that "what we're really talking about is censorship more than anything else." He went on to say, "This is the military's attempt to control the imagery of what is actually happening on the ground." Journalists covering the activities of Canada's armed forces in Afghanistan have often been held back from going to the site of direct conflict, or their requests for information are denied or delayed. Is this for their own safety, or for the protection of information related to military operations?

- Why might the Canadian government place restrictions on the type and amount of information that Canadian soldiers shared with their family members?
- How might governments handle dilemmas that involve the disclosure of information (other than with openness and truthfulness) during times of war, crisis, or emergency?

One controversial example of a liberal democratic government seemingly violating liberal principles is the US Army's "stop-loss" provision. Between 2002 and 2008, it is estimated that 70 500 soldiers were issued stop-loss orders by the US military. The controversial stop-loss policy can force soldiers to involuntarily extend their terms of service for their enlistment in the army for up to 15 extra months. There are many different perspectives regarding this policy, such as those of: army officials, who generally feel that the policy is necessary to maintain leadership by experienced soldiers; and some "stop-lossed" soldiers, who wish for the army to honour its original agreements. (Source: Julian E. Barnes, "Army 'stop-loss' orders up dramatically over last year", *Los Angeles Times*, May 09, 2008, p. A-16. http://articles.latimes.com/2008/may/09/nation/na-stoploss9.)

- To what extent do democratic governments have a responsibility to adhere to the principles of liberalism during times of conflict?

PAUSE AND REFLECT

If the federal government were to remove any of your rights for the perceived common good, what individual or collective rights would you be most concerned about losing? What individual rights or collective rights would you be most willing to temporarily suspend for the perceived common good? To what extent would your beliefs and values be conflicted during your decision making?

Liberal democracies face myriad situations in which their adherence to the principles of liberalism is tested. During times of war, emergency, and environmental crisis, liberal democracies have restricted people's movement, controlled people's access to information, and limited people's rights, freedoms, and choices. While these actions are often short term, some illiberal policies have remained in effect for years or even decades after they were implemented in an emergency situation. Furthermore, illiberal policies are often not universally applied to citizens; rather, certain groups or individuals receive differential treatment.

The War Measures Act

The **War Measures Act** was first passed in 1914 in response to Canada's involvement in the First World War. It has been invoked only three times in Canada's history. The actions that were taken by the Canadian government when it invoked the Act were atypical of the day-to-day actions of governments in liberal democracies. In each case, the federal government stated reasons for its actions to suspend, restrict, and limit rights, freedoms, and the basic principles of liberalism. The following reasons have been given in the past to justify the Act's use:

- It was necessary for the overall good of society.
- It was justified because of the threat or severe nature of the situation.
- It was essential to protect, retain, or secure other principles of liberalism.

The War Measures Act gave the federal cabinet emergency powers for circumstances where it determined that the existence of war, invasion, or insurrection, real or apprehended, existed. The real distinction of this Act was that it allowed the cabinet to govern by decree rather than through discussion and debate in Parliament. The federal government had increased powers under this Act: powers that could be used immediately once the Act was invoked. The following sections outline the circumstances and repercussions of using the War Measures Act. Which instances of its use, if any, do you consider to be necessary, justified, and essential?

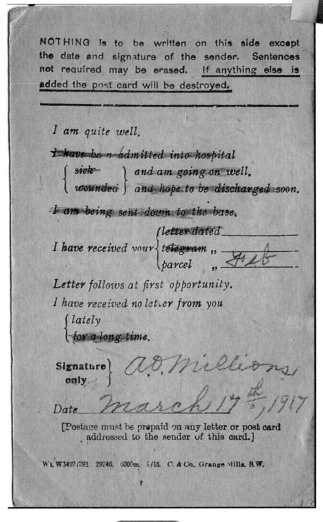

Figure 11-13 ▲

During times of war, governments might introduce the illiberal practice of censorship for concerns related to safety and security. This postcard is from a First World War soldier to his family in Saskatchewan. All correspondence home was subject to being opened and read by censors to make sure no additional information was being added.

Canada's Anti-Terrorism Act

Something to Think About: Canada is known for its Charter of Rights and Freedoms; specifically, civil liberties that every Canadian citizen is entitled to, such as the legal rights

- not to be arbitrarily detained and imprisoned
- to be informed of the reasons of arrest or detention
- to be released if the detention is found not to be justified

However, in the aftermath of the terrorist attacks on September 11, 2001, the federal government in Canada quickly fast-tracked the Anti-Terrorism Act (Bills C-36 and C-42), which defined what **terrorism** is and made it a punishable offence in Canada's Criminal Code. The Act created much controversy in Parliament as some questioned if this legislation had adequate debate in the House of Commons. The Anti-Terrorism Act became part of the Criminal Code on December 18, 2001, and gave police new powers, including the ability to arrest people and withhold them without charge for up to 72 hours if they are suspected of planning a terrorist act. As well, police can make preventative arrests, and can now more easily access electronic surveillance during their investigations.

When this legislation was introduced in 2001, many Canadians felt that the government was taking basic civil liberties away. Today that is still the case. Others, however, argue that the legislation is needed to protect and ensure security for Canadian citizens from the threat of terrorism.

An Example: Abdullah Almalki, a Syrian-born Canadian from Ottawa, was at the centre of an RCMP national security investigation. He ran a company as a supplier to an electronics manufacturer in Pakistan, and often traveled throughout Asia and the Middle East. He came under suspicion of the RCMP and The Canadian Security Intelligence Service (CSIS), partly because of his business travel to places such as Pakistan and Afghanistan. The RCMP raided his home in Ottawa in early 2002, looking for evidence to his connection to terrorism. While on a trip to visit his mother in Syria in April 2002, he was detained by the Syrian police at the airport, and spent the next 22 months in a Syrian jail. He was beaten and tortured. He was told by the prison's chief interrogator that agents from the RCMP and CSIS wanted information about Canadian Muslim men, and thought that he had collaborated with terrorist organizations. He was released and sent back to Canada in August 2004, and was cleared by a Syrian judge of a being a terrorist threat for lack of evidence.

There are questions that remain unanswered, however, such as the role Canadian intelligence played in his detention in Syria, and whether his torture was part of an unwritten Canadian policy to send terrorist

Abdullah Almalki at a news conference on Parliament Hill in Ottawa, December, 2006.

suspects to Syria for interrogation. As well, there was the issue of why he did not receive any Canadian consular help in prison.

Many believe that Abdullah Almalki's arrest and detention in Syria is connected to Canada's Anti-Terrorism Act, as it gave sweeping powers to the RCMP and CSIS to extensively search and investigate Almalki in an effort to identify evidence tying him to terrorist activities. Moreover, because of the legislation, Almalki—and other Canadian citizens who have been detained overseas on suspicion of terrorism—have yet to find out why they were targeted by the RCMP and CSIS because information can be withheld in confidentiality by the government.

Many feel that the Anti-Terrorism Act gives too much power to organizations like CSIS and the RCMP, and that it takes away certain civil rights. It operates on the assumption that a person is guilty, and the due course of process to individual freedoms is overruled by the need for security.

QUESTIONS FOR REFLECTION

1. Is the Anti-Terrorism Act a rejection of liberal principles?

2. To what extent is the Anti-Terrorism Act placing the perceived common good of citizens above individual rights?

3. Do you believe this is appropriate or inappropriate? Explain your position.

The First World War and Enemy Aliens

The first use of the War Measures Act in Canada came during the First World War. Canada and Newfoundland were part of the British Empire at the time, and Britain and the Allied Powers were at war against the Central Powers: Germany, Austria-Hungary (which included parts of Ukraine), and the Ottoman Empire. Under the War Measures Act (1914) immigrants from these countries already residing in Canada were considered **enemy aliens**.

As a result, all enemy aliens were required to register with the Canadian government and carry their government-issued ID cards at all times. In addition, they were not permitted to publish or read anything in a language other than English or French, to leave the country without exit permits, to possess firearms, or to join any group the government deemed inappropriate, dangerous, or seditious.

Several thousand enemy aliens were deported or sent to **internment** camps (Figure 11-16 shows one of these camps). Their property was confiscated and often went missing during their internment or was not returned afterwards. The internment camps did

October Crisis, 1970

The third and final time the War Measures Act was invoked was in October 1970. Canada and the world underwent significant political, social, and cultural changes during the 1960s. Many reforms were prompted by individuals and groups seeking less government control, greater freedoms, and increased power over decisions affecting their lives. Examples include the women's liberation movement, the anti-war movement, and pressures to end poverty, discrimination, and abuses of power.

Some Francophone Québécois strongly desired greater protection of their language and culture and wanted equal opportunities for participation in the economy of Québec, which was dominated by an Anglophone minority. The **Quiet Revolution (*la Révolution tranquille*)** was a time of rapid social, economic, and political modernization in Québec: a revolution without violence, force, or direct conflict, aimed at enhancing opportunities for Francophone Québécois within Québec society.

Some people felt the pace of change was too slow, however. These people supported the use of violence, terrorism, or other illegal means to achieve their goals. *The Front de libération du Québec* (the FLQ, or the Quebec Liberation Front), founded in 1963, and committed to the independence of Québec, was a group that was willing to resort to terrorism.

During the 1960s, the FLQ used a series of bombings and armed robberies to further its goals. On October 5, 1970, the FLQ abducted British trade commissioner James Cross, an act that shocked Canadians. Ransom demands were made, most of which were not met. On October 10, 1970, the kidnapping and subsequent murder of Pierre Laporte, a popular Québec cabinet minister, generated strong reactions from Canadians as well as citizens of other countries. Within days, the Canadian Armed Forces were sent to protect politicians in Ottawa. Québec premier Robert Bourassa requested that troops be sent to support local police. The military and police presence was either disquieting or reassuring to Canadians, depending on their points of view.

Prime Minister Trudeau invoked the War Measures Act on October 16, 1970, explaining that a state of "apprehended insurrection" existed in Québec. Civil liberties were suspended, and the FLQ was formally outlawed. Anyone attending an FLQ meeting or speaking favourably of the organization was presumed to be a member. Nearly 500 people were arrested without warrants for expressing their pro-FLQ views and could be held in prison for up to 90 days; many of the people arrested were artists, journalists, unionists, teachers, and other supporters of **Québécois nationalism**.

The actions of the federal government during the October Crisis raised a great deal of controversy. Although an overwhelming number of Canadians supported the government's actions, many Québec

We deplore that recourse... was made to the War Measures Act; in its possible applications, it far exceeds the scope of the problem that the authorities faced... However, we can only reaffirm the right of a democracy to defend itself and the obligation that it has to judge severly and to put down those that unjustly threaten the freedom and the life of their fellow citizens.

—Claude Ryan, "The War Measures Act: Three Questions", editorial in *Le Devoir*, October 17, 1970.
http://faculty.marianopolis.edu/
c.belanger/quebechistory/docs/
october/ryan.htm

nationalists and advocates of civil rights criticized the use of the War Measures Act as excessive and too broad, especially for a case involving two kidnappings and a murder, issues that would normally be dealt with by the police and existing laws. One major criticism was that the government acted on limited information and treated all separatist supporters as potential terrorists.

There are a lot of bleeding hearts around who just don't like to see people with helmets and guns. All I can say is go and bleed…It is more important to keep law and order in society than to be worried about weak-kneed people…Society must take every means at its disposal to defend itself against the emergence of a parallel power which defies the elected power.

—Pierre Elliott Trudeau, impromptu interview with Tim Ralfe of the CBC and Peter Reilly of CJON-TV, October 13, 1970.

The actions of the federal government during the October Crisis can appear very different to us today than it did to Canadians at the time.

- Under the circumstances in October 1970, do you believe the federal government's actions were appropriate?
- What other alternatives could Trudeau have used to deal with the FLQ without rejecting the principles of liberalism during this crisis?

Emergencies and Security Legislation Today

Following the introduction of the Canadian Charter of Rights and Freedoms in 1982, the Canadian government introduced a new law, the Emergencies Act, in 1988, in order to harmonize this law with the articles of the Charter.

The Emergencies Act includes more safeguards protecting the rights of Canadians. First, the Emergencies Act clearly defines an emergency situation:

A public welfare emergency is defined as one that is caused by real or imminent:
- *natural catastrophe*
- *disease in humans, animals or plants*
- *accident or pollution*
resulting in danger to life or property, social disruption or a breakdown in the flow of essential goods, services or resources so serious as to constitute a national emergency.

—Source: Government of Canada, Emergencies Act.
http://dsp-psd.tpsgc.gc.ca/Collection-R/LoPBdP/BP/prb0114-e.htm#A. Preamble(txt)

Second, the Emergencies Act limits the powers of the government during the time of the crisis. Any measures implemented under the Emergencies Act are subject to the approval of Parliament. Under the new Emergencies

Figure 11-19 ▲

How does the presence of troops in a Canadian city affect the citizens? What possible responses are there to such government actions?

PAUSE AND REFLECT

To what extent does the Emergencies Act respect the principles of liberalism?

Act, the government is obliged to specify to which part or parts of Canada the emergency measures apply, if it is not a national issue.

Third, any temporary emergency measures taken under the Emergencies Act must take into account the rights of Canadians, as outlined in the Charter of Rights and Freedoms. The Emergencies Act even includes a section requiring the government to award compensation to anyone who has suffered injury or damages as a result of the Act's application.

In addition to the Emergencies Act, the Parliament of Canada passed the Anti-Terrorism Act in 2001 to deal with perceived security threats, and is "aimed at disabling and dismantling the activities of terrorists groups and those who support them." Similar to the Emergencies Act, the Anti-Terrorism Act (about which you read in the Investigations feature on pages. 396–397) allows the government to impose limits to Canadians' freedoms in order to ensure security during times of crisis or perceived threat.

Restricting Freedoms in Subtle Ways

Following the events of 9/11 (the terrorist attacks on the United States, September 11, 2001), governments, individuals, and groups have developed a different understanding of security, terrorism, and mobility. Your own experiences with travel, especially through airports and border crossings, are different from those of Canadians prior to 9/11. Yet many people raise concerns about the appropriateness as well as the effectiveness of increased security measures in Canada and around the world. Supporters of increased security often point out that the restrictions are minor and certainly not as serious as the potentially devastating consequences.

The USA PATRIOT Act

The United States government has responded to the need for increased security by introducing the Uniting and Strengthening America by Providing Appropriate Tools Required to Intercept and Obstruct Terrorism Act (USA PATRIOT **Act,** 2001). This act's preamble states that its purpose is to "deter and punish terrorist acts in the United States and around the world, to enhance law enforcement investigatory tools, and for other purposes." (Source: USA PATRIOT Act, October 24, 2001. Electronic Privacy Information Center, http://www.epic.org/privacy/terrorism/hr3162.html.)

Negative reaction to this legislation quickly emerged. Groups as diverse as the American Civil Liberties Union (ACLU) and Utah's conservative *Deseret News* openly opposed the USA PATRIOT Act because of its potential threat to personal liberties. Many groups have lobbied the government, posted websites, and employed the media to raise public awareness of their perceptions of the intended and unintended consequences of this centralization of government power.

Jeff Stahler: © Columbus Dispatch/Dist. by Newspaper Enterprise Association, Inc.

Figure 11-20 ▲

What does the cartoonist suggest regarding the balance between security and freedom?

In addition, in September 2004, the ACLU challenged the federal government's power to issue National Security Letters, a provision of the USA PATRIOT Act, and won in court. National Security Letters permitted the government to obtain sensitive customer records from Internet service providers and other businesses without first obtaining a search warrant from a judge. The court ruled that this was an unconstitutional limit to the freedom from unreasonable searches. The court also ruled against the so-called gag provisions of the USA PATRIOT Act that allowed the government to censor protestors' complaints against the Act as "unconstitutional prior restraint" on free speech. (Source: "ACLU Case, Federal Court Strikes Down Patriot Act Surveillance Power As Unconstitutional." American Civil Liberties Union, http://www.aclu.org/safefree/spying/18589prs20040929.html, September 29, 2004.)

The intention of the USA PATRIOT Act was to protect the security of the American people from acts of terrorism. However, some feel that the act undermines the civil liberties of the American people and subverts the rights of minorities, especially those who share the same ethnic heritage as those who perpetrated the 9/11 attacks.

Canada's No-Fly List

One of the increased security measures in Canada is a **no-fly list** called Transport Canada's "Specified Persons" list. This is a list of people the government has identified as potentially posing an immediate threat to aviation security. People on the list are barred from flying on domestic flights in Canada (see Investigation, pages 396–397). Figure 11-21 lists the criteria for determining who may be placed on the list. Canada's initiative is modelled after a similar one created in the United States. The US list has been highly criticized because of its extent (it contains more than 44 000 names) and for the arbitrary way in which people are placed on the list. While it is believed that the Canadian list contains fewer than 1000 names, it is not publicly available, so many people on the list will not know that they have been barred from flying until they try to do so. What is known about the list is included in the chart in Figure 11-21. To what additional information would you like to have access in order to better understand and evaluate the list's appropriateness?

Maher Arar, whom you read about in the chapter opener, is one Canadian who has been affected by the American no-fly list. Arar arrived in New York on a stopover during his return to Canada from Tunisia. American officials detained Arar, claiming he had links to al Qaeda. Arar was questioned, held, and eventually deported to Syria, even though he was carrying a Canadian passport. He was tortured and held in Syria until October 2003.

PAUSE AND REFLECT

What is your reaction to legislation such as the USA PATRIOT Act? Why do you think the courts ruled that some aspects of the act were unconstitutional? Is there a better way to address the need for national security that does not involve actions that infringe on individual rights?

PAUSE AND REFLECT

How would you deal with this issue if you were the government minister responsible for safety, security, and transportation? Do you think a no-fly list is the best or only solution?

Figure 11-21 ▶

Do you think the rules for who may be placed on the no-fly list are fair and adequate? Are they too vague, leaving room for innocent people to be wrongly placed on the list? Are they too limited, meaning that some potential terrorists will not be listed?

—Source: information from "Passenger Protect program now in effect," Transport Canada. http://www.passengerprotect.gc.ca/

Who may be placed on Transport Canada's Specified Persons list:
• An individual who has been involved in a terrorist group and who, it can reasonably be suspected, will endanger the security of any aircraft or aerodrome, or the safety of the public, passengers, or crew members.
• An individual who has been convicted of one or more serious and life-threatening crimes against aviation security.
• An individual who has been convicted of one or more serious and life-threatening offences and who may attack or harm an air carrier, passengers, or crew members.

Maher Arar questioned the actions of the Canadian and American governments in his deportation. Should individuals expect governments to respect the principles of liberalism under all circumstances? Does Arar's case prove that the no-fly list is doing more damage than good?

Arar sought redress for the actions of Canadian and American officials. Among other criticisms, he accused American officials of knowing that Syria practises torture, and of endangering his life by deporting him. The Canadian inquiry resulted in Arar being vindicated by the federal government and compensated financially. However, Arar remains on the US no-fly list.

The Canadian government's post-9/11 security measures are less intrusive and restrictive than the examples from Canada's history when the War Measures Act was invoked. The restrictions still constrain people's freedoms and challenge the principles of liberalism, however, although in less obvious ways. Despite this subtlety, the new policies are clearly illiberal measures.

Explore the Issues

Concept Review

1. a) Identify and describe five examples from this section of situations where the government chose to reject principles of liberalism.
   b) For each of the examples, identify the specific liberal principle or individual or collective right that was violated.

Concept Application

2. *You Be the Judge.* In a group of five, analyze the issue in *United States V. Brown* and its relevance to Section 7 of the Charter. Your teacher will provide you with the case. Research it and simulate a Supreme Court of Canada judges' deliberation. Discuss the extent to which the government in your case either promoted or protected individual or collective rights or rejected the principles of liberalism. Produce a written verdict on the case, and have your chosen Chief Justice read it to the class.

3. Write a letter to your Member of Parliament explaining your views on how the government has rejected the principles of liberalism in a specific situation that you have read about in the news. Assess the manner in which the government dealt with the situation and how the government might better protect citizens' individual or collective rights in the future.

Reflect and Analyze

In this chapter you have seen how complex it can be to apply the values of liberalism to many real-life situations. Often, promoting an individual's or a group's rights can mean minimizing or infringing on another individual's or group's rights. We have started to explore the interplay between government and citizens, which will give you some insight into the Chapter Issue: *To what extent should democratic governments promote and protect individual and collective rights?*

Respond to Ideas

1 In groups of at least six people, research one of the current or classic precedent-setting Charter cases provided by your teacher. Discuss and debate the judges' verdict, their reasons for the verdict and relevant legislation involved, and different perspectives on the ruling. Simulate a Supreme Court of Canada courtroom proceeding to demonstrate your group's position on the verdict, providing evidence during the proceeding and in the judgement to support agreement or disagreement with the Court's actual ruling.

Current Cases:
- *R. v. D.B.:* Reverse onus provisions and Section 7 of the Charter
- *R. v. White:* Publication Ban Upheld
- *R v. Kapp:* Supreme Court Approves Affirmative Action Program
- *Canada (Attorney General) v. Lameman:* Papaschase Land Claim Resolved
- *R. v. Ferguson:* Supreme Court Upholds Mandatory Minimum Sentence and Refuses to Grant Constitutional Exemption
- *Morrow v. Zhang:* Alberta Court Strikes Down Damages Cap

Classic Cases:
- *R. v. Oakes:* The Oakes Test
- *R. v. Sparrow:* Aboriginal Rights
- *Law v. Canada:* Equality Rights
- *R. v. Morgentaler:* Women's Rights
- *Re B.C. Motor Vehicle Act:* The Right to Not be Arbitrarily Detained
- *Vriend v. Alberta:* Equality Rights (sexual orientation)
- *Hunter v. Southam Inc.:* Government Use of Search Warrants
- *Andrews v. Law Society of British Columbia:* Equality Rights
- *R. v. Collins:* The Collins Test
- *R. v. Stinchcombe:* Burden of Proof
- *R. v. Askov:* Trial in a Timely Manner

Case law summaries can be found at the University of Alberta's Centre for Constitutional Law website. Cases and verdicts can be found at the Supreme Court of Canada's website.

Bear in mind that these cases often deal with controversial topics that invite a variety of responses. They were not selected because they provide a definitive perspective on an issue but rather, because each verdict established an important legal precedent.

2 Create a short poem, prose piece, photo essay, or video to illustrate the challenges governments face in promoting individual and collective rights—"liberalism in practice"—in society.

Recognize Relationships among Concepts, Issues, and Citizenship

3 In groups of five, examine the Charter of Rights and Freedoms. Create a report card for the current federal or Alberta government on how well it has promoted and protected individual and collective rights as outlined in the Charter. As this activity will require a fair bit of research, your teacher might divide the 34 statutes of the Charter among groups.

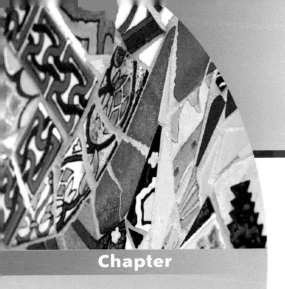

The Viability of Contemporary Liberalism

KEY SKILLS

Evaluating personal assumptions and opinions to develop an expanded appreciation of an issue

KEY CONCEPTS

Exploring how well the principles of liberalism provide a framework for addressing challenging contemporary issues

Key Terms

Consumerism
Environmental change
Extremism
Pandemics
Postmodernism

Why I Am Not a Postmodernist by Edward R. Friedlander, M.D.

I'm an honest doctor. I have chosen science over prejudice, health over disease, opportunity over slavery, and love and kindness over mean-minded make-believe.

There was a time when people were openly grateful to scientists and physicians who dedicated their lives to making us healthier and happier. There was a time when it was fashionable to express appreciation for the system of government and the practice of dispassionate inquiry which have brought us the unparalleled health, freedom, and prosperity that we enjoy today.

There was a time when people thought that a proposition was "valid" or "true" if, and only if, it ultimately squared with the observable world around us.

There was a time when people thought that respecting the beliefs and experiences of others, even when they differed from your own, was the mark of an educated, decent person.

There was a time when people enjoyed discovering how much we all have in common, and how most of us wanted the same things despite the superficial differences. There was even a time when we thought the best way to overcome misunderstanding, prejudice, and hate was by means of reason, common sense, clear-thinking, and good-will.

We called this being scientific. *We called this being* rational. *We called this being* enlightened. *We called this being* liberal.

We called this being modern.

—Edward R. Friedlander, Kansas City University of Medicine and Biosciences, "Why I Am Not a Postmodernist." *Kairos*, **vol 3, issue 1, Spring 1998**
http://www.technorhetoric.net/3.1/index.html

In this quotation, Dr Friedlander launches a defence of modernism, a philosophical school of thought closely associated with liberalism. He laments the current attitude against modernism, which he refers to as **postmodernism**—a movement that largely began as a reaction to modernism after the First and Second World Wars. Friedlander, later in his article, quotes philosopher Michael Fegan's definition of postmodernism:

Postmodernism calls into question enlightenment values such as rationality, truth, and progress, arguing that these merely serve to secure

Figure 12-1

Classical liberalism allowed for the rampant economic growth of the Industrial Revolution. The structures of modern liberalism attempt to find solutions to many of the problems caused by economic growth. Seen here are former US president Bill Clinton and Canadian prime minister Paul Martin addressing the 2005 UN Conference on Climate Change.

the monolithic structure of modern capitalistic society by concealing or excluding any forces that might challenge its cultural dominance.

—Michael Fegan, quoted in James Gerrand, "Feminist amnesia." *The Skeptic* **18, 1 (Autumn, 1998): p. 37.**

According to Friedlander, to what extent are modern liberal values being challenged and is this challenge appropriate? Postmodernism is developed more fully and given context on pages 408–410.

Chapter Issue

In this book you have explored the ideology of liberalism, from its conceptual beginnings to its practice in modern-day society. Throughout its long history, certain principles of liberalism have remained the same—individualism, economic freedom, and political freedom, to name a few. However, as the social, environmental, political, and technological conditions of liberal democracies have changed over time, as you saw in Chapter 6, liberalism has shifted with them. Many issues facing liberal democracies in the 21st century did not exist when the ideology was first conceived. Those issues create new challenges for both individuals and governments. Exploring how liberal principles provide a framework for addressing contemporary issues as well as examining various perspectives on that framework will help you address the Chapter Issue, *To what extent do contemporary issues challenge the principles of liberalism?*, and the Related Issue for Part 3, *To what extent are the principles of liberalism viable?*

It can be argued that the contemporary Western world is a product of early liberal principles in action, which makes the modern industrialized world also the result of the implementation of liberal principles. But the **modern industrial complex** (that is, the structure of industry in our Western society) has given us disparity as well as the gifts of scientific and technological progress. Access to resources, health care, and the subsequent quality of life available to individuals varies greatly in liberal societies and throughout the world. This modern industrialized world is faced with environmental issues and must deal with the impact of economic development. Debt and poverty exist amid wealth within liberal democracies, and there is significant disparity among countries. Not all individuals and groups are treated equally in liberal democratic countries—racism and censorship exist in some form in all countries. If liberal principles have resulted in the modern industrialized world, can they also be harnessed to solve the problems of the industrialized world?

In this chapter you will examine examples of how liberal democracies respond to contemporary challenges and determine how effective liberalism has been in adapting to these challenges.

Figure 12-2 ▶

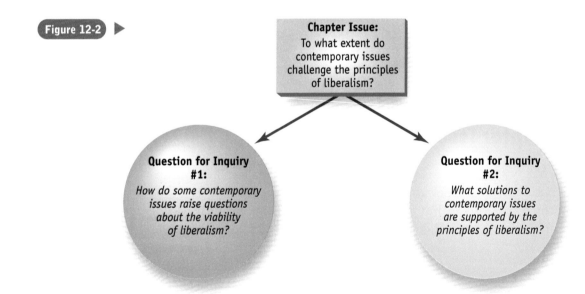

Chapter Issue:
To what extent do contemporary issues challenge the principles of liberalism?

Question for Inquiry #1:
How do some contemporary issues raise questions about the viability of liberalism?

Question for Inquiry #2:
What solutions to contemporary issues are supported by the principles of liberalism?

The Horseshoe Debate

We have a long way to go before we are able to hear the voices of everyone on earth, but I believe that providing voices and building bridges is essential for the World Peace we all wish for.

—Joichi Ito (American-educated Japanese activist, entrepreneur, and venture capitalist), "Season's Greetings and Global Voices," December 25, 2004.

http://joi.ito.com/weblog/2004/12/25/seasons-greetin.html

If you have lived your entire life in a liberal democracy, it may be difficult for you to imagine any other form of government or ideology. Discussion and debate with others, especially those whose views differ from yours, can be important for gaining insight and understanding. Engaging in an informal debate, one with structure yet without the formality of competitive debates, is important for developing the essential skills for appraising information from multiple perspectives. Debate is like entering a "marketplace of ideas." This Skill Path is designed to assist you in using evidence skilfully in an argument. It will help you explore the various perspectives on the challenges facing the principles of liberal democracies. In addition, you will have the opportunity to examine the possible means of addressing those challenges, as an individual, and a citizen of a liberal democracy.

Your Task: Responses to two different issues are presented as horseshoe debate topics (at the top of the right-hand column). Half the class will debate Issue 1 and the other half will debate Issue 2. For your issue, independently research the different sides of the debate and prepare your own informed response to the issue. Each individual in the group will present his or her position and will also have the opportunity to modify that position. A horseshoe debate is a non-confrontational, open-forum arrangement where each participant is seated along a large U-shaped arrangement of desks facing his or her classmates. After the debate, you will independently prepare a written reflection on the issues that were explored in the debate.

Issue 1: Be it resolved that the liberalism of the West is responsible for global terrorism.

Issue 2: Be it resolved that human beings will be able to control and reduce global warming.

Steps:

1. Thoroughly research your issue using appropriate information sources.

2. Share your information and conclusions on a "meeting board" (electronic or paper). This board will allow all group members to better examine the issue.

3. After examining the information other students have posted on the meeting board, prepare a personal position or opinion on the issue for sharing. This sharing will occur in a horseshoe debate in which you will present your information and opinion *one time.* You will present only once because this format gives each opinion or position the same presence and weight in the debate. Listen carefully to the information and positions of others to make an informed decision about the issue.

4. An important characteristic of an informal debate or sharing of information is the opportunity for participants to change their positions based on what they hear from others. Confirming your position or opinion is also an important characteristic of an informal debate. When you have confirmed your position, you can prepare a written summary of the debate and your own position for submission to your teacher. You can use the Questions to Guide You to reflect on your experience.

Questions to Guide You

1. What reasons have participants provided to support their points of view in response to the issue?

2. Other than your own initial point of view, what responses did you hear during the process that most strongly influenced your original position?

3. In a debate, what are the benefits of considering the views of others when forming or modifying your response to an issue?

The Viability of Liberalism

Question for Inquiry

• **How do some contemporary issues raise questions about the viability of liberalism?**

Even though modern liberalism is imperfect, as you have read about in previous chapters, many people in liberal democracies consciously or unconsciously assume that the principles of liberalism themselves are beyond criticism. People who live in liberal democracies generally have a bias in favour of such liberal concepts as the worth of every individual, the power of human reason, the limits of a government's reach into individual lives, and a belief in human progress. This type of conscious or unconscious bias could be considered normal for a person living in a society or a community that is based on a particular liberal democratic ideological system of beliefs. Nonetheless, modern liberalism is not necessarily embraced by all peoples or groups living within liberal democracies or by everyone living outside of liberal democracies.

For example, as you examined in Chapter 8 (and to some extent in Chapters 9 and 10), modern liberalism and its ideological principles can sometimes be challenged by alternative thought, such as environmentalism, Aboriginal collective thought, religious perspectives, and neo-conservatism. Additional challenges to liberal principles can be found in the examples of postmodernism and extremism. These two additional examples of alternative thought will be examined in this Question for Inquiry.

Postmodernism

Postmodernism is another ideological school of thought that challenges liberalism. You will recall that you were introduced to postmodernism at the beginning of this chapter.

Up till now the car and the house, and various "commodities" have somehow or other succeeded in soaking up the disposable physical and mental capacities of individuals. What would happen if all disposable wealth was redistributed amongst them? Quite simply, the bottom would drop out of their lives—they would lose the fabric and even tempo of a well-tempered economy, lose a sense of self-interest and of purpose…

We are in a universe where there is more and more information, and less and less meaning…

—**Jean Baudrillard, *In the Shadow of the Silent Majorities* (Cambridge, MA: MIT Press, 1983).**

PAUSE AND REFLECT

What aspects of contemporary life does Baudrillard critique in these quotations? How does his criticism mirror the quotation at the beginning of this chapter by Michael Fegan? What challenge do these two thinkers pose for liberalism?

Postmodernism is the period that follows *modernism* in the fields of art, literature, and philosoph, largely in Western societies. It is also a school of thinking that questions and rejects the principles of modernism and liberalism. Some of the central concepts of modernism, which began during the Enlightenment, include the following:

- Science provides universal and eternal truths.
- Knowledge will lead to progress.
- Freedom consists of obedience to laws that are based on reason.
- Reason and rational thinking are the ultimate means of establishing what is true.

Modernity, then, is about order, universal truths, reason, and rationality. In this view, by using science and rationality to establish truths, an organized society can emerge.

Postmodernism calls into question the central ideas of modernism. It argues that, rather than a process for discovering truth, modernism has constructed "governing narratives" that tell us stories about our modern society and provide us with ideas around which we can organize society. Postmodernism claims that most of us are under a "veil of deceit" that hides alternative ways of thinking from us. Postmodernism does not necessarily deny any of the claims of modernism, but it does see many of the "truths" of modernism—and liberal ideology—as mere constructions— as convenient "lies" we tell ourselves so we do not have to think too much.

Although many see postmodernism as a mixture of related ideas rather than any sort of organized ideology or belief system, there are recurrent themes in postmodernist thinking. Some of these are:

- a belief that there is no set of moral or political ideas that can dominate cultural, ethnic, and gender differences. For example, postmodernists criticize what they see as the dominance of modern liberal ideology over many aspects of life to the exclusion of other ways of thinking.
- skepticism about the modern liberal idea that society can be "improved," that there is "progress" in civilization
- a critique of the nature of knowledge: knowledge claims are relative to linguistic, social, and historical contexts. A simple example of this is the idea that Columbus "discovered" the New World. Another example is that we are often unaware of our own prejudices or biases until we step outside of our normal lives, such as when we travel to another country.
- a concern for issues of gender, race, and other parts of culture previously marginalized by the "grand governing narrative" (that is, the mainstream line of thinking in society). Groups that have traditionally been left out of the dominant social structure have their own legitimate ways of making sense of the world, and these ways of making sense may make more sense than those prescribed by liberal tradition.

Figure 12-3 ▲

Etch-a-Sketch portrait of French thinker Jean Baudrillard (1929–2007). Baudrillard, a major postmodern thinker, believed there is no "true" reality in Western liberal culture. What we think of as reality is actually constructed for us by our culture and our media, and can be changed, just as the Etch-a-Sketch portrait can be changed, to create new versions of reality and truth.

Examining Postmodernism

Postmodernist critiques of our society's governing narratives generate many questions. At times, the answers to these questions threaten the values on which modern liberal democracies are based. Central to the postmodernist challenge is the following question: If we claim that there are no universal truths that transcend cultural boundaries and traditions, how can we expect all members of society to adhere to a dominant set of (liberal) principles?

American political scientist Peter Berkowitz suggests that the postmodern challenge of the authority of liberal values is an inevitable outcome of liberalism itself—that liberalism contains the seeds of its own destruction.

At every turn, the spread of freedom emboldens the liberal spirit's inclination to expose and overthrow the claims of arbitrary authority. However, as the claims of freedom themselves acquire authority in a free society, the liberal spirit has difficulty limiting its campaign against authority to that which is arbitrary. Or rather, with each new success, the liberal spirit comes closer to viewing all authority as arbitrary. Eventually, the liberal spirit turns upon the authority of freedom itself, attacking the very source of its moral standing. Thus does postmodernism arise out of the sources of liberalism.

—**Peter Berkowitz, "Liberal Spirit in America,"** *Liberalism for a New Century* **eds. Neil Jumonville and Kevin Mattson (Berkeley, CA: University of California Press, 2007), p. 25.**

Francis Fukuyama raises the concern that the idea of valuelessness associated with postmodernism will challenge the grand governing narrative of liberalism.

…the rise of relativism [the belief that no absolute standards of rightness or wrongness exist and that all beliefs and value systems are equally defendable] has made it impossible for postmodern people to assert positive values for which they stand, and therefore the kinds of shared beliefs they demand as a condition for citizenship. Postmodern societies, particularly those in Europe, feel that they have evolved past identities defined by religion and nation and have arrived at a superior place. But aside from their celebration of endless diversity and tolerance, postmodern people find it difficult to agree on the substance of the good life to which they aspire in common.

—**Francis Fukuyama, "Identity, Immigration and Democracy,"** *Journal of Democracy* **17, 2 (April, 2006): pp. 18–19.**
http://www.journalofdemocracy.org/articles/gratis/Fukuyama-17-2.pdf

1 What, according to Fukuyama, is postmodernism's weakness? How might this weakness affect a multicultural country such as Canada?

2 In what ways can believers in the principles of modern liberalism respond to the criticisms of postmodernism?

Extremism

What is objectionable, what is dangerous about extremists is not that they are extreme, but that they are intolerant. The evil is not what they say about their cause, but what they say about their opponents.

—Robert F. Kennedy, quoted in Thomas A. Hopkins, ed., *Rights for Americans: The Speeches of Robert F. Kennedy* **(Indianapolis, IN: Bobbs-Merrill, 1964), p. 237.**

Unlike other terms related to the subject of ideology, such as *democrat, socialist,* or *anarchist,* the term *extremist* is normally used to refer only to other people, usually in a pejorative sense. Whereas someone might readily call himself or herself an environmentalist, those who are considered extremists by others generally do not see themselves as extremists.

In common parlance, *extremism* refers to a belief system that is outside the mainstream spectrum of beliefs, and it may advocate actions that are considered socially or morally unacceptable, such as the violent targeting of those perceived as innocent civilians. Sometimes the mainstream absorbs extremist views, however, and views that were considered extreme in one era become conventional in another (for example, women's right to vote and desegregation). Thus the judgement of "extremist" depends entirely on one's point of view. A group that violates the moral codes of a segment of society as a means to an end is judged as "extremist" by that social segment, but not necessarily by others.

- Can you think of other ideas related to individual or collective rights that are now part of liberal democracies but were once considered extreme?

It is important to note that extremists avoid referring to themselves as extremists not because they do not view their actions as intolerant or extreme but rather because they believe that they are acting out of principled beliefs. There can be extremist views on both the right and the left of the political spectrum, but in many cases, labelling a group or ideology as extremist is a political act to make a group's beliefs appear to challenge the status quo. An example of this might be labelling people as eco-terrorists if they threaten to spike trees (that is, embed metal spikes that will damage forestry equipment in large trees; an action that can also injure loggers) that are to be logged in an environmentally sensitive area. For some, this is an act of desperation in defence of a principle; for others it is an act of extremism.

Terrorism as practised by groups such as al Qaeda, however, is clearly extremist. Even the supporters of al Qaeda may agree that their organization uses extreme measures. They might claim, however, that in a world of injustice where military, political, and economic power is

Figure 12-4 ▲

A rejection of liberalism? Members of Bangladeshi group Ahaly Babeya burn an American flag during their anti-US rally in Dhaka, Bangladesh, on September 26, 2001. The protesters were condemning the idea that the US would invade Afghanistan following the September 11 attacks.

concentrated in the hands of a small group (Western powers) and used to keep others powerless, extreme measures are the only way to arrive at justice. They may argue that systemic injustice leads inevitably to extremism. How should liberalism respond to this argument?

As suggested by the earlier quotation by Robert Kennedy, extremism is perceived as intolerance. A religious ideology may be declared extremist if it is intolerant of and advocates violence against those who follow other belief systems. Extremism does not have to be religious, however. The *Front de libération du Québec* (Quebec Liberation Front) kidnappings and bombings in Québec during the October Crisis of 1970 are considered by many people to be examples of extremism. Nonetheless, the individuals involved in such actions normally believe that they are acting on principle.

One major challenge that extremism presents to modern liberalism is that governments threatened by extremist actions may curtail civil liberties of all citizens in an effort to maintain security. This may include limiting such rights as the freedom of association, the freedom of expression, and the right to privacy. Examples of this are the use of the War Measures Act in Canada during the October Crisis in 1970 and the creation of the USA PATRIOT Act in the United States, which was discussed in the previous chapter. In the case of the October Crisis, the limiting of individual rights was temporary. Most of the provisions of the USA PATRIOT Act, however, eventually became permanent. Some would argue that such limits on liberal values are necessary for the preservation of public security. Others claim that by limiting some liberal values in response to extremist threats, governments encourage extremists by giving them what they want.

- Why might some people adopt positions and actions that are so far from what is considered acceptable by most people? How does this challenge liberalism?
- To what extent is the use of the label *extremism* dependent on one's ideological point of view on a given situation?
- Under what circumstances would you define an act as *extreme*?

Extremism and Intolerance

Extremism challenges liberal beliefs about the structure of society, interpretations of history, and even liberal visions of the future. Extremism also challenges liberalism's tolerance. A liberal belief in freedom of expression is challenged when extremists profess intolerant views that sometimes promote hatred toward others. Sections 318 and 319 of the Criminal Code of Canada define promoting hate as a crime. In the United States, the First Amendment of the Bill of Rights protects people's freedom of expression.

The Canadian Charter of Rights and Freedoms guarantees (among other things) the freedom of thought, belief, opinion, and expression "subject only to such reasonable limits" that "can be demonstrably justified in a free and democratic society." In your opinion, is it acceptable for a liberal democracy to enact laws that prevent intolerance at the expense of freedom of expression? Which specific values of modern liberalism are in potential conflict here?

Economic Extremism

Extremism is also used by some people to characterize economic activities that strictly adhere to a set of principles despite their perceived adverse effects on a population. For example, during the Cold War, the economic practices of communist countries were seen as extremist by the United States government and some other free-market countries.

More recently, critics of free-market policies have claimed that some forms of capitalism have become extremist forms of economics. Canadian author Naomi Klein sees the ideas of economist Milton Friedman (about whom you read in chapters 6 and 8) of the Chicago School of Economics as central to this "economic extremism": "Friedman dreamed of depatterning societies, or returning them to a state of pure capitalism, cleansed of all interruptions—government regulations, trade barriers and entrenched interests." (Excerpted from *The Shock Doctrine: The Rise of Disaster Capitalism* by Naomi Klein, p. 50. Copyright © 2007 Naomi Klein. Reprinted by permission of Knopf Canada.)

According to Klein, the Chicago School of Economics, supported by the American government, educated many economists from less developed countries—the countries most likely to lean toward communism. When these economists returned to their native countries, they would then introduce "extreme" free-market economic policies, such as mass privatizations of public companies, agencies, and educational institutions; government deregulation; unrestricted free-market access for foreign corporations; and large cuts in social spending.

Sometimes these policies had devastating effects on local economies, while benefiting entrepreneurs: "Friedman's free-market rule book…[has] made some people extremely prosperous, winning for them something approximating complete freedom—to ignore borders, to avoid regulation and taxation and to amass new wealth." (Source: Klein, p. 59.) Friedman encouraged such policies because he was convinced that they were the most effective way to increase economic prosperity and political freedom.

- Milton Friedman considered his thinking to be classical liberalism. What specific values of modern liberalism do Friedman's ideas challenge?

Explore the Issues

Concept Review

1 a) Summarize what postmodernism is and how it seems to question the viability of modern liberalism.

b) Describe briefly the forms of extremism discussed in this section. How do the beliefs and values of extremism seem to challenge the viability of modern liberalism?

Concept Application

2 Debate the following in small groups: Be it resolved that liberalism is the ultimate evolution in economic and political development. Identify a specific location (for example, your community, Canada, or globally), time period (for example, today or over a particular period in history), and context or events to help guide your research into this topic and to focus your response to the issue. You may also use the Skill Path to help you.

3 Review examples of alternative thought that challenge modern liberal principles provided in chapter 8 (for example, environmentalism, Aboriginal collective thought, religious perspectives, and neo-conservatism) and in this section of chapter 12 (postmodernism and extremism). Create a collage that depicts liberalism on one side and alternative thought or forces in the 21st century that challenge the principles of liberalism on the other. Which example of alternative thought do you believe provides the strongest challenge to modern liberal principles?

4 Identify what you believe to be the most important issue in the world or in Canada, today. What principles of liberalism and/or aspects of alternative thought do you believe might best shape a response to this issue? Does this issue raise questions about the viability of liberalism?

Contemporary Issues and Liberalism

Question for Inquiry

• **What solutions to contemporary issues are supported by the principles of liberalism?**

Consumerism, a product of the success of following classical liberal principles, apparently poses another challenge to liberal principles. Like postmodernism and extremism, consumerism calls into question the viability of liberal principles. As the charts on consumption patterns show (Figures 12-5 and 12-6), the values and beliefs of liberalism may not necessarily lead to reasonable outcomes.

In this second section of this chapter, we will extend the discussion beyond postmodernism and forms of extremism that challenge the viability of liberal thought. We will explore some of the solutions liberal governments have proposed to address other contemporary issues that challenge the principles of liberalism. We will also explore the continuing tension between the principles of classical and modern liberalism and the different beliefs and values that guide their differing responses to issues in the world today.

Classical liberalism can be seen as the original engine for economic growth while modern liberalism can be seen as an attempt to suggest solutions to the problems caused by laissez-faire principles and economic growth. First, we will look at some of the unanticipated consequences of liberalism and the effects they have had on less developed countries as well as on industrialized liberal democracies. Then, we will also explore a few of the solutions proposed by liberal governments to address several global issues, including concerns with resource use and development; debt and poverty; the environment; and pandemics.

Consumerism as a Liberal Issue

The following table shows the annual expenditures on various products around the world.

The table on the following page shows an estimate of how much money it would cost, on top of what is already being spent, to achieve universal access to the certain social services in all less developed countries.

The impacts of consumerism, both positive and negative, are very significant to all aspects of our lives, as well as to our planet. But equally important in discussing consumption patterns is the underlying system that promotes certain types of consumption and not other types.

Figure 12-5

Compare the figures in Figure 12-5 to the estimates of the additional costs of achieving universal access to basic social services in Figure 12-6.

Area of Spending	US$ Billions per year
Cosmetics in the United States	8
Ice cream in Europe	11
Perfumes in Europe and the United States	12
Pet foods in Europe and the United States	17
Business entertainment in Japan	35
Cigarettes in Europe	50
Alcoholic drinks in Europe	105
Narcotic drugs in the world	400
Military spending in the world	780

Figure 12-6 ▶

Compare the figures in Figure 12-5 to the estimates of the additional costs of achieving universal access to basic social services in Figure 12-6.

Source: both tables adapted from United Nations Development Programme, *Human Development Report* (New York: United Nations and Oxford University Press, 1998), p. 37. http://hdr.undp.org/en/media/ hdr_1998_en_chap1.pdf By permission of Oxford University Press, Inc. www.oup.com

Area of Spending	US$ Billions per Year
Basic education for all	6
Water and sanitation for all	9
Reproductive health for all women	12
Basic health and nutrition for all	13

- What do the dollar amounts in Figure 12-5 and Figure 12-6 tell you about consumption priorities? Is there anything wrong with spending money on cosmetics or pet food?
- Do you think the principles of liberalism helped create the disparity that is apparent in the tables? Do you think liberal governments should do something to address this disparity?

Liberal democracies do take some actions to address issues related to consumerism. Since 2005, Albertans buying new televisions and computers pay a provincial electronics recycling fee of $45 per new television and $12 for computer components. The fees cover the costs of collection, transportation, recycling, public awareness programs, and electronics-related research. Each year, Albertans throw out over 200 000 televisions and 100 000 computers. The electronic trash contains harmful chemicals and few facilities exist that can properly dispose of those chemicals. In this case, the government has chosen a policy of charging a fee to the consumer. While the fees collected assist in addressing some negative consequences of consumerism, government actions do not directly discourage or prohibit the purchasing of goods by individuals.

We will further explore some of the solutions liberal governments have proposed to address contemporary issues that challenge the principles of liberalism. First, we will look at some of the unanticipated consequences of liberalism and the effects they have had on less developed countries as well as on industrialized liberal democracies. We will also explore some of the solutions liberal governments have proposed to address environmental issues and pandemics.

Unanticipated Consequences of Liberalism

In the brief history of liberal democracies, economic freedom has helped create some very powerful individuals and companies. Beginning with the colonization of Africa, Asia, and South America, consumers in liberal democracies were given greater access to increasing varieties and amounts of goods. Bananas, coffee, chocolate, silk, and cotton are examples of such goods. In more recent decades, companies from liberal democracies have entered into economic relationships with countries such as China, Japan, Korea, and Mexico

PAUSE AND REFLECT

Are such actions of liberal democratic governments a workable means of addressing issues such as consumerism, use of resources, and disposal of associated waste products? What other actions might governments take to address these issues more directly?

to make technological gadgets, toys, and entertainment goods available in large quantities at relatively low cost. The pursuit of economic freedom in liberal democracies has brought increased personal choice for consumers in some countries but not in all. And within most countries these benefits are not equally distributed.

Therefore, unanticipated consequences of economic freedom and development have developed within countries and on a worldwide scale. First, the wealth and resource development produced by economic liberalism did not benefit many of the people in former colonies in Asia, Africa, and South America to the same degree as they benefited people in more industrialized countries. In fact, many colonized countries were forced to reduce their own food production in order to grow cash crops such as coffee and bananas for export. These crops provided little benefit to most of the citizens of the countries where they were grown. As many of these countries became independent, they were faced with world markets dominated by trade arrangements among liberal democracies, making it difficult for them to participate in the economic gains from world trade. This, and many other factors, led to greater debt and poverty on a large scale for less developed countries.

Second, citizens of colonized countries were not treated in ways that reflected the principles of liberalism. Differential laws governing ownership of property and land, access to education and health care, and other aspects of life often restricted the pace of development in these countries. Such treatment led to negative sentiments within these countries between members of various races or ethnic groups. A legacy of racism, alienation, instability, and anger resulted.

Third, such feelings have also created conditions that support violence, illiberalism, and terrorism. The unequal treatment of some countries and their citizens by liberal democracies—especially those most closely associated with the principles of democracy—has left a troubling legacy in many former colonies. Liberal democracies have become targets of this dissatisfaction. The United States, Great Britain, France, and other European Union countries have experienced terrorist threats and attacks. Canada has also been included in the group of liberal democratic countries whose policies and practices have been criticized.

PAUSE AND REFLECT

What particular aspects of liberalism helped create these unanticipated outcomes? Do you think leaders of liberal democracies have learned anything from the decisions and issues related to past liberal leaders?

Environmental Change and Activism

A $120 000 lawsuit filed by Syncrude Canada Ltd. [see Figure 12-7] earlier this month aims to financially cripple the environmental group and intimidate other oilsands critics, charged a Greenpeace activist yesterday.

But a company spokesman is defending the legal proceedings, saying the lawsuit is a way to preserve safety at the massive Aurora oilsands operation near Fort McMurray.

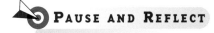

Figure 12-7 ▶

Greenpeace activists entered Syncrude's Aurora North oil sands facility in July 2008 and erected a banner that transformed the opening of a tailings pond pipe into the mouth of a giant skull. The pipe was transporting bitumous waste into the same tailings pond where 500 migrating ducks died earlier in 2008.

Eleven Greenpeace members were each handed a $287 fine at the time for trespassing at the company's mine site.

Activists said they were planning to block a pipe which flows into a toxic tailings pond where 500 ducks died in April.

—Source: "Syncrude suit 'punitive': Greenpeace."
***Edmonton Sun*, August 30, 2008.**
© 2008 The Canadian Press.

http://www.edmontonsun.com/News/Alberta/2008/08/30/6614991-sun.html

How might environmental direct action campaigns and companies' protection of workers' safety and rights be viewed both as an expression of liberalism and a solution to some of the problems caused by liberalism?

In response to **environmental change** (that is, the changes in the natural world around us) many individuals and groups have resorted to activism to focus media attention on problems caused by industry and societal practices (for example, air pollution from cars and consumerism). Environmental groups have been exposing some of the offences that threaten the well-being of our planet.

We each share a significant relationship with all other people on earth through the environment. The environment is a shared system; changes in one part of the world affect all other parts. As noted in Figure 12-8, the interconnections between human health and water, air, vegetation, animal life, and climate mean that each region of the earth is dependent on all others. During the latter part of the 20th century, scientists, environmental activists, and other groups began to place increasing pressure on governments around the world to consider the quality of the environment and to limit the human impact on the environment. Liberal democracies now face a dilemma: How can they

PAUSE AND REFLECT

How do you think liberal governments should address the issue of protecting the environment? Which principles of liberalism does your answer challenge? Why is this challenge acceptable to you?

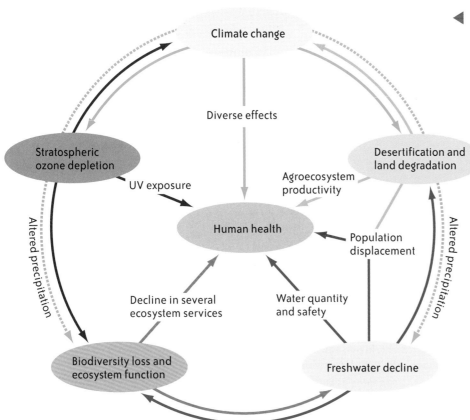

Figure 12-8

The interconnected nature of the world's environment links all individuals in ways that are not always obvious. Actions taken by one person will affect all people, creating conditions of interdependence that may strongly influence how governments address issues.

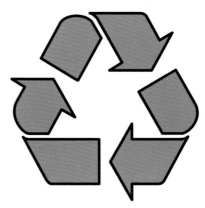

Figure 12-9

The 3Rs—"Reduce, Reuse, and Recycle"—has become a symbol of conscientious response to waste in a consumer society. When the concept was originally introduced, however, people were resistant. Even today, because of economic considerations or longstanding customs, some communities do not consider environmental efforts a priority. In some cases poverty and other issues take precedence. In 2008, for example, economic turmoil affected many countries and environmental considerations took a back seat for many. To what extent are efforts at environmental stewardship consistent with liberal principles? How can green choices be balanced with economic sustainability and convenience in order to better safeguard global and environmental success?

support principles of liberalism such as economic and personal freedom while also promoting the modern liberal principle of a high quality of life for all members of society?

While there is a long-standing tradition among some citizens of liberal democracies of promoting care for the environment and treating nature with respect, the environmental movement began to be influential only during the 1970s. Several notable publications, scientific and popular best sellers, and significant environmental disasters served to increase public awareness and pressure on governments to make changes. Oil spills off the Pacific Coast, an increasing awareness of water shortages, and the Exxon Valdez oil spill in 1989 brought environmental concerns to the forefront for the governments of Canada and the United States. Since the 1970s, governments have passed legislation concerning clean air, water, endangered species, the Arctic, forests, and disposal of toxic substances other forms of hazardous waste.

There is, according to Greenpeace, approximately a 30-year delay in the impact of emissions. In other words, we are only now feeling the effects of the greenhouse gas emissions of the 1970s. (**Greenhouse gas emissions** are gases, from both natural and artificial sources, that are released into the earth's atmosphere. They change the way the earth's atmosphere absorbs and emits radiation, which affects the temperature of earth.)

The views of politicians, ecologists, environmental activists, their supporters, and critics all contribute to the range of perspectives on environmental issues. All these perspectives affect the roles of individuals and governments and social expectations during the early part of the 21st century. How have the principles of liberalism provided people with a way of addressing the issue of environmental change?

Environmentalism through the Years

Before 1985, mankind will enter a genuine age of scarcity…in which the accessible supplies of many key minerals will be facing depletion.

—Paul Ehrlich, American biologist, environmentalist and author of *The Population Bomb* (1968), speaking at Earth Day, 1976.

Traditional people of Indian nations have interpreted the two roads that face [European settlers] as the road to technology and the road to spirituality. We feel that the road to technology…has led modern society to a damaged and seared earth. Could it be that the road to technology represents a rush to destruction, and that the road to spirituality represents the slower path that the traditional native people have traveled and are now seeking again? The earth is not scorched on this trail. The grass is still growing there.

—William Commanda, Algonquin (Mamiwinini) leader and elder, 1991.

I want to argue that it is now time for us to make a major shift in our thinking about the environment, similar to the shift that occurred around the first Earth Day in 1970, when this awareness was first heightened. We need to stop the mythic fantasies, and we need to stop the doomsday predictions. We need to start doing hard science instead…It's time to abandon the religion of environmentalism, and return to the science of environmentalism, and base our public policy decisions firmly on that.

—Michael Crichton (medical doctor and novelist), from "Environmentalism as Religion" speech, September 15, 2003.
http://www.crichton-official.com/speech-environmentalismaseligion.html

1 Does each speaker present a distinct view of environmental issues? Are there similar themes?

2 Which principles of liberalism are challenged by the speakers' views?

3 There are many other points of view, opinions, and ideas related to this issue. How might we address the variety of responses to this challenge?

The Kyoto Protocol

As environmental issues are not limited by national borders, international co-operation and joint approaches seem essential. Yet all countries are careful to protect their sovereignty and promote national interests. In addition, various individuals and groups within countries express their desires, demands, and preferences to their own governments and to those of other countries. The **Kyoto Protocol**—an agreement reached at an international convention at which world leaders met to discuss climate change and create a plan for reducing greenhouse gases—is an example of how liberal democracies and other countries have approached the challenges of **climate change** (that is, the change in global weather patterns). The concept of climate change was, up to the early 2000s, rejected by neo-conservative governments and business leaders. It has recently been almost universally supported by scientific studies and is now no longer a matter of much debate. Science has shown, beyond reasonable doubt, that human economic activities are affecting the climate of the earth.

There is new evidence that climate change is a reality. The North Pole was an island for the first time in 2007, with alarming rates of sea ice melt. Low-lying inhabited islands in the Pacific and Indian oceans have had to be evacuated because of flooding caused by climate change and increased melting ice at the poles. Closer to home, the spread of the mountain pine beetle in British Columbia and Alberta is attributed to climate change. The insect is now better able to survive our milder winters, which is a problem because the beetle eats the bark of many trees, devastating whole forests.

The Kyoto Protocol is the first, and to date the only, binding international agreement that includes specific goals for individual countries to reduce their greenhouse gas emissions. It came into effect on February 16, 2005, but the countries ratifying the protocol have undertaken their goals with varying approaches and degrees of commitment.

In 2004, the government of Canada, led by Liberal prime minister Paul Martin, announced a broad plan for dealing with greenhouse gases, one that was based on voluntary participation and tax incentives for companies that complied. The plan also included mandatory emissions reductions for factories and power plants, improved fuel efficiency in Canadian vehicles, a climate fund to purchase emission reduction credits, and funding for infrastructure projects that would decrease greenhouse gas emissions.

One of the complicating factors in most liberal democracies is that when different political parties come to power, changes to international agreements can and do occur. Such a situation occurred in Canada in 2006 when the newly elected Conservative government, led by Prime Minister Stephen Harper, altered funding to climate change programs and instituted a new climate change plan focusing on additional consultations with industries and businesses, two groups that are traditionally not very enthusiastic about government guidance or restrictions. It is highly unlikely that Canada will meet its **Kyoto targets** (that is, the reduced levels of greenhouse gas emissions for each country set by the Kyoto Protocol). Canada's emissions in 2004 were 27 percent above our 1990 level, and our Kyoto target for 2008 was 6 percent below the 1990 level. Since the ratification of the Kyoto Protocol, very little progress has been made by either political party leading Canada.

Friends of the Earth is an international non-profit environmental group that was founded in 1978. It focuses on many issues, one of which is the campaign to stop **global warming**, which is an increase in the average temperature of the earth's atmosphere and a potential indicator of climate change. Friends of the Earth Canada has a three-point plan that addresses this global issue:

1. the Kyoto Protocol Implementation Act Lawsuit
2. the Climate Protection Plan (a carbon tax for big polluters)
3. the Energy Greenbox Program (the donation of energy-saving devices to underprivileged households through food bank Greenbox donations)

The Friends of the Earth Lawsuit against the Government of Canada, first launched in the courts in June, 2008, is described as follows:

The Kyoto Protocol Implementation Act (KPIA) is a federal law that requires the Government of Canada to take serious action on climate change. This law set out a series of legal requirements and deadlines with which the government must comply, including the creation of a climate change plan and enactment of regulations that ensure that Canada meets its international obligations.

The federal government did not comply with these requirements or meet the deadlines set out in the Act.

On behalf of Friends of the Earth, Ecojustice and lawyer Chris Paliare launched legal proceedings in September 2007 for a Judicial Review of the government's non-compliance with the Act. We are seeking a declaration from the Court that the government has not complied with the law and an order in the nature of mandamus (a court order) requiring it to do so.

The application was heard in Federal Court in Toronto in June and a decision was released on October 20, 2008. The Court ruled that the legislation itself is not justiciable—meaning it is not an issue the courts can resolve.

The same parties launched an appeal on November 25, 2008, seeking to have the Federal Court decision set aside and asking the Court of Appeal to declare that the Minister of the Environment and the Governor

PAUSE AND REFLECT

One of the ironies of liberal democracy is that its liberal principles are directly responsible for the level of economic development, abundance, and the consumer lifestyle we enjoy. Yet it is the uncontrolled consumerism of countries such as Canada and the United States that results in, among other things, disproportionate amounts of greenhouse gases in the atmosphere. Can those same principles of liberalism somehow control the damage our lifestyle is causing the planet?

Figure 12-10

In Montréal in November 2005, outside the United Nations Climate Change Conference, Friends of the Earth International created a mosaic 50 metres tall asking negotiators from many countries to formally accept and enforce the Kyoto Protocol.

in Council are violating the KPIA. A hearing is expected in Summer 2009.

—Source: "Kyoto Protocol Implementation Act Lawsuit", Ecojustice Canada.

http://www.ecojustice.ca/cases/kyoto-protocol-implementation-act-lawsuit

On December 11, 2008, Canada's environment minister, Jim Prentice, addressed a UN climate summit in Poznan, Poland. He said that Canada wanted to work with other countries to cut greenhouse gas emissions in half by 2050.

"Canada, like the rest of the world, worries about the health of our planet, and is already living with the impacts of a changing climate," Prentice said in a prepared address to the conference. "We must bring to these negotiations a sense of urgency and a shared vision for long-term co-operation that places us on the path to a low carbon future. And we must ensure that our vision is informed by the best science and also by the traditional knowledge and voices of Aboriginal people."

Scientists and governments from around the world have reached a consensus that heat-trapping gases in the atmosphere from human activity are causing potentially irreversible changes to the climate that could damage the earth's ecosystems and cause billions of dollars worth of losses to the global economy.

Delegates at the conference from other countries as well as environmental groups have suggested that Canada is causing delays in negotiations by refusing to endorse targets recommended by scientists that industrialized countries must cut greenhouse gas emissions by 25 to 40 per cent below 1990 levels by 2020 in order to avoid dangerous climate change. Although the Harper government has proposed to cut domestic emissions by three per cent below 1990 levels by 2020, Prentice said that Canada was willing to take actions "comparable with those of other developed countries."

"We believe that effective global measures regarding climate change and the economy can only occur with the commitment and contribution of all

major economies," Prentice said in the speech. "In the meantime, we must increase our support for the poorest and most vulnerable countries to help them become more resilient to climate change and to adapt to its worst effects." …

UN Secretary General Ban Ki-moon, who met privately with Prentice, also urged delegates at the conference to push for a "Green New Deal" by ensuring that global stimulus measures for the economy would also address pollution from fossil fuels and spur growth in clean energy technology…

—Source: Mike De Souza, "Canada urges climate-change battle", Canwest News Service, December 11, 2008. Material reprinted with the express permission of: "CANWEST NEWS SERVICE", a Canwest Partnership.
http://www.canada.com/topics/news/national/story.html?id=1062783

- What does economic expansion mean for the environment? Is economic expansion necessarily harmful to the environment?
- To what extent do the Canadian government's responses above reflect liberal principles and a willingness to address climate change?

Perspectives on Green Policies in Canada

As you read in Chapter 8, a carbon tax is one proposed strategy to fight climate change that Canadian politicians and other interested parties have discussed. Read the following viewpoints on the carbon tax and other climate change strategies.

The Liberal Party of Canada's "Green Shift" and Carbon Taxes

Liberal Leader Stéphane Dion revealed his party's carbon tax plan in June of 2008, telling reporters that Canada needs to make a "green shift" to help save the environment.

At the heart of the energy plan is an energy tax on carbon fuels, which will be based on consumption.

New taxes are expected to generate about $15.4 billion annually in revenue in four years. But the Liberals say their plan will be revenue neutral because it will cut income taxes and increase family support payments.

Alberta Conservative MP Jason Kenney claimed new taxes on jet fuel, diesel, and home heating will hurt average Canadians.

Prime Minister Stephen Harper accused Dion of making a tax grab and of flip flopping on a commitment against a carbon tax. "Mr. Dion has already broken his promise," Harper told reporters following a press conference in Huntsville, Ontario. Dion said "he would not have a carbon tax…when he gets into office he'll put a carbon tax on gasoline and everything else. And it will not be revenue neutral," Harper said.

Figure 12-11 ▲

Following his speech about the carbon tax plan, Stéphane Dion wears a Green Shift baseball cap while greeting supporters on Parliament Hill.

Jack Layton of the NDP dismissed the Tories' intensity-based approach, which the party says won't reduce carbon emissions. Layton has also rejected the concept of a carbon tax. Instead, the NDP has called for a "cap and trade" system that puts a strict limit on greenhouse gas emissions by "big polluters."

—Source: "Dion introduces 'green shift' carbon tax plan." CTV.ca, June 19, 2008.
http://www.ctv.ca/servlet/ArticleNews/story/CTVNews/20080619/dion_green_plan_080619

Sophisticated economic liberalism would consider the total picture of real costs including environmental cleanups, additional health-care costs due to unfettered pollution, and actually, in the long run, the economic benefit of cleaner power generation.

—William Lehtinen, design engineer in Montréal, interview with author, September 2008.

We may soon have no choice but to move away from an oil-obsessed economy.

Shot in 13 countries over a four-year period, Oil Apocalypse Now? reveals the myths and conspiracy theories surrounding the future of our world's oil supplies. It includes interviews with over 30 of the most influential people on both sides of the argument to examine if the oil age is coming to an end.

—Source: Andrew Evans, "New peak oil film on CBCNewsworld." Energy Bulletin, August 21, 2008.
http://www.energybulletin.net/node/46332

Is there a conspiracy of silence to keep the truth from us? In the last four years world oil prices have tripled. Alberta is being looked to as a new source of oil as it moves from 20th position to 2nd position (behind Saudi Arabia) on the world oil production charts. The US in particular, which burns a quarter of the world's supply, is desperately seeking new sources of oil as the pressure is on to try to sustain the "American way of life" while world supplies reach their peak.

—Source: "Supply and demand: World oil markets under pressure." CBC News, April 28, 2005.
http://www.cbc.ca/news/background/oil/supply_demand.html

But our oil takes up to ten times more energy and money to produce than "cheap" Saudi oil extracted from traditional oil wells. Alberta's oil then stands as a perfect example of an economic miracle that is also a huge environmental problem that requires a solution.

—Mike Hudema, Greenpeace Canada campaigner stationed in Alberta, interview with author, October 3, 2008.

1 What are some of the issues around climate change being identified in these excerpts? What are some of the solutions being proposed? Which solutions seem to be most in keeping with the principles of liberalism?

2 Based on these sources and your own past research and experience, how do you believe Canada can best work towards reducing greenhouse gas emissions and addressing climate change?

China and India: 21st Century Economic Miracles

As Western civilization contends with the looming world oil crisis and the environmental by-products of an oil-consuming society, in other parts of the world things are just starting to take off. China and India are rapidly modernizing and have recently experienced tremendous economic growth. They have both experienced remarkable reductions in poverty and increases in the numbers of people in the middle class.

However, China and India are not travelling the same development path. While China has introduced reforms quickly, India has been more deliberate. China has followed the traditional route, becoming a centre for low-wage manufacturing and exporting clothing, toys, electronics, and other goods. Because of its large, relatively well-educated English-speaking labour force, India has concentrated on providing services, such as call centres and data-processing operations.

Today's rapid globalization has been vital to the countries' climb up the income ladder. As they opened their economies and began to grow, both saw trade boom and became magnets for foreign investment. China's surging goods production laid the foundation for a rapidly expanding export sector, while India built up its niche in the global services market…

…India expects even greater success selling its services in the future. The Federation of Indian Chambers of Commerce and Industry, the country's largest business group, estimates services exports will more than triple in the next five years, growing much faster than goods shipments and reaching more than 50 percent of total exports in 2012.

—Source: "Economic Letter—Insights from the Federal Reserve Bank of Dallas." *Federal Reserve Bank of Dallas* 3, 8 (August, 2008).
http://dallasfed.org/research/eclett/2008/el0808.html

Figure 12-12 ▼

Since 1978, when reform began opening up the communist economy to more free market practices, China has been rapidly modernizing, changing the cityscape of many of its largest industrial centres.

Both countries have had to face similar political, social, and environmental problems as a result of their accelerated economic expansion.

India has also created Special Economic Zones (SEZs) that provide new infrastructure and a tax holiday to foreign companies making products for export using Indian workers. Today, India has more than 200 SEZs, which generate more than US$15 billion in annual exports and provide jobs for more than half a million Indian workers. The vitality of these SEZs is partly responsible for India's soaring economic growth rate of 9 per cent a year, second only to China among comparable market economies.

Some downsides to this miraculous economic expansion include loss of farmland and traditional ways of life, the exploitation of underpaid workers, and environmental issues. The most pressing environmental and health problems in China and India are caused by automobiles and urban air pollution. There is increasing evidence that motor vehicles are now the primary source of urban air pollution in China, which was not the case even in the late 1990s. Heating, cooking, power generation, and industrial coal consumption were formerly the main contributors to urban air pollution, but in the biggest cities coal was mostly replaced by natural gas for residential uses during the 1990s. Seven of the ten most polluted cities on earth are located in China: a statistic that is largely caused by growing auto emissions.

For decades India was subject to an embargo from the members of the Nuclear Suppliers Group, an international body that controls the export of nuclear materials. This prevented India from obtaining commercial nuclear fuel, nuclear power plant components, and services from the international market. Now that this embargo is lifted, India hopes to increase its nuclear power generation and decrease its reliance on "dirty" coal-powered thermal plants.

Figure 12-13 ▲

With the completion of India's new Golden Quadrilateral superhighway, which connects the country's four largest cities, there has been a surge in automobile manufacturing and sales. This increase in car culture has also contributed greatly to air pollution.

India now is going to be the home of making cheap cars for the rest of the world. But every car then requires land, which is grabbed from tribals, peasants. It requires aluminum and steel, which needs to be mined. It requires coal, which needs to be mined.

And just as when the first colonization took place, it was assumed that the earth was empty, terra nullius, no matter how many indigenous people existed. India, a land of 1.2 billion people, is being treated as an empty land for global capital, making 80 per cent of India redundant.

But people are fighting back. And place after place, in Dadri, in Nandigram, in Singur, people are just getting together in a new earth democracy and saying, "This land is our land. We will decide what we do with it. You cannot force a polluting industry on us. Globalization cannot force it."

—Source: Vandana Shiva Decries the "Outsourcing of Pollution to the Third World", Democracy Now!, September 14, 2007.

http://www.democracynow.org/2007/9/14/vandana_shiva_decries_the_outsourcing_of

According to a report from China's official news agency, the Chinese State Environmental Protection Agency (SEPA) is set to evaluate the environmental impact of development plans in five regions and five heavily polluted industries: the steel, petrochemical, power, paper making, and the coal chemical industries.

"China has started to pay the price for industrial development entered into without taking account of the environmental impact," said Pan Yue, deputy director of SEPA.

...Pan said that 26 of the 75 largest steel plants in China are located in cities with population of more than 1 million. "The conflict between the development of steel plants and cities is more and more obvious. There is an urgent need to adopt environmental impact evaluations on regional and industrial development plans. Some industries and local governments oppose implementing such a policy, based on their own interests, which made our work harder," Pan said.

—Source: "China to evaluate environmental impact of development plans." Xinhua News Agency, November 4, 2007.

http://www.china.org.cn/english/MATERIAL/230762.htm

As with China, India seems to be facing an ongoing conflict between economic development and environmental degradation. Sustainable economic development and environmental protection are luxuries that these developing countries do not think they can afford. India may have a slight advantage over China with its focus on a service-based economic expansion as this economic sector tends to pollute less.

The push to grow each country's economy has created increased competition for resources and international markets for goods and services. In many cases, this push for economic growth has been at the expense of the environment.

- What solutions has economic liberalism brought to each country? What problems have resulted from such liberalism?

Pandemics

A **pandemic** is an outbreak of a disease on a global scale. It is another example of how the principles of liberalism may be challenged but how, at the same time, they may also offer solutions. From the Greek *pan* (all) and *demos* (people), a pandemic is a rapidly spreading, highly virulent disease that creates a borderless path of infection from which people have little or no immunity and for which there is presently no vaccine. Pandemics usually spread easily from person to person, cause serious and sometimes fatal illness, and infect a country, continent, or even several continents in a relatively short time. You have likely heard of historical pandemics such as the Black Plague, which occurred in the 1350s in Europe. More recent examples, such as the avian (bird) flu and SARS (Severe Acute Respiratory Syndrome), have also threatened modern societies. While mass communication has increased our awareness of pandemics, the ease of international travel has also precipitated their spread.

Figure 12-14 ▲

Air quality was a major concern for athletes competing in the 2008 Summer Olympics, held in Beijing, China.

Liberal democracies are faced with a difficult situation when attempting to address pandemics. On the one hand, limiting travel and restricting visitors, tourists, and new immigration to a country can provide greater protection against pandemics. On the other hand, such actions will hamper trade and development, severely restrict the basic freedoms of citizens and potentially create other issues related to human rights violations. Determining the best course of action is a complex matter because of the need for international co-operation, negotiation, and compromise. Each country must work with others for a common purpose, forgoing some aspects of its own national interests for those of the world community.

International health organizations such as the **World Health Organization (WHO)** as well as national health organizations (such as Health Canada and the Centers for Disease Control in the United States) monitor established protocols and work on disseminating the most up-to-date information regarding pandemics and other forms of disease. The dissemination of information, tracking of outbreaks, and establishment of means of treatment become a shared responsibility for all countries under this system, regardless of their form of government. While globalization of business and international travel are both important activities for millions of people, and though countries may seek to support personal and economic freedom of movement, restricting the movement of human beings is one important step in addressing pandemics and limiting their spread.

> *Our greatest concern must always rest with disadvantaged and vulnerable groups. These groups are often hidden, live in remote rural areas or shantytowns and have little political voice.*

> **—Margaret Chan (director-general of the World Health Organization), quoted in *Working for Health: An introduction to the World Health Organization* (Geneva, Switzerland: WHO, 2007), p. 1.**
> http://www.who.int/about/brochure_en.pdf

In the 21st century, health is a shared responsibility, involving equitable access to essential care and collective defence against transnational threats.

> **—Source: "World Health Organization." Global Alliance for Improved Nutrition.** http://www.gainhealth.org/world-health-organization

- How can liberal democracies and organizations such as WHO balance people's freedoms with the need to curb the spread of disease?

The Four Horsemen of the Apocalypse, 31" x 48", Ed. 30, 1995. Artist - Daniel O. Stolpe

Figure 12-15

Societies have often used metaphor and symbols to explain the negative forces of nature and humankind; for example, the spread of disease or pandemics. The Four Horseman of the Apocalypse depicted in this image—Famine, Pestilence, War and Death—is one such example. What does the symbol of the four horsemen convey about the negative forces facing humans? To what extent can the principles of liberalism combat these forces?

PAUSE AND REFLECT

Should all countries be equal partners in decisions related to the control of pandemics, or should one or more countries take the lead? Do you think there is a point at which individual freedom should be restricted by governments in dealing with pandemics?

SARS in Toronto

Something to Think About: Pandemics spread rapidly in the modern world, because individuals and groups travel freely throughout most countries. Canada faced a potential pandemic in 2003 with the confirmation of SARS cases in Toronto. The response of health-care professionals and their preparedness illustrate the challenges pandemics pose to liberal societies.

An Example: **Severe Acute Respiratory Syndrome (SARS)** is a new disease with no evidence of spreading within the general population of Canada. Although it is understood as a respiratory disease spread through close contact with an infected person, much about the disease remains unknown. The only known risk factors for developing SARS are recent travel to areas where SARS is spreading locally, or recent close contact with someone who has SARS or is ill and has been in an area where SARS is spreading locally. The symptoms of the disease include a fever of 38.0 degrees Celsius or more, and respiratory problems such as coughing, shortness of breath, or difficulty breathing. Other symptoms may include muscle aches, headaches, a sore throat, or diarrhea.

In March 2003, the first Canadian cases were identified in people who had travelled to Hong Kong. The WHO briefly issued a travel advisory warning for Toronto, as it believed the city was a hotspot for the spread of the disease (the travel advisory was lifted approximately a week after it was issued). Although most cases were identified in Ontario, cases were also reported in British Columbia, Alberta, Saskatchewan, New Brunswick, and Prince Edward Island. By September 2003, 438 cases of SARS had been reported in Canada.

Figure 12-16 ▼

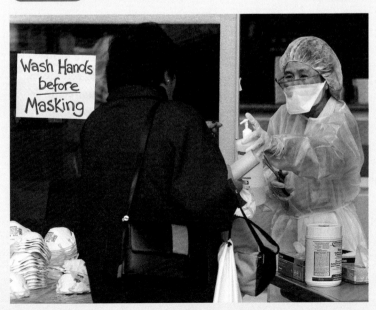

Canada's Response:

When SARS was first detected in Canada, health officials responded by isolating individuals with the disease and by issuing public announcements about preventative measures that individuals could take. In Toronto, where most SARS cases were reported, hospitals and medical facilities instituted strict rules to minimize the risk of further spreading the disease. All visitors or patients were required to have their temperatures taken and to wash their hands before entering, and were given a face mask to wear while inside the building. For a brief time, doctors and nurses were required to wear full protective clothing while they were at work.

Even with these preventions in place, the disease continued to spread during April and May 2003, causing many to criticize health officials' inability to contain the disease quickly enough. The SARS outbreak in Toronto helped teach health officials how to deal with highly infectious diseases and forced them to develop better emergency preparedness plans for the future.

Highlights of Steps Taken by Governments since SARS:

There has been significant progress in public health since the SARS outbreak in 2003, particularly in the areas of networks and collaboration, planning and emergency preparedness, infectious disease surveillance and response, and laboratory capacity. Officials claim that Canada is better prepared today to respond to a public health emergency than it was in 2003.

A key accomplishment has been the establishment of the Public Health Agency of Canada (PHAC), and the appointment of this country's first chief public health officer, Dr David Butler Jones. Progress is also being achieved through increased partnerships and collaboration. And since public health challenges do not respect borders, PHAC participates in various international forums to advance its public health agenda.

The federal government also committed $1 billion over five years to support Canada's avian and pandemic influenza preparedness efforts. Further, multi-disciplinary health emergency response teams have been set up to be deployed across the country to provide extra medical services in the event of a public health crisis.

In addition to emergency preparedness, preventative measures have also been put in place. In particular, greater surveillance of global health concerns has become increasingly important. The Global Public Health Intelligence Network, a system that tracks thousands of media stories in multiple languages in order to quickly identify and monitor potential emerging public health events around the world, has been established. In Canada, PHAC has developed a cutting-edge web-based framework of applications and resources called the Canadian Network for Public Health Intelligence (CNPHI). CNPHI has the capability to gather information from various sources, such as pharmacy sales, emergency room visits, and various other surveillance systems; analyze the information; and provide alerts when significant trends emerge.

Furthermore, a new Quarantine Act, enacted in December 2006, established quarantine services at airports in Halifax, Montréal, Ottawa, Toronto, Calgary, and Vancouver, where 95 per cent of international air travellers arrive to or depart from Canada. The purpose of these quarantine services is to reduce and prevent the spread of serious infectious diseases from ill travellers by identifying them before they actually enter or leave the country.

QUESTIONS FOR REFLECTION

1 Canada has taken a series of steps to address the potential outbreak of a pandemic. SARS, like other pandemics, presents a serious (but not necessarily immediate) risk to individuals and countries. What steps has Canada taken to address the outbreak of a pandemic? In what ways do these steps reflect liberal principles? To what extent do these steps support the common good as the more important value than individual rights and freedoms?

2 Is there a possible danger to individual privacy with the increased surveillance of citizens under systems such as CNPHI? Is the potential for abuse of this information by governments a challenge to liberal principles? Is this an acceptable risk, given the potential danger?

3 Two important principles of liberalism are social autonomy and protection of individual rights and freedoms. How might our federal, provincial, and municipal governments be challenged to demonstrate these principles when addressing pandemics in Canada?

4 What role should liberal democracies play in addressing pandemics that arise in other countries? Should liberal democracies ever engage in practices that restrict the principles of liberalism to protect their own societies' interests and their citizens?

Water Availability

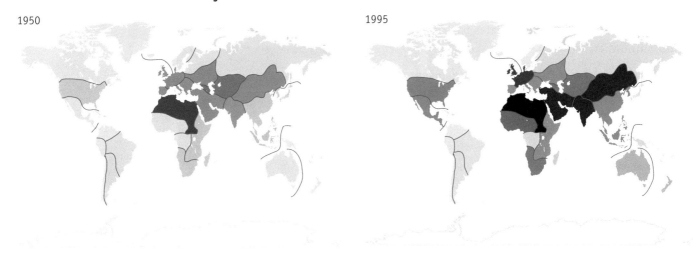

1950

1995

2025

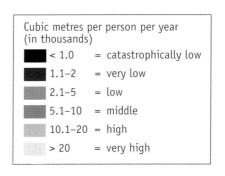

Cubic metres per person per year
(in thousands)

■	< 1.0	= catastrophically low
■	1.1–2	= very low
■	2.1–5	= low
■	5.1–10	= middle
▨	10.1–20	= high
░	> 20	= very high

Source: Graph on Water Consumption, website of UN
International Year of Freshwater, 2003. © United Nations.
http://www.un.org/events/water/

Figure 12-18 ▲

Consider the changes shown in the three maps. What other sources of information would be helpful when investigating this issue? What other factors are important in this issue?

Like oxygen, water is an essential resource to life on earth. In 2003, the United Nations focused world attention on the growing problem of fresh water availability. As you can determine from the maps in Figure 12-16, that availability has decreased over the past 50 years. Within your lifetime, if the trend continues, access to fresh water could become one of the most pressing global issues. How have liberal democracies addressed this issue in the past decade?

You have read about the competing rights of individuals, groups, and the larger society throughout this text. The regulation and control of water represent a dilemma—whose rights take precedence and who makes decisions? Land owners, farmers, municipalities, and businesses all need readily available, consistent sources of fresh water. The growth of cities as well as changing precipitation patterns over the past several decades have placed increased demands on water supplies. You may live in a community where the use of fresh water is controlled through water meters, non-watering days, low-flow fixtures, restrictions on car washes, and other regulations designed to limit consumption. For several regions of Canada, including southern Alberta, the threat of **drought**—a severe lack of precipitation in a given area, which often affects crops—is an ongoing concern. Water management by governments can create issues and tensions over who owns, and controls, the flow of and access to fresh water. In addition, agreements with the United States over access to fresh water by states bordering Canada complicate matters regarding water management.

One such example can be found in Manitoba with the Garrison Diversion project. This project includes a proposal to transfer treated water from the Missouri River to Minot, North Dakota, and from there to have it flow into the Red River Basin with eventual dispersal into Hudson Bay. The project involves the movement of water from one water basin to another, diverting the natural flow of water. It also presents environmental concerns with the likely introduction of foreign species into Canadian waters. This project could create a precedent for future large-scale water transfers from other parts of the United States into Hudson Bay or other water basins. The potential disruption to plant and animal life (since new plant and animal life not native to the Hudson Bay Basin could be introduced), as well as the changes to water levels, are of great concern to Canada.

The damming of the Old Man River in Alberta has also been discussed for a number of years. Some believe that this may be part of a long-range plan to sell Alberta water to the United States under the North American Free Trade Agreement. In what ways could this be a challenge to liberal principles in Canada and to Alberta in particular?

The issues related to water in other countries have different causes and circumstances. In China, the rapid industrialization and growth of the economy has put tremendous pressure on clean water. The Yangtze River has provided the surrounding population with more than a sufficient supply of water for consumption and hydroelectric power. Yet the use of the river to dispose of industrial, human, and animal waste is creating an unhealthy water source. Throughout much of Africa and Asia the green revolution that began in the 1970s to provide more food for famine-stricken areas has saved millions of lives, but it has also strained the water sources to drought conditions. India faces a different problem. The priority placed on the creation of dams to irrigate crops has turned almost 90 per cent of India's water over to farms. Obtaining clean water for other uses is difficult, and reducing agricultural dependency on water means switching to crops that use less water. For many in the Middle East, the supply of water is very limited. This limitation is further complicated by the flow of underground water that crosses national boundaries and can be

Figure 12-19 ▲

As you read in Chapter 6, a massive drought in the Canadian Prairies and the Great Plains of the United States set in during the 1930s, resulting in the **Dust Bowl** (so named because of the dust storms that swept the area). The economic effects of the drought deepened the Great Depression, which had just begun. In 2002, drought conditions were also faced by farmers and others in the Western provinces in Canada. To what extent could liberal principles be used to support a response to issues related to drought in Canada?

PAUSE AND REFLECT

What do you think the Canadian government should do when it comes to moving water between countries? Who are the parties that would be most affected by a project such as the Garrison Diversion? In what ways are liberal principles being challenged by this issue?

accessed only by the countries in which the water collects in underground reservoirs. Political tensions and scarcity add to pressures over control and access to water.

- What actions might countries take to improve the accessibility of fresh water for more people?
- What solutions to world water shortages and the control over Canada's fresh water resources can liberalism offer?

Explore the Issues

Concept Review

1 a) Identify five contemporary world issues that present challenges to liberalism.

b) Identify the solutions that liberalism proposes to the issues you identified in question 1a.

Concept Application

2 Debate the following: *Be it resolved that liberalism offers the means to address contemporary issues.* Use the Skill Path to guide your debate.

3 Please read the following quotation and respond to the questions that follow:

The global financial crisis, brewing for a while, really started to show its effects in the middle of 2007 and into 2008. Around the world stock markets have fallen, large financial institutions have collapsed or been bought out, and governments in even the wealthiest nations have had to come up with rescue packages to bail out their financial systems.

On the one hand many people are concerned that those responsible for the financial problems are the ones being bailed out, while on the other hand, a global financial meltdown will affect the livelihoods of almost everyone in an increasingly inter-connected world...

Many blame the greed of Wall Street for causing the problem in the first place because it is in the US that the most influential banks, institutions and ideologues that pushed for the policies that caused the problems are found.

The crisis became so severe that after the failure and buyouts of major institutions, the Bush Administration offered a $700 billion bailout plan for the US financial system.

This bailout package was controversial because it was unpopular with the public, seen as a bailout for the culprits while the ordinary person would be left to pay for their folly. The US House of Representatives initially rejected the package as a result, sending shock waves around the world...

In Europe, starting with Britain, a number of nations decided to nationalize, or part-nationalize, some failing banks to try and restore confidence. The US resisted this approach at first, as it goes against the rigid free market view the US has taken for a few decades now.

Eventually, the US capitulated and the Bush Administration announced that the US government would buy shares in troubled banks.

This illustrates how serious this problem is for such an ardent follower of free market ideology to do this...

Perhaps fearing an ideological backlash, Bush was quick to say that buying stakes in banks "is not intended to take over the free market, but to preserve it."

—Source: Anup Shah, "Global Financial Crisis 2008" December 07, 2008.
http://www.globalissues.org/article/768/global-financial-crisis

Reflect in writing on the point of view shared by the author regarding the global financial crises in 2008. According to this author, to what extent has following the ideological principles of liberalism been able to successfully guide proposed solutions to global economic issues in 2008? In your response, consider to what extent the United States and Britain have strayed from the liberal ideals of a free market economy in order to address the issues created by debt and some free market practices.

Reflect and Analyze

In this chapter you have explored some ideologies that question liberalism. You have seen how liberalism has promoted economic growth and individual rights. You have also seen how liberalism has caused major social and environmental problems for which we now seek solutions. Ironically, liberalism is, in some cases, providing solutions to the very problems it helped create. These observations will hopefully give you some insight into the Chapter Issue: *To what extent do contemporary issues challenge the principles of liberalism?*

Respond to Ideas

1 Explain, in your own words, why liberalism can be seen as a solution to a lot of the world's problems. This may take the form of a fictional piece, such as a story or poem, or a non-fiction piece, such as a newspaper article or a blog entry.

Respond to Issues

2 Debate the following response as a class: Be it resolved that liberalism is a failed ideology due to all the challenges it creates. Use the chapter examples to support and inform your position.

Recognize Relationships among Concepts, Issues, and Citizenship

3 Suppose you had to pass an exam to earn full-fledged Canadian citizenship with all its rights. New Canadians must prove that they have learned things about Canada before being sworn in. So, in this instance, all 18-year-old Canadian teenagers would be required to pass a citizenship exam.

The real citizenship exam tests prospective citizens' knowledge of Canada. Thus, our citizenship exam in this chapter will let you demonstrate your understanding of liberalism and its viability. Please respond to the following questions:

a) What is the most critical question that you would ask on a citizenship exam? Consider the following aspects when you develop your answer:
   - identifies a specific issue in Canada that needs to be addressed
   - reflects a clear link to the viability of the principles of liberalism
   - reflects active and responsible citizenship

b) Share your question with the class.

c) Rank the questions shared to identify what you believe to be the most critical question. Share your rankings and come to consensus as a class as to which question is the most critical, based on the criteria provided above.

d) Respond individually to the question that was identified as the most critical. Choose the best format for your response.

Ideology and Citizenship

PART

4

Never underestimate the power of a few committed people to change the world. Indeed, it is the only thing that ever has.

**—Anthropologist Margaret Mead
(1901–1978)**

In this part of your course, you will have the opportunity to consider ways of applying the understandings you have gained from previous chapters. Having explored ideologies in general and liberalism in particular—its principles, its evolution, its critics, its successes and failures, and its contributions to and implications for democratic citizenship—you are now in a position to think about the relationship between ideology and active citizenship.

Consider the story of American Greg Mortenson. In 1993, he tried to climb the Himalayan peak "K2" and failed. Weak and barely able to descend the mountainside, Mortenson was nursed back to health by people living in a Muslim village nearby in Pakistan. As a result, he made a personal commitment to act and to make a difference: he promised the men and women who rescued him that he would build them a school.

Back at home, Mortenson's fund-raising campaign got off to a dismal start. According to an article in the *New York Times*, "his 580 fundraising letters to prominent people generated one check, from Tom Brokaw—and Mr. Mortenson ended up selling his beloved climbing equipment and car."

But Mortenson built the school as promised, and then continued to build more schools in the isolated regions of Pakistan and Afghanistan. For each project, villagers supplied the land and employed locals so that the school would involve a sense of local effort and ownership. Mortenson provided the funding. So far, the Taliban seems uninterested in attacking these schools built by local labour.

Mortenson points out, "Schools are a much more effective bang for the buck than missiles…" He believes that educated women will be less likely to support their sons being recruited by the Taliban and that educated young men will be less attracted by Taliban ideology (Source: Nicholas Kristof, "It Takes a School, Not Missiles", *New York Times*, July 13, 2008).

To what extent are the choices and actions of Greg Mortenson an expression of his having embraced an ideology? In what ways do his actions demonstrate responsible citizenship?

Part 4 of this course investigates the issue ***To what extent should my actions as a citizen be shaped by an ideology?*** In order to begin to answer this question you'll need to develop an understanding of the term "citizenship." Most likely you already have a sense of what is meant by this term.

- A citizen lives in and is a member of a country.
- A citizen votes.
- A citizen has certain responsibilities like usually obeying laws and paying taxes.
- A citizen also has certain rights like protection from arbitrary arrest and freedom of speech.

But surely citizenship is much more than legal status. In the next chapter you will read that Andrew Coyne, a well known Canadian columnist, believes that being a citizen of a country means being part of a *moral project*. What does this involve and on what ideology is this moral project based? Can you be part of many moral projects—in your community or country, or globally?

Mark Kingwell, a University of Toronto professor of philosophy, based his book *The World We Want* on similar ideas. Kingwell states that the purpose of his book "is to provoke reflection on the idea of citizenship at a time when such reflection is in painfully short supply, whether from pressures of time or from assumptions of certainty— whether from *busyness* or from *knowingness*, the twin distracting deities of our day." (Mark Kingwell, *The World We Want* [Lanham, Maryland: Rowman & Littlefield], p. 4.) What is the world you want? What roles and responsibilities might you have in taking action to achieve this world? How does your personal ideology make sense of Andrew Coyne's "moral project"? Does your personal ideology allow you to reflect on the idea of citizenship? Like Greg Mortenson, does your personal ideology lead you to consider a citizenship that is driven by responsible and informed action geared toward making the world a better place?

There are many examples of young people who decide to take responsible action to practise their citizenship and to make a difference. In 2001, Christine Jairamasingh, 16, and Eryn Fitzgerald, 15, sued the Alberta government to change the Municipal Election Act to lower the voting age from 18 to 16, allowing youth to vote for city councillors and school trustees. Others join groups such as Amnesty International or attend conferences to address social issues such as HIV/AIDS or homelessness. The involvement of these young people is necessarily based on an ideology or worldview. As you explore the following two chapters, reflect on how your ideology shapes your view on issues and your decision to take action. Consider also how this section helps you to answer the Key Issue for this course, ***To what extent should we embrace an ideology?***

Visit the Learn Alberta site www.LearnAlberta.ca and click on the *Perspectives on Ideology* learning object for fully interactive learning scenarios entitled ExCite (Exploring Citizenship). These scenarios related to issues and concepts in the Student Resource enhance learning.

Part 4
To what extent should my actions as a citizen be shaped by an ideology?

Chapter 13
Reflecting on Worldview, Ideology, and Citizenship
To what extent should ideology shape responses to issues in times of peace and times of conflict?

Chapter 14
Reflecting on Ideology, Action, and Citizenship
To what extent should ideology shape your thinking and action as a citizen?

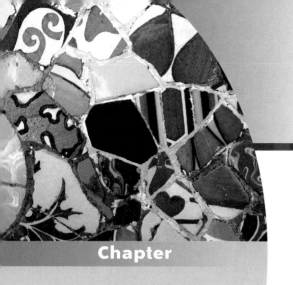

Reflecting on Worldview, Ideology, and Citizenship

KEY SKILLS

Demonstrating leadership by employing strategies to resolve issues and create a plan of action

KEY CONCEPTS

Exploring the relationship between worldviews and ideology and how ideologies shape understandings of citizenship

Analyzing the rights, roles, and responsibilities of individuals in democratic societies or during times of conflict.

Key Terms

Citizen advocacy
Citizenship
Individual rights, roles, and responsibilities
Political Participation

Have you ever crossed an international border and been asked by an official what your citizenship is? Given the situation, likely you answered with your legal country of origin—the place where you were born—such as "Canadian." What exactly did the official mean when he or she asked about your citizenship? What did you mean by your response? Answering the question "What is your citizenship?" is complex, and your answer is shaped in several ways by **worldviews** and ideology. If you were a citizen of Israel or Burma, for example, you would likely have different ideas about citizenship.

Statements about citizenship, whether in historical or contemporary official government documents or in other public writing, provide an opportunity to analyze the range of beliefs about what it means to be a citizen in a particular time and place. Consider the quotations regarding some legal and personal understandings of citizenship in the next section. As you read each, look for evidence of a worldview and an ideology. What understanding of citizenship is reflected in each source? What worldview or ideology seems to underlie this understanding of citizenship? To what extent could this worldview and/or ideology inform a citizen's response to issues in their country and in the world?

Canadian Citizenship

Canada's Oath of Citizenship reads as follows:

I swear (or affirm) that I will be faithful and bear true allegiance to Her Majesty Queen Elizabeth the Second, Queen of Canada, Her Heirs and Successors, and that I will faithfully observe the laws of Canada and fulfil my duties as a Canadian citizen.

—**Source: "The Citizenship Ceremony." Citizenship and Immigration Canada.**
http://www.cic.gc.ca/English/citizenship/cit-ceremony.asp#oath

According to a recent national survey of public attitudes conducted by EKOS, more than eight in ten Canadians feel that national volunteer service creates a culture of active citizenship and civic participation. Almost nine in ten feel that a term of full time national volunteer service improves the communities where youth volunteer. Moreover, three in four Canadians feel that volunteer service provides youth with clearer direction for post-secondary education.

—**Source: "Canadians Deem National Volunteer Service Indispensable in Engaging Youth", Katimavik Press Release, June 26, 2008.**
http://www.katimavik.org/files/File/press%20release%20EKOS%20%20final.pdf

We are citizens, not just consumers. Our environment requires citizen preferences, not just consumer preferences. As citizens, we need to protect nature, not just buy, sell, and consume it. It has a dignity, not just a price.

—Source: Mark Sagoff, Director, Institute for Philosophy and Public Policy, University of Maryland
http://www.cep.unt.edu/citizen.htm

National Definition of Métis

Métis means a person who self-identifies as Métis, is of historic Métis Nation Ancestry, is distinct from other Aboriginal Peoples, and is accepted by the Métis Nation…

"Historic Métis Nation" means the Aboriginal people then known as Métis or Half-Breeds who resided in Historic Métis Nation Homeland;

"Historic Métis Nation Homeland" means the area of land in west central North America used and occupied as the traditional territory of the Métis or Half-Breeds as they were then known;

"Métis Nation" means the Aboriginal people descended from the Historic Métis Nation, which is now comprised of all Métis Nation citizens and is one of the "aboriginal peoples of Canada" within [section] 35 of the Constitution Act of 1982;

"Distinct from other Aboriginal Peoples" means distinct for cultural and nationhood purposes.

—Source: "Who Are the Métis? National Definition of Métis." Métis National Council.
http://www.metisnation.ca/who/definition.html

Burma's Constitution

The 1982 constitution of Burma contains the following description of citizenship:

Nationals such as the Kachin, Kayah, Karen, Chin, Burman, Mon, Rakhine or Shan and ethnic groups as have settled in any of the territories included within the State as their permanent home from a period anterior to 1185 B.E., 1823 A.D. are Burma citizens.

The Council of State may decide whether any ethnic group is national or not.

Every national and every person born of parents, both of whom are nationals are citizens by birth.

A person who is already a citizen on the date this Law comes into force is a citizen. Action, however, shall be taken under section 18 for infringement of the provision of that section.

—Source: "Burma Citizenship Law of 1982." Online Burma/Myanmar Library.
http://burmalibrary.org/docs/Citizenship%20Law.htm

Figure 13-1 ▲

In 2008, Aung San Suu Kyi started a hunger strike to protest her long detention under house arrest in Myanmar. Suu Kyi was elected the leader of the opposition in Myanmar and her party, the National League for Democracy, won the majority vote in the general election of 1990; however, the military government ignored the election result.

However, recently the military government of Myanmar (as Burma is now known), introduced a new constitution, as reported below:

[On] February 19, 2008, Burma's military government announced that work had been completed on writing the draft of the proposed new constitution…Aung Toe said the draft was drawn up with the objective of ensuring a leading role in politics for the military. The guidelines for a new constitution were adopted…after 14 years of on-and-off meetings, where the militarily hand-picked delegates have attended.

In fact, the draft constitution contains all the provisions to glorify the militarism in the governance in the guise of so-called "disciplined democracy." It is a blue-print for the army to legitimize its grip on power for an indefinite period and where the head of the army will be the most powerful person in the country, with the ability to appoint key cabinet figures and suspend the constitution in the event of an emergency that he defines.

—**Source: Ahmedur Rahman Farooq,**
"The Draft Constitution of Burma's Military Rulers."
Burma Digest **March 20, 2008.**
http://burmadigest.info/2008/03/20/
the-draft-constitution-of-burmas-military-rulers/

Israeli Citizenship

Israel grants its state membership based on Jewish identity or ancestry, but it also provides citizenship to Palestinian Arabs living in Israel…Jews in Israel participate in a citizenship model that expects them to contribute to the common good. Israeli Arabs, on the other hand, are excluded from the common good although they are formally entitled to equal rights under the law. One avenue of exclusion relates to the fact that military service is obligatory for Jews, is seen as a fundamental contribution to the common good, and entitles those who perform it to a range of social benefits. Arab citizens of Israel are barred from military service, from the social, cultural, political and economic benefits that accompany it, and hence from…full membership in the society.

—**Source: Sheila L. Croucher,**
Globalization and Belonging: The Politics of Identity in a Changing World
(Lanham, MD: Rowman & Littlefield, 2004), p. 50.

Chapter Issue

Part 1 of this text explored the relationship between identity and ideology; Part 2 assessed impacts of, and reactions to, principles of liberalism as they emerged and were applied in the world; and Part 3 considered the extent to which the principles of liberalism are viable in a contemporary world. In Part 4, you will respond to the following issue: *To what extent should my actions as a citizen be shaped by an ideology?*

The two chapters of Part 4 focus on relationships among worldview, ideology, citizenship, and action. Part 4 will assist you in furthering your understandings related to the Key Issue in the book and in formulating a response to this issue: *To what extent should we embrace an ideology?*

As we continue our exploration of ideology in this chapter, you will consider citizenship and the relationships between ideology and how societies and individuals respond to issues during times of peace and times of crisis. You will explore how citizenship may be defined and how individuals and societies act on their understanding of the term. You will also examine how people define their roles, rights, and responsibilities as citizens in particular circumstances. These considerations will be the focus of this chapter as you address the Chapter Issue: *To what extent should ideology shape responses to issues in times of peace and times of conflict?*

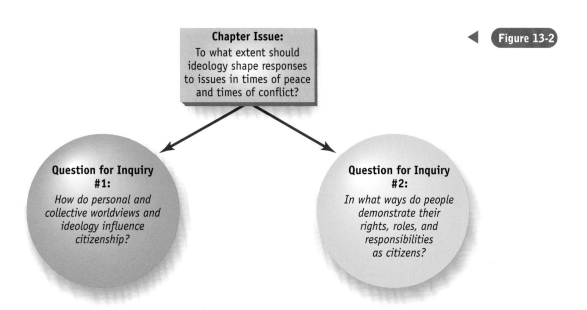

◀ Figure 13-2

Chapter Issue:
To what extent should ideology shape responses to issues in times of peace and times of conflict?

Question for Inquiry #1:
How do personal and collective worldviews and ideology influence citizenship?

Question for Inquiry #2:
In what ways do people demonstrate their rights, roles, and responsibilities as citizens?

Influences of Worldview and Ideology on Citizenship

Question for Inquiry

- **How do personal and collective worldviews and ideology influence citizenship?**

As you saw in Part 1 of this book, your worldview may lead you toward an ideology that influences the ways you think and act. As you will explore in this chapter, worldview and ideology shape your evolving role as a citizen. For example, when you react to an issue in your community or respond to an event that you see on the news, there are different factors that may influence your response:

- your worldview (your view of how the world is and how it should be, based on your experiences, beliefs, and values)
- your ideology (ideology is the application of your worldview to a current issue or crisis situation. Your ideology suggests to you what should be done next to bring about the kind of society you envision through your individual and collective worldviews.)

Your contributions to your community and society—which is one way in which you might demonstrate your understanding of citizenship—rest in part on where you come from and what your worldview is, what ideologies have helped to shape your thoughts, and the kinds of events and issues to which you and your society have had to respond.

For example, consider these two photos.

Both photos are of Canadian soldiers involved in the NATO mission in Afghanistan. How do you respond to what you see in each of the photos?

Figure 13-3

Figure 13-4 ▼

In the Figure 13-3 and Figure 13-4 photo exercise, your worldview helps you understand and interpret what you see. Your personal ideology is shaped in part by the ideologies that surround you. Personal ideology suggests how you should respond to particular issues, based on your worldview. With this explanation in mind and with respect to the soldiers in Afghanistan, think about how you could describe your worldview and how you could describe your personal ideology.

Legal and Political Understandings of Citizenship

Your answer to the question asked on page 442, What is your citizenship?, may be quite simple and straightforward to you. In the most basic terms, *citizenship* is a form of identification or a label that you might use to describe yourself in relation to a country: *Canadian, American, Chinese, French*, or some other term. This label is based on where you were born, who your parents are, or some combination of these and additional factors. However, how a country and society define and identify its citizens suggests a collective worldview, and how you think of, feel about, and express your citizenship is influenced by your worldview and ideology. As you read through this section and consider the concept of citizenship, note the various ways in which it is viewed and expressed through action. Note the ideologies you see demonstrated.

From a legal perspective, citizenship is based on two key principles:

- *jus soli* (right of the soil)—a person's citizenship or nationality is determined by place of birth
- *jus sanguinis* (right of blood)—the citizenship and nationality of a child is the same as the natural parents, wherever the child is born

Most countries use a combination of jus soli and jus sanguinis as well as **naturalization**—the process of applying for citizenship—to determine who may (and may not) legally identify oneself as a citizen of the country.

Jus soli has been used as the basis for determining citizenship among many countries that want to increase their citizenship or that, like Canada and the United States, historically increased their population through settlement. Some countries base citizenship on jus sanguinis to maintain national and cultural identity, and for historical reasons (for example, past wars or complex cultural or ethnic issues). For example, Finland applies jus sanguinis in that it offers a "right of return" to ethnic Finns who live in the former Soviet Union and who pass a Finnish language examination. The modern state of Israel offers an automatic right to citizenship to any immigrant who is Jewish by birth or conversion, or who has a Jewish parent or grandparent. Israel also grants Israeli citizenship to all ethnic and religious groups based on

The modern state of Israel was formed in 1948 as a Jewish state in accordance with a United Nations decision.

birth in Israel (but with the limitations regarding military service noted on page 444) and allows naturalization after living in the country for five years and acquiring a basic knowledge of Hebrew.

In comparison to other European countries, France was early to adopt the principle of jus soli. Germany and many other European countries used jus sanguinis; for example, until 2000, German citizenship was granted primarily on the basis of jus sanguinis, which seriously limited the naturalization of foreigners living in Germany and their children. This had a tremendous impact on *Gastarbeiter*, the "guest workers" recruited from places such as Italy, Turkey, Greece, and Portugal for industrial jobs in West Germany during the 1950s, 1960s, and 1970s. Significant revisions in 2000, however, included the following:

Children born in Germany to foreign parents may acquire German nationality if certain conditions are met. They must however decide between the ages of 18 and 23 whether to retain their German nationality or the nationality of their parents…

As a general rule, foreigners now have the right to become naturalized after eight years of habitual residence in Germany, provided they meet the relevant conditions, instead of the fifteen years previously required. The minimum period of residence for spouses of German nationals is usually shorter. For naturalization, it is necessary to prove adequate knowledge of German. A clean record and commitment to the tenets of the Basic Law (Constitution) are further criteria. The person to be naturalized must also be able to financially support him/herself.

The aim of avoiding multiple nationality remains a key feature of the German law on nationality. In general, those applying for naturalization must give up their foreign nationality.

—Source: "Law on Nationality."
Welcome to the Federal Foreign Office, September 16, 2005.
http://www.diplo.de/diplo/en/WillkommeninD/EinreiseUnd
Aufenthalt/Staatsangehoerigkeitsrecht.html

The German example points to some critical issues about how citizenship is defined and what it entails: the situation of children born to foreigners, multiple citizenship, and the relationships between economic roles and political rights in a country.

For example, if you are born in Canada, you are most likely a Canadian citizen, regardless of your parents' nationality, because Canada applies the principle of jus soli. Children born outside Canada but to one Canadian citizen can be Canadian citizens also—thus jus sanguinis also applies to some extent. Canada also allows for citizenship by naturalization—granting citizenship to applicants who meet certain requirements (for example, permanent residency, basic ability in spoken English or French, and knowledge of Canada).

Even Canada's relatively unrestrictive citizenship policies can have potentially negative implications, however. Take the example of a Canadian child whose parent is being deported as an illegal immigrant. In the case of *Baker v. Canada* (Ministry of Citizenship and Immigration), 1999, Mavis Baker was to be deported because she immigrated to Canada from Jamaica illegally. Baker appealed her deportation on the basis of "humanitarian and compassionate" grounds because the deportation would affect her four children who were born in Canada during her 11 years of working and living in Canada. Mavis Baker's appeal was denied.

The United States applies the principle of jus soli; thus, generally, children born in the United States are American citizens. However, the United States has been concerned about the rising number of children of illegal immigrants attending public schools in the United States. Some authorities have argued that providing school, as well as health care and social services, for children of illegal immigrants is too costly and essentially rewards families for the parents' illegal immigration. Although a 1982 US Supreme Court ruling overturned a Texas law that denied public school education to undocumented children, and declared that children of illegal immigrants are entitled to free public education, California and other states have introduced propositions to restrict access to education and services. In 2004, it was estimated that the state of California spent US$7.7 billion educating undocumented children. Critics, however, say that allowing states to refuse public education to children of illegal immigrants creates a second class of citizenship.

Australia formerly used jus soli as the basis for citizenship but modified its laws so that children born in Australia to foreign parents who are not permanent residents become Australian citizens at the age of 10 if they meet certain requirements. Again, this has been criticized as making the children of foreign parents second-class citizens, in this case, until the age of 10.

Ireland also considered modifying its laws that automatically granted citizenship to children born in Ireland. The goal of the change was to end what was described as "citizenship tourism": pregnant women travelling to Ireland to give birth so that their children would gain Irish citizenship, and thus a European Union passport.

Rather than modify its jus soli laws, India moved to abolish jus soli and use jus sanguinis instead. The change started in 1987 and meant that children born in the country are citizens only if one parent is also an Indian citizen. In 2004, India further modified the laws so that a child cannot become a citizen of India if one parent immigrated to India illegally. India also grants citizenship through naturalization. India does not, however, allow citizens to hold Indian citizenship as well as the citizenship of another country; it does allow for a person to be recognized as a citizen of another country and an "Overseas Citizen of India," but this is not full Indian citizenship.

Why is multiple citizenship an issue for some countries? While some countries might view dual (or even triple) citizenship as a citizen's right to recognize his or her heritage as well as his or her present and future home—and might even see it as an advantage to a country's businesspeople—others view it as a potential source of conflicting loyalties or legal confusions. Germany, as already noted, allows dual nationality in only limited circumstances. Denmark does not allow dual nationality at all. The United States takes the following stance:

> …*The US Government recognizes that dual nationality exists but does not encourage it as a matter of policy because of the problems it may cause. Claims of other countries on dual national US citizens may conflict with US law, and dual nationality may limit US Government efforts to assist citizens abroad. The country where a dual national is located generally has a stronger claim to that person's allegiance.*

—**Source: "Dual Nationality." US Department of State.**
http://travel.state.gov/travel/cis_pa_tw/cis/cis_1753.html

Broader Understandings of Citizenship

The question of multiple citizenship highlights diverse and sometimes conflicting worldviews of what being a citizen means. What does the term *citizenship* mean to you?

To some individuals, citizenship is a matter solely of where you are born, where your parents were born, your heritage, and your past. To others, it is a matter of where you live and work, your present loyalty, and where you see your future. Additionally, citizenship can reflect what kind of society you wish to support, what society offers the greatest benefits to you, and what obligations and duties society requires of you.

As noted in the Canadian Oath of Citizenship, being a citizen in Canada means, among other things, accepting the laws of the country. Canada's laws, like laws of all countries, reflect the ideals of the country. However, the requirement that citizens observe the country's laws is a minimal requirement of citizenship. In ancient Athens, citizenship involved a moral right and duty to actively participate in the politics of the city. This republican understanding of citizenship seeks to create a sense of belonging to a community. The citizen becomes a stakeholder in the well-being of the republic. Civic and **political participation**, in this context, is understood as the obligations that citizens have to the state and society as a result of being granted rights.

According to a literature review conducted by Canadian Policy Research Networks,

Citizenship is composed of three dimensions: (1) rights and responsibilities, (2) access to these rights and responsibilities, and (3) feelings of belonging, that is, identity. Being a citizen, therefore, is more than possessing formal, theoretical rights to citizenship. It involves the capacity of the individual citizen to exercise actively the three dimensions of citizenship. Being a citizen is defined as having the resources, capacity and opportunity to participate in the different areas of adult life.

—Source: Canadian Policy Research Networks, "Youth and Citizenship: Overview" September 2004, p. 1.
http://www.cprn.org/documents/34016_en.pdf

Civic participation can be direct or indirect and there is a minimalist conception as well as an activist understanding of one's role as a citizen. People can get involved in their communities directly by attending town hall meetings, protesting or demonstrating, participating in non-governmental organizations (NGOs), and so on. They can also get involved indirectly by writing letters to the editors of newspapers or by contributing money to social organizations. Getting involved in these ways can be called **citizen advocacy**. Figures 13-5 and 13-6 show examples of people being involved in their communities through protest. Keep in mind that protest is just one way in which citizens can become involved in their communities.

In one study of citizenship, the following understandings of citizenship were presented:

- *Liberal/Individualistic—Citizenship is a status. It is a function of the political realm to protect and maximise individual interests. Individuals are urged to take up their civic responsibilities rather than to rely on governments.*
- *Communitarian—Citizenship is a practice. It arises from a sense of belonging to a community, and wishing to work with others to achieve the common good. An individual's identity is produced through its relations with others—creating a sense of group identity.*
- *Civil republican—Citizenship is a practice. It is concerned with developing an overarching sense of civic identity. It is shaped by a common public culture and a sense of belonging to a particular nation state. In particular it desires to create a reciprocal relationship between the individual and the state. It is sometimes referred to as "civic morality."*

—Julie Nelson and David Kerr, "Active Citizenship: Definitions, Goals, and Practices" (Qualifications and Curriculum Authority/National Foundation for Educational Research, background paper, September 2005). International Review of Curriculum and Assessment Frameworks Internet Archive.
http://www.inca.org.uk/pdf/Active_citizenship_background_paper.pdf

University of New Brunswick Social Studies Education professor Alan Sears, having studied various models of citizenship, notes that there are four elements that all of the models studied have in common:

1. *A sense of membership or identity with some wider community, from the local to the global.*

2. *A set of rights and freedoms, such as freedom of thought or the right to vote.*

3. *A corresponding set of duties or responsibilities, such as an obligation to respect the rights of others or a duty to obey the law.*

4. *A set of virtues and capacities that enable a citizen to effectively engage in and reflect upon questions and concerns of civic interest.*

—Source: Mark Evans and Cecilia Reynolds, "Introduction: Educating for Global Citizenship in a Changing World", pp. 4-5.
http://cide.oise.utoronto.ca/projects/globalcitizenship/intro.pdf

Which of the ideas above reflect your view of citizenship in Canada? What ideologies underlie each of the above understandings? Following your completion of the Voices activity that follows, identify which of these understandings would be most in agreement with the ideas of Alain Renaut cited in Voices.

Figure 13-5 ▶

In 2006, daycare operators protest the federal government's plan for daycare funding on the steps of the Alberta Legislature Building.

◀ **Figure 13-6**

In March 2008, protesters in Montréal demonstrated against alleged police brutality.

Understandings of Citizenship

In the following excerpts, three writers seek to describe and differentiate *citizenship*. What definition best matches your current understanding of your citizenship? Does any definition expand on or challenge your own definition?

In writing about the French ideas of republicanism, Sophie Duchesne notes the following:

Citizenship and national identities are central elements of political systems. They account for the political link, i.e., for the relationship between the citizens as well as between citizens and rulers. Citizenship is often analyzed through the notions of rights and obligations…They also encompass a set of values or moral qualities as well as a series of social roles…

> —**Dr Sophie Duchesne, Coordinator of the European Research Group "European Democracies", Department of Politics and International Relations, University of Oxford.**

In a paper entitled "Is Citizenship Enough?" Antonio N. Álvarez Benavides of the Universidad Complutense de Madrid outlined the important link between civic participation and identity.

…civic participation (obtained through legal equality) creates civic identity…Participation gives rise to civic links between individuals, as well as between them and the community they are participating in. Therefore…we can claim that dynamics of participation generate a type of civic identity that is not based on belonging to any nationality or nation…Civic participation, understood as a basic element of citizenship, creates a sense of belonging (to feel like a member) of a community.

> —**Antonio N. Álvarez Benavides, "Is Citizenship Enough?" (European Conference on Equal Opportunities, Antwerp, Belgium, paper, September 13–15, 2006), p. 4.**
> www.equalisnotenough.org/followup/papers/AntonioAlvarezBenavides.pdf

Reviewing the works of Alain Renaut (a contemporary thinker from France), Peter Berkowitz (a philosopher from Harvard University) suggests that Renaut has solved the dilemma that seems to exist within modern liberalism— finding the right balance between individualism and rights (supporting the supremacy of the individual) and collectivism and responsibilities (providing for the needs of the community). Renaut, according to this article, has redefined liberal democratic citizenship:

…Renaut provides principled means for distinguishing autonomy from individualism.

- *Individualism stands for the independence of the individual, in the sense of the right to be left alone, to be free from the will of the collectivity, to do one's own thing.*

- *Autonomy involves grasping the necessary limits of freedom and imposing them on oneself.*

- *Individualism is accidental, what an individual happens to be doing.*

- *Autonomy is an achievement, what an individual sets out, freely and with his powers, to do.*

- *Individualism is the flight from constraint.*

- *Autonomy is a discipline by which one freely accepts laws and norms, not because one has invented them but because they are reasonable and right…*

- *"Individualism," as Tocqueville argued, is a disease marked by slackness of soul.*

- *Autonomy, like the "individuality" of Mill, is a virtue based on the education of the heart and the mind. [bullets added]*

—Peter Berkowitz, "Liberalism Strikes Back,"
The New Republic December, 15, 1997, p. 37.
http://www.peterberkowitz.com/liberalismstrikesback.htm

Active citizenship cannot be limited to its formal limits. It is as diverse as the persons who get involved and covers everything from loaning [a] neighbour milk to organizing an international sporting event. It depends on an individual's personal obligations.

—Source: Comment from "Taskforce on Active Citizenship consultation meeting, Sept. 24, 2006, Galway, Ireland.
http://www.activecitizen.ie/index.asp?locID=123&docID=-1

… Me to We has sparked a movement. It's a way of thinking and acting at every level, and a global network of social enterprises, options and ideas unlike any other.

Ask yourself: how does your lifestyle truly affect others? How do the ways you vote, shop and think leave a mark on your community, your society, your world? Can the T-shirt on your back reflect your role within this world?

Me to We is about a shift in our thinking. It's about spreading positive messages and letting your voice be heard. It's about stirring your soul from complacency. It's about embracing our shared humanity and thinking globally.

—Source: Me to We, Philosophy.
http://www.metowe.com/aboutus/philosophy/

1. What worldview or ideology might lead a person to view citizenship as involvement in the community?

2. What worldview or ideology might lead a person to view citizenship as embracing a shared humanity?

3. What worldview or ideology might lead a person to say of citizenship, "Our environment requires citizen preferences, not just consumer preferences" (page 441).

4. Using an example of a specific quotation from this Voices feature or from pages 448–451 as the basis for discussion, state what the quotation suggests about the ideal or model citizen.

Multiple Citizenship

Something to Think About: As transportation has advanced, people have become more and more mobile. In greater numbers and with greater frequency, people migrate in search of peace, prosperity, and freedom. One result is a greater likelihood of multiple citizenship in a legal or political context. As noted earlier in the chapter, however, possessing citizenship in more than one country raises questions about the nature of citizenship:

- Can an individual be a citizen of more than one country?
- What should countries expect from citizens?
- What can citizens expect from countries?

An Example: As war raged in Lebanon during the summer of 2006, the Canadian government sent ships to remove people from the war zone. At a cost to Canadian taxpayers of $85 million, around 15 000 Lebanese citizens were hurried aboard Canadian ships and taken to safety. Why would the Canadian government go to such measures to rescue Lebanese citizens? It did so because the Lebanese citizens were also Canadian citizens.

Andrew Coyne wrote the following in the *National Post*:

Here's a statistic guaranteed to set your teeth on edge: Of the 15 000 Lebanese citizens evacuated from Beirut by Canadian Forces…some 7000 are reported to have returned home. Home, as in Lebanon.

…That is, they are dual citizens, beneficiaries of a 1977 change in immigration legislation, and as such, though many have not lived or paid taxes in this country for several years, are entitled to all the protections the Canadian state affords.

Despite the public outrage this aroused at the time, the Harper government wisely decided the middle of a war was not the time to revisit the principle of dual citizenship: They were Canadian citizens, and that was that. But the war being now ended, the government is said to be considering whether to abolish this strangely ambivalent status, to which at least four million foreign-born Canadians, plus an uncounted number of native-born, lay claim.

If so, this would be an event of enormous symbolic importance. Moreover, it would fit this Prime Minister's broader aim, which is nothing less than to recast the meaning of Canadian nationhood—as a moral project, in which we are collectively and individually engaged, rather than a simple dispenser of services; something that lays claims upon us, as much as it confers entitlements. And the very least claim it can make upon us is that we commit ourselves to it, to the exclusion of all others.

Figure 13-7 ▲

Lebanese civilians who lost their homes in Israeli bombing raids share food at a shelter set up in Beirut University.

Hezbollah is an Islamic political and paramilitary organization based in Lebanon. In July 2006, Hezbollah forces fired rockets at Israeli targets and attacked an Israeli patrol of seven soldiers, killing three, wounding two, and capturing two. Israel responded with air, ground, and sea attacks.

1 Why would Canada allow multiple citizenship?

2 How might the idea of a "moral project" change the relationship between the citizen and the state?

3 What view do you hold of citizenship: is it a service relationship or a moral project?

This asks no more of us than that we make a choice. It does not bind us permanently, nor does it impose any barrier to entry. We can be citizens of Lebanon first and then of Canada, or of Canada and then Lebanon. The only thing we can't do is be a citizen of both countries at the same time.

What's wrong with that? Nothing, if your view of nationhood is essentially service-based—just as you can belong to two frequent-flier programs at the same time. But if you incline to a view of the nation as moral project, as a moral order we are in the process of constructing, then a higher degree of commitment is implied.

…But higher purpose is not achieved without reciprocal obligation. If a nation is something we do together, with and for each other, it requires us to make certain commitments to one another: to pay our taxes, to accept decisions that don't go our way, in extremis to lay down our lives for one another—in short, to put each other first. The associations that inspire our fiercest loyalties—our team, say, or our unit—are not those that give things to us, but those that ask things of us. What, if anything, have we asked of ourselves?

—Andrew Coyne, "What you can do for your country: Why dual citizens should be forced to choose." *National Post* September 23, 2006.

Material reprinted with the express permission of:
"The National Post Company", a Canwest Partnership.
http://andrewcoyne.com/columns/2006/09/what-you-can-do-for-your-country.php

Impacts of Worldview and Ideology on Citizenship

Now that you have a better understanding of citizenship, how do you think worldview can affect it? What about ideology? Consider the effect that worldview and ideology can have on

- conceptions of citizenship in a country
- conceptions of rights granted to people
- understandings of responsibilities people have to a country
- benefits a person can expect from a country
- the role a person can play within a society

In fact, worldview and ideology can have an impact on all of these. Let's take a look at some examples of citizens. In each example, how does (or might) the individual describe his or her citizenship? How would you describe each person's citizenship? What worldviews do you see informing their understandings of citizenship? What ideology informs their understanding?

Ngam Cham

My name is Ngam Cham. I am the President of the Cambodian Buddhist Association. I came to Calgary in April 1983. I was a rice farmer back home in Battambang, Cambodia. During the civil war with the Khmer Rouge it was very dangerous in my region.

My wife, my two children, and I escaped overland across the border into Thailand in 1979.

When we arrived in Calgary, the Immigration people found us a house. We found it very cold and different. It took a long time to get comfortable here.

Now I work as a cleaner in downtown office buildings.

I am very proud of the Cambodian Buddhist temple that we have built in Calgary.

Now, we have three monks that we brought from Cambodia to give us spiritual advice and leadership. It is important that our young people have access to their culture, their faith, and their language.

In Canada, we have freedom and it is easier to find a job. We must work very hard, but there is no fighting and there are lots of opportunities for the next generation.

—**Ngam Cham, Seven Stories, www.glenbow.org/sevenstories**

Thomas King's "Borders"

Thomas King was born to a Cherokee father and a mother of Greek and German descent. He grew up in northern California. He has spent much of his adult life in Canada, including Alberta and Ontario, and is both a professor and writer. In King's short story "Borders" the narrator says the following:

When I was twelve, maybe thirteen, my mother announced that we were going to go to Salt Lake City to visit my sister who had left the reserve, moved across the line, and found a job…I was seven or eight when Laetitia left home. She was seventeen. Our father was from Rocky Boy on the American side.

The short story describes attempting to cross "the line."

My mother got a coffee at the convenience store, and we stood around and watched the prairies move in the sunlight. Then we climbed back in the car. My mother straightened the dress across her thighs, leaned against the wheel, and drove all the way to the border in first gear, slowly, as if she were trying to see through a bad storm or riding high on black ice…
"Citizenship?"
"Blackfoot," my mother told him.
"Ma'am?"
"Blackfoot," my mother repeated.
"Canadian?"
"Blackfoot."
It would have been easier if my mother had just said "Canadian" and been done with it, but I could see she wasn't going to do that…

The narrator and mother bounce back and forth between the American border guards and the Canadian border guards, during which the mother identifies herself as "Blackfoot." Unless she identifies herself and her child as "Canadian" or "American," the border guards will not let them pass. Thus, the narrator and mother continue this for two days, sleeping two nights in their car between the border guard offices. On the third morning, after television vans roll up to interview the family and the mother has a talk with a "good-looking guy in a dark blue suit and an orange tie with little ducks on it," they are allowed to cross the line:

"Citizenship?"

"Blackfoot."

The guard rocked back on his heels and jammed his thumbs into his gun belt. "Thank you," he said, his fingers patting the butt of the revolver. "Have a pleasant trip."

—Source: Thomas King, excerpts from "Borders," From *One Good Story, That One*. (HarperCollins, 1993; New Edition, 1999). Copyright © 1993 Dead Dog Café Productions Inc. With permission of the author.

International Protective Accompaniment and Christian Peacemaker Teams

PAUSE AND REFLECT

Christian Peacemakers see themselves as "world citizens and citizens of the Kingdom of God," and therefore as citizens whose citizenship extends beyond national boundaries. How might their worldview and ideology broaden the concept of citizenship?

When political systems are unable to function on behalf of the entire populace, outsiders may be invited to step into the vacuum, performing the critical roles of observing and reporting on the conflict in general, and on human rights in particular. Some international observers take on the added role of attempting to deter human rights violations and thereby provide both symbolic and real protection to those whose rights are under threat...

In the last 20 years, some NGOs have refined a particular aspect of the observer role that is based on interposition principles and is known as "international protective accompaniment." The foremost practitioners of protective accompaniment have been small teams of international observers from Peace Brigades International, Christian Peacemaker Teams, Witness for Peace, and related groups. These largely non-partisan initiatives enter a conflict upon the invitation of a local nonviolent organization that is working to secure human rights and conflict transformation, but that is perceived to be under considerable threat for those activities.

—Source: Coy, Patrick G. "Protective Accompaniment", *Beyond Intractability*, ed. Guy Burgess and Heidi Burgess (Conflict Research Consortium, University of Colorado, Boulder), June 2003.
http://www.beyondintractability.org/essay/protect/

Christian Peacemaker Teams (CPT) is a group that

arose from a call in 1984 for Christians to devote the same discipline and self-sacrifice to nonviolent peacemaking that armies devote to war...

[CPT] emphasizes creative public witness, nonviolent direct action and protection of human rights.

—Source: "About CPT." Christian Peacemaker Teams.
http://www.cpt.org/about_cpt, 2007

CPT participates in actions that place violence-reduction teams—primarily from the United States and Canada—in crisis situations and militarized areas around the world. They do so when invited by local peace and human rights workers and knowingly risk injury and death "in bold attempts to transform lethal conflict through the nonviolent power of God's truth and love." (Source: http://www.cpt.org/about_cpt, 2007) CPT is part of a movement of third-party non-violent intervention groups, some of which are religious and some of which are not.

CPT is often asked why they are anti-United States. CPT's answer is as follows:

We aren't. In fact, most CPTers are from the United States, and wish that the US would consistently live up to the ideals of justice and freedom it proudly proclaims. Sadly, US actions at home and throughout the world have run counter to these ideals, and as responsible world citizens and citizens of the Kingdom of God, we need to confront those roots of violence that grow within the United States. CPTers who are US citizens are uniquely positioned, and have a responsibility, to speak to US decision-makers about the violence that results from US actions.

—Source: "Frequent Questions." Christian Peacemaker Teams.
http://www.cpt.org/about/faq, 2007

Figure 13-8 ▲

Christian Peacemaker Teams (CPT) have acted in Colombia, Palestine, Uganda, Congo, along the United States/Mexico border, and with Indigenous peoples in Canada and the United States. In Iraq, one CPT effort in 2005 ended with a hostage-taking. Of the four-member team, the American CPT member (Tom Fox, shown here) was found shot dead, and the two Canadians and one Briton were rescued in March 2006 by a coalition force including American and British troops.

Explore the Issues

Concept Review

1 a) Identify and define three principles used as the basis for citizenship policies in various countries.

b) For each of the principles identified in 1a, name one country that uses the principle as the basis for its citizenship policy.

c) Identify three ways in which worldview and/or ideology can influence conceptions of citizenship.

Concept Application

2 Consider your own citizenship and use the terminology and concepts you have explored so far in this chapter to examine and describe it. For example,

- On what principles is your citizenship based?
- What role, rights, and responsibilities are associated with your citizenship?
- What understanding of citizenship (liberal/individualistic, communitarian, civil republican) seems to best describe your citizenship?
- What worldview is reflected in this understanding of citizenship?

- What questions does your citizenship raise?
- To what extent does your understanding of citizenship include the concept of **global citizenship** (being a citizen of the world)?

Using your answers to these questions about citizenship to help inform your response, answer the following question: How do personal and collective worldviews and ideology influence your citizenship?

3 In small groups, discuss the issue of multiple citizenship and try to reach a conclusion as to whether Canada should allow multiple citizenship. Why do you think it should or should not?

After the discussion, explore the ideological differences that were expressed in the Investigation. Try to develop a list and description of several different ideologies and how they impact the idea of citizenship. Following your small group discussion, conduct a horseshoe debate on the same topic to see if your ideas are similar to those of your classmates.

Understandings of Rights, Roles, and Responsibilities

> **Question for Inquiry**
>
> • **In what ways do people demonstrate their rights, roles, and responsibilities as citizens?**

History

The idea of human rights has a long history that extends back to 500 BCE in Persia. Some believe that a document called the Cyrus Cylinder outlined rights such as religious freedom and the abolition of slavery. If laws reflect rights, then you can go back even further to the Code of Hammurabi (1780 BCE), which outlined rules regarding the rights of women, children, and enslaved people. Religious documents such as the Bible (Christianity), the Quran (Islam), the Vedas (Hinduism), and the Analects (Confucianism) all address the idea of rights as well as duties and responsibilities. The Magna Carta, issued in England in 1215 CE, and the Manden Charter, issued in Mali, Africa, in 1222 CE, are also examples of documents that outlined rights.

As you discovered in earlier chapters, in more recent times, the European Enlightenment of the 1600s and 1700s spawned an exploration of justice and human rights. You will recall that such philosophers as John Locke, Thomas Hobbes, and Jean-Jacques Rousseau explained their ideas about rights, but even these ideas varied greatly.

Inspired by these philosophies, two major revolutions occurred in the latter part of the 1700s—the American and French revolutions. Each revolution included in its philosophy an idea of individual rights. The American Declaration of Independence and the French Declaration of the Rights of Man and of the Citizen both outline a set of individual rights.

Continuing into the 20th century, documents outlining human rights have been created as a way to encourage their universal recognition. The United Nations Universal Declaration of Human Rights (1948) is one of the most recent attempts to outline the rights to which all people are entitled.

In most documents, the two main types of rights include

- negative human rights—obliging inaction, including liberties that the government may not infringe upon, such as those freedoms found in the Canadian Charter of Rights and Freedoms

Figure 13-9 ▲

Cyrus the Great conquered large areas of the Middle East and is famous for his good government. The Cyrus Cylinder, pictured here, tells his story.

- positive human rights—obliging action, including entitlements that the government is required to provide, such as education or health care

Despite the long history of rights and their place in the political culture of countries and supranational organizations, a common understanding of rights remains contested. Critics point out that our understanding of rights in Canada is based on Western philosophies and values that are not necessarily applicable in other societies. This argument is supported when you look at the differences between more developed and less developed countries.

The Rights, Roles, and Responsibilities of Citizens

In Canada, legal citizenship is made up of several significant elements.

Rights and Responsibilities	
Rights and Freedoms Some rights and freedoms are:	**Responsibilities** Some responsibilities are:
• legal rights • equality rights • mobility rights • Aboriginal peoples' rights • freedom of thought • freedom of speech • freedom of religion • the right to peaceful assembly	• to obey Canada's laws • to express opinions freely while respecting the rights and freedoms of others • to help others in the community • to care for and protect our heritage and environment • to eliminate discrimination

◀ Figure 13-10

—Source: "Rights and responsibilities in Canada." Citizenship and Immigration Canada, March 24, 2005. http://www.cic.gc.ca/english/celebrate/rights-fs.asp.

Review the first two sections of the Canadian Charter of Rights and Freedoms in Get to the Source on the next page. In some ways, section 1 seems to limit activism. To what extent are these limits reasonable? What criteria would you consider appropriate for limiting citizen participation?

Citizens of Canada are guaranteed all the rights outlined in the Charter.

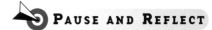

PAUSE AND REFLECT

What evidence is there that the principles of liberalism and collectivism underlie the rights and responsibilities listed in Figure 13-10?

The first two sections of the Canadian Charter of Rights and Freedoms read as follows:

1. *The Canadian Charter of Rights and Freedoms guarantees the rights and freedoms set out in it subject only to such reasonable limits prescribed by law as can be demonstrably justified in a free and democratic society.*

2. *Everyone has the following fundamental freedoms:*

   a) *freedom of conscience and religion;*

   b) *freedom of thought, belief, opinion and expression, including freedom of the press and other media of communication;*

   c) *freedom of peaceful assembly; and*

   d) *freedom of association.*

—**Source: "Canadian Charter of Rights and Freedoms."**
Department of Justice Canada.
http://laws.justice.gc.ca/en/charter/

Some Aboriginal peoples do not regard Canadian citizenship in the same way as other Canadians—as evidenced by the definition of Métis on page 443 and in Thomas King's short story "Borders" on pages 457–458. Indeed, a key right sought by many Aboriginal people is the right finally to define one's own citizenship. In the following, Anishinabek Nation Grand Council Chief John Beaucage challenges one definition of citizenship:

The right to determine our own citizenship is at the heart of our self-government negotiations…The government needs to move beyond limiting our rights and thwarting our Nationhood…We challenge Canada to work with us to achieve the inevitable—a prosperous and sovereign Anishinabek Nation within Canada.

—**John Beaucage, quoted in Tehaliwaskenhas**
(Bob Kennedy), "No More Status Indians? Anishinabek Nation
Grand Council Chief defines citizenship."
Turtle Island Native Network, October 4, 2007.
http://www.turtleisland.org/discussion/viewtopic.php?p=8619

Similarly, in June 2007, Henri Chevillard of Winnipeg noted the following:

We were never given an opportunity to say whether we wanted to be Canadian citizens or not. We were never given the opportunity to enjoy the riches of our lands. We were never given the opportunity to be free! We are still under the Indian Act, without even having a say on our own self-determination.

—**Henri Chevillard, quoted in "Phil Fontaine takes your questions."** *The Globe and Mail*, **June 28, 2007.**
http://www.theglobeandmail.com/servlet/story/RTGAM.20070627.wlive
fontaine0628/BNStory/specialComment/home/?pageRequested=3

An Aboriginal right to determine citizenship would be in sharp contrast to the past. As you read in Chapter 9, the Indian Act defined who could and could not be identified as a registered Indian, and thus defined who could benefit from the rights and freedoms extending from treaties with First Nations people. Status (as a registered Indian under the Indian Act) could be lost in ways that are now considered unfair. For example, before 1960, a status Indian had to give up status to gain the right of a Canadian citizen to vote in a federal election, and, before 1985, a status Indian woman would lose status if she married a non-status husband. The determination of Indian status has been challenged in cases such as the following:

- In the 1970s, the Supreme Court of Canada ruled that Jeannette Corbiere Lavell and Yvonne Bedard were not discriminated against when they lost their status by marrying non-status husbands; according to the ruling, they gained the rights of non-Aboriginal women by marrying, so their loss of Indian status was not discriminatory.
- In 1981, the case of Sandra Lovelace went to the United Nations Human Rights Commission. Lovelace challenged the Canadian law that would have revoked her status as a registered Indian if she married a non-status man, and thus lose, among other benefits, her right to live on reserve lands. The success of that case resulted in the 1985 amendment to the Indian Act to partially address the discrimination.

In essence, the Lovelace case took the issue of rights and citizenship beyond Canada to the arena of global citizenship to determine the rights of First Nations citizenship and Canadian citizenship.

For many Canadians, the right and responsibility of Canadian citizenship that they exercise most often and overtly is the democratic right to vote. For example, voter turnout for the October 2008 federal election was about 59 per cent or 13 832 972 votes cast of the 23 401 064 registered electors.

Other rights that Canadian citizens exercise with regularity are their legal rights, including the right to a fair trial and due process. As you read earlier in the chapter, Canadian citizens are expected to obey the law and they have certain legal rights. Additionally, as you read earlier in this chapter and in other chapters, Canadian citizens sometimes challenge Canadian law and its interpretations.

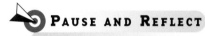 **PAUSE AND REFLECT**

Why would Canada have required a status Indian to give up his or her legal status as a citizen of a First Nation to vote in Canada's federal elections? What worldview is reflected in that law? What ideology is evident?

Figure 13-11 ▶

Mitchell Chernovsky (left) and Faisal Mirza are defence lawyers. Here they talk to reporters outside Ontario Superior Court in Brampton, Ontario, in 2008. The two lawyers were representing a young man charged with taking part in a homegrown terrorist conspiracy. How do defence lawyers demonstrate the rights, roles, and responsibilities of the justice system?

Court challenges such as the Lovelace challenge are not everyday occurrences, but Canadian citizens do demonstrate their rights, roles, and responsibilities in the justice system every day. For example, in 1996–1997, youth courts alone heard 110 065 cases involving 208 594 federal offences. Almost 50 per cent of the cases involved property offences, and 21 per cent were violent offences. (Source: "A Graphical Overview of Crime and the Administration of Justice in Canada, 1997." Statistics Canada, http://www.statcan.ca/english/kits/justic/5-1.pdf.) In a criminal court case, what rights, roles, and responsibilities of citizens can you imagine would be at play? How would these rights, roles, and responsibilities be evident in a minimalist understanding of citizenship? How does that compare with an understanding of citizenship as a "moral project"? What understandings of citizenship do you see evident in the following news story excerpt?

> The BC Court of Appeal has backed BC Supreme Court Chief Justice Don Brenner's decision to kill the Canadian Bar Association's landmark attempt to force governments to provide adequate civil legal aid to poor people...
>
> Susan McGrath, past president of the bar association, said she was saddened because the decision means access to justice will continue being denied to those least able to help themselves.
>
> "We're disappointed we continue to confront procedural hurdles trying to bring this case," the Ontario lawyer said in an interview. "We're going to have to study the ruling and consider our options...We're not giving up the fight."...
>
> "Although the action is intended to assist low-income members of the pubic and its spirit is commendable, I do not consider that the altruistic nature of the action should be afforded much weight until at least the [bar association] has established it can meet the minimal test of disclosing a reasonable claim," Justice Mary Saunders wrote.

Supported by Justice Peter Lowry, she quoted the Supreme Court of Canada saying there is no fundamental right to access to legal services:

"Access to legal services is fundamentally important in any free and democratic society. In some cases, it has been found essential to due process and a fair trial. But a review of the constitutional text, the jurisprudence and the history of the concept does not support the respondent's contention that there is a broad general right to legal counsel as an aspect of, or precondition to, the rule of law."…

—Source: Ian Mulgrew, "Legal aid not a right, court rules."
Vancouver Sun, March 4, 2008.
Material reprinted with the express permission of:
"Vancouver Sun", a CanWest Partnership.
http://www.canada.com/vancouversun/news/story.html?
id=455d6db3-5a42-459d-9173-2f86bf21d25d&k=93890

Another area in which some Canadian citizens manifest a particular understanding of citizenship in times of peace is through **philanthropy** (concern and effort to improve the state of humankind) and volunteerism. By giving money, time, or expertise, citizens act on their worldview and demonstrate an ideology. According to the 2004 Canada Survey of Giving, Volunteering, and Participating (CSGVP),

- *Over 22 million Canadians—85% of the population aged 15 and over—made a financial donation to a charitable or other nonprofit organization in the 12-month period covered by the CSGVP.*
- *Almost 12 million Canadians or 45% of the population aged 15 and older volunteered during the one-year period preceding the survey.*
- *Their contributions totalled almost 2 billion hours, an amount equivalent to 1 million full-time jobs.*
- *Canadians donate money and volunteer time to support the arts, local sports clubs, medical research, food banks, shelters, international relief efforts, and their places of worship, among many other causes. They help their neighbours and friends in a variety of ways, by doing work around their homes, doing shopping or driving people to appointments, or providing health-related or personal care. Canadians also participate in community life by joining a host of organizations and groups. They are active in rural areas, in towns and cities and they reach beyond their communities to support regional, national and global causes.*

—Statistics Canada, "Caring Canadians, Involved Canadians: Highlights from the Canada Survey of Giving, Volunteering and Participating", Catalogue 71-542-X, 2004.
http://www.statcan.gc.ca/bsolc/olc-cel/olc-cel?lang=eng&catno=71-542-X

In recent years, giving in Canada has changed with regards to the people who give and the context in which they give.

PAUSE AND REFLECT

- Recalling the distinctions between individualism and autonomy described by Berkowitz earlier in the chapter, how can individuals' charitable giving be seen as an act of citizenship?

- Since 1999, Ontario high school students have been required to perform 40 hours of community service to graduate from high school. What understanding of citizenship does this demonstrate?

Philanthropy—once a responsibility reserved for the black-tie and ballroom set—is undergoing a significant transformation in Canada…With new techniques and ideas, charities are making their ways into the kitchens and consciousness of Canadians across the economic spectrum. According to Dr. Keith Seel, director of the Institute for Non Profit Studies at Mount Royal College, Canada is just beginning to move beyond a 400-year old philanthropic culture that put the responsibility of charitable spending on the shoulders of the wealthy merchant class.

Significant reductions in government funding starting in the '90s, the consequential proliferation of non-profits, plus society's growing financial and social sophistication have begun to change this traditional model, says Dr. Seel…

In its most familiar guise, philanthropy is represented by the large (sometimes literally and figuratively) cheque that suit- and stiletto-clad donors present a worthy charity at some fine reception. In its less obvious form, it's the sidewalk bake sale the 11-year-old down the street holds one Saturday morning. How and what people give is, in part, a function of the generation they belong to. According to those who have made it their business to understand differences in generational giving, almost anyone who believes in a cause will give to that cause. But where older donors may quietly write cheques made out to the same organization year after year, younger donors are proving to be more fickle, more demanding and more willing to get involved personally…Mary Beth Taylor, director of World Wildlife Fund's planned giving and living planet circle [says,] "We see lots of interest in engagement—more desire to make a commitment. There is an increased interest in having knowledge, they want access to the experts, and they want to see fiscal accountability."

—Source: This article originally appeared in "The Future of Philanthropy"—a special information supplement published in *The Globe and Mail* newspaper on June 26, 2008, produced by RandallAnthony Communications Inc. Reprinted with permission.

To view the full report, please visit: http://www.randallanthony.com/the-future-of-philanthropy

What kind of worldview or ideology is reflected in the actions of citizens who volunteer or contribute financially to various social causes?

Natural Disasters and World Responses

As the *Globe and Mail* article on philanthropy notes, sometimes community participation—in the form of charitable donations and volunteerism—steps in where government service provision leaves off, where a new need develops, or where personal worldviews and ideologies encourage such participation; however, sometimes individuals, organizations, and governments from around the world work together to respond to a global crisis. Such situations can be a challenge to individual and collective understandings of citizenship. A crisis might not only expand the definition of citizen from, for example, "Canadian citizen" to "world citizen" or "global citizen", but may also ask global citizens about their roles and responsibilities to their fellow humans. As you read the following examples of global crises, consider what motivates citizens to choose to act or not to act.

When a powerful tsunami devastated countries along the coasts of the Indian Ocean in December 2004, citizens around the world were motivated to help.

The world response was unprecedented (over 9 billion dollars), yet even this overwhelming support created almost as many problems and issues as it solved. What would the money be spent on? How would goods and services get to the region? What did the victims need?

In Canada, the response was immediate. Over $500 million was donated by the end of January 2005. This figure included money given by government, NGOs, and individual Canadians. It also included the use of support services that were donated to assist in the recovery projects. Canada's DART (Disaster Assistance Response Team) was sent to Sri Lanka with four water purification units. After the disaster, basics such as drinking water were in high demand.

Canada's Doctors Without Borders (*Médecins Sans Frontières*, or MSF) received $2.7 million for tsunami relief, and the worldwide organization collected almost $150 million. MSF needed only $25 million for tsunami relief, so it made the unprecedented announcement that it did not need any more donations for tsunami relief. Instead, MSF asked donors to give their money freely in support of other areas worldwide, which were in need for reasons unrelated to the tsunami. This approach was in sharp contrast to what was happening with other NGOs around the globe.

A UN News Centre reporter interviewed United Nations Emergency Relief Coordinator Jan Egeland in May 2005 and noted the following:

...donations for some other crises had slowed. [Egeland] pointed in particular to low responses to appeals for the Central African Republic, Djibouti and Somalia, which were suffering some of the highest child mortality rates in the world...

Concerned that 90 per cent of the world's attention was focused on 10 per cent of the world's disasters and wars, Egeland noted that five times more money than had been requested for all the forgotten emergencies combined was spent annually in Europe on ice cream, and that an amount equal to the UN's combined humanitarian appeals was spent each year in North America on chewing gum.

—Source: "New UN website to track pledge for tsunami relief." UN News Centre, May 24, 2005. © United Nations, 2005. Reproduced with permission.
http://www.un.org/apps/news/story.asp?NewsID=14371&Cr=tsunami&Cr1=

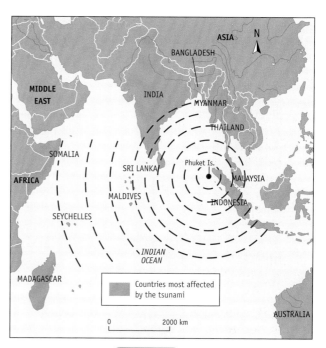

Figure 13-12 ▲

In late December 2004, an underwater earthquake measuring 9.0 on the Richter scale occurred about 160 kilometres west of the Indonesian island of Sumatra. The resulting tidal wave (tsunami) killed over 280 000 people and left over 3 million homeless and destitute.

- **When a disaster of great magnitude occurs, why do you think that individuals, governments, and NGOs can put aside differences and focus on providing aid to those in distress? What can get in the way of such a co-operative response?**

- **How do you think Egeland, the UN's emergency relief coordinator, would define the roles and responsibilities of individual global citizens?**

- **How do you think Berthelsen (quoted in Josh Katz's article here) would define a citizen's rights in relation to government?**

To explore further the Chapter Issue—*To what extent should ideology shape responses to issues in times of peace and times of conflict?*—let's look at some additional crises and responses.

As you read in the Investigation in Chapter 1, when Cyclone Nargis hit Myanmar (Burma) in May 2008, relief workers within Myanmar and foreign relief workers struggled to get information about and access to affected areas. However, internal and international responses were frustrated by the Myanmar government. The United Nations asked the International Charter on Space and Major Disasters for help mapping the crisis for disaster relief workers and the result was that maps created by ENVISAT (the European Space Agency's Earth-monitoring satellite) were used to aid relief workers.

In contrast, in that same month, China's Sichuan province suffered a devastating earthquake and the Chinese government responded with troops, frank communication, a welcome to international relief efforts, and a visit to the area by Chinese premier Wen Jiabao, who saw the impact and met with citizens.

John Berthelsen [writing for the Asia Sentinel*] contrasts Myanmar's response to Cyclone Nargis with China's reaction to the earthquake. "Nothing underscores the criminal nature of the Burmese junta more than the contrast between its neglect of its people and China's immediate reaction to the massive earthquake that devastated large parts of Sichuan province on Monday, killing as many as 10 000 people," he writes. Even the Southeast Asian countries hit by the tsunami in 2006 handled their crises better than Myanmar has dealt with the cyclone, because they allowed the international community help.*

—Source: Josh Katz, "Assessing China's Earthquake Response."
*Finding Dulcinea,***May 14, 2008.**
http://www.findingdulcinea.com/news/Asia-Pacific/May-June-08/
Assessing-China-s-Earthquake-Response.html

Figure 13-13 ▶

According to US Defense Secretary Robert Gates, the Burmese government contributed to thousands of deaths by delaying aid in May 2008. Gates said that "American ships and aircraft were ready to provide help, but Burma rejected it, 'at a cost of tens of thousands of lives.'" However, according to Burmese state radio, the aid from US warships would come with "strings attached" and this was "not acceptable to the people of Myanmar." What understanding of global citizenship does Gates's response reveal? What ideologies are evident? (Source: "Burmese government cost lives by delaying aid, U.S. defense secretary says." CBC News, May 30, 2008, http://www.cbc.ca/world/story/2008/05/30/burma-gates.html)

The Call to War

In this chapter's Investigation feature you read an understanding of citizenship that included the commitment "in extremis to lay down our lives for one another." By engaging in armed conflict, including war, governments go to just such an extreme. In such times of conflict, what are the citizen's rights, roles, and responsibilities? And does that change if he or she does not accept the government's decision or reasons for going to war?

Pacifism, the commitment to peace and opposition to war, is practised in a variety of ways, but one definition is outlined in the following article, which was written in July 2008.

It's become particularly popular to…proclaim non-pacifism: I'm not against all wars—just the dumb ones.

*Well, let me step off the bandwagon and ask the question: What war is **not** dumb? When is it really intelligent to send off huge numbers of people to kill and destroy the homes of huge numbers of other people?*

Every now and then, in rare circumstances, it's necessary to commit violent acts of self-defense. That doesn't make the violence something honorable or otherwise praiseworthy. It just makes it a terrible thing that sometimes has to be done. But when does that violence have to be committed? Almost never.

Yes, I'm a pacifist. That doesn't mean that if flesh-eating Martians invade the Earth and try to eat my children, I won't defend them. It means that even as I defend my kids from the flesh-eating Martians, I won't love the violence, and I won't celebrate it, and I won't continue the violence after it's necessary.

Besides, the flesh-eating Martians are just theoretical. They don't really exist.

A pacifist is someone with the kooky idea that hurting and killing people is a bad thing. …Pacifism is not a popular idea these days, but popularity has been a poor indicator of what makes an idea worth considering.

—J. Clifford, "You Bet I'm a Pacifist." *Irregular Times*, **July 27, 2008.**
http://irregulartimes.com/index.php/archives/2008/07/27/you-bet-im-a-pacifist/

Pacifists include members of many diverse non-religious peace groups and of religious groups that have traditions of opposing war, such as Mennonites; Amish; Brethren; Quakers; the Roman Catholic group *Pax Christi*; the Jewish "Voice for Peace"; the *Shministim* (Israeli high school student conscientious objectors); the Gulen Movement, a pacifist Islamic organization; the Bahai faith (a religion deriving from Islam, with strongly pacifist views); Hindus; Buddhists; and Jains. Pacifists vary in how they interpret and act on their pacifism. Some are pacifist in an absolute sense, rejecting violence of all sorts, while others are specifically anti-war or against a certain war but not all wars. For example, physicist Albert Einstein and philosopher Bertrand Russell both described themselves as pacifists yet believed that the Second World War was necessary.

In times of conflict, a government might call on citizens to participate in the war effort. Citizens opposed to the government's action may declare themselves pacifist and be prepared to accept the consequences, which could include going to jail. As you read further about pacifism, consider what ideology would motivate someone to embrace pacifism.

Despite differences in interpretations of pacifism, as Dennis R. Hoover notes, media coverage in the wake of an event such as 9/11 is often simplistic, treating pacifists as undifferentiated.

Overall it was liberal activist Quakers—best known for their longstanding opposition to US war making—who got the most ink. On September 11 several Quaker organizations put out a "Joint Statement" press release saying, "The Religious Society of Friends, since its inception in the 1650s, has been led to eschew war and all forms of violence for any end whatsoever." Two days later, the 84-year-old American Friends Service Committee spearheaded a "No More Victims" campaign…An ad that ran in the New York Times *and* Washington Post *October 7 read:*

> *"Dear President Bush, We, the undersigned, join the American Friends Service Committee in urging you to look for diplomatic means to bring to justice the people who are responsible for this crime against humanity. Now is the time to break the cycle of violence and retaliation. Do not respond to these terrible acts by waging war. War will lead to additional deaths and the suffering of many people in the US and abroad."*

Quakers were not without their internal debates, however. "We're a peace church," Tom Ryan, a Quaker from State College, Pennsylvania, told the AP's Tina Moore September 26. "But there are some people who are worried whether that's enough, or whether some sort of police action is consistent with our beliefs." Similarly, 24-year old Matt Reilly told the Philadelphia Inquirer's *Lini Kadaba September 24 that he felt war might be justified in these unusual circumstances…*

Kadaba was the only journalist to notice that, in contrast to the largely liberal strand of Quakerism that predominates in the Philadelphia area, the more conservative Evangelical Quakers (located mostly on the West Coast, and who represent something like 30 percent of all US Quakers) do not oppose all forms of violence in all cases. "There may be a need for violent action in order for there to be justice," said Jim LeShana, an Evangelical Quaker pastor from Yorba Linda, California.

The AP's Richard N. Ostling found other religious pacifists feeling similarly conflicted. In an excellent September 28 article on peace church traditions, Ostling quoted Albert Keim, an historian at Eastern Mennonite University in Harrisonburg, Virginia, who admitted, "We pacifists know how to behave in war, but we're still learning how to react to terrorism. We're finding it very, very difficult."…

Arguing that "pacifism" equals appeasement and surrender, [Michael Kelly, in a Washington Post *column] quoted George Orwell, who in the midst of World War II wrote, "Pacifism is objectively pro-Fascist. This is elementary common sense. If you hamper the war effort of one side you automatically help out that of the other." On October 3 Kelly…declared that if "the United States did as the pacifists wish—if it eschewed war even when attacked—it would, at some point, be conquered by a foreign regime."*

Denunciations were delivered by a clutch of anti-pacifist opinion writers, among them Rocky Mountain News *columnist Mike Rosen…Many seemed to have the secular left in mind rather than religious pacifists, but the distinction wasn't often kept clear. "We protect the right of pacifists and other anti-war militants to assemble and advance their cause," wrote Rosen. "But I don't respect such people and I don't shrink from exposing their ideas as destructive and suicidal. Pacifists are my enemy because wittingly or not, they serve the purposes of my enemy and jeopardize my freedom."…*

On its web page, the Mennonite Central Committee posted this modest proposal for responses to September 11: "At a time when emotions are running high and there are no simple answers, perhaps the best role for advocates of nonviolence is to ask good questions."

Source: Dennis R. Hoover, "Religion after 9-11: Pacifism on the Record." *Religion in the News* **(Fall 2001).**
http://www.trincoll.edu/depts/csrpl/RINVol4No3/peace%20churches.htm

In contrast to its policies during the Vietnam War (which we will explore in the next chapter), the United States has not drafted young Americans into the military to serve in Afghanistan and Iraq. However, in case the American government decides it needs additional citizens for military service, it does maintain a registry of young men. Pacifists can apply to be classified as conscientious objectors.

Almost all male US citizens, and male aliens living in the US, who are 18 through 25, are required to register with Selective Service. It's important to know that even though he is registered, a man will not automatically be inducted into the military. In a crisis requiring a draft, men would be called in sequence determined by random lottery number and year of birth. Then, they would be examined for mental, physical and moral fitness by the military before being deferred or exempted from military service or inducted into the Armed Forces…

Men who would be classified as Conscientious Objectors if they were drafted must also register with Selective Service. If a draft begins and they are called, they would have the opportunity to file a claim for exemption from military service based upon their religious or moral objection to war.

—Source: "Who Must Register", United States Selective Service System.
http://www.sss.gov/FSwho.htm, July 23, 2008

 **PAUSE AND REFLECT**

This section provides some perspectives on expressions of pacifism. In what ways do these perspectives demonstrate different understandings of the rights, roles, and responsibilities of citizens during times of conflict?

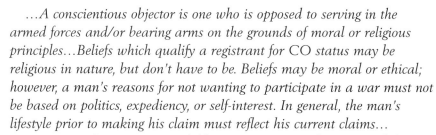

PAUSE AND REFLECT

What understandings of citizenship are expressed by pacifists, those who object to pacifism, governments that require citizens to complete military service, conscientious objectors and war resisters? What rights and responsibilities are at play?

…A conscientious objector is one who is opposed to serving in the armed forces and/or bearing arms on the grounds of moral or religious principles…Beliefs which qualify a registrant for CO status may be religious in nature, but don't have to be. Beliefs may be moral or ethical; however, a man's reasons for not wanting to participate in a war must not be based on politics, expediency, or self-interest. In general, the man's lifestyle prior to making his claim must reflect his current claims…

Two types of service are available to conscientious objectors, and the type assigned is determined by the individual's specific beliefs. The person who is opposed to any form of military service will be assigned to Alternative Service…The person whose beliefs allow him to serve in the military but in a noncombatant capacity will serve in the Armed Forces but will not be assigned training or duties that include using weapons.

…This [Alternative Service] program attempts to match COs with local employers. Many types of jobs are available, however the job must be deemed to make a meaningful contribution to the maintenance of the national health, safety, and interest. Examples of Alternative Service are jobs in:

- *conservation*
- *caring for the very young or very old*
- *education*
- *health care*

Length of service in the program will equal the amount of time a man would have served in the military, usually 24 months.

—**Source: "Conscientious Objection and Alternative Service," United States Selective Service System.**
http://www.sss.gov/FSconsobj.htm, April 30, 2002.

The United Nations supports the right to **conscientious objection** (the refusal on moral or religious grounds) to military service and monitors how conscientious objectors are treated. Some countries, such as Finland, Germany, and Israel, require military service but offer alternative service options.

Figure 13-14 ▲

Since the early days of the war in Iraq in 2003, about 40 "war resisters" have fled to Canada from the United States. American Corey Glass joined the US National Guard "hoping to carry out humanitarian and disaster relief work, but was deployed to Iraq in 2005 as a military intelligence officer north of Baghdad. He told his commanding officer that he couldn't continue fighting in a war he didn't believe in and was sent home for two weeks. But instead of rejoining his unit, Glass deserted." In Canada, he applied for refugee status. However, the Canadian government argued "that Glass and the others did not exhaust legal alternatives in the US and have not made a case that they face persecution should they return home…Those fleeing to Canada now are in a different situation to those who came during the Vietnam war. 'Those coming to Canada now volunteered for military service,' said the citizenship and immigration spokeswoman."…

"'When I joined the National Guard, they told me the only way I would be in combat is if there were troops occupying the United States,' Corey said. 'I signed up to defend people and do humanitarian work filling sandbags if there was a hurricane; I should have been in New Orleans, not Iraq.'" (Sources: Dan Glaister, "US 'war resister' faces key asylum decision in Canada." The Guardian Weekly, June 20, 2008, p. 8, © Guardian News and Media 2008; and "Corey Glass." War Resisters Support Campaign, http://www.resisters.ca/resisters_stories.html#Corey.)

Creating an Action Plan

One way of looking at how ideology can affect your citizenship is to look at the options for action in a particular situation and then to decide what you would choose to do. When governments respond to crises, their responses are rarely supported by every citizen. Some citizens will feel that the government made a poor decision, that the rights of some segment of society have been violated, or that the decision addresses only a special-interest group or agenda. As you read in Chapter 11, in the aftermath of 9/11, the American government decided to limit citizens' freedoms in the interest of safety. The police and other agencies gained more powers to monitor communications and address the issues of terrorism. New restrictions were introduced in public places such as airports. Many people accepted these inconveniences as the price of safety in a free society. Others felt that government was using terrorism as a justification to crack down on segments of society and fulfill an agenda that had little to do with public security.

In a small group of five to six students, choose a crisis situation of global significance currently (or recently) in the news. For example, you could examine

- an environmental disaster, such as an oil spill

- a natural disaster, such as a hurricane that caused flooding or widespread damage

- an escalating conflict between two or more countries

- a medical disaster, such as a famine or pandemic

- a terrorist action, such as a series of bombings

Research facts about the situation from a range of sources, and summarize the facts of the situation. Next, consider the impact of this situation and explore various possible perspectives on it.

Brainstorm with the group possible actions in response to the situation. Flesh out details by considering some basic questions such as What? How? When? Who? and Why? Then, individually, note your choice of action.

As a group, consider the pros and cons of each possible response, who would benefit and who might not, the short- and long-term impact, what worldview and ideology the response is consistent with, what understanding of citizenship the response implies, and possible objections to the response action. Choose an action by consensus. Next, plan the steps of the action.

Present your situation summary, action plan, and explanation to your class. Then, discuss the plans and your initial reactions to them.

Questions to Guide You

1. As Canadians and world citizens, what should be your informed response to the issue?

2. Who is involved? How are they affected? What perspectives and positions do they have (or might they have) on the situation?

3. What rights, responsibilities, and roles does the possible action address? What is the best option—or best possible combination of actions?

4. What worldviews and ideologies are evident in the action plan? What understandings of citizenship are evident?

5. Was your individual choice of action changed by considering and critically evaluating options in a group? Why or why not?

6. What is the impact of evaluating options from several different perspectives?

Explore the Issues

Concept Review

1. a) List at least 10 of the rights, roles, or responsibilities of Canadian citizens that were discussed in this section.
   b) For three of the rights, roles, and responsibilities you identified in 1a, outline two differing perspectives on each term.

Concept Application

2. American president John F. Kennedy famously said, "And so, my fellow Americans, ask not what your country can do for you; ask what you can do for your country." What is less well known is that Kennedy followed that sentence with "My fellow citizens of the world, ask not what America will do for you, but what together we can do for the freedom of man." What definitions of *citizenship* are implicit in the two statements? In what ways would a citizen, as Kennedy defined one, act?

3. In a small group, contact an NGO in your community and investigate the organization's beliefs about democratic responsibilities. Contact your local Member of the Legislative Assembly or Member of Parliament to determine his or her beliefs. Develop a list of questions to ask both of your contacts. Present your research in a visual form to compare and contrast the results.

4. In a small group, discuss the idea that citizens are made, not born. Consider the following topics:

   - What are understandings of citizenship in Canada?
   - To what extent should understandings of global citizenship inform your understanding of citizenship in Canada?
   - What institutions promote certain understandings of citizenship?
   - How do the institutions promote these understandings?
   - What ideology is most commonly reflected in their actions?
   - Do you agree or disagree with the ideology that is promoted?

   Use this information to develop a policy statement expressing your conception of Canadian citizenship for a new political party. Present this statement to the class.

5. Research an understanding of citizenship from a citizen or group of citizens in a country or community in Africa, Latin America, or Asia. In what ways does this person demonstrate his or her rights, roles, and responsibilities as a citizen? To what extent does his or her understanding of citizenship appear to be influenced by ideology?

Reflect and Analyze

In this chapter you have read about how citizenship is identified by nation-states, how it might be understood by individuals and groups, and various ways in which citizenship is demonstrated through rights, roles, and responsibilities—in times of peace and in times of conflict. Throughout, you have reflected on the worldviews and ideologies evident in various understandings or expressions of citizenship. These considerations have helped you address the Chapter Issue: *To what extent should ideology shape responses to issues in times of peace and times of conflict?* In so doing, these considerations have helped you focus on the relationships among worldview, ideology, citizenship, and action—relationships that you will continue to explore in the next chapter.

Respond to Ideas

1 Of the citizenship models presented in this chapter, which most closely resembles your own worldview, ideology, and understanding of citizenship? Which most challenges you? Why? Write a journal entry reflecting on this.

Respond to Issues

2 Consider the statement "almost anyone who believes in a cause will give to that cause" and list possible causes to which you could give time or money. Identify what issue or cause would (or does) motivate you to action. Finally, write a personal response to the Chapter Issue: *To what extent should ideology shape responses to issues in times of peace and times of conflict?*

Recognize Relationships among Concepts, Issues, and Citizenship

3 In Canada, you are exposed to a range of ideologies. Political ideologies range from conservative to socialist within a democratic structure. Religions promote ideologies, and the laws of the land also express an ideology. The issue for Part 4 of this text is *To what extent should my actions as a citizen be shaped by an ideology?* Consider your role as a citizen of this country. Evaluate the extent to which ideology and worldview shape your responses to issues and influence your citizenship. Cite examples from the chapter, research, and your own experiences that relate to issues of citizenship and nationality and the rights, roles, and responsibilities of citizens. For example, you could use evidence from the "Borders" excerpt (pages 457–458) to help you support your position. During your analysis of the issue, address the question: "To what extent should liberalism and/or other ideologies shape your individual and collective citizenship?"

a) Create a graphic organizer that illustrates what you believe are the most important issues in Canada or the world today, and which ideology or ideologies you believe would best respond to these issues.

b) Consider if you embrace an ideology (or ideologies—you may have more than one). How does embracing or not embracing an ideology (or ideologies) help you respond to the world around you? Draw a picture that shows how your choice to embrace or not embrace an ideology responds to social issues in society.

Reflecting on Ideology, Action, and Citizenship

KEY SKILLS

Demonstrating leadership by engaging in acts of citizenship

KEY CONCEPTS

Evaluating the extent to which ideology should shape responses to contemporary issues

Exploring opportunities to demonstrate active and responsible citizenship through individual and collective action

Developing strategies to address local, national or global issues that demonstrate individual and collective leadership

Key Terms

Anti-war movements

Civility

Pro-democracy movements

Figure 14-1 ▲

In late 2004, the world watched as the citizens of Ukraine led their country in a **pro-democracy movement**. Members of the crowd wore something orange, the campaign colour of the political candidate Viktor Yushchenko.

Orange Crush

The crowd chanted, *"Razom nas bahato! Nas ne podolaty!"* ("Together, we are many! We cannot be defeated!"). The words filled Kiev's Independence Square on the evening of November 22, 2004.

> *Emerging from a sea of orange, the mantra signaled the rise of a powerful civic movement, a skilled political opposition group, and a determined middle class that had come together to stop the ruling elite from falsifying an election and hijacking Ukraine's presidency.*

> **—Source: Adrian Karatnycky, "Ukraine's Orange Revolution."** *Foreign Affairs* **(March/April, 2005).**
> http://www.foreignaffairs.org/20050301faessay84205/
> adrian-karatnycky/ukraine-s-orange-revolution.html

November 22, 2004, was the beginning of a spontaneous, massive protest, called the Orange Revolution, against the results of the Ukraine presidential election on November 21. The declared winner, Viktor Yanukovych, had been hand-picked by the outgoing president, Leonid Kuchma, an anti-democratic and pro-Russian politician.

Yanukovych's opponent, Viktor Yushchenko, was pro-democratic, pro-Western, and the favoured candidate of the middle class.

The Yanukovych campaign was accused of **election fraud** that included voter intimidation, multiple voting in areas favouring Yanukovych, and the burning of ballot boxes in areas with strong Yushchenko support. There was even a report that the pens for ballot-marking had been filled with disappearing ink in some areas of strong Yushchenko support so that ballots would be blank when counted. During the campaign, Yushchenko was poisoned with dioxin and almost died. Evidence suggested that pro-Kuchma operatives had poisoned Yushchenko in an effort to remove him from the presidential race.

Yushchenko publicly declared himself president on November 22 and issued a call for people around the country to come to the capital to demand a re-election. Hundreds of thousands of people descended on central Kiev that day to peacefully state their objections to the election. For 17 days, thousands of protesters stood their ground, demanding that a new election be held. The world watched these events unfold. The Yanukovych government sat back, hoping the opposition would go away, but it did not. On November 27, Parliament declared the election invalid and six days later the Supreme Court pronounced the election null and void.

A new election was held on December 26, 2004. Over 12 000 election monitors from around the world travelled to Ukraine to watch the voting process closely. Canada showed its support for the process by appointing former prime minister John Turner to oversee a group of 500 Canadian volunteer monitors. This time the results gave Yushchenko the win. A peaceful protest by a large number of citizens was enough to change the course of Ukraine's history.

How was it that ordinary citizens could cause the reversal of an election? What prompted them to take action? Several conditions helped make this protest successful.

Ukraine had benefited from more than a decade of civil-society development, a good deal of it nurtured by donor support from the United States, European governments, the National Endowment for Democracy, and private philanthropists such as George Soros. Although such sponsorship was nonpartisan, it reinforced democratic values and deepened the public's understanding of free and fair electoral procedures...

Another factor that promoted a dynamic civic sector was increasing awareness of the ruling elite's corruption. The country's emerging Internet news sites...were an integral part of this process. By November 2004, Ukraine, with a population of 48 million people, boasted some 6 million distinct users accessing the Internet.

—Source: Adrian Karatnycky, "Ukraine's Orange Revolution." *Foreign Affairs* **(March/April, 2005).**
http://www.foreignaffairs.org/20050301faessay84205/
adrian-karatnycky/ukraine-s-orange-revolution.html

Figure 14-2

On September 5, 2004, after a dinner with the chief and deputy chief of the Ukrainian Security Service, Viktor Yushchenko (shown here in July 2004 and in December 2004) became ill. His symptoms and a blood test indicated that he had been poisoned with tetrachlorodibenzoparadioxin (TCDD), a key ingredient of Agent Orange, a herbicide used in the Vietnam War.

Following the Orange Revolution, citizens in the Ukraine are still fighting to see the promised reforms realized in their society.

Since 2004, Ukraine has been confronted with recurrent internal political turmoil and parliamentary gridlock which have tarnished its image as a reforming country and the prospects of deepening relations with the enlarged [European] Union…The 2004 Orange Revolution failed to deliver domestically. The years since then have been marked by political infighting, personal rivalries among its political elite and government incompetence. As a result, Ukraine has stumbled from crisis to crisis…The newly-elected [2007] government of Our Ukraine (OU) and the Yulia Tymoshenko Bloc (BYuT) offers a second chance for the Orange forces to deliver on the promises they made [to the citizens] in 2004…

—Source: Amanda Akçakoca and Richard Whitman,
"Ukraine and the EU after the elections: more of the same?",
European Policy Centre, December 2007.
http://www.epc.eu/TEWN/pdf/444589015_Ukraine%20and%20the%20EU.pdf

PAUSE AND REFLECT

To what extent do you believe liberal democratic ideology shaped citizens' actions, the government's actions, or both in the Ukraine during the Orange Revolution?

Chapter Issue

When you began this course you were introduced to the concept of ideology. You were encouraged to explore how your identity, beliefs, and values may attract you toward one ideology and repel you from others. Throughout the course you explored several ideologies and liberalism in particular—its origins, guiding principles, various forms, opponents, and complexities. In Chapter 13 you focused on understandings of citizenship and how citizenship in a liberal democratic society is more than the guarantee of certain rights: citizenship also asks citizens to consider their responsibilities and actions, and to what extent their identity and beliefs and values play a role in their actions.

In this final chapter you will reflect on the relationship between ideology and your responsibilities and actions as a citizen. You will consider the following Chapter Issue:

To what extent should an ideology shape your thinking and actions as a citizen?

Figure 14-3 ▼

Chapter Issue:
To what extent should an ideology shape your thinking and actions as a citizen?

Question for Inquiry #1:
To what extent do citizens have a right, role, or responsibility to take action?

Question for Inquiry #2:
How do your ideology and your citizenship affect how you demonstrate leadership in responding to local, national, and global issues?

Responding to Issues

- **To what extent do citizens have a right, role, or responsibility to take action?**

As you read through this first section of the chapter, bear the Orange Revolution in mind and decide for yourself to what extent you are able to fulfill your obligations to yourself, your country, the citizens of the world, and the planet. Do your responses to environmental, social, economic, or political issues confirm your chosen ideologies, or do they cause you to reconsider or adjust the ideologies you have chosen to embrace? Reading about the responses of others to issues they have confronted will help you consider and evaluate your own responses.

The Anti-Apartheid Movement in South Africa

For over 300 years, the interaction of Africans (black) and European settlers (white) created a legacy of violence, distrust, and hate in South Africa, reflected in **apartheid**, a strict, legislated system of racial segregation and discrimination against Black South Africans set in place by the National Party of South Africa from 1948 to 1994.

Apartheid consisted of numerous laws that allowed the ruling white minority in South Africa to segregate, exploit and terrorize the vast majority: Africans, mostly, but also Asians and Coloureds—people of mixed race. In white-ruled South Africa, black people were denied basic human rights and political rights. Their labour was exploited, their lives segregated.

Under Apartheid, racist beliefs were enshrined in law and any criticism of the law was suppressed. Apartheid was racism made law. It was a system dictated in the minutest detail as to how and where the large black majority would live, work and die. This system of institutionalized racial discrimination defied the principles of the United Nations Charter and the Universal Declaration of Human Rights. [emphasis added]

—Source: "Human Rights: Historical images of Apartheid in South Africa," © United Nations. Reproduced with permission.
http://www.un.org/av/photo/subjects/apartheid.htm

The struggle of black South Africans to end apartheid was led by a number of organizations, which viewed themselves as **liberation movements**. One of these organizations was the African National Congress (ANC).

Figure 14-4 ▼

Disproportionate treatment in South Africa, circa 1978.

Apartheid and the People of South Africa	Blacks	Whites
Population	19 million	4.5 million
Land allocation	13%	87%
Share of national income	< 20%	75%
Ratio of average earnings	1	14
Doctors/population	1/44 000	1/400
Infant mortality rate	20% (urban) 40% (rural)	2.7%
Annual expenditure on education per pupil	US$ 45	US$ 696
Teacher/pupil ratio	1/60	1/22

Source: Richard Leonard, *Computers in South Africa: A Survey of US Companies* (New York: Africa Fund, November 1978).

Figure 14-5 ▲

These young men are watching a soccer game at an all-white school in Johannesburg during the apartheid era. Spending per child in schools for black South Africans was less than one-tenth that for white South Africans. If black South African children had any schooling at all, it was often in overcrowded classrooms that were led by poorly trained teachers.

PAUSE AND REFLECT

Under apartheid, all black South Africans were required to carry identification papers at all times that detailed where they lived and worked. The only way that a black South African could travel outside his or her community was with a special pass, which was required by the Pass Laws. How does this compare with your right to mobility in Canada?

One of the ANC leaders, Nelson Mandela, began his career as a lawyer. He rose to prominence and eventually became the president of the organization. Initially attempting to use the law and **civil disobedience** to protect black Africans, the ANC eventually resorted to acts of violence in retaliation for similar acts by the South African government.

Another African liberation organization was the Pan-Africanist Congress (PAC), which had split from the ANC. The schism occurred because the ANC did not focus specifically on blacks, but also worked to improve the situation of the other non-white groups discriminated against in South Africa. Led by Robert Sobukwe, the PAC focused exclusively on black power.

Following the principles of **civility** and non-violence, the resistance movement's tactics of protest were sit-ins, boycotts, and strikes, and the tactic used by the South African government was repression. Dissidents were arrested, tortured, and jailed. A defining moment in the struggle against apartheid occurred on March 21, 1960. Prior to this, the PAC had encouraged large groups to stand peacefully outside local police stations to demand to be arrested for not having official passes with them. It was impossible to arrest thousands of people, and the government ignored these protests. For March 21, however, the PAC announced that it would conduct a mass non-violent protest of the Pass Laws by holding a national strike.

On March 21, numerous groups of Africans surrounded police stations as part of the nation-wide protest. The South African government was determined to disperse the crowds using military flyovers, tear gas, and riot police. In the township of Sharpeville, some 5000 to 7000 people had gathered by 10:00 AM in a peaceful demonstration. The crowd did not disperse in spite of the government measures, and a standoff developed. Finally, a shot was fired and then many more. At first, the protesters thought a vehicle had backfired, but then people began to fall. Almost immediately, people began to run. First-person accounts tell stories of police officers on the roofs of vans spraying wide arcs of machine-gun fire directly into the panicked crowd. By the time the shooting ended, 69 people were dead and nearly 200 were wounded—men, women, and children. Most had been shot in the back as they ran.

The government of South Africa claimed that the gathered people were becoming aggressive and throwing rocks. Within days, the government passed new laws. The ANC and PAC were outlawed, and their leaders were sought and imprisoned. A state of emergency was declared and thousands of black South Africans were arrested. In response to international protests, South Africa withdrew from the Commonwealth and declared itself a republic.

Both the ANC and PAC eventually turned to more extreme actions, including attacks on government buildings, bombings, and

Non-Violence

Non-violence as a philosophy and strategy has been practised by such leaders as Mahatma Gandhi (in British colonial India's struggle for independence), Martin Luther King Jr (in the American civil rights movement), and César Chavez (in the struggle for farm workers' rights in California). Non-violence is not passive acceptance of oppression; instead, it can include civil disobedience, media campaigns, and targeted direct (non-violent) action. As Chavez noted,

Non-violence is not inaction. It is not discussion. It is not for the timid or weak... Non-violence is hard work. It is the willingness to sacrifice. It is the patience to win.

—César Chavez, quoted in "Applying the Principles of Nonviolence in Our Lives." Carry the Vision.
http://www.carrythevision.org/CTV-NV-final.pdf

Just before the 1960 campaign to protest the Pass Laws in South Africa, PAC leader, Robert Sobukwe spoke to other PAC leaders, imploring them to follow the practice of non-violence.

My instructions, therefore, are that our people must be taught now and continuously that in this campaign we are going to observe absolute non-violence.

—Robert Sobukwe, quoted in David M. Sibeko, "The Sharpeville Massacre: Its historic significance in the struggle against apartheid." African National Congress.
http://www.anc.org.za/ancdocs/history/misc/sharplle.html

Why did Sobukwe originally insist on non-violence? Do citizens ever have a right to resort to violence against their civil authorities?

other terrorist tactics. While the struggle against apartheid continued within South Africa, it continued in world opinion as well. Countries began to impose sanctions and embargos on South Africa. Trade was reduced. Banks refused loans to the country, South Africa was barred from participation in the Olympics from 1964 onward, and South Africa became isolated from the world. By the late 1980s, it became obvious to the white rulers of the republic that apartheid was indefensible, and successive South African governments began the slow reduction of the policies of apartheid.

Mandela became a symbol of the fight to end apartheid and his cause was taken up around the world. After months on the run, Mandela was arrested in 1962 and sentenced to five years' hard labour for inciting a workers' strike and leaving the country illegally. In 1964, he was tried along with other ANC leaders for "plotting to overthrow the government with violence." In April 1964, Nelson Mandela made a statement in his own defence at his trial, in which he said:

During my lifetime I have dedicated myself to the struggle of the African people. I have fought against white domination, and I have fought against black domination. I have cherished the ideal of a democratic and free society in which all persons live together in harmony and with equal opportunities. It is an ideal which I hope to live for and to achieve. But if needs be, it is an ideal for which I am prepared to die.

—**Nelson Mandela, "I Am Prepared to Die" (statement at the Rivonia Trial, April 20, 1964). African National Congress.**

http://www.anc.org.za/ancdocs/history/mandela/1960s/rivonia.html

As apartheid declined, so did the government's resolve to keep Mandela imprisoned. On February 11, 1990, he was freed from prison. That same year the ANC was once again free to exist in South Africa. Mandela continued the struggle to abolish apartheid. In 1994, the first free interracial election occurred in South Africa. The ANC won the election, and Mandela became the first black president of South Africa. Apartheid was now a thing of the past.

Taking Action: Post-Apartheid South Africa

After apartheid was abolished in South Africa, the Truth and Reconciliation Commission (TRC) was created to address the country's racist past, including the discriminatory policies of the government. It was hoped that by establishing such a commission, the victims of apartheid would come forward to describe their personal experiences. In many respects, the TRC has been viewed as the process that helped South Africa take the last steps toward democracy.

The aim of the commission and its chairman, Archbishop Desmond Tutu, was to promote reconciliation in South Africa's divided society through truth about its dark past.

One of the Truth commissioners, Dr Faizal Randera said: "If we cannot understand what made people think and do what they did these conflicts will arise again within our society."

In the turbulent final decade of South Africa's last white government, few sections of society were left untouched by violence...

"I and many other leading figures in our party have already publicly apologised for the pain and suffering caused by former policies of the National Party. I reiterate these apologies,"[Former President F.W. de Klerk] told the commission...

It has been an unprecedented experiment in trying to heal the wounds of the apartheid era, but after more than two years of hearings and investigations some people are asking how much reconciliation has been achieved by exposure of dark truth from South Africa's dark past...

Figure 14-6 ▲

After his conviction, Nelson Mandela (centre) was sentenced to life in prison and was imprisoned from 1962 to 1990. In 1993, the Nobel Peace Prize was awarded jointly to Nelson Mandela and F.W. de Klerk (the leader of South Africa's National Party and the country's president at the time) for "their work for the peaceful termination of the apartheid regime, and for laying the foundations for a new democratic South Africa." The Nobel committee noted, "From their different points of departure, Mandela and de Klerk have reached agreement on the principles for a transition to a new political order based on the tenet of one man-one vote. By looking ahead to South African reconciliation instead of back at the deep wounds of the past, they have shown personal integrity and great political courage." (Source: "The Nobel Peace Prize 1993," October 15, 1993. Nobelprize.org, http://nobelprize.org/nobel_prizes/peace/laureates/1993/press.html.)

The trauma of the past

Much of the criticism of the commission stems from a basic misunderstanding about its mandate.

It was never meant to punish people, just to expose their role in crimes committed under apartheid.

It is in this respect that the achievements of the Truth and Reconciliation Commission stand out.

Only by revisiting the trauma of the past can people look to a better future—but with the truth comes pain and a reminder that reconciliation may still be a distant goal in the new South Africa.

—"South Africans reconciled?", BBC News, October 30, 1998.

http://news.bbc.co.uk/1/hi/special_report/1998/10/98/
truth_and_reconciliation/142673.stm

Voices

Destiny's Children: "Born Free" in South Africa

JOHANNESBURG, SOUTH AFRICA—At 23, Joy Methula is too young to fully remember the dark days of apartheid. Too young to remember her mother risking her life to demonstrate against oppression. Too young to recall her elder brother's treason trial and two-year prison stint for organizing student protests. "To me," she says with a shrug, "they sound like folk tales."

Methula is a "born free," part of the generation of 17 million post-liberation blacks who came of age after Nelson Mandela's release from prison in 1990 and inherited a free, though deeply troubled South Africa. Theirs is a South Africa where 1 in 10 blacks is malnourished, 1 in 4 black children are stunted, and 1 of every 2 blacks lives below the poverty line. Despite such statistics, theirs is also a nation where, for the first time, large numbers of young blacks are getting a good education, finding a good job, and joining the middle and upper classes.

Their journey from shantytowns, mud hovels, and modest brick homes to the suburbs demonstrates how far this country has come toward egalitarianism and nonracialism in a remarkably short time—and how much remains to be done. Their challenges arise from a legacy of 300 years of colonialism and four decades of apartheid that will continue to plague this nation for generations to come. And their aspirations show how young South Africans are breaking with past traditions and cultural norms to remake their country...

Young blacks, however, are looking forward. To them, the political struggle that so consumed their elder siblings and parents is ancient history. Now, they believe, is the time to enjoy the fruits of their elders' struggle...

Though her brother and mother risked their lives to win the right to vote, Methula, like many young people, doesn't plan to cast her ballot in this *week's contests for the national Parliament—only the third time South Africa has held democratic, nonracial elections. Just half of 18- to 25-year-olds are registered to vote, a significantly lower rate than that of any other age group…Now, the preoccupation is with making money: More than 90 percent of youth think money makes people happy, the same survey shows. In the new South Africa, people are judged not by the color of their skin, many of these young people say, but by how much is in their wallets…*

While many lament the growth of consumerism and conspicuous consumption, it is in some ways a measure of the success of South Africa's transition. Black graduates are now receiving more than half of all university diplomas each year. In 1991, they received fewer than one quarter of the diplomas…The black middle class, once almost nonexistent, is now bigger than the white middle class.

Luceth Nzima, 22, a first-year student at the University of the Witwatersrand, plans to become a chartered accountant. One of apartheid's legacies is that only 337 of South Africa's 20 000 accountants are black…Maxwell Nqeno, a classmate of Nzima's, returns each night after class to his parents' home in an abandoned building in a squatter camp. He studies by candlelight, fetches water from a nearby communal tap to wash each morning, and uses public toilets.

The government is trying to bridge these two worlds: the rich, western world previously reserved for whites and the traditional, poor world where the vast majority of blacks remain trapped…People like Nzima, who have come into adulthood in the past decade, are acutely aware of the challenges that remain. Their materialism is not without conscience. They dream of mansions and fast cars but also of community centers and clinics for those left behind. "A lot of people died for us so that I can have better opportunities," says Nzima…

—Source: Rena Singer, "Destiny's Children: 10 Years After The End Of Apartheid", US News and World Report, April 11, 2004.
© 2004 U.S. News & World Report, L.P. Reprinted with permission.
http://www.usnews.com/usnews/culture/articles/040419/19apartheid.htm

Consider the different young people identified in this feature as you answer these questions.

1 What would you identify as the most important legacies of the apartheid era in South Africa today? In what ways is an ideology a part of the causes and effects of these legacies?

2 To what extent do citizens in South Africa have the right, role, or responsibility to take action in response to these legacies? What beliefs and values may most strongly motivate their actions? In what ways can a citizen's generation have an impact on his or her beliefs and values and actions?

3 In what ways has apartheid had an impact on the beliefs and values of Black South Africans? White South Africans?

The War against the Vietnam War

Just as the fight to end apartheid in South Africa lasted decades, so did the war in Vietnam. After the Second World War, the former colonial power in southeast Asia, France, was allowed to return to the country. Many Vietnamese, however, wanted control of their own country and so they fought the French army. By 1954, the French were defeated. According to the Geneva Accords of 1954, Vietnam was to be independent, and it was temporarily divided into two zones, North and South Vietnam, in preparation for an election that was to be held in 1956. In the frenzy of the Cold War, the election never happened. The northern part of the country was supported by communist countries, including the USSR and China, while the south was supported by Western powers led by the United States. As you read in Chapter 7, this American support was part of the larger US policy of containment, which was practised in the Cold War in an effort to "contain" or limit the spread of communism.

The United States first sent military advisors to Vietnam in 1950. By 1961, the United States was beginning to bring American troops to South Vietnam to defend the Saigon government from attacks from within the country and from North Vietnam. By 1963, however, the mission (containment of communism in Vietnam) was looking less and less viable. Some leaders in the United States were looking for ways to get out. Arthur Schlesinger recalls in his book *Robert Kennedy and His Times* that American president John F. Kennedy asked Canadian prime minister Lester B. Pearson (1957 Nobel Peace Prize winner for diplomacy) for advice about Vietnam. "Get out," is what Pearson replied. Kennedy apparently responded, "That's a stupid answer. Everyone knows that. The question is: How do we get out?" (Source: Arthur M. Schlesinger, Jr, *Robert Kennedy and His Times* (New York: Ballantine, 1978), p. 767.)

When American vice-president Lyndon B. Johnson took over as president after John F. Kennedy was assassinated on November 22, 1963, Johnson seemed initially more concerned with domestic policy than foreign policy. Johnson sought election as president in 1964 and won in a landslide victory. He is credited with a strong domestic policy, which he called "The Great Society." This included civil rights legislation, the "war on poverty," and health care for people living in poverty and those who were elderly. The US involvement in Vietnam, however, soon took on tremendous importance for Johnson and millions of other Americans. During his leadership, as the American casualties in southeast Asia increased, protests against American involvement grew and protesters would often taunt the president over how many young men had died in the war that day. Johnson announced in March 1968 that he would not seek re-election and withdrew from public service. Richard Nixon was elected president in the next election.

Figure 14-7 ▲

Estimates vary for the numbers who died in the Vietnam conflict, but they include: 58 159 American soldiers, 3–4 million Vietnamese (both sides), and 1.5–2 million people from the border states of Laos and Cambodia.

What happened in the United States over the course of its involvement in Vietnam is enlightening not only in terms of the actions of political leaders, but also in terms of the kinds of actions ordinary citizens can take to effect change in society.

An **anti-war movement** began slowly. When the American phase of the war began in the late 1950s and early 1960s, the anti-war movement existed largely among academics at universities. American involvement at that time was very limited. As the 1960s progressed, however, the number of American soldiers in the conflict increased until, by the end of 1968, there were over 500 000 US troops engaged in the war. The troops were overwhelmingly young (often reported as having an average age of 19, but this has been disputed; the average age of a US solider who died in the conflict was 22.8 years of age) and a one-year tour of duty was required. This short tour of duty meant that few of the combatants gained experience, their basic training was brief, and they often served under inexperienced leadership. Many of these American combatants were not volunteers; they had been drafted into service through the American registry for selected service (you read about the **draft** in Chapter 13).

Some young men joined the National Guard or the Peace Corps rather than serve in Vietnam. Others were exempt because they were married or for "physical, mental, or moral grounds." Some young men asked for deferments for college or university education. Others fled the United States as **draft dodgers** to countries such as Sweden and Canada. All told, low-income Americans and African-Americans were disproportionately represented among draftees. By the late 1960s, the anti-war movement was in full force, and the times were characterized by unprecedented student activism and political engagement of young people, and a popular culture that encouraged both free expression and questioning authority.

Free expression and questioning authority had a particularly strong impact during a time of war. In any war, there will be mistakes. There may also be aggressive overreactions and atrocities. Until the advent of modern communications, these events were usually revealed only after the war was over in books and the occasional magazine or documentary. In the 1960s and 1970s, however, reporters and photographers had relatively few restrictions on what they filmed and reported in Vietnam. In turn, most Americans routinely watched the evening news—which was both relatively new as an information source and less varied than it is today, since most people had access to only three television channels. Many Americans also read newsmagazines such as *Life, Look, Time,* and *Newsweek,* which had powerful photography and reports on the war. The news of Vietnam was a shared, almost unavoidable, and disturbing experience for Americans. Some of the images that Americans saw—of American soldiers, Vietnamese combatants, and civilians in the region—

quickly became iconic and are credited with shaping public opinion against the war. At the same time, popular music and movies were delivering a steady stream of arguments to support the position that the war was not a "**just war.**"

Throughout the war, television news and newsmagazines focused on the stories of young American soldiers. According to Daniel C. Hallin, professor of communications at the University of California, Los Angeles, in the early years of television news from Vietnam

...the emphasis was on the visual and above all the personal: "American boys in action" was the story, and reports emphasized their bravery and their skill in handling the technology of war...In the early years, when morale was strong, television reflected the upbeat tone of the troops.

However, as the war continued and casualties grew in number, and

...as withdrawals continued and morale declined, the tone of field reporting changed. This shift was paralleled by developments on the "home front." Here, divisions over the war received increasing air time, and the anti-war movement, which had been vilified as Communist-inspired in the early years, was more often accepted as a legitimate political movement.

—Source: Daniel Hallin, "Vietnam on Television."
Museum of Broadcast Communications.
http://www.museum.tv/archives/etv/V/htmlV/vietnamonte/vietnamonte.htm

No one was used to viewing the realities of war so immediately and in such an unfiltered way. No one could ignore the sacrifice that young men were making for a questionable exercise. Additionally, the scope of the draft brought the seriousness and the inescapability of the war right to the main streets of every town in America. Over time, almost 3 million Americans served in the Vietnam conflict. Everyone knew someone who had served.

Support for the war was widespread in the early years, but it waned, especially after 1968. Opposition in the United States and around the world to the war in Vietnam was loud and varied. The following are some of the many individual voices and actions in protest. As you read them, consider how the individuals involved demonstrate their ideologies.

Among the student groups and anti-war protesters, perhaps the Students for Democratic Society (SDS) was the best known. SDS became famous for the slogans "Make Love, Not War" and "Burn the card, not people," which encouraged young men to burn their draft cards. In April 1965, Paul Potter, president of SDS, gave the following speech in front of the Washington Monument before a crowd of 25 000 anti-war protesters.

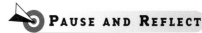

PAUSE AND REFLECT

If ordinary citizens have an increased knowledge of a war, how might that affect their right, role, or responsibility to act on that knowledge?

Figure 14-8

In this *Life* magazine photo taken in 1966, American medic Thomas Cole tends to fellow American soldiers despite his own injury. The Vietnamese-born, French photographer Henri Huet covered the Vietnam War for Associated Press. He died in 1971 on a battlefront inspection with three other photojournalists and the commanding officer of the South Vietnamese force invading Laos. The group's helicopter pilot lost his way and flew into heavily defended areas.

Figure 14-9 ▲

In this photo taken near the end of the war, a Vietnamese woman carries her wounded daughter away from the fighting. What impact do you think this photo would have on American readers?

Most of us grew up thinking that the United States was a strong but humble nation, that involved itself in world affairs only reluctantly, that respected the integrity of other nations and other systems, and that engaged in wars only as a last resort. This was a nation with no large standing army, with no design for external conquest, that sought primarily the opportunity to develop its own resources and its own mode of living. If at some point we began to hear vague and disturbing things about what this country had done in Latin America, China, Spain and other places, we somehow remained confident about the basic integrity of this nation's foreign policy. The Cold War with all of its neat categories and black and white descriptions did much to assure us that what we had been taught to believe was true.

But in recent years, the withdrawal from the hysteria of the Cold War era and the development of a more aggressive, activist foreign policy have done much to force many of us to rethink attitudes that were deep and basic sentiments about our country. The incredible war in Vietnam has provided the razor, the terrifying sharp cutting edge that has finally severed the last vestige of illusion that morality and democracy are the guiding principles of American foreign policy…

The President says that we are defending freedom in Vietnam. Whose freedom? Not the freedom of the Vietnamese…

—Paul Potter, "Naming the System" (SDS anti-war speech), April 17, 1965.

http://mrzine.monthlyreview.org/potter150106.html

Figure 14-10 ▶

In 1968, the United States itself felt like a war zone to some. Martin Luther King, Jr was assassinated in April 1968. This event was soon followed by the assassination of Robert Kennedy, the brother to John F. Kennedy, Jr and an anti-war candidate for the Democratic Party's presidential campaign. In August 1968, the successor to President Lyndon B. Johnson was to be nominated at the Democratic Convention in Chicago. While the convention took place indoors, it seemed like the whole world watched as 10 000 demonstrators outdoors faced off against 23 000 Chicago police officers and Illinois National Guard soldiers in dramatic confrontations.

In 1967, American civil rights leader Martin Luther King, Jr addressed a meeting of Clergy and Laymen Concerned About Vietnam, with the following:

...We still have a choice today: nonviolent coexistence or violent coannihilation. We must move past indecision to action. We must find new ways to speak for peace in Vietnam and justice throughout the developing world, a world that borders on our doors. If we do not act, we shall surely be dragged down the long, dark, and shameful corridors of time reserved for those who possess power without compassion, might without morality, and strength without sight...

—Martin Luther King, Jr, "Beyond Vietnam"
(speech delivered at Riverside Church,
New York City), April 4, 1967.
http://www.vietnamwar.com/beyondvietnammlk.htm

The anti-war movement had a profound impact on foreign policy for the United States. President Johnson and, later, President Nixon both had to deal with widespread negative public sentiment. Rallies and protest marches, which had limited participation early in the war, grew to immense proportions. By November 15, 1969, the largest peace march in US history brought as many as 500 000 protesters to Washington. In the two days before this event, 40 000 protesters marched past the White House, each carrying the name of a different US soldier who had been killed in Vietnam. All this was seen on television.

In the mid-1950s, it had appeared that communism could be held back at the border between North and South Vietnam in much the same way as North and South Korea had been divided; however, in hindsight, the Vietnam War was an unwinnable war, for France and later for the United States, and particularly in American public opinion. In January 1973, a peace treaty was signed by all parties, but fighting continued within the region. In June 1973, the US Congress signed the Case-Church Amendment, which disallowed any American military intervention in Vietnam. By April 1975, the Northern forces captured Saigon, and the two regions were reunited in 1976 as a communist country.

Figure 14-11 ▲

In 1969, this protest against US involvement in Vietnam was held in Washington, DC.

The Vietnam Veterans Memorial

In 1982, the Vietnam Veterans Memorial was completed in Washington, DC. It honours the American soldiers who died in Vietnam and those who are still missing in action. All of the names are listed in chronological order. When the wall was first unveiled, many found it too plain and uninspiring. However, the memorial has since become one of the most admired and visited landmarks in the United States.

In 1998 a virtual wall was created to extend the legacy of the Vietnam Veterans Memorial. Through the Internet, anyone in the world can look up the name of a veteran and find its location on the wall. Visitors to the website can choose a name on the wall and post images, text, or audio as a remembrance of that person. By late 2008, more than 100 000 remembrances had been posted to the site. The Virtual Wall

Figure 14-12

Visitors to the Vietnam Veterans Memorial wall pause to remember the fallen.

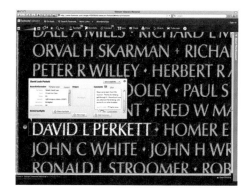

Figure 14-13 ▲

Anyone can view the memorial Wall online, search for a name, and leave a remembrance.

also can provide digital versions of name "rubbings", similar to what someone could make if they visited the Wall itself.

Canada and Afghanistan

Canada's military involvement in Afghanistan has steadily increased since the fall of the Taliban regime in late 2001 (see page 320). Canada has had a major role in many military operations throughout the country, and has been involved in many offensive battles with insurgents, resulting in Canadian military casualties. Canada has also been involved in providing humanitarian assistance and supporting development activities. Originally, Canada intended for its troops to be pulled out of Afghanistan in February 2009, but debates arose in Parliament and among Canadians on the future of the mission. Prime Minister Stephen Harper has extended the mission until 2011. Some Canadians have been opposed to the mission, as they believe that Canada will not be able to make a difference in such a volatile area, and that Canadian actions in the area are building more resistance in insurgent groups, rather than making the area more peaceful. Ordinary Canadian citizens have taken action and organized anti-war peace rallies across Canada to make their opinions known:

Peace activists are holding anti-war protests across the country, calling on the government to end Canada's combat operations in Afghanistan...

"I'm happy with the turn out," Matthew Abbott of the Fredericton Peace Coalition...

"We can see there are a number of people in Fredericton willing to brave the bad weather to show their opinion about what's happening in Afghanistan, despite the climate that isn't very friendly to dissent."

In Montréal, hundreds of people attended a peace march in equally rainy weather, many of them carrying colourful banners and chanting anti-war slogans.

Mary Walsh, an activist with the Raging Grannies, said she was concerned by Prime Minister Stephen Harper's comments that the mission should be extended to 2011—two years beyond the current completion date of February 2009.

"This is why we're here today, because 2009 is bad enough but 2011 just isn't going to go down well with the Canadian public," she told CTV Montréal.

Another march in Toronto had more than 300 attendants and began at the US Consulate…

Michael Skinner, a Toronto academic and anti-war activist, said NATO and Canadian actions in Afghanistan are building resistance rather than the peace.

"Certainly the reason I went to Afghanistan is that I'm quite skeptical of the claims of the government," said Skinner, who is a PhD candidate at York University.

"We're involved in a counter-insurgency war that's very similar to what occurred in Vietnam and Central America."

Skinner, a researcher at the York Centre for International and Security Studies, said he visited four provinces. He found Afghans to be skeptical about the role of foreign troops in Afghanistan and that they saw very little progress in reconstruction.

"Up to this point, thousands of Afghans have been killed. We really have no idea how many have been injured, how many people have been made homeless or become refugees and how many people are arbitrarily arrested or detained," he said.

"All of these things are creating resistance rather than support," he said.

The Afghanistan situation is undermining the United Nations' traditional peacekeeping role, he said.

Public opinion polling has found that most Canadians oppose Canada's military role in Afghanistan…

John Holmes, the UN's undersecretary-general for humanitarian affairs and emergency relief coordinator, has said recently that Canada is making a difference on the ground in Afghanistan and that it should maintain its commitment there.

Afghanistan's President Hamid Karzai has asked foreign troops to stay, but he has also expressed frustration at the number of civilian deaths as a result of NATO and US clashes with the Taliban.

—Source: "Anti-war activists hold peace rallies across Canada", CTV.ca News, October 27, 2007.
http://www.ctv.ca/servlet/ArticleNews/story/CTVNews/
20071027/afghan_protests_071027/20071027

Active Citizens Recognized by OneWorld.net

As you have been reading, citizens in various countries have been able to effect change through their actions, such as civil rights and anti-war demonstrations. The responsibilities of these individuals and how they have embraced beliefs and values that have guided them to take action on national or local crisis or conflicts are featured in the following examples. Each of these individuals has been nominated as a finalist by OneWorld.net for its people awards which recognize their work as active citizens through their humanitarian efforts. OneWorld is a global information network and nonprofit organization that highlights various ongoing economic, environmental and human rights issues around the world.

Pamela Adoyo

Pamela Adoyo stands calmly and resolutely at the epicenter of Kenya's AIDS epidemic. Her women's group is helping care for the sick, impede the disease's spread, and stitch back together a community torn apart by the epidemic...

"HIV/AIDS has affected all facets of Kenyan society with devastating economic consequences," says the United Nations. The disease has deprived rural areas in particular of many of their most productive members of the community, and made it very difficult for families to earn a sufficient living, further entrenching poverty.

Children orphaned by AIDS increase the economic burden on the families or community organizations that take over their care. Plus, AIDS orphans are likely to miss out on education, and so are more prone to end up engaged in risky behaviors like prostitution and drug abuse. "This completes the vicious cycle of poverty and HIV/AIDS," adds the UN report.

But the Dago Women's Group, which Adoyo helped found in 1996, is pushing back against those trends in the country's southwestern Nyanza province.

About half of Kenya's 1.4 million annual HIV/AIDS cases originate in Nyanza, says Alexandra Moe, in a recent profile of Adoyo for New America Media.

"For Adoyo and dozens of other Dago women, the generations-long fight for family survival includes leading the battle against HIV and AIDS, one house at a time, in a region that has been ravaged by the epidemic," writes Moe.

And in this traditionally patriarchal community, Adoyo's steadfast leadership is also starting to redefine what women "can" and "can't" do.

Adoyo is most proud of the orphanage the women built, Dago Dala Hera ("Home of Love"), with fundraising assistance from Dago's first Peace Corps volunteer. On September 24, 20 girls were moved in, cared for by "volunteer mothers," most of whom are AIDS widows. Plans are being made to take in the first group of boys...

—**Source: Jeffrey Allen, OneWorld.net and Alexandra Moe, New America Media "People of 2008 Finalist: Pamela Adoyo", OneWorld, November 26, 2008.**

http://us.oneworld.net/perspectives/peopleof2008/358715-pamela-adoyo

Figure 14-14 ▲

Adoyo (middle) consults with two caregivers from the Dago Women's Group.

Francisco Soberón

Francisco Soberón has worked to find justice for Peruvians for over 25 years, and the human rights group he founded has been instrumental in bringing former Peruvian President Alberto Fujimori to trial for alleged crimes against humanity.

A young lawyer with a background in education and agricultural cooperatives, Soberón founded the Asociacion Pro Derechos Humanos (APRODEH) in 1982 to help protect ordinary Peruvians caught in the crossfire between the Shining Path guerrilla group, the Túpac Amaru Revolutionary Movement (MRTA), and the Peruvian armed forces.

Beatings, torture, "disappearances," and arbitrary detentions were common during the almost 20 years of active conflict. During APRODEH's first two years of work alone, the group documented over 2,000 forced disappearances. Over 600,000 people were forced from their homes and villages by the fighting. Some 30,000 were killed.

In 1985, Soberón helped found the National Coordination Network of Human Rights, an umbrella organization that now brings together 70 human rights organizations in Peru. He has worked at every level to help promote justice—from educating peasants about their rights, to working within the country's beleaguered judicial system, to petitioning international human rights bodies and the United Nations.

In the past 25 years, APRODEH has come to play an increasingly central role in monitoring and documenting rights violations.

APRODEH has been the driving force behind the current trial of [former president Alberto] Fujimori. While in power from 1990 to 2000, Fujimori was accused of human rights violations in what he described as a campaign to uproot terrorism in Peru. Fujimori was allegedly involved in the 1991 Barrios Altos massacre of 15 men, women, and children as well as the disappearance and murder of eight students and a professor from La Cantuta University in 1992, according to Amnesty International.

APRODEH led the international pressure campaign that saw Fujimori extradited last year from Chile, where he had taken refuge...Several of Soberón's colleagues have been attacked, killed, threatened, exiled, or have simply disappeared over the years, most likely because of their work to expose human rights violations in the country...

Speaking at the awards ceremony, Soberón reflected back on his group's 25 years of work. "Human rights abuses and crimes against humanity were a common thing in my country...In these 25 years a lot of things have happened in Peru. [The country is] not perfect yet. We have to keep struggling against impunity. There are obstacles that we have to confront nowadays...[But] I think the future is of hope, the future is of peace, and the future is of justice. Our work will continue in that respect."

**—Source: Brittany Schell and Jeffrey Allen, OneWorld.net,
"People of 2008 Finalist: Francisco Soberón",
OneWorld, December 3, 2008.**
http://us.oneworld.net/perspectives/peopleof2008/358675-francisco-soberon

Figure 14-15 ▲

Francisco Soberón

Waseem Mahmood

With the signatures of over 62 million Pakistanis committed to the Yeh Hum Naheen Foundation's anti-terrorism campaign, founder Waseem Mahmood has become a leader in a movement promoting Islam as a peaceful, tolerant faith.

It started with a simple observation by his children—that the radical depiction of the Muslim faith was inaccurate, and dangerous. One song, 6 000 volunteers, and all those signatures later, he is changing perceptions of the Muslim religion worldwide and helping to build peace in one of the more volatile—and he says misunderstood— countries of the world.

Mahmood is a British author and media producer. After his sons raised their concerns about the radicalization of young Muslims in England, he used his professional skills to help put together a catchy tune with some powerful words [which translate into] English: "The name by which you know us—we are not that. The eyes with which you look at us—we are not that. This is not us, this is not us, this is not us." Another part of the song says: "The stories that are being spread in our name are lies—this is not us."…

Now, the phrase "yeh hum naheen," meaning "this is not us," is being repeated all over Pakistan. In October 2007, Mahmood founded the Yeh Hum Naheen Foundation with the aim of changing the negative image of Islam. He captured the attention of some of Pakistan's biggest young stars, and their version of the song quickly rose to the top of the charts in the country. From there the song—and its message—have spread like wildfire across the nation of 172 million, 95 per cent of whom are Muslim…

Even Mahmood has been surprised by the overwhelming response of Pakistanis agreeing that "this is not us!"

—Source: Jeffrey Allen, OneWorld.net and Alexandra Moe, New America Media, "People of 2008 Finalist: Waseem Mahmood", OneWorld, December 8, 2008.
http://us.oneworld.net/perspectives/peopleof2008/358674-waseem-mahmood

Figure 14-16 ▲

Waseem Mahmood

Explore the Issues

Concept Review

1 Identify two examples from this section of a citizen who took action. Describe the method the person used to take action and the ideology that you think shaped that action. For one action, give your personal response, and explain your reasons for responding that way.

Concept Application

2 In this section of the chapter, you have read of the actions of citizens against some form of oppression or perceived wrong. Some ideologies support the use of force as a means of achieving political results. Given that Canada is a pluralistic country, it is reasonable to assume that there will be a range of ideologies that guide people's decision making. Consider again the Question for Inquiry for this section: To what extent do citizens have a right, role, or responsibility to take action? Express your thoughts about the extent to which violent or non-violent action is a proper response to a perceived unjust situation.

3 The Vietnam War and apartheid in South Africa have had powerful and lasting impacts on countries involved in those conflicts and globally. Research a current relevant issue that has a link to one of these events and explore various perspectives and/or points of view of citizens in response to this issue. What beliefs in the rights, roles, and responsibilities of citizenship are evident? What beliefs most closely align with your own, and best inform and support your response to the issue?

Leading for Change

*Question for **Inquiry***

- **How do your ideology and your citizenship affect how you demonstrate leadership in responding to local, national, and global issues?**

As you know, Canadians vote in a federal election at least every five years. They also vote in regular local and provincial or territorial elections. That vote, according to philosopher John Ralston Saul, is the *minimal act* of a citizen.

To believe in the possibility of change is something very precise. It means that we believe in the reality of choice. That there are choices. That we have the power to choose in the hope of altering society for the greater good…The conviction that citizens have such power lies at the heart of the idea of civilization as a shared project. And the more people are confident that there are real choices, the more they want to vote—a minimal act—and of greater importance, the more they want to become involved in their society.

—From *The Collapse of Globalism* by John Ralston Saul.
© John Ralston Saul, 2005. Reprinted by permission of Penguin Group (Canada), a Division of Pearson Canada Inc.

Historian Peter C. Newman, another Canadian, says, "One reason I want to be a Canadian citizen is that it seems the closest I can come…to being a world citizen." (Source: Peter C. Newman, quoted in "Our Work at the ICC." Institute for Canadian Citizenship, http://www.icc-icc.ca/en/projects/.)

As you read the remainder of this chapter, think about the leadership you see in response to issues and how you personally might demonstrate leadership as a citizen, in response to issues. What worldviews and ideologies in this chapter best inform and support your actions, identity, and citizenship in response to important issues?

Believing in the Possibility of Change

In 1968, two athletes knew they had a shot at winning Olympic medals and, as a result, an opportunity to express to an international audience their strongly held belief about an issue. The issue was racial discrimination in the United States; they felt that the American civil rights movement had not yet eradicated the injustices that they and other black Americans faced. In the lead-up to the 1968 Olympic Games, a young sociologist named Harry

PAUSE AND REFLECT

What does Saul believe is an important ingredient of a civilized society? What might Newman mean by his statement?

Figure 14-17 ▼

This cartoon indicates some ways in which a citizen can act. In what additional ways can citizens take action?

© 2008, Jeff Parker, Florida Today, and PoliticalCartoons.com

Tommie Smith later told the media that he "raised his right, black-glove-covered fist in the air to represent black power in America while Carlos' left, black-covered fist represented unity in black America. Together they formed an arch of unity and power. The black scarf around Smith's neck stood for black pride and their black socks (and no shoes) represented black poverty in racist America." (Source: John Gettings, "Civil Disobedience: Black medallists raise fists for Civil Rights Movement." Infoplease, http://www.infoplease.com/spot/summer-olympics-mexico-city.html.)

Edwards approached athletes Tommie Smith and John Carlos, along with other black American athletes and civil rights leaders, with the idea of boycotting the Games in Mexico City to bring attention to the issue. The boycott did not gather sufficient support, but Smith and Carlos secretly planned a non-violent protest. After their win, as they stood on the podiums at the Olympic medal ceremony, the two men bowed their heads and raised their fists in protest as the American flag rose and the anthem was played.

Today the protest might seem mild compared with many, but Smith and Carlos were suspended from the US Olympic team, banned from the Olympic Village, and sent home during the Games. Some observers thought the men were brave. Some critics thought that the Olympics, which was then considered apolitical, was no place for their political protest. Others thought their protest was a disgrace to the United States. Smith, Carlos, and their families faced death threats. While many Olympic medalists have followed their wins with endorsements and job offers, these two athletes had trouble finding jobs for several years.

Protest from the Podium

John Carlos and Tommie Smith recalled the protest as follows:

It (a protest) was in my head the whole year. We first tried to have a boycott (of the games) but not everyone was down with that plan. A lot of athletes thought that winning medals would supercede or protect them from racism. But even if you won the medal, it ain't going to save your momma. It ain't going to save your sister or children. It might give you fifteen minutes of fame, but what about the rest of your life? I'm not saying that they didn't have the right to follow their dreams, but to me the medal was nothing but the carrot on a stick.

—**John Carlos, quoted in Dave Zirin, *What's My Name, Fool?* (Chicago:Haymarket Books, 2005), p. 86.**

I did what I thought was necessary…But who is Tommie Smith to go tell someone that this is how you should act or feel about human rights? Look in the mirror, have a conversation with that person in the mirror and act accordingly.

—**Tommie Smith, quoted in Jeff Duncan, "Tommie Smith says not everyone should feel obligated to protest."** *The Times-Picayune* **August 4, 2008.**
http://blog.nola.com/olympics/2008/08/tommie_smith_says_not_everyone.html

PAUSE AND REFLECT

- **Should athletes use the international stage to try to bring about change?**

- **If you believed in a cause very strongly, what would best define what you would be willing to risk to attempt to address the issue?**

Change from Inside or Outside

Some citizens who choose to question a society or organization in an attempt to change it do so from *outside* that society or organization; others question from *within*. For example, Tommie Smith and John Carlos chose not to boycott the Olympics but to participate in them and raise their concerns there.

Adam Werbach is an example of someone who has worked for change both from the outside and from within. As you read about him and those who reflect on him, consider what worldviews, ideologies, choices, and actions are evident. Also examine the language used to describe Werbach, Wal-Mart, and the company's chief executive officer (CEO). What questions and concerns does the language raise for you?

Werbach first got involved in environmental activism at the age of 9. In high school, he founded the Sierra Student Coalition. By the age of 23, he had become the youngest-ever president of the Sierra Club, one of the oldest and most influential environmental organizations in North America. Ten years later, in 2006, he began working as a consultant for Wal-Mart, helping the chain develop more environmentally friendly retail practices. That same year, he was elected to the international board of directors of Greenpeace.

The truly unexpected—even revolutionary—idea contained in Mr. Werbach's speech is that Wal-Mart might be sustainability's most powerful advocate. With 4100 stores in the U.S. and more than 300 in Canada, Wal-Mart, he notes, is the continent's largest trucking company, its most voracious consumer of electricity and—with a workforce of 1.3 million in the U.S. and 75 000 in Canada—its biggest employer.

His belief is that changing the mindset of Wal-Mart's employees from within will have a catalytic effect on this century's newborn sustainability movement as powerful as conservation organizations like the Sierra Club had on 20th-century environmentalism.

In lieu of consciousness-raising, he argues, the key to sustainability is changing how people think about the everyday products they buy—toilet paper, for instance…

The company's 60 000-plus suppliers, meanwhile, have begun scrambling to reduce their packaging to comply with Wal-Mart's new "sustainability scorecard." To underscore the commitment, [Wal-Mart CEO Lee] Scott called a meeting of 250 of the retail world's most prominent CEOs in October, at which he warned that companies with failing grades might be denied space in Wal-Mart's massively influential circulars and in-store promotional displays. Wal-Mart, as Advertising Age noted, had become "a sort of privatized [US] Environmental Protection Agency, only with a lot more clout."

—Source: Chris Turner, "Environment: Thinking Outside the Big Boxes." *The Globe and Mail*, March 15, 2008, p. F7.

- **What is the issue being presented? Identify the two ideologies that are reflected in the points of view.**

- **How would you evaluate Adam Werbach's actions? Do you think he has found an effective way to pursue environmental goals, or do you think he has betrayed his principles? Explain how you arrived at your answer.**

One critic of Adam Werbach and Wal-Mart, however, wrote:

Let's face it, Wal-Mart has engaged in greenwashing here and we've fallen for it, hoping that the world's largest retailer would miraculously grow a conscience. Instead, Wal-Mart has only distracted environmentalists from the company's woeful record while they pursue their bottom line—cutting costs and making profits…

I wonder what groups like Environmental Defense—organizations that claimed to be working with Wal-Mart to fix their problems from the inside—will do now that Scott's greedy intentions are out in the open. I wonder how Adam Werbach, the former Sierra Club sell-out, will try to spin this one. Wal-Mart isn't just "a new breed of toxin," as Werbach once said (before hypocritically taking on Wal-Mart, and a huge salary from them, as a client through Act Now Productions); they just brought their toxic breed to a whole new insidious level…

—**Z.P. Heller, Editorial Director, Brave New Films, "Lee Scott: It's Not Easy Being Green."** *The Huffington Post*, **March 20, 2008.**

http://www.huffingtonpost.com/zp-heller/lee-scott-its-not-easy-_b_92679.html

Wal-Mart itself states on its website:

At Wal-Mart, we know that being an efficient and profitable business and being a good steward of the environment are goals that can work together. Our environmental goals at Wal-Mart are simple and straightforward: To be supplied 100 percent by renewable energy; to create zero waste; and to sell products that sustain our resources and the environment.

"Sustainability", Wal-Mart.

http://walmartstores.com/FactsNews/FeaturedTopics/?id=6

PAUSE AND REFLECT

Quite likely you have found that there are things in your own community or somewhere else in the world that don't fit with your ideal vision of the world. How could you take a leadership role to get involved—that is, to act on an issue important to you? As you read the rest of this chapter, consider the issues that engage you and what that means for you as a citizen.

Acting Accordingly

As you read earlier in this chapter, Tommie Smith, the banished Olympian, did what he thought was necessary and encouraged people to consider their own beliefs and values, and then "act accordingly." Irish politician Edmund Burke (1727–1797) expressed a similar idea. He believed that *not* acting has a profound impact:

All that is necessary for the triumph of evil is that good men do nothing.

—**attributed to Edmund Burke, quoted in the *Oxford Dictionary of Political Quotations*, 2nd edition. (Oxford: Oxford University Press, 2004), p. 255.**

As mentioned earlier in the chapter, John Ralston Saul stated that to vote was the minimal act of the citizen but being involved in society is much more important. Burke's quotation warns us against doing nothing.

Rwanda

While some issues may seem far removed from our own reality, or difficult to influence, it is important to realize that there are consequences when individuals do not act. Consider this example from 1994. That year, in Rwanda, 800 000 people were killed in ethnic violence in 100 days.

Rwanda's population consists of two major ethnic groups—the majority Hutu and the minority Tutsi. Since colonial times, the Tutsi were favoured by the Belgian governors, who encouraged them to become educated and prepared them for governing. When the Rwandan president, a Hutu, was killed in a suspicious plane crash in 1994, some Hutu leaders incited their followers to seek revenge by attacking Tutsis. A massive and rapid killing campaign resulted.

Roméo Dallaire, the Canadian general in charge of the United Nations (UN) peacekeeping forces in Rwanda, saw the potential for violence and pleaded with the United Nations to increase the number of troops and to empower them to deal with the crisis. Dallaire felt that he needed only 2500 UN troops to stop the killing. He was repeatedly turned down. In fact, the United States undertook a campaign within the UN to remove the peacekeepers as quickly as possible. Dallaire was left with only 500 troops in Rwanda. It could be perceived that the leaders of the world did not have the political will to stop this genocide in the making. Although journalists reported on the actions taken in Rwanda, the people of the world and their governments chose to turn away from the conflict.

In her 2003 book *A Problem from Hell: America and the Age of Genocide*, American author Samantha Power claims that disbelief in the totality of a horror and a genuine hope that a problem will just go away are typical responses to horrific crimes against humanity. Power states that we can be "bystanders" or "upstanders," and if we generate the political will, governments will change their policies.

After speaking of the United States' unwillingness to do anything to stop the horror in Rwanda, Samantha Power says the following:

The story of U.S. policy during the genocide in Rwanda is not a story of willful complicity with evil. U.S. officials did not sit around and conspire to allow genocide to happen. But whatever their convictions about "never again," many of them did sit around, and they most certainly did allow genocide to happen. In examining how and why the United States failed Rwanda, we see that without strong leadership the system will incline toward risk-averse policy choices.

—Samantha Power, "Bystanders to Genocide."
***The Atlantic*, September 2001.**
http://www.theatlantic.com/doc/200109/power-genocide

PAUSE AND REFLECT

Compare Power's thoughts to the quote attributed to Burke on page 498. In what ways are these two thinkers saying the same thing? How might Power and Burke answer the Question for Inquiry for this section: How do your ideology and your citizenship affect how you demonstrate leadership in responding to local, national, and global issues?

Celebrities Speak Out

Something to Think About: Sometimes, musicians, actors, and other public figures use their place in the media spotlight to express their personal views on current issues and events. Actor Leonardo DiCaprio, for example, has used his celebrity to promote environmental causes.

Celebrities who publicly take ideological stands sometimes find their views to be unpopular. In 1972, at the height of her popularity, actress Jane Fonda travelled to North Vietnam and spoke out against the United States' war with the Vietnamese communists. She was harshly criticized by many in the United States for years after the incident.

To what extent do celebrities have the power to influence others? If you have a strong opinion about an issue that concerns the general public, should you share your position with others? If you are the object of public attention, should you use your celebrity to communicate your views to others? Looking at it from a different point of view, if a public figure believes something strongly, is it that person's responsibility as a citizen to voice that belief?

Figure 14-19 ▲

The Dixie Chicks found themselves in the media spotlight for their criticism of President Bush on the eve of the American invasion of Iraq.

An Example: In March 2003, the United States was about to invade Iraq. A country band from Texas, the Dixie Chicks, was giving a live performance in London, England, that same month and during the concert the lead singer, Natalie Maines, said the following:

Just so you know, we're on the good side with y'all. We do not want this war, this violence, and we're ashamed that the president of the United States is from Texas.

> **—Source: "'Shut Up and Sing': Dixie Chicks' Big Grammy Win Caps Comeback from Backlash Over Anti-War Stance."** *Democracy Now!* **February 15, 2007.**
> http://www.democracynow.org/2007/2/15/shut_up_and_sing_dixie_chicks

Public reaction to the comment was immediate. American radio stations stopped playing Dixie Chicks' songs, album sales dropped, and some fans crushed their CDs in protest. Also, the band reported receiving death threats.

President George W. Bush commented on the incident in an interview with American television journalist Tom Brokaw.

…the Dixie Chicks are free to speak their mind. They can say what they want to say…They shouldn't have their feelings hurt just because some people don't want to buy their records when they speak out…Freedom is a two-way street…I…don't really care what the Dixie Chicks said. I want to do what I think is right for the American people, and if some singers or Hollywood stars feel like speaking out, that's fine. That's the

great thing about America. It stands in stark contrast to Iraq…

—George W. Bush, quoted in "Full Text of Brokaw's Interview with Bush," *The New York Times* April 25, 2003.

http://www.nytimes.com/2003/04/25/international/worldspecial/25BUSHTEXT.html?
pagewanted=10&ei=5070&en=a9c7e13d49ebf120&ex=1206504000

Fellow musician Bruce Springsteen defended the Dixie Chicks' right to express themselves in a statement on his website.

The pressure coming from the government and big business to enforce conformity of thought concerning the war and politics goes against everything that this country is about—namely freedom. Right now, we are supposedly fighting to create freedom in Iraq, at the same time that some are trying to intimidate and punish people for using that same freedom here at home.

—Bruce Springsteen, quoted in "Springsteen: Dixie Chicks 'Getting a Raw Deal.'" NBC 6 News Team, April 24, 2003.

http://www.nbc6.net/entertainment/2156255/detail.html

After the response they received, the Dixie Chicks issued a new song that included the following lyrics:

I made my bed and I sleep like a baby
With no regrets and I don't mind sayin'
It's a sad sad story when a mother will teach her
Daughter that she ought to hate a perfect stranger
And how in the world can the words that I said
Send somebody so over the edge
That they'd write me a letter
Sayin' that I better shut up and sing
Or my life will be over

Source: "Not Ready to Make Nice" by Dan Wilson, Martie Maguire, Emily Robison, and Natalie Maines © 2006 Chrysalis Music (ASCAP), Sugar Lake Music (ASCAP), Scrapin' Toast Music (ASCAP) and Woolly Puddin' Music (BMI). All rights for Sugarlake Music administered by Chrysalis Music. All rights reserved. Used by permission. International copyright secured.

QUESTIONS FOR REFLECTION

1 Identify the ideologies you find in Maines' comment and in the different responses to it. What understanding of citizenship is implicit in each?

2 Find other examples of celebrities taking a stand on an issue. For each, comment on the issue, the celebrity's ideology, and the effectiveness of the celebrity's action. Compare your results with those of your classmates.

Part 4 Issue: *To what extent should my actions as a citizen be shaped by an ideology?*   501

Some activists believe that even the smallest action—from buying a ribbon-campaign product to drinking bottled water or buying a fair-trade product—can have an impact. In the choice between bottled water and tap water, some consumers and activists point not only to the environmental costs of making plastic bottles and transporting them, but also to the waste and recycling problem that bottles can become for some local areas. For some stores and consumers, making purchases can mean ensuring a fair income for people around the world.

For example, the Mennonite Central Committee runs stores in the United States and Canada called Ten Thousand Villages, which sell products to "provide a vital, fair income to Third World people…who would otherwise be unemployed or underemployed. This income helps pay for food, education, health care and housing." (Source: "Our Mission Statement." Ten Thousand Villages, http://www.tenthousand villages.ca)

What worldview and ideology would encourage a store to sell fair-trade products—ranging from coffee, tea, and chocolate to jewellery and pottery? Why would a consumer buy them? What small actions have you undertaken based on your worldview and ideology?

Whatever choices citizens (including activists and consumers) make, choice—or belief in the reality of choice—is key to leadership.

The stories of civilization in any place at any time have this in common—individuals feel they understand the mechanisms of their society. This sense of understanding implies that each of us has the self-confidence to wish to change our society for the better. Or at least we have the self-confidence to accept the possibility that we could change it for the better. Think of those who worked for clean water systems, public education, against slavery.

Do all of us have that self-confidence? Perhaps not…[However this] understanding may come in many forms and at many levels. It may be conscious or unconscious or a bit of both.

To believe in the reality of choice is one of the most basic characteristics of leadership. Curiously enough, many individuals who think of themselves as leaders find this reality very difficult. They believe that their job is to understand power and management and perhaps make minor corrections to what they accept to be the torque of events. But they take for granted the reigning truths of the day and so are fundamentally passive.

As a result, change is eventually thrust upon them by reality. Or they are replaced. In either case, the strength of that particular civilization—its ability to choose—is weakened.

—From *The Collapse of Globalism* by John Ralston Saul. © John Ralston Saul, 2005. Reprinted by permission of Penguin Group (Canada), a Division of Pearson Canada Inc.

PAUSE AND REFLECT

One characteristic of leadership, according to Saul, is believing in the ability to make meaningful choices to bring about change. Think of a situation or an issue that you think needs to be changed. List all the choices that exist, however unlikely their success might be, that could change that situation or issue. What would be the likelihood of you attempting that change? How does your willingness or lack of willingness to attempt a change indicate the extent to which you have embraced an ideology?

Raising Awareness

As a student nearing the end of high school, you are perhaps in the process of making choices about a career or further education, or both. What aspects of a career are most important to you? Are you focused on achieving financial success, attaining personal satisfaction, doing something purposeful and meaningful, having personal growth opportunities through travel, education, and experiences, meeting interesting people, having variety, or something else?

As a young adult, Sam Singh co-created Northscape Productions Inc. with Jessica Hall in order to produce insightful, entertaining, and exciting documentary films with social, political, and environmental themes. Their first project, *Land Unlocked*, which is about the impact of climate change on Aboriginal communities in the Yukon and Bolivia, aired February 2007 on the Aboriginal Peoples Television Network.

When interviewed, this was Singh's explanation for why he chose this career:

I turned to journalism because of an inherent curiosity with how the world works and a desire to know why things happen the way they do. The first step in bringing change to the world starts when the public knows what's wrong with it and that's where journalists come in. Most reporters embody a mix of hope and cynicism; the questions they ask often lead to answers we're not usually accustomed to in mainstream society. It's been said that "journalists should comfort the afflicted and afflict the comfortable," so it's not surprising that many reporters are left-leaning. After all, the status quo may be okay at times, but it's definitely not interesting for long when others are telling you how things can be better.

Documentary filmmaking offers me a unique way to be a storyteller by looking at stories behind the headlines and "digging deeper," both here and at home. Land Unlocked, *my first film, examined how climate change was impacting Aboriginal communities in the Yukon and in Bolivia. I wanted to know more about these two ecosystems and the people who lived within them. In the process, I learned it was occurring in a couple of ways I'd never really considered and that gave me new insights into how we affect the environment and how it affects us. The highlight of my new career so far has been interviewing the President of Bolivia, Evo Morales. As a result of the film, an Aboriginal group from the Yukon is now working with an Indigenous community in Bolivia to preserve the main river that runs through their community. That's the greatest satisfaction: in bringing other realities to light, documentaries offer a chance for myself and others to change those realities for the better.*

—**Sam Singh, Interview with author,
October, 2007.**

PAUSE AND REFLECT

- **What ideology appears to have informed Singh's values?**

- **Singh chose to make a career choice based on his passions. How important do you think passion is for you when considering possible careers?**

- **Check the newspaper career postings or other sites that offer job and career descriptions or opportunities and see what is available. Are there ideas you had not considered before that may interest you? What ideological beliefs and aspects of leadership and citizenship best inform the career choice you are most interested in?**

Organizing for Change

Taking action by creating an organization dedicated to an issue may seem like a daunting task; however, often extraordinary efforts are initiated by everyday people. The following story about Simon Jackson is an example of this.

At the age of 7, Jackson began contributing to efforts to protect the Alaskan Kodiak bear. At the age of 13, he started a successful initiative to protect the habitat of the endangered Kermode, or spirit bear, in British Columbia. This became the most supported conservation initiative in Canadian history. He was recognized by *Time* magazine as one of its 60 Heroes for the Planet; he was one of only six youths selected. CTV made a movie about his life called *Spirit Bear: The Simon Jackson Story,* and Jackson is currently working to produce *Spirit Bear,* a major animated Hollywood movie, as well as continuing the fight to protect the spirit bear. He founded the Spirit Bear Youth Coalition, a youth-run environmental organization of over 6 million people in 65 countries.

From a more philosophical perspective, the story of this campaign—from me selling lemonade at the age of 7 to help save Alaska's Kodiak bear to helping produce a Hollywood movie—may seem, well, impossible for the "average" kid to duplicate. But it's not. Anybody and everybody could have done what I've been doing for any issue they believe in—whether it's trying to protect a peregrine falcon's nest in their neighborhood or trying to rid the world of cancer.

If the Youth Coalition can help prove to our global audience that they saved the spirit bear and that they can do the same thing for anything that they believe in, my hope is that in the years to come we'll see 6 million Youth Coalitions start up to help address 6 million additional issues. For every person there is a passion: if we can help begin to restore hope to the many young people who have lost it, I believe we will turn the tides of apathy and empower a generation to follow their passions in order to create a better world…

It doesn't matter what type of action is taken—as long as it is positive. There are no insignificant endeavours for the sum total of all our acts will be the solutions to our unsolvable problems and our legacy to all life for generations to come.

—Simon Jackson, Interview with author, 2007.

PAUSE AND REFLECT

- **Would you support Simon Jackson's organization? Why or why not? What criteria did you use to make your decision?**

- **Is there any connection between what Jackson has done and embracing an ideology?**

Ways toward Action

One concern many social activists have is that a perceived growth of individualism in our society has led to a preoccupation with the self, and consequently people are less concerned with the welfare of others. In Samantha Power's terms, this leads to fewer "upstanders" and more "bystanders."

The following article addresses this issue by examining the nature of responsible citizen action.

PAUSE AND REFLECT

Of the five "ways" described in this article, explain which you feel is the most important.

• Is there anything in this excerpt with which you disagree or that raises questions?

• Does the extent to which a person believes in an ideology affect an individual's level of involvement as a citizen?

Wake Up: 5 Ways to Raise Citizen Awareness

1. Take Part

In *The Malaise of Modernity*, the 1991 Massey Lectures, Charles Taylor observed that "individualism...names what many people consider the finest achievement of modern civilization. We live in a world where people have a right to choose for themselves their own pattern of life, to decide in conscience what convictions to espouse."

However, individuals, happy to "stay at home and enjoy the satisfactions of private life," as Taylor puts it, may close themselves off to public engagement, pursuing only their own interests (notably material gain). By pursuing democratic freedom to its logical end, citizens might abandon public systems altogether. Some would say that recent Alberta history has affirmed Taylor's concerns. Low voter turnout; stagnation in public office; materialism; intolerance of dissent.

...Democracy not only empowers the individual, but also makes individuals responsible...Individuals who realize their citizenship will apply their power to common pursuits and the public good.

2. Question

A democracy is alive only if its members are willing to question. Citizens must ask what is working and what is failing within their society...How do we balance the needs of the individual with that of the collective? How do we balance rights and responsibilities? Whose interests are served by a particular government policy? Whose interests are served by the status quo?

3. Include All

...Let us ensure that all segments of society have the wherewithal to participate—opportunities for education and employment; opportunities to be heard...Do the decisions of the government serve the best interests of all the people?

4. Insist on Accurate Information

We need access to truth rather than propaganda so that we give truly informed consent to decisions that affect us. The Freedom of Information & Protection of Privacy Act is meant to allow people to see public documents...We depend on the media to inform us. Insist on intelligent and objective journalism.

5. Focus on the Local and the Living

...A healthy democracy, with accountable citizens, is rooted in local culture and face-to-face interaction. Many of us spend more time with our computers than with people, online rather than in conversation. Democracy is social. Interaction stokes the diverse voices a democracy needs. The system works when citizens pipe up, express their beliefs and actively encourage others to do the same. Only by listening to each other can we create a mutually beneficial shared life.

—"**Wake Up: 5 Ways to Raise Citizen Awareness.**"
Alberta Views, January/February 2008, p. 33.

Figure 14-20 ▶

These children are spending their days involved in a program of play, art, music, storytelling, and drama at the Butterfly Peace Garden in Batticaloa, Sri Lanka. The Garden opened in 1996 as a retreat that brings together local Tamil and Muslim children traumatized by decades of civil war and more recently the tsunami of 2004. The creative director is Paul Hogan (pictured here, left), a Canadian artist who helped found a garden-based arts program at Bloorview Macmillan Centre in Toronto for children with physical disabilities and chronic illness. Hogan was invited to Sri Lanka after the Centre for Peace Studies and Health Reach (both at McMaster University in Hamilton, Ontario) examined the impact of war on children in Sri Lanka, the former Yugloslavia, and the West Bank in the Middle East. Butterfly Peace Garden became not only a place for healing and reconciliation but also a literal refuge after the December 2004 tsunami. Research this example about the garden and other humanitarian organizations of a similar nature, and explain which organization or cause best reflects your understanding of what it means to demonstrate global citizenship.

"5 Ways to Raise Citizen Awareness" seems to focus on making change at the local or the provincial level; however, the personal or local response often has an impact on even global issues. For example, Tzeporah Berman's actions grew from local Vancouver Island actions to those on a global scale. As you think back on the examples of choices made and actions taken in this chapter, think again about the global impact of citizens believing in the possibility of change and acting accordingly—or doing neither.

Explore the Issues

Concept Review

1. Is there any relationship between citizenship and the extent to which one accepts and demonstrates belief in an ideology? Explore the question through examples from the chapter, the news, or your own experience.

Concept Application

2. Use the Skill Path to think through an informed response to, and plan of action for, what you see as the most important issue in your community, province, nation, country, or the world. Outline: the issue and why you selected it; the action or series of actions that you would recommend; perspectives and evidence used to best support and inform your response; and the impact that your actions could have regarding this issue.

Taking Action to Bring About Change in the Community

We have a choice—choosing to act or to accept things as they are. As a conclusion to what you have learned about ideology, this chapter encourages you to translate thinking into action.

Once you have identified your own beliefs and values, and have formed an idea of how the world should be, you may find that the world *as it is* does not live up to your idea. Assume that you can create the change you want to see. Active citizenship means acting with integrity and responsibility to carry out actions that work toward fulfilling your goals. In this Skill Path, you will have the opportunity to practise this process by embarking on a plan for change.

Identify an issue that matters most to you and that best reflects your beliefs and values and consider:

- What is the issue (for example, what should be done about climate change or about farming and food scarcity)? Focus on particular ways the issue is impacting your school or community.
- What is your position on the issue? What are the reasons and evidence that best support your position?
- What need could your potential actions address? Why should this need be addressed?

Your choice of project will reflect your own beliefs and values. It reflects an ideology that you personally embrace.

For the issue you identified, using the skills you learned previously, form a clear, defendable position on the issue.

Once you have decided that an issue is important and have formed a responsible position, determine what you can do about it.

- Brainstorm a list of possible projects or solutions that might be undertaken (for example, a fundraiser or a public awareness campaign about the issue).
- Narrow down the possibilities to two or three projects.
- Research widely to see how others have worked to create change around an issue such as yours.

Narrow your options. In choosing an action, you should consider whether you have the necessary commitment, time, and energy. Think about the steps to take and resources you would need, including materials, assistance from others, advertising, and so on. What challenges or barriers might prevent the plan from succeeding?

To take action, the following ideas might be useful:

Team Up

There may be agencies or organizations whose focus is either similar to yours or overlapping with yours. Explore the possibilities of working with or through them.

Create a Project Plan

Set goals; identify your tactics; determine roles and responsibilities. Consider the questions: Who? What? When? Where? Why? How? What specific tactics will you use to raise awareness about the problem or effect change? Do you need money to implement your project? Do you need to get a permit? Who is going to take care of those things and when?

Take Action

Promote your plan however you can. For example, hit the streets, hit the airwaves, put pen to paper, speak out at a school assembly, and put up an exhibit.

Document Your Efforts

Keep good notes as you go along. A record of events will help you keep track of remaining tasks, as well as your (personal or group) accomplishments. Clip stories from school and community newspapers. Take pictures or video your "action event."

Assess Progress

Debrief after you finish your action project. What worked? What did not work? What should be done differently—or the same—next time?

Share Your Experiences

Students all across Canada and other countries are looking for good ideas about how to be responsible citizens. Share your ideas, your successes, and even the pitfalls you encountered. Write a story, create an online photo-essay exhibit, publish a booklet, or produce a documentary short film about your efforts.

Look Long Range

As you celebrate the completion of your project, start planning for the future. What is next?

—Source: adapted from "10 Steps to Take Action." Teaching Tolerance.
http://www.tolerance.org/teens/10ways.jsp

1. What will best inform your decisions, actions and leadership in response to the issue? What perspectives, ideology, worldview, and elements of individual and collective identity will best support your response?

2 Think about what you believe in and value. Will your actions in response to the issue be consistent with what you want for yourself, for the people who are important to you, and for your community locally, nationally, and globally?

3 Think about the kind of future you want for yourself and others. How will your actions contribute to creating the kind of community and future you want?

4 What will be the consequences of your actions? What are the possible consequences for various groups—businesses, legislators, various age groups, and others? Are you prepared to accept those consequences?

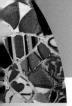

Reflect and Analyze

In this chapter we have explored the following question: *To what extent should an ideology shape your thinking and actions as a citizen?* Even as we analyzed this challenging question, the Key Issue—*To what extent should we embrace an ideology?*—must still be considered. Through what you have learned about ideology, that question should no longer be so overwhelming. Ideology and its role in your thinking and actions will change and grow as you learn and experience things. What is most important is that you continue to choose to be an active, informed, and responsible citizen—an integral participant in our liberal democratic society.

Respond to Ideas

1 Reflect on what you have read, thought about, and researched in this chapter. Express your thoughts on the following question: *To what extent should an ideology shape your thinking and actions as a citizen?*

2 Consider what you have examined in this chapter and draw some conclusions about the responsibilities and benefits of citizenship. To what extent is it important to make responsible and active decisions that respect the principles of liberalism when living in a liberal democratic society? Think about how embracing an ideology may affect your thinking and your openness to creative solutions to problems and challenges.

Respond to Issues

3 Choose one outstanding "upstander" (from this book, the news, or someone else you know) who you would like to research. Prepare a class presentation about this person that identifies

- his or her worldview, perspective, and point of view

- his or her ideology
- the issue
- the action
- evidence of how he or she demonstrated citizenship and leadership in response to that issue

Finally, comment on what makes this person outstanding in your eyes.

Recognize Relationships among Concepts, Issues, and Citizenship

4 Identify and research a contemporary issue that you believe is most critically in need of global leadership and action. Use this chapter's Skill Path and your knowledge of how to best develop informed responses to issues in order to

- explore the issue and its importance to you and globally
- research the issue by exploring and identifying support from different perspectives and from valid and relevant sources
- explore your position by considering possible actions in response to the issue
- focus your response to the issue and organize your evidence in an effective and engaging manner

Consider what action should be taken and to what extent an ideology, and possibly the principles of liberalism, shape your thinking and actions about the issue.

The Promise of Citizenship

Citizen Cube, by Brenda Guyton, a sculpture made of found computer parts. What ideas about citizenship are evident in this sculpture?

Any group of people—a society—that has ever had the luxury of being able to think about its existence eventually arrives at a general understanding of how the world is and how the world ought to be. Such an understanding can be called an ideology. *Ideologies grow out of the honest and serious contemplation of several fundamental questions:*
- *What are humans like, and why do they act as they do?*
- *What is the nature of society?*
- *What is the role of the individual in society?*

Do you remember these questions? They opened *Perspectives on Ideology*. Now that you have completed this course and have worked and shared with others while encountering the many ideas, stories, concepts, perspectives, and ideologies found in this book, you may have some tentative answers to these questions.

You have had the opportunity to explore how your identity—your essential self—prepares you to embrace an ideology, a belief about how the world should be. You have examined a group of ideologies that concern the place of the individual in society, as well as those that focus on collective beliefs and values. You have had the chance to assess the viability of the principles of different ideologies, especially liberalism. Finally, you have been asked, in response to this assessment, to consider what your citizenship means in light of the issues you have explored and the questions listed above.

To What Extent Should We Embrace an Ideology?

A central part of being "Canadian" is living in a democracy. This means that everyone in Canada—both individuals and collectives—has a stake in considering what would be best for Canada and the world.

We can shape our future.

This course and this book are grounded in the idea that the beliefs and values of individual citizens and groups *matter*. Therefore, we must all be equipped with the skills, attitudes, and knowledge to make informed and responsible decisions. Canadian citizenship demands that we thoughtfully consider our own identities, the perspectives of others, and the impact of our decisions and our actions on others and the world around us. Canadian citizenship requires that we all take part, that we all play a role, and that we all practise "engaged, active, informed, and responsible citizenship."

These thoughts are echoed in the Inaugural Address of President Barack Obama to his country on 20 January 2009:

Our journey has never been one of short-cuts or settling for less. It has not been the path for the faint-hearted, for those that prefer leisure over work, or seek only the pleasures of riches and fame. Rather, it has been the risk-takers, the doers, the makers of things—celebrated, but more often men and women obscure in their labor—who have carried us up the long rugged path towards prosperity and freedom…

We honor them, those brave Americans who at this very hour patrol far-off deserts and distant mountains, not only because they are the guardians of our liberty, but because they embody the spirit of service—a willingness to find meaning in something greater than themselves.

And yet at this moment, a moment that will define a generation, it is precisely this spirit that must inhabit us all. For as much as government can do, and must do, it is ultimately the faith and determination of the American people upon which this nation relies. It is the kindness to take in a stranger when the levees break, the selflessness of workers who would rather cut their hours than see a friend lose their job which sees us through our darkest hours. It is the firefighter's courage to storm a stairway filled with smoke, but also a parent's willingness to nurture a child that finally decides our fate...

What is demanded, then, is a return to these truths. What is required of us now is a new era of responsibility—a recognition on the part of every American that we have duties to ourselves, our nation and the world; duties that we do not grudgingly accept, but rather seize gladly, firm in the knowledge that there is nothing so satisfying to the spirit, so defining of our character than giving our all to a difficult task.

This is the price and the promise of citizenship.

—Barack Obama, 44th President of the United States, Inaugural Address, Washington, DC, 20 January 2009.

http://www.whitehouse.gov/blog/inaugural-address/

Michael Ignatieff, speaking at the University of Ottawa in 2006, said

In understanding Canada's place in the world, we need to think of ourselves not just as defenders of our own sovereignty, but as stewards of the global commons...The 21st century will be convulsed by vast global flows of labour and capital. As a result, all societies are becoming multicultural. All societies are opening to the world. All societies are struggling with the challenge of maintaining stable and democratic political orders among peoples from different faiths, ethnicities and national origins. Canada is uniquely placed to show the world how to do this better...

When I was in the classroom, I always knew I was not just in the business of teaching a subject. I was teaching hope and self-belief, the key engines of productivity...Our society lives by the promise of opportunity equally distributed to all. We know how far short we fall. Aboriginal Canadians, visible minorities new to our country, and the working poor lack opportunity, security and skills...Let us commit ourselves to a Canada where no one goes hungry at night, where no one is denied a world-class education because of their race or ancestry; where we bet the future of our country on the proposition that if we can unlock the hidden talent of every citizen, we will always pay our way in the world...

My Canada is held together by a spine of citizenship, common rights, responsibilities and common knowledge so that we truly feel we are one people.

—Michael Ignatieff, "Canada in the World",
***Ottawa Citizen*, Thursday, March 30, 2006.**
http://www2.canada.com/ottawacitizen/news/story.html?
id=5164baa5-0041-4d92-9344-233607ff1529&k=26279

President Obama's appeal to American citizens to accept responsibility for themselves, their country, and the world is equally an appeal to all citizens of all liberal democratic countries. Michael Ignatieff's comments also appeal to this idea about citizenship. It is an appeal for each citizen to embrace an ideology. To embrace an ideology means to act on the basis of that ideology.

The question for all of us remains: ***To what extent should we embrace an ideology?***

To what extent should we be willing to make the commitment and fulfill the promise of citizenship?

To what extent will you take responsible actions to achieve the kind of society and the kind of world in which you want to live?

Glossary

A

Aboriginal Healing Fund: an Aboriginal-managed, Ottawa-based, not-for-profit private corporation with the mission to help Aboriginal people build healing processes that address the legacy of abuses such as the residential school system

adherence to collective norms: faithful observance of the norms or standards imposed on members of a group as a condition of membership in the group. These norms can relate to conduct, values, or appearance.

alignment: an alliance or agreement. During the Cold War, some countries aligned themselves with either the United States or the Soviet Union to gain political, economic, and security benefits.

American Bill of Rights: the first 10 amendments to the US Constitution. Ratified by the original 13 states by 1791, it is based primarily on John Locke's concept of "natural rights" for all individuals, including life, liberty, and the protection of property.

Anti-Terrorism Act: a set of laws passed in December 2001, in response to the September 11, 2001 attacks. It gave the Canadian government special powers, such as surveillance and detention, for dealing with people carrying out activities thought to be associated with terrorism. Some of the act's measures, such as that of preventative arrest, expired in March 2007.

anti-war movements: organized campaigns against war. The Vietnam anti-war movement gained public support during the late 1960s and contributed to the United States ending that war. These movements can be pacifist in general, and aimed at ending or restricting the military policy options, or they can be movements opposing specific military campaigns.

apartheid: a strict, legislated system of racial segregation and discrimination against Black and other "coloured" South Africans set in place by the National Party of South Africa from 1948 to 1994

autarky: self-sufficiency or independence from other countries. During the 1930s, the German government worked to achieve autarky in the country's economy.

authoritarianism: a form of government with authority vested in an elite group that may or may not rule in the interests of the people. Authoritarian political systems take many forms, including oligarchies, military dictatorships, ideological one-party states, and monarchies.

autonomy: a state of individual freedom from outside authority

B

bank run: a situation in which too many depositors try to withdraw their savings from a financial institution, endangering it with bankruptcy

beliefs and values: important aspects of identity that influence behaviour and choices, and that guide people in their interactions with others and how they view the world

boycott: a refusal to do business with or to associate with a person, organization, or country as an expression of protest

brinkmanship: international behaviour or foreign policy that takes a country to the brink of war; pushing one's demands to the point of threatening military action; usually refers to the showdown between the United States and the Soviet Union over Cuba in October 1962

C

Canadian Charter of Rights and Freedoms: a document entrenched in the Constitutional Act, 1982 that lists and describes the fundamental rights and freedoms guaranteed to Canadians

capital: the money or other assets with which an entrepreneur starts in business; any tool or mechanism used in the creation of wealth. A hammer may be considered capital for a carpenter opening a business, or a fridge may be considered capital for an ice-cream vendor.

capitalism (laissez-faire capitalism): an economic system based on free markets, fair competition, wise consumers, and profit-motivated producers; a minimum of government involvement is favoured

censorship: the act of restricting freedom of expression or freedom of access to ideas or works, usually by governments, and usually to protect the perceived common good; may be related to speech, writings, works of art, religious practices, or military matters

Chartism: a working-class movement in Britain that focused on political and social reform from 1838 to 1848

citizen advocacy: a movement to strengthen citizen action and motivation to participate in community and civic affairs; often focuses on bringing the marginalized back into the community

citizenship: membership by birth or naturalization in a society, community, or country that entails definable rights of participation and protection, and certain responsibilities and duties to the society, community, or country

civil disobedience: the refusal to obey a law because it is considered to be unjust; a form of non-violent political protest

civility: thoughtfulness about how our actions may affect others, based on the recognition that human beings live together

civil rights movements: popular movements, notably in the United States in the 1950s and 1960s, that work to extend rights to marginalized members of society. Often these struggles aim not only for legal and civic rights, but also for respect, dignity, and economic and social equality for all.

classical conservatism: an ideology that says government should represent the legacy of the past as well as the well-being of the present, and that society should be structured in a hierarchical fashion, that government should be chosen by a limited electorate, that leaders should be humanitarian, and that the stability of society is all important

class system: the division of a society into different classes of people, usually based on income or wealth

climate change: the change in global weather patterns

Cold War: the political, economic, and social struggle between the Soviet Union and its allies, and the United States and its allies, conducted using propaganda, economic measures, and espionage rather than military means

collective identity: the identity that you share with other people as a member of a larger social group, such as a linguistic, faith, cultural, or ethnic group. Individuals have both individual identities and collective identities.

collective interest: the set of interests that members of a group have in common. The principle of collective interest states that while individual members may have individual interests, these interests are often better addressed by making them a common set of interests that the group can address together. Individuals have both individual interests and collective interests.

collective responsibility: holding a whole group or collective responsible for the actions of individuals (or individual groups) within the group or collective

collectivism: a current of thinking that values the goals of the group and the common good over the goals of any one individual

collectivization: an economic policy where all land is taken away from private owners and combined in large, collectively worked farms

command economy: an economic system based on public (state) ownership of property in which government planners decide which goods to produce, how to produce them, and how they should be distributed (for example, at what price they should be sold); also known as a centrally planned economy; usually found in communist states

common good: the good of a community; something that benefits the public health, safety, and/or well-being of society as a whole

communism: a system of society with property vested in the community and each member working for the common benefit according to his or her capacity and receiving according to his or her needs

competition: the act or an instance of competing or contending with others (for example, for supremacy, a position, or a prize). Competition is seen as an incentive for individuals and groups to work harder and more efficiently.

conscientious objection: the refusal to perform military service on moral or religious grounds

consensus decision making: a process whereby a group of individuals share ideas, solutions, and concerns to find a resolution to a problem that all members of the group can accept

consumerism: consumer spending; a preoccupation with consumer goods and their acquisition; a set of values focused on the acquisition and display of things in order to denote status

containment: the American Cold War foreign policy of containing the spread of communism by establishing strategic allies around the world through trade and military alliances

co-operation: working together to the same end; a principle emphasized by collectivist ideologies

D

deficit: a deficiency; an excess of liabilities or expenditures over income or assets in a given period. Deficit spending by a government is spending that is financed by borrowing and may occur in order to "kick-start" a stagnant economy.

democracy: a form of government in which power is ultimately vested in the people

détente: a period of the Cold War during which the major powers tried to lessen the tensions between them through diplomacy, arms talks and reductions, and cultural exchanges

deterrence: the Cold War foreign policy of both major powers aiming to deter the strategic advances of the other through arms development and arms build up. Deterrence depends on each combatant creating the perception that each is willing to resort to military confrontation.

dictatorship of the proletariat: the theoretical organization of a communist society in the early stage of communism. The centralized government of the state, which would be elected by the workers, would control all aspects of life.

direct democracy: a form of government in which the people participate in deciding issues directly. A direct democracy operates on the belief that every citizen's voice is important and necessary for the orderly and efficient operation of society.

dissent: the political act of disagreeing; the right to disagree. Sometimes dissent takes the form of popularly organized opposition to a tradition or an official policy or statute.

dissuasion: the French word for deterrence

draft: conscription or compulsory military service

draft dodger: someone who avoids conscription or compulsory military service, usually by fleeing to another country

drought: a severe lack of precipitation in a given area, which often affects crops

Dust Bowl: the regions of the Canadian Prairies and the Great Plains of the United States that were devastated by the drought and dust storms of the 1930s

E

economic equality: a principle common to collectivist ideologies which can have different meanings depending on the person or the ideology. Governments may try to foster economic equality through tax policies and by ensuring that all people earn equal wages for work of similar value.

economic freedom: the freedom to buy what you want and to sell your labour, idea, or product to whomever you wish

egalitarianism: a political principle that holds that all people should be treated as equals and allowed equal civil, social, political, and economic rights under the law

election fraud: changing the true results of an election by various means, including voter intimidation, multiple voting, destruction of ballots, tampering with ballots, or changing electoral boundaries to change the composition of a riding

emancipation: freeing from restraint, especially legal, social, or political

Emergencies Act: a set of laws that permits the Canadian government to invoke special measures to deal with emergencies. It replaced the War Measures Act in 1988. Emergencies can include those that affect public welfare and order, Canadian security, or war or other armed conflict. The legislation is designed to protect Canadians' fundamental rights and freedoms even in a time of crisis.

enclosure: the act of enclosing. Land that had been held in common becomes the private property of an individual.

enemy aliens: non-citizens who come from an enemy country

enfranchisement: granting people the rights of citizens, especially the right to vote

Enlightenment: An intellectual movement of the 17th and 18th centuries when classical liberalism spread through Europe and changed some people's beliefs about religion, reason, nature, and human beings; also called the Age of Reason

environmental change: the changes in the natural world around us

environmentalism: a political and ethical ideology that focuses on protecting the natural environment and lessening the harmful effects that human activities have on the ecosystem

espionage: the practice of spying or of using spies, especially to obtain secret information

expansionism: a country's foreign policy of acquiring additional territory through the violation of another country's sovereignty for reasons of defence, resources, markets, national pride, or perceived racial superiority

extremism: a term used by others to describe the beliefs and actions of those perceived to be outside of the accepted norms of political or social behaviour. Extremism may be a response adopted by those for whom ordinary political means of redressing perceived wrongs are deemed ineffective.

F

fascism: an extreme, right-wing, anti-democratic nationalist movement which led to totalitarian forms of governments in Germany and Italy from the 1920s to the 1940s

feminism: the belief in the social, political, and economic equality of the sexes. The term also stands for the movement that advocates for these equalities.

foreign policy: the course of action taken by a country in its relations with other countries

free market: a market that operates with limited government intervention. In a free-market economy, questions regarding production and marketing of goods and services are decided through the free interaction of producers and consumers.

G

global citizenship: being a citizen of the world; a feeling of responsibility, beyond a country's borders, toward humanity

global warming: an increase in the average temperature of the earth's atmosphere and a potential indicator of climate change

Great Depression: an economic crisis that began in late 1929 with the stock market crash and continued through the 1930s. During this period, banks failed, factories closed, many people became unemployed, and international trade declined.

greenhouse gas emissions: gases, from both natural and (primarily) human-made sources, that are released into the earth's atmosphere and change the way the atmosphere absorbs and emits radiation, which in turn affects the temperature of the earth

H

hot war: a traditional war which includes troops in direct conflict, as opposed to a cold war

humanist: someone who believes in the supremacy of reason of individuals over faith and who has developed an interpretation of history and beliefs about human nature, the structure of society, and the purpose of life, based on reason rather than religion

humanitarianism: trying to improve the lives of others and to reduce their suffering through various means, including social reform and aid

human rights: also known as "natural rights", the rights and freedoms to which all humans are entitled. These rights are enshrined in Bills and Declarations of Rights in many countries including Canada and the United States, and in the United Nations Universal Declaration of Human Rights.

I

ideology: a set of principles or ideas that explains your world and your place within it, which is based on certain assumptions about human nature and society and provides an interpretation of the past, an explanation of the present, and a vision for the future

illiberal: ideologies opposed to the values, beliefs, and principles of liberalism; usually refers to undemocratic actions but may be found in democratic countries during times of crisis.

income disparity: difference in earnings between the rich and the poor

Indian Act: an act of Parliament first passed in 1867, since amended many times, dealing with the governance of reserves and the rights and benefits of registered individuals. Included under the act are those First Nations peoples (and their descendants) who signed treaties or were otherwise registered in the act.

individualism: a current of thinking that values the freedom and worth of the individual, sometimes over the security and harmony of the group

individual rights and freedoms: a key principle of individualism and an important feature of liberal democracies; examples include freedom of religion, freedom of association, and the right to life, liberty, and the security of the person

industrialization: the stage of economic development during which the application of technology results in mass production and mass consumption within a country. This is accompanied by urbanization and changes in national living standards.

inflation: an increase in the general price level of products, the cost of labour, and interest rates

internment camp: detention facilities used to confine political prisoners and people of specific national or minority groups

iron curtain: a phrase coined by Winston Churchill in 1947 that refers to the barrier in Europe between self-governing, pro-democratic, pro-capitalist countries of the West and countries in pro-Soviet Eastern Europe under communist Soviet control

J

jus sanguinis: the right by blood; one of the two key legal principles of citizenship: the citizenship and nationality of a child is the same as the natural parents, wherever the child is born

jus soli: the right of the soil; one of the two key legal principles of citizenship: a person's citizenship or nationality is determined by place of birth

"just war": the idea that a country is right to go to war for certain reasons, including self-defence, defence of another country that is under attack, protection of innocents, and punishment for serious crimes

K

Kyoto Protocol or Kyoto Accord: an agreement reached at an international convention at which world leaders met to discuss climate change and create a plan for reducing greenhouse gases

Kyoto targets: the reduced levels of greenhouse gas emissions for each country set by the Kyoto Protocol

L

labour movement: the effort by organized labour to improve conditions for workers. Collective interest is the basis for the organized labour movement, which began during, and as a result of, the Industrial Revolution.

labour standards: government-enforced rules and standards aimed at safe, clean working environments, and the protection of workers' rights to free association, collective bargaining, and freedom from discrimination

labour unions: associations of workers engaged in a similar function who unite to speak with management about their concerns. Their purpose is to provide a united voice that speaks for the rights of its members.

laissez-faire: non-interference or non-intervention. Laissez-faire economics theory supports free markets and an individual's right to own private property.

Language legislation: laws regarding the official language of a state. In the Canadian context, such legislation is related either to Canada's official languages (for example, the Official Languages Act, 1969) or to Québec's *Charte de la langue française* (Charter of the French Language, such as Bill 101, 1977).

liberalism: a collection of ideologies all committed to the principle of the dignity and freedom of the individual as the foundation for society. Liberalism has faith in human progress and tends to favour decentralized power, both in political and economic affairs, and respect for the sovereignty of the reasoning individual.

liberation movements: military and political struggles of people for independence from countries that have colonized or otherwise oppressed them

limited government: the principle of little government involvement in the affairs of an economy, in the belief that this results in more efficient self-regulating markets

Luddism: a protest movement of the early 1800s against industrialization and mechanization. Protesters broke into factories and destroyed machines.

M

Marxism: a radical form of socialism, often called scientific socialism or communism to distinguish it from other socialist ideologies

McCarthyism: an anti-communist movement in the United States during the 1950s, led by Republican senator Joseph McCarthy. It was intended to uncover and persecute those with perceived ties to communism within the US government, universities, and entertainment industries.

mercantilism: an economic theory that says the aim of all economic pursuits should be to strengthen the power and wealth of the state

military dictatorship: a form of government in which political power resides with the military leadership. Some countries in Latin America, Africa, and the Middle East have presented many examples of military dictatorships.

mixed economy: an economic system based on free-market principles but with some government intervention, usually to regulate industry, to moderate the boom-and-bust nature of the free-market business cycle, and to offer social welfare programs. In some mixed economic systems, the government owns some key industries (such as communications, utilities, or transportation).

moderate socialism: a term used to distinguish the non-violent, non-revolutionary character of socialism from the communist idea of revolutionary change; sometimes referred to as democratic socialism

modern industrial complex: the structure of industry in Western society alluding to the partnership of industry and government

monopoly: the exclusive ownership or control of trade in a particular good or service

mutually assured destruction (MAD): a situation that would result from an unwinnable nuclear war. MAD ideally deters each side from entering into direct conflict.

N

naturalization: the process of applying for citizenship and becoming a citizen

neo-conservatism: an ideology that emerged in the United States during the 1950s and 1960s as a reaction against modern liberal principles. Some aspects of neo-conservatism challenge modern liberal principles and favour a return to particular values of classical liberalism. Other neo-conservative ideas challenge both classical and modern liberal principles and favour values identified as "family values" and traditional values, often resting on a religious foundation.

New Deal: economic policies put in place by US president Franklin D. Roosevelt in 1933. The policies gave government a more significant role in the regulation of the economy and in providing social "safety net" programs.

Nisga'a Final Agreement: a land claims settlement signed in 2000 between the Canadian and British Columbian governments and the Nisga'a First Nation. The agreement gives the Nisga'a control over their land, including the forestry and fishery resources contained in it.

no-fly list: a list of people whom the Canadian government has identified as potentially posing an immediate threat to aviation security. People on the list are barred from flying on domestic flights in Canada.

non-alignment: the position taken during the Cold War by those countries in the United Nations that did not form an alliance with either the United States or the Soviet Union. This group of countries became a third voting bloc within the UN and pushed for more aid for the developing world.

non-violence: a philosophy and strategy used to bring about political change. It may include civil disobedience, media campaigns, and targeted direct (non-violent) action.

nouveau riche: from French, meaning "newly wealthy"; factory owners, bankers, retailers, lawyers, engineers, and other professionals and entrepreneurs who gained their wealth during the Industrial Revolution. The term also generally refers to those people who are relatively new to wealth.

O

oligarchy: a form of government in which political power rests with a small elite segment of society. An oligarchy often consists of politically powerful families who pass on their influence to their children.

one-party state: a form of government where only one party forms the government and no other parties are permitted to run candidates for election

P

pacifism: a commitment to peace and opposition to war

pandemics: outbreaks of disease on a global scale

party solidarity: in the Canadian system, a requirement that all party members vote with their party, except in rare instances when the party leadership explicitly frees them from this obligation, in what is known as a free vote

personal identity: the idea you have of yourself as a unique individual; the collection of traits that you think of as distinguishing you from other people

perspective: the outlook of a particular group of people with the same age, culture, economics, faith, language, or other shared quality

philanthropy: a concern for, and an effort to improve, the state of humankind through donations of money, time, or talents

physiocrats: a group of Enlightenment philosophers in France who criticized the prevailing economics of mercantilism. Physiocrats believed that government should leave business entrepreneurs alone to follow their natural self-interest.

point of view: an individual's opinion, based on that individual's personal experience and values

political dissidents: people who disagree with the policies and actions of their government

Political participation: any number of ways a citizen can be involved in the political process, such as voting, running as a candidate, supporting a candidate, attending constituency meetings, speaking out, demonstrating, protesting, writing letters to elected representatives.

postmodernism: a movement of thought, art, and criticism that raises questions about the faith that moderns have in reason and in progress, and tries to get people to rethink their assumptions about the meaning of modern life

private property: something that is owned by an individual, including real estate, other forms of physical possessions, and intellectual property. The right to the protection of private property is a central principle of liberalism and is seen as a natural extension of the concept of the worth of each individual.

pro-democracy movements: movements or campaigns in favour of democracy

progressivism: a 1920s movement in the United States, usually associated with President Theodore Roosevelt, that reacted to the perceived abuses of laissez-faire capitalism by large corporations. Progressives favoured "a square deal" for average citizens and used legislation and some regulation of the marketplace to achieve this.

propaganda: exaggeration and misrepresentation of information to rally support for a cause or an issue

proportional representation: a system of government where citizens vote directly for a party, and then representatives are assigned based on the amount of popular support obtained. This results in a fairly accurate representation within the legislature of the will of the people.

protest: a statement of dissent; a public demonstration against the policies of a government or other organization

proxy wars: conflicts in which one superpower provides support to a group or state that opposes the rival superpower. The support may consist of money, arms, and personnel.

Public Health Agency of Canada (PHAC): a federal agency founded in 2006 to promote and protect the health and safety of Canadians with a focus on preventing chronic diseases and injuries, and responding to public health emergencies and infectious disease outbreaks

public property: anything (for example, land, buildings, or vehicles) not privately owned by individuals. Generally speaking, public property is owned by the state or the community, and managed according to the best interests of the community.

Q

Quebec Charter of Human Rights and Freedoms *(La Charte des droits et libertés de la personne)*: a statutory bill of rights and human rights code that was passed by the National Assembly of Québec in 1975

Quiet Revolution *(la Révolution tranquille)*: a time of rapid social, economic, and political modernization in Québec; a revolution without violence, force, or direct conflict, aimed at enhancing opportunities for Francophone Québécois within Québec society

R

radical: extreme; revolutionary. A radical change in a political regime often rejects the political and economic traditions of the past.

reactionary: tending to oppose change. A reactionary change in a political regime often idealizes the past and accepts economic inequality.

Reaganomics: the economic policies of the Ronald Reagan US presidency, which advocated less government intervention in the economy and pro-industry, anti-labour, anti-regulation, anti-environmental regulations policies

Red Paper: the name given to the National Indian Brotherhood's "Citizens Plus" which outlined their objections to the policy changes recommended in the Trudeau government's White Paper

red scare: an intense fear of communism that overcame the majority of the American population during and after the Second World War, influencing everything from movies and television to national security

Renaissance: a period in European history from about 1350 to 1600 that was characterized by a renewed interest in classical Greek and Roman culture, which included a renewed interest in humanism, the power of human reason and human creative potential, and the concept of the worth of the individual

representative democracy: a form of government in which a small group of politicians are elected by a larger group of citizens. The people participate in deciding issues through elected officials who represent them and make laws in their interests.

republican: a form of government where governing authority is vested in the hands of the representatives of the citizens and not a ruling monarch. Generally, a president is the head of state and the head of government.

residential school system: a school that provides dormitories for its students. As part of Canada's program for the assimilation of the Aboriginal peoples under the original Indian Act of 1867, Aboriginal children were removed from their communities and housed and taught in church-run residential schools.

Respect for law and order: one of the responsibilities of citizens in a liberal democratic society, where people enjoy a high degree of individual rights and freedoms. Failure on the part of the population to demonstrate this type of respect could result in a state of chaos.

responsible government: in the Canadian system, a form of representative democracy in which the branch of government that proposes laws, the executive branch of government (the prime minister and the cabinet ministers), is dependent on the direct or indirect support of elected members of the legislative branch (a majority of MPs in the House of Commons)

rule of law: a key principle in liberal democracies that states that every individual is equal before the law and all citizens are subject to the law

S

same-sex marriage: a marriage between two people of the same sex

satellite state: a state that is formally independent but is dominated by another more powerful state. Satellite states of the former Soviet Union included Bulgaria, Romania, Poland, Hungary, and East Germany.

self-interest: one's personal interest or advantage

self-reliance: the quality of being solely responsible for one's own well-being

Severe Acute Respiratory Syndrome (SARS): a respiratory disease spread through close contact with an infected person

single-member constituency: an electoral process whereby each constituency sends a single representative to the legislature; if there are more than two candidates competing in a constituency, the winner of the election may be supported by fewer than half the voters; also known as the "first past the post" system

socialism: any ideology that contains the belief that resources should be controlled by the public for the benefit of everyone in society, and not by private interests for the benefit of private owners and investors

social programs: programs that affect human welfare in a society. Social programs are intended to benefit citizens in areas such as education, health, and income support. Supporters base their support both on humanitarian principles and on economic principles.

sphere of influence: the territories and countries over which a powerful country dominates

stagflation: an economic condition where stagnation and high inflation occur at the same time. In the 1970s, stagflation was caused by a rapid increase in the price of oil.

superpower: a state that has great power and influence. The term was used to describe the United States and the Soviet Union because of their great influence and economic and military strengths.

T

terrorism: the policy of various ideological groups to disrupt the affairs of an enemy state or culture by the use of violent acts against non-combatants, in order to create debilitating terror and confusion

totalitarianism: a government system that seeks complete control over the public and private lives of its citizens

traditional economy: an economic system usually practised by a pre-industrialized society, where needs are met through agriculture, hunting, and fishing, and where there tends to be a division of labour based on custom and tradition

trickle-down economics: government economic policies that include reduced income and business taxes, reduced regulation (controls on business), and increased government spending on the military; also known as supply-side economics. Generally these policies favour industry, assuming that if industry prospers then everyone will prosper as wealth "trickles down" to the ordinary workers and consumers.

U

Universal Declaration of Human Rights (UDHR): a resolution adopted by the General Assembly of the United Nations in 1948. The declaration outlines the human rights to which all people are entitled.

universal suffrage: the right of all members of society, once they reach the age of accountability, to fully participate politically. This participation begins with the right to vote.

urbanization: an increase in the number of people residing in cities and an extension of urban boundaries to include areas that were previously rural

USA PATRIOT Act (the Uniting and Strengthening America by Providing Appropriate Tools Required to Intercept and Obstruct Terrorism Act): controversial legislation passed by the United States government in 2001 to deter and punish terrorist acts in the United States. Some Americans argue that the act is a threat to personal liberties.

Utopian socialists: humanitarians who advocated an end to the appalling conditions of the average worker in the industrial capitalist countries of the 19th century; people who believe it is possible to work to bring about a better world and that obvious evils can be eradicated

W

War Measures Act: a Canadian law that gave the federal cabinet emergency powers for circumstances where it determines that the threat of war, invasion, or insurrection, real or apprehended, exists. It was replaced by the Emergencies Act (1988).

"war on terror": a military, political, and ideological conflict headed by the United States, which was a direct result of the September 11, 2001, terrorist attacks on that country. There is some debate about whether terrorism can be defeated through military means.

water shortage: a lack of access to clean and safe drinking water. According to the United Nations, more than one billion people suffer from this shortage. Some people believe that this may also become a very significant issue for many societies in the near future.

welfare capitalism: initiatives by industrialists to provide workers with non-monetary rewards to head off the growing demand for labour unions; also refers to government programs that would provide social safety nets for workers

welfare state: a state in which the economy is capitalist, but the government uses policies that directly or indirectly modify the market forces in order to ensure economic stability and a basic standard of living for its citizens, usually through social programs

White Paper: an official government document that outlines that government's policies. In 1969, the government of Prime Minister Trudeau issued a controversial White Paper that proposed to abolish treaties, the Department of Indian Affairs, and everything else that had kept the First Nations and Inuit people distinct from the people of Canada.

World Health Organization (WHO): the directing and coordinating authority for health within the United Nations system

worldview: a collection of beliefs about life and the universe held by an individual or group; the lens through which the world is viewed by an individual or group; the overall perspective from which the world is interpreted

People, Organizations, and Places Index

Wal-Mart, 497–498
Walsh, Mary, 490
Wappel, Tom, 375–376
Weinstein, Michael M., 320
Wells, H.G., 138
Wen Jiabao, 468
Werbach, Adam, 497–498
Wiegand, Steve, 338
Wilson, Charlie, 259
Wilson, Karina, 45–46
Wilson, Stuart, 95
Wilson, Woodrow, 319
Wollenberger, Vera, 261
Wollstonecraft, Mary, 73, 158

Wood, Chris, 434
Woolf, Virginia, 138
Workers' Party, 155–156
Workers Unity League, 146
Works Progress Administration, 209
World Health Organization (WHO), 431
World Trade Organization (WTO), 285
Worldwatch Institute, 282

Y

Yanukovych, Viktor, 476–477
Yeh Hum Naheen Foundation, 494

Yugoslavia, and Non-Aligned Movement, 247–248
Yunus, Muhammad, 90–91
Yushchenko, Viktor, 477

Z

Zakaria, Fareed, 328
Zambia, *humanism*, 223
Zola, Émile, 122

Subject Index

A

Aboriginal justice, 295
Aboriginal peoples
　and assimilationist policies, 308–311
　and citizenship, 457–458, 462–463
　collectivism, 12–13, 15, 81–82
　constitutional rights of, 312, 370, 377, 379–380, 386–387, 389
　contact with Europeans, 106
　enfranchisement, 308–309, 310
　entrepreneurialism, 96–97
　environmental degradation and, 434–435
　government, 116
　holistic learning models, 23, 25–26
　Indian Act, 309–310, 312
　"Indian" status, 308–309, 310, 463
　land, relationship to, 39–41, 74, 422
　land claims, 312–313, 389
　land dispute, 384–385
　land holding, concept of, 307–308
　language, 42
　laws of relationships, 306
　political activism, 55–56
　repatriation, 40
　residential schools, 308
　self-governance, 75, 296, 313
　suffrage, 157, 204
　treaties, 307–308, 310, 387–388
　worldview, 23–24
Abortion, decriminalized, 371
Absolute monarchy, 358
Activism. *See* Civic participation
Adherence to collective norms, 85–86
Affirmative action, 377
Age of Reason, 106. *See also* Enlightenment
Agricultural Adjustment Act, 209
Air traffic controllers strike, 220
Albania, and Soviet bloc, 239

Alignment, 249–250
American Bill of Rights, 378
American Revolution, 114, 117, 141, 460
An Inconvenient Truth (film), 87, 282
Anti-apartheid movement, 479–484
Anti-communism, 210, 212, 216. *See also* Red scare
Anti-Semitism, 177, 188–189
Anti-Terrorism Act, 396, 402
Anti-trust legislation, 200
Anti-war movement, 486–489, 490–491
Apartheid, 479. *See also* Anti-apartheid movement
Argentina, authoritarianism in, 364
Arms race, 239, 256
Assimilation, 42, 303, 308–312
Atlantic Charter, 237
Autarky, 188
Authoritarianism, 356–366
　controlled participation, 363
　defined, 357
　directing public discontent, 363–364
　military dictatorships, 360–361
　oligarchies, 359
　one-party states, 359–360
　political systems, 357–561
　propaganda, 362, 363
　strengths and weaknesses of, 365–366
　terror, 364–365
　vision, 361–362
Auto industry, 204
Autonomy, 65

B

Bandung Conference, 249–250
Bank runs, 206
Barriere Lake Algonquin First Nation, 75

Bay of Pigs Invasion, 255
Beliefs and values, 23, 28–30
Berlin airlift, 244–245
Berlin Wall, 246–247
Bible, 34, 70, 460
Bicameral legislature, 340
Bill 101. *See* Charter of the French Language
Bill C-150. *See* Criminal Code revision, sexual preference
Blacklisting, 267
Bloody Sunday, 164–165
Boycott, 200, 256, 267, 321, 480, 496–497,
Brave New World (Huxley), 8, 27–28, 272
Breast cancer, ending, 503–504
Bretton Woods Agreement, 216
Brinkmanship, 254–255
"Bystanders" (inaction), 498, 499

C

Canada Pension Plan, 78, 215
Canadian Charter of Rights and Freedoms, 42, 46, 73, 370–373, 377–379, 382, 383, 386, 389, 401, 402, 414, 461–462
Canadian Citizenship Act, 46
Canadian Constitution, 42, 117, 309–312, 338, 370, 373, 375, 377, 379, 386, 389
"Cap and trade" system, 282–283
Capital, 121
Capitalism, 102, 110–113, 119–120, 156, 276, 415. *See also* Welfare capitalism
reactions to, 131–141
Capital punishment, abolition of, 351
Carbon tax, 282–283, 426
Case-Church Amendment, 489
Celebrities, and social issues, 500–501

freedom of religion, 288–289
Great Depression and, 144–145,
    205–212
Keynesian economics, 148–149,
    208–209, 219
limitations on religious practices
    and symbolism, 288–289,
    292–293, 390–392
limited government, 202–203,
    220–221
monetarism, 217–219
and positive freedoms, 278–279
postwar consensus, 214
problems in spreading democracy,
    328–329
progressivism, 199
state intervention, 198, 205–216,
    225–227
welfare state, 78, 144–145, 209,
    215
Molotov Plan, 243
Monetarism, 217–219
Monetary policy, 148–149
Monopoly, 107, 136, 200
Mujahedeen, 259
Multiculturalism Policy, 46
Multiple citizenship, 455–456
Mutually assured destruction (MAD),
    251–252

N

Nation, 51
National Housing Act, 211
National security, and civil liberties,
    368, 395–404, 414
National Security Letters, 403
Nativism, 202–203, 205
Naturalization, 447–448
Neo-conservatism, 284–286
New Deal, 150, 208–210, 213
New Economic Policy, 181
"Night of the Long Knives," 187
Nineteen Eighty-Four (Orwell), 7–8, 86,
    272
Nisga'a Final Agreement, 313
No-fly lists, 403–404
Non-alignment, 250–251
Non-confidence vote, 333, 339
Non-governmental organizations
    (NGOs), 94–95
Non-smokers, rights of, 393
Non-violent protest, 480, 481, 495–496
North American Free Trade Agreement
    (NAFTA), 229, 437
Nouveau riche, 122
Nuclear war, threat of, 263–264
Nuclear weapons, 239–240, 251, 252,
    253–254

Nunavut government, 294–295,
    353–354
Nuremberg Laws, 190

O

October Crisis, 1970, 400–401, 414
Oil sands, 419–420, 434
Old Age Security, 215
Oligarchy, 359
One-party state, 359–360
On-to-Ottawa Trek, 208
Orange Revolution, in Ukraine, 476–478
Osoyoos Indian Band, 96–97
Our Ukraine (OU), 478

P

Pacifism, 469–471
Padlock Law, 212, 216
Pandemics, 430–433
Parliamentary democracy, 332–333,
    339–341
Party solidarity, 332
Passing of the Great Race, The (Grant),
    205
Pass Laws, 480
Peacekeeping, 253, 326
Peace movement. *See* Anti-war
    movement
People's Charter, 132–133
Personal identity, 23
Perspective, 5, 297–298
Philanthropy, 465–466
Physiocrats, 111–112
Pietà (Michelangelo), 69
Plebiscites, 338. *See also* Referendums
Pluralism, 46
Point of view, 5, 297–298
Polder Model, 223
Political dissidents, 169, 364, 480
Political doctrines, 318
Political participation, 450–452
Political philosophy, 65
Polygamy, 292–293
Positive freedoms, 278–279
Postmodernism, 406–407, 410–412
Postwar consensus, 214
Potsdam Conference, 239
Private property, 74–77, 107
Privatization, 221
Pro-democracy movement, in Ukraine,
    476–478
Progress, ideal of, 305–306
Progressive taxation, 80
Progressivism, 51, 143, 199–200
"Proletarian internationalism," 239
Propaganda, 178, 185–186, 362, 363
Proportional representation, 343–345

protest, 131–133, 164–165, 208, 210,
    279, 288–289, 303, 313–314,
    326–327, 365, 372, 385, 391, 413,
    444, 451–452, 476–478, 479–482,
    483, 485–489, 490–491, 495–496,
    500–501
Protestant Reformation, 70, 106, 114
Proxy war, 258–260
Public property, 82–83
Pure Food and Drug Act, 199

Q

Quakerism, 469–471
Quarantine Act, 433
Québec Act, 43
Québec Charter of Human Rights and
    Freedoms, 281, 373
Québécois nationalism, 400
Quiet Revolution (la Révolution
    tranquille), 400
Quran, 460

R

Race, 51
Radical (totalitarian regimes), 167
Reactionary (totalitarian regimes), 167
Reagonomics, 220–221
Recall election, 338
Red Paper, 311–312
Red scare, 202, 265–267
Referendums, 338, 351
Reform Acts, 133
Regina Manifesto, 138–139
Regina Riot, 208
Reichstag Fire Decree, 187
Reign of Terror, 115
Religion, 34, 36, 51, 287–293
Renaissance, 68–70, 106
Repatriation, 40
Representation by population, 339,
    340, 341
Representative democracy, 18, 338–339
Representative recall, 338
Republican government, 117, 337–338,
    341–343
Residential schools, 308
Responsible government, 332–333, 339
Restorative justice, 295
Revenue Acts, 202, 203
Rising Tide of Color, The (Stoddard), 205
Road to Serfdom (Hayek), 275
Royal Proclamation of 1763, 310
Rule of law, 71–72
Russian Revolution, 164–165, 168–172,
    202

Photo Credits

t=top; c=centre; b=bottom; l=left; r=right

2 (t) Pablo Picasso, *Jacqueline Rocque* (1954), oil and charcoal on canvas, Picasso Estate. © Pablo Picasso Estate / SODRAC (2009). Photo: Online Picasso Project (Dr. Enrique Mallen, Director), (bl) Pablo Picasso, *Jacqueline* (1960), oil on canvas, Private Collection. © Pablo Picasso Estate / SODRAC (2009). Photo: Online Picasso Project (Dr. Enrique Mallen, Director), (br) Pablo Picasso, *Jacqueline Rocque* (1954), oil and charcoal on canvas, Private Collection. © Pablo Picasso Estate / SODRAC (2009). Photo: Online Picasso Project (Dr. Enrique Mallen, Director); 4 © Ted Horowitz/CORBIS; 8 © Photos 12 / Alamy; 9 © Jason Love/www.Cartoon Stock.com; 11 © Ronaldo Dias/www.CartoonStock.com; 14 (tl) CP (David Boily), (tr) CP/Charlottetown Guardian(Brian McInnis), (bl) Victor Last Geographical Visual Aids, (br) Bill Ivy/Ivy Images; 15 CP(Adrian Wyld); 17 (l) Spencer Grant\PhotoEdit, Inc., (r) © David Stoecklein/ CORBIS; 19 © Copyright 2002 Mark Stivers; 20 (c) CP/Toronto Star Syndicate, (br) CP/Rex Features; 25 Canadian Council on Learning, "Redefining how success is measured in Aboriginal learning." http://www.ccl-cca.ca/NR/rdonlyres/93F93D9E-9CD4-482D-987D-8009D1DC088D/0/CCLLearningModelMET.pdf; 26 Canadian Council on Learning, "Redefining how success is measured in Aboriginal learning." http://www.ccl-cca.ca/CCL/Reports/RedefiningSuccessInAboriginal Learning/RedefiningSuccessModelsMétis.htm; 27 © John Wang/ maxximages.com; 29 Holly Harris/Getty Images; 31 © Betsy Streeter/ www.CartoonStock.com; 35 Larry MacDougal/First Light; 36 (tl) © Mike Baldwin /www.CartoonStock.com, (b) UN Photo; 37 (tl) CP/Edmonton Sun (Darryl Dyck), (cr) © Fran/www.CartoonStock.com; 41 Wikipedia Commons; 44 (t) © Mike Shapiro/www.CartoonStock.com, (b) Copyright © 2006 Off the Wahl Productions; The Granger Collection, New York; 69 (tl) © Francis G. Mayer/CORBIS, (tr) © Araldo de Luca/CORBIS, (c) © Priamo Melo/iStock; 82 Talking Circle (2005), Leah Marie Dorion. Metis artist, Prince Albert, SK. Used by permission of the artist and Feather Child Gallery; 84 © Catherine Karnow/CORBIS; 87 Amy Graves/ WireImage/Getty Images; 90 © Karen Kasmauski/Corbis; 92 CP/ Maclean's (Phil Snel); 94 © Ricki Rosen/CORBIS SABA; 95 HFHI/ Gregg Pachkowski; 97 Courtesy of the Nk'Mip Desert Cultural Centre; 100 (bl) Paul Gauguin, French, 1848–1903. *Where Do We Come From? What Are We? Where Are We Going?* (detail), 1897–98. Oil on canvas. Image: 139.1 x 374.6 cm (54 3/4 x 147 1/2 in.). Framed: 171.5 x 406.4 x 8.9 cm (67 1/2 x 160 x 3 1/2 in.). Museum of Fine Arts, Boston. Tompkins Collection—Arthur Gordon Tompkins Fund, 36.270. Photograph © 2009, Museum of Fine Arts, Boston, (br) © Yetish Yetish / Alamy; 102 The Granger Collection, New York; 106 The Granger Collection, New York; 108 *The Battle of Edgehill in 1642* (engraving), Gucht, Michael van der (1660-1725) / National Army Museum, London / The Bridgeman Art Library International; 109 Thomas Coex/AFP/Getty Images; 110 The Granger Collection, New York; 112 © stockcam/ iStockphoto.com; 115 The Granger Collection, New York; 120 Science Museum; 121 (t) © Underwood & Underwood/CORBIS, (b) © Mary Evans Picture Library / Alamy; 122 MPI/Getty Images; 124 CP/Everett Collection; 128 (t) The Granger Collection, New York, (b) AP Photo/The Journal of New Ulm, Steve Muscatello; 132 *Workmen take out their anger on the machines*, Doughty, C.L. (1913-85) / Private Collection / © Look and Learn / The Bridgeman Art Library International; 135 © Worldwide Picture Library / Alamy; 140 © The Art Archive/Corbis; 142 "Mother Goose & Grimm" used with the permission of Grimmy, Inc. and the Cartoonist Group. All rights reserved.; 144 CBC/Library and Archives Canada / C-013236; 146 A Gushul Photograph courtesy Gushul Collection Crowsnest Museum; 160 (l) & (c): Reproduced with permission of Punch, Ltd., www.punch.co.uk; (r) Bibliothèque nationale de France; 161 © Bettmann/CORBIS; 164 ©Topham / The Image Works; 165 Copyright by Bill Mauldin (1958). Courtesy of the Bill Mauldin Estate LLC. Photo: Library of Congress, Prints & Photographs Division, LC-USZ62-116324; 169 *From Lodging to Lodging*, 1876 (oil on canvas), Vasnetsov, Victor Mikhailovich (1848-1926) / Tretyakov Gallery, Moscow, Russia / RIA Novosti / The Bridgeman Art Library International; 171 CP/Everett Collection; 173 © CORBIS; 175 Hulton Archive/Getty Images; 178 (r) © Ann Ronan Picture Library / Heritage-Images / The Image Works; 179 © Topham / The Image Works; 181 Courtesy of the Gareth Jones Website, www.garethjones.org. Original Research, Content & Site Design by Nigel Linsan Colley; 183 © SV-Bilderdienst / The Image Works; 185 National Library of Russia; 189 Imagno/Getty Images; 192 ©

Dr. George J. Wittenstein; 196 Library of Congress, Prints & Photographs Division, LC-USZ62-126046; 202 Wikipedia Commons; 206 © Hulton-Deutsch Collection/CORBIS; 209 © CORBIS; 210 North Carolina Collection, University of North Carolina Library at Chapel Hill; 214 CP; 219 (l) George Rose/Getty Images, (r) © J.L. Atlan/Sygma/CORBIS; 220 Yvonne Hemsey/Getty Images; 221 ©Peter Arkell / Impact / HIP / The Image Works; 223 © K.M. Westermann/CORBIS; 224 © Lynsey Addario/ Corbis; 230 Stan Honda/AFP/Getty Images; 232 Cleland Rimmer/ Evening Standard/Getty Images; 242 The Granger Collection, New York; 246 United States Air Force; 247 © 1952 Time Inc.; 250 AP Photo/Henry Griffin; 255 Central Intelligence Agency (www.cia.org); 256 © Amerika Haus / Sueddeutsche Zeitung Photo / The Image Works; 261 American Stock/Getty Images; 265 AP Photo; 266 Catechetical Guild Educational Society of St. Paul, Minnesota; 273 ANGLO ENTERPRISE/VINEYARD / THE KOBAL COLLECTION; 277 The Granger Collection, New York; 279 CP(Bullit Marquez); 280 © Copyright 2006 Eric Allie; 281 AP Photo/Greenpeace, Miller, HO; 285 AP Photo; 286 © GARY HERSHORN/Reuters/Corbis; 287 © Bettmann/CORBIS; 290 Cynthia Johnson//Time Life Pictures/Getty Images; 294 CP(Paul Chiasson); 300 (l) © Mike Dobel / Alamy, (c) Reg Lancaster/Express/Getty Images, (r) CP/Everett Collection; 303 CP(Fred Chartrand); 304 © Syracuse Newspapers/John Berry/ The Image Works; 309 Pittaway & Jarvis/Library and Archives Canada/C-003812; 311 CP; 314 CP(Tom Hanson); 315 © Copyright 2009 Barb Cranmer; 318 CP/Maclean's(Phill Snel); 319 CP(Matthew Fearn); 322 © Claudio Furnier / www.CartoonStock.com; 323 CP(Kevin Frayer); 324 CP (Tsvangirayi Mukwazh); 326 CP(Ariana Cubillos); 327 By permission of Gary Markstein and Creators Syndicate, Inc.; 332 CP(Tom Hanson); 333 (l) CP(Derek Oliver), (r) CP(Tom Hanson); 335 © Bettmann/CORBIS; 337 Steve Dykes/Getty Images; 348 © Joe Heller/Green Bay Press-Gazette; 350 © 2006 Brian Fairrington and PoliticalCartoons.com; 351 Harley Schwadron/Artizans.com; 357 © Bettmann/CORBIS; 360 © Bettmann/CORBIS; 362 Valentina Kulagina, *8 Million Tons of Pig Iron* (1931), Lithograph. © Estate of Valentina Kulagina / SODRAC (2009). Photo: Collection International Institute of Social History, Amsterdam; 363 (l) © Lisa Young / Alamy, (r) ; 369 © JIM YOUNG/Reuters/Corbis; 372 DAVID BOILY/AFP/Getty Images; 375 Norm Betts/Bloomberg News /Landov; 377 CP; 381 © Gregory Davies / Alamy; 383 Bado/Artizans.com; 384 CP (Dave Chidley); 390 © Fred de Noyelle/Godong/Corbis; 392 © Annie Griffiths Belt/CORBIS; 393 © Roy McMahon/Corbis; 395 Courtesy Keith Millions; 396 REUTERS/Chris Wattie /Landov; 398 Glenbow Archives NA-1870-6; 399 (l) National Film Board of Canada/Library and Archives Canada/C-024452, (r) Vancouver Public Library, Special Collections, VPL 12851; 401 CP; 402 Jeff Stahler: © Columbus Dispatch/Dist. by Newspaper Enterprise Association, Inc.; 407 (l) The Granger Collection, New York, (r) © CHRISTINNE MUSCHI/Reuters/Corbis; 411 The Etchasketchist; 413 AP Photo/Pavel Rahman; 420 © Greenpeace; 421 Wikipedia Commons; 425 © CHRISTINNE MUSCHI/Reuters/Corbis; 426 CP(Tom Hanson); 428 © Ryan Pyle/Corbis; 429 Soham Banerjee/Wikipedia Commons; 430 © Copyright 2008 Tab, The Calgary Sun, and PoliticalCartoons.com; 431 *The Four Horsemen of the Apocalypse*, 31" x 48", Ed. 30, 1995. Artist - Daniel O. Stolpe; 432 CP (Kevin Frayer); 434 (l) © David Gray/Reuters/ Corbis, (c) AP Photo/Michael Reilly, (r) © Diego Azubel/epa/Corbis; 437 Glenbow Archives NA-2928-26; 440 Image courtesy Central Asia Institute; 444 CP(Charles Dharapak); 446 (l) CP(Les Perreaux), (r) Source: AR2005-A01-369 Combat Camera, http://www.combatcamera. forces.gc.ca/netpub/server.np?original=62105&site=combatcamera&catalo g=photos. Reproduced with the permission of the Minister of Public Works and Government Services, 2009; 452 (l) CP(Graham Hughes), (r) CP/Edmonton Sun(Jason Franson); 455 Laura Boushnak/AFP/Getty Images; 459 CP PHOTO/HO, Christian Peacemaker Teams; 460 © British Museum / Art Resource, NY; 464 CP(Colin Perkl); 468 © epa/Corbis; 472 CP(Colin Perkel); 476 CP(Efrem Lukatsky); 477 AP Photo/Efrem Lu; 480 UN Photo; 482 CP(Jerome Delay); 487 AP Photo/Henri Huet; 488 (tl) AP Photo/Nick Ut, (br) © BettmannCORBIS; 489 AP Photo; 490 (l) Courtesy of Footnote.com, (r) CP (Khue Bui); 492 Alexandra Moe, New America Media; 493 YURIKO NAKAO/Reuters /Landov; 494 Courtesy of Waseem Mahmood; 495 © 2008, Jeff Parker, Florida Today, and PoliticalCartoons.com; 496 CP; 500 © J.P. Moczulski/Reuters/Corbis; 508 © CIDA Photo: Stephanie Colvey; 512 *Citizen Cube*, Brenda Guyton. Reprinted by permission of the artist.

Text Credits

8 "Foreword", from *Amusing Ourselves to Death* by Neil Postman, copyright © 1985 by Neil Postman. Used by permission of Viking Penguin, a division of Penguin Group (USA) Inc. 13 originally drawn by Mike Martin for Native Council of Nova Scotia Mi'kmaq Language Program, PO Box 1320, Truro, Nova Scotia B2N 5N2 13 Marie Battiste and James Youngblood Henderson, *Protecting Indigenous Knowledge and Heritage*, Purich Publishing Ltd., Saskatoon, p. 55 15 Marie Battiste and James Youngblood Henderson, *Protecting Indigenous Knowledge and Heritage*, Purich Publishing Ltd., Saskatoon, p. 56 21 "Shunning materialism saves money", Candice Choi, The Associated Press, July 19, 2008 © The Associated Press 2008 25 Canadian Council on Learning, "Redefining how success is measured in Aboriginal learning." http://www.ccl-cca.ca/NR/rdonlyres/93F93D9E-9CD4-482D-987D-8009D1DC088D/0/CCLLearningModelMET.pdf 26 Canadian Council on Learning, "Redefining how success is measured in Aboriginal learning." http://www.ccl-cca.ca/CCL/Reports/RedefiningSuccessInAboriginal Learning/RedefiningSuccessModelsMétis.htm 32 Reverend John E. Gibbons, "Simpson Family Values" (Unitarian minister, the First Parish in Bedford, Massachusetts, excerpt from sermon, October 28, 2001), http://www.uubedford.org/sermons/JEG-SimpsonsValues-10-28-01.htm 39 Sam Metcalfe, quoted in *Report of the Royal Commission on Aboriginal Peoples*, Vol. 4, Perspectives and Realities, Chapter 3, "Elders' Perspectives", 1996. http://www.aincinac.gc.ca/ap/pubs/sg/cg/cj3-eng.pdf, p. 2. 40 Cynthia Chambers and Narcisse Blood, Publication Date: 2009, Source: *International Journal of Canadian Studies*, Issue 39 40-41 Clayton Thomas-Müller, "Tar Sands: Environmental Justice and Native Rights." Tar Sands Watch, http://www.tarsandswatch.org/tar-sands-environmental-justice-and-native-rights, March 25, 2008 41 Oscar Kistabish, Val d'Or, Québec, November 30, 1992, quoted in *Report of the Royal Commission on Aboriginal Peoples*, 1,2, Chapter 11, "Relocation of Aboriginal Communities," http://www.ainc-inac.gc.ca/ch/rcap/sg/sg41_e.html 43 Statistics Canada, "Population by mother tongue, by province and territory (2006 Census)", http://www40.statcan.gc.ca/l01/cst01/demo11 c-eng.htm 45-46 Karina Wilson, MediaKnowAll, "Ideology." www.mediaknowall.com/alevkeyconcepts/ideology.html 48 Shelley Boettcher, "Green Wedding: Calgary couples hitch their nuptials to the eco-movement." *Calgary Herald* 2007. Material reprinted with the express permission of: "Calgary Herald Group Inc.", a CanWest Partnership 52-53 Tommy Douglas, "On His Legacy: to a NDP audience in Prince Albert, Saskatchewan—November 27, 1970." Tommy Douglas Research Institute. http://www.tommydouglas.ca/speeches/legacy-1970 54-55 Milton Friedman, quoted in Micheline Ishay, *The Human Rights Reader* (NewYork: Routledge, 2007), pp. 343–346. Used with permission of: The Smith Center for Private Enterprise Studies College of Business and Economics California State University, East Bay, http://thesmithcenter.org 55-56 Ovide Mercredi, quoted in *Saskatchewan Indian*, 21, 3 (May, 1992), p. 7. 58 Sukhpal Singh, "Myanmar condemns foreign aids for linking aid money to have full access in the region." MindTalks.org, May 30, 2008. http://www.mindtalks.org/misc/myanmar-condemns-foreign-aids-for-linking-aid-money-to-have-full-access-in-the-region.html 58-59 C. Moore (Reuters), "A month after Nargis, junta still under fire." June 1, 2008 59 "Burmese Endure in Spite of Junta, Aid Workers Say." From *The New York Times*, June 18, 2008 © 2008 The New York Times. All rights reserved. Used by permission and protected by the Copyright Laws of the United States. The printing, copying, redistribution, or retransmission of the Material without express written permission is prohibited. www.nytimes.com 64 Yung Suk Kim (theology professor at Virginia Union University), The Roots of Individualism. http://www.youaregood.com/rootsof individualism.pdf 64 Albert Einstein, "An Ideal of Service to Our Fellow Man," from *This I Believe* (essay collection). David Domine [trans.]. Essay courtesy of the Albert Einstein Archives at the Hebrew University of Jerusalem. *This I Believe*, http://www.npr.org/templates/story/story.php? storyId=4670423, May 31, 2005.1954, AEA 28-1067 66-67 Mary Anulik Kutsiq, "An Elder Offers Advice." Inuktitut magazine 79 (Fall 1995): 11, 14–15. , www.itk.ca 75 "A Call for Endorsements and Solidarity", Barriere Lake Solidarity Collective 76 Ronald A. Cass, Chairman, Center for the Rule of Law, http://www.ruleoflaw.org/Issues.html 77 "Woman Faces the Music, Loses Download Case." The Associated Press, October 4, 2007, © The Associated Press 2007 77 University of Ottawa, "File-sharing." Canadian Internet Policy and Public Interest Clinic, June 2, 2007. http://www.cippic.ca/

file-sharing/ 86 *Nineteen Eighty Four* by George Orwell (Copyright © George Orwell, 1949) Reprinted by permission of Bill Hamilton as the Literary Executor of the Estate of the Late Sonia Brownell Orwell and Secker & Warburg Ltd. 90 Brian Bergman, "John Stanton." *Maclean's*, July 1, 2004. http://www.macleans.ca/article.jsp?content=20040701_83575_83575 92 Canadian Child Care Federation, "CCCF Urges New Government to Work Together to Solve Child Care Crisis in Canada." January 24, 2006. http://www.cccf-fcsge.ca/pressroom/pr_32_en.htm 93 CBC News Online, "Day Care." CBC.ca, July 5, 2006. © CBC 2006 http://www.cbc.ca/news/ background/daycare/ 93 Based on Figure 5.3. Public expenditure on ECEC services (0-6 years) in selected OECD countries (%),Starting Strong II: Early Childhood Education and Care, OECD 2006 94-95 John Ralston Saul, "Struggling for Balance: Public Education and Civil Society," a speech given at the University of Calgary, March 25, 2003. Governor General of Canada. http://www.gg.ca/media/doc.asp?lang=e&DocID=4026 95 Stuart Wilson (a South African from the gated community adjacent to Ethembeni, site of the 2002 Jimmy Carter Work Project), quoted on Habitat World http://www.habitat. org/hw/june-july04/notes.html 96-97 Proceedings of the Standing Senate Committee on Aboriginal Peoples. Issue 13, "Evidence," meeting on October 26, 2005. http://www.parl.gc.ca/38/1/parlbus/commbus/senate/Com-e/abor-e/13evb-e.htm?Language=E&Parl=38&Ses=1&comm_id=1 97 Proceedings of the Standing Senate Committee on Aboriginal Peoples. Issue 13, "Evidence," meeting on October 26, 2005. http://www.parl.gc.ca/38/1/parlbus/commbus/ senate/Com-e/abor-e/13evb-e.htm?Language=E&Parl=38&Ses=1&comm_id=1 105 Gaus, Gerald and Shane Courland, "Liberalism", Stanford Encyclopedia of Philosophy (Fall 2008 Edition), Edward N. Zalta (ed.), URL: http://plato. stanford.edu/entries/liberalism/#DebAboLib 125 "IRWeb: Information Page." Oracle Education Foundation ThinkQuest. http://library.thinkquest.org/4132/ info.htm 125 Europe and their cultural offshoots, such as the United States, the most powerful in the world in the eighteenth Joseph A. Montagna, "The Industrial Revolution." Yale-New Haven Teachers Institute. http://www.yale. edu/ynhti/curriculum/ units/1981/2/81.02.06.x.html 155 The Universal Declaration of Human Rights © United Nations, 1948. Reproduced with permission. 156 *How Capitalism Saved America: The Untold History of our Country, from the Pilgrims to the Present* by Thomas J. DiLorenzo, copyright © 2004 by Thomas J. DiLorenzo. Used by permission of Crown Forum, an imprint of Crown Publishers, a division of Random House, Inc. 183 Nadezhda Joffe, *Back in Time: My Life, My Fate, My Epoch* trans. Frederick S. Choate (Oak Park, MI: Labor Publications, 1995), p. 237. 190 Liselotte Katscher from Women in Nazi Germany (Seminar Studies in History) by Jill Stephenson, publisher: Longman 191 David Crossland, "'Himmler was mygodfather'." The Times Online November 6, 2006. http://www.timesonline. co.uk/tol/news/world/europe/article626101.ece 193-194 Martha Dodd, My Years in Germany,1939, quoted on Spartacus Educational. http://www.spartacus.schoolnet.co.uk/GERwomen.htm 196-197 Website of the PBS series *American Experience*, "Emma Goldman" episode, "People & Events: Henry Clay Frick (1849–1919)", March 2004. http://www.pbs.org/ wgbh/amex/goldman/peopleevents/p_frick.html 201 John Dos Passos, *Manhattan Transfer* (1925), p. 21, Houghtan Mifflan. Used with permission. French translation by Maurice-Edgar Coindreau © Editions Gallimard 205 "Ashes To Ashes, Dust To Dust" written by Woody Guthrie and Hans-Eckardt Wenzel © Copyright Secured WOODY GUTHRIE PUBLICATIONS (BMI) ADMINISTERED BY BUG MUSIC. ALL RIGHTS RESERVED. USED BY PERMISSION 213 Mike Denos and Roland Case, *Teaching about Historical Thinking*,eds. Peter Seixas and Penny Clark(Vancouver: University of British Columbia, 2006). 217 James Callaghan, speech at a Labour Party conference, quoted in Michael Starks, *Not for Profit, Not for Sale*, (New Brunswick, NJ: Transaction Books, Rutgers University,1992) p. 10. 220 & 221 Excerpted from *The Shock Doctrine: The Rise of Disaster Capitalism* by Naomi Klein. Copyright © 2007 Naomi Klein. Reprinted by permission of Knopf Canada. 222 "UK Politics: What is the Third Way?" BBC News, September 27, 1999. http://news.bbc.co.uk/2/hi/uk_news/politics/458626.stm 226-227 Reprinted with permission from *Utne Reader* (May-June 2003); www. Utne.com, Copyright © 2003 Ogden Publications, Inc. 229 "Free-Market Upheaval Grinds Mexico's Middle Class" From *The New York Times*, September 3, 2002 © 2002 The New York Times. All rights reserved. Used by permission and protected by the Copyright Laws of the United States. The printing, copying, redistribution, or retransmission of the Material without express written permission is prohibited. www.nytimes.com 237 The Yalta Accords, "Part II: Declaration on Liberated Europe," February 11, 1945, quoted in Richard Sakwa, The Rise and Fall of the Soviet Union, 1917–1991 (New York: Routledge, 1999), p. 280 **241** N. Novikov (Soviet Ambassador to the United States), telegram to the Soviet Leadership, September 27, 1946. Cold War International History Project, http://www.wilsoncenter.org/index.cfm?topic_id=1409&fuseaction=va2.document&identifier=952E8C7F-423B-763D-D5662C42501C9BEA&sort=Collection&item=US-Soviet%20Relations, www.cwihp.org **243** Divine, Robert A.; Breen, T.H.H.; Fredrickson, George M.; Williams, R. Hal; Gross, Arielaj; Brands, H.W.; *America Past and Present,* 8th Edition, © 2007, p. 815. Reprinted by permission of Pearson Education, Inc., Upper Saddle River, NJ. **243** National Center for Policy Analysis Idea House, "Marshall Plan: Freer Markets Restored Europe," June 2, 1997. http://www.ncpa.org/pd/pdint140.html **249** http://users.erols.com/mwhite28/coldwar1.htm, http://users.erols.com/mwhite28/coldwar2.htm **262** Patria Rivera "Cold War 1957 Manila Philippines" in *Puti/White* (Calgary: Frontenac House, 2005) **264** Vladimir Pozner (Russian television commentator), interview for background material for *Red Files,* "Soviet Propaganda Machine," Abamedia and PBS, first broadcast in September 1999. Red Files, 1999. http://www.pbs.org/redfiles/prop/deep/prop_deep_inter_frm.htm **275** Friedrich Hayek, *The Road to Serfdom* (London: Routledge Press, 1944), p. 21. **278** The Universal Declaration of Human Rights © United Nations, 1948. Reproduced with permission. **281** Terence Corcoran, "Good sense to prevail over enviro-alarmism," *National Post*, March 1, 2007. Material reprinted with the express permission of: "The National Post Company", a Canwest Partnership. **286** Excerpted from *The Shock Doctrine: The Rise of Disaster Capitalism* by Naomi Klein. Copyright © 2007 Naomi Klein. Reprinted by permission of Knopf Canada. **289** Kristin Norget, "How Islam Evolved." CBC News, January 20, 2004 © CBC 2004 http://www.cbc.ca/news/background/islam/evolved.html **293** Melissa Leong, "Legal experts recommend Canada legalize polygamy." *National Post,* January 13, 2006. Material reprinted with the express permission of: "The National Post Company", a Canwest Partnership. **296** Darren Bernhardt, "Treaty Six chiefs promote Native health-care system." The Star Phoenix July 25, 2008. Material reprinted with the express permission of: "Saskatoon Star Phoenix Group Inc.", a Canwest Partnership. **297** Friedrich Nietzsche,Twilight of the Idols, 1895. English translation: Wordsworth Editions, Ware, Hertfordshire: 2007, p. 71. **297-298** Reprinted with the permission of Scribner, a Division of Simon & Schuster, Inc., from *And More by Andy Rooney* by Andrew A. Rooney. Copyright © 1979, 1980, 1981, 1982, 1986 by Essay Productions, Inc. All rights reserved. **304-305** Edward J. Cross (chairman, Kanien'kehaka Raotitiohkwa Cultural Centre, Kahnawake, Québec), quoted in *Report of the Royal Commission on Aboriginal Peoples,* Vol. 4, "Perspectives and Realities", Chapter 3, "Elders' Perspectives", 1996, p. 120 http://www.ainc-inac.gc.ca/ap/pubs/sg/cg/cj3-eng.pdf **305-306** Ronald Wright, *A Short History of Progress* (Toronto: House of Anansi, 2004), p. 3. **307** Mi'kmaq chief in a declaration to the English, who assumed they owned mainland Nova Scotia under the Treaty of Utrecht, 1749, quoted in *Report of the Royal Commission on Aboriginal Peoples,* Vol. 1, "Looking Forward, Looking Back", Chapter 5, "Stage Two: Contact and Co-operation", 1996, p. 126. http://www.ainc-inac.gc.ca/ap/pubs/sg/cg/cg5-eng.pdf **309** *Report of the Royal Commission of Aboriginal Peoples,* Vol. 1, "Looking Forward, Looking Back", Chapter 9, "The Indian Act", 1996, p. 272. http://www.ainc-inac.gc.ca/ap/pubs/sg/cg/cg9-eng.pdf **311** "Citizens Plus, also known as the Red Paper, 1970" Early Canadiana Online linked from "1951–1981: Aboriginal Rights Movement" Canada in the Making, produced by canadiana.org. Copyright © 1998-2009 Canadiana.org (Formerly Canadian Institute for Historical Microreproductions) **312** Harold Cardinal, *The Unjust Society* (Edmonton: M.G. Hurtig Publishers, 1969), p. 140. **316** "Namgis Nation," Treaty Commission Annual Report 2006: Six perspectives on treaty making. Indian and Northern Affairs Canada, December 21, 2001. http://ainc-inac.gc.ca/bc/treapro/mreinf/pub/bctcr6/namgis_e.html **317** Mike Denos and Roland Case, *Teaching about Historical Thinking,* eds. Peter Seixas and Penny Clark (Vancouver: University of British Columbia, 2006), p. 2 **318** Lord Bhikhu Parekh (professor of political theory), "What is multiculturalism?" *Seminar Magazine*, December 1999. http://www.india-seminar.com/1999/484/484%20parekh.htm **321-322** Sean M. Lynn-Jones, "Why the United States Should Spread Democracy" , Belfer Center for Science and International Affairs **322** Gaus, Gerald and Shane Courland, "Liberalism", Stanford Encyclopedia of Philosophy (Fall 2008 Edition), Edward N. Zalta (ed.), URL: http://plato.stanford.edu/entries/liberalism/#DebAboLib **323** Michael Byers, "Afghanistan: Wrong Mission for Canada." *The Tyee*, October 6, 2006. http://thetyee.ca/Views/2006/10/06/Afghanistan/ **325** William Anthony Hay, "Democratization, Order, and American Foreign Policy," April 2006. Foreign Policy Research Institute, http://www.fpri.org/enotes/200604.americawar.hay.democratizationorderforeignpolicy.html **325** Yoweri Museveni, quoted in

Robert D. Kaplan, "Was Democracy Just a Moment?," *The Atlantic Monthly* December 1997. Third World Traveller, http://www.thirdworldtraveler.com/Democracy/DemocracyMoment_AM.html **326-327** Haiti in better shape because of UN: Canadian diplomat." CBC News, April 25, 2007 © CBC 2007 http://www.cbc.ca/world/story/2007/04/25/mission-haiti.html **327** "Pettigrew: Canada will stay the course in Haiti," CTV.ca, January 3, 2006. http://www.ctv.ca/servlet/ArticleNews/story/CTVNews/20060103/staying_Haiti_060103/20060103?hub=Canada **328** Yoweri Museveni, quoted in Robert D. Kaplan, "Was Democracy Just a Moment?," *The Atlantic Monthly* December 1997. Third World Traveller, http://www.thirdworldtraveler.com/Democracy/DemocracyMoment_AM.html **328** From *The Future of Freedom: Illiberal Democracy at Home and Abroad* by Fareed Zakaria © 2003 by Fareed Zakaria. Used by permission of W.W. Norton & Company Inc. **329** William Anthony Hay, "Democratization, Order, and American Foreign Policy," April 2006. Foreign Policy Research Institute, http://www.fpri.org/enotes/200604.americawar.hay.democratizationorderforeignpolicy.html **346** Peter Levine, "A blog for civic renewal," October 14, 2005. http://www.peterlevine.ws/mt/archives/000707.html **347** Turnout rate in federal elections (1945–2006) in "Estimation of Voter Turnout by Age Group at the 39th Federal General Election, January 23, 2006," p. 2. http://www.elections.ca/loi/res/rep39ge/estimation39ge_e.pdf **347** "Estimation of Voter Turnout by Age Group at the 39th Federal General Election, January 23, 2006." http://www.elections.ca/loi/res/rep39ge/estimation39ge_e.pdf **348-349** interview between Mac Harb and the Frontier Centre for Public Policy, October 4, 2005. Frontier Centre for Public Policy, http://www.fcpp.org/main/publication_detail.php?PubID=1178 **355** Tom Christiano, "Democracy." The Stanford Encyclopedia of Philosophy,July 27, 2006. http://plato.stanford.edu/entries/democracy/ **355-356** Gary J. Bass, "Clueless." *New York Times Magazine* May 27, 2007, p. 18. From The New York Times, May 27, 2007 © 2008 The New York Times. All rights reserved. Used by permission and protected by the Copyright Laws of the United States. The printing, copying, redistribution, or retransmission of the Material without express written permission is prohibited. www.nytimes.com **356** Scott L. Althaus, "False Starts, Dead Ends, and New Opportunities in Public Opinion Research," *Critical Review* 18, 1–3 (2006): 75–104. **368** Patrick Leahy, "The Time 100 List: Maher Arar." *Time* Magazine, May 3, 2007. http://www.time.com/time/specials/2007/time100/article/0,28804,1595326_1615754_1616006,00.html **376** Mike Boon, "Civil Marriage Act Tabled." TorontoMike, http://www.torontomike.com/2005/02/civil_marriage_act_tabled.html, February 1, 2005 **378** Stéphane Dion, "The Canadian Charter of Rights and Freedoms at Twenty: The Ongoing Search for Balance Between Individual and Collective Rights" (speech given at the Woodrow Wilson International Center for Scholars), April 2, 2002. Reproduced with the permission fo the Minister of Public Works and Government Services, 2009, and courtesy of the Privy Council Office. **381** "Irish pub, French language watchdog battle over vintage signs, service" by Sidhartha Banerjee © 2008 The Canadian Press **384** Diana Breti, "Canada's Concentration Camps—The War Measures Act." *The Law Connection,* Simon Fraser University, 1998. http://www.britishcolumbia.com/general/details.asp?id=44 , Centre for Education, Law & Society, SFU, www.lawconnections.ca **384-385** Ipperwash Public Inquiry Transcript, September 8, 2004. The Ipperwash Inquiry. http://www.attorneygeneral.jus.gov.on.ca/inquiries/ipperwash/transcripts/sep_08_04/text.htm **385** "Submissions on behalf of the Aazhoodena and George Family Group", The Ipperwash Inquiry, pp. 13, 14. http://www.attorneygeneral.jus.gov.on.ca/inquiries/ipperwash/closing_submissions/pdf/AazhoodenaAndGeorgeFamilyGroup_ClosingSubmissions.pdf **387** "Human Rights Council adopts the UN Declaration on the Rights of Indigenous Peoples." International Work Group for Indigenous Affairs, http://www.iwgia.org/sw21486.asp **387-388** Copyright © Province of British Columbia. All rights reserved. Reprinted with permission of the Province of British Columbia. Www.ipp.gov.bc.ca **388** Treaty Negotiations in British Columbia www.ainc-inac.gc.ca/bc/fnbc/mps/trynega_e.pdf **393** "Stop Hate Crimes and Social Exclusion of Smokers"(online petition to end government bans on smoking). http://www.ipetitions.com/petition/CanadianSmokersRights/ **406** Edward R. Friedlander, Kansas City University of Medicine and Biosciences, "Why I Am Not a Postmodernist." *Kairos*, vol 3, issue 1, Spring 1998. http://www.technorhetoric.net/3.1/index.html **415** Excerpted from *The Shock Doctrine: The Rise of Disaster Capitalism* by Naomi Klein. Copyright © 2007 Naomi Klein. Reprinted by permission of Knopf Canada. **417-418** both tables adapted from United Nations Development Programme, Human Development Report (c) 1998 (New York: United Nations and Oxford University Press, 1998), p. 37. http://hdr.undp.org/en/media/hdr_1998_en_chap1.pdf. By permission of Oxford University Press, Inc. www.oup.com **419-420** "Syncrude suit 'punitive': Greenpeace." *Edmonton Sun* August 30, 2008, © 2008 The Canadian Press

421 http://www.who.int/globalchange/en/ 424-425 "Kyoto Protocol Implementation Act Lawsuit", Ecojustice Canada. http://www.ecojustice.ca/cases/kyoto-protocol-implementation-act-lawsuit 425-426 Mike De Souza, "Canada urges climate-change battle", Canwest News Service, December 11, 2008. Material reprinted with the express permission of: "CANWEST NEWS SERVICE", a Canwest Partnership. 426-427 "Dion introduces 'green shift' carbon tax plan." CTV.ca, June 19, 2008 429 Vandana Shiva Decries the "Outsourcing of Pollution to the Third World", *Democracy Now!,* September 14, 2007. http://www.democracynow.org/2007/9/14/vandana_shiva_decries_the_outsourcing_of 430 "China to evaluate environmental impact of development plans." Xinhua News Agency, November 4, 2007. http://www.china.org.cn/english/MATERIAL/230762.htm 434 Chris Wood, *Dry Spring: The Coming Water Crisis of North America* (Vancouver, BC: Raincoast Books, 2008), pp. 17–18, 21 436 Graph on Water Consumption, website of UN International Year of Freshwater 2003, http://www.un.org/events/water/images/WaterYearGraph.jpg 444 Ahmedur Rahman Farooq, "The Draft Constitution of Burma's Military Rulers." *Burma Digest* March 20, 2008, http://burmadigest.info/2008/03/20/the-draft-constitution-of-burmas-military-rulers/ 444 Sheila L. Croucher, *Globalization and Belonging: The Politics of Identity in a Changing World* (Lanham, MD: Rowman & Littlefield, 2004), p. 50 451 Nelson, J. and Kerr, D. (2005). Active Citizenship: Definitions, Goals and Practices [online]. Available: http://www.inca.org.uk/pdf/Active_citizenship_background_paper.pdf 24, November, 2008] 453-454 Peter Berkowitz, "Liberalism Strikes Back," The New Republic December, 15, 1997, p. 37. http://www.peterberkowitz.com/liberalismstrikesback.htm 454 Me to We, Philosophy. http://www.metowe.com/aboutus/philosophy/ 455-456 Andrew Coyne, "What you can do for your country: Why dual citizens should be forced to choose." *National Post* September 23, 2006. Material reprinted with the express permission of: "The National Post Company", a Canwest Partnership. 456-457 Ngam Cham, Seven Stories, www.glenbow.org/sevenstories © Glenbow Museum, 2006. All rights reserved. 457-458 From *One Good Story, That One.* (HarperCollins, 1993; New Edition, 1999). Copyright © 1993 Dead Dog Café Productions Inc. With permission of the author. 458 Coy, Patrick G. "Protective Accompaniment." *Beyond Intractability*. Eds. Guy Burgess and Heidi Burgess. Conflict Research Consortium, University of Colorado, Boulder. Posted: June 2003 http://www.beyondintractability.org/essay/protect/ 464-465 Ian Mulgrew, "Legal aid not a right, court rules." *Vancouver Sun,* March 4, 2008. Material reprinted with the express permission of: "Vancouver Sun", a CanWest Partnership. 465 Statistics Canada, "Caring Canadians, Involved Canadians: Highlights from the Canada Survey of Giving, Volunteering and Participating", Catalogue 71-542-X, 2004. (http://www.statcan.gc.ca/bsolc/olc-cel/olc-cel?lang=eng&catno=71-542-X) 466 This article originally appeared in "The Future of Philanthropy" — a special information supplement published in *The Globe and Mail* newspaper on June 26, 2008, produced by RandallAnthony Communications Inc. Reprinted with permission. To view the full report, please visit: http://www.randallanthony.com/the-future-of-philanthropy 467

"New UN website to track pledge for tsunami relief" UN News Centre, © United Nations, 2005. Reproduced with permission. 469 J. Clifford, "You Bet I'm a Pacifist." *Irregular Times,* July 27, 2008, http://irregulartimes.com/index.php/archives/2008/07/27/you-bet-im-a-pacifist/ 470-471 Dennis R. Hoover, "Religion after 9-11: Pacifism on the Record." *Religion in the News* (Fall 2001): http://www.trincoll.edu/depts/csrpl/RINVol4No3/peace%20churches.htm 472 Dan Glaister, "US 'war resister' faces key asylum decision in Canada," *The Guardian Weekly,* June 20, 2008, p. 8, © Guardian News and Media 2008 479 Richard Leonard, *Computers in South Africa: A Survey of US Companies* (New York: Africa Fund, November 1978) 479 "Human Rights: Historical images of Apartheid in South Africa." © United Nations, http://www.un.org/av/photo/subjects/apartheid.htm. Reproduced with permission. 482-483 "South Africans reconciled?", BBC News, October 30, 1998. http://news.bbc.co.uk/1/hi/special_report/1998/10/98/truth_and_reconciliation/142673.stm Reprinted by permission of Penguin Group (Canada), a Division of Pearson Canada Inc. 483-484 Rena Singer, "Destiny's Children: 10 Years After The End Of Apartheid", *US News and World Report,* April 11, 2004. http://www.usnews.com/usnews/culture/articles/040419/19apartheid.htm © 2004 U.S. News & World Report, L.P. Reprinted with permission. 490-491 "Anti-war activists hold peace rallies across Canada", CTV.ca News, October 27, 2007. http://www.ctv.ca/servlet/ArticleNews/story/CTVNews/ 20071027/afghan_protests_071027/20071027 492 Jeffrey Allen, OneWorld.net and Alexandra Moe, New America Media 493 Brittany Schell and Jeffrey Allen, OneWorld.net 494 Brittany Schell and Jeffrey Allen, OneWorld.net 495 From *The Collapse of Globalism* by John Ralston Saul. Copyright © John Ralston Saul, 2005. 496 *What's My Name, Fool?* by Dave Zirin (Chicago: Haymarket Books 2005), p. 86 497 Chris Turner, "Environment: Thinking Outside the Big Boxes." *The Globe and Mail,* March 15, 2008, p. F7 498 ZP Heller, Editorial Director, Brave New Films, "Lee Scott: It's Not Easy Being Green." *The Huffington Post,* March 20, 2008, http://www.huffingtonpost.com/zp-heller/lee-scott-its-not-easy-_b_92679.html 501 "Not Ready to Make Nice" by Dan Wilson, Martie Maguire, Emily Robison and Natalie Maines © 2006 Chrysalis Music (ASCAP), Sugar Lake Music (ASCAP), Scrapin' Toast Music (ASCAP) and Woolly Puddin' Music (BMI). All rights for Sugarlake Music administered by Chrysalis Music. All rights reserved. Used by permission. International copyright secured. 502 Bob Bossin, "The Clayoquot Women." http://www3.telus.com/oldfolk/women.htm 503 "Where did the pink ribbon come from?" Breast Cancer Action. http://bcaction.org/index.php?page=politics-faq#Q4 504 From *The Collapse of Globalism* by John Ralston Saul. Copyright © John Ralston Saul, 2005. Reprinted by permission of Penguin Group (Canada), a Division of Pearson Canada Inc. 507 "Wake Up: 5 Ways to Raise Citizen Awareness." Alberta Views, January/February 2008, p. 33 509-510 adapted from "10 Steps to Take Action." *Teaching Tolerance,* http://www.tolerance.org/teens/10ways.jsp, www.tolerance.org 514-515 Michael Ignatieff, "Canada in the World", *Ottawa Citizen,* Thursday, March 30, 2006. http://www2.canada.com/ottawacitizen/news/story.html?id=5164baa5-0041-4d92-9344-233607ff1529&k=26279